BUSINESS LAW
An Introduction

BUSINESS LAW
An Introduction

Victor D. López, J.D.
State University of New York at Delhi

GLENCOE
McGraw-Hill

New York, New York   Columbus, Ohio   Woodland Hills, California   Peoria, Illinois

Send all inquiries to:
Glencoe/McGraw-Hill
21600 Oxnard St. Suite 500
Woodland Hills, CA 91367-4906

The material in the end-of-part cases and computer screen images in Chapter 21 are reprinted with the permission of Mead Data Central, Inc., provider of the LEXIS®/NEXIS® services.

Library of Congress Cataloging-in-Publication Data

López, Victor D.
    Business law : an introduction / Victor D. López.
      p.   cm.
    Includes index.
    ISBN 0-256-12389-6 (alk. paper)
      1. Commercial law—United States. 2. Business law—United States.
    I. Title.
    KF889.3.L64 1993
    346.73'07—dc20   92–28448
    [347.3067]

Printed in the United States of America.
   7 8 9   071   02 01

For my parents,
Manuela and Felipe
López, for a lifetime of
sacrifice, support, and
love.

PREFACE

An unvoiced question for many Business Law students is, "How does Business Law relate to me personally; how will knowing this material be useful in my career?" *Business Law: An Introduction*, is my answer to them, and to other students who undoubtedly ask the same questions. The study of Business Law should be exciting, challenging, enjoyable, and above all relevant. After all, Business Law affects the way all of us live our lives. In writing this book I've addressed the need for a comprehensive yet concise text that is highly relevant to students' daily lives and the world of work. Designed to provide basic fluency in Business Law, this text presents accessible, thorough coverage of the field.

The 21 chapters included in this text cover the same basic ground as other Business Law texts. Topics covered in a greater number of very short chapters in some texts are unified here to achieve logical simplicity and ease of understanding. *Business Law: An Introduction* provides in-depth coverage of those topics most relevant to students. Every chapter and section in the text can be used—until the neccesary material for a one or two semester Business Law course is covered. After completing a course based on *Business Law: An Introduction*, students are prepared to apply their knowledge of Business Law inside and outside of the classroom.

In addressing the needs of students, I've concentrated on demystifying the language of Business Law. Complex and potentially intimidating topics such as Tort Law, Contract Law, and Commercial Paper are explained through the use of realistic examples familiar to readers. Brief hypothetical cases are used throughout the text to illustrate legal concepts. My students have responded positively to this direct and uncluttered approach.

The emphasis on concise language and focused coverage in *Business Law: An Introduction*, I believe, enhances the usefulness of the text's other pedagogical features:

Learning Objectives

Every chapter opens with a list of the most important concepts explained in that chapter. Students are provided with shared goals to work toward in learning the chapter material. These objectives also provide a preview of the chapter.

Illustrative Cases

In every chapter, difficult concepts are clarified through the use of brief, illustrative hypothetical cases indicated by the graphic symbol ➤. These cases refer to experiences that students will find familiar. For instance, a short hypothetical case used to illustrate necessary conditions for fraud describes a car purchase that went sour. Students can relate to the case descriptions, realize that a seemingly complex issue may not be so complex after all, and move on with confidence to the next concept.

Judge for Yourself

Hypothetical case descriptions and accompanying questions occur at the end of each chapter. These illustrate and clarify salient chapter topics while giving students the opportunity to assess their comprehension. These sample cases not only provide an important self-check before moving on to the next chapter, but can also be used as the basis of take-home assignments and as a catalyst for class discussion.

Case Studies

Extended *Case Studies* are actual court cases and questions occurring at the end of each of the book's first five Parts. These are real cases, such as those involving Baby M, Bernard Goetz, and the rap group *Fat Boys*, in their original format and language. By placing these Cases after groups of related chapters, rather than within chapters, students can test their assimilation and understanding of a substantial body of material. Each Case Study challenges students to apply both their analytical skills and knowledge of the law in answering questions related to the cases.

Contemporary Focus

Business Law is a dynamic field. Evolving technolgies and changing social mores often leave their impact on the law. *Business Law: An Introduction* reflects some of these changes in its coverage of computer crime, ethics, and computer-assisted legal research using the LEXIS®/NEXIS® services.

A Glossary at the end of the text defines business law terms. Appendix A is the *Constitution of the United States*. Appendixes B and C are selections from the Uniform Commercial Code on Sales and Commercial Paper that supplement the text's coverage of these topics.

The *Instructor's Resource Manual* offers, for each chapter, objectives, outlines, answers to the Judge for Yourself and Case Studies and approximately 40 test items with answers. A computerized test bank of more than 800 test items is available.

Acknowledge-
ments

This text owes its existence to the concerted efforts of many individuals to whom I am most grateful. I would like to formally acknowledge the important contribution of Mead Data Central for generously providing me with access to the LEXIS ® services.

I would also like to thank my publisher and friend, David Helmstadter, president of Mirror Press. His guidance and support throughout this project have been simply invaluable. Thanks also to Carla Tishler of Mirror Press and Jean Lou Hess of Richard D. Irwin, Inc.

I am very grateful to the following individuals whose reviews provided useful feedback, guidance, and support:

Paul Bittner, *Southwestern College of Business, Cincinnati, Ohio.*

Marilyn Chernoff, *Sawyer School, Pittsburgh, Pennsylvania.*

Darnel Cole, *Indiana Vocational Technical School, Gary, Indiana.*

Judy Peterson, *Northeast Metro Technical College, White Bear Lake, Minnesota.*

Clovie Quick, *Columbus Area Technical College, Columbus, Georgia.*

Paul Sedlacek, *National College, Rapid City, South Dakota.*

Esther Tremblay, *Duff's Business Institute, Pittsburgh, Pennsylvania.*

Donald Wiesner, *University of Miami, Coral Gables, Florida.*

A special thanks to my wife Alice Z. López, for her editing of various portions of the manuscript and her astute and helpful comments—and also for keeping the coffee flowing late into the night.

I am grateful to United University Professions for its support in awarding me a faculty development grant to help defray some of my research costs, and to my colleagues at the State University of New York College of Technology at Delhi and Plaza College for Business, along with the administration of both institutions, who have offered heartening encouragement from the project's inception through its conclusion.

Finally, and most importantly, I would like to thank all of my students, past, present, and future, whom it is truly a privilege to serve, and who provide more joy, challenge, and enlightenment to me than they will ever know.

Victor López

CONTENTS

PART 6

COMPUTERIZED LEGAL RESEARCH

21   Computerized Legal Research Using LEXIS® 395

BUSINESS LAW
An Introduction

I

THE LEGAL ENVIRONMENT OF BUSINESS

The study of law as it affects business is essential for every businessperson. We live in the most litigious society on earth. Thus, business owners, managers, and employees need to be aware of legal issues that affect business. They also must have a solid grasp of basic legal principles so they can spot potential problem areas and seek expert legal advice before problems grow into costly and time-consuming impediments. The question most persons involved with business need to ask is not *whether* they are likely to be involved in litigation, but rather *when* they are likely to encounter it. Consequently, awareness of basic legal principles is probably the best (and cheapest) risk management tool available to any businessperson. Indeed, an employee who fully understands basic legal principles and can recognize potential legal problems before they arise can be a company's greatest asset.

In Unit I, we begin our journey into practical legal training by examining the sources of American law, our court system, and the basic principles of tort and criminal law.

1

SOURCES OF THE LAW AND THE COURT SYSTEM

Learning Objectives

After studying this chapter, you will be able to:

1. Recognize sources of modern law.
2. Distinguish between common law and civil law.
3. Define jurisdiction and its implications.
4. Describe the level and function of courts in the federal court system.
5. Describe the level and function of courts in the state court system.

Introduction

Law, distilled to its essence, can be described as rules of conduct decreed and enforced by government for the benefit of its citizens. Laws are by no means the only type of rules that regulate conduct: a restaurant may require patrons to wear ties and jackets when dining in its premises, a college professor may demand that students refrain from talking in class, and a religious institution may command that its members abstain from using certain types of contraceptives. In all three cases, a penalty may be imposed for failure to observe the rules: the restaurant may deny entrance to anyone not wearing the proper attire, the professor may expel a student who talks during class, and the church may ostracize any member who admits using prohibited contraceptives. Nevertheless, these rules do not rise to the level of laws simply because the state does not enact and enforce them.

In this chapter, we will trace the law to its various sources and explore an overview of the federal and state court systems to gain a better understanding of our justice system.

Sources of the Law

It is a common misconception to think of the law as a set of rules written down in old, dusty books that show little change over time. Such a vision makes the law seem stagnant and inflexible. The reality, however, is quite different. Law in the United States is vibrant, adaptable, and ever changing (albeit slowly). Statutes passed by legislative bodies such as the U.S. Congress and the various states' legislatures are an important part of the law, as are decisions handed down by federal and state judges and the regulations and administrative decisions of state and federal agencies. All of these taken together make up what we commonly refer to as *the law*. We will examine each of these important sources of the law separately to gain a better understanding of how they help to shape our law.

The Civil Law Tradition

There are two basic legal systems in the Western world: civil law and common law. Civil law is the dominant legal system, favored by most non–English-speaking countries in Europe, Asia, Africa, and Latin America. The civil law system is based on a tradition dating back to the Code of Hammurabi (2100 B.C.) of reducing the law to written codes that the general citizenry could understand and abide by. This tradition continued with Roman law, which traces its recorded origin to the Twelve Tables (450 B.C.)—bronze tablets setting down the law that were attached to the orator's platform in the Roman Forum so that all citizens could read and know the law. Finally, the tradition reached its zenith around 533 A.D. when the Byzantine emperor Justinian I recorded and integrated 1,000 years of existing law into a single code—the *Corpus Juris Civilis* (literally, the body of the civil law), more commonly referred to as the *Justinian Code*. That 1,459-year-old code forms the most important pillar of the civil law system and is still widely studied today in civil law jurisdictions as a starting point in understanding the law.

The tradition of writing down the law into a code that the general populace can read, understand, and know continues today in most civil law jurisdictions. The emphasis is very much on the *black-letter law*, or on what the statute says, not on its interpretation. Civil law reduces all law into a writing that gives people a clear understanding of their rights and obligations as citizens. Judges have very little leeway in interpreting the law and little room for debating the meaning and application of it in a given circumstance. On the positive side, civil law jurisdictions make it simpler for citizens to know the law. As a result, there is less need for attorneys in civil law societies, with paralegals handling many routine tasks. On the negative side, civil law leaves judges little leeway in making distinctions between the letter and spirit of the law. Societal opinions, changing values, or the cumulative wisdom of judicial interpretation of the law gleaned from legal precedent have little, if any, place in common law. Therefore, the law tends to be inflexible and unchanging. That is the price paid for civil law's predictability and accessibility to the average person.

The Common Law Tradition

The common law system traces its roots to England, in particular to the Norman Conquest of 1066 A.D. William I (1066–87) began the attempts to consolidate what were at times conflicting laws throughout England into a unified common law that would apply throughout the realm. By the 13th century, magistrates traveled throughout the countryside, hearing cases from town to town. The law applied by magistrates and justices was based on common customs and traditions; since jurists had no great body of written law to rely on, they in essence created the law as they decided cases by applying basic principles of fairness drawn from the customs, traditions, and ethics of the time. Ultimately, these decisions were written down and used as *precedent*, or guidelines, in similar cases in the future. Under the doctrine of *stare decisis* (to stand by decided cases), courts today still follow precedent closely, deciding cases in ways consistent with similar, past case decisions. The role of the legal advocate largely requires arguing how existing precedent should be applied to a particular set of facts.

The distinguishing characteristic of common law is that it is primarily judge-made law. That is not to say that only judges make law. Today, there are large bodies of statutes not unlike those of civil law jurisdictions that seek to codify important areas of the law. Unlike civil law jurisdictions, however, statutes do not form the foundation of the law in most areas but merely alter or clarify the common law. Even in areas where the law has been largely modified by statute, the courts still retain the power of interpreting, modifying, and generally fine-tuning the law through legal decisions. In a common law jurisdiction, it can never be said that a statute embodies the law; the courts always have the final say on both the validity of statutes and on their interpretation. Unlike civil law jurisdictions, where for the most part the courts interpret the law literally as defined in statutes, in our common law system of jurisprudence the statutory law is always subject to judicial interpretation. To know what a given statute means, one must always look to see how it has been interpreted and applied by the courts.

Courts even have the power to declare any statute invalid if they believe it to go against either the federal or a state's constitution; this power is known as *judicial review*. For this reason, it is very difficult for the average lay person to know with any certainty what the law is in any specific situation. In many instances, even experienced attorneys can only venture an educated guess on how a court is likely to apply the law to a given set of facts. This uncertainty is perhaps the most negative aspect of common law. On the positive side, common law is not as inflexible as civil law; judges have a considerable amount of power to change, adapt, and mold the law to fit particular cases to ensure that justice is done and that the law reflects society's changing social values.

Constitutional Law

A constitution is the most fundamental source of law. It establishes a state's or nation's form of government and sets out its most fundamental principles. In the United States, we find a federal constitution as well as state constitutions for each of the 50 states. In addition, local municipalities have their own local constitutions, known as charters. The United States Constitution is the supreme law of the land: no other law passed by a state or by the federal government may contradict it. Article VI, Section 2, of the United States Constitution (see Appendix I) specifically states that the United States Constitution "shall be the supreme law of the land." If a conflict arises between the United States Constitution and any other law, including a state constitution or city charter, the federal Constitution rules, rendering the conflicting law unconstitutional, which means it has no force or effect.

Constitutions are of necessity rather broad documents stating the basic principles a government must follow. The interpretation of a constitution is left to the courts. Every court has the power to interpret the United States and state constitutions, but the Supreme Court of the United States has the final say on the meaning of the United States Constitution. All other courts are bound by the highest court's interpretation of the Constitution. To put it another way, the United States Constitution says whatever the Supreme Court of the United States says it says.

> James is a New York City resident who would like to own a handgun. He knows that under the city's strict handgun laws he will be unable to legally obtain a permit. During a business trip to Florida, he purchases a handgun from a private citizen in that state and brings it with him back to New York City. He later uses it to defend himself against a mugger and is arrested for illegal possession of a handgun, a felony under New York City criminal law. Facing a mandatory jail sentence, he defends himself by claiming that the city's gun law is unconstitutional, since it clearly violates the second amendment to the United States Constitution, which reads: "A well-regulated militia, being necessary to the security of a free state, the right of the people to keep and bear arms, shall not be infringed." Will he succeed?

Despite his logical argument, James is going to jail. The Supreme Court of the United States has said that the second amendment does not grant the right to bear arms to individuals but merely gives states the right to raise state militias. Is this what the founding fathers intended? Perhaps not, but the Supreme Court's interpretation of the Constitution is binding and cannot be challenged, and all lower state and federal courts must adhere to it. The Court always reserves the right to change its mind, however. If it chose to, it could hear an appeal by James on his illegal handgun possession conviction and overturn it, in effect changing the law and giving everyone the right to bear arms. But, because of the doctrine of *stare decisis* (letting decided opinions stand), it is unlikely to do so.

Courts also have the power of judicial review, through which they interpret statutes by legislative bodies such as Congress and state and local legislatures. Every court has the power to declare a legislative act unconstitutional, and judgments of lower courts exercising judicial review can be appealed to higher appellate courts. The final say as to constitutionality is reserved for the Supreme Court. If, for example, Congress decided to pass a bill that established the Church of the United States, such an act would be held to violate the First Amendment, which reads in part: "Congress shall make no law respecting an establishment of religion." As such, the act would be unconstitutional.

What can Congress do if it disagrees with the Supreme Court's interpretation of the Constitution? Only one thing: amend the Constitution. Under Article V, Congress has the right to amend the Constitution by a two-thirds vote by the House of Representatives and the Senate. If the proposed amendment receives the required two-thirds vote in Congress, the various state legislatures must approve it. If three-fourths of the states' legislatures approve the amendment, it becomes law and the Constitution is changed to include it. An amendment to the United States Constitution can also be made if three fourths of the states approve it in a constitutional convention. There is no limit to the extent of change an amendment may bring to the Constitution, other than that the right of each state to equal representation in the Senate may not be revoked.

Statutory Law

Another important source of law in the United States are statutes enacted by federal, state, and local legislatures. In general, the federal government can legislate over any area that it has been granted the power to regulate by the United States Constitution. Because ours is a government of limited powers, Congress can only legislate in an area over which it has specific jurisdiction.

Article I enumerates the powers of Congress, which include the power to levy taxes, borrow money, regulate international and interstate commerce, regulate naturalization and bankruptcy, mint money, punish counterfeiting, establish a post office and post roads, award patents and copyrights, set up inferior federal courts, punish crimes on the high seas, declare war, raise armed forces, and so forth (see Appendix A). Under the 10th Amendment, "The powers not delegated to the United States by the Constitution, nor prohibited by it to the states, are reserved to the states respectively, or to the people." For example, the Constitution does not give the federal government the power to pass social legislation for the common good. Where, then, does Congress get the power to legislate in these areas? From Article I, Section 8, Clause 3 (the *commerce clause*), which gives Congress the power "To regulate commerce with foreign nations, and among the several states, and with the Indian tribes."

In a long series of decisions concerning the commerce clause, the Supreme Court has interpreted it in the broadest possible sense, in effect giving Congress the power to regulate any activity that either directly or indirectly may affect or burden interstate commerce. As strange as it may sound, the 1964 Civil Rights Act enacted by Congress owes its existence to the commerce clause; Congress had the power to pass the act because discrimination based on sex, race, color, religion, or national origin can burden interstate commerce. In passing the legislation, Congress was merely exercising its right to regulate commerce. Without such a broad interpretation of the Constitution, Congress would lack the power to pass any social legislation that did not come under any of the areas specifically reserved to it in the Constitution.

Administrative Law

One other source of law comes from outside the court system. Administrative law has risen from the steady increase of governmental regulation since the 1930s, both at the state and federal levels. Administrative agencies are empowered by either the legislative or executive branches of the federal and state governments to carry out governmental processes entrusted to these branches of government.

Often, the executive or legislative branches lack the technical expertise or even the time to regulate and control an area over which it has jurisdiction. Consider the plight of Congress, entrusted with regulating commercial aviation in the United States. A great deal of technical expertise and a substantial amount of time is required to develop adequate regulations and then oversee their enforcement. Members of Congress clearly lack the expertise necessary to determine, for example, how often commercial planes should be inspected, how airline personnel should be trained, or what safety features airplanes need to adopt. Only aviation experts can make such determinations. Congress, recognizing its limitations, wisely created the Federal Aviation Administration to act on its behalf; it empowered the agency to both create regulations affecting commercial flight and to enforce these through the administrative process. Other common federal agencies include the Securities and Exchange Commission, Nuclear Regulatory Commission, National Labor Relations Board, Equal Employment Opportunity Commission, Federal Communications Commission, and the Environmental Protection Agency. Like the federal government, state and local governments also set up administrative agencies to assist with the administration of local government. There are thousands of such agencies set up by state legislatures, local city councils, governors, and mayors to assist them in implementing their legislative and executive responsibilities.

When taken together, the various federal and state agencies make up the important body of administrative law. In empowering agencies to perform legislative or executive functions, the empowering authority (e.g., Congress or the president) must outline the purpose, function, and scope of the agency's power in creating and enforcing regulations. Agencies have enormous power over the areas that they control. In many situations, agencies are given legislative, judicial, and executive powers in that they are entrusted with creating regulations, enforcing them, and investigating and punishing those who violate them. The administrative process requires that those subject to agency regulation be given the opportunity to be heard before any new regulation is passed; the process tries to ensure that agencies do not act in a vacuum but rather remain responsive to the needs and concerns of those they regulate. If, for example, the Federal Aviation Administration were to propose a new rule affecting the airline industry (e.g., prohibiting flight personnel from drinking any alcoholic beverage 48 hours prior to a flight), it would have to go through public hearings giving all interested individuals the right to testify and make their point of view known before the new rule could be adopted.

Agencies also exercise judicial-like powers through hearings and administrative decisions. Persons accused of violating agency rules are brought before the agency for a hearing resembling a trial. Administrative law judges preside over such hearings. They are not true judges but rather employees of the agency empowered to decide administrative hearings. Administrative hearings generally resemble trials with two important differences: there are no juries involved (the administrative law judge decides all questions of law and fact) and they are much less formal. Finally, appeal from an administrative law judge's decision is generally available to an intermediary appeal court at either the state or federal level.

The Court System

As we've seen, the courts interpret and implement laws. There are, in effect, 52 court systems in the United States: the federal courts, state courts for each of the 50 states, and a court system for Washington, D.C. Even though there are some differences between court systems, they are similar enough that we can make some generalizations about them. In the following discussion, we will examine working models of state and federal court systems to better understand how the judicial system works. But first, we'll examine the power of the courts to hear and decide cases.

Jurisdiction of State and Federal Courts

Before a court can hear and decide a case, it must have *jurisdiction* over both the subject matter and the parties involved. Jurisdiction refers to the power a court has to hear and decide a case brought before it (from the Latin *juris*, law, and *diction*, to speak: literally, the power to speak the law). A court has *subject matter jurisdiction* to hear and decide cases that it is empowered by statute to decide. For example, a traffic court clearly has subject matter jurisdiction to hear a case involving a speeding ticket or the running of a red light, but it lacks jurisdiction to hear a divorce or breach-of-contract action. Even when a court has the required subject matter jurisdiction, it cannot hear a case unless it also has *personal jurisdiction* over the litigants. Consider the following example:

➤ A resident of Rhode Island is injured in a car accident in Texas. Several months later, while visiting a relative in Vermont, he decides to bring an action against the Texas domiciliary in Vermont. Can he do so? The answer is clearly no: the Vermont court will have jurisdiction over the subject matter, since the appropriate trial court in Vermont can hear a personal injury suit, but not over the parties, since the Texas resident in particular has no contacts with the state.

For a court to have personal jurisdiction over the parties in a lawsuit, the parties must either voluntarily submit themselves to the court's jurisdiction by appearing before it or have significant contacts with the state to justify the court hearing the case. Significant contacts include living in the state, working in the state, carrying out business in the state, or committing either a tort, breach of contract, or crime while in the state.

Courts generally have jurisdiction to hear cases either for the first time, called *original jurisdiction,* or on appeal, called *appellate jurisdiction,* but not both. A notable exception is the Supreme Court of the United States, which has both original and appellate jurisdiction (see Article III, Section 3, in Appendix A). A court with appellate jurisdiction can only hear cases on appeal to review whether any error was made in the application of the law; it cannot hear testimony or consider any question of fact.

Venue

A court with subject matter and personal jurisdiction may still refuse to hear a case on the grounds that the action should be brought in a different county in the state with closer ties to the litigants or the subject matter of the action. If a New York domiciliary who lives in New York City's Queens County injures a resident of New York City's Kings County in an automobile in Kings County, the action could be brought in either Queens or Kings county, but not in, say, upstate New York's Otsego County. If both parties decide to travel 225 miles to Cooperstown, New York, to have their case tried in Otsego County (where it would take considerably less than the 4–5 years to get to trial that it would in Queens or Kings county), the Otsego County court of general original jurisdiction could, and would, refuse to hear the case on grounds that Otsego is not the proper venue for it to be brought, even though it would have both personal and subject matter jurisdiction over the litigants.

Federal Courts: Jurisdiction and Organization

Access to the federal courts is more restrictive than that of state courts. Under Article III, Section 2, of the United States Constitution, subject matter jurisdiction of the federal courts is restricted to:

1. Cases involving federal laws or the United States Constitution.
2. Cases affecting ambassadors, other public ministers, and consuls.
3. Cases involving maritime law.
4. Cases in which the U.S. government is a party.
5. Cases involving different states or the citizens of different states.
6. Cases involving states and foreign governments or their subjects, or between a U.S. citizen and foreign governments or their subjects.

Unless a case involves one of the preceding criteria, access to the federal courts will be denied. In addition, civil cases litigated in the federal courts must be for amounts in excess of $50,000.

Cases involving diversity of citizenship or a federal question (the two primary means of gaining access to the federal courts) can also be brought in state courts. In these areas, the federal and state courts share *concurrent jurisdiction*. Thus, if a citizen of Texas wants to bring an action for a breach of contract involving more than $50,000 in damages against a citizen of Wyoming, she can to do so in federal court, since diversity of citizenship exists (a case between citizens of two or

FIGURE 1–1   **Diagram of the Federal Court System**

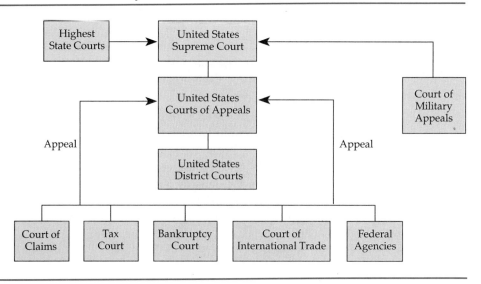

more states is involved); the same lawsuit could be brought in the state courts of either Texas or Wyoming. But if two residents of Utah want to sue each other for $100,000 in damages arising out of an automobile accident in Utah, they cannot do so in federal court, since the case does not involve diversity of citizenship or a federal question (e.g., a case arising out of the U.S. Constitution or any federal law).

Federal Court System.   The federal court system contains trial courts called district courts, intermediate appeals courts known as courts of appeals, and the Supreme Court of the United States. Figure 1–1 presents a diagram of the Federal Court system.

Federal Courts of Limited Jurisdiction.   As is the case in many state systems, the federal court system contains a number of courts of limited original jurisdiction that try specific types of cases. These include the U.S. Tax Court, Bankruptcy Court, Court of Claims (tries cases in which the U.S. government is a party), Court of International Trade (tries civil cases involving trade tariffs and related trade issues), and the territorial courts. A special Court of Military Appeals also exists to hear appeals from military tribunals.

U.S. District Courts.   The U.S. district courts are the federal trial courts and have general original jurisdiction over any case involving federal jurisdiction (e.g., diversity of citizenship and federal question). There is at least one U.S. district court in every state, with a current

FIGURE 1–2 **U.S. Courts of Appeals by Circuit**

First Circuit	*Second Circuit*	*Third Circuit*	*Fourth Circuit*	*Fifth Circuit*	*Sixth Circuit*	*Seventh Circuit*
Maine	Connecticut	Delaware	Maryland	Louisiana	Kentucky	Illinois
Massachusetts	New York	New Jersey	North Carolina	Mississippi	Michigan	Indiana
New Hampshire	Vermont	Pennsylvania	South Carolina	Texas	Ohio	Wisconsin
Rhode Island		Virgin Islands	Virginia		Tennessee	
Puerto Rico			West Virginia			

Eighth Circuit	*Ninth Circuit*	*Tenth Circuit*	*Eleventh Circuit*	*District of Columbia*	*Federal District*	
Arkansas	Alaska	Colorado	Alabama			
Iowa	Arizona	Kansas	Florida			
Minnesota	California	New Mexico	Georgia			
Missouri	Hawaii	Oklahoma				
Nebraska	Idaho	Utah				
North Dakota	Montana	Wyoming				
South Dakota	Nevada					
	Oregon					
	Washington					
	Guam					
	N. Mariana Islands					

total of 96 judicial districts. Congress can change the number and location of judicial districts according to changes in population and the load of district court calendars.

U.S. Courts of Appeal.   The U.S. courts of appeals are intermediate appellate courts that hear appeals from specialized federal courts, the federal district courts, and many federal agency decisions. There are 11 judicial districts, each encompassing more than one state, plus the District of Columbia and the Federal District (see Figure 1–2). In general, decisions of the U.S. courts of appeals are final. At its discretion, the Supreme Court may take appeals from these courts.

Supreme Court of the United States.   The Supreme Court is the only U.S. court specifically established under the Constitution (Article III, Section 1), which gives Congress the power to create all other inferior federal courts. Article III, Section 3, of the Constitution vests the Court with the following original and appellate jurisdiction:

1. Original jurisdiction over all cases affecting ambassadors, other public ministers, and consuls, and those in which a state shall be a party.

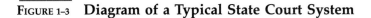

FIGURE 1-3   **Diagram of a Typical State Court System**

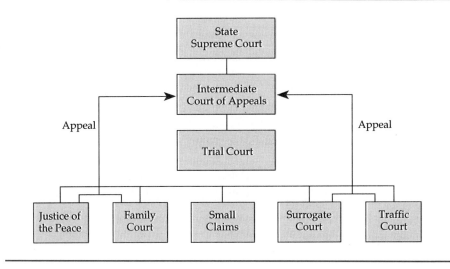

2. Appellate jurisdiction over all other cases over which the federal courts have jurisdiction.

Litigants who are unhappy with the decision of a state's highest court or with a district court of appeals decision may appeal to the Supreme Court, provided they meet the jurisdictional requirements of the federal courts (e.g., litigation involving a federal question, diversity of citizenship, etc.). Whether or not the Supreme Court hears a case on appeal is completely within its discretion. If the Supreme Court believes that a sufficiently important constitutional issue exists requiring it to render a final opinion, it will issue a *writ of certiorari* to the lower federal court or to the state's highest court where the case was last decided; the writ is an order demanding that the lower court forward the record of the case in question to the Supreme Court for its review. If the Court refuses to issue a writ of certiorari, the lower court's decision is left standing. A refusal by the Supreme Court to issue such a writ does not necessarily indicate that it supports the lower court's position; it merely means that at the time the case was appealed, the Supreme Court didn't find a sufficiently pressing issue for it to decide.

State Courts: Jurisdiction and Organization

As previously noted, state court systems can vary somewhat, but they generally conform to the following model (see Figure 1–3):

1. Lower courts of limited jurisdiction.
2. Trial courts of general, original jurisdiction.
3. Intermediate appeals courts.
4. The state's highest appellate court (generally, the state's supreme court).

Lower Courts.   Most states have one or more lower courts of limited jurisdiction where minor criminal offenses are tried and civil litigation involving small dollar amounts is heard. Such courts include *small claims courts,* which hear any civil case involving small dollar amounts— typically not to exceed $5,000; *justice of the peace courts,* where minor criminal offenses are adjudicated; *traffic courts,* where traffic violations are adjudicated; *surrogate courts,* where matters relating to trusts and estates are heard; and *family courts,* where child custody, divorce, separation, and a variety of other matters pertaining to families is adjudicated.

The advantage of lower courts of limited jurisdiction is that they often provide quick and relatively informal means of resolving civil disputes and minor criminal infractions. By bringing action in small claims court, a litigant can have a case resolved in months, instead of years, and without the need of retaining legal counsel. On the downside, appeal from small claims court is generally not available, and the dollar amounts for which one can sue are relatively low.

Trial Courts.   As the name implies, trial courts, or courts of original general jurisdiction, try almost any type of criminal or civil case. They have the widest trial jurisdiction available. Typical cases heard by trial courts include crimes, breach-of-contract actions, and torts. This is where nearly all cases affecting business are litigated.

Intermediate Appeals Courts.   Intermediate appeals courts have jurisdiction to hear appeals from most trial and some limited jurisdiction courts as well as some rulings of administrative agencies. These courts provide parties who feel that a legal error was made by the original trial judge with the opportunity to have their trial court record reviewed. As previously noted, appeals or appellate courts only review questions of law and do not review findings of fact. Thus, for example, a losing party could successfully appeal on the grounds that the trial judge improperly instructed the jury on a point of law or failed to sustain a valid objection by the losing litigator (both questions of law), but an appeal based on a contention that a witness lied at the trial (a question of fact) would not be valid.

State Supreme Court.   The state's highest court—usually named the State Supreme Court—has the final say on all appeals from trial and intermediate appeals courts. Whether a state's highest court hears a case on appeal is usually by its own discretion. If the court does hear a case on appeal from a lower court, its decision is final and can only be overturned by the Supreme Court of the United States if a federal question is involved.

Judge for Yourself

Case 1.   Ted, a domiciliary of Connecticut travels to California on business. While in California, he purchases a defective cigarette lighter. When he returns to Connecticut, the lighter explodes, causing him severe injuries. Ted knows that juries in Kings County (Brooklyn), New York, have a reputation for awarding some of the highest personal injury judgments in the country, so he asks his attorney to sue the seller and the manufacturer of the lighter there.

  a. Can an action be brought in Kings County, New York? Explain.
  b. If the parties appear in Kings County willing to have the court adjudicate the case, will the court have subject matter and personal jurisdiction over the parties?
  c. Assuming that the New York court does have jurisdiction in the last example, will it hear the case? Explain.

Case 2.   Assume the same facts as in Case 1.

  a. In which state or states can the plaintiff sue the defendant?
  b. Assume that the plaintiff will sue the defendant for $100,000 in damages. Can the suit be brought in federal court? Explain.
  c. If the plaintiff only wants to sue for $9,000 for his medical costs and pain and suffering, can he do so in federal court? Explain.
  d. Assume that the suit can be brought in federal court. What court and in which federal district(s) can the suit be brought?

Case 3.   Ephraim, a nearsighted college student who likes to drive very fast, decides to travel from Maine to California over spring break. On the way, he manages to get into automobile accidents in New Hampshire, Vermont, New York, Pennsylvania, Ohio, Indiana, Illinois, and Missouri, where he finally totals his car and flies on to California to enjoy the rest of his vacation.

  a. Assume that plaintiffs in each of the states mentioned begin legal actions in their states against Ephraim. Will he have to defend himself in each of those states? Will the various state courts be able to obtain personal jurisdiction over him once he has left the state?

b. Would it make any difference if Ephraim had never been to any of the states noted prior to the automobile accidents and has no other contact with the states?

c. If the plaintiffs in Pennsylvania and Indiana decide to sue in federal court for $100,000, will they be able to do so? In which districts will each be able to bring his suit?

Case 4.   The town of Pious in your state decides to pass a local ordinance that reads as follows:

> Sunday is hereby decreed a day of rest. The performing of work of any kind, whether for oneself, for pay, or gratuitously is hereby forbidden to all citizens. For purposes of this statute, *work* shall not include essential medical services or the conducting of religious services. Violation of this statute shall carry with it a fine not to exceed $500 and or a jail sentence not to exceed 30 days in the county jail.

Two days after the statute is passed and published in the local newspapers and broadcast on radio and television stations, you are arrested by police for washing your car. You defend yourself at trial on two grounds: (1) that you were not washing your car and (2) that the statute is unconstitutional. You are, nevertheless, convicted and fined $500. You decide to appeal.

a. What is your best argument on appeal as to the unconstitutionality of the statute? (e.g., what part of the constitution does it possibly violate?)

b. What court in your state could you appeal to? Could you appeal to the federal courts?

c. Can you argue on appeal that you were not washing your car if the trier of fact at the trial level found that you were? Why?

d. If the intermediate appeals court and your state's highest court affirm the lower court's decision, do you have any other recourse? Explain.

e. If an identical case in a neighboring state has recently been affirmed by the highest state court, does it mean that you will definitely lose your appeal? Explain.

2

TORT LAW

Learning Objectives

After studying this chapter, you will be able to:
1. Define torts.
2. Describe the difference between torts and crimes.
3. Define common torts against persons and property.
4. Differentiate between intentional torts, negligence and strict liability.

Introduction

The law of torts concerns itself with private wrongs or injuries (other than a breach of contract) for which a court will award damages. A tort is committed when a person fails to observe a *duty of care*, or responsibility not to infringe on another's rights, by either intentionally or carelessly causing him injury. The harm could be physical, emotional, or to one's property. There are many different torts covering a variety of wrongful acts that individuals commit upon one another. If Bill purposely and without provocation punches Denise in the nose, he is guilty of the tort of battery. If Sue takes Christina's book and sells it to Ranji, she is guilty of the torts of trespass to property and conversion. Likewise, if Barry tells his friends that Rachel is a thief when it is untrue, and his friends believe him, Barry is guilty of the tort of defamation. Three different wrongs are involved, and there are three different torts covering them.

As you might suspect, in at least two of the above examples, crimes are also committed. Bill and Sue have committed criminal acts (simple assault and larceny, respectively), for which they could be tried and, if convicted, fined or sent to jail. Many of the torts we examine in this chapter are also crimes. The difference is that in a tort, one *individual* is suing another to recover money damages, where in a crime, the *state*, acting through a prosecutor, is suing the alleged wrongdoer to try to punish her for the wrong done. It is possible for someone to be guilty of both a crime (a wrong against society as a whole) and a tort (a private or civil wrong) at the same time; in that case, the wrongdoer is sent to jail and must pay compensatory damages to the person he has harmed.

The law of torts exists to let wrongfully injured people collect damages from those who have injured them. Tort law doesn't punish wrongdoers (that is the primary objective of criminal law), but rather compensates people for legal wrongs they suffer at the hands of others. The ultimate goal of tort law is to put the wronged party back in the position he or she was in before becoming the victim of a tort.

Legal Duty

Before we can examine the various types of torts, it is imperative that the idea of a legal duty be understood. A fundamental principle of all civilized societies is that individuals have certain rights and obligations in their dealings with one another. In general, people have the right to enjoy their property, their health, and their privacy, free of undue interference from others. It follows logically that along with these rights comes a corresponding *duty* to respect the same prerogative of others. When someone disregards this duty and infringes on the rights of another, liability in tort arises.

A tort will not arise unless there are two elements present:

1. The existence of a legal duty.
2. A breach of that duty.

Keep in mind that when no legal duty is breached, no liability in tort will arise.

> Howard, while taking a leisurely stroll by his town's railroad tracks, notices that his neighbor, Deidra, is lying down on the tracks, fast asleep. He also notices that a train is approaching a mile away. He considers waking her, but remembers that he has never been particularly fond of this neighbor. In fact, he decides that he'd be quite happy to see her dead. So he moves approximately 10 yards away, sits down, and waits for the inevitable to happen, smiling broadly in anxious anticipation of his poor neighbor's demise.

Howard's conduct in the rather gruesome example is deplorable. His actions are clearly immoral, and his behavior monstrous. But did he commit a tort? Before we answer, we must consider whether he has breached a duty that he owed Deidra. The answer to that question is no. He did not bring about Deidra's plight, and did not violate any legal duty owed her. She has the right to be left alone, and he has left her alone; she does not have the right to be rescued by him. Therefore, Howard is not guilty of a tort. Howard is a scoundrel and a miserable human being, but not a *tort feasor*—one who has breached a tort.

If Howard were a police officer, or Deidra's husband, he would have a legal duty to act imposed by the nature of his job or his relationship to the unfortunate Deidra. The law demands that police take reasonable measures to protect the health and safety of members of our society; likewise, spouses must take reasonable steps to prevent one another from coming to harm. Not so for complete strangers, or even neighbors, who are free to help or ignore each other as they see fit.

Types of Torts

There are basically three types of torts:

1. Intentional torts.
2. Negligence torts.
3. Strict liability torts.

Intentional torts, as the name implies, arise out of an intentional or willful breach of duty. If Jack throws a stone at Pepe's car, intending to break its windshield, and the stone causes harm, Jack is guilty of at least one intentional tort (trespass to property). Negligence torts, on the other hand, occur when a duty of care is breached unintentionally, causing harm. An example would be Rudy going through a red light he did not notice and hitting Genine's car as she drove through the intersection. The breach of duty here is Rudy's failure to exercise due care while driving his automobile so as not to injure the persons or property of others; it would not be an intentional tort, since Rudy did not intend to run the light, he was only careless in not noticing it. Finally, strict liability in tort arises where someone suffers an injury not from anyone's willful or negligent act, but rather out of some intrinsically dangerous activity or, under certain circumstances, through the manufacturing of an unsafe product. For example, if Barry decides to keep a tiger as a pet and it escapes and injures someone, he will be liable to the injured person regardless of how many precautions he had taken to ensure that the tiger could not escape. Keeping a wild animal is considered so dangerous that a person who does so is responsible for any and all damage the animal causes, regardless of fault.

Intentional Torts against a Person

Battery.   *Battery* is intentionally touching someone in either a harmful or offensive manner without the person's consent. If Judy intentionally slaps Henry without his consent, she has battered him and could be sued for damages. Likewise, if Jemal throws a crumpled piece of paper at Irma that bounces off her head, he has battered her; he has intentionally caused the paper to "touch" her head without her consent, and the touching, while not harmful, is offensive (i.e., most reasonable people would object to being hit by crumpled pieces of paper thrown at them). In both of these examples, no serious harm is done, yet tort liability would arise. The damages a jury will award will reflect the severity of the harm done by the unconsented-to touching. Almost any intentional touching is deemed to be offensive as long as a reasonable person under the circumstances would object to it. Where no real harm is done, a court normally awards only *nominal damages,* or damages in name only, usually $1.

Assault.   The tort of *assault* consists of intentionally causing someone to reasonably fear that they are about to be the victim of a battery. In battery, a harmful or offensive touching must take place; in assault, there is no actual touching, only the fear that one is about to be touched without one's consent. If Linda points a gun at Irving and causes him to fear that he is about to be shot, she is guilty of assault— even if she never intended him any harm. It is enough that she purposely pointed the gun at him and that he was justifiably frightened by the incident. If she goes on to shoot him and the bullet "touches" him, she will also be guilty of battery. In the second case, Irving could sue Linda for both assault and battery, since they are separate torts, and could recover damages for each.

False Imprisonment.   One of our most fundamental rights is that of moving about freely. Whenever anyone intentionally and unjustifiably prevents another from moving about, he commits the tort of *false imprisonment.* The defendant must have intentionally restrained the plaintiff to be considered having committed this tort. Obviously, tying someone to a chair against their will fulfills the requirements. But so will other methods. Both physical and psychological barriers can give rise to the tort. People can use walls, doors, ropes, and locks to prevent another from leaving. But words can also have the same result when they issue threats. A person standing in the middle of an open field who reasonably believes some harm will come to him, to his property, or to his loved ones if he leaves is as much the victim of false imprisonment as someone locked in a room against her will.

Note that false imprisonment only applies if the restraining action is unjustified. If a burglar is apprehended by his would-be victim, tied, locked in a room, and threatened with serious bodily injury if he tries to escape before police arrive, the tort will not apply, since the person being restrained is a suspected felon and the imprisonment is justifiable.

Even when a person is justifiably detained, the tort of false imprisonment may apply if the period of the detention is unreasonable. Keeping a suspected thief tied up while police arrive is not false imprisonment, but holding him tied in the basement for several days before calling the police is.

Intentional Infliction of Emotional Distress.   The tort of *intentional infliction of emotional distress* arises when one person intentionally causes another to suffer extreme emotional distress. A statement that upsets someone is not enough; the conduct must be extreme and outrageous before this tort will ensue. If Jerry calls Violet a "fat slob" and she is devastated by the comment, she cannot sue Jerry. His statement may have been unkind and have caused her great pain, but the comment will not qualify as an outrageous or abominable act. But if Jerry phones Violet every night for a month at 3:00 A.M. and calls her a fat slob, this would, in all likelihood, fall to the level of conduct that gives rise to the tort.

A problem with this tort is that mental suffering is hard to prove. Where there is no physical manifestation of the emotional harm, damages are not likely to be awarded. Thus, in the last example, Violet would need to show some physical manifestation of her suffering to recover damages in many courts. If she can show that her hair is falling out as a result of grief suffered from the calls, or that she has gained 50 pounds since the calls began or has had to undergo therapy for a sleep disorder, her chances of recovery in every court would be quite good. But if these calls have simply upset her without any physical effects, she is unlikely to recover damages.

Invasion of Privacy.   Another important tort concerns a person's fundamental right to privacy and offers protection against unreasonable interference with this right. The tort of *invasion of privacy* is commonly narrowed down into four categories:

1. Appropriation of a person's name or likeness for commercial use.
2. Intrusion into a person's seclusion.
3. Placing a person in a false light by facts told to others.
4. Public disclosure of private facts about an individual.

In the first type of situation, one person attempts to profit by using another's name or picture for commercial purposes. The most obvious example is using a person's name in connection with a product without the person's permission. "John Doe [a famous movie star] uses our product, shouldn't you?" If Mr. Doe has not approved of the use of his name or picture in connection with that product, he can sue for invasion of privacy. The mere unpaid mention of a person's name in a non-newsworthy context may lead to an action for invasion of privacy.

The second type of situation, intrusion into a person's seclusion, essentially entails unreasonably prying into another's privacy. The classic example is that of a peeping Tom. If Thomas climbs Stacy's fire escape and watches her through her bedroom window, he is clearly guilty of the tort. But what if Stacy stands in front of her bedroom window on the first floor and Thomas watches her as he walks by her sidewalk? Then there is no invasion of privacy; Stacy is engaging in a public act by standing by an open window in plain view, and anyone may glance at her who wishes to. For the tort to arise, there must be three separate conditions: (1) the act observed must be private; (2) the intrusion must be willful; and (3) the nature of the intrusion must be objectionable to a reasonable person.

The third type of situation, placing someone in a false light, occurs when facts about someone are published that either attribute unpopular views to her or depict actions that she did not take. Again, for the tort to arise, the action or views attributed must be objectionable to a reasonable person. Claiming that a person is a fascist or communist, for example, might give rise to damages under the tort if it is untrue. Reporting facts that are true but are likely to be misconstrued can also give rise to the tort.

> Henry writes a letter to all his friends in which he states that Erika, his ex-girlfriend, has been seen frequenting a drug rehabilitation center for crack addicts for the past three months. Erika has, in fact, been visiting the center, but as a volunteer counselor, a fact that Henry omits. Erika has a valid cause of action against Henry, if she proves that the letter that was "published" (sent out to others) implies she is a crack addict.

Finally, the publication of private facts about someone that a reasonable person would find objectionable can also lead to liability. If Phil tells others that Cassandra is a bed wetter, a fact Cassandra had not made public, he could be liable to her. Being a bed wetter is something a reasonable person would consider objectionable if Cassandra is 30 years old, but not if she is 3. If Cassandra is 30, she can sue Phil for invasion of privacy, even if the statement Phil made is true, as long as it was not public knowledge. In essence, the law holds that we have the right to keep certain matters to ourselves.

Defamation.   Publishing a false statement about someone that tends to harm the person's reputation gives rise to the tort of *defamation*. If the statement is spoken, it is *slander*; if it is written, it is *libel*. If the false statement is made about a person who is a public figure, then that person needs to show that the defamatory statement was made with *malice*. Malice, for purposes of defamation, is the making of a statement either knowing it to be false or with reckless disregard for its truth or falsity. The requirement of malice applies only in the case of public figures or public officials.

For the tort of defamation to arise, a statement made about an individual or corporation must (1) be false, (2) negatively affect the person's reputation, and (3) be published, which simply means it must be communicated to at least one person other than the person defamed. Examples of defamatory language would include, but not be limited to, false statements relating to a person's honesty, integrity, or sanity. The statement must also be reasonably traceable to the individual bringing the suit. Saying that "all lawyers are liars and thieves" is not slander because it is too broad and does not sufficiently affect any one lawyer; but falsely calling attorney Sandra Jones "a lying thief" is slander, since an individual is clearly specified.

In general, truth is an absolute defense to the tort of libel. If the defendant to a libel suit can show that the damaging statement about the plaintiff is true, he will not be liable for damages. Keep in mind that if the published fact relates to a private matter that the plaintiff has not made public, the defendant may still be liable for the separate tort of invasion of privacy as discussed above.

> Oswaldo, a 45-year-old investment banker, likes to collect dolls and occasionally plays with them. He confides in his best friend, Sylvia, that he has been collecting and playing with dolls most of his life and asks her whether she thinks there is anything wrong with his hobby. Sylvia finds this information amusing and calls up several of Oswaldo's friends to tell them about it. This causes Oswaldo great embarrassment and a loss of several clients who think his eccentric hobby a negative reflection on his judgment. Oswaldo sues Sylvia for defamation. Will he prevail? What if he also sues for invasion of privacy?

Oswaldo cannot recover under a theory of defamation as long as Sylvia can show that the statement is true. The extent of damage done by the publication of the embarrassing material is irrelevant, since truth is an absolute defense. This would be true even if it can be shown that Sylvia acted with malice. Oswaldo has a much better chance of proving that Sylvia is guilty of invasion of privacy. Oswaldo's hobby is a personal matter that is not public knowledge, and the information is of a type that Oswaldo may be able to show would be found objectionable by a reasonable person.

The above *fact pattern*—a brief synopsis of the essential facts of a case—illustrates an important aspect of the law in general: a person seeking relief for a wrong very often has more than one legal theory under which he can seek a remedy. It is up to an attorney to explore every avenue available for relief in a given case and then to pursue the best ones for her client to obtain the desired relief.

Fraud.   Intentional misrepresentation, or *fraud,* occurs when one person makes a false statement about an important fact to induce another to take action that causes harm. For this tort to come into existence, five elements must be met.

To put it plainly, whenever a person is (1) lied to (2) about an important fact (3) to be convinced to undertake a specific action, (4) and the person undertakes that action, relying on the false statement, (5) thereby suffering some material loss, then that person has suffered the tort of misrepresentation, or fraud, and may sue to recover damages.

Consider the following example of fraud:

> Dan wants to sell his old car to his friend, Ken. He knows that Ken wants an automobile in good condition with less than 50,000 miles. Dan calls up Ken and tells him he is willing to sell him the car for $2,000. He further states that it is in excellent condition with only 35,000 miles on the odometer. In fact, the car has engine, transmission, and electrical problems; it also has 135,000 miles (the odometer reads 35,000). Ken purchases the car after a cursory inspection, relying on his friend's statements. A week later, Ken takes the car in to a mechanic for a tune-up and discovers the truth about the vehicle's condition. He wants to sue his ex-friend for damages under a theory of fraud. Will he succeed?

The answer to the above example is apparent. Dan intentionally lied to Ken about the car's condition to get him to buy it. Ken relied on the misrepresentations and purchased the car, losing money as a result. Ken will easily prevail in court, provided he can prove that Dan knowingly lied.

What if Dan had said nothing about the automobile and Ken had not asked? Could Ken sue for fraud? Generally, the answer would be no; silence of itself will not constitute misrepresentation unless there is either a duty to speak or the defects in question would not be discovered in the course of a reasonable inspection. A duty to speak generally exists only if there is a special relationship of trust and confidence between the parties.

If someone says nothing when they have a duty to speak, they are guilty of *passive fraud*. Relationships in which a duty to speak might arise would include those between close friends, parents and children, brothers and sisters, or attorneys and clients and other such fiduciary relationships (relationships of trust).

Hiding a material fact to make its discovery difficult can also give rise to *active fraud*, which has the same effect as a misrepresentation, even if no special relationship of trust exists between the parties.

Intentional Torts Against Property

Trespass to Land.   The tort of *trespass to land* requires an intentional physical act that results in an intrusion into the land of another without the owner's consent. Thus, walking on another's property, throwing a stone that lands in another's property, or shooting a gun over someone's property are all examples of trespass to land.

There are certain circumstances when entering someone else's land without their permission will not be considered trespass. Entering into another's land by mistake or by accident does not constitute trespass, provided that the person leaves as soon as she becomes aware of her mistake. Furthermore, trespass is excused if it occurs under emergency circumstances, such as entering the land of another while fleeing from a wild animal or to render emergency assistance to someone on the land.

In an action for trespass to land, damages will be awarded even if no harm was caused to the land. In the absence of harm to the land, and where the trespass was of brief duration, courts will generally only award nominal damages—usually the sum of $1. Where the trespass is of a continuing nature, however, substantial damages can be awarded, even if no harm is done to the land. The property owner can also receive an *injunction* from the court requiring the defendant to cease trespassing on the plaintiff's land.

> ➤ On his way to work every morning, Henry cuts across Abigail's lawn to save himself from having to walk an extra 200 yards on the sidewalk. He does no damage to the property. The first time he does it, Abigail sues and recovers $1.00. If the behavior continues, she can either sue for a greater amount of money (a jury will determine appropriate damages) or ask the judge to issue an injunction prohibiting Henry from trespassing on her land, or do both. If the judge issues an injunction (an order demanding that the improper activity cease) and Henry continues to trespass over the land, he will be held in contempt of court and either fined or jailed, in addition to having to pay damages to Abigail.

Trespass to Personal Property.   Just as people have the right to exclusive possession and enjoyment of real estate, they also have the right to exclusively possess and enjoy their personal property. Any intentional interference with that right will bring about an action for *trespass to personal property* (also known as *chattels*). Personal property, or chattels, can be defined as any tangible property that can be owned other than real estate. A car, a watch, a pair of shoes, a cow, a dog, and a mobile home are all examples of chattels.

➤ Bill borrows his neighbor Henry's lawnmower without his permission and mows his lawn. After he is done, he returns the same to its rightful place in Henry's garage. Even if no damage is done to the lawnmower, and even if Bill replaces the gasoline used in mowing his lawn, Bill is liable to Henry for trespass to personal property and must pay the reasonable value of the use of the lawnmower (e.g., its rental value). Bill is also liable for trespass to real estate in having entered Henry's property to retrieve the mower without his permission.

If Bill damages the mower in the above example, he must pay the reasonable cost for its repair in addition to damages for trespass.

Conversion.   The tort of *conversion* is closely related to trespass to personal property. As in the case of trespass, the owner of the personal property is deprived of its use and enjoyment, but on a permanent basis due to the property being either stolen or destroyed. If, in the previous example, Bill takes the lawnmower from Henry with the intent of permanently depriving him of its use (e.g., intends to keep it himself or to sell it to another or otherwise dispose of it), Bill would be guilty of conversion. The same is true if he intentionally or unintentionally destroyed the lawnmower, thus permanently depriving Henry of its use.

In the last example, Bill is also guilty of a crime and could be fined or jailed. Here, we are only concerned with the civil consequences of the wrongful act and the wronged party's ability to recover damages for his loss. We will discuss criminal liability in the next chapter.

Negligence

The law states that everyone has the duty to act with reasonable care to avoid creating undue risk of harm to others. Everyone is charged with taking the precautions that a reasonably prudent person would take to prevent bringing about foreseeable harm to others. If a person fails to observe such care and another person suffers harm as a result, *negligence* can be charged.

For a defendant to be liable for negligence, there must be (1) a breach of duty (2) owed plaintiff to by the defendant (3) that brings about a foreseeable harm (4) and is the direct cause of that harm. Keep in mind that the nature of negligence does not require intent. If a harmful act is done intentionally, it is covered under one of the many intentional torts such as assault, battery, or trespass. Harm done negligently is, by definition, done unintentionally. The reason for tort liability is not that a defendant meant to cause another harm, but rather that he harmed another through carelessness—that he failed to observe reasonable care under the circumstances.

Let's look at several examples:

➤
1. Bill punches Tom in the mouth, causing him severe injury.
2. Bill pushes Tom, causing him to lose his balance and fall, breaking a leg.
3. Bill, while running to catch a bus, runs into Tom as he rounds a corner.
4. Bill, a juggler, practices his knife-juggling act while walking along the street. One of the knives gets away from him and impales the luckless Tom.
5. Bill suffers a heart attack and staggers into Tom, who loses his balance and falls, breaking an arm.

In each of the above examples, Bill caused Tom's injuries. But only two of the examples involve the tort of negligence, while another involves no tort at all. In examples 1 and 2, Bill intentionally commits an act—punching and pushing Tom—that results in Tom's injuries. In both examples, Bill is guilty of an intentional tort, namely battery (and probably assault as well). In examples 3 and 4, Bill is guilty of negligence. He did not intend to injure Tom, but he acted in a negligent manner under the circumstances: he breached a duty of care owed to Tom by acting carelessly and thereby directly caused Tom's injuries, which were foreseeable under the circumstances. Running without looking where one is going and juggling knives in public are clearly not acts a reasonably prudent person would undertake. In example 5, however, Bill is not guilty of any tort, since the act that brought about Tom's injuries—Bill's heart attack—was neither intentional nor negligent. Bill had no reason to know he would have a heart attack, nor did he intentionally have one. In the last example, Tom's harm is caused accidentally, which is to say without anyone's fault. He therefore cannot be compensated for his injuries.

Once the defendant's negligence is established, the plaintiff is entitled to damages that will compensate her for her loss. Compensable damages in negligence actions include property damage, medical expenses, pain and suffering, and loss of present or future earnings. In essence, any damage that the plaintiff can prove she has suffered as a result of defendant's negligence is compensable—except for attorney's fees, which, as is usually the case in American jurisprudence, each party must bear. In example 4 above, for example, Tom can recover from Bill the following: the cost of repairing or replacing his clothes ruined by the knife wound; any medical bills in treating his injuries;

any lost wages caused by his inability to work after the incident; a reasonable award to compensate him for his "pain and suffering"; and any loss of future income resulting directly from the injury.

Defenses to Negligence

There are certain circumstances under which a negligent defendant may avoid liability or have the extent of his liability reduced. Recognized defenses to a negligence action include contributory negligence, comparative negligence, and assumption of risk.

At common law, a party suing under a theory of negligence could only recover damages if she were without fault herself. Where both parties were partly to blame for damages caused by their negligence, each was said to be guilty of *contributory negligence,* and neither party could recover. The basic rationale for the rule is that the negligence of both parties contributed to the resulting harm and that were it not for the failure of both parties to observe reasonable care under the circumstances, the resulting damage would have been avoided. Problems arise under contributory negligence when parties are not equally negligent; barring both parties from recovering any damages when one of them is much more negligent than another can bring about some rather unfair results. Consider the following example:

> ▶ Dana approaches an intersection in which there is a stop sign. She slows down, looks both ways, and continues. Mario races across the intersection at a high rate of speed, ignoring a stop sign. Dana sees Mario coming too late to get out of his way, and an accident occurs that completely destroys Dana's 1992 Ferrari, worth $190,000, and Mario's 1975 Buick Skylark, worth $190. A jury finds that Dana was approximately 10 percent at fault in bringing about the accident and Mario 90 percent at fault.

In the above example, neither Dana nor Mario would be able to recover any part of their damages under the common law rule. Hence, Dana, who was only one-tenth responsible for the accident, will lose $190,000 as a result, while Mario, who was nine-tenths responsible for causing the accident, will only lose $190.

While some jurisdictions still cling to the common law rule that contributory negligence bars any recovery in a negligence suit, most states have abandoned this view in favor of a less harsh *comparative negligence* theory. Under comparative negligence, a plaintiff who is contributorily negligent can still bring a suit to recover damages for the portion of the harm suffered for which he was not responsible. The trier of fact (the jury, if the case is being tried by a jury) must determine the percentage of each party's negligence in bringing about the harm being litigated. Once the percentage of fault is allocated, each party can recover damages equal to the total amount of their actual damages for which they were not responsible. In the above example, Dana would be able to recover from Mario 90 percent of her $190,000 damage. Since she bears 10 percent of the responsibility for the accident, she cannot recover for the 10 percent of the damages that were "her fault."

Most jurisdictions limit recovery under comparative negligence to cases in which a party's contributory negligence is less than 50 percent. A small number of states will permit recovery even by parties who are more than 50 percent negligent under what is commonly called *pure comparative negligence.* In such states, a party who is 90 percent negligent can still recover 10 percent of his damages, the portion of his damages for which he was not at fault. This can also have some unfair results. What if Mario were driving the Ferrari and Dana the old Buick? In a state that observes pure comparative negligence, Dana would recover 90 percent of her damages, or $171, and have to pay Mario, who was 90 percent responsible for the accident, 10 percent of his damages, or $19,000!

Finally, if an injury is caused by engaging in an activity that is likely to cause such an injury, the injured party is said to have *assumed the risk* of the injury and cannot recover damages. Thus, a boxer who is injured by his opponent cannot recover damages. Neither can a hockey goalie who is hit by a puck, or a baseball player injured by a line drive.

Strict Liability

There are a few instances in which someone can be found guilty of a tort and made to pay damages, even though the person had neither intentionally nor negligently breached a duty owed another. Such liability is termed *strict liability,* or *liability without fault.* It generally occurs in three separate types of situation: those involving animals, ultrahazardous activities, or product liability.

An owner is strictly liable for damage done by a trespassing animal, as long as the type of damage caused was reasonably foreseeable or predictable. Thus, the owner of a pet rabbit who gets out of its cage and eats all of the vegetables in a neighbor's garden is liable to the neighbor for the harm done. It doesn't matter that the owner did not intend the damage to be done and that he may have taken all reasonable precaution to prevent its happening. A rabbit eating vegetables given the chance is perfectly foreseeable, thus the owner would have to pay for the damage, regardless of fault.

With regard to personal injuries caused by domestic animals considered to be nondangerous, an owner is not responsible absent negligence—unless she has reason to know about the animal's dangerous tendencies. If an owner knows that an animal is prone to attacking others, however, he will also be held strictly liable for bodily injuries it causes. An owner is always strictly liable for bodily injury or property damage caused by a wild animal, unless such injury was provoked by the party injured; a wild animal is defined as any animal that can never be fully tamed, such as a wolf, lion, panther, or rattlesnake. Thus, if Cynthia shows Esther her pet rattler, and the snake bites Esther without provocation, Cynthia will be strictly liable for Esther's injuries—even if she shows that she was not negligent and did not intend the act to happen.

Manufacturers and retailers of commercial products can be held strictly liable for damages caused by products they manufacture or sell, provided the product is so defective as to be unreasonably dangerous to intended users. This would include spoiled food and unreasonably dangerous power tools and appliances. Merely the fact that a product is unsafe, or even highly dangerous, does not necessarily give rise to strict product liability whenever a consumer is injured using it. Guns, knives, razor blades, and sewing needles are all highly likely to cause varying degrees of injury in their everyday use. Yet, accidents arising from using these items will generally not give rise to strict liability by the manufacturer or retailer, since they are among products that cannot be made absolutely safe to use. Generally, though, where a reasonable alternative exists for making an unsafe product safe, a manufacturer and retailer will be held strictly liable for any injury during the ordinary use of that product.

Judge for Yourself

Case 1. At the end of one of his business law classes, Professor Strange noticed that his students were gathering their books before being dismissed. He reached into his briefcase and pulled out a replica handgun, which he waved in the air while yelling out: "Don't even think about moving from your chairs. The period is not over until I say it is." The gun was not real, but it looked exactly like a .38 caliber snub-nosed revolver. Upon seeing the gun, three of his students fainted, while two others grinned broadly, realizing the professor was simply pulling one of his usual jokes. The remainder of the class was simply confused, not believing the professor would shoot them but afraid to push the issue by leaving. After continuing his lecture for an hour past the usual class time, Professor Strange dismissed his class and told them that he had only been joking about shooting them and that the gun was a fake.

The following day, three students decide to sue their professor and ask you, the brightest student in the class, to advise them on their rights. The students are Jill, who fainted from fear during the incident; Bob, who knew Professor Strange was joking all along but stayed until the dismissal just to "see what would happen"; and Lydia, who didn't faint during the incident but, not being sure whether the instructor was joking or not, decided not to test the issue by leaving early. Advise the students on the following matters:

    a. What tort or torts might Professor Strange have committed? Give concrete reasons for your answers.

    b. What are each of the three students' chances of obtaining a judgment against their instructor?

    c. Whether or not each student has one or more causes of action in tort against the professor, might they be able to file criminal complaints against him? Is there any other legal recourse they might have against the professor?

    d. Should you advise each or any of the students to speak with an attorney about their possible legal remedies in this case? Even if you don't think they have a case? Why?

Case 2.   John decides to spend a week at his friend Don's summer home in New York's Catskill mountains. On the drive up from New York City, he loses control of his car on a tight turn and drives off the road into a farmer's cornfield. After some maneuvering, he manages to get back onto the road, but not before trampling several hundred yards of growing corn. Since he can't stand waste, John gets out and fills his trunk with as many ripe ears of corn that he finds on the ground as he can. When he finally arrives at Don's house, he decides to go to sleep.

    Unknown to him, Don has wired the guest bedroom with microphones and hidden cameras, hoping that John, who walks and talks in his sleep, will say or do something funny at night so they can share a laugh the next morning. That night, John dreams he is having a fight with his friend, Rhoda, and while talking in his sleep, accuses her of being a liar, a thief, and a woman of loose morals. (Rhoda is none of those things.) He also discloses that she is suffering from Acquired Immune Deficiency Syndrome (AIDS) and that she acquired the HIV virus through her intravenous drug use. The latter statement is true, and Rhoda has confided it to John, asking him never to reveal that fact to anyone.

    The next day, when learning that Don taped his sleep-talking, John storms out of the house. Don, incensed at his friend's lack of a sense of humor, chases him with a baseball bat and strikes him on the head from behind. John, who never saw him coming, falls to the ground, seriously injured.

    A few days later, John calls you, asking your advice. Answer the following questions for him:

    a. What intentional torts is John definitely guilty of? Why?

    b. Is John guilty of libeling Rhoda? Explain.

    c. Is John guilty of slandering Rhoda? Explain.

    d. Is John guilty of invasion of privacy? Explain.

    e. Is Don guilty of invasion of privacy? Explain.

f. Is Don guilty of assault? Explain.

g. Is Don guilty of battery? Explain.

Case 3.   Edward keeps a lion, a collie, and an aquarium full of piranhas as pets. He hires Dominick to walk the dog and lion every day. Yesterday, Dominick celebrated his 21st birthday and, before going to work at his pet-walking job, he stopped by his neighborhood bar to enjoy a couple of legal drinks with his friends. By the time he got to Edward's house, he was quite drunk. He decided to walk the dog and lion to sober up a bit but forgot to put on their collars and chains. Almost as soon as they'd left the house, the dog lunged at the mailman and nipped him several times—despite never having bitten a human being in the past. Meanwhile, the lion snacked on the neighbor's three cats and severely injured the neighbor when she tried to save them. After rounding up the stray pets, Dominick decided to wash his hands in the piranhas' aquarium. The fish, who had not as yet been fed, were quickly drawn to his immersed arms and took several bites before Dominick could withdraw them.

Several days later, the mailman, the neighbor, and Dominick want to know their rights. Advise them as to the following:

a. Under what theory can the neighbor successfully sue Edward for the loss of her cats and her personal injuries? Explain fully.

b. Can the neighbor also sue Dominick? If so, under what theory?

c. Can the mailman sue Edward under a theory of strict liability for the dog bite? Explain fully.

d. Can the mailman sue Dominick? If so, under what theory?

e. Can Dominick sue Edward for his piranha-bite injuries? If so, under what theory?

3

CRIMINAL LAW

Learning Objectives

After studying this chapter, you will be able to:

1. Describe the difference between felonies, misdemeanors, and violations.
2. Define the elements of a crime.
3. Define the crime of attempt and distinguish it from other crimes.
4. List and define the main defenses to criminal liability.
5. Describe major crimes against persons, property, and judicial procedure.

Introduction

Criminal law deals with punishing people who commit wrongs against society. When a person steps outside of the bounds of permissible conduct and voluntarily, or willfully, engages in conduct prohibited by the state, he has commited a crime.

In general, individuals in a free society have the right to conduct themselves in any way they see fit, so long as they do not unduly interfere with the rights of others to do the same. As we have seen in the preceding chapter, when an individual willfully breaches a duty of care he owes another, the individual harmed by that breach can sue to recover monetary damages or ask a judge to issue an injunction, an order prohibiting the defendant from continuing the wrongful activity. Some types of conduct, however, are seen as being so dangerous to society as a whole that the governing body itself (a state, a municipality, or the federal government) may decide to prohibit such conduct to preserve the common good. Criminal law is, essentially, a set of rules that a local, state, or federal government has decided must be followed by all members of a society for the good of that society as a whole. The violation of one of these rules is a *crime*.

There is a strong relationship between torts and crimes. Indeed, many torts are also crimes, as noted in the previous chapter. What distinguishes the two is the nature of the offense: a tort is a wrong against an *individual*, while a crime is a wrong against *society as a whole*. The criminal is sued by a state or federal prosecutor; if she is found guilty, she can be punished with jail, a fine, or both.

➤ Harriet, upset at her low midterm grade, pulls out a gun and aims it at her professor. She sneers and pulls the trigger. The bullet misses the professor, and fellow students apprehend Harriet before she can take another shot. Under the circumstances, Harriet is quite possibly guilty of the *crime* of attempted murder. She is also guilty of the tort of assault for placing her professor in reasonable apprehension that he was about to be battered. If Harriet is tried for the crime of attempted murder (at the state's criminal court), she can also be sued for the tort of assault in a separate legal action (in the state's civil court). Whether or not the state proves that Harriet was guilty of attempted murder, the professor can sue her for the tort of assault. Harriet, by the way, cannot defend on the constitutional safeguard against double jeopardy, since she is not being sued twice for the same crime, but rather she is being sued for a crime and a separate tort arising out of the same incident.

Classification of Crimes

Crimes are usually divided into categories related to their seriousness. From most to least serious, these are felonies, misdemeanors, and violations.

Felonies

Felonies, the most serious types of crime, are punishable by more than one year in a state or federal penitentiary. Common felonies include treason, murder, arson, burglary, embezzlement, grand larceny, aggravated assault, rape, and manslaughter. Many states further categorize felonies by their seriousness, such as:

1. Capital felonies: crimes punishable by death.
2. Class A felonies: crimes punishable by maximum imprisonment of more than 15 years.
3. Class B felonies: crimes punishable by imprisonment for 7 to 15 years.
4. Class C felonies: crimes punishable by imprisonment for one to seven years.

Misdemeanors

Misdemeanors are less serious offenses, punishable by a fine or imprisonment for a period of up to one year. Common misdemeanors include petty larceny, simple assault, reckless endangerment, and disorderly conduct. Like felonies, misdemeanors are also sometimes classed into more than one category in some states. For example:

1. Class A misdemeanors: crimes punishable by a fine or imprisonment of six months to one year.
2. Class B misdemeanors: crimes punishable by a fine or imprisonment of up to six months.

Violations

The least serious types of criminal conduct are classified as *violations.* Unlike most felonies or misdemeanors, violations are usually not punishable by imprisonment (although they can be) but are punishable by fines. Common violations include the breaking of traffic and health regulations such as speeding, failing to stop at a red light, failing to inspect one's automobile on time, spitting on the sidewalk, and littering.

Legislatures have very broad powers in classifying what types of behavior are to be prohibited and what punishment will be levied on criminal offenders. And legislatures in different states do not always agree on what constitutes a crime or on what is an appropriate punishment. For example, casino gambling is legal in New Jersey, and both casino gambling and prostitution are legal in Nevada. These two activities are prohibited in nearly every other state. Thus, the definition of a crime and its punishment depends very much on the jurisdiction one is in. Every state makes it a crime to knowingly take the life of another human being without just cause; that constitutes the crime of murder, which is a felony in every state. Yet the punishment for the crime of murder, and its classifications, vary from state to state. Some states exact the death penalty for certain kinds of murder, while in others, such as New York, the murderer of anyone but a police officer may be eligible for parole in less than 15 years.

Elements of a Crime

Before finding any criminal defendant guilty of a crime, the prosecution must prove the following two elements:

1. The existence of a physical act or wrongful omission by the defendant.
2. A wrongful state of mind, or *intent,* at the time of the commission of the prohibited act.

Let's examine some sample situations:

1. Fred steals Matilda's purse for money to buy himself his daily "fix" of crack cocaine.
2. Linda steals a pound of hamburger meat from a supermarket to feed her three starving children.
3. Mario steals a carton of cigarettes from Shirley and throws it away to prevent her from smoking and damaging her health.

In the three examples above, the same crime has been committed: *larceny.* It is true that the motives of Fred, Linda, and Mario are quite different, nevertheless all three are equally guilty of the same crime. The crime of larceny requires a wrongful act (the wrongful taking of another's property) and the intent to commit that act. All three examples involve the same wrongful act—the taking of another's property—and the requisite intent, since the acts were purposely committed. It is completely irrelevant that Fred's motivation for committing the crime—his need to buy illicit drugs—was quite different from Linda's motivation to feed her children or Mario's concern for his friend's health. All three knowingly engaged in an illegal act and are, thus, criminally liable for the same crime.

It should be noted here that criminal motive is not an element of a crime. This may sound strange to most of us who grew up watching television attorneys and detectives searching for a motive to ferret out the culprit from among their suspects. While the existence of a motive is always an important tool to detectives and prosecutors alike, none need be shown to convict a defendant of any crime–including capital offenses (those for which the maximum penalty is death).

Criminal liability can arise even when a criminal act is not fully performed. An intentional, substantial step towards the commission of a crime constitutes the crime of *attempt.* To prove someone guilty of attempting to commit a crime, the prosecution must show the presence of the following two elements:

1. *Intent* to commit a crime.
2. An *overt act* towards the commission of the crime.

When someone is prosecuted for a criminal attempt, it generally means she has tried to commit a crime but fallen short for one reason or another. For example, Darlene pulls a gun on Brigitte with the intent of killing her. She aims the gun and fires, but the gun jams and does not shoot. As a result, Brigitte is unharmed. Had Darlene succeeded in her attempt, she could be tried for murder. Since Brigitte is unhurt, Darlene obviously cannot be tried for murder, but she can be tried for the lesser offense of *attempted murder,* a crime in and of itself. She will be found guilty of that crime if the prosecution can show that she intended to kill Brigitte and that she took some act to carry out her intent. Pointing the gun at Brigitte will suffice as an overt act taken to fulfill her intended crime, and Darlene will be found guilty of attempted murder. The same would be true if Darlene had shot at Brigitte but missed, and Brigitte had managed to escape unharmed. The act of shooting the gun would suffice, provided that Darlene also had the criminal intent to kill Brigitte.

Problems arise when would-be criminals are apprehended before they can take a step towards carrying out their plans. Most often, the crucial question in cases of attempt is whether a sufficient step has been undertaken towards the commission of the intended crime. For example, if Darlene tells Marvin that she intends to buy a gun tomorrow and kill Brigitte, and Marvin informs the police, who arrest her the following day *before* she has purchased the gun, Darlene would not be guilty of a crime. She may have had the criminal intent but had not yet taken any overt action towards carrying it out, and intent in and of itself will not bring about criminal liability without an accompanying criminal act.

Limitations on Statutes Creating New Crimes

Congress and state legislatures have a great deal of power in determining what types of conduct constitute crimes. There are, however, some constitutionally mandated ground rules for determining crimes. In essence, legislatures must do the following:

1. Be specific as to what types of conduct constitute crimes so that people are given reasonable notice of the types of conduct they must avoid.

2. Refrain from passing *ex post facto laws,* or retroactive laws. This means that a law cannot be passed making an act illegal that was legal when committed or changing either substantive or procedural law to negatively affect a defendant who has already committed a criminal act; and,

3. Refrain from passing *bills of attainder.* A bill of attainder is a legislative act that punishes without a judicial trial.

4. As always, legislatures cannot contradict the United States Constitution. Any criminal statute that contradicts the Constitution is of no force.

As long as legislatures follow the above rules, they have nearly a free hand in deciding what type of conduct they can label as illegal and what type of punishment to attach to it. For example, the state legislature in the state of Moot passes the following criminal statutes:

➤   1. It shall be a class A misdemeanor, punishable by a fine of $5,000, incarceration for a period of time not to exceed one year, or both, for any person under the age of 35 to purchase or consume alcoholic beverages as of January 1, 1993.

2. Effective immediately, all persons who have smoked cigarettes within the past two months will be subject to a fine of $100.

3. Effective January 1, 1993, any person who ridicules an elected official shall be guilty of a class A misdemeanor and be subject to a fine not to exceed $5,000 and/or incarceration not to exceed one year.

Of the above, which are valid and which invalid? The Moot legislature has the power to legislate who, if anyone, may consume alcoholic beverages and to punish those who illegally consume alcohol. If it decides that the state's interests would best be served by preventing anyone under the age of 35 from drinking, it could so decree. Such a law might be unusual but is well within the legislature's power to proclaim. The second and third laws, however, are unconstitutional and therefore void. The second example above is an ex post facto law, since it seeks to retroactively punish cigarette smokers. The third example is in direct violation of the liberally interpreted First Amendment right to free speech; in addition, it is overly broad, since a reasonable person would have difficulty in determining what type of behavior would constitute "ridiculing a public official."

Specific Crimes

Now that we've examined the characteristics and elements of crimes, let's take a look at some common types of crimes. As is usually the case, there are significant differences in the penal codes of most states regarding the type of behavior prohibited as "criminal" and its punishment. Despite these differences, however, all states prohibit certain kinds of conduct, among which are the following criminal offenses. Note that many of these crimes are also torts, as discussed in Chapter 2, and can give rise to civil liability as well as criminal liability.

Crimes against a Person

Battery.   *Battery* consists of harmfully or offensively touching a person. Simple battery is a misdemeanor. Aggravated battery, which is commonly defined as a battery performed with the use of a deadly weapon or any battery that results in serious injury, is punishable as a felony in most states.

➤ Jill, without provocation, slaps Rudy on the face, causing him embarrassment but no real harm. Jill is guilty of simple battery, a misdemeanor.

Jill, without provocation, repeatedly beats Rudy with a telephone, causing him to be hospitalized with a concussion. Jill is guilty of aggravated battery, a felony.

Assault.   Criminal *assault* is commonly defined as either (1) an attempted battery or (2) intentionally placing a person in reasonable fear of imminent bodily harm. Simple assault is a misdemeanor. Assault with a dangerous weapon, or in some jurisdictions, with the intent to commit a rape, is deemed aggravated assault and carries a greater penalty.

> ➤ Rudy, without provocation, screams at Jill that he's going to punch her lights out, lunges at her, but is stopped by a police officer before he can touch her. He is guilty of simple assault.
>
> Rudy, without provocation, tells Jill he's going to kill her, takes out a handgun and tries to shoot her, but the gun jams. He is apprehended before he can carry out his threat. He is guilty of aggravated assault.

Homicide.   The unjustified taking of a human life can constitute one of three different criminal offenses: murder, voluntary manslaughter, involuntary manslaughter.

Murder.   *Murder* is the unjustified killing of a human being with malice aforethought. Malice here can be actual or implied. Actual malice is present when a person intentionally takes another's life. *Aforethought* means premeditated, or acting to bring about a preplanned result. Murder can also result where there is no actual intent to cause death in three circumstances: (1) where the death results from an act intended to bring about serious injury; (2) where the death results from purposely subjecting a person to an unjustifiably high risk of death or serious injury; and (3) where death occurs in the course of the commission of a felony. In these cases, malice is implied from the surrounding circumstances. All of the following examples would result in the crime of murder:

> ➤ 1. Charlene shoots at Francesco with the intent to kill him so that she can steal his wallet. Francesco dies. (Malice aforethought.)
> 2. Charlene beats Francesco with a baseball bat, intending to cause him serious injury not to kill him. He dies. (Act intended to bring about serious injury.)
> 3. Charlene cuts Francesco's car's brake lines, not intending to kill him but only to scare him. He subsequently dies when he is unable to control the car and drives off a cliff. (Subjecting a person to an unjustifiably high risk of death or serious injury.)
> 4. Charlene chases Francesco with a gun, trying to rob him of his wallet. He runs into the street and is killed when hit by a truck. (Felony–murder–even though Charlene did not intend the death to occur, she is guilty of murder because the death resulted from her commission of a felony.)

Voluntary Manslaughter. *Voluntary manslaughter* consists of intentionally taking a human life with adequate provocation. Voluntary manslaughter, although still a felony, is a less serious crime than murder and results in less stringent punishment. What is "adequate provocation" under particular circumstances is a question of fact to be determined by the jury.

> ➤ Roy comes home early from work and finds his wife, Esther, in bed with the milkman. He becomes enraged and immediately chokes both to death.

Even though Roy intentionally killed his wife and her lover, he is probably not guilty of murder since he acted in the heat of passion and with adequate provocation. A person in such circumstances is deemed less culpable than one who acts with cool, dispassionate premeditation. Revenge, however, does not qualify to lower a murder to voluntary manslaughter; if Roy, after witnessing his wife and the milkman in bed, plots their deaths and kills them the next day, he will be guilty of murder. A day is sufficient time for the rage of the moment to subside, so that such a killing would not be done under the heat of passion and would constitute murder.

Involuntary Manslaughter. *Involuntary manslaughter* involves a death resulting from a criminally negligent act or a killing that occurs in the commission of a misdemeanor.

> ➤ Yvonne, upset that John has decided to break up with her, punches and kicks him, intending to hurt but not kill him. He runs out into the street to escape her and is killed by a passing trolley car. Yvonne is guilty of involuntary manslaughter, since the death occurred during her commission of a misdemeanor. (Simple battery.)

False Imprisonment.   The unlawful confinement of a person against her will constitutes the misdemeanor of *false imprisonment*. The requirements for this crime are identical for the tort of false imprisonment discussed in Chapter 2.

Kidnapping.   *Simple kidnapping*, a misdemeanor, consists of unlawfully confining a person against his will and either transporting him or hiding him. *Aggravated kidnapping*, a felony, consists of a kidnapping committed for the purpose of obtaining ransom, committing a sexual assault, or for any other criminal purpose.

Rape.   Engaging in sexual intercourse with a woman by a man, not her husband, without her effective consent constitutes the crime of *rape*, a felony. Note that a woman whose husband engages in sex with her against her will is not the victim of rape under the common statutory definition of the crime. She can, however, be the victim of a battery under the common law definition of the crime. This is still the statutory definition of the crime in most jurisdictions, although, fortunately, there has been legislative movement in recent years to expand rape to include forced sexual intercourse between spouses. Rape further requires penetration of the female sex organ by the male sex organ—other types of sexual intercourse do not qualify as rape but constitute the separate crime of *sodomy.* Lack of effective consent includes sex obtained through force or the use of threats.

Statutory Rape.   Engaging in sexual intercourse with a female under the age of consent constitutes the crime of *statutory rape.* Whether the victim gave her consent or not is irrelevant. Generally, the age of consent is 18, although it is lower in some states. It is usually irrelevant that a person may reasonably appear older than the age of consent; this is a strict liability crime in most states, so that the willful commission of the offense will suffice to raise criminal liability.

> ➤ Sandra, a 17-year-old college student, consents to engaging in sexual intercourse with Howard, a 21-year-old fellow student, whom she has been dating for months. Howard honestly believes Sandra to be at least 20, since she looks much older than her age. Assuming the age of consent is 18, Howard is guilty of statutory rape. Sandra's consent is irrelevant, as is Howard's honest mistake as to her age.

Statutory rape is a strict liability crime for which liability is imposed regardless of actual "fault." All that needs to be shown for criminal liability to attach is that the sexual act occurred and that the female was under the age of consent. In many states, even if the woman lied about her age and consented to the sexual act, the male would still be found guilty. A judge, however, in sentencing the defendant, would take into consideration whether or not the male obtained consent and whether or not he was honestly mistaken about the victim's age.

Crimes against Property

Crimes against property are of particular importance since they are the likeliest to be encountered in the daily operation of any business.

Larceny.   Taking and carrying away the property of another without consent, or by consent fraudulently obtained, with the intent to steal it constitutes the crime of *larceny.*

> ➤ Annette borrows a company car overnight without permission. Bill, Annette's boss, discovers it missing and informs police. If police apprehend Annette before she has returned the automobile, can she be successfully prosecuted for larceny? No, since she did not take the car with the intent of stealing it. (She is, however, guilty of criminal trespass.)

Embezzlement.   *Embezzlement* is the conversion or improper use of another's property lawfully in one's possession. Embezzlement differs from larceny in that in embezzlement, the property is already in the possession of the wrongdoer, who abuses a position of trust by converting it to his own use. The following examples all involve embezzlement:

➤   1. Ariel, the comptroller for ABC Corporation, misdirects funds that he controls into a Swiss bank account.
      2. Marsha, a bank teller, takes $500 from her cash drawer and puts it in her pocket.
      3. Jack, a construction laborer, takes home a band saw with the intent to keep it.

Robbery.   *Robbery* is the taking of another's property by force or threat of force with the intent to permanently deprive its owner of it. In general, threats must be of physical harm to the person, her family, or any other person present.

➤   1. Larry lifts Philip's wallet from his pocket without Philip noticing, then walks away. Is he guilty of robbery? No, since there was no force or threat of force used. (Larry is guilty of larceny, however.)
      2. Henry tells Loretta, who is walking her daughter home from school, "If you don't give me $100, I'll see to it your daughter never makes it home from school today." Loretta gives him the $100. Is this an example of robbery? Yes. Here there is a clear implied threat of immediate force against Loretta's daughter if she does not comply with Henry's demand.
      3. Susan pulls out a knife and tells Marvin, "Give me your watch or I'll cut you." This is the most obvious example of robbery.

Extortion.   Obtaining property through the use of threats is *extortion,* commonly called blackmail. Although the crime is obviously similar to robbery, it is distinguished from it in that the threat need not be of physical harm, nor does it have to be an immediate threat. "If you don't pay me $1,000 a month from now on, I'll show your wife the pictures of you and your secretary at last month's convention" is an example of extortion. In some states, making the statement in and of itself constitutes the crime, while others require that property actually be turned over to the defendant by the person being extorted before the crime is complete.

Forgery.   Writing or altering any document that has legal significance is *forgery.* Thus, placing the signature of another on a check without the person's permission is, as everyone knows, forgery, since it alters a legal document (the check itself). But forgery is not limited to a fraudulent use of another's signature. All of the following examples constitute the crime of forgery, since they materially alter a legal document:

1. Changing the date in one's birth certificate.
2. Altering the amount a check is made out for.
3. Changing a contractual provision without the consent of the other contracting party.
4. Altering the date in one's driver's license.

Burglary.   At common law, the crime of *burglary* consisted of breaking and entering another's home at night with the intent of carrying out a serious crime inside. Today, it is not necessary in most states for the crime to occur at night nor for the structure to be a home. It is also sufficient for the intended crime to be a misdemeanor and not just a "serious crime." A modern definition of burglary would be *breaking and entering any structure with the intent to commit a crime inside.*

Any use of force to enter a building will suffice. Forcing a lock, breaking down a door, or just turning an unlocked doorknob will be enough to satisfy the requirement of a breaking.

➤ Irma picks a lock to a warehouse, then opens the door, enters, and beats up the security guard inside, who happens to be her boyfriend whom she recently learned has been cheating on her. She then leaves, not taking anything from the structure. Is she guilty of burglary? Yes. If her intention was to beat up the guard when she entered, the crime is complete as soon as she opened the door (pushing it in suffices) and entered the structure. It is immaterial that she did not intend to steal anything from inside—the crime she intended to commit was battery.

It is a common misconception that burglary is synonymous with "stealing something from a house." True, a person breaking and entering a home with the intention of committing the crime of larceny is guilty of burglary, but the intent to commit larceny is not necessary to have burglary present; breaking into any building with the intent to commit any crime therein will bring about criminal liability for burglary, a felony.

Arson.   The traditional common law definition of *arson*, a felony, is the malicious burning down of another's dwelling. The common law definition has been expanded today in most jurisdictions to include the malicious burning down of any structure belonging to another. Some jurisdictions have gone so far as to include personal property in the classification subject to arson, so that burning another's automobile or boat can be considered arson. Maliciously burning one's own home was not traditionally considered arson, but the lesser misdemeanor offense of *house burning.* Likewise, burning down one's home in order to collect insurance was not deemed arson at common law. Today, however, every state makes it a crime to commit arson of one's own or another's house to defraud an insurer.

Crimes against Judicial Procedure

The law tries to protect the integrity of the legal system by punishing behavior that seeks to undermine it. Perjury and bribery are two important crimes against the judicial process.

Perjury.   *Perjury,* a misdemeanor, consists of willfully and maliciously taking a false oath in regard to a material fact in a judicial proceeding. False information presented at trial as a result of a mistake will not give rise to the crime, nor will maliciously giving false testimony as to facts that do not affect some aspect of the judicial proceeding.

➤   1. Raymond, who is suing Martha for assault and battery, asks his friend José to testify on his behalf. José, who was out of state on business at the time of the incident, testifies that he saw the incident. He is guilty of perjury.

  2. If José truthfully testifies that he saw the incident in question take place but then lies under oath about Martha dying her hair and hating dogs, his testimony will not amount to perjury since Martha's natural hair color and feelings about canines are irrelevant.

Bribery.   Traditionally, *bribery* is defined as the corrupt payment or receipt of anything of value in return for official action. Today, many jurisdictions have expanded the common law definition to include people who are not public officials, such as business people and sports officials. Also, while bribery has traditionally been considered a misdemeanor, many state and federal statutes today have elevated this crime to a felony.

➤   1. Lorraine, the owner of a restaurant, offers the state's health inspector $2,000 to ignore several health code violations in her establishment. She is guilty of bribery in every state, since a public official is involved.

  2. Lorraine offers the umpire of her daughter's Little League baseball team $500 if he'll refrain from calling her out on strikes when she comes up to bat. She is guilty of bribery in only some states, since the umpire is not a public official.

Computer Crime

Personal computers have become indispensable business tools over the past decade. A relatively modest system purchased for business use and costing under $2,000 today offers far greater computing power and ease of use than the expensive and cumbersome minicomputers available 10 years ago. Like any tool, however, the computer can be used for good as well as evil purposes. Along with the benefits wrought by the ongoing computer revolution of the 1980s and 1990s, there has been a rise in the use of computers to assist in the commission of traditional crimes, and the age of electronic enlightenment has led to the commission of new crimes with the aid of this most versatile tool.

Definition of Computer Crime

Computer crime is defined as any crime accomplished through the use of a computer or special knowledge of computer technology. The mere fact that a computer is used as an incidence to the commission of a crime does not in and of itself make that crime fall within the definition of computer crime, as the following examples illustrate:

1. Jill, using a word processor, writes an extortion note demanding that the intended victim pay $100,000 in cash
2. John, a crooked accountant, uses a spreadsheet program to keep track of money he embezzles from his employer
3. Pete throws a computer through a plate glass window in order to enter a jewelry store and steal precious gems

None of the examples just cited constitutes a computer crime, since the use of a computer is merely incidental to the underlying crimes of extortion, embezzlement and burglary. In order to rise to the level of a computer crime, the crime must be such that it cannot be accomplished without the use of computer technology, or must be accomplished through the use of such technology.

Application of Existing Criminal Statutes

States and the federal government can use existing criminal statutes to punish the use of computers to perpetrate traditional crimes. Thus, where the mails or telephone lines are used in the perpetration of mail or wire fraud through the use of a computer, the wrongdoer can be prosecuted for these crimes without the need to use special legislation specifically aimed at computer crime.

➤ Harold, a computer hacker, dials up a neighbor's bank and electronically transfers $1,000 from his neighbor's checking account to his own savings account at the same bank. Since Harold has used his computer hooked up via modem through telephone lines to perpetrate his crime, he is guilty of wire fraud and also of larceny and can be prosecuted for both crimes under existing criminal law statutes.

Specific Legislation Concerning Computer Crime

Most states and the federal government have enacted specific criminal statutes to combat computer crime. At the federal level, two acts passed by congress are worthy of brief mention:

> **The Counterfeit Access Device and Computer Fraud and Abuse Act of 1984:** The act covers national defense, financial institutions, government computers and interstate commerce. It specifically prohibits the unauthorized use of computers to gain access to secret information that could compromise national security and prohibits unauthorized access to the computer records of financial institutions. The act also specifically prohibits access to computers used expressly by the federal government to conduct its business. The act also prohibits the transfer of information that will facilitate the unauthorized use of any computer with the intent to defraud when such a transfer of information affects interstate commerce. This last prohibition is the broadest and can serve as a catchall provision prohibiting the unauthorized access to computers in general, since almost any criminal access to computers used in business or government can arguably have some effect on interstate commerce.

Electronic Funds Transfer Act of 1979: This act makes it a federal offense to use any device involved in an electronic fund transfer to steal money, goods or services.

As the use of computers continues to proliferate, new legislation covering criminal use of computers and protecting sensitive data in government and private computerized databases is certain to be introduced. In the meantime, prosecutors and police will use existing legislation and increasingly sophisticated computer technology to apprehend and punish those who use computers to perpetrate crimes, while criminals continue to find new ways to manipulate the same technology to further their own ends.

Defenses to Criminal Liability

As previously noted, criminal liability requires two elements: (1) the commission of a prohibited act, or failure to act when one has a duty to act, and (2) a wrongful state of mind. Unless both elements are present in a given case, no criminal liability will arise. Unless the prosecutor convinces the trier of fact "beyond a reasonable doubt" that the defendant has met both elements, there can be no criminal conviction. The defense attorney at trial will try to disprove the existence of a criminal act by the defendant or, where it is clear that the act was committed, that the defendant lacked the required mental state to be guilty of a crime. In other words, the defendant's lawyer will try to show that either the defendant did not commit the criminal act or that, if he committed it, he was incapable of criminal intent. If she can succeed at either argument, the defendant will be acquitted.

Consider the following examples:

1. Before leaving work, Rita, an employee at Impressive Computer Company, picks up a $5,000 notebook-sized computer from her desk and places it in her attaché case. A security guard observes the behavior and follows her out of the building. As soon as she exits into the street, the guard apprehends her and holds her until police arrives.

2. Marianne, angered that she has been fired for stealing office supplies, marches into the office with an axe and chases her supervisor and the personnel director around the office for 20 minutes before being subdued by building security.

3. Harry, a precocious five-year-old child, sets fire to his parent's bed while they are asleep. He later tells firefighters and police that he wanted to punish his parents for refusing to buy him a new video game system.

Assuming that Rita is tried for larceny, Marianne for attempted murder, and Harry for arson, what defenses can each raise? All three can defend on grounds that they did not commit the act in question. Suppose there are plenty of reliable witnesses willing to testify that each in fact committed the acts with which they are charged. Would they have any other defense open to them? The answer for all three would be yes. Each would be able to claim that they did not have the required criminal intent. Rita could argue that she placed the computer in her attaché by mistake, not intending to steal it. Marianne might claim that she was temporarily insane—that the stress and grief of being fired made her lose control of her ability to tell right from wrong. Harry, of course, would be able to raise the defense of infancy—that he is too young to understand the difference between right and wrong. A five-year-old child is incapable of framing a criminal intent in the eyes of the law, regardless of how intelligent she or he may be.

Valid defenses to criminal culpability include insanity, intoxication, infancy, self-defense, defense of others, defense of property, and entrapment. A defendant who either admits or fails to refute that she has committed a criminal act will avoid criminal liability if she can assert one of the foregoing defenses.

Insanity

The *insanity* defense has received a great deal of bad press in recent years. The perception in many people's minds is that any criminal with a good lawyer can avoid criminal liability by pleading insanity. While the reality is, fortunately, not as bleak, there is undeniably an appreciable margin for abuse in this area due to the imprecise nature of psychiatry.

The basic premise of the insanity defense is a sound one: A person who is insane cannot form the criminal intent (or what is technically referred to as *scienter*) that is a prerequisite to criminal liability. States use a variety of tests for determining when a defendant's actions are exempt from criminal liability due to insanity:

M'Naughten Rule.   A defendant who suffers from a mental illness that prevented him at the time of the crime from either knowing the wrongfulness or understanding the nature of his actions will be excused from criminal liability. Under M'Naughten, it is not enough that a defendant may be suffering from mental illness; the test is whether such illness prevents him from understanding that his actions are wrong.

> Rafael suffers from a mental illness that causes him to honestly believe that all left-handed people are unworthy of life. As a result, every time he encounters left-handed persons, he follows an irresistible impulse to kill them. If at trial it is found that he understands murder to be wrong, and that he has committed murder, the fact that he acted under a delusion will not excuse his conduct.

Irresistible Impulse Test.   A person who establishes that he acted as a result of an irresistible impulse due to mental illness is entitled to acquittal.

> In a jurisdiction that follows the irresistible impulse test, Rafael would not be found guilty of murdering a left-handed person in the previous example as long as he established that, due to his mental illness, he felt an irresistible need or impulse to kill all left-handed people. Unlike the M'Naughten rule, the irresistible impulse test excuses criminal conduct even if the mentally ill person understands that his actions were illegal and wrong but simply "could not help himself."

New Hampshire Rule.   Under the New Hampshire Rule, also known as the Durham Rule, a court cannot find a defendant criminally liable if she establishes that her crime was a product of a mental defect or disease. For a crime to be the product of mental illness, the defense must show that the defendant would not have committed the crime but for the mental illness. This is a much broader test than either the M'Naughten or the irresistible impulse tests, and very few jurisdictions currently use it.

Model Penal Code Test.   The model penal code test, adopted by the American Law Institute, excuses criminal conduct if the defendant suffers from a mental disease or defect that prevents him from recognizing the wrongfulness of his conduct or prevents him from conforming his conduct to the requirements of the law. This, the most commonly used test of insanity today, essentially combines the M'Naughten and irresistible impulse theories.

Under all of the above tests, the mental defect or illness must have existed at the time of the criminal act in question. The court generally institutionalizes defendants acquitted by reason of insanity in some type of long-term mental health facility until such time as they can prove to the satisfaction of a judge that they have been cured of the mental defect.

Intoxication

The defense of *intoxication* is very similar to that of insanity. In essence, persons intoxicated to such an extent that they cannot understand the nature of their actions cannot be found guilty of a crime, since they are unable to frame the necessary criminal intent. Intoxication can arise from a variety of sources, including the use of alcohol, medication, or illicit drugs.

Intoxication can be either voluntary or involuntary. Voluntary intoxication results when someone intentionally uses an intoxicating substance, while involuntary intoxication can result from a mistake (such as taking a hallucinogenic drug believing it to be aspirin), by trick (such as drinking from a glass into which someone has surreptitiously slipped an intoxicating substance), or by force (such as being forced to drink a bottle of brandy at gunpoint). Involuntary intoxication is treated exactly as insanity and measured by whatever rule the jurisdiction employs. Voluntary intoxication, on the other hand, is treated somewhat differently depending on the nature of the offense—it is treated the same as insanity when the offense requires the presence of criminal intent, such as murder; but is not a defense for crimes involving negligence, recklessness, or strict liability.

➤ Kim knowingly drinks a dozen tequila sunrises. She becomes so intoxicated she loses the ability to tell right from wrong. When her friend Sandy rings the doorbell, she answers it and then plunges a butcher knife into the unsuspecting woman, killing her. Then feeling a bit queasy, she decides to drive to the nearest drugstore to buy some stomach-relieving medicine. She is found several hours later fast asleep in the middle of a busy intersection and is arrested for driving while intoxicated, a felony in her state. She will be able to successfully raise the defense of intoxication with regard to her friend's stabbing, since she will be deemed to have been incapable of framing the required intent for murder. But she will not be able to defend against the driving-while-intoxicated charge, since it is a strict liability offense. Had she been involuntarily intoxicated, she would not have been found guilty of either offense.

Infancy

As previously noted, *infancy* can be a defense to criminal liability. Under traditional common law, a child under the age of 7 was deemed incapable of framing the necessary intent to commit a crime; one between 7 and 14 was presumed to be incapable of framing the intent to commit a crime (a prosecutor could overcome the presumption in a given case by showing that the child in fact did understand the difference between right and wrong and intentionally engaged in a criminal act); and a child over 14 was treated the same as an adult. Many states today retain the common law rule, while others have adopted statutes that specify the age at which a child will be deemed capable of committing a crime (usually 13 or 14).

Whether a state retains the traditional common law rule or has adopted a different age standard for criminal responsibility, all states today have enacted some type of juvenile delinquency laws. The state's family court often handles cases involving minors who commit offenses while they are too young to be tried for crimes. Such courts have the power to waive their jurisdiction over a child's case and allow the child to be treated as an adult. Some jurisdictions permit some children to be charged as adults in cases of serious crimes such as murder and rape.

Self-Defense

A person may use reasonable force to protect himself against another's aggression, so long as such aggression was not initiated or provoked by him. For the defense of *self-defense* to be available, the defendant must have responded to physical aggression or the reasonable threat of aggression. If faced with imminent death or risk of serious bodily harm, a person is justified to use any force, including deadly physical force (defined as that likely to cause death). A person defending himself from the use of force that is not likely to result in death or serious bodily harm may never use deadly physical force.

➤ Roseanne, without provocation, punches and kicks Julian repeatedly. Julian punches her back, breaking her jaw in the process. Julian cannot be be sued successfully for the tort of battery, nor is he guilty of the crime of battery, since he was using reasonable force to defend himself from an unprovoked attack. Would the answer be the same if Julian shot Roseanne after she slapped him across the face without provocation? No, since the use of deadly force (shooting the gun) under the circumstances was not warranted. Even though the attack was unprovoked and Julian is entitled to defend himself using reasonable force, shooting Roseanne is not reasonable force when her attack did not threaten him with serious injury.

It should be noted that people have an absolute right to protect themselves against intrusion in their homes and that cases involving the use of deadly force in defense of one's home are almost always deemed justified. One's right to protect one's home and loved ones is nearly sacred.

Defense of Others

In general, a person who comes to the assistance of a victim of a crime has the right to use as much force as the victim himself can use under the circumstances. A person who aids the victim of a crime, then, is not subject to civil or criminal liability for injuries caused to the victim's attacker, as long as the victim herself had the right to inflict such injuries in self-defense.

> Harry is being robbed at gunpoint by Joe. Maria, who happens by the scene, sees the robbery taking place and strikes Joe with her mahogany cane, cracking his skull and killing him instantly. Maria is guilty of no crime, since in coming to Harry's assistance, she is entitled to use as much force as Harry himself could use under the circumstances. Harry, in this case, could use any force including deadly force to fend off the armed robbery attempt; Maria, in coming to his assistance, has the same right to use force as Harry himself and is therefore justified in killing Joe.

Problems arise when, as is often the case, things are not what they seem. Consider the following example:

> Marlene, dressed as a police officer, attempts to hold up a convenience store clerk. Isaac, an undercover police officer dressed in dirty, tattered clothing, wrestles the gun away from her, identifies himself as a police officer, and orders her to raise her hands. She kicks him in the midsection and runs out, screaming for help; he follows her out the door, yelling at her to stop while waving her gun in the air. Angelina, a passerby, sees what appears to be a police officer being chased by a vagrant and shoots Isaac with her licensed handgun.

In the above example, the fate of Angelina will vary from state to state. In some jurisdictions, a person who comes to the assistance of another is held to "stand in that person's shoes," and has exactly as much right to use force as the apparent victim had under the circumstances. If this is the rule in the state where the above facts took place, then Angelina is in trouble; she will have exactly no more right to use force in Marlene's defense than Marlene had. Since Marlene was a criminal escaping from justice, she had no right to defend herself from Isaac; Angelina, therefore, also had no right to use any force, let alone deadly force, against Isaac. As a result, Marlene will be guilty of intentional manslaughter (she will not be guilty of murder since she lacked the requisite criminal intent to wrongfully deprive Isaac of life). This may seem unfair, but it serves as a warning that in a significant number of jurisdictions, before prematurely rushing to someone's rescue, one had better be sure that the apparent victim is, in fact, a victim of another's unlawful aggression.

In a majority of jurisdictions, however, a person who tries to prevent what appears to be a crime will not be guilty of a crime so long as she reasonably believed that the other was the victim of a crime.

Defense of Property

A person may defend his property by using reasonable force short of deadly force. One is never justified in using deadly force when the only purpose is to protect property. The law will not sanction the taking of a human life merely to prevent larceny or trespass.

➤ Nelya catches Thomas in the act of stealing her radio from her car. She runs to get her husband's 12-gauge shotgun and shoots him. The killing is unjustified since it represents the taking of a life merely to protect property. If, however, she tells Thomas to get out of the car slowly and he quickly reaches into his inside breast pocket, she will most probably be justified in shooting him, since she would be acting not only to protect her property but also herself if he reasonably appeared to be reaching for a hidden weapon.

Entrapment

Undercover sting operations have been much in the news in recent years and have netted some prominent politicians engaged in a variety of illegal acts, including the use of illegal drugs, soliciting sex, and influence peddling. In many of these cases, as well as the less-publicized daily arrests of drug dealers who sell drugs to undercover law enforcement officers, the defense of *entrapment* is often raised. To raise such a defense, a defendant must prove that the law enforcement official convinced or manipulated him into committing the crime and that he was not otherwise predisposed to commit the crime.

➤ An undercover police officer poses as a drug dealer and stands in a street corner in an area known for drug activity. He offers crack cocaine to passersby and arrests everyone who attempts to buy drugs from him. Roselinda buys a vial of crack and is arrested. She defends on grounds of entrapment. Will she succeed? No. Even though the police officer offered her the drugs, there is no evidence that he convinced or manipulated her into the illicit purchase. Under the facts given, it is clear that she was predisposed to purchase the drugs and would have bought them from someone else had the police officer not offered them. Merely giving the defendant the opportunity to commit a crime is not wrongful conduct by police and will not constitute entrapment.

Successful entrapment defenses usually result from overzealous law enforcement officials who convince a hesitant defendant to commit a criminal act. If the jury feels the defendant would not have committed the act but for the pressure exerted by police, it will acquit on grounds of undue influence.

➤ Marcia, a secretary with no history of criminal activity, is approached by Shawn, a new employee, and asked if she would be interested in earning some extra cash by selling him office supplies that she purchases with company funds. She refuses and threatens to tell her boss. But Shawn persists and, upon his 20th proposal to the same effect, convinces her that the company would not miss the extra supplies, that there is no way for her to get caught, and that she is grossly underpaid for the job she does and the taking of the supplies would only be a sort of raise to which she is entitled. She finally agrees, and when she turns over $25 worth of office supplies to him, he arrests her, explaining that he is an undercover police officer who has been investigating a rash of recent reported thefts at the company. If she is prosecuted for embezzlement, Marcia will be able to successfully raise the defense of entrapment. It is clear from the facts given that she was not predisposed to commit the crime and would not have committed it but for the pressure exerted by the police officer.

Judge for Yourself

Case 1. Ines comes home early from work one afternoon and finds her husband, Darren, in bed with her best friend, Rita. In a fit of rage, she runs to the kitchen, grabs a butcher knife, and stabs Darren and Rita repeatedly. Darren dies immediately, and Rita suffers serious injuries requiring hospitalization. Answer the following questions relating to this case:

a. Will Ines be found guilty of murder? Why?

b. Will Ines be found guilty of intentional manslaughter? Why?

c. With regard to Rita's injuries, will Ines be found guilty of attempted murder? Of attempted manslaughter? Of battery?

d. Can Ines defend herself under a theory of self-defense? How about a theory of defense of others? Might she be able to raise an insanity defense? Is she likely to succeed under an insanity theory? Would it make a difference if Rita were her eight-year-old daughter, instead of her best friend? How?

Case 2. Change the facts in Case 1 as follows: Rita is 17 years old, and the age of consent in this state is 18. To a reasonable person, however, she looked at least 25 years old. Darren shot Ines to death with a licensed handgun when she lunged at him with the butcher knife.

  a. Is Darren guilty of murder?

  b. Is Darren guilty of manslaughter?

  c. If Darren is prosecuted for murder, will he have a valid defense?

  d. If Darren is prosecuted for statutory rape, will he have a valid defense?

Case 3. William, without provocation, slaps Mary. Mary punches and kicks him to the ground. William, angered by her spirited reaction, takes out a gun and shoots at Mary, missing her. A policewoman who happens to be passing by arrests both. William is charged with criminal battery and attempted murder; Mary is charged with criminal battery. Are Mary and William guilty of the crimes they are charged with? Explain.

CASE STUDY 1-1
FREEDOM OF SPEECH

UNITED STATES, APPELLANT v. SHAWN D. EICHMAN, DAVID GERALD BLALOCK AND SCOTT W. TYLER; UNITED STATES, APPELLANT v. MARK JOHN HAGGERTY, CARLOS GARZA, JENNIFER PROCTER CAMPBELL AND DARIUS ALLEN STRONG

Nos. 89–1433, 89–1434

SUPREME COURT OF THE UNITED STATES

110 S. Ct. 2404; 1990 U.S. LEXIS 3087; 110 L. Ed. 2d 287; 58 U.S.L.W. 4744

May 14, 1990, Argued
June 11, 1990, Decided*
*Together with No. 89–1434, United States v. Haggerty et al., on appeal from the District Court for the Western District of Washington.

PRIOR HISTORY:

ON APPEAL FROM THE UNITED STATES DISTRICT COURT FOR THE DISTRICT OF COLUMBIA.

ON APPEAL FROM THE UNITED STATES DISTRICT COURT FOR THE WESTERN DISTRICT OF WASHINGTON.

DISPOSITION: No. 89–1433, 731 F. Supp. 1123; No. 89–1434, . . . F. Supp. . . . affirmed.

JUDGES: Brennan, J., delivered the opinion of the court, in which Marshall, Blackmun, Scalia, and Kennedy, JJ., joined. Stevens, J., filed a dissenting opinion, in which Rehnquist, C. J., and White and O'Connor, JJ., joined.

OPINION: In these consolidated appeals, we consider whether appellees' prosecution for burning a United States flag in violation of the Flag Protection Act of 1989 is consistent with the First Amendment. Applying our recent decision in Texas v. Johnson, 491 U.S. . . . (1989), the District Courts held that the Act cannot constitutionally be applied to appellees. We affirm.

I.

In No. 89–1433, the United States prosecuted certain appellees for violating the Flag Protection Act of 1989, 103 Stat. 777, 18 U.S.C.A. § 700 (Supp. 1990), by knowingly setting fire to several United States flags on the steps of the United States Capitol while protesting various aspects of the Government's domestic and foreign policy. In No. 89–1434, the United States prosecuted other appellees for violating the Act by knowingly setting fire to a United States flag while protesting the Act's passage. In each case, the respective appellees moved to dismiss the flag-burning charge on the ground that the Act, both on its face and as applied, violates the First Amendment. Both the United States District Court for the Western District of Washington, F. Supp. (1990), and the United States District Court for the District of Columbia, 731 F. Supp. 1123 (1990), following Johnson, supra, held the Act unconstitutional as applied to appellees and dismissed the charges.[1] The United States appealed both decisions directly to this Court pursuant to 18 U.S.C.A. § 700(d) (Supp. 1990).[2] We noted probable jurisdiction and consolidated the two cases. 494 U.S. (1990).

II.

Last Term in Johnson, we held that a Texas statute criminalizing the desecration of venerated objects, including the United States flag, was unconstitutional as applied to an individual who had set such a flag on fire during a political demonstration. The Texas statute provided that "[a] person commits an offense if he intentionally or knowingly desecrates . . . [a] national flag," where "desecrate" meant to "deface, damage, or otherwise physically mistreat in a way that the actor knows will seriously offend one or more persons likely to observe or discover his action." Tex. Penal Code Ann. § 42.09 (1989). We first held that Johnson's flag-burning was "conduct 'sufficiently imbued with elements of communication' to implicate the First Amendment." 491 U.S., at . . . (citation omitted). We next considered and rejected the State's contention that, under United States v. O'Brien, 391 U.S. 367 (1968), we ought to apply the deferential standard with which we have reviewed Government regulations of conduct containing both speech and nonspeech elements where "the governmental interest is unrelated to the suppression of free expression." Id., at 377. We reasoned that the State's asserted interest "in preserving the flag as a symbol of nationhood and national unity," was an interest "related 'to the suppression of free expression' within the meaning of O'Brien" because the State's concern with protecting the flag's symbolic meaning is implicated "only when a person's treatment of the flag communicates some message." Johnson, supra, at . . . . We therefore subjected the statute to " 'the most exacting scrutiny,' " id., at . . ., quoting Boos v. Barry, 485 U.S. 312, 321 (1988), and we concluded that the State's asserted interests could not justify the infringement on the demonstrator's First Amendment rights.

After our decision in Johnson, Congress passed the Flag Protection Act of 1989.[3] The Act provides in relevant part:

"(a) (1) Whoever knowingly mutilates, defaces, physically defiles, burns, maintains on the floor or ground, or tramples upon any flag of the United States shall be fined under this title or imprisoned for not more than one year, or both.

"(2) This subsection does not prohibit any conduct consisting of the disposal of a flag when it has become worn or soiled.

"(b) As used in this section, the term 'flag of the United States' means any flag of the United States, or any part thereof, made of any substance, of any size, in a form that is commonly displayed." 18 U.S.C.A. § 700 (Supp. 1990).

The Government concedes in this case, as it must, that appellees' flag-burning constituted expressive conduct, Brief for United States 28; . . ., but invites us to reconsider our rejection in Johnson of the claim that flag-burning as a mode of expression, like obscenity or "fighting words," does not enjoy the full protection of the First Amendment. Cf. Chaplinsky v. New Hampshire, 315 U.S. 568, 572 (1942). This we decline to do.[4] The only remaining question is whether the Flag Protection Act is sufficiently distinct from the Texas statute that it may constitutionally be applied to proscribe appellees' expressive conduct.

The Government contends that the Flag Protection Act is constitutional because, unlike the statute addressed in Johnson, the Act does not target expressive conduct on the basis of the content of its message. The Government asserts an interest in "protect[ing] the physical integrity of the flag under all circumstances" in order to safeguard the flag's identity " 'as the unique and unalloyed symbol of the Nation.' " Brief for United States 28, 29. The Act proscribes conduct (other than disposal) that damages or mistreats a flag, without regard to the actor's motive, his intended message, or the likely effects of his conduct on onlookers. By contrast, the Texas statute expressly prohibited only those acts of physical flag desecration "that the actor knows those acts of desecration that "cas[t] contempt upon" the flag.

Although the Flag Protection Act contains no explicit contest-based limitation on the scope of prohibited conduct, it is nevertheless clear that the Government's asserted interest is "related 'to the suppression of free expression,' " 491 U.S., at . . ., and concerned with the content of such expression. The Government's interest in protecting the "physical integrity" of a privately owned flag[5] rests upon a perceived need to preserve the flag's status as a symbol of our Nation and certain national ideals. But the mere destruction or disfigurement of a particular physical manifestation of the symbol, without more, does not diminish or otherwise affect the symbol itself in any way. For example, the secret destruction of a flag in one's own basement would not threaten the flag's recognized meaning. Rather, the Government's desire to preserve the flag as a symbol for certain national ideals is implicated "only when a person's treatment of the flag communicates [a] message" to others that is inconsistent with those ideals.[6] Id.

Moreover, the precise language of the Act's prohibitions confirms Congress' interest in the communicative impact of flag destruction. The Act criminalizes the conduct of anyone who "knowingly mutilates, defaces, physically defiles, burns, maintains on the floor or ground, or tramples upon any flag." 18 U.S.C.A. § 700(a) (1) (Supp. 1990). Each of the specified terms—with the possible exception of "burns"—unmistakably connotes disrespectful treatment of the flag and suggests a focus on those acts likely to damage the flag's symbolic value.[7] And the explicit exemption in § 700(a)(2) for disposal of "worn or soiled" flags protects certain acts traditionally associated with patriotic respect for the flag.[8]

As we explained in Johnson, . . .: "[I]f we were to hold that a State may forbid flag-burning wherever it is likely to endanger the flag's symbolic role, but allow it wherever burning a flag promotes that role—as where, for example, a person ceremoniously burns a dirty flag—we would be . . . may burn the flag to convey one's attitude toward it and its referents only if one does not endanger the flag's representation of nationhood and national unity." Although Congress cast the Flag Protection Act in somewhat broader terms than the Texas statute at issue in Johnson, the Act still suffers from the same fundamental flaw: it suppresses expression out of concern for its likely communicative impact. Despite the Act's wider scope, its restriction on expression cannot be "justified without reference to the content of the regulated speech." Boos, 485 U.S., at 320 (citation omitted); see Spence v. Washington, 418 U.S. 405, 414, nn. 8, 9 (1974) (State's interest in protecting the flag's symbolic value is directly related to suppression of expression and thus O'Brien test is inapplicable even where statute declared "simply . . . that nothing may be affixed to or superimposed on a United States flag"). The Act therefore must be subjected to "the most exacting scrutiny," Boos, supra, at 321, and for the reasons stated in Johnson, supra, at the Government's interest cannot justify its infringement on First Amendment rights. We decline the Government's invitation to reassess this conclusion in light of Congress' recent recognition of a purported "national consensus" favoring a prohibition on flag-burning. Brief for United States 27. Even assuming such a consensus exists, any suggestion that the Government's interest in suppressing speech becomes more weighty as popular opposition to that speech grows is foreign to the First Amendment.

III.

" 'National unity as an end which officials may foster by persuasion and example is not in question.' " Johnson, . . ., quoting West Virginia Board of Education v. Barnette, 319 U.S. 624, 640 (1943). Government may create national symbols, promote them, and encourage their respectful treatment.[9] But the Flag Protection Act goes well beyond this by criminally proscribing expressive conduct because of its likely communicative impact.

We are aware that desecration of the flag is deeply offensive to many. But the same might be said, for example, of virulent ethnic and religious epithets, see Terminiello v. Chicago, 337 U.S. 1 (1949), vulgar repudiations of the draft, see Cohen v. California, 403 U.S. 15 (1971), and scurrilous caricatures, see

Hustler Magazine, Inc. v. Falwell, 485 U.S. 46 (1988). "If there is a bedrock principle underlying the First Amendment, it is that the Government may not prohibit the expression of an idea simply because society finds the idea itself offensive or disagreeable." Johnson, supra, at. Punishing desecration of the flag dilutes the very freedom that makes this emblem so revered, and worth revering. The judgments are Affirmed.

DISSENT: JUSTICE STEVENS, with whom THE CHIEF JUSTICE, JUSTICE WHITE and JUSTICE O'CONNOR join, dissenting.

The Court's opinion ends where proper analysis of the issue should begin. Of course "the Government may not prohibit the expression of an idea simply because society finds the idea itself offensive or disagreeable." Ante, at 7. None of us disagrees with that proposition. But it is equally well settled that certain methods of expression may be prohibited if (a) the prohibition is supported by a legitimate societal interest that is unrelated to suppression of the ideas the speaker desires to express; (b) the prohibition does not entail any interference with the speaker's freedom to express those ideas by other means; and (c) the interest in allowing the speaker complete freedom of choice among alternative methods of expression is less important than the societal interest supporting the prohibition.

Contrary to the position taken by counsel for the flag burners in Texas v. Johnson, 491 U.S. . . . (1989), it is now conceded that the Federal Government has a legitimate interest in protecting the symbolic value of the American flag. Obviously that value cannot be measured, or even described, with any precision. It has at least these two components: in times of national crisis, it inspires and motivates the average citizen to make personal sacrifices in order to achieve societal goals of overriding importance; at all times, it serves as a reminder of the paramount importance of pursuing the ideals that characterize our society.

The first question the Court should consider is whether the interest in preserving the value of that symbol is unrelated to suppression of the ideas that flag burners are trying to express. In my judgment the answer depends, at least in part, on what those ideas are. A flag burner might intend various messages. The flag burner may wish simply to convey hatred, contempt, or sheer opposition directed at the United States. This might be the case if the flag were burned by an enemy during time of war. A flag burner may also, or instead, seek to convey the depth of his personal conviction about some issue, by willingly provoking the use of force against himself. In so doing, he says that "my disagreement with certain policies is so strong that I am prepared to risk physical harm (and perhaps imprisonment) in order to call attention to my views." This second possibility apparently describes the expressive conduct of the flag burners in these cases. Like the protesters who dramatized their opposition to our engagement in Vietnam by publicly burning their draft cards—and who were punished for doing so—their expressive conduct is consistent with affection for this country and respect for the ideals that the flag symbolizes. There is at least one further possibility: a flag burner may intend to make an accusation against the integrity of the American people who disagree with him. By burning the embodiment of America's collective commitment to freedom and equality, the flag burner charges that the majority has forsaken that commitment—that continued respect for the flag is nothing more than hypocrisy. Such a charge may be made even if the flag burner loves the country and zealously pursues the ideals that the country claims to honor.

The idea expressed by a particular act of flag burning is necessarily dependent on the temporal and political context in which it occurs. In the 1960s it may have expressed opposition to the country's Vietnam policies, or at least to the compulsory draft. In Texas v. Johnson, it apparently expressed opposition to the platform of the Republican Party. In these cases, the respondents have explained that it expressed their opposition to racial discrimination, to the failure to care for the homeless, and of course to statutory prohibitions of flag burning. In any of these examples, the protestors may wish both to say that their own position is the only one faithful to liberty and equality, and to accuse their fellow citizens of hypocritical indifference to—or even of a selfish departure from—the ideals which the flag is supposed to symbolize. The ideas expressed by flag burners are thus various and often ambiguous.

The Government's legitimate interest in preserving the symbolic value of the flag is, however, essentially the same regardless of which of many different ideas may have motivated a particular act of flag burning. As I explained in my dissent in Johnson, 491 U.S., at . . ., the flag uniquely symbolizes that ideas of liberty, equality, and tolerance—ideas that Americans have passionately defended and debated throughout our history. The flag embodies the spirit of our national commitment to those ideals. The message thereby transmitted does not take a stand upon our disagreements, except to say that those disagreements are best regarded as competing interpretations of shared ideals. It does not judge particular policies, except to say that they command respect when they are enlightened by the spirit of liberty and equality. To the world, the flag is our promise that we will continue to strive for these ideals. To us, the flag is a reminder both that the struggle for liberty and equality is unceasing, and that our obligation of tolerance and respect for all of our fellow citizens encompasses those who disagree with us—indeed, even those whose ideas are disagreeable or offensive.

Thus, the Government may—indeed, it should—protect the symbolic value of the flag without regard to the specific content of the flag burner's speech. The prosecution in this case does not depend upon the object of the defendants' protest. It is, moreover, equally clear that the prohibition does not entail any interference with the speaker's freedom to express his or her ideals by other means. It may well be true that other means of expression may be less effective in drawing attention to those ideas, but that is not itself a sufficient reason for immunizing flag burning. Presumably a gigantic fireworks display or a parade of nude models in a public park might draw even more attention to a controversial message, but such methods of expression are nevertheless subject to regulation.

This case therefore comes down to a question of judgment. Does the admittedly important interest in allowing every speaker to choose the method of expressing his or her ideas that he or she deems most effective and appropriate outweigh the societal interest in preserving the symbolic value of the flag?

This question, in turn, involves three different judgments: (1) The importance of the individual interest in selecting the preferred means of communication; (2) the importance of the national symbol; and (3) the question whether tolerance of flag burning will enhance or tarnish that value. The opinions in Texas v. Johnson demonstrate that reasonable judges may differ with respect to each of these judgments.

The individual interest is unquestionably a matter of great importance. Indeed, it is one of the critical components of the idea of liberty that the flag itself is intended to symbolize. Moreover, it is buttressed by the societal interest in being alerted to the need for thoughtful response to voices that might otherwise go unheard. The freedom of expression protected by the First Amendment embraces not only the freedom to communicate particular ideas, but also the right to communicate them effectively. That right, however, is not absolute—the communicative value of a well-placed bomb in the Capitol does not entitle it to the protection of the First Amendment.

Burning a flag is not, of course, equivalent to burning a public building. Assuming that the protester is burning his own flag, it causes no physical harm to other persons or to their property. The impact is purely symbolic, and it is apparent that some thoughtful persons believe that impact, far from depreciating the value of the symbol, will actually enhance its meaning. I most respectfully disagree. Indeed, what makes this case particularly difficult for me is what I regard as the damage to the symbol that has already occurred as a result of this Court's decision to place its stamp of approval on the act of flag burning. A formerly dramatic expression of protest is now rather commonplace. In today's marketplace of ideas, the public burning of a Vietnam draft card is probably less provocative than lighting a cigarette. Tomorrow flag burning may produce a similar reaction. There is surely a direct relationship between the communicative value of the act of flag burning and the symbolic value of the object being burned.

The symbolic value of the American flag is not the same today as it was yesterday. Events during the last three decades have altered the country's image in the eyes of numerous Americans, and some now have difficulty understanding the message that the flag conveyed to their parents and grandparents—whether born abroad and naturalized or native born. Moreover, the integrity of the symbol has been compromised by those leaders who seem to advocate compulsory manipulate the symbol of national purpose into a pretext for partisan disputes about meaner ends. And, as I have suggested, the residual value of the symbol after this Court's decision in Texas v. Johnson is surely not the same as it was a year ago.

Given all these considerations, plus the fact that the Court today is really doing nothing more than reconfirming what it has already decided, it might be appropriate to defer to the judgment of the majority and merely apply the doctrine of stare decisis to the case at hand. That action, however, would not honestly reflect my considered judgment concerning the relative importance of the conflicting interests that are at stake. I remain persuaded that the considerations identified in my opinion in Texas v. Johnson are of controlling importance in this case as well.

Accordingly, I respectfully dissent.

Questions for Case Study 1–1
1. What are the basic facts of the case?
2. What are the most important issues in this case?
3. What is the decision of the court?
4. What is the dissenting opinion of the court?
5. Discuss whether you agree with the majority's opinion or with the dissent.

Footnotes
1. The Seattle appellees were also charged with causing willful injury to federal property in violationof 18 U.S.C. §§ 1361 and 1362. This charge remains pending before the District Court, and nothing in today's decision affects the constitutionality of this prosecution. See n. 5, infra.
2. (1) An appeal may be taken directly to the Supreme Court of the United States from any interlocutory or final judgment, decree, or order issued by a United States district court ruling upon the constitutionality of subsection (a).
   "(2) The Supreme Court shall, if it has not previously ruled on the question, accept jurisdiction over the appeal and advance on the docket and expedite to the greatest extent possible." 18 U.S.C.A. § 700(d) (Supp. 1990).
3. The Act replaced the then-existing federal flag-burning statute, which Congress perceived might be unconstitutional in light of Johnson, Former 18 U.S.C. § 700(a) prohibited "knowingly cast[ing] contempt upon any flag of the United States by publicly mutilating, defacing, defiling, burning, or trampling upon it."
4. We deal here with concededly political speech and have no occasion to pass on the validity of laws regulating commercial exploitation of the image of the United States flag. See Texas v. Johnson, 491 U.S. n. 10 (1989); of, Walter v. Nebraska, 205 U.S. 34 (1907).
5. Today's decision does not affect the extent to which the Government's interest in protecting publicly owned flags might justify special measures on their behalf. See Spence v. Washington, 418 U.S. 405, 408–409 (1974); cf, Johnson, supra at n. 8.
6. Aside from the flag's association with particular ideals, at some irreducible level the flag is emblematic of the Nation as a sovereign entity. Appellant's amicus asserts that the Government has a legitimate non–speech-related interest in safeguarding this "eminently practical legal aspect of the flag, as an incident of sovereignty." Brief for the Speaker and the Leadership Group of the United States House of Representatives [as] Amicus Curiae 25. This interest has firm historical roots: "While the symbolic role of the flag is now well-established, the flag was an important incident of sovereignty before it was used for symbolic purposes by patriots and others. When the nation's founders first determined to adopt a national flag, they intended to serve specific functions relating to our statute as a sovereign nation." Id., at 9; see id., at 5 (noting "flag's 'historic function' for such sovereign purposes as marking 'our national presence in schools, public buildings, battleships and airplanes' ") (citation omitted).

   We concede that the Government has a legitimate interest in preserving the flag's function as an "incident of sovereignty," though we need not address today the extent to which this interest may justify any laws regulating conduct that would thwart this core function, as might a commercial or like appropriation of the image of the United States flag. Amicus does not, and cannot, explain how a statute that penalizes anyone who knowingly burns, mutilates, or defiles any

American flag is designed to advance this asserted interest in maintaining the association between the flag and the Nation. Burning a flag does not threaten to interfere with this association in any way; indeed, the flag-burner's message depends in part on the viewer's ability to make this.

7. For example, "defile" is defined as "to make filthy; to corrupt the purity or perfection of; to rob of chastity; to make ceremonially unclean; tarnish; dishonor." Webster's Third New International Dictionary 592 (1976). "Trample" is defined as "to tread heavily so as to bruise, crush, or injure; to inflict injury or destruction; have a contemptuous or ruthless attitude." Id., at 2425.

8. The Act also does not prohibit flying a flag in a storm or other conduct that threatens the physical integrity of the flag, albeit in an indirect manner unlikely to communicate disrespect.

9. See, e.g., 36 U.S.C. §§ 173–177 (suggesting manner in which flag ought to be displayed).

Case Study 1-2
Criminal Law

The People of the State of New York, Appellant, v. Bernhard
Goetz, Respondent

Court of Appeals of New York

68 N.Y.2d 96; 497 N.E.2d 41; 506 N.Y.S.2d 18

May 28, 1986, Argued July 8, 1986, Decided

COUNSEL: Robert M. Morgenthau, District Attorney (Robert M. Pitler, Mark Dwyer and Gregory L. Waples of counsel), for appellant. Mark M. Baker, Barry Ivan Slotnick and Michael Shapiro for respondent.

JUDGES: Chief Judge Wachtler. Judges Meyer, Simons, Kaye, Alexander, Titone and Hancock, Jr., concur.

A Grand Jury has indicted defendant on attempted murder, assault, and other charges for having shot and wounded four youths on a New York City subway train after one or two of the youths approached him and asked for $5. The lower courts, concluding that the prosecutor's charge to the Grand Jury on the defense of justification was erroneous, have dismissed the attempted murder, assault and weapons possession charges. We now reverse and reinstate all counts of the indictment.

I.

The precise circumstances of the incident giving rise to the charges against defendant are disputed, and ultimately it will be for a trial jury to determine what occurred. We feel it necessary, however, to provide some factual background to properly frame the legal issues before us. Accordingly, we have summarized the facts as they appear from the evidence before the Grand Jury. We stress, however, that we do not purport to reach any conclusions or holding as to exactly what transpired or whether defendant is blameworthy. The credibility of witnesses and the reasonableness of defendant's conduct are to be resolved by the trial jury.

On Saturday afternoon, December 22, 1984, Troy Canty, Darryl Cabey, James Ramseur, and Barry Allen boarded an IRT express subway train in the Bronx and headed south toward lower Manhattan. The four youths rode together in the rear portion of the seventh car of the train. Two of the four, Ramseur and Cabey, had screwdrivers inside their coats, which they said were to be used to break into the coin boxes of video machines.

Defendant Bernhard Goetz boarded this subway train at 14th Street in Manhattan and sat down on a bench towards the rear section of the same car occupied by the four youths. Goetz was carrying an unlicensed .38 caliber pistol loaded with five rounds of ammunition in a waistband holster. The train left the 14th Street station and headed towards Chambers Street.

It appears from the evidence before the Grand Jury that Canty approached Goetz, possibly with Allen beside him, and stated "give me five dollars." Neither Canty nor any of the other youths displayed a weapon. Goetz responded by standing up, pulling out his handgun and firing four shots in rapid succession. The first shot hit Canty in the chest; the second struck Allen in the back; the third went through Ramseur's arm and into his left side; the fourth was fired at Cabey, who apparently was then standing in the corner of the car, but missed, deflecting instead off of a wall of the conductor's cab. After Goetz briefly surveyed the scene around him, he fired another shot at Cabey, who then was sitting on the end bench of the car. The bullet entered the rear of Cabey's side and severed his spinal cord.

All but two of the other passengers fled the car when, or immediately after, the shots were fired. The conductor, who had been in the next car, heard the shots and instructed the motorman to radio for emergency assistance. The conductor then went into the car where the shooting occurred and saw Goetz sitting on a bench, the injured youths lying on the floor or slumped against a seat, and two women who had apparently taken cover, also lying on the floor. Goetz told the conductor that the four youths had tried to rob him.

While the conductor was aiding the youths, Goetz headed towards the front of the car. The train had stopped just before the Chambers Street station and Goetz went between two of the cars, jumped onto the tracks and fled. Police and ambulance crews arrived at the scene shortly thereafter. Ramseur and Canty, initially listed in critical condition, have fully recovered. Cabey remains paralyzed, and has suffered some degree of brain damage.

On December 31, 1984, Goetz surrendered to police in Concord, New Hampshire, identifying himself as the gunman being sought for the subway shootings in New York nine days earlier. Later that day, after receiving Miranda warnings, he made two lengthy statements, both of which were taped [in which] Goetz admitted that he had been illegally carrying a handgun in New York City for three years. He stated that he had first purchased a gun in 1981 after he had been injured in a mugging. Goetz also revealed that twice between 1981 and 1984 he had successfully warded off assailants simply by displaying the pistol.

According to Goetz's statement, the first contact he had with the four youths came when Canty, sitting or lying on the bench across from him, asked "how are you," to which he replied "fine." Shortly thereafter, Canty, followed by one of the other youths, walked over to the defendant and stood to his left, while the other two youths remained to his right, in the corner of the subway car. Canty then said "give me five dollars." Goetz stated that he knew from the smile on Canty's face that they wanted to "play with me." Although he was certain that none of the youths had a gun, he had a fear, based on prior experiences, of being "maimed."

Goetz then established "a pattern of fire," deciding specifically to fire from left to right. His stated intention at that point was to "murder [the four youths], to hurt them, to make them suffer as much as possible." When Canty again requested money, Goetz stood up, drew his weapon, and began firing, aiming for the center of the body of each of the four. Goetz recalled that the first two he shot "tried to run through the crowd [but] they had nowhere to run." Goetz then turned to his right to "go after the other two." One of these two "tried to run through the wall of the train, but . . . he had nowhere to go." The other youth (Cabey) "tried pretending that he wasn't with [the others]" by standing still, holding on to one of the subway hand straps, and not looking at Goetz. Goetz nonetheless fired his fourth shot at him. He then ran back to the first two youths to make sure they had been "taken care of." Seeing that they had both been shot, he spun back to check on the latter two. Goetz noticed that the youth who had been standing still was now sitting on a bench and seemed unhurt. As Goetz told the police, "I said '[you] seem to be all right, here's another,' " and he then fired the shot which severed Cabey's spinal cord. Goetz added that "if I was a little more under self-control . . . I would have put the barrel against his forehead and fired." He also admitted that "if I had had more [bullets], I would have shot them again, and again, and again."

II.

After waiving extradition, Goetz was brought back to New York and arraigned on a felony complaint charging him with attempted murder and criminal possession of a weapon. The matter was presented to a Grand Jury in January 1985, with the prosecutor seeking an indictment for attempted murder, assault, reckless endangerment, and criminal possession of a weapon. Neither the defendant nor any of the wounded youths testified before his Grand Jury. On January 25, 1985, the Grand Jury indicted defendant on one count of criminal possession of a weapon in the third degree (Penal Law § 265.02), for possessing the gun used in the subway shootings, and two counts of criminal possession of a weapon in the fourth degree (Penal Law § 265.01), for possessing two other guns in his apartment building. It dismissed, however, the attempted murder and other charges stemming from the shootings themselves. . . . Presentation of the case to the second Grand Jury began on March 14, 1985. Two of the four youths, Canty and Ramseur, testified. Among the other witnesses were four passengers from the seventh car of the subway who had seen some portions of the incident. Goetz again chose not to testify, though the tapes of his two statements were played for the grand jurors, as had been done with the first Grand Jury.

On March 27, 1985, the second Grand Jury filed a 10-count indictment, containing four charges of attempted murder (Penal Law §§ 110.00, 125.25 [1]), four charges of assault in the first degree (Penal Law § 120.10 [1]), one charge of reckless endangerment in the first degree (Penal Law § 120.25), and one charge of criminal possession of a weapon in the second degree (Penal Law § 265.03 [possession of loaded firearm with intent to use it unlawfully against another]). Goetz was arraigned on this indictment on March 28, 1985, and it was consolidated with the earlier three-count indictment.[1]

On October 14, 1985, Goetz moved to dismiss the charges contained in the second indictment alleging, among other things, that the evidence before the second Grand Jury was not legally sufficient to establish the offenses charged (see, CPL 210.20 [1] [b]), and that the prosecutor's instructions to that Grand Jury on the defense of justification were erroneous and prejudicial to the defendant so as to render its proceedings defective (see, CPL 210.20 [1] [c]; 210.35 [5]).

On November 25, 1985, while the motion to dismiss was pending before Criminal Term, a column appeared in the New York Daily News containing an interview which the columnist had conducted with Darryl Cabey the previous day in Cabey's hospital room. The columnist claimed that Cabey had told him in this interview that the other three youths had all approached Goetz with the intention of robbing him. The day after the column was published, a New York City police officer informed the prosecutor that he had been one of the first police officers to enter the subway car after the shootings, and that Canty had said to him "we were going to rob [Goetz]." The prosecutor immediately disclosed this information to the court and to defense counsel, adding that this was the first time his office had been told of this alleged statement and that none of the police reports filed on the incident contained any such information. Goetz then orally expanded his motion to dismiss, asserting that People v Pelchat (62 NY2d 97) because it appeared, from this new information, that Ramseur and Canty had committed perjury.

In an order dated January 21, 1986, Criminal Term granted Goetz's motion to the extent that it dismissed all counts of the second indictment, other than the reckless endangerment charge, with leave to resubmit these charges to a third Grand Jury. The court, after inspection of the Grand Jury minutes, first rejected Goetz's contention that there was not legally sufficient evidence to support the charges. It held, however, that the prosecutor, in a supplemental charge elaborating upon the justification defense, had erroneously introduced an objective element into this defense by instructing the grand jurors to consider whether Goetz's conduct was that of a "reasonable man in [Goetz's] situation." The court, citing prior decisions from both the First and Second Departments (see, e.g., People v Santiago, 110 AD2d 569 [1st Dept]; People v Wagman, 99 AD2d 519 [2d Dept]), concluded that the statutory test for whether the use of deadly force is justified to protect a person should be wholly subjective, focusing entirely on the defendant's state of mind when he used such force. It concluded that dismissal was required for this error because the justification issue was at the heart of the case.[2]

Criminal Term also concluded that dismissal and resubmission of the charges were required under People v Pelchat (supra) because the Daily News column and the statement by the police officer to the prosecution strongly indicated that the testimony of Ramseur and Canty was perjured. Because the additional evidence before the second Grand Jury, as contrasted with that before the first Grand Jury, consisted largely of the testimony of these two youths, the court found that the integrity of the second Grand Jury was "severely undermined" by the apparently perjured testimony.

On appeal by the People, a divided Appellate Division affirmed Criminal Term's dismissal of the charges. The plurality opinion by Justice Kassal, concurred in by Justice Carro, agreed with Criminal Term's reasoning on the justification issue, stating that the grand jurors should have been instructed to consider only the defendant's subjective beliefs as to the need to use deadly force. Justice Kupferman concurred in the result reached by the plurality on the ground that the prosecutor's charge did not adequately apprise the grand jurors of the need to consider Goetz's own background and learning. Neither the plurality nor the concurring opinion discussed Criminal Term's reliance on Pelchat as an alternate ground for dismissal. . . . On the justification question, he opined that the statute requires consideration of both the defendant's subjective beliefs and whether a reasonable person in defendant's situation would have had such beliefs. Accordingly, he found no error in the prosecutor's introduction of an objective element into the justification defense. On the Pelchat issue, Justice Asch noted the extensive differences between the Grand Jury evidence in that case and the case at bar and concluded that the out-of-court statements attributed to Cabey and Canty did not affect the validity of the indictment. In a separate dissenting opinion, Justice Wallach stressed that the plurality's adoption of a purely subjective test effectively eliminated any reasonableness requirement contained in the statute.

Justice Asch granted the People leave to appeal to this court. We agree with the dissenters that neither the prosecutor's charge to the Grand Jury on justification nor the information which came to light while the motion to dismiss was pending required dismissal of any of the charges in the second indictment.

III.

Penal Law article 35 recognizes the defense of justification, which "permits the use of force under certain circumstances" (see, People v McManus, 67 NY2d 541, 545). One such set of circumstances pertains to the use of force in defense of a person, encompassing both self-defense and defense of a third person (Penal Law § 35.15). Penal Law § 35.15 (1) sets forth the general principles governing all such uses of force: "[a] person may . . . use physical force upon another person when and to the extent he reasonably believes such to be necessary to defend himself or a third person from what he reasonably believes to be the use or imminent use of unlawful physical force by such other person."[3]

Section 35.15 (2) sets forth further limitations on these general principles with respect to the use of "deadly physical force": "A person may not use deadly physical force upon another person under circumstances specified in subdivision one unless (a) He reasonably believes that such other person is using or about to use deadly physical force[4] or (b) He reasonably believes that such other person is committing or attempting to commit a kidnapping, forcible rape, forcible sodomy or robbery."

Thus, consistent with most justification provisions, Penal Law § 35.15 permits the use of deadly physical force only where requirements as to triggering conditions and the necessity of a particular response are met (see, Robinson, Criminal Law Defenses § 121 [a], at 2). As to the triggering conditions, the statute requires that the actor "reasonably believes" that another person either is using or about to use deadly physical force or is committing or attempting to commit one of certain enumerated felonies, including robbery. As to the need for the use of deadly physical force as a response, the statute requires that the actor "reasonably believes" that such force is necessary to avert the perceived threat.[5]

Because the evidence before the second Grand Jury included statements by Goetz that he acted to protect himself from being maimed or to avert a robbery, the prosecutor correctly chose to charge the justification defense in section 35.15 to the Grand Jury (see, CPL 190.25 [6]; People v Valles, 62 NY2d 36, 38). The prosecutor properly instructed the grand jurors to consider whether the use of deadly physical force was justified to prevent either serious physical injury or a robbery, and, in doing so, to separately analyze the defense with respect to each of the charges. He elaborated upon the prerequisites for the use of deadly physical force essentially by reading or paraphrasing the language in Penal Law § 35.15. The defense does not contend that he committed any error in this portion of the charge.

When the prosecutor had completed his charge, one of the grand jurors asked for clarification of the term "reasonably believes." The prosecutor responded by instructing the grand jurors that they were to consider the circumstances of the incident and determine "whether the defendant's conduct was that of a reasonable man in the defendant's situation." It is this response by the prosecutor—and specifically his use of "a reasonable man"—which is the basis for the dismissal of the charges by the lower courts. As expressed repeatedly in the Appellate Division's plurality opinion, because section 35.15 uses the term "he reasonably believes," the appropriate test, according to that court, is whether a defendant's beliefs and reactions were "reasonable to him." Under that reading of the statute, a jury which believed a defendant's testimony that he felt that his own actions were warranted and were reasonable would have to acquit him, regardless of what anyone else in defendant's situation might have concluded. Such an interpretation defies the ordinary meaning and significance of the term "reasonably" in a statute, and misconstrues the clear intent of the Legislature, in enacting section 35.15, to retain an objective element as part of any provision authorizing the use of deadly physical force. . . . These provisions have never required that an actor's belief as to the intention of another person to inflict serious injury be correct in order for the use of deadly force to be justified, but they have uniformly required that the belief comport with an objective notion of reasonableness. The 1829 statute, using language which was followed almost in its entirety until the 1965 recodification of the Penal Law, provided that the use of deadly force was justified in self-defense or in the defense of specified third persons "when there shall be a reasonable ground to apprehend a design to commit a felony, or to do some great personal injury, and there shall be imminent danger of such design being accomplished."

In Shorter v People (2 NY 193), we emphasized that deadly force could be justified under the statute even if the actor's beliefs as to the intentions of another turned out to be wrong, but noted there had to be a reasonable basis, viewed objectively, for the beliefs. We explicitly rejected the position that the defendant's own belief that the use of deadly force was necessary sufficed to justify such force regardless of the reasonableness of the beliefs (id., at pp 200–201).

In 1881, New York reexamined the many criminal provisions set forth in the revised statutes and enacted, for the first time, a separate Penal Code (see generally, 1937 Report of NY Law Rev Commn, Communication to Legislature Relating to Homicide, at 525, 529 [hereafter cited as Communication Relating to Homicide]). The provision in the 1881 Penal Code for the use of deadly force in self-defense or to defend a third person was virtually a reenactment of the language in the 1829 statutes,[6] and the "reasonable ground" requirement was maintained.

The 1909 Penal Law replaced the 1881 Penal Code. The language of section 205 of the 1881 code pertaining to the use of deadly force in self-defense or in defense of a third person was reenacted, verbatim, as part of section 1055 of the new Penal Law. Several cases from this court interpreting the 1909 provision demonstrate unmistakably that an objective element of reasonableness was a vital part of any claim of self-defense. In People v Lumsden (201 NY 264, 268), we approved a charge to the jury which instructed it to consider whether the circumstances facing defendant were such "as would lead a reasonable man to believe that [an assailant] is about to kill or to do great bodily injury" (see also, People v Ligouri, 284 NY 309, 316, 317). We emphatically rejected the position that any belief by an actor as to the intention of another to cause severe injury was a sufficient basis for his use of deadly force, and stated specifically that a belief based upon "mere fear or fancy or remote hearsay information or a delusion pure and simple" would not satisfy the requirements of the statute (201 NY, at p 269). In People v Tomlins (213 NY 240, 244), justified the defendant as a reasonable man in believing that he was about to be murderously attacked."

Accordingly, the Law Revision Commission, in a 1937 Report to the Legislature on the Law of Homicide in New York, summarized the self-defense statute as requiring a "reasonable belief in the imminence of danger," and stated that the standard to be followed by a jury in determining whether a belief was reasonable "is that of a man of ordinary courage in the circumstances surrounding the defendant at the time of the killing" (Communication Relating to Homicide, op. cit., at 814). The Report added that New York did not follow the view, adopted in a few States, that "the jury is required to adopt the subjective view and judge from the standpoint of the very defendant concerned" (id., at 814).

In 1961 the Legislature established a Commission to undertake a complete revision of the Penal Law and the Criminal Code. The impetus for the decision to update the Penal Law came in part from the drafting of the Model Penal Code by the American Law Institute, as well as from the fact that the existing law was poorly organized and in many aspects antiquated (see, e.g., Criminal Law Revision Through A Legislative Commission: The New York Experience, 18 Buff L Rev 213; Note, Proposed Penal Law of New York, 64 Colum L Rev 1469). Following the submission by the Commission of several reports and proposals, the Legislature approved the present Penal Law in 1965 (L 1965, ch 1030), and it became effective on September 1, 1967. The drafting of the general provisions of the new Penal Law (see, Penal Law part I), including the article on justification (id., art 35), was particularly influenced by the Model Penal Code (see, Denzer, Drafting a New York Penal Law for New York, 18 Buff L Rev 251, 252; Wechsler, Codification of Criminal Law in the United States: The Model Penal Code, 68 Colum L Rev 1425, 1428). While using the Model Penal Code provisions on justification as general guidelines, however, the drafters of the new Penal Law did not simply adopt them verbatim.

The provisions of the Model Penal Code with respect to the use of deadly force in self-defense reflect the position of its drafters that any culpability which arises from a mistaken belief in the need to use such force should be no greater than the culpability such a mistake would give rise to if it were made with respect to an element of a crime (see, ALI, Model Penal Code and Commentaries, part I, at 32, 34 [hereafter cited as MPC Commentaries]; Robinson, Criminal Law Defenses, op. cit., at 410). Accordingly, under Model Penal Code § 3.04 (2) (b), a defendant charged with murder (or attempted murder) need only show that he "[believed] that [the use of deadly force] was necessary to protect himself against death, serious bodily injury, kidnapping or [forcible] sexual intercourse" to prevail on a self-defense claim . . . If the defendant's belief was wrong, and was recklessly, or negligently formed, however, he may be convicted of the type of homicide charge requiring only a reckless or negligent, as the case may be, criminal intent (see, Model Penal Code § 3.09 [2]; MPC Commentaries, op. cit., part I, at 32, 150).

The drafters of the Model Penal Code recognized that the wholly subjective test set forth in section 3.04 differed from the existing law in most States by its omission of any requirement of reasonableness (see, MPC Commentaries, op. cit., part I, at 35; LaFave & Scott, Criminal Law § 53, at 393–394). The drafters were also keenly aware that requiring that the actor have a "reasonable belief" rather than just a "belief" would alter the wholly subjective test recognized years earlier by the New York Law Revision Commission and continues to be noted by the commentators (Communication Relating to Homicide, op. cit., at 814; Robinson, Criminal Law Defenses, op. cit.; Note, Justification: The Impact of the Model Penal Code on Statutory Reform, 75 Colum L Rev 914, 918–920).

New York did not follow the Model Penal Code's equation of a mistake as to the need to use deadly force with a mistake negating an element of a crime, choosing instead to use a single statutory section which would provide either a complete defense or no defense at all to a defendant charged with any crime involving the use of deadly force. The drafters of the new Penal Law adopted in large part the structure and content of Model Penal Code § 3.04, but, crucially, inserted the word "reasonably" before "believes."

The plurality below agreed with defendant's argument that the change in the statutory language from "reasonable ground," used prior to 1965, to "he reasonably believes" in Penal Law § 35.15 evinced a legislative intent to conform to the subjective standard contained in Model Penal Code § 3.04. This argument, however, ignores the plain significance of the insertion of "reasonably." Had the drafters of section 35.15 wanted to adopt a subjective standard, they could have simply used the language of section 3.04. "Believes" by itself requires an honest or genuine belief by a defendant as to the need to use deadly force (see, e.g., Robinson, Criminal Law Defenses, op. cit. § 184 (b), at 399–400). Interpreting the statute to require only that the defendant's belief was "reasonable to him," as done by the plurality below, would hardly be different from requiring only a genuine belief; in either case, the defendant's own perceptions could completely exonerate him from any criminal liability.

We cannot lightly impute to the Legislature an intent to fundamentally alter the principles of justification to allow the perpetrator of a serious crime to go free simply because that person believed his actions were reasonable and necessary to prevent some perceived harm. To completely exonerate such an individual, no matter how aberrational or bizarre his thought patterns, would allow citizens to set their own standards for the permissible use of force. It would also allow a legally competent defendant suffering from delusions to kill or perform acts of violence with impunity, contrary to fundamental principles of justice and criminal law.

We can only conclude that the Legislature retained a reasonableness requirement to avoid giving a license for such actions. The plurality's interpretation, as the dissenters below recognized, excises the impact of the word "reasonably." This same conclusion was recently reached in Justice Levine's decision for a unanimous Third Department in People v Astle (117 AD2d 382), in which that court declined to follow the First Department's decision in this case (see also, People v Hamel, 96 AD2d 644 [3d Dept]).

The change from "reasonable ground" to "reasonably believes" is better explained by the fact that the drafters of section 35.15 were proposing a single section which, for the first time, would govern both the use of ordinary force and deadly force in self-defense or defense of another. Under the 1909 Penal Law and its predecessors, the use of ordinary force was governed by separate sections which, at least by their literal terms, required that the defendant was in fact responding to an unlawful assault, and not just that he had a Penal Law §§ 42, 246 [3]; People v Young, 11 NY2d 274; 7 Zett, New York Criminal Practice para. 65.3). Following the example of the Model Penal Code, the drafters of section 35.15 eliminated this sharp dichotomy between the use of ordinary force and deadly force in defense of a person. Not surprisingly then, the integrated section reflects the wording of Model Penal Code § 3.04, with the addition of "reasonably" to incorporate the long-standing requirement of "reasonable ground" for the use of deadly force and apply it to the use of ordinary force as well (see, Zett, New York Criminal Practice, § 65.3 [1], [2]; Note, Proposed Penal Law of New York, 64 Colum L Rev 1469, 1500).

The conclusion that section 35.15 retains an objective element to justify the use of deadly force is buttressed by the statements of its drafters. The executive director and counsel to the Commission which revised the Penal Law have stated that the provisions of the statute with respect to the use of deadly physical force largely conformed with the prior law, with the only changes they noted not being relevant here (Denzer & McQuillan, Practice Commentary, McKinney's Cons Laws of NY, Book 39, Penal Law § 35.15, p 63 [1967]). Nowhere in the legislative history is there any indication that "reasonably believes" was designed to change the law on the use of deadly force or establish a subjective standard. To the contrary, the Commission, in the staff comment governing arrests by police officers, specifically equated "[he] reasonably believes" with having a reasonable ground for believing (Penal Law § 35.30; Fourth Interim Report of the Temporary State Commission on Revision of the Penal Law and Criminal Code at 17–18, 1965 NY Legis Doc No. 25).

Statutes or rules of law requiring a person to act "reasonably" or to have a "reasonable belief" uniformly prescribe conduct meeting an objective standard measured with reference to how "a reasonable person" could have acted (see, e.g., People v Cantor, 36 NY2d 106; Donovan v Kaszycki & Sons Contrs., 599 F Supp 860, 871; Klotter, Criminal Law, at 312; Fletcher, The Right and the Reasonable, 98 Harv L Rev 949; 57 Am Jur 2d, Negligence, §§ 67, 68). In People v Cantor (supra), we had before us a provision of the Criminal Procedure Law authorizing a police officer to stop a person "when he reasonably suspects that such person is committing, has committed or is about to commit [a crime]" (CPL 140.50 [1]. We held that this section authorized "stops" only when the police officer had "the quantum of knowledge sufficient to induce an ordinarily prudent and cautious man under the circumstances to believe criminal activity is at hand" (People v Cantor, 36 NY2d, at pp 112–113, supra).

In People v Collice (41 NY2d 906), we rejected the position that section 35.15 contains a wholly subjective standard. The defendant in Collice asserted, on appeal, that the trial court had erred in refusing to charge the justification defense. We upheld the trial court's action because we concluded that, even if the defendant had actually believed that he was threatened with the imminent use of deadly physical force, the evidence clearly indicated that "his reactions were not those of a reasonable man acting in self-defense" (id., at p 907). Numerous decisions from other States interpreting "reasonably believes" in justification statutes enacted subsequent to the drafting of the Model Penal Code are consistent with Collice, as they hold that such language refers to what a reasonable person could have believed under the same circumstances (see, e.g., State v Kelly, 97 NJ 178, 478 A2d 364, 373–374; Weston v State, 682 P2d 1119, 1121 [Alaska]).

In People v Miller (39 NY2d 543) . . . a defendant charged with homicide could introduce, in support of a claim of self-defense, evidence of prior acts of violence committed by the deceased of which the defendant had knowledge. The defense, as well as the plurality below, place great emphasis on the statement in Miller that "the crucial fact at issue [is] the state of mind of the defendant" (id., at p 551). This language, however, in no way indicates that a wholly subjective test is appropriate. To begin, it is undisputed that section 35.15 does contain a subjective element, namely that the defendant believed that deadly force was necessary to avert the imminent use of deadly force or the commission of certain felonies. Evidence that the defendant knew of prior acts of violence by the deceased could help establish his requisite beliefs. Moreover, such knowledge would also be relevant on the issue of reasonableness, as the jury must consider the circumstances a defendant found himself in, which would include any relevant knowledge of the nature of persons confronting him (see, e.g., People v Taylor, 177 NY 237, 245; Communication Relating to Homicide, op. cit., at 816). Finally, in Miller, we specifically recognized that there had to be "reasonable grounds" for the defendant's belief.

Goetz's reliance on People v Rodawald (177 NY 408) is similarly misplaced. In Rodawald, decided under the 1881 Penal Code, we held that a defendant who claimed that he had acted in self-defense could introduce evidence as to the general reputation of the deceased as a violent person if this reputation was known to the defendant when he acted. We stated, as emphasized by Goetz, that such evidence, "when known to the accused, enables him to judge of the danger and aids the jury in deciding whether he acted in good faith and upon the honest belief that his life was in peril. It shows the state of his mind as to the necessity of defending himself" (177 NY, at p 423). Again, such language is explained by the fact that the threshold question, before the reasonableness issue is addressed, is the subjective beliefs of the defendant. Nowhere in Rodawald did we hold that the only test, as urged by Goetz, is whether the defendant honestly and in good faith believed himself to be in danger. Rather, we recognized that there was also the separate question of whether the accused had "reasonable ground" for his belief, and we upheld the trial court's refusal to charge the jury that the defendant's honest belief was sufficient to establish self-defense (177 NY, at pp 423, 426–427).

Goetz also argues that the introduction of an objective element will preclude a jury from considering factors such as the prior experiences of a given actor and thus, require it to make a determination of "reasonableness" without regard to the actual circumstances of a particular incident. This argument, however, falsely presupposes that an objective standard means that the background and other relevant characteristics of a particular actor must be ignored. To the contrary, we have frequently noted that a determination of reasonableness must be based on the "circumstances" facing a defendant or his "situation" (see, e.g., People v Ligouri, 284 NY 309, 316, supra; People v Lumsden, 201 NY 264, 268, supra). Such terms encompass more than the physical movements of the potential assailant. As just discussed, these terms include any relevant knowledge the defendant had about that person. They also necessarily bring in the physical attributes of all persons involved, including the defendant. Furthermore, the defendant's circumstances encompass any prior experiences he had which could provide a reasonable basis for a belief that another person's intentions were to injure or rob him. . . .

Accordingly, a jury should be instructed to consider this type of evidence in weighing the defendant's actions. The jury must first determine whether the defendant had the requisite beliefs under section 35.15, that is, whether he believed deadly force was necessary to avert the imminent use of deadly force or the commission of one of the felonies enumerated therein. If the People do not prove beyond a reasonable doubt that he did not have such beliefs, then the jury must also consider whether these beliefs were reasonable. The jury would have to determine, in light of all the "circumstances," as explicated above, if a reasonable person could have had these beliefs.

The prosecutor's instruction to the second Grand Jury that it had to determine whether, under the circumstances, Goetz's conduct was that of a reasonable man in his situation was thus essentially an accurate charge. It is true that the prosecutor did not elaborate on the meaning of "circumstances" or "situation" and inform the grand jurors that they could consider, for example, the prior experiences Goetz related in his statement to the police. We have held, however, that a Grand Jury need not be instructed on the law with the same degree of precision as the petit jury (see, People v Valles, 62 NY2d 36, 38; People v Calbud, Inc., 49 NY2d 389, 394; compare, CPL 190.25 [6], with CPL 300.10 [2]). This lesser standard is premised upon the different functions of the Grand Jury and the petit jury: the former determines whether sufficient evidence exists to accuse a person of a crime and thereby subject him to criminal prosecution; the latter ultimately determines the guilt or innocence of the accused, and may convict only where the People have proven his guilt beyond a reasonable doubt (see, People v Calbud, Inc., 49 NY2d, at p 394, supra).

In People v Calbud, Inc. (supra, at pp 394–395), we stated that the prosecutor simply had to "[provide] the Grand Jury with enough information to enable it intelligently to decide whether a crime has been committed and to determine whether there exists legally sufficient evidence to establish the material elements of the crime." Of course, as noted above, where the evidence suggests that a complete defense such as justification may be present, the prosecutor must charge the grand jurors on that defense, providing enough information to enable them to determine whether the defense, in light of the evidence, should preclude the criminal prosecution. The prosecutor more than adequately fulfilled this obligation here. His instructions were not as complete as the court's charge on justification should be, but they sufficiently apprised the Grand Jury of the existence and requirements of that defense to allow it to intelligently decide that there is sufficient evidence tending to disprove justification and necessitating a trial. The Grand Jury has indicted Goetz. It will now be for the petit jury to decide whether the prosecutor can prove beyond a reasonable doubt that Goetz's reactions were unreasonable and therefore excessive.

IV.

Criminal Term's second ground for dismissal of the charges, premised upon the Daily News column and the police officer's statement to the prosecutor, can be rejected more summarily. The court relied upon People v Pelchat (62 NY2d 97, supra), the facts of which, however, are markedly different from those here. In Pelchat, the defendant was one of 21 persons arrested in a house to which police officers had seen marihuana delivered. The only evidence before the Grand testimony of a police officer listing defendant as one of 21 persons he had observed transporting the drug. After defendant was indicted, this same police officer told the prosecutor that he had misunderstood his question when testifying before the Grand Jury and that he had not seen defendant engage in any criminal activity. Although the prosecutor knew that there was no other evidence before the Grand Jury to establish the defendant's guilt, he did not disclose the police officer's admission, and instead, accepted a guilty plea from the defendant. We reversed the conviction and dismissed the indictment, holding that the prosecutor should not have allowed the proceedings against defendant to continue when he knew that the only evidence against him before the Grand Jury was false, and thus, knew that there was not legally sufficient evidence to support the indictment.

Here, in contrast, Canty and Ramseur have not recanted any of their Grand Jury testimony or told the prosecutor that they misunderstood any questions. Instead, all that has come to light is hearsay evidence that conflicts with part of Canty's testimony. There is no statute or controlling case law requiring dismissal of an indictment merely because, months later, the prosecutor becomes aware of some information which may lead to the defendant's acquittal.

There was no basis for the Criminal Term Justice to speculate as to whether Canty's and Ramseur's testimony was perjurious (see, CPL 190.25 [5]), and his conclusion that the testimony "strongly appeared" to be perjured is particularly inappropriate given the nature of the "evidence" he relied upon to reach such a conclusion and that he was not in the Grand Jury room when the two youths testified.

Moreover, unlike Pelchat, the testimony of Canty and Ramseur was not the only evidence before the Grand Jury establishing that the offenses submitted to that body were committed by Goetz. Goetz's own statements, together with the testimony of the passengers, clearly support the elements of the crimes charged, and provide ample basis for concluding that a trial of this matter is needed to determine whether Goetz could have reasonably believed that he was about to be robbed or seriously injured and whether it was reasonably necessary for him to shoot four youths to avert any such threat.

Accordingly, the order of the Appellate Division should be reversed, and the dismissed counts of the indictment reinstated.

Questions for Case Study 1–2

1. What are the basic facts of the case?
2. What are the most important issues in this case?
3. What is the decision of the court?
4. Discuss whether you agree or disagree with the court's decision based on the facts given in the case.
5. What is it that the jury will need to decide at Goetz's trial?
6. From the facts given, how do you think a jury should decide the guilt or innocence of Bernard Goetz with regard to the following charges?
   a. Attempted murder.
   b. Assault.
   c. Reckless endangerment.
   d. Criminal possession of a weapon.
7. If you were Bernard Goetz's defense attorney, what arguments would you make on Mr. Goetz's behalf as a defense to each of the above charges?
8. If you were the prosecuting attorney, what arguments would you make for Mr. Goetz's guilt on each of the above charges?
9. For further study: Any or all of the following activities can be engaged in at the instructor's discretion either during class time, assigned as a group or individual project, or as extra credit.
   a. Moot court trial: Prepare the defense and prosecution of Bernard Goetz on any of the five charges against him. Assume that Mr. Goetz will not testify at his trial. Have a team of three students serve as co-counsel for the defense and a team of three students serve a co-prosecutors. Argue to a jury made up of the remainder of the class why Mr. Goetz should be convicted or acquitted. The instructor (or a student) can serve as the judge and ensure that the

discussion is kept to the relevant issues. The jury will vote to convict or acquit by a unanimous vote, and the judge will pass sentence (if appropriate) assuming the following maximum penalties: up to a maximum of 25 years to life for attempted murder, 1–25 years for the assault, 1–5 years for the reckless endangerment, and a minimum of 1–5 years for the criminal possession of a deadly weapon.

b. Pretrial preparation: Assume that you are a defense or prosecuting attorney working on this case. Prepare your best arguments for acquittal or conviction of Mr. Goetz on each of the above charges. Base your arguments on your understanding of criminal law, and make sure to note why you think the elements of each crime have been met in this case, or why the elements have not been met.

c. Using *The New York Times Index,* research the Goetz case. Write a paper about the case's final determination and substantiate it with a series of photocopied articles using your college's or local public library's microfilm version of *The New York Times.* (You may also use other newspapers, provided your local library carries them on microfilm.) Discuss how the newspaper coverage of the facts differs from those contained in this official court record. The Goetz case received a great deal of national and international attention. Compare coverages of different newspapers and news magazines; in particular, try to find any slant or bias either in favor of or against the accused in different reported accounts.

Footnotes

1. On May 14, 1985, Goetz commenced an article 78 proceeding in the Appellate Division seeking to prohibit a trial on the charges contained in the second indictment on the ground that the order allowing resubmission of the charges was an abuse of discretion. The Appellate Division dismissed the proceeding on the ground that prohibition did not lie to review the type of error alleged by Goetz (111 AD2d 729, 730), and this court denied a motion for leave to appeal from the Appellate Division order (65 NY2d 609). The propriety of the resubmission order is not before us on this appeal.

2. The court did not dismiss the reckless endangerment charge because, relying on the Appellate Division decision in People v McManus (108 AD2d 474), it held that justification was not a defense to a crime containing, as an element, "depraved indifference to human life." As our reversal of the Appellate Division in McManus holds, justification is a defense to such a crime (People v McManus, 67 NY2d 541). Accordingly, had the prosecutor's instructions on justification actually rendered the Grand Jury proceedings defective, dismissal of the reckless endangerment count would have been required as well.

3. Subdivision (1) contains certain exceptions to this general authorization to use force, such as where the actor himself was the initial aggressor.

4. Section 35.15 (2) (a) further provides, however, that even under these circumstances a person ordinarily must retreat "if he knows that he can with complete safety as to himself and others avoid the necessity of [using deadly physical force] by retreating."

5. While the portion of section 35.15 (2) (b) pertaining to the use of deadly physical force to avert a felony such as robbery does not contain a separate "retreat" requirement, it is clear from reading subdivisions (1) and (2) of section 35.15 together, as the statute requires, that the general "necessity" requirement in subdivision (1) applies to all uses of force under section 35.15, including the use of deadly physical force under subdivision (2) (b).

6. The 1881 provision expanded the class of third persons for whose defense an actor could employ deadly force from certain specified persons to any other person in the actor's presence.

II

CONTRACTS

Contract law is of great importance in business and in everyday life. Even though most of us are unaware of it, we enter into a large number of binding contracts every day. Ordinary business transactions such as buying a pack of gum at the corner grocery store, purchasing a ticket at a movie theater, or ordering a meal at a restaurant all involve valid contracts that provide the concerned parties with certain rights and duties. In this unit, we will explore the nature of contracts, the requirements for their valid formation, and the consequences for their breach.

A *contract* is a legally enforceable promise between two or more people. Although all contracts contain enforceable promises, not all promises between people result in contracts. There are many promises made between people that the courts will not enforce.

Consider the following:

➤ Henry invites Ericka to dinner, and Ericka accepts. Henry is looking forward to the date and can think of little else all day long. A half hour before Henry was to pick her up, Ericka calls him and tells him that she will not be able to keep their date since Ron has invited her to go dancing and she has accepted. Henry is upset, hurt, and quite angry. He'd like to sue her for breach of contract, since she has clearly broken a promise made to him earlier that day. Will he succeed?

Ericka may not be a very nice person; she has broken a promise to a friend and needlessly hurt his feelings in the process. She may have had a *moral* obligation to attend the dinner date; nevertheless, she had no *legal* obligation to do so. The agreement she breached was not a contract, but merely a social obligation that the courts will not enforce.

For there to be a valid contract, five basic criteria must be present: (1) a valid offer, (2) a valid acceptance, (3) consideration, (4) legality, and (5) genuine assent. Some cases further require that the contract be in a particular form to be enforceable. We will examine each of these requirements in this unit. Briefly, the five criteria are:

1. Offer: An invitation for another to enter into a contract.
2. Acceptance: Acquiescence to enter into a contract under the terms of the offer.
3. Consideration: Anything of legal value that is asked for and received as the price for entering into a contract.
4. Legality: To be enforceable, a contract cannot be for an illegal purpose or require the performing of an illegal act, nor can a contract violate the public policy of a state.
5. Genuineness of assent: For a valid contract to be formed, both parties must willingly enter into the agreement. There are a variety of circumstances that can invalidate what appears to be consent by part of both parties. Examples are a signed agreement entered into at gunpoint (duress) or those involving persons who are insane, intoxicated, minors, or tricked into entering into an agreement by misrepresentations of the other party.

Each of us enters into many contracts every day without giving the matter any thought. On the way to work, you stop at a newsstand and buy a newspaper and a pack of gum. You also go into a diner and buy a cup of coffee and a doughnut. Afterwards, you stop at a discount ticket counter and purchase two tickets to a Broadway show. Finally, you arrive at the subway station and buy a token. In each of these examples, a contract was made. In each case, there was a valid offer and acceptance, consideration, mutual assent, and legality. No documents were signed, and no contract negotiations took place, yet valid contracts were formed giving each party certain rights and imposing on each some responsibilities as well.

Most contracts are routinely completed without a problem and without the interested parties giving the matter much thought. Problems arise when parties to a contract fail to live up to their agreements or misunderstand what it is they agreed to do. The law of contracts is called upon to settle the dispute between the parties in accordance with established rules of law that determine each party's rights and obligations under a valid contract. Parties can avoid many misunderstandings and disagreements between contracting parties, as well as costly, time-consuming litigation, if they have a basic understanding of the law of contracts. The following chapters will explore the requirements for the formation of valid contracts and the remedies available when they are breached.

Some of the rules about contract formation that we learn here will be modified somewhat when regarding *sales contracts* (see Chapters 11–13). Nevertheless, the common law of contracts is very much in effect today and is crucial to the running of every business, regardless of size.

4

CONTRACTS: OFFER AND ACCEPTANCE

Learning Objectives

After studying this chapter, you will be able to:

1. Describe the difference between express, implied, simple, and formal contracts.
2. Explain the requirements for a valid offer and acceptance.
3. Explain the provisions for revoking an offer.
4. Define the five requirements for a valid contract.
5. Distinguish unilateral from bilateral contracts.

Introduction

A contract is, as previously noted, a legally enforceable *agreement*. As this definition implies, a contract arises from the voluntary assent of two or more individuals to enter into a legally binding agreement. Mutual accord is crucial to the formation of a contract. One party makes an offer—a business proposition—to another; the other accepts. Provided that the other three requirements are present (consideration, legality, and mutual assent), there is a valid contract. Let's look at a simple example:

➤ Manuela offers to sell Linda her car for $1,000. Linda accepts the offer. A valid contract is formed since there is a valid offer and acceptance, consideration (something of value is given and received by each party—the car and the $1,000), mutual assent (both parties are of sound mind and are freely entering into the agreement), and the contract is for a legal purpose.

The above seems simple enough. But few matters of the law are truly simple, as we shall see when examining the various types of contracts and trying to determine what constitutes a *valid* offer and acceptance.

Types of Contracts

Contracts can be classified as express, implied, bilateral, unilateral, simple or formal. We will briefly examine each type below.

Express Contracts

Express contracts are formed by the express language of the parties—the actual words they use in their agreement—and can be either written or oral. Whenever parties either verbalize or put in writing what they are obligating themselves to do, they enter into an express contract. It is a popular misconception that contracts are not binding unless they are in writing, witnessed, or notarized. It is always a good idea to reduce business agreements to writing to avoid future misunderstandings—and to keep the parties honest about what they have obligated themselves to do—but most contracts are legally valid whether they are oral or written. While some contracts, such as those transferring an interest in land, are required to be written, witnessed, notarized, and sealed in most jurisdictions, the vast majority of contracts do not need to follow any of those formalities in order to be binding.

Implied Contracts

Implied contracts are formed not by the words of the parties but by their actions. Both parties must clearly show their assent to enter into an agreement of which the terms are clear to both. As long as the parties' actions plainly indicate an intention to enter into a contract, and the terms of that contract can clearly be implied from those actions, the contract is binding, without a single word being spoken.

Consider the following examples:

1. Harold goes to a movie theater where only one movie is showing. He puts down $10 at the cashier's window. The cashier takes the money, gives him a ticket and returns $3 to him.
2. Dana walks into a newsstand and places a quarter and a dime on the counter, taking a copy of *The New York Times* from a rack to her right.
3. Steve enters Nilda's hardware store. He picks up a Phillips head screwdriver from a rack and, looking over at Nilda, who is taking care of a line of people at the moment, waves the screwdriver in the air. She recognizes Steve, a long-time customer, and understands that he intends to pay for it later. She signals her consent by nodding in his direction. He leaves, taking the screwdriver with him.

In each of the above examples, the parties have entered into an implied contract. Harold has implicitly agreed to pay $7 for the privilege of watching a movie, Dana has paid 35 cents for a copy of *The New York Times*, and Steve has agreed to pay the selling price of the screwdriver to Dana at a later time.

Bilateral Contracts

If the two parties exchange promises to perform some act in the future, they have formed a *bilateral contract*. A bilateral, or two-sided, contract results from an exchange of promises whereby both parties bind themselves to undertake some future action, as in the following examples:

➤ 1. Bruce offers to sell his car to Irving if he will pay him $2,000. Irving accepts the offer.
2. Lina offers to baby-sit for Inga every Saturday for the next three months if Inga will pay her $4 per hour. Inga accepts.
3. Tina offers to sing at Charles's nightclub next Friday, Saturday, and Sunday if he will pay her $5,000 per night. He agrees.

In each of the above examples, both parties are obligating themselves to take some action in the future. As soon as both accept the offer, a valid contract comes into existence. Thus, the contracts formed are bilateral: both parties are exchanging promises to perform some future act. Once both parties accept a valid offer, they are obligated to perform the agreed-upon act in the future. If either party fails to live up to the agreement, a suit for damages can result.

Unilateral Contracts

In a bilateral contract, the parties exchange promises with each other. In a *unilateral contract*, one party makes a promise to the other that can only be accepted by the other's performance. The acceptance of a unilateral contract does not come about by giving a promise in return but by beginning the performance of the requested act. The following examples should clarify the distinction:

➤ 1. Larry promises to pay Moe $500 if Moe will paint Curley's house. Moe goes over to Curley's house and begins painting it. He has accepted Larry's unilateral promise by undertaking the desired task.
2. Bill promises his son, Michael, that he will pay him $100,000 if he can stop smoking cigarettes for two years. Michael immediately stops smoking. Michael has accepted his father's unilateral offer, who must pay the $100,000 if Michael in fact does not smoke a cigarette for two years.
3. Jenine promises to pay Olga $1,000 if she will begin painting her portrait within the next six months. Three months later, Olga goes to Jenine's house with her paint supplies and tells Jenine that she is ready to begin the portrait. She has accepted the contract through her actions.

In each of the above examples, the offeree (the person to whom the offer is made) is not obligated to do anything; only the offeror is obligated to do some act (pay a specific sum of money in the above examples) if the offeree takes the specified action. The offeree is free to accept the offer by performing the desired act or to reject it by doing nothing. The acceptance of the offer, and thereby the formation of the contract, comes about by the offeree beginning to perform the required act.

Simple Contracts

A *simple contract* is any oral or written agreement that is not required to follow a specific form or to be signed, witnessed, or sealed. The vast majority of contracts entered into by businesses and private individuals are simple contracts, even though some may seem rather complex and go on for many pages.

Formal Contracts

A *formal contract* at common law was one that needed to be written, signed, witnessed, and sealed by the parties. At common law, a person's seal on a contract (usually a mark made by a signet ring on sealing wax—but a seal could be any symbol adopted by an individual or a company) gave that contract special significance. The seal legitimized a contract to such an extent that a contract not supported by consideration (see next chapter) would still be binding if sealed.

Today, the Uniform Commercial Code—the most important statute affecting business, drafted by the National Conference of Commissioners on Uniform State Laws and adopted in every state save Louisiana—has abolished the significance of the seal for contracts involving the sale of goods (UCC §2–203), and many states have likewise abolished the significance of the seal for contracts in general. Where the formality of the seal is retained, most states permit any mark to take the place of the seal or simply the word *Seal* or the initials *L.S.* (for *locus sigilli*—Latin for *in place of seal*) to be used instead of an actual seal.

Characteristics of an Offer

An offer must contain a clear promise to enter into a contract and must be communicated by the promisor (the person making the promise) to the promisee (the person to whom the promise is made). What may on its face appear to be a valid offer may not meet this simple test upon close examination. Examine the following three statements to see which, if any, meet the test of a valid offer by being an unequivocal promise communicated to the offeree.

➤   1. Seller tells buyer, "I am considering selling my car for $1,000."
    2. Seller tells buyer, "I'd sure like to sell my car for $1,000."
    3. Seller tells buyer, "If you give me $1,000, I'll sell you my car."

The first two examples are not valid offers since neither makes a clear, unequivocal offer nor a promise. In example 1, the seller simply says he is considering selling his car; he does not promise to or imply that he will sell it to the buyer. Likewise, in example 2 the seller says he'd like to sell his car but does not promise to sell it to the buyer. Example 3, however, does contain a valid offer. The seller makes a clear offer that cannot be misinterpreted: he is willing to sell his car to the buyer for $1,000. If the buyer accepts, the parties have formed a valid contract.

Clear Intent: An Unequivocal Promise

An offer does not need to contain specific language such as "I promise to sell you" or "I offer to sell you" to be effective. What matters is that a reasonable person under the same circumstances would clearly understand that the party intended an offer. The language used is always important in helping to determine the intent of the parties, but a valid offer can be made even when no words are spoken, simply by the actions of the parties. If, for example, Muhammad holds out $20 and tells Carol, "I'll give you this for that fountain pen on your desk," and Carol takes the money and puts it in her pocket without saying a word, she will have clearly accepted his offer by her actions. What is important in determining whether a valid offer or acceptance existed is the objective intent of the parties as communicated through their words or actions.

Since an offer must contain a clear intent to enter into a contract, an offer not seriously intended is not valid. It can be difficult at times to determine whether an offer is seriously intended. The subjective intent of the offeror and offeree are irrelevant, and a court will not examine it in determining the validity of an offer. What is important is not whether an offeror subjectively made an offer in jest, but rather whether the person to whom the offer was made, the offeree, should have realized that the offeror was only joking when he made the offer. It must be clear to an average person that the offer was not seriously intended; otherwise, the offeree can accept it and form a valid contract. Examine the following illustrations:

➤ 1. Alvin offers to sell his brand new Porsche to Margaret for $1. Margaret, knowing that he just paid $65,000 for the automobile, promptly accepts.
2. Laverne tells Ernest, "If you kiss me, I will give you $1 million." Ernest, knowing a good deal when he hears it, runs to her and gives her a quick smooch before she can change her mind.
3. Deborah, exasperated at Gabe's incessant chatter, tells him, "If you can keep your mouth shut for five minutes, I'll give you an all-expense-paid cruise around the world." He remains silent for the required period.

If, in each of the above examples, the offerees seek to enforce the offerors' promises, they will have a difficult time. Albert, Laverne, and Deborah will most likely prevail if they say they did not seriously intend the offer. Under the circumstances, a reasonable person should have realized the offers were in jest and not serious proposals. But consider the following examples:

➤   1. Glenda offers to sell Richard her brand new Ferrari for $1. Richard knows the car is worth in excess of $180,000, so he replies, "I wish you were serious. I'd take you up on the offer in a minute!" Glenda insists that she is serious, that the car has given her nothing but headaches since she bought it, and that she'd be much better off without it. Richard, after questioning the seriousness of the offer several times, finally accepts.

2. Rufus shows his friend Donald a new painting he has just purchased. Donald, knowing nothing about art, does not recognize that it is a genuine Picasso, worth several million dollars. Nevertheless, he is intrigued by the bizarre images on the canvas and offers to buy it from Rufus for $100. Rufus, thinking his friend is kidding, accepts in a serious tone, playing along with what he thinks is a joke.

In both of the above examples, Glenda and Rufus will have a hard time trying to get out of the contracts by claiming the offers were not seriously intended. In Glenda's case, her insistence that she was serious after Richard specifically asked her so will make it unlikely that a court will hold her offer to have been made in jest. If a reasonable person under the circumstances would have thought the offer seriously made, she will be bound by it. Rufus is also in trouble. If Donald can convince the trier of facts that he did not realize the painting was an expensive artwork, then he would have been justified in thinking the offer seriously made and could bind Rufus with his acceptance. (As you will see in the next chapter, the mere fact that the consideration given by one party is much less than that of the other will not ordinarily invalidate the contract.)

Provisions for Revocation

Generally, an offer can be accepted at any time until it is revoked.

➤ Tawana makes the following offer to Jerome: "I will sell you my 1990 Oldsmobile Cutlass Supreme for $8,000." Jerome tells Tawana that he'll think about her offer. Two days later, he calls her and agrees to buy the car under her terms.

Tawana's statement to Jerome constituted a valid offer since it clearly conveyed to him her unequivocal willingness to sell him her automobile. Once Jerome accepts the offer, a valid contract is formed and neither party will be able to back out of it without the other's consent. After Jerome accepts, he is obligated to buy her car and she to sell it to him. If either one refuses to perform his or her part of the agreement, the other party may sue for damages (we will fully explore the consequences of breach of contract in Chapter 10). But if Tawana had changed her mind in the above example *before* Jerome accepted her offer, no contract would come into existence. Once the offeror revokes an offer, the offeree no longer has the power of accepting it and thereby entering into a contract.

Unless the offer itself states otherwise, the offeree can accept it within a reasonable time until the offeror revokes it. What is a reasonable time varies depending on the circumstances of each case. Jerome's acceptance of Tawana's offer two days after it was made would be deemed timely (within a reasonable time) by most courts. But if Tawana's offer to Jerome was for pork belly futures, his acceptance two days later would not be deemed timely by most courts. What is the difference in these situations? The futures market is very volatile, with prices in such commodities as pork bellies and soybeans capable of wide fluctuations in a short period of time. But the same is not true for the automobile market. For this reason, courts are very likely to hold that the passing of several days is a reasonable time in which to accept an offer to buy a car but not to accept an offer to buy pork belly futures.

What if Jerome had waited a year before accepting Tawana's offer and she had not revoked the same in that period? Would the offer still be valid? No. A year is not a reasonable period for an offer to remain open. What about four days? A week? A month? Where does one draw the line? It is very difficult to determine with certainty in any given case what a court might determine to be a reasonable time for acceptance. For that reason, the offeror should expressly state in the offer itself an outside time limit for its acceptance. For example, if Tawana tells Jerome that she is willing to sell him her car for $8,000 provided he accepts the offer before 5:00 P.M. that afternoon, then the offer will automatically be revoked at 5:00 P.M. if Jerome has not accepted it by then. She can still revoke the offer before 5:00 P.M. simply by telling Jerome that she has changed her mind and is no longer willing to sell him her car. Unless she does so, Jerome will have the power to accept the offer and bind her to a contract until 5:00 P.M.

The offeree can also revoke an offer in two ways. First, any statement by the offeree that he is unwilling to accept the offer automatically revokes it and removes his ability to accept it. In addition, if the offeree makes a counteroffer containing significantly different terms than those of the original offer, the original offer is automatically revoked.

➤ Tawana offers to sell her automobile to Jerome for $8,000. Jerome accepts, provided she is willing to take $7,500 for her car. Jerome has made a counteroffer that automatically revoked Tawana's original offer. If Tawana refuses to sell her car for $7,500, Jerome will no longer have the power to accept the original offer. When he made a counteroffer, he revoked her original offer and can no longer accept it. If he offers her $8,000 and she still wishes to sell him the car, it is *she* who will be accepting *his* new offer to buy the car for $8,000. If she no longer wishes to sell him her car, she will not be obligated to do so, even though he is willing to pay what she originally required.

Provisions for Acceptance

Acceptance of an offer is the clear manifestation of assent to the terms of the offer. For an acceptance to be valid, it must be (1) made by the offeree, (2) unequivocal, and (3) communicated to the offeror. The first requirement is simple: only a person to whom an offer was made may accept it. If Harry offers to sell Sally his stereo for $200, but Nancy overhears the offer, she will not have the power to accept it, since it was not intended for her. Consider the following example:

➤ Professor Smith, an attorney, offers to draft a will for anyone in his business law class for $25. Bill Jones, who is not a student in Professor Smith's class, overhears the offer while walking outside of the class and promptly walks in and accepts. Bill's acceptance is not valid since Professor Smith's offer was only made to students in his class and could only be validly accepted by them. Bill Jones, not being a member of the class, does not have the power to accept an offer not made to him.

The requirement that the offer be unequivocal is also rather straightforward: For the acceptance to be valid, it must be clear from the offeree's words or actions that he intends to accept the offer under the offeror's terms. At common law, under the *mirror image rule,* an acceptance was deemed valid only if it mirrored the offer exactly. Any substantial deviation, such as a difference in price or other material terms, served to revoke the original offer. Today, the Uniform Commercial Code has modified the mirror image rule in transactions involving the sale of goods between merchants (Article 2 of the U.C.C.). In contracts between merchants for the sale of goods, acceptance is valid even if it contains terms different from the original offer. Inconsistent terms that would materially alter the contract are ignored, while consistent terms that do not materially change the terms of the contract become part of the agreement unless these are objected to within a reasonable time. The mirror image rule is still very much in force in transactions not involving merchants.

Finally, and not surprisingly, an acceptance is not valid until it is communicated to the offeror. Generally, the offeree may communicate her acceptance to the offeror in any manner, so long as the offeror is given a clear, unmistakable indication that the offeree accepts the offer. In face-to-face transactions, acceptance is usually communicated verbally. But acceptance can also be communicated by telegram, telephone, videotape, letter, or in some circumstances, actions such as the nod of the head to indicate assent. As soon as assent is given, a contract is formed that obligates both parties to render whatever performance was promised.

Since a contract comes into existence as soon as the offeree accepts the offer, problems can arise when the acceptance is not made face to face. What happens when an offeree decides to accept by a medium other than in person? Consider the following situation:

➤ Joan offers to sell Matilda a used television set for $100. Matilda decides to accept the offer and writes Joan a letter in which she accepts Joan's offer. She mails the letter at 5:00 P.M. The next morning, before the mail is delivered, Joan calls Matilda and tells her that she wishes to revoke her offer. Can she do so?

This example illustrates the *mailbox rule*, which states that an offer accepted by mail forms a binding contract as soon as a properly addressed, stamped envelope is mailed. Matilda's acceptance was complete and binding as soon as she mailed her letter to Joan. Joan attempted to revoke too late, since Matilda had validly accepted the offer the previous day as soon as she dropped the letter into the mailbox. Unless the offer limits acceptance to a specific mode, such as in person or by telephone, acceptance may be made in any reasonable fashion. It makes no difference that the offeror may not receive the acceptance for a day or two; indeed, if the postal service loses the letter and the offeror never receives it, a valid contract still exists. The offeree needs only to prove that he properly addressed, stamped, and mailed the letter. If he can do so, the offeror will be bound to the contract even though he will never receive actual notification of acceptance. This may seem unfair, but keep in mind that the offeror can easily protect himself by requiring as part of the offer that acceptance be made in a particular way (e.g., in person or by telephone). If an offeror states, "I will sell you my car for $1,000 provided you accept this offer by coming to my office prior to 3:00 P.M. tomorrow and informing me of your acceptance in person," then the offeree can *only* accept in person, at the place and time designated in the offer. An acceptance by telephone, fax, telegram, or mail will be invalid and no contract will arise; the nonconforming acceptance will be deemed a counteroffer that the offeror is free to accept or reject. If acceptance is not required in a particular form, however, any one of these methods of acceptance would suffice, since each is reasonable.

Judge for Yourself

Case 1.   Jonas tells Candide, "You know, I might consider paying you $100 if you would wash and wax my car." Candide says nothing but goes out and begins washing and waxing the car. Four hours later, she calls Jonas over, shows him the gleaming car, and demands the $100.

   a. Was there a valid contract that Jonas must honor? Why or why not?
   b. If there was a valid contract, was it bilateral or unilateral? Why?

Case 2.   Bertha telephones Anita and offers her an oriental rug for $400. Anita says she'll think about it. Later that day, she writes Bertha telling her that she accepts her offer. After Anita returns from mailing the letter, Bertha calls to revoke her offer, since she's found someone who is willing to pay $800 for the rug.

   a. Has Bertha revoked her offer in a timely manner? Why?
   b. If Bertha sells the rug to the third person for $800, can Anita successfully sue Bertha for breach of contract? Explain.
   c. Is it true that the contract between Bertha and Anita came into existence as soon as she mailed the letter?
   d. If Anita mailed the letter but forgot to put a stamp on it, will Bertha's telephone call later that day successfully revoke the offer?
   e. Assume that Anita's letter was properly addressed and contained the proper postage. Will a valid contract come into existence if the letter contained the following language: "I accept your offer to sell me your oriental rug provided you will take $350 for it instead of $400"? What effect would this letter have on Bertha's offer?

Case 3.   Angela offers Tai Chang $1,000 if he will paint her house while she is away on vacation. While she is away, Tai Chang buys the paint and begins painting the house.

   a. Is this an example of a unilateral or a bilateral contract?
   b. If Angela calls Tai Chang 10 minutes after he has begun painting the house and tells him she has changed her mind, will she successfully revoke her offer?

    c. If Angela returns from her trip to find that the house has not been painted, can she successfully sue Tai Chang?

    d. If Tai Chang began painting the house and then changed his mind after completing half of the work, would Angela be able to sue him for breach of contract?

Case 4.   Curt asks Michelle to the senior prom. She accepts. On the night of the prom, Curt calls Michelle and tells her that he will not be able to escort her to the prom, since he has been asked to go with Gretchen and has accepted.

    a. Can Michelle sue Curt for breach of contract?

    b. What are the five basic criteria that need to be present for there to be a contract? Which of the five seems to be missing here?

    c. If Curt had offered to take Michelle to the prom in exchange for her paying him $100, and if she had accepted, would a valid contract have existed? What is different between the two situations?

5

CONTRACTS: CONSIDERATION

Learning Objectives

After studying this chapter, you will be able to:

1. Define consideration.
2. Explain why past consideration, preexisting duties, and illusory promises do not contain valid consideration.
3. Distinguish requirement and output contracts from illusory promises.
4. Provide examples of forbearance as valid consideration.

Introduction

Consideration is defined as "some right, interest, profit or benefit accruing to one party, or some forbearance, detriment, loss or responsibility given, suffered or undertaken by the other" (*Richman v. Brookhaven Servicing Corp.*, 80 Misc. 2d 563, 363 N.Y.S. 2d 731, 733). Another way of defining consideration is as whatever is given or received to persuade someone to enter into a contract. To put it yet another way, consideration is simply the price of the contract.

➤ Norma offers to sell Leopold her stamp collection for $1,000. Leopold accepts. A valid contract is formed, the consideration for which is as follows: the $1,000 that Leopold must pay to Norma, and the stamp collection that Norma must turn over to Leopold.

In the above case, both parties are getting something of obvious value out of the bargain. This is the simplest type of consideration and the easiest to understand. It is not always so easy to determine whether both parties have received consideration under a given agreement or whether what was given suffices as consideration. Fortunately, we have some guidelines to help us determine whether consideration was given and received in any given case.

Constraints on Valid Consideration

Two elements must be present for consideration to exist in a contract: (1) there must be a bargained-for exchange, and (2) something of value to the receiver or of detriment to the giver must have been exchanged as the basis of the bargain. In the contract between Norma and Leopold, the $1,000 that Leopold promises to pay Norma for her stamp collection is a detriment to Leopold (something of value he is giving up) and a benefit to Norma (she will get $1,000 that she is not otherwise entitled to). Likewise, the stamp collection that Norma promises in exchange for Leopold's $1,000 represents a detriment to her (she must give it up) and a benefit to him (he will receive it in the bargain). In the same example, the parties clearly bargained for, or negotiated, the consideration given by each. Therefore, both elements of consideration are satisfied, and we can say that there was valid consideration in that case.

Based on these requirements, is there valid consideration in the following case?

> Darren, after winning the lottery, promises his friend Gustav that he will invest $250,000 in a business they will run as equal partners. A month later, the friends have a falling-out, and Darren informs Gustav that he has changed his mind about the planned joint venture and will give the money that was to be the start-up capital for their business to charity instead. Gustav is understandably annoyed and wishes to sue his former friend for breach of contract. Will he succeed?

In this case, Darren's promise to Gustav is not supported by consideration. Neither element of consideration is present: Darren neither asked for nor received anything of value in exchange for his promise. Thus, there was neither a bargained-for exchange nor something of value given to him, or of detriment to Gustav, as the basis of the bargain. Darren simply intended to make a gift to Gustav, and a promise to make a gift is unenforceable since it lacks consideration (a gift is, by definition, something that is given without the expectation of receiving anything in return).

Past Consideration

As a general rule, courts will not enforce contracts that cite past consideration as the basis of the contract, even if the word *consideration* is specifically used. Look at following examples:

> 1. Helen, the owner of ABC Company, wishes to reward the loyal service of Matthew, an employee. She drafts an agreement that reads as follows: "In consideration of Matthew's faithful service to ABC Company throughout the past 30 years, ABC Company hereby promises to pay to Matthew a yearly pension of $20,000 per year."

2. Yin, grateful for Mark having saved his life, tells him, "In consideration of your bravery in rescuing me from the path of an oncoming truck, I promise to give you $50,000."

In both of the above examples, past consideration is given as the basis of the contract. Such consideration is invalid and the contract is unenforceable. In reality, the persons citing past consideration want to make a *gift* to reward a good deed. Matthew's 30 years of faithful service are certainly valuable, as is Mark's good deed. But there is no present value in such services. Neither Yin nor Helen will receive any benefit at the time of making the offer, nor will their benefactors suffer any loss as a result of the proposed contracts. If the grateful givers wish to bestow a gift on their benefactors, they are free to do so. But if they change their minds prior to giving the promised money, they cannot be forced to do so; the agreements in question are unenforceable for lack of consideration.

Preexisting Duty

It is not consideration to do what one is already obligated to do. Contracts in which one of the parties promises to perform a duty he is already obligated to perform are, therefore, not enforceable. Consider the following examples:

➤ 1. At the scene of a fire, a firefighter agrees to rescue the homeowner's son from the burning building in return for the homeowner paying him $20,000.
   2. A company's accountant agrees to recheck the company's tax returns in exchange for a percentage of the tax savings he can realize for the company.
   3. A college professor agrees to teach during the second year of his two-year contract only if he is given a 50 percent raise in salary.

In each of the above examples, the contracts are unenforceable because the professionals involved are already obligated to perform the duties for which they seek additional compensation: the firefighter has a preexisting duty to save the child; the accountant, to find the largest legal refund he can for his employer; and the college professor, to teach during the second year of his contract. In each of these situations, the parties involved are not giving anything in return for the benefit they are to receive under the contract, since they are already obligated to do what they are agreeing to do under the new agreements.

A notable exception to the preexisting duty rule is found in contracts for the sale of goods under the Uniform Commercial Code (U.C.C.). Agreements modifying a contract under the U.C.C. need no new consideration to be binding, as long as the modifications are made in good faith [U.C.C. §2–201(1)].

The preexisting duty rule commonly comes into play to invalidate agreements modifying a preexisting debt. In general, a person who owes a debt to another cannot enter into an agreement to pay a lesser amount, since there is no consideration for the new agreement.

▶ Daniel owes Victor $100,000. Daniel is unable to pay back the debt but would like to avoid bankruptcy. Victor, on the other hand, knows that Daniel is unable to pay back the debt and will declare bankruptcy unless they agree to settle for less than the full amount. Both men draft an agreement whereby Daniel is to pay Victor $50,000 in full payment of the preexisting debt. Daniel pays the $50,000 as per the new agreement; Victor then sues him for the remaining $50,000. Will he succeed?

In most states, Victor would succeed in the above example. Daniel was under a preexisting duty to pay $100,000. That he paid part of that amount under a new agreement will not invalidate the old one, since there is no valid consideration for the new agreement. (Most states would hold differently if there was a good faith dispute as to the amount of the debt between the parties.)

Illusory Promises

For consideration to be valid, each party to an agreement must be obligated under the contract. If neither party is obligated to do anything, or if the obligation under the contract falls only on one party, then there is failure of consideration and the contract is unenforceable.

There are situations in which both parties to a contract appear to be giving consideration, but in fact, only one is obligated to perform under the contract. If promises under a contract are not mutually obligatory, such agreements are unenforceable for lack of consideration. A promise that does not obligate action is termed an *illusory promise*. Such promises wrap themselves in promissory language but, when examined, show that the promisor has not obligated herself to do anything.

Consider the following example:

▶ XYZ Company promises to buy from the ABC Oil Company "All the heating oil we want for the next year at a price of $1.30 per gallon."

XYZ's promise is illusory, since XYZ is not obligated to buy any oil from ABC. Under the agreement, only ABC is obligating itself to do anything—to provide XYZ with all the oil it wants at a set price of $1.30 per gallon. If prices drop and XYZ prefers to buy its oil from someone else, it is free to do so. If, on the other hand, oil prices increase, XYZ will be able to take advantage of its "contract" with ABC and buy as much oil as it wants for the $1.30 per gallon price. Since only ABC is bound to do anything under this agreement (sell oil to XYZ at $1.30 per gallon), the agreement fails for want of consideration. XYZ's promise is illusory since it does not obligate it to do anything under the agreement. Agreements obligating a party to buy any amount it *wishes, chooses, desires, or wants* are always illusory since there is no explicit or implied promise that the promisor will wish, choose, desire, or want to buy anything in the future.

What if the above example were to read, "In consideration of a $10,000 cash payment by XYZ to ABC, ABC promises to sell to XYZ all the oil it may want in the coming year for $1.30 per gallon." Is there now some binding obligation for XYZ that will make this a valid contract? Yes, since XYZ is now paying ABC a cash amount (valid consideration) for what amounts to an option contract where XYZ can buy any oil it needs during the coming year for a set price. The consideration given to ABC now is the $10,000 payment, and the consideration received by XYZ is the security in knowing that it will have a secure source of oil at a set price during the coming year despite fluctuations in the oil market.

Requirement Contracts

If promises to buy anything one wishes, chooses, desires, or wants are illusory, then how about a promise to buy as much of a given item as one will *need* or *require?* Consider the following examples:

> 1. The ABC Company promises to buy from the XYZ Company "all the heating oil it needs next winter for $1.30 per gallon."
> 2. Carl, a carpenter, promises to buy from Nails-R-Us "all the hardware supplies he *needs* for his business during the next year at a discount of 25 percent below retail prices."
> 3. Gabriela, the owner of a car rental fleet, promises to buy all the auto parts that her fleet might *need* during the next year from Fleece-M Auto Parts at prices 5 percent over wholesale.

Each of the above examples represents a *requirement contract*. Even though they look suspiciously similar to illusory promises, requirement contracts where one party agrees to buy all the supplies they may require or need are held to contain valid consideration. In enforcing these contracts, the courts impose an implied duty of good faith on the parties. As long as the promisor is likely to need the goods, materials, or services contracted for during the period in question, the courts hold that there is valid consideration for the promise and will enforce it. In the above examples, ABC is likely to need some heating oil next winter, and Carl will need hardware supplies to practice his trade. Likewise, Gabriela's fleet is likely to need some repairs. Since it is reasonable that the promisors will in fact need the supplies contracted for, and they are agreeing to purchase them from the promisees, valid consideration exists. If any one of the promisors refuses to purchase *any* supplies from the promisees, or they purchase the supplies in question from a third party, they will breach their duty of good faith under the contract and must pay damages. Note that if the promisor is not likely to need the goods or services contracted for, the promise would be illusory and unenforceable. If, for example, the ABC company uses gas heat and obligates itself to purchase all the heating oil it needs, the promise is illusory and the agreement unenforceable, since ABC is not likely to need any oil.

Forbearance and Adequacy of Consideration

As previously noted, consideration includes (1) anything of value promised by one party to another in a contract and (2) any detriment or forbearance to be borne by the promisor. It is easy enough to understand the idea of something of value as consideration but not as easy for detriment or forbearance. The following examples should help:

> 1. Jonas promises to pay his daughter, Jane, $100,000 if she will stop smoking cigarettes for five years. She forbears smoking for five years as a result of the promise.
> 2. Ricky promises to pay Claudia $50 if she will not go to the movies with Henry. She breaks the date and stays home.
> 3. Irma promises to cook a 12-course meal for Michael if he will agree not to watch the football game next Sunday.

In each of the above examples, the promisees are giving up the right to do something that they otherwise have the right to do. Jane stops smoking for five years, Claudia breaks her date with Henry, and Michael does not watch the ball game. The forbearance by each of these promisees is valid consideration, and the promisors must pay the agreed-upon consideration for the forbearance they have bargained for. It does not matter that Jane will benefit from quitting smoking or that there is no tangible benefit to her father from her quitting. What matters is that she gave up an activity that she had the legal right to engage in as part of the bargained-for exchange. At the end of the five years, her father will have to pay her the $100,000; should he refuse to, she can successfully sue him for breach of contract. All that is necessary for the forbearance to be valid consideration is that the promisee had the right to engage in the activity given up either temporarily or permanently as the basis of the contract. If, for example, Bill agrees to stop smoking crack cocaine in exchange for his father paying him $100,000, Bill is not giving valid consideration and the agreement is unenforceable, since Bill does not have the legal right to smoke the illicit drug and is, therefore, not giving up an activity that he has the right to engage in.

In general, courts do not look into the adequacy of consideration unless there is some evidence of fraud or undue influence by one of the contracting parties. As long as it appears that both parties willingly entered into the contract and that both have the capacity to understand the nature of the contract, then it will not matter that one party's consideration is disproportionate to the other's. The courts are generally uninterested in whether one or both parties made a bad bargain. If, as an example, a reasonably intelligent person agrees to pay $25 for a ballpoint pen worth $1, the courts will not examine the adequacy of the consideration unless the buyer can show that there was some improper conduct on the seller's part (e.g., that the buyer told the seller the pen was solid silver when, in fact, it was made of stainless steel).

Judge for Yourself

Case 1.   Theo tells Rena, "If you agree to come with me to the movies tomorrow, I will pay for the tickets and give you $50." Rena accepts the offer. The following day, Rena changes her mind and tells Theo that she will not go to the movies with him.

- *a.* Was there a valid contract between the parties? If so, what was the consideration each was to receive?
- *b.* Was this a social obligation as opposed to an enforceable contract? Explain.

Case 2.   Todd, the president of BCA Corp., tells Rebecca, "In consideration of your 30 years of faithful service to this company, BCA Corp. promises to pay you $1,500 per month for the rest of your life when you retire next week."

- *a.* If Todd changes his mind and refuses to pay Rebecca the promised pension, can she successfully sue for breach of contract? Explain.
- *b.* Would your answer to the previous question be the same if the agreement read: "In consideration of Rebecca's 30 years of faithful service, BCA Corp. promises to pay her $1,500 per month for the rest of her life, provided she continues to work for BCA for at least 3 more years"? Explain.

Case 3.   Clifford works for A&B Company as a sales associate under a one-year contract. After six months, he is offered a better paying position by C&D Company, A&B's competitor. After learning of C&D's proposal, A&B offers Clifford a $20,000 bonus if he will stay until the end of his one-year contract. Clifford agrees, then quits as soon as the year is up, intending to go to work for C&D.

- *a.* If A&B refuses to pay Clifford the promised $20,000 and Clifford sues for breach of contract, will he recover? Explain.
- *b.* Would your answer to the previous question be the same if Clifford had not quit his job after the one-year term?

    c. If A&B offered Clifford a bonus of $20,000 after six months of employment if he agreed to extend his original contract for two years, would that promise be enforceable? Why?

Case 4. John Notsobright, a greedy but less-than-brilliant business law professor, demands to draft his own employment contract at the college where he teaches. It reads: "In consideration for his teaching any courses that he might desire at the XYZ College, XYZ College promises to pay Dr. John Notsobright the sum of $52,000 per year for the next five years." He is fired at the start of the next semester, when, citing the contract, he refuses to teach more than one class.

    a. If John sues XYZ College for breach of contract, will he succeed? Explain.

Case 5. Brutus, a 22-year-old high school senior, drafts an agreement with his classmates wherein he promises "to forbear from punching, kicking, biting, harassing, or otherwise terrorizing my classmates in consideration of their paying me the sum of $2 per day."

    a. Leaving aside problems of illegality for the moment, is there valid consideration for this contract? Explain.

    b. Would your answer to the previous question be the same if Brutus had agreed not to "talk to or come near any of my classmates"?

6

CONTRACTS: GENUINE ASSENT

Learning Objectives

After studying this chapter, you will be able to:

1. Define valid, voidable, and void contracts.
2. Distinguish fraud in the execution from fraud in the inducement and explain their effects on the validity of a contract.
3. Define genuine assent.
4. List the categories of lack of capacity and provide an example of each.
5. Explain the rights of minors in entering into a contract.
6. Define the effect of insanity and intoxication on genuine assent.

Introduction

Assuming that an offer and acceptance are valid and that there is valid consideration, for an agreement to be binding, both parties must show genuine assent. To put it another way, the parties must fully understand that they are entering into a contract, and they must willingly enter into a contractual relationship with each other. There are a variety of circumstances that will invalidate what might appear to be valid, binding agreements between two or more parties. Consider the following situations:

➤ 1. Fausto, an adult, enters into a contract with Enrique, a 15-year-old boy, wherein Enrique promises to buy Fausto's Rolls-Royce automobile for $100,000.
   2. Felicia forces Henrietta to sign a contract at gunpoint through which Felicia will purchase Henrietta's home for $10,000.
   3. Claude agrees to purchase Cathy's boat for $10,000. Unknown to them, at the time of the signing of the contract, the boat has sunk in a storm and is at the bottom of the bay.

4. Ray, who has been judicially declared to be mentally incompetent, contracts with Sohair to buy 1,000 pairs of gloves.

In each of the above examples, one of the parties has not given genuine assent. There is a defect in the contracts that either renders them *void* (unenforceable, or having no validity) or *voidable* (able to be invalidated at the option of one of the parties). In the first example, the contract is voidable at the option of Enrique, the 15-year-old boy. Generally, persons under the age of consent can at their option avoid contracts they enter into, since they are held not to have full capacity to understand the nature of a contract and therefore cannot give their binding consent to enter into a contractual relationship. The contract in the second example is void, since contracts entered into under the threat of force are unenforceable (duress). The third example contains another void contract; a mutual mistake as to the matter contracted for renders the agreement unenforceable. Because both parties are mistaken as to the existence of the boat at the time of entering into the contract, the contract is void. The final example also involves a void contract, since a person judicially declared to be incompetent cannot give his consent to enter into a contract.

In every one of the above examples, there is a defect in the formation of the contract that makes each agreement either void or voidable. This chapter will concentrate on the types of problems that can arise in contract formation that prevent a binding contract from coming into existence. The common thread of all these impediments to contract formation is that the assent of at least one of the parties was not genuine due to factors outside of his or her control.

Mutual Mistake

If contracting parties make a mutual mistake that is vital to the agreement, there is no genuine assent, hence no valid contract. Common examples of mutual mistakes include situations in which both parties are mistaken as to the existence of the subject matter (in example 3 above, the boat the parties have agreed on, unbeknown to them, has sunk) or where both parties are mistaken as to the identity of the subject matter.

➤ Christopher offers to sell his car to Lisandra for $2,000. He owns a 1985 Toyota Corolla and a 1990 Nissan 240 SX. Christopher intends to sell the Toyota, but Lisandra thinks he intends to sell the Nissan. Both parties are mistaken in identifying the property to be sold, so no valid contract can come into existence.

Only mutual, or bilateral, mistakes will prevent a contract from being formed. Where only one party is mistaken as to the subject matter, a valid contract will come into existence despite the party's unilateral mistake. To put it another way, unilateral mistakes will *not* prevent a contract from coming into existence.

▶ Christopher offers to sell Lisandra his car; he owns a 1985 Toyota Corolla. Lisandra examines the car and mistakenly believes it to be a 1990 Nissan 240 SX (she does not ask Christopher about the car's year or make and he does not offer the information). Lisandra's unilateral mistake will not invalidate the contract, even if she can prove that she would not have purchased the car had she realized its make and year.

Fraud

As discussed in Chapter 2, the tort of fraud, or intentional misrepresentation, entails one party willfully making a false statement about an important fact to induce the second party to take some action that causes them a loss. Like mutual mistake, fraud invalidates genuine assent and prevents a valid contract from coming into existence. With regard to contracts, one party misrepresents the facts to induce the other contracting party to enter into a contract. The consequences of the intentional misrepresentation vary, depending on what the defrauding party is misrepresenting in the contract:

Fraud in the inducement: When one party to a contract intentionally misrepresents a material fact to the other party to induce them to enter into the contract, the first party has perpetrated fraud in the inducement on the innocent party. The misrepresentation is not about the nature of the transaction but rather about the subject matter of the contract. In other words, the defrauded party knows he is entering into a contract but thinks the bargain he is making is more beneficial to him than in fact it is due to the other party's misrepresentations.

Fraud in the execution: When the first party's intentional misrepresentation makes the innocent party unaware that she is entering into a contract, it is fraud in the execution of the contract.

The distinction between fraud in the execution and fraud in the inducement is both simple and crucial. When fraud is in the execution of a contract, the party harmed by the misrepresentation is simply not aware that she entered into a contract, since the transaction itself was misrepresented as being other than a contract. When fraud in the inducement is involved, the defrauded party knows he is entering a contract, but he has been misled into thinking that the terms of the agreement benefit him more than in fact they do. As a result, the contract resulting from fraud in the execution is void since there was no mutuality of agreement and, obviously, no genuine assent by the defrauded party; such agreements cannot rise to the level of a contract since they are fatally flawed. When agreement is reached as a result of fraud in the inducement, a contract will come into existence since the parties knew they were entering into a contract and both assented to its terms.

Nevertheless, such agreements are voidable, which means they are flawed and can be set aside at the option of the deceived party. Two quick examples will illustrate:

➤ 1. Michelle asks Laurent to witness her will. She places the document in front of him, after signing it herself, and asks him to sign in a given place. As he signs, she covers up the document with her hands so that he is unable to read it. (He thinks she is merely trying to hide the provisions of the will and signs the document, trusting in Michelle's word that it is what she purports.) In fact, the document is a contract whereby Laurent agrees to sell his house to Michelle for $100. This is an example of fraud in the execution, since Laurent was misled as to the very nature of the transaction. This "contract" is void and of no force or effect, since Laurent made no genuine assent to enter into a contract.

2. Rinaldo offers to sell Katrina his automobile for $20,000, after telling her it is a genuine 1969 Rolls-Royce. The sales contract simply states that Rinaldo promises to sell his "1969 automobile" to Katrina for the stated amount. In fact, Rinaldo's 1969 automobile (the only one he owns) is a Volkswagen Beetle that has been customized with a Rolls-Royce hood. When Katrina discovers the fraud, she will have the option of avoiding the contract. If she does not act within a reasonable time after discovering the material misrepresentation, however, the contract will be valid.

In the second example, a voidable contract came into existence; in the first, the contract was void. The main difference between both kinds of fraud is that in fraud in the inducement, the parties agreed to enter into a contract, where in fraud in the execution, one of the parties was not even aware that he was entering into a contract.

Lack of Capacity

Only parties who fully understand the nature of a contract and freely agree to enter into a contractual relationship can be bound to their agreement by genuine assent. It stands to reason that people who lack full mental capacity to understand the nature of a contract cannot be said to have given their genuine assent to enter into a contractual relationship. Contracts involving minors, mental incompetents, and intoxicated persons lack genuine assent. Consent given by these types of people is flawed, and the resulting agreement is either void or voidable at the option of the person who does not possess full capacity.

Minor's Contracts

In general, contracts entered into by a minor are voidable at the minor's option. In other words, minors are given the legal right to invalidate any contract they enter into at their option. A minor's exercise of this right is called *disaffirmance.* A minor is simply a person who has not reached the age of consent, generally 18 or 21. In most states, a person under the age of consent when entering into a contract has the option of voiding the contract until she reaches her majority (the age of consent).

If a minor disaffirms a contract, he must return whatever benefit he had received under it and will be refunded his payment. This creates problems for merchants and others who deal with minors, since the minor can get out of the contract at any time and demand the return of any money or other consideration he has paid. In exchange, the minor in most states need only give back whatever consideration he has received under the contract—in whatever condition it is in when he disaffirms the contract. Consider the following example:

> Rena, a 16-year-old girl with a valid driver's license, agrees to buy a 1991 Mercedes from Jeremiah, a Mercedes-Benz dealer, for $83,000 cash. She uses the car for 23 months and, a day before her 18th birthday, decides she'd much rather have $83,000 than a two-year-old car with various dents and scratches. She informs Jeremiah that she'd like to return the car and get her money back. When Jeremiah stops laughing, he calls up his lawyer who informs him that Rena is within her rights to disaffirm the contract and that he'll have to refund the full amount of the car's original value.

The above example may seem grossly unfair and unjust. It is, nevertheless, the law in most states. Some states, however, will offset the minor's right to receive a refund by the reasonable value of the benefit she has derived from the use of the subject matter of the contract—but this is a minority view. Other states would allow Rena to recover the full $83,000, but they would give Jeremiah the right to sue her for any damage she had caused the automobile under a tort theory (e.g., negligence). In many states, however, Jeremiah would have to absorb the entire loss, and Rena would only be responsible for returning the car, whatever its present condition.

The right of minors to disaffirm contracts at will can place a heavy burden on merchants who regularly sell goods to minors. Yet most merchants are quite happy to deal with minors. The reason? It makes good business sense to bear the risk that a minor may disaffirm a contract, since only a very small percentage of minors ever do so. One way around this potential risk is to have an adult cosign any contract with a minor. If this is done, the adult contracting with a minor has a greater measure of protection, since she may recover the full price of the contract from the cosigner in the event the minor decides to avoid the contract. It should also be noted here that only the minor has the right to avoid a contract entered into during minority—the adult who contracts with a minor is fully bound by his contract. (If both parties to the contract are minors, than either may avoid the contract at her option.)

Ratification.   A minor can ratify any contract she has entered into during minority as soon as she reaches the age of consent. Upon ratification, the contract becomes fully binding and is no longer voidable by the minor. Ratification may be either active or passive. Active ratification involves some overt act by the minor that expresses the wish to honor the contract once he has reached his majority. Passive ratification comes about if a minor does not exercise his right to disaffirm a contract entered into during his minority; once majority is reached, the contract is deemed ratified after passage of a reasonable time (e.g., several days or weeks, depending on the circumstances).

> ➤ Susan purchases a car from Sam on credit when she is 17 years old, agreeing to pay for it over the next three years at $100 per month. The age of consent in her state is 18. On her 18th birthday, she tells Sam, "Even though that car you sold me last year is a real lemon, I want you to know that I intend to keep making payments on it." She has ratified the contract and lost her right to disaffirm it. If she had said nothing but sent Sam her regular car payment after her 18th birthday, the act of sending the check would also be deemed a ratification of the contract. If she does not send her monthly payment upon reaching her 18th birthday and does not expressly disaffirm the contract within a reasonable time thereafter, she will have passively ratified the contract.

Business Contracts.   In most states, a minor's right to avoid contracts entered into during minority is not applicable to those entered into in the course of conducting a business he owns. In essence, minors who go into business are treated as adults for purposes of contracts they enter into in conducting that business.

> ➤ Jerome, a minor, owns and operates a gasoline station. He contracts with Moxxon Oil to deliver 10,000 gallons of gasoline per week to his station for one year. A month after signing the agreement, he finds that Texobil Oil will supply him with the same amount and grades of gasoline at a 10 percent savings over his current contract with Moxxon. He will not be able to avoid his contract with Moxxon, since the contract related to his business.

In the above example, if Jerome buys a Porsche from his local dealer for personal use, will he be able to avoid that contract before reaching his majority or within a reasonable time thereafter? Yes, since the contract for the Porsche is not one entered into during the regular course of his business and will, therefore, not be covered by the business exception to the general rule.

Contracts for Necessities.   Another exception to the general rules for minors involves necessities purchased by the minor. A *necessity* can be defined as anything that a minor reasonably needs to live and covers such essential items as food, clothing, shelter, and medical care. There is also some precedent that education be considered a necessity. If a minor's contract involves an item deemed essential, thus a necessity, it is generally enforceable against the minor for the reasonable value of the goods or services.

> Mario, a 17-year-old minor, goes into a general store and purchases a pair of jeans, a gold watch, potato chips, apple juice, a $3,000 stereo system, and a dozen CDs. Several weeks later, while still a minor, he returns to the store with all the merchandise and demands a refund. Is he entitled to get his money back?

Mario can return the gold watch, the stereo system, and the CDs and get the full amount he paid for these items refunded to him. The potato chips, jeans, and apple juice, however, are necessities (food and clothing), so the store need not refund his money for these items.

What constitutes a necessity depends in part on the facts of each case. There is often a fine line dividing a necessity and a luxury item. In part, the distinction will depend on the minor's background, or her family's status in life. For example, if the daughter of parents of modest means purchases a $10,000 mink coat from Bloomingdales, it will be deemed a luxury, not a necessity, and she will be able to return it at any time during her minority (or within a reasonable time after reaching the age of consent) and get a full refund. But the mink coat might be deemed a necessity for the daughter of wealthy parents; she might reasonably be expected to buy such a coat to keep warm, so she might not be able to return it. Likewise, an automobile can be a necessity for a person with a physical handicap who needs a car to get around or go to work, although a car is usually considered a luxury.

Insanity

A contract entered into by a person suffering from some mental condition that prevents him from understanding the nature of the contract is voidable; he may disaffirm it at his option when his disability ends, or his legal representative may do so at any time. The key question involved is whether the mental infirmity prevents the person from understanding the nature of a contract. Merely that a person suffers from mental delusions or is under psychiatric care is not enough in and of itself to give him the right to avoid contracts. A person who believes himself to be Napoleon is quite able to enter into binding contracts, as long as he can understand that he is entering into a valid agreement. As in the case of minors, persons who were unable to comprehend the nature of a contract due to some mental illness can ratify such voidable contracts once cured of that illness; the legal guardians of such persons can also ratify such contracts. Whether or not a person's mental condition prevented him from comprehending the nature of a contract must be decided by the trier of fact after hearing testimony by expert witnesses. On the other hand, contracts made by persons judicially declared to be incompetent are void, not merely voidable.

> Norma, who believes she is Cleopatra and has been transported to the present by space travelers from a faraway galaxy, purchases 1,000 wigs from Wigs-B-Us in preparation for the day when the interstellar travelers

return to take her home. If Norma had been judicially declared insane prior to entering into the contract, it would be void. If she has not been declared insane, the contract is voidable only if she can show that the nature of her delusion prevented her from understanding the nature of a contract.

Intoxication

A contract entered into by a person so intoxicated that he cannot understand its nature is voidable. It doesn't matter whether the intoxication is from alcohol or another drug. The question is whether the person was capable of understanding that she was entering into a binding agreement at the time the contract was formed. As with insanity and minority, contracts entered into by intoxicated persons are voidable; and the trier of facts must decide whether or not the person was so intoxicated as to be unable to comprehend the nature of a contract.

It should come as no surprise that many business contracts are entered into while one or both parties are drinking; three martini lunches were, after all, popular much before President Jimmy Carter ever made an issue of them and remain so today. It would be a mistake to assume that any contract entered into where one or both parties had been drinking is voidable; most are not. The issue is not the blood alcohol level of each party (although such information, if available, is very relevant) but the ability of each party to know that they were entering into a contract and to comprehend its terms. If the contract is voidable, the intoxicated party, upon recovering sobriety, may disaffirm it at his option within a reasonable time of discovering his entry into the contract.

> Marvin, after drinking six extra-dry martinis, offers to sell his house to Bertha for $100,000. Bertha, who has drunk half a glass of wine, accepts. At the time of the offer and acceptance, Marvin seemed perfectly sober, spoke clearly, sat perfectly erect, and otherwise seemed normal; he is someone who drinks heavily and regularly. Bertha, on the other hand, never drinks, and was under the table singing Christmas carols (in July) and laughing hysterically at the time she signed the contract. The following day, Marvin changes his mind and wants to back out of the deal. Can he?

In the above example, Marvin will have a relatively hard time proving that he was so intoxicated as to not understand the nature of the contract. From all appearances, he was perfectly sober, despite heavy drinking; the heavy drinking by itself, although very relevant, is not the only factor the jury will weigh in determining his ability to understand what he was getting into. Bertha, on the other hand, can present a lot of evidence to a jury to the effect that she did not understand the nature of the contract at the time of its formation, despite an extremely low level of alcohol consumption. Hence, she would easily be able to avoid the contract should she choose to; but not so Marvin, who will not be able to present as much convincing evidence (e.g., testimony of witnesses) that he was too intoxicated to understand the nature of the contract he proposed.

Judge for Yourself	**Case 1.** Neil agrees to buy Pepe's 1986 Buick Skylark for $2,000. Unknown to both men, the automobile has been struck by lightning and burned five minutes before they entered into the contract.

    a. Is the contract valid? Why?

    b. Would the answer be the same if the car was struck by lightning five minutes after the contract was formed?

Case 2. Sally offers to sell Jimmy her automobile for $10,000, telling him that it is a 1991 Nissan. In fact, the car is a 1989 Nissan. Jimmy, who knows very little about cars, accepts the offer, trusting in Sally's word.

    a. Is the contract valid, void, or voidable?

    b. Can Jimmy get out of this contract? Why?

    c. Can Sally get out of this contract? Why?

Case 3. Lorraine, a 15-year-old girl, buys a blue fox coat from Simple Simon for $5,000. Two years later, while still a minor, she wants to return the coat and get a refund, since she feels that wearing animal furs promotes cruelty to animals.

    a. If Lorraine is the daughter of unemployed construction workers at the time she buys the coat, will she be able to return it? Why?

    b. Is the fact that her father is an unemployed laborer relevant to her ability to return the coat? Why?

    c. If the coat is sprayed with red paint by an animal rights activist before she tries to return it and she is the daughter of parents of modest means, will she be able to get her money back in most states?

    d. If Simple Simon the furrier wanted to protect himself against the dangers of dealing with minors, what could he do?

Case 4. During a business lunch, Lynn and Sue discuss a merger of their two companies over several cocktails. After protracted negotiations, they agree to a contract for the merger and write the basic agreement, which they both sign. On the way home, Sue gets into an automobile accident and a Breathalyzer test shows she was driving while intoxicated. A week later, she wants to get out of the merger agreement and contacts you, her attorney, for advice.

    a. Under what theory can you try to have the contract invalidated?

    b. Will you definitely succeed? Why?

    c. What type of evidence would you like to have available for trial?

7

Contracts: Legality

Learning Objectives

After studying this chapter, you will be able to:
1. Describe the effect of illegality on contracts.
2. Define the different types of illegal contracts.
3. Name and briefly explain the major federal antitrust legislation.
4. Distinguish illegal contracts from contracts that are against public policy.

Introduction

Legality is the final requirement that every agreement must meet before it can rise to the level of a contract. Simply put, the subject matter of any agreement sought to be enforced as a binding contract must not involve the commission of an illegal act and, furthermore, must not oppose the state's public policy.

A court can deem a contract illegal if it is inconsistent with any state or federal law. Common examples of illegal agreements include gambling contracts, usurious contracts, contracts that call for the commission of a crime or tort, contracts involving restraint of trade, contracts involving obstruction of justice, and contracts deemed to be against public policy as declared by the courts. We will briefly examine each of these below. Keep in mind that parties to nearly all illegal contracts are guilty of committing a crime simply by entering into them; but here we are concerned with the enforceability of such contracts rather than the criminal liability of parties to them. In that regard, contracts not meeting the requirement of legality are deemed void; as such, they are unenforceable in the courts.

Gambling Contracts

Perhaps the most common type of illegal contract involves gambling. Although gambling was legal at common law, every state today has legislatively outlawed or severely restricted and controlled gambling. To be valid, a contract involving gambling must conform to the state's gambling regulations. Therefore, the purchase of a state-run lottery ticket gives rise to an enforceable contract, as does the placing of a bet in a racetrack or state-sanctioned bingo hall. A court would deem any other type of contract involving gambling illegal, hence void.

Consider the following examples:

➤
1. Sally buys a $1 Lotto ticket.
2. Sally places a $2 bet at the racetrack.
3. Sally places a $2 bet with her bookie.
4. Sally puts up $10 towards a Super Bowl pool at work.
5. Sally bets Jenine $100 that the Mets will win the National League pennant in 1992.
6. Sally loses $50 at her weekly poker game with her friends.
7. Sally bets $1,000 on number 123 in her state's daily numbers game.

Assuming that Sally's state, like most, sanctions state-run lotteries and allows bets at racetracks but outlaws all other forms of gambling, the bets in examples 1, 2, and 7 are legal and the contracts they involve are enforceable. The rest of the examples involve illegal gambling contracts and are, as such, unenforceable. Betting with a bookie, gambling on a Super Bowl pool, betting on sports (unless sanctioned by the state), and playing cards for money with friends all involve illegal contracts. As such, agreements involving these gambling activities are illegal and unenforceable. As previously noted, Sally may well be guilty of a crime for engaging in illegal gambling, but here we are concerned with the civil effect of such contracts. In terms of contract law, the illegal gambling contracts are unenforceable. This means that if Sally refuses to pay on all the illegal bets she has made, neither her bookie, her friend Jenine, nor her poker friends may collect on such bets in a court of law. The courts will generally not intervene when illegal contracts are involved. Sally's bookie may, of course, seek other illegal means to collect his bet. The only point here is that he will not be able to sue her for the gambling loss, be it $2, $200, or $2 million.

Usurious Contracts

At common law, parties could lend money at any interest rate they mutually agreed upon. Today, every state has modified the common law by passing statutes that limit the highest interest rate that parties may agree to in contracts involving credit. The maximum rate that states allow lenders to charge varies, generally between 16 percent and 25 percent. Contracts involving credit in which the borrower agrees to pay a greater rate of interest than the law allows are termed *usurious* and are void. Unlike with illegal gambling contracts, however, a court will not generally "leave the parties as it found them" and refuse to enforce the contract. Although there is a split of opinion across the various states, most states enforce the usurious contracts but *reform*, or judicially change, them to reflect a rate of interest allowed by law. Most states will simply reduce usurious rates of interest to the highest level the state law allows. A minority of states seek to punish lenders who attempt to enter into usurious contracts with borrowers; they do not allow lenders to recover any interest at all on those loans and require borrowers to pay back only the principal amount of the loan over the life of the loan agreed to by both parties. Let's look at an example:

> ▶ Emma signs an agreement for a new car loan with Greedy Savings and Loan. She borrows $15,000 and agrees to pay back the loan over a period of five years at an interest rate of 25 percent per year. Emma's state has a usury statute that makes 20 percent the highest rate of interest that lenders may charge on consumer loans. After making several payments, Emma is told about the state's usury law and refuses to make any further payments. The bank sues her to recover the full amount of the loan principal plus the interest it would have received over the five-year period of the loan.

Emma's original loan of $15,000 at 25 percent for five years carried a monthly payment of $440.27. If Emma lives in a state whose usury laws conform to the majority view, she will be forced to pay back her loan at a rate of interest equal to the state's maximum allowable interest rate. Assuming that such a rate is 20 percent, Emma will have to pay back the loan at a rate of $397.41 per month for five years (a savings of $42.86 per month). If her state is in the minority of states that do not allow usurious lenders to recover any interest at all for the life of the loan, she can pay back her loan with no interest for its five-year term, making her monthly payments $250 per month (a monthly savings of $190.27).

Commission of a Tort or Crime

Contracts involving the commission of a tort or a crime as part of their subject matter are unenforceable. Consider the following examples:

> ▶ 1. Tammy pays Pete $500 to beat up Angela, with whom she has had a disagreement.
>   2. Ron agrees to pay Lucy $50 for two vials of crack cocaine.
>   3. Harry offers to pay Susan $1,000 if she gets a letter published in the local paper that falsely accuses the town's mayor of being a thief.

In each of the above examples, the underlying agreement is void for illegality. If the money promised under the above agreements has already been paid, the offerors will not be able to sue offerees to return the money to them. A court will simply leave parties to illegal contracts where it finds them, neither enforcing the underlying contracts nor forcing parties to return any benefit they have received under them. For the same reason, if the promisees have performed as agreed, they also will not be able to sue in court to receive the promised reward.

Restraint of Trade

Agreements to restrain trade through unlawful means are void for illegality. Such agreements include those involving unfair competition, price-fixing, monopolies, and violations of either state or federal antitrust legislation, such as the following:

- *Sherman Antitrust Act of 1890:* This Congressional act makes it a felony to enter into contracts that result in the restraint of trade among the states or with foreign countries. The act also makes it a felony to monopolize or attempt to monopolize any part of interstate or international trade or commerce. The Department of Justice enforces the act's criminal penalties, but the act also gives individuals civil remedies. Persons harmed by the illegal antitrust activities of others can sue to recover *treble damages*—three times their actual damages—and attorney's fees in civil court.
- *Clayton Act of 1914:* In passing the Clayton Act, Congress intended to strengthen antitrust legislation by bolstering the Sherman Act. The Clayton Act prohibits sellers from charging buyers different prices unless the differences are related to differences in selling or transportation costs. The act also makes it illegal to restrict buyers from dealing with competitors' products and for one company to hold stock in a competing company when the effect is to lessen competition. It also places some restrictions on persons serving on the board of directors of competing companies (other than most financial institutions).
- *Federal Trade Commission Act of 1914:* Congress created the Federal Trade Commission (FTC) through the Federal Trade Commission Act and empowered it to prevent unfair competition and unfair or deceptive trade practices. Subsequent amendments have substantially broadened the powers of the FTC, including the power to investigate allegations of violations of any federal antitrust statutes, as well as defining specific unfair or deceptive trade practices. The FTC has the power to issue *cease and desist* orders to businesses that violate federal antitrust laws and can fine them up to $10,000 per day that violations are allowed to continue.

· *Robinson-Patman Act of 1936:* Congress passed this act as a supplement to the Clayton Act. It prohibits businesses from discriminating in price charged to buyers of goods of similar grade and quality when such discrimination tends to lessen competition or create a monopoly. Price discrimination is only allowed if the seller can show that price differences are due to higher shipping costs or a good faith effort to meet a competitor's lower price. Like the Sherman Act, Robinson-Patman allows injured businesses to sue for three times their actual losses. Most antitrust litigation under the act is instituted by businesses seeking treble damages rather than direct intervention by the FTC.

Obstruction of Justice

Agreements to interfere with the administration of justice include bribery of public officials, influence peddling, and jury tampering. Contracts with the underlying purpose of obstructing justice are illegal and void. Naturally, those who enter into such contracts are guilty of a crime. Examples of contracts with the purpose of obstructing justice would include the following:

➤ 1. Barbara promises to pay Michael, a state inspector, $5,000 if he overlooks several health code violations in her restaurant.
2. Robert offers $50 to Tom, a police officer, if he'll "forget about the speeding ticket."
3. Justin, a lieutenant in the John Doe organized crime syndicate, offers to pay $100,000 to Patrick if he votes to acquit Mr. Doe of the racketeering charges with which he is charged.

Against Public Policy

Finally, there are a variety of situations under which a contract may not technically be for an illegal purpose, but the courts will still refuse to enforce the agreement on public policy grounds. In such situations, although a contract may otherwise be enforceable, courts argue that enforcement would not be in the interest of society or will otherwise harm the common good. Instances of agreements void as against public policy include unconscionable contracts, where the subject matter is so outrageous or the relative benefit to one of the parties is so grossly unfair as to "shock the conscience of the court." The following are examples of contracts that many courts would refuse to enforce as against public policy, even when the subject matter of the contract is not specifically prohibited by statute:

➤ 1. Juan, a poor family man who speaks no English, agrees to purchase a refrigerator under a valid installment purchase agreement. The fair market value of the refrigerator is $350. Juan agrees to pay a retail price of $1,000 plus interest at the highest rate allowed by law. After Juan pays most of the purchase price, the refrigerator breaks down and he refuses to continue making payments.

2. Raymond, a luckless gambler deeply in debt, agrees to sell his eyes to Lina, a wealthy person in need of a cornea transplant, for $10,000. Before the operation takes place, he changes his mind and wants to have the contract declared void.

3. Harry, a livery cab driver, offers to drive Suyitno from Kennedy Airport to downtown Manhattan for $500 (the trip normally costs under $30).

Assuming that no laws have been broken in the above examples, a court would still be free to declare each of the agreements void as against public policy if it finds them grossly unfair. A court could also reform any of the above agreements to make them fall within acceptable limits (e.g., it could award Harry the $30 reasonable fee for his services, instead of the $500 agreed-upon fee.). Courts are under no obligation to hold any given contract void as against public policy simply because it is unfair to one of the parties, or even grossly unfair. Under its equity jurisdiction, a court can exercise that power at its discretion. Generally, courts are very reluctant to declare contracts void as against public policy and will do so only under extreme situations.

Judge for Yourself

Case 1.   Susanne bets her friend Orlando $100 that the number drawn in her state's legalized Daily Numbers Game that evening will be a combination of the numbers 739. Orlando agrees to the bet. That night, the number 937 is drawn.

a. If Orlando refuses to pay off on their bet, can Susanne sue him? Why?

b. If Orlando had given her his money at the time of the bet and the combination does not come up, can he sue her to have her return the money to him?

c. Change the facts as follows: Susanne asks Orlando to bet $100 for her through the state's legal Daily Numbers agent and promises to give him 10 percent of her winnings for his effort. Orlando takes the money but does not make the bet, electing to keep it for himself. Can Susanne successfully sue him for the return of her money?

d. In question *c*, if the number that Orlando was to bet on "hits," can Susanne sue him for her lost winnings?

Case 2.   Mark asks his friend Phil to lend him $1,000 to buy a used car. He says he will pay him back $1,500 in one year when one of his

CDs matures. The maximum rate of interest their state allows is 20 percent per year.

 a. Is this contract usurious? Why?

 b. If Mark refuses to pay the loan back at the end of the year, can Phil sue him? If he does, how much money will he recover if his state adheres to the majority rule? What if his state follows the minority rule?

Case 3. John, Ken, and Robin are all involved in the sale of used cars in the same state. John and Ken agree to cut their car prices by 30 percent for four months to drive Robin out of business. Three months later, Robin goes bankrupt, not having been able to sell any automobiles.

 a. Does the agreement between John and Ken satisfy all of the elements for a valid contract? If not, which element(s) is (are) missing?

 b. Regardless of whether or not the agreement is enforceable, is there valid consideration by John and Ken under the agreement? If so, what is it?

 c. If, a month after entering into the agreement, John decides to raise his prices back to their original level, can Ken sue under the contract? Why?

Case 4. Sadam, a well-known Wall Street broker specializing in corporate takeovers, is indicted for federal securities fraud and insider-trading violations. The chief prosecution witness is Husne, a long-time associate of Sadam's working in the same firm. Just as the case goes to trial, Sadam offers Husne an all-expense-paid cruise around the world plus $50,000 in cash if he will agree to house-sit his villa in the south of France for six months, until "the trial winds down." Husne accepts and promptly leaves for France a day before the trial begins.

 a. If, upon Husne's return after the trial, Sadam is unwilling to pay him the promised consideration for Husne's service, can he successfully sue? Why?

 b. Assume that Sadam paid Husne the $50,000 in advance and gave him the requisite cruise tickets, and Husne then decides to testify against his former colleague. Can Sadam sue him for the return of his money and the reasonable cost of the cruise? Why?

8

CONTRACTS: STATUTE OF FRAUDS

Learning Objectives

After studying this chapter, you will be able to:

1. Explain the basic purpose of the statute of frauds.
2. Define the types of contracts that come within the statute of frauds.
3. Explain what constitutes a contract that cannot be performed within one year.
4. Give examples of contracts that constitute a transfer of an interest in realty.
5. Give examples of specially manufactured goods and explain when they do not fall within the statute of frauds.

Introduction

As we have seen in previous chapters, a variety of requirements must be met before an agreement gains the status of an enforceable contract. Some types of agreements are subject to one additional condition: they must be evidenced by a signed writing to be enforceable.

In general, contracts need not be in any particular form to be enforceable; binding contracts can be formed orally, in writing, and under special circumstances, simply by the action of the parties involved. Not surprisingly, the flexibility available to parties in forming contracts leaves much room for abuse. It should come as no surprise that many people are not above lying to further their own ends and that oral contracts and contracts arising out of the specific behavior of the parties (implied-in-fact contracts) are particularly susceptible to false claims. Consider the following common example:

➤ Enrique offers to buy Mary's car for $2,000 provided she has the car tuned up and replaces a worn tire. Mary accepts the offer and tells Enrique that she will have the car ready for him in two days. Two days later, Enrique gives Mary $2,000 and demands that she turn over the car.

Chances are quite high that Mary will give the car to Enrique as promised and that she will have had it tuned up and replaced the worn tire. The vast majority of contracts are honored by both parties without a problem arising. But what would happen if any of the following situations arises?

➤ 1. Mary denies having agreed to sell Enrique the car and refuses to turn it over.
2. Mary is willing to turn over the car but denies having agreed to replace the old tire or to get it tuned up.
3. Mary claims that Enrique promised to pay $3,000 for the car.
4. Mary is willing to comply with the contract, but Enrique claims that she had agreed to paint the car as well as purchase four new tires for it and tune it up previous to its transfer.

The potential problems that can arise out of a misunderstanding by one of the parties, or from a fraudulent claim, are nearly limitless. If one or both of the parties refuses to perform as agreed, the only remedy is a lawsuit—which is expensive, time-consuming, and impractical in many cases. If one or both parties sue, there will be a problem with proof. Since there is no objective written evidence of the contract, each party will have to try to convince the trier of facts that his or her version of the facts is correct, and the trier of facts will determine which party is telling the truth and which is lying; unfortunately, the process of determining whom to believe is not infallible, and crafty, dishonest wrongdoers sometimes prevail over honest but unconvincing victims.

Fraudulent lawsuits are not new. The British Parliament first attempted to deal with them in 1677 by passing the Act for the Prevention of Fraud and Perjuries. This statute, which became to be commonly known as the *statute of frauds,* sought to prevent fraudulent contracts by requiring certain types of contracts to be in writing and signed by the parties (at least by the party being sued) to be enforceable. A modern version of the statute of frauds is applicable today in every state, requiring a signed writing as a prerequisite to the enforceability of six types of contracts:

1. Contracts that by their terms cannot be performed within one year.
2. Contracts for the sale of an interest in real property.
3. Contracts for the sale of personal property worth $500 or more.

4. Contracts promising to answer for the debt of another.
5. Contracts of executors and administrators.
6. Contracts in consideration of marriage.

An *executory contract* (one that has not yet been fully performed by both parties) falling within one of the above enumerated categories must be in writing and signed by the person being sued for its breach before it is enforceable. Oral contracts covering the six areas in question are not enforceable. An *executed contract* (one which has been fully performed by all parties), on the other hand, is not the subject of the statute of frauds. Once an oral contract that by its terms needed to be evidenced by a signed writing under the statute of frauds has been fully performed, it cannot be invalidated. In other words, the statute of frauds makes certain types of oral contracts unenforceable unless they are evidenced by a signed writing. Once an oral contract is fully performed, however, whether or not it needed to be in writing to be enforceable becomes a moot point.

Contracts That Cannot Be Performed within One Year

A contract that by its terms cannot be fully performed within one year must be in writing and signed by the parties before it is enforceable. Common examples would include:

1. Professor Wong promises to teach business law at State University for two years in exchange for a yearly salary of $40,000.
2. Mohammed promises to sell Noxxe Oil one million barrels of crude oil per year for the next three years at the benchmark price set by OPEC at the time delivery is made.
3. Carla agrees to lease an automobile from Auto Wrecks for five years at a monthly cost of $157.

In each of the above examples, the contract by its very terms cannot be completed within one year, since it must run for the specified period of from two to five years. To be enforceable then, each of these contracts must be evidenced by a signed writing. If the parties orally agreed to the contracts, the underlying agreements would be unenforceable and either party could refuse the promised performance without penalty. Keep in mind that if the parties orally entered into the contracts and performed as agreed, the statute of frauds would be irrelevant. The significance of the statute is that it makes certain kinds of agreements unenforceable unless there is a signed writing to evidence them; nothing in the statute prevents parties from honoring oral contracts that it requires to be in writing. Furthermore, the statute of frauds applies only to executory contracts (those not yet fully performed by both parties). Once oral contracts are fully executed by each party performing as agreed, the statute no longer applies. In other words, the statute of frauds will permit parties to refuse to perform contracts they have orally entered into when such contracts needed to be in writing, but it will not invalidate oral contacts that have been fully carried out.

Contracts that by their terms may last less than one year do not fall within the statute of frauds and are fully binding whether they are oral or in writing. Consider the following examples:

➤ 1. Professor Wong promises to teach at State University for two semesters (10 months) at a salary of $40,000.
2. Mohammed agrees to deliver one billion barrels of light sweet crude oil to Noxxe Oil within the next six months at the current OPEC benchmark price.
3. Carla agrees to lease a car from Auto Wrecks for the next three months at $200 per month.
4. Victor López promises to handle any and all legal matters for the BCA Corporation for the rest of his life in exchange for a yearly retainer of $100,000.

None of the above examples need to be in writing to be enforceable, since each contract is capable of being fully discharged within one year. The first three examples are obvious, since by their terms the contracts will be fully executed within 10, 6, and 3 months, respectively. The last example is a little harder to understand at first blush, but is also quite simple: although Victor has agreed to represent BCA "for the rest of his life," the contract must not necessarily be performed for one year or more. Even assuming that Victor is 34 years old and is likely to live at least another 40 years, there is no guarantee that he will. He could die at any time from an accident during the first year; this contract, then, is not one that cannot be performed within one year. The rationale may seem somewhat strange, but it is logical. As a result, any contract that is to run for a person's lifetime is enforceable even though it is verbally agreed to and is not evidenced by a signed writing.

Contracts That Transfer an Interest in Realty

A contract that transfers an interest in land must be evidenced by a signed writing to be enforceable. That a contract concerns real estate in and of itself does not mean that it must be in writing; only contracts that transfer *an interest in realty* fall within this section of the statute of frauds. A contract to lease an apartment for less than one year, for example, need not be in writing to be enforceable; although a lease obviously involves real estate, it does not transfer an ownership interest in realty and therefore need not be in writing to be enforceable. If the lease runs for one year or more, however, it does need to be in writing—not because it transfers an interest in realty, but because it is a contract that cannot be performed within one year and hence is covered by the statute of frauds.

Common examples of contracts that must be in writing because they transfer an interest in realty include:

1. Contracts for the sale of real estate.
2. Easements.
3. Contracts transferring mineral rights.
4. Contracts transferring air rights.
5. Mortgages.

The above will be covered in Chapter 16 on real property.

Contracts for the Sale of Personal Property Worth $500 or More

Personal property can be defined as anything capable of being owned other than real estate. Personal property can be either tangible or intangible. Tangible personal property has a physical existence and can be touched; common examples of tangible personal property would include a car, a book, a pair of slacks, and a computer. Intangible personal property does not have a physical existence, but rather represents an ownership right of something that cannot be touched or seen; common examples include copyrights, trademarks, and stock ownership. (See Chapter 15 on personal property for a fuller discussion of personalty.)

Under the statute of frauds, any contract involving the sale of personal property for a price of $500 or more must be in writing to be enforceable. Consider the following examples:

1. Charles agrees to sell his butterfly collection to Sandra for $600.
2. Harry agrees to sell his motorcycle to Jessica for $500.
3. Mark agrees to sell his piano to Robin for $1,900.
4. Kim agrees to sell the rights to her copyrighted song "A Bird in Hand Can Be Messy" to XYZ Records for $1,000.
5. Lena agrees to sell her 12 shares of IBM common stock for $100 per share to Ron.
6. Dan phones ABC Department Store and orders a microwave oven priced at $200 and a 19-inch color television priced at $300.

Each of the above examples involves the sale of personal property for $500 or more and must as such be evidenced by a signed writing to be enforceable. Where more than one item is purchased as part of the same transaction, the total cost of the items is considered as a single sale, so that the $500 requirement is met in example 6, even though the price of each separate item is less than $500. (Sales taxes or shipping costs are not considered as part of the sale price.)

An important exception exists for specially manufactured or custom-made goods. Contracts for such goods are enforceable even without a writing regardless of their price, provided the goods are not readily salable in the manufacturer's regular course of business and the manufacturer has taken some steps to begin producing the special-order goods.

➤ Lenny enters into an oral contract with Cindy whereby she agrees to crochet a bedspread for him in exchange for $500. Even though there is no writing, Lenny will be bound to the contract as soon as Cindy takes some substantial steps to fulfill her part of the agreement, such as buying the necessary materials or starting to crochet the bedspread.

Note that if Cindy owns a store where she regularly sells hand-made bedspreads, her contract with Lenny would have to be in writing, since she could sell the crocheted bedspread to another customer in the regular course of business if Lenny refuses to take it.

Contracts Promising to Answer for the Debt of Another

A contract whereby one person binds herself to answer for the debt of another must be evidenced by a signed writing to be enforceable. This section of the statute of frauds applies to agreements guaranteeing payment, such as the following:

➤ Susan tells Sam, a car dealer, "Sell the car to Suyitno and I promise to pay you for it if she can't." If Sam sells Suyitno the car and she defaults on the payments, Sam will not be able to demand that Susan pay unless the agreement was in writing and signed by Susan.

It is important to distinguish a contract to answer for the debt of another from a contract entered into for another's benefit; only the former need be in writing.

➤ Alice tells Sam, a car dealer, "Please deliver this car to Victor and I will pay for it." This agreement need not be in writing (unless the car is sold for $500 or more, of course), since it is not a contract to answer for the debt of another—Alice is a principal party to this agreement, and the debt created is her own, not Victor's.

Contracts of Executors and Administrators

A contract by an executor or an administrator of an estate to pay the estate's debts out of his own funds must be evidenced by a signed writing to be enforceable. This is clearly a variation on a contract to answer for the debt of another, which we've just examined. Note that not all contracts by executors and administrators on behalf of the estates they represent need be in writing—only those in which the administrator or executor agrees to pay for estate debts out of his own pocket. If, for example, an executor agrees to pay for funeral expenses out of his own funds, rather than from estate funds, the contract would have to be in writing and signed by him to be enforceable.

Contracts in Consideration of Marriage

Finally, any promise made in consideration of marriage must be in writing and signed by the promisor to be binding. The following examples would all need to be in writing and signed by the promisor to be enforceable:

> 1. John promises to employ Dana as a vice president for advertising if she will marry his son, Harold.
> 2. Damon promises to give a gift of $1 million to Cathleen's favorite charity if she agrees to marry him.
> 3. Jemel agrees to marry Gretel if she will buy him a new Ferrari.

Each of the above promises is fully enforceable, but only if it is made in writing and is signed by the promisor.

Judge for Yourself

Case 1.   Arti Runsalot, a famous track star, promises to be a lifetime spokesperson for Runfast Shoes in exchange for a salary of $100,000 per year.

    a. Does the contract need to be in writing and signed by Arti to be enforceable?

    b. Would your answer be the same if Arti agreed to be Runfast Shoes' spokesperson for the next two years at the same salary?

    c. If Arti orally agreed to be Runfast Shoes' spokesperson for six months for a payment of $50,000, would this contract need to be in writing?

Case 2.   Vincent, the owner of an oil exploration company, offers to pay Sari $1 million for the exclusive right to drill for oil on her land forever; he also agrees to pay her $2 per barrel for any oil his company extracts from the land in the event oil is found.

    a. Does this agreement need to be evidenced by a signed writing?

    b. If Vincent offers to lease Sari's land for six months to store oil drilling equipment on it, does that agreement need to be in writing?

    c. Would your answer to the previous question be the same if the contract was to run for 12 months? Explain.

Case 3. Pablo, a painter, agrees to sell Margaret one of his paintings, "Boy Eating Spaghetti through His Ear," for $500. If he later changes his mind and refuses to part with the painting for the agreed-upon consideration, can Margaret sue to enforce the contract if it was orally entered into?

Case 4. Renata wants to buy an automobile on credit from the Rip-M-Off Used Car Company. The salesman refuses to sell her the car on credit because she is 19 and has no prior credit history. Renata's friend, Rhoda, assures the salesman that she will pay for the car if Renata is unable to do so, whereupon he agrees to sell Renata the car, a 1978 Fiat X 1/9, for $10,000. The salesman writes on the credit agreement: "Rhoda Sirlin, guarantor for Renata Schmidt." Renata signs the agreement, but Rhoda is not asked to sign it.

   a. If Renata is unable to keep up with the car payments after the first year, can Rip-M-Off sue Rhoda for the balance of the payments? Explain.
   b. Would your answer be the same if the car was sold for $499?

Case 5. Tyrone Tycoon, a wealthy industrialist and doting father of a very spoiled brat, wishes to have Teenage Idol, of whom his daughter is horrendously fond, marry his daughter, Minnie Tycoon. Mr. Tycoon orally promises to give Mr. Idol his own film studio if he will marry his precious Minnie. Mr. Idol, who is immediately stricken with Minnie's intelligence, beauty, and grace upon hearing the offer, accepts. After the wedding ceremony the next day, Mr. Tycoon informs Mr. Idol that he was only kidding about setting him up with his own studio but is willing to get him a job in one of his companies' mailrooms if his screen popularity ever fades. Can Mr. Idol sue for breach of contract? Explain.

9

CONTRACTS: THIRD-PARTY BENEFICIARIES AND ASSIGNMENT OF CONTRACTS

Learning Objectives

After studying this chapter, you should be able to:

1. Define and distinguish between intended and incidental beneficiaries.
2. State the general rule on assignment of rights and delegation of duties.
3. Name the types of duties that are not generally delegable.
4. State the general rights and obligations of parties when assignment or delegation is involved.
5. Define obligor, obligee, delegator, delegatee, assignor, and assignee.

Introduction

There are situations in which persons or companies who are not parties to a valid contract are affected by it. In such cases, it is necessary to determine whether such third parties have legally recognized rights stemming from contracts made by others that directly affect them. As an example, if George takes out a life insurance policy with the CBA Insurance Company and names Barbara as his beneficiary, George and CBA are clearly the parties to the contract. Barbara, the contract's beneficiary, has an economic interest in the contract but is not a party to it. When George dies, his executor or executrix can sue CBA for breach of contract if it fails to honor the policy and pay Barbara the death benefit. But suppose the executor or executrix refuses to sue CBA for any reason. Can Barbara sue CBA herself for the breach, even though she is not a party to the contract? To answer the question with certainty, we must first explore the law of contracts as it relates to third-party rights.

There are also many situations in which parties wish to assign their rights or delegate duties under a valid contract. In general, the law allows parties to assign their rights under contracts rather freely, but delegation of duties is more difficult to achieve. A *contractual right* can be defined as the entitlement a party is to receive as the bargained-for consideration under the contract. A contract by definition is a binding agreement between two or more parties under which each receives some benefit. If, for example, John agrees to paint Mary's house for $1,000, Mary's rights under the contract would include having her house painted (in a reasonable manner), and John's rights would include being paid $1,000 for his labor. With a few exceptions to be noted shortly, contractual rights are freely assignable.

Along with each party's contractual rights, there are also contractual duties that each is obligated to perform. In the last example, John's duty under the contract is to paint Mary's house in a competent manner, whereas Mary's duty is to pay John the agreed-upon consideration for his work. Contractual duties can be delegated, but not as freely as contractual rights can be assigned, for reasons that will soon become apparent.

Third-Party Beneficiaries

Whether third parties to a contract have the right to enforce it depends largely on the intention of the principal parties in entering into it.

Intended Beneficiaries

Where contracts between parties are entered into for the express benefit of another, the intended beneficiary has the right to sue on his own behalf to enforce the contract. Several criteria are used to determine whether a third party to a contract was an intended beneficiary of that contract. These include the following:

1. Does the contract expressly name the third party as beneficiary?
2. Was the contract entered into by the principal parties primarily for the benefit of the third party?
3. Is there a relationship between the third party and the principal parties to the contract (e.g., the offeror and offeree) such that it is likely that the principals intended the contract to be for the third party's benefit?

If the third party is determined to be the intended beneficiary of the contract, then he has the right to enforce that contract in court if it is breached. A classic example of a third-party beneficiary is the beneficiary of a life insurance policy alluded to in this chapter's introduction. Even though the beneficiary is not involved in the contract as a party, such a contract is clearly entered into for his benefit.

Incidental Beneficiaries

Third parties to contracts who are not intended as the primary beneficiaries but nonetheless have an economic interest in the contracts cannot enforce them if they are breached. The following illustrates an incidental beneficiary to a contract who has a great stake in the contract but is unable to enforce it since the principal parties did not primarily enter into it for the third party's benefit.

➤ Big Defense Firm (BDF, Inc.) enters into a contract to produce a production model ashtray suitable for use in an F-16 fighter. Since the contract calls for the development of only three prototypes, the cost is rather high—$6,000 for each ashtray. After the contract is entered into, the Pentagon decides that allowing pilots to smoke during the middle of a dogfight might not be a good idea and informs BDF that it no longer wants the ashtrays. BDF decides not to sue for breach of contract, since it wants to maintain good relations with the Pentagon and thinks it has an excellent chance of winning an even more lucrative defense contract for 100 high-tech screwdrivers at a price of $5,000 each. Windfall Contractors, a company to which BDF was considering awarding much of the work to be done on the ashtrays, is not as understanding as BDF; it only produces state-of-the-art ashtrays and will not benefit from the screwdriver deal. Windfall would like to sue the Pentagon to enforce its contract with BDF. Can it do so?

Although it is clear that BDF could sue the Pentagon for breach of contract under the facts given, Windfall Contractors could not sue either on its own behalf or to enforce BDF's contractual rights. Windfall has a clear economic interest in the contract, but it is not a party to it and was clearly not intended as a beneficiary of the contract between BDF and the Pentagon. Windfall is merely an incidental beneficiary who has no rights under the contract.

Contract Assignment

Every party to a contract has certain rights and responsibilities under the contract. There are instances when one or both of the parties to a contract wish to assign their rights under the contract for the benefit of a third party or would like to delegate performance of their duties under the contract to a third party. Generally, both assignment of rights and delegation of duties under a contract are allowed, provided certain guidelines are met.

Assignable Rights

In general, rights under a contract are freely assignable, unless the assignment would substantially change the burden to the obligor. Keep in mind that in every bilateral contract, each party is an obligor—a person obligated to perform under a contract—and an obligee—a person who receives the benefit of another's performance in a contract. When parties exchange mutual promises, each is an obligor in that each has promised to perform some duty, and an obligee, since each has also been promised the performance of some duty by the other party.

Consider the following examples:

➤ 1. Sally lends $10,000 to Oscar, which he promises to repay in one year, along with interest at a rate of 10 percent. After entering into the contract, Sally loses her job and would like to transfer her right to receive the $10,000 plus interest to the ABC Bank, which is willing to pay her $9,750 in cash for Oscar's note.

2. Ricardo agrees to paint a portrait of Maggie for $1,000. After the contract is entered into, Ricardo's landlord threatens to evict him if he does not pay $1,000 in back rent immediately. Ricardo offers to assign his right to collect the $1,000 from Maggie to the landlord, and he accepts.

3. Vincent, a writer, is asked to make a contribution to UNICEF, one of his favorite charities. He has very little cash on hand but would like to give the charity the royalties from a short story he has just sold. UNICEF gratefully accepts the assignment.

Each of the above examples involves the assignment of a right: Sally's right to collect her $10,000 principal plus 10 percent interest from Oscar, Ricardo's right to the $1,000 payment from Maggie, and Vincent's right to royalties from his publisher. Each of these assignments would be valid, since they do not substantially change the burden of the obligor. It is just as easy for Vincent's publisher to send a royalty check to UNICEF as it is to send it to Vincent; likewise, Maggie will not be unduly burdened by having to pay Ricardo's landlord instead of Ricardo; nor will Oscar's burden under the contract be any greater because he must now repay his debt to ABC Bank rather than to Sally. In short, each of these assignments would be valid.

There are circumstances, however, under which contract rights cannot be assigned. Briefly, they are as follows:

1. When the assignment will substantially change the nature of the obligor's duty.

2. When the assignment substantially changes the risk to the obligor under the contract.

3. When the contract itself prohibits assignment.

4. When personal service contracts of a unique nature are involved. (Routine personal service contracts may be freely assigned. In determining whether a personal service contract is for unique or routine services, the question to ask is whether it makes a significant difference that one competent individual performs the services over another. Professional services

deemed to be of a personal or unique nature would include those of a physician, a lawyer, an accountant, a teacher, or an artist. Routine services would include skilled or unskilled labor performed under a universal code or standard, such as the services of plumbers, electricians, and contractors, all of whom work in accordance to an existing code for their trade under which personal differences in performance are deemed to be insubstantial.)

5. When the assignment is prohibited by law. (Most states, for example, prohibit the assignment of wages beyond a set limit. If a worker attempts to assign his wages beyond that limit, the assignment is invalid.)

Delegable Duties

Duties under a contract may generally be delegated, just as rights under a contract may be freely assigned. As with assignment of rights, the delegation of duties is also subject to some notable exceptions. Instances in which delegation of duties under a contract is not permitted include the following:

1. Duties that require the exercise of personal judgment or special skill. In general, these include duties performed by such professionals as doctors, lawyers, actors, and artists. Duties to be performed by some skilled professionals, such as plumbers and electricians, however, are freely delegable. The reason is that the duties performed by such professionals is deemed to be standardized in accordance to an approved set of guidelines (e.g., a city's electrical code), and competent performance by any member of such a trade or profession is deemed the equivalent of any other member's performance.

2. Duties involving a relationship of trust. Classic examples of such relationships include services performed by an accountant, physician, or attorney. Even though these services may be fairly standard (e.g., any competent accountant can file an accurate tax return following standard accounting principles and the guidelines of the Internal Revenue Code), a relationship of trust between the obligee client and obligor professional is crucial to the contractual relationship. For this reason, such contractual duties cannot generally be delegated.

3. Delegation that changes the burden of the obligee. If the obligor's duty might be significantly changed by a delegation, the delegation is invalid.

Consider the following examples:

➤ 1. Victor, a business law professor, is under contract to teach courses in the management department for State University. He is also under contract to write several books for a leading publisher. Victor would like to take off two semesters to devote himself to writing full time and wants to assign his teaching duties to a good friend and fellow attorney, Pearse, who is at least as well qualified to teach business law as he.

2. Ricardo, who has agreed to paint Maggie's portrait for $1,000, finds that he will be unable to finish the task in time, since two previous portraits he had committed himself to painting are taking longer than expected. He'd like to assign his painting duties to Maria, an artist who is at least as talented as he.

3. Cindy, after signing a contract to rewire Vincent's house, finds that she will not be able to honor the contract on time due to other electrical contracting duties. She would like to delegate her duty to wire Vincent's home to Brian, a licensed electrical contractor who is willing to undertake the responsibility.

The first two examples involve contracts that cannot be delegated, whereas delegation of duties in the third example would be allowed. In the first example, Victor cannot delegate his duties because teaching clearly requires the exercise of personal judgment and special skills. Regardless of the competence of his friend Pearse, the latter's teaching would be *materially different* from that of Victor. The same would be true if Victor tried to delegate to Pearse his client's cases; unless the clients agreed to it, such a delegation would be invalid. The practice of law, like teaching, involves special skills and the exercise of personal judgment. In addition, the attorney-client relationship is also a relationship of trust, so it is not delegable.

In the second example, Ricardo's duty to paint Maggie's portrait is also of a personal nature and requires the exercise of special (artistic) skills, making it nonassignable; Maria's talent as an artist is irrelevant, since a portrait painted by Maria, regardless of artistic merit, would not be the same as one painted by Ricardo.

Finally, in the third example we find a delegable duty. Cindy's duty to wire Vincent's house calls for standardized performance in accordance with the applicable electrical code in their jurisdiction. As long as Brian is a licensed electrician who will perform the work according to code, Cindy will be able to delegate the work to him without needing Bertha's consent. The same would be true if Cindy were a plumber who had agreed to install a new bathroom for Vincent or to convert his home heating system from oil to gas heat. Even in the case involving standardized performance, however, delegation will not be allowed if the contract between the parties specifically forbids it. Anyone concerned about a contract for standardized performance being delegated to an unknown third party can guard against it by insisting that the contract includes a clause prohibiting delegation.

Rights and Responsibilities of Parties when Delegation or Assignment Are Involved

The third parties to whom a valid assignment or delegation is made inherit certain rights and obligations under the contract. In essence assignees (persons to whom rights under a contract are assigned) and delegatees (persons to whom duties under a contract are delegated) inherit the respective rights and responsibilities of their assignors or delegators (persons under contract who delegate their duties to third parties). In a manner of speaking, assignees and delegatees "stand in the shoes" of the assignors and delegators whose rights or responsibilities they take over. Even when a valid assignment or delegation takes place, however, the original parties to the contract still retain certain obligations, as will be seen in the following discussion.

Obligee's Duties

The obligee (the person to whom the obligor owes a duty under a contract) has the duty to accept performance from the delegatee if the duties may lawfully be delegated under the contract. The obligee need not accept performance from the delegatee if the duties are nondelegable.

Delegator's Duties

The delegator, or the original obligor, remains personally responsible for performance on the contract. If the delegatee's performance is inadequate, the obligee can sue the original obligor for breach of contract. In such an event, the delegatee would, of course, be liable to the delegator for the breach.

Delegatee's Duties

The delegatee's duties depend on the nature of the delegation. If the delegatee receives consideration from the delegator for her promise to perform his duties under the contract, a contractual relationship will exist between them, and the delegatee will be obligated to perform the delegator's duties or be liable for breach of contract. In such a case, the delegatee is also liable to the obligee, who is a third-party intended beneficiary of the delegation contract; the obligee will be able to sue the delegatee directly to enforce the contract if the latter breaches. The obligee will have the option of suing the delegator or the delegatee individually or jointly, since both will be liable for performance of the contract. If the delegator has given no consideration to the delegatee, the delegatee will be under no enforceable obligation to perform the delegator's duties and neither the delegator nor the obligee will be able to bring suit against him for breach of contract. Finally, if the obligee agrees to allow the delegatee to perform the contract in an instance where the delegation is not otherwise valid, the delegatee will take the place of the delegator as the primary party to the contract and the delegator's duties under the contract will end. When that happens, it is called a *novation*. In a novation, the delegatee replaces the delegator as the obligee in a contract. Consider the following example:

> ➤ Helen, an attorney, promises to handle Laura's uncontested divorce for a fee of $750. After entering into the retainer contract, Helen becomes ill. To avoid needlessly delaying the divorce action, she offers to delegate her duties to Margaret, an attorney who also practices in the family law area. Helen cannot delegate her duties under the retainer to Margaret without Laura's consent, since the practice of law is not deemed to be a standardized duty, and Laura has the right to demand that Helen perform her agreed-upon responsibilities personally. Nevertheless, Laura agrees to the delegation of duties, since she also trusts Margaret and doesn't want her divorce action to be delayed. As soon as she gives her consent to the delegation, Margaret will take the place of Helen as Laura's attorney, and Helen's responsibility under the agreement will end. The transfer of duties from Helen to Margaret is not a delegation; it's a novation. As such, Helen will not be responsible for any breach of contract (including malpractice) that Margaret may be guilty of.

Judge for Yourself

Case 1.   Larry wants to surprise Eileen by having her house painted while she is away on vacation. He contracts with Sue to do the job and pays her $3,000 in advance for the work. Sue takes the money but does not do the work.

   a. Can Eileen bring an action against Sue for breach of contract? Explain.
   b. Can Sue subcontract the work to Tawana, a housepainter, for $2,500 without getting Larry's approval first? Why?
   c. If Larry's check to Sue bounces, can Sue collect the $3,000 from Eileen? Why?

Case 2.   Manuel asks Daniel to draft his will and offers to pay Daniel his standard fee of $150. Six months later, Daniel, who has been busy with a variety of projects, remembers Manuel's will and, feeling guilty, delegates the duty of its drafting to his colleague Gabriel, paying him $200 for the task.

    a. If Manuel objects to the delegation of the duty to Gabriel, can he insist that Daniel draft the will himself? Why?

    b. Would your answer to the above question be the same if Gabriel specializes in trusts and estates and is the foremost expert on wills in the country?

Case 3.   Angela takes out a $10,000 guaranteed student loan from State Bank to help finance her college education. Under her agreement with State Bank, she must pay back her loan over a 10-year period at an interest rate of 9 percent. A year after Angela graduates from State Community College, State Bank notifies Angela that it has sold the note covering the unpaid balance of her student loan to the Student Loan Marketing Association (SLMA) and that Angela must now make her monthly payments to that organization.

    a. If Angela objects to the assignment from State Bank to SLMA, will she nonetheless have to send her monthly payments to SLMA? Why?

    b. Assuming that the assignment is valid, can the assignee (SLMA) demand that Angela make all future payments to it by certified mail if that requirement was not part of the original contract between Angela and State Bank? Explain.

    c. Assuming once again that the assignment is valid, can SLMA demand that Angela make each monthly payment to SLMA in person at its offices in Angela's city, as opposed to mailing the payments as she had previously done to State Bank?

Case 4.   Solomon enters into a valid requirements contract with the XYZ Oil Company whereby XYZ is to provide to Solomon all the oil he needs to heat his home over the next five years at a price of $1.10 per gallon. After the first year of the contract, Solomon decides to convert his home's heating system from oil to natural gas.

    a. If Solomon tries to assign his right to receive the home heating oil for the remaining four years under his contract to Harriet, his neighbor, will XYZ be bound by the assignment? Explain.

10

Contracts: Discharge and Remedies for Breach

Learning Objectives

After studying this chapter, you will be able to:

1. List the various ways in which contracts can be discharged.
2. Distinguish between impossibility and impracticability of performance.
3. Define nominal and compensatory damages.
4. Define specific performance and explain when it is available as a remedy.
5. Explain what is meant by election of remedies.

Introduction

Once a valid contract comes into existence, parties to the agreement are obligated to render the promised performance. Until all parties to a contract have fully performed their obligations under it, the contract is said to be *executory*. This means that there are obligations still to be met under the agreement or performance still to be rendered. As soon as all parties to a contract have fully performed their contractual obligations, the contract is deemed an executed agreement and the obligations of all parties are thereby discharged. In the overwhelming majority of contracts, parties render the agreed-upon performance and the contract is discharged without a problem. But there are obviously a notable number of instances in which one or more of the parties to a contract is either incapable of rendering the promised performance or simply refuses to do so. Whenever this happens, it is necessary to determine whether the failure to perform is excusable, in which case the contract is discharged, or whether the failure is inexcusable, in which case a breach of contract occurs, with the nonbreaching party having the right to recover damages. In this chapter we will examine first what constitutes a valid discharge of contractual duties and then what remedies are available to the victims of a breach of contract.

Discharge of Contracts

Once a valid contract is formed, the parties to it are absolutely obligated to render the agreed-upon performance. Failure to do so results in breach of contract and gives rise to remedies, as will be discussed shortly. But not every instance in which parties fail to perform gives rise to an action for breach of contract. As will be seen, there are a variety of instances in which contracts are deemed to be fully discharged even when the promised performance has not been rendered or has been rendered only in part. Once a contract has been discharged, rights and duties of parties to the agreement end. In general, valid contracts can be discharged many ways, as you'll see.

Performance

As previously noted, parties perform exactly as promised in the vast majority of contracts. Once each party to a contract has done what she or he has agreed to do under it, the contract is discharged and the obligation of each party to perform ends. The following example is typical of a contractual obligation discharged through performance:

➤ Yin offers to buy Almeda's sailboat for $2,000 provided she buys new rigging for it prior to delivering it to him; Almeda agrees. The next day, Almeda turns over the boat to Yin along with the new rigging, and Yin gives Almeda $2,000 in cash. As soon as the boat is delivered and the cash is paid, the contract is discharged; each party has performed as promised and nothing more remains to be done.

Objective Impossibility of Performance

If, after a valid contract is formed, circumstances change so that it is impossible for one or both of the parties to perform as promised through no fault of their own, the contract is discharged and both parties are excused from performing as agreed. For a contract to be discharged for impossibility of performance, it must be shown that circumstances beyond the control of the parties render promised performances physically impossible, not just that one of the parties is herself unable to perform as agreed. Consider the following examples:

➤ 1. Roberta promises to sculpt a bust of Marcel out of granite for $5,000. After entering into the contract, Roberta realizes that it is impossible for her to perform as promised since she lacks any talent or skill as a sculptor. Roberta will not be excused from performing as promised. Her inability to perform is purely subjective. It is possible for someone to sculpt a bust of Marcel out of granite if the person has the necessary skills; that Roberta does not have the skills will not render her failure to perform excusable. She will be liable for the breach.

2. Roberta, a sculptor, promises to sculpt a miniature bust of Marcel out of ivory for $5,000. After the contract is entered into, the United States passes a law prohibiting the importation or sale of ivory into the United States, and Roberta is unable to procure the necessary ivory to sculpt Marcel's bust. In this situation, the contract between Roberta and Marcel would be discharged, since it is objectively impossible for the contract to be performed due to its subsequent illegality.

Death or Incapacity

In situations involving personal service contracts, the death or incapacity of either party will discharge the contract. This involves only contracts for services of a personal nature that cannot be delegated as discussed in Chapter 9. If the contract is delegable, then the death or incapacity of the promisor or promisee will not discharge it; rather, the executor or executrix of the deceased must either accept the performance under the contract (if the deceased was the promisee) or delegate the deceased promisor's duties to a third party. Consider the following examples:

1. Darlene, a business law professor, signs a two-year contract to teach at State University. She dies after the first year of the contract. Darlene's contract with State University is discharged.
2. Darlene, a plumber, contracts with State University to install a new gas heat furnace. She dies after the contract is entered into but before she has had the opportunity to perform (while the contract is still executory). Darlene's executor must find another plumber to do the job or be liable for breach of contract.

The difference in the above situations is that duties under a plumbing contract may be delegated, but not under a teaching contract; the former are, therefore, not discharged by the death of the obligor, whereas the latter are.

Impracticability of Performance

The courts in some, but not all, states hold that a contract is discharged when its performance becomes commercially impracticable. Performance under a contract is deemed impracticable when it is either highly difficult or expensive to carry out and neither party foresaw such difficulty or expense when entering into the contract. Under Article 2 of the Uniform Commercial Code, contracts for the sale of goods (to be discussed in detail in the following chapter) may be discharged if their performance is commercially impracticable. The following example illustrates a commercially impracticable contract:

> ▶ Albert contracts with Nastasia to excavate a foundation for a new home on his land for $1,000. Both Nastasia and Albert assume that his land consists of sandy soil, as is common in his area. In fact, Albert's land contains only two feet of topsoil over several hundred feet of solid rock. To excavate the foundation to the agreed-upon depth of 10 feet, Nastasia would have to blast through solid rock at an expense to her of tens of thousands of dollars. Since the cost involved in completing this contract is much greater than anticipated *by both parties,* and the unusual solid rock foundation was not foreseeable at the time the contract was entered into, many courts would deem this contract commercially impracticable.

The elements of unforeseeability and extreme expense are crucial to a case in which one of the parties is seeking to have the contract declared discharged for commercial impracticability. Merely that the contract will be more costly than anticipated is not enough; nor will extreme cost be the basis for discharging a contract where the parties could have found out the special circumstances through a reasonable inspection.

Frustration of Purpose

There are instances in which an unforeseeable event takes place after parties enter into a valid contract but before performance is rendered (while the contract is still executory) that destroys the purpose of the contract. Under such circumstances, the parties are able to perform, but performance would be pointless. For the contract to be discharged for frustration of purpose, the following circumstances must exist:

1. An unforeseeable act or event takes place after the contract is entered into but before performance is due.
2. The intervening act or event is not caused by any party to the contract.
3. The intervening act destroys the purpose of the contract.
4. Both parties to the contract were aware of the contract's purpose at the time they entered into the contract.

The following examples illustrate situations in which valid contracts would be discharged by frustration of purpose:

> ▶ 1. Juan pays Jacob $300 to paint his car and makes an appointment to take the car to his shop three days later. The next day, a severe storm causes a tree to fall on Juan's car, causing damage far in excess of the car's market value. The contract is discharged, since

its purpose has been frustrated by an unforeseeable intervening event (the damage caused by the storm). Jacob could still paint the car and may even wish to do so; but to allow this contract to be carried out would be wasteful and unreasonable.

2. Peter agrees to build an attached garage on Cindy's land. On the day before Peter was to begin work on the project, a severe earthquake causes structural damage to Cindy's house, rendering it unsafe and requiring it to be torn down. Even though Peter could still build the attached garage, the purpose of the contract has been frustrated, since the house will have to be torn down and an attached garage to a condemned house is useless. Therefore, either Peter or Cindy could ask a court to declare the contract discharged.

Rescission and Release

Parties are always free to discharge a contract by their mutual consent, provided the contract is executory. The mutual agreement to rescind, or nullify, the contract is binding, provided the parties freely entered into it. This is called *rescission.*

A *release,* or contract not to sue, serves to discharge a contract, provided it is supported by new consideration.

➤ Tina agrees to buy 1,000 widgets from Tom for $1 each. When the widgets are delivered, she refuses to accept them and wants to cancel the contract. She knows she is guilty of a breach and wants to avoid being sued for Tom's lost profits under their agreement. If she offers Tom $50 in exchange for a release of his right to sue her for breach of contract, and if Tom accepts the offer, their original contract involving the sale of widgets will be discharged.

Accord and Satisfaction

An *accord* is an agreement supported by new consideration to discharge a contractual duty. *Satisfaction* is the performance of an accord. Once accord and satisfaction have taken place by an agreement to discharge a contract having been carried out, the underlying contract is discharged. Consider the following example:

➤ Hans owes Lillian $5,000. He offers to perform handyman's chores around Lillian's house for six months if she will agree to discharge his $5,000 debt to her. If she agrees, the new contract will be deemed an accord. Once he has fully performed as promised by rendering his services for the six-month period, a valid satisfaction of the accord will take place, and the previous contract will be discharged. Note that the accord itself does not discharge the previous contract until the satisfaction has taken place.

Bankruptcy

Bankruptcy is a process that allows debtors in financial difficulty to make a fresh start by having most debts discharged, while at the same time protecting the rights of creditors by ensuring that the available assets of an individual who files for bankruptcy protection are distributed equitably among all creditors. Individuals, associations and corporations whose liabilities exceed their total assets can file for protection under the bankruptcy laws. A brief examination of the major sections of the Bankruptcy Code, Title 11 of the *United States Code,* will be helpful here since bankruptcy proceedings can serve to discharge contractual obligations.

General Provisions

Bankruptcy in the United States is a matter of federal law. Title 11 of the United States Code contains all statutes pertaining to bankruptcy and is divided into nine chapters. Chapters 1, 3, 5, and 15 contain the basic rules affecting all bankruptcy proceedings, while Chapters 7, 9, 11, 12, and 13 create specific types of bankruptcy. Of these, Chapters 7 and 11 merit a closer look since they contain, respectively, the basic rules on ordinary bankruptcy and reorganization affecting business.

Chapter 7: Under Chapter 7 (Liquidation), the property owned by a debtor is sold by a trustee and the proceeds are then used to pay off creditors. Under Chapter 7, certain types of personal and real property are exempt from attachment. Exempt property includes: the equity in the debtor's principal place of residence up to $7,500, and household items not to exceed $4,000 in total value; up to $1,200 of the value of an automobile; professional tools or books up to $750 in value; and support payments, such as alimony and child support. Most personal and real property owned by the debtor, however, is attached and sold to satisfy the outstanding debt. Liquidation can be either voluntary or involuntary. In *voluntary liquidation,* the debtor petitions the federal district court for his district for protection under Chapter 7. Under *involuntary liquidation,* it is the creditors who petition the court to institute the bankruptcy proceedings. Creditors can seek involuntary liquidation whenever the debtor fails to pay bills as they become due. A single creditor can file the petition if there are fewer than 12 creditors combined, and at least three creditors must file the petition if the debtor owes money to 12 or more creditors. In either case, the combined debt must exceed $5,000 before involuntary liquidation proceedings are commenced. The debtor is free to contest any petition for involuntary liquidation, and such petitions cannot be brought against cities, farmers, or charities.

Chapter 11: Under Chapter 11 (Reorganization), a business can continue to operate with court approval under its existing management or under the direction of a court-appointed trustee while its creditors' claims are frozen until a plan for the payment of debts is approved by the court. With the approval of the court, a business operating under Chapter 11 protection can continue to conduct business, its debts can be modified, and the disposition of assets, recapitalization of the business or even plans for mergers or takeovers can be carried out if approved by the court. Individuals, partnerships and corporations can all avail themselves of Chapter 11 protection of their businesses. When businesses file for Chapter 11 protection, they have 120 days to come up with a reorganization plan that must be approved by both at least 50% of each class of creditors and the court.

Once either a liquidation or reorganization is approved under Chapters 7 or 11 of the Bankruptcy Code, part or all of the debtor's debts are forgiven and need never be repaid. Not surprisingly, debtors whose debts are discharged under Chapters 7 or 11 find it difficult to obtain credit in the future. Bankruptcy makes it both difficult and expensive to obtain credit for at least seven years after a discharge in bankruptcy occurs.

Remedies for Breach

Whenever a promisor who is under an absolute duty to perform fails to render the promised performance, a breach occurs. The available remedies for breach of contract depend on the nature of the breach. Generally, when the breach by the promisor is minor, or not going to the heart of the contract, the promisee must honor her end of the bargain but can sue for damages. If the breach by the promisor is major, the promisee's duties under the contract are discharged, and she may also sue for damages.

There are basically two types of remedies available to a party who suffers a breach of contract: compensatory damages and specific performance. Compensatory damages include various types of money awards meant to compensate the injured party for monetary losses suffered as a result of the breaching party's failure to perform or imperfect performance. Specific performance, on the other hand, is not a monetary award; it is a court order forcing the breaching party to actually honor the terms of his contract by rendering the promised performance. Specific performance is only awarded in exceptional cases where money damages would not properly compensate the victim of a breach. The specific remedies are examined in greater detail below.

Compensatory Damages

Compensatory damages is the most commonly available remedy to the victim of a breach. It is a money award meant to place the nonbreaching party in the same condition he would have been in had the breaching party performed as agreed. Compensatory damages include the cost of curing the breaching party's defective performance and the cost of any damages the nonbreaching party suffered that the breach caused directly and the breaching party should have foreseen. The following example will illustrate:

> Mark contracts with Darren to renovate his club. The agreement calls for Darren to finish the work within 30 days of the contract. At the end of the 30 days, Darren has not finished the work and can give no assurance as to when he will be able to complete it. Mark is unable to open the club on time and must pay $2,000 to "The Screaming Knees," a new group he'd contracted to play at the club's previously scheduled reopening day. He can also prove that he is losing $1,000 per day in lost profits and must pay $2,000 to Jane's Contracting Co. to finish the work.

Mark's compensatory damages include the cost of having the new contractor finish the work and all other foreseeable expenses that resulted directly from the breach, including "The Screaming Knees" contract and the loss of profits.

Nominal Damages

Nominal damages are small monetary damages awarded when a breach does not cause any actual harm to the nonbreaching party. A common nominal damage award is $1. In awarding nominal damages, a court recognizes that a legal injury has been done but that it has caused no real harm.

> Victor, a business law professor, begins his lecture on torts at State University by walking up to a student and gently tapping her on the head. He then asks what tort he has just committed, and the student correctly responds "The tort of battery." If the student then sues the professor for the tort, she will only be entitled to recover nominal damages, such as $1, since she has not suffered any real harm.

Specific Performance

There are instances in which money damages are simply incapable of properly compensating a nonbreaching party for the other party's breach. In such situations, a court has the power to force the breaching party to actually perform the contract as promised. For a party to successfully seek *specific performance* as a remedy, he must show that the following circumstances exist:

1. The subject matter of the contract is unique, and a replacement unobtainable.
2. Money damages would not properly compensate the nonbreaching party for his loss.

Contracts for which courts typically award specific performance include those involving real estate and the sale of art or antiques, all of which are unique; no two pieces of real estate are the same, even though they may be of similar value and location, and the same holds true for artwork, rare coins, antiques, and similar articles. Personal service contracts, however, are not subject to specific performance, even though they are unique by their very nature. Courts will simply not force anyone to work for another against her will; only money damages are available to nonbreaching parties in such circumstances. Consider the following examples:

➤ 1. Rosario, an artist, contracts to sell one of her paintings to Carl for $5,000. She then changes her mind. Carl can seek specific performance, since the painting is unique and money damages will not adequately compensate him for his loss.
   2. Rosario contracts to paint Carl's portrait for $5,000. She then changes her mind. Specific performance is unavailable as a remedy to Carl since a court will not force Rosario to paint the portrait against her will. His only remedy is compensatory damages; he can recover from Rosario the difference between the contract price and what he will have to pay another artist of similar skill to Rosario's to paint his portrait. If another artist of equal or better skill is willing to paint his portrait for the same or a lower price, his only remedy would be nominal damages.

Election of Remedies

There are circumstances in which the aggrieved party in a breach of contract action has more than one remedy available. When that is the case, the victim of the breach must select the remedy that he wants the court to award. Depending on the subject matter of the contract and the state involved, a person may have the option of asking for *alternative remedies*—such as asking for specific performance with compensatory damages as the alternative—or he may have to make a final binding selection from the several available remedies. Since the basic purpose of contract law is to compensate aggrieved parties for losses suffered as a result of breaches of contract, punitive damages are generally not available in contract actions. For the same reason, courts will not grant more than one remedy when a single remedy will suffice to put the aggrieved party in the same condition she would have been in had there not been a breach of contract. If both specific performance and compensatory damages are available, as in the case of a breach of a contract for the sale of real estate, a court will award either specific performance or compensatory damages, but not both.

Judge for Yourself

Case 1. Cynthia, the owner of a large chain of gasoline stations, contracts with Big Oil Company to buy all the gasoline she needs for her business for the next three years at a wholesale price of $1 per gallon. After the first six months of her contract, hostilities are renewed in the Persian Gulf and the price of crude oil rises by 50 percent.

    a. Is the contract between Cynthia and Big Oil discharged due to impossibility of performance? Why?

    b. Is the contract discharged due to commercial impracticability? Explain.

Case 2.   Ramón, owner of Ramón's Home Contracting Company, contracts to build Jemal and Patty a new home for $85,000. After entering into the contract but before beginning work, Ramón dies.

    a. Does Ramón's death discharge the contract? Why?

    b. If Ramón were an attorney who died prior to completing a will for Jemal and Patty, would the retainer agreement (the contract for Ramón's professional services) be discharged by his death? What is the crucial difference between the two types of contracts?

Case 3.   Francois, a housepainter, agrees to paint the outside of Carol's house light green with dark green trim. Because of a clerical error, he mixes up Carol's order with that to paint a day-care center and paints Carol's house in a bright and cheerful rainbow motif.

    a. If Francois offers to refund 50 percent of the cost of the contract price to Carol in exchange for a signed release, and if Carol agrees, will the contract be discharged? Why?

    b. What is Carol's consideration for signing the release?

    c. If Carol signs the release but decides she can't live with the paint job several days later, can she sue Francois? Why?

    d. If Carol refuses to sign the release, what legal recourse does she have?

Case 4.   Renee agrees to sell an original wood sculpture she has purchased in Kenya from a local artist to Francene for $500. Before turning over the sculpture, Renee has a local gallery owner examine it and is delighted when the latter offers her $2,000 for the piece. Deciding that she has made a bad bargain, she calls up Francene and tells her that she has changed her mind and decided to keep the sculpture after all.

    a. If Francene agrees to allow her friend to back out of the deal, what will be the legal effect on their contract?

    b. If Francene agrees to allow Renee to rescind the contract and subsequently changes her mind, will she be able to sue Renee for the breach? Why?

    c. If Francene does not agree to allow Renee to rescind the contract, what legal remedies is she entitled to sue for?

    d. Will a court be likely to award specific performance in this case? Explain.

CASE STUDY 2-1
ILLEGAL CONTRACTS

IN THE MATTER OF BABY M, A PSEUDONYM FOR AN ACTUAL PERSON
No. A–39
Supreme Court of New Jersey
109 N.J. 396; 537 A.2d 1227; 1988 N.J. LEXIS 1;

September 14, 1987, Argued
February 3, 1988, Decided

COUNSEL: Harold J. Cassidy and Alan J. Karcher argued the cause for appellants, Mary Beth and Richard Whitehead. . . . Gary N. Skoloff argued the cause for respondents, William and Elizabeth Stern. . . . Lorraine A. Abraham, Guardian ad litem, argued the cause *pro se.*

JUDGES: For affirmance in part, reversal in part and remandment—Chief Justice Wilentz and Justices Clifford, Handler, Pollock, O'Hern, Garibaldi and Stein. Opposed—None. The opinion of the Court was delivered by Wilentz, C.J.

OPINION: In this matter the Court is asked to determine the validity of a contract that purports to provide a new way of bringing children into a family. For a fee of $10,000, a woman agrees to be artificially inseminated with the semen of another woman's husband; she is to conceive a child, carry it to term, and after its birth surrender it to the natural father and his wife. The intent of the contract is that the child's natural mother will thereafter be forever separated from her child. The wife is to adopt the child, and she and the natural father are to be regarded as its parents for all purposes. The contract providing for this is called a "surrogacy contract," the natural mother inappropriately called the "surrogate mother."

We invalidate the surrogacy contract because it conflicts with the law and public policy of this State. While we recognize the depth of the yearning of infertile couples to have their own children, we find the payment of money to a "surrogate" mother illegal, perhaps criminal, and potentially degrading to women. Although in this case we grant custody to the natural father, the evidence having clearly proved such custody to be in the best interests of the infant, we void both the termination of the surrogate mother's parental rights and the adoption of the child by the wife/stepparent. We thus restore the "surrogate" as the mother of the child. We remand the issue of the natural mother's visitation rights to the trial court, since that issue was not reached below and the record before us is not sufficient to permit us to decide it de novo.

We find no offense to our present laws where a woman voluntarily and without payment agrees to act as a "surrogate" mother, provided that she is not subject to a binding agreement to surrender her child. Moreover, our holding today does not preclude the Legislature from altering the current statutory scheme, within constitutional limits, so as to permit surrogacy contracts. Under current law, however, the surrogacy agreement before us is illegal and invalid.

I. FACTS

In February 1985, William Stern and Mary Beth Whitehead entered into a surrogacy contract. It recited that Stern's wife, Elizabeth, was infertile, that they wanted a child, and that Mrs. Whitehead was willing to provide that child as the mother with Mr. Stern as the father.

The contract provided that through artificial insemination using Mr. Stern's sperm, Mrs. Whitehead would become pregnant, carry the child to term, bear it, deliver it to the Sterns, and thereafter do whatever was necessary to terminate her maternal rights so that Mrs. Stern could thereafter adopt the child. Mrs. Whitehead's husband, Richard,[1] was also a party to the contract; Mrs. Stern was not. Mr. Whitehead promised to do all acts necessary to rebut the presumption of paternity under the Parentage Act. N.J.S.A. 9:17 43a(1),–44a. Although Mrs. Stern was not a party to the surrogacy agreement, the contract gave her sole custody of the child in the event of Mr. Stern's death. Mrs. Stern's status as a nonparty to the surrogate parenting agreement presumably was to avoid the application of the baby-selling statute to this arrangement. N.J.S.A. 9:3–54.

Mr. Stern, on his part, agreed to attempt the artificial insemination and to pay Mrs. Whitehead $10,000 after the child's birth, on its delivery to him. In a separate contract, Mr. Stern agreed to pay $7,500 to the Infertility Center of New York (ICNY). The Center's advertising campaigns solicit surrogate mothers and encourage infertile couples to consider surrogacy. ICNY arranged for the surrogacy contract by bringing the parties together, explaining the process to them, furnishing the contractual form,[2] and providing legal counsel.

The history of the parties' involvement in this arrangement suggests their good faith. William and Elizabeth Stern were married in July 1974, having met at the University of Michigan, where both were Ph.D. candidates. Due to financial considerations and Mrs. Stern's pursuit of a medical degree and residency, they decided to defer starting a family until 1981. Before then, however, Mrs. Stern learned that she might have multiple sclerosis and that the disease in some cases renders pregnancy a serious health risk. Her anxiety appears to have exceeded the actual risk, which current medical authorities assess as minimal. Nonetheless that anxiety was evidently quite real, Mrs. Stern fearing that pregnancy might precipitate blindness, paraplegia, or other forms of debilitation. Based on the perceived risk, the Sterns decided to forego having their own children. The decision had special significance for Mr. Stern. Most of his family had been destroyed in the Holocaust. As the family's only survivor, he very much wanted to continue his bloodline.

Initially the Sterns considered adoption, but were discouraged by the substantial delay apparently involved and by the potential problem they saw arising from their age and their differing religious backgrounds. They were most eager for some other means to start a family.

The paths of Mrs. Whitehead and the Sterns to surrogacy were similar. Both responded to advertising by ICNY. The Sterns' response, following their inquiries into adoption, was the result of their long-standing decision to have a child. Mrs. Whitehead's response apparently resulted from her sympathy with family members and others who could have no children (she stated that she wanted to give another couple the "gift of life"); she also wanted the $10,000 to help her family.

Both parties, undoubtedly because of their own self-interest, were less sensitive to the implications of the transaction than they might otherwise have been. Mrs. Whitehead, for instance, appears not to have been concerned about whether the Sterns would make good parents for her child; the Sterns, on their part, while conscious of the obvious possibility that surrendering the child might cause grief to Mrs. Whitehead, overcame their qualms because of their desire for a child. At any rate, both the Sterns and Mrs. Whitehead were committed to the arrangement; both thought it right and constructive.

Mrs. Whitehead had reached her decision concerning surrogacy before the Sterns, and had actually been involved as a potential surrogate mother with another couple. After numerous unsuccessful artificial inseminations, that effort was abandoned. Thereafter, the Sterns learned of the Infertility Center, the possibilities of surrogacy, and of Mary Beth Whitehead. The two couples met to discuss the surrogacy arrangement and decided to go forward. On February 6, 1985, Mr. Stern and Mr. and Mrs. Whitehead executed the surrogate parenting agreement. After several artificial inseminations over a period of months, Mrs. Whitehead became pregnant. The pregnancy was uneventful and on March 27, 1986, Baby M was born.

Not wishing anyone at the hospital to be aware of the surrogacy arrangement, Mr. and Mrs. Whitehead appeared to all as the proud parents of a healthy female child. Her birth certificate indicated her name to be Sara Elizabeth Whitehead and her father to be Richard Whitehead. In accordance with Mrs. Whitehead's request, the Sterns visited the hospital unobtrusively to see the newborn child.

Mrs. Whitehead realized, almost from the moment of birth, that she could not part with this child. She had felt a bond with it even during pregnancy. Some indication of the attachment was conveyed to the Sterns at the hospital when they told Mrs. Whitehead what they were going to name the baby. She apparently broke into tears and indicated that she did not know if she could give up the child. She talked about how the baby looked like her other daughter, and made it clear that she was experiencing great difficulty with the decision.

Nonetheless, Mrs. Whitehead was, for the moment, true to her word. Despite powerful inclinations to the contrary, she turned her child over to the Sterns on March 30 at the Whiteheads' home.

The Sterns were thrilled with their new child. They had planned extensively for its arrival, far beyond the practical furnishing of a room for her. It was a time of joyful celebration—not just for them but for their friends as well. The Sterns looked forward to raising their daughter, whom they named Melissa. While aware by then that Mrs. Whitehead was undergoing an emotional crisis, they were as yet not cognizant of the depth of that crisis and its implications for their newly-enlarged family.

Later in the evening of March 30, Mrs. Whitehead became deeply disturbed, disconsolate, stricken with unbearable sadness. She had to have her child. She could not eat, sleep, or concentrate on anything other than her need for her baby. The next day she went to the Sterns' home and told them how much she was suffering.

The depth of Mrs. Whitehead's despair surprised and frightened the Sterns. She told them that she could not live without her baby, that she must have her, even if only for one week, that thereafter she would surrender her child. The Sterns, concerned that Mrs. Whitehead might indeed commit suicide, not wanting under any circumstances to risk that, and in any event believing that Mrs. Whitehead would keep her word, turned the child over to her. It was not until four months later, after a series of attempts to regain possession of the child, that Melissa was returned to the Sterns, having been forcibly removed from the home where she was then living with Mr. and Mrs. Whitehead, the home in Florida owned by Mary Beth Whitehead's parents.

The struggle over Baby M began when it became apparent that Mrs. Whitehead could not return the child to Mr. Stern. Due to Mrs. Whitehead's refusal to relinquish the baby, Mr. Stern filed a complaint seeking enforcement of the surrogacy contract. He alleged, accurately, that Mrs. Whitehead had not only refused to comply with the surrogacy contract but had threatened to flee from New Jersey with the child in order to avoid even the possibility of his obtaining custody. The court papers asserted that if Mrs. Whitehead were to be given notice of the application for an order requiring her to relinquish custody, she would, prior to the hearing, leave the state with the baby. And that is precisely what she did. After the order was entered, ex parte, the process server, aided by the police, in the presence of the Sterns, entered Mrs. Whitehead's home to execute the order. Mr. Whitehead fled with the child, who had been handed to him through a window while those who came to enforce the order were thrown off balance by a dispute over the child's current name.

The Whiteheads immediately fled to Florida with Baby M. They stayed initially with Mrs. Whitehead's parents, where one of Mrs. Whitehead's children had been living. For the next three months, the Whiteheads and Melissa lived at roughly twenty different hotels, motels, and homes in order to avoid apprehension. From time to time Mrs. Whitehead would call Mr. Stern to discuss the matter; the conversations, recorded by Mr. Stern on advice of counsel, show an escalating dispute about rights, morality, and power, accompanied by threats of Mrs. Whitehead to kill herself, to kill the child, and falsely to accuse Mr. Stern of sexually molesting Mrs. Whitehead's other daughter.

Eventually the Sterns discovered where the Whiteheads were staying, commenced supplementary proceedings in Florida, and obtained an order requiring the Whiteheads to turn over the child. Police in Florida enforced the order, forcibly removing the child from her grandparents' home. She was soon thereafter brought to New Jersey and turned over to the Sterns. The prior order of the court, issued ex parte, awarding custody of the child to the Sterns pendente lite, was reaffirmed by the trial court after consideration of the certified representations of the parties (both represented by counsel) concerning the unusual sequence of events that had unfolded. Pending final judgment, Mrs. Whitehead was awarded limited visitation with Baby M.

The Sterns' complaint, in addition to seeking possession and ultimately custody of the child, sought enforcement of the surrogacy contract. Pursuant to the contract, it asked that the child be permanently placed in their custody, that Mrs. Whitehead's parental rights be terminated, and that Mrs. Stern be allowed to adopt the child, i.e., that, for all purposes, Melissa become the Sterns' child.

The trial took thirty-two days over a period of more than two months. It included numerous interlocutory appeals and attempted interlocutory appeals. There were twenty-three witnesses to the facts recited above and fifteen expert witnesses, eleven testifying on the issue of custody and four on the subject of Mrs. Stern's multiple sclerosis; the bulk of the testimony was devoted to determining the parenting arrangement most compatible with the child's best interests. Soon after the conclusion of the trial, the trial court announced its opinion from the bench. 217 N.J. Super. 313 (1987). It held that the surrogacy contract was valid; ordered that Mrs. Whitehead's parental rights be terminated and that sole custody of the child be granted to Mr. Stern; and, after hearing brief testimony from Mrs. Stern, immediately entered an order allowing the adoption of Melissa by Mrs. Stern, all in accordance with the surrogacy contract. Pending the outcome of the appeal, we granted a continuation of visitation to Mrs. Whitehead, although slightly more limited than the visitation allowed during the trial.

Although clearly expressing its view that the surrogacy contract was valid, the trial court devoted the major portion of its opinion to the question of the baby's best interests. The inconsistency is apparent. The surrogacy contract calls for the surrender of the child to the Sterns, permanent and sole custody in the Sterns, and termination of Mrs. Whitehead's parental rights, all without qualification, all regardless of any evaluation of the best interests of the child. As a matter of fact the contract recites (even before the child was conceived) that it is in the best interests of the child to be placed with Mr. Stern. In effect, the trial court awarded custody to Mr. Stern, the natural father, based on the same kind of evidence and analysis as might be expected had no surrogacy contract existed. Its rationalization, however, was that while the surrogacy contract was valid, specific performance would not be granted unless that remedy was in the best interests of the child. The factual issues confronted and decided by the trial court were the same as if Mr. Stern and Mrs. Whitehead had had the child out of wedlock, intended or unintended, and then disagreed about custody. The trial court's awareness of the irrelevance of the contract in the court's determination of custody is suggested by its remark that beyond the question of the child's best interests, "[a]ll other concerns raised by counsel constitute commentary." 217 N.J. Super. at 323.

On the question of best interests—and we agree, but for different reasons, that custody was the critical issue—the court's analysis of the testimony was perceptive, demonstrating both its understanding of the case and its considerable experience in these matters. We agree substantially with both its analysis and conclusions on the matter of custody.

The court's review and analysis of the surrogacy contract, however, is not at all in accord with ours. The trial court concluded that the various statutes governing this matter, including those concerning adoption, termination of parental rights, and payment of money in connection with adoptions, do not apply to surrogacy contracts. Id. at 372–73. It reasoned that because the Legislature did not have surrogacy contracts in mind when it passed those laws, those laws were therefore irrelevant. Ibid. Thus, assuming it was writing on a clean slate, the trial court analyzed the interests involved and the power of the court to accommodate them. It then held that surrogacy contracts are valid and should be enforced, id. at 388, and furthermore that Mr. Stern's rights under the surrogacy contract were constitutionally protected. Id. at 385–88.

Mrs. Whitehead appealed. This Court granted direct certification. 107 N.J. 140 (1987). The briefs of the parties on appeal were joined by numerous briefs filed by amici expressing various interests and views on surrogacy and on this case. We have found many of them helpful in resolving the issues before us.

Mrs. Whitehead contends that the surrogacy contract, for a variety of reasons, is invalid. She contends that it conflicts with public policy since it guarantees that the child will not have the nurturing of both natural parents—presumably New Jersey's goal for families. She further argues that it deprives the mother of her constitutional right to the companionship of her child, and that it conflicts with statutes concerning termination of parental rights and adoption. With the contract thus void, Mrs. Whitehead claims primary custody (with visitation rights in Mr. Stern) both on a best interests basis (stressing the "tender years" doctrine) as well as on the policy basis of discouraging surrogacy contracts. She maintains that even if custody would ordinarily go to Mr. Stern, here it should be awarded to Mrs. Whitehead to deter future surrogacy arrangements.

In a brief filed after oral argument, counsel for Mrs. Whitehead suggests that the standard for determining best interests where the infant resulted from a surrogacy contract is that the child should be placed with the mother absent a showing of unfitness. All parties agree that no expert testified that Mary Beth Whitehead was unfit as a mother; the trial court expressly found that she was not "unfit," that, on the contrary, "she is a good mother for and to her older children," 217 N.J. Super. at 397; and no one now claims anything to the contrary.

One of the repeated themes put forth by Mrs. Whitehead is that the court's initial ex parte order granting custody to the Sterns during the trial was a substantial factor in the ultimate "best interests" determination. That initial order, claimed to be erroneous by Mrs. Whitehead, not only established Melissa as part of the Stern family, but brought enormous pressure on Mrs. Whitehead. The order brought the weight of the state behind the Sterns' attempt, ultimately successful, to gain possession of the child. The resulting pressure, Mrs. Whitehead contends, caused her to act in ways that were atypical of her ordinary behavior when not under stress, and to act in ways that were thought to be inimical to the child's best interests in that they demonstrated a failure of character, maturity, and consistency. She claims that any mother who truly loved her child might so respond and that it is doubly unfair to judge her on the basis of her reaction to an extreme situation rarely faced by any mother, where that situation was itself caused by an erroneous order of the court. Therefore, according to Mrs. Whitehead, the erroneous ex parte order precipitated a series of events that proved instrumental in the final result.[3]

The Sterns claim that the surrogacy contract is valid and should be enforced, largely for the reasons given by the trial court. They claim a constitutional right of privacy, which includes the right of procreation, and the right of consenting adults to deal with matters of reproduction as they see fit. As for the child's best interests, their position is factual: given all of the circumstances, the child is better off in their custody with no residual parental rights reserved for Mrs. Whitehead.

Of considerable interest in this clash of views is the position of the child's guardian ad litem, wisely appointed by the court at the outset of the litigation. As the child's representative, her role in the litigation, as she viewed it, was solely to protect the child's best interests. She therefore took no position on the validity of the surrogacy contract, and instead devoted her energies to obtaining expert testimony uninfluenced by any interest other than the child's. We agree with the guardian's perception of her role in this litigation. She appropriately refrained from taking any position that might have appeared to compromise her role as the child's advocate. She first took the position, based on her experts' testimony, that the Sterns should have primary custody, and that while Mrs. Whitehead's parental rights should not be terminated, no visitation should be allowed for five years. As a result of subsequent developments, mentioned infra, her view has changed. She now recommends that no visitation be allowed at least until Baby M reaches maturity.

Although some of the experts' opinions touched on visitation, the major issue they addressed was whether custody should be reposed in the Sterns or in the Whiteheads. The trial court, consistent in this respect with its view that the surrogacy contract was valid, did not deal at all with the question of visitation. Having concluded that the best interests of the child called for custody in the Sterns, the trial court enforced the operative provisions of the surrogacy contract, terminated Mrs. Whitehead's parental rights, and granted an adoption to Mrs. Stern. Explicit in the ruling was the conclusion that the best interests determination removed whatever impediment might have existed in enforcing the surrogacy contract. This Court, therefore, is without guidance from the trial court on the visitation issue, an issue of considerable importance in any event, and especially important in view of our determination that the surrogacy contract is invalid.

II. INVALIDITY AND UNENFORCEABILITY OF SURROGACY CONTRACT

We have concluded that this surrogacy contract is invalid. Our conclusion has two bases: direct conflict with existing statutes and conflict with the public policies of this State, as expressed in its statutory and decisional law.

One of the surrogacy contract's basic purposes, to achieve the adoption of a child through private placement, though permitted in New Jersey "is very much disfavored." Sees v. Baber, 74 N.J. 201, 217 (1977). Its use of money for this purpose—and we have no doubt whatsoever that the money is being paid to obtain an adoption and not, as the Sterns argue, for the personal services of Mary Beth Whitehead—is illegal and perhaps criminal. N.J.S.A. 9:3–54. In addition to the inducement of money, there is the coercion of contract: the natural mother's irrevocable agreement, prior to birth, even prior to conception, to surrender the child to the adoptive couple. Such an agreement is totally unenforceable in private placement adoption. Sees, 74 N.J. at 212–14. Even where the adoption is through an approved agency, the formal agreement to surrender occurs only after birth (as we read N.J.S.A. 9:2–16 and –17, and similar statutes), and then, by regulation, only after the birth mother has been offered counseling. N.J.A.C. 10:121A–5.4(c). Integral to these invalid provisions of the surrogacy contract is the related agreement, equally invalid, on the part of the natural mother to cooperate with, and not to contest, proceedings to terminate her parental rights, as well as her contractual concession, in aid of the adoption, that the child's best interests would be served by awarding custody to the natural father and his wife—all of this before she has even conceived, and, in some cases, before she has the slightest idea of what the natural father and adoptive mother are like.

The foregoing provisions not only directly conflict with New Jersey statutes, but also offend long-established State policies. These critical terms, which are at the heart of the contract, are invalid and unenforceable; the conclusion therefore follows, without more, that the entire contract is unenforceable.

A. Conflict with Statutory Provisions

The surrogacy contract conflicts with: (1) laws prohibiting the use of money in connection with adoptions; (2) laws requiring proof of parental unfitness or abandonment before termination of parental rights is ordered or an adoption is granted; and (3) laws that make surrender of custody and consent to adoption revocable in private placement adoptions.

(1) Our law prohibits paying or accepting money in connection with any placement of a child for adoption. N.J.S.A. 9:3–54a. Violation is a high misdemeanor. N.J.S.A. 9:3–54c. Excepted are fees of an approved agency (which must be a non-profit entity, N.J.S.A. 9:3–38a) and certain expenses in connection with childbirth. N.J.S.A. 9:3–54b.[4]

Considerable care was taken in this case to structure the surrogacy arrangement so as not to violate this prohibition. The arrangement was structured as follows: the adopting parent, Mrs. Stern, was not a party to the surrogacy contract; the money paid to Mrs. Whitehead was stated to be for her services—not for the adoption; the sole purpose of the contract was stated as being that "of giving a child to William Stern, its natural and biological father"; the money was purported to be "compensation for services and expenses and in no way. . . a fee for termination of parental rights or a payment in exchange for consent to surrender a child for adoption"; the fee to the Infertility Center ($7,500) was stated to be for legal representation, advice, administrative work, and other "services." Nevertheless, it seems clear that the money was paid and accepted in connection with an adoption.

The Infertility Center's major role was first as a "finder" of the surrogate mother whose child was to be adopted, and second as the arranger of all proceedings that led to the adoption. Its role as adoption finder is demonstrated by the provision requiring Mr. Stern to pay another $7,500 if he uses Mary Beth Whitehead again as a surrogate, and by ICNY's agreement to "coordinate arrangements for the adoption of the child by the wife." The surrogacy agreement requires Mrs. Whitehead to surrender Baby M for the purposes of adoption. The agreement notes that Mr. and Mrs. Stern wanted to have a child, and provides that the child be "placed" with Mrs. Stern in the event Mr. Stern dies before the child is born. The payment of the $10,000 occurs only on surrender of custody of the child and "completion of the duties and obligations" of Mrs. Whitehead, including termination of her parental rights to facilitate adoption by Mrs. Stern. As for the contention that the Sterns are paying only for services and not for an adoption, we need note only that they would pay nothing in the event the child died before the fourth month of pregnancy, and only $1,000 if the child were stillborn, even though the "services" had been fully rendered. Additionally, one of Mrs. Whitehead's estimated costs, to be assumed by Mr. Stern, was an "Adoption Fee," presumably for Mrs. Whitehead's incidental costs in connection with the adoption.

Mr. Stern knew he was paying for the adoption of a child; Mrs. Whitehead knew she was accepting money so that a child might be adopted; the Infertility Center knew that it was being paid for assisting in the adoption of a child. The actions of all three worked to frustrate the goals of the statute. It strains credulity to claim that these arrangements, touted by those in the surrogacy business as an attractive alternative to the usual route leading to an adoption, really amount to something other than a private placement adoption for money.

The prohibition of our statute is strong. Violation constitutes a high misdemeanor, N.J.S.A. 9:3–54c, a third-degree crime, N.J.S.A. 2C:43–1b, carrying a penalty of three to five years imprisonment. N.J.S.A. 2C:43–6a(3). The evils inherent in baby-bartering are loathsome for a myriad of reasons. The child is sold without regard for whether the purchasers will be suitable parents. N. Baker, Baby Selling: The Scandal of Black Market Adoption 7 (1978). The natural mother does not receive the benefit of counseling and guidance to assist her in making a decision that may affect her for a lifetime. In fact, the monetary incentive to sell her child may, depending on her financial circumstances, make her decision less voluntary. Id. at 44. Furthermore, the adoptive parents[5] may not be fully informed of the natural parents' medical history.

Baby-selling potentially results in the exploitation of all parties involved. Ibid. Conversely, adoption statutes seek to further humanitarian goals, foremost among them the best interests of the child. H. Witmer, E. Herzog, E. Weinstein, & M. Sullivan, Independent Adoptions: A Follow-Up Study 32 (1967). The negative consequences of baby-buying are potentially present in the surrogacy context, especially the potential for placing and adopting a child without regard to the interest of the child or the natural mother.

(2) The termination of Mrs. Whitehead's parental rights, called for by the surrogacy contract and actually ordered by the court, 217 N.J. Super. at 399–400, fails to comply with the stringent requirements of New Jersey law. Our law, recognizing the finality of any termination of parental rights, provides for such termination only where there has been a voluntary surrender of a child to an approved agency or to the Division of Youth and Family Services (DYFS), accompanied by a formal document acknowledging termination of parental rights, N.J.S.A. 9:2–16, –17; N.J.S.A. 9:3–41; N.J.S.A. 30:4C–23, or where there has been a showing of parental abandonment or unfitness. A termination may ordinarily take one of three forms: an action by an approved agency, an action by DYFS, or an action in connection with a

private placement adoption. The three are governed by separate statutes, but the standards for termination are substantially the same, except that whereas a written surrender is effective when made to an approved agency or to DYFS, there is no provision for it in the private placement context. See N.J.S.A. 9:2–14; N.J.S.A. 30:4C–23.

N.J.S.A. 9:2–18 to –20 governs an action by an approved agency to terminate parental rights. Such an action, whether or not in conjunction with a pending adoption, may proceed on proof of written surrender, N.J.S.A. 9:2–16, –17, "forsaken parental obligation," or other specific grounds such as death or insanity, N.J.S.A. 9:2–19. Where the parent has not executed a formal consent, termination requires a showing of "forsaken parental obligation," i.e., "willful and continuous neglect or failure to perform the natural and regular obligations of care and support of a child." N.J.S.A. 9:2–13(d). See also N.J.S.A. 9:3–46a, –47c.

Where DYFS is the agency seeking termination, the requirements are similarly stringent, although at first glance they do not appear to be so. DYFS can, as can any approved agency, accept a formal voluntary surrender or writing having the effect of termination and giving DYFS the right to place the child for adoption. N.J.S.A. 30:4C–23. Absent such formal written surrender and consent, similar to that given to approved agencies, DYFS can terminate parental rights in an action for guardianship by proving that "the best interests of such child require that he be placed under proper guardianship." N.J.S.A. 30:4C–20. Despite this "best interests" language, however, this Court has recently held in New Jersey Div. of Youth & Family Servs. v. A.W., 103 N.J. 591 (1986), that in order for DYFS to terminate parental rights it must prove, by clear and convincing evidence, that "[t]he child's health and development have been or will be seriously impaired by the parental relationship," id. at 604, that "[t]he parents are unable or unwilling to eliminate the harm and delaying permanent placement will add to the harm," id. at 605, that "[t]he court has considered alternatives to termination," id. at 608, and that "[t]he termination of parental rights will not do more harm than good," id. at 610. This interpretation of the statutory language requires a most substantial showing of harm to the child if the parental relationship were to continue, far exceeding anything that a "best interests" test connotes.

In order to terminate parental rights under the private placement adoption statute, there must be a finding of "intentional abandonment or a very substantial neglect of parental duties without a reasonable expectation of a reversal of that conduct in the future." N.J.S.A. 9:3–48c(1). This requirement is similar to that of the prior law (i.e., "forsaken parental obligations," L. 1953, c. 264, @ 2(d) (codified at N.J.S.A. 9:3–18(d) (repealed))), and to that of the law providing for termination through actions by approved agencies, N.J.S.A. 9:2–13(d). See also In re Adoption by J.J.P., 175 N.J. Super. 420, 427 (App. Div. 1980) (noting that the language of the termination provision in the present statute, N.J.S.A. 9:3–48c(1), derives from this Court's construction of the prior statute in In re Adoption of Children by D., 61 N.J. 89, 94-95 (1972)).

In Sees v. Baber, 74 N.J. 201 (1977) we distinguished the requirements for terminating parental rights in a private placement adoption from those required in an approved agency adoption. We stated that in an unregulated private placement, "neither consent nor voluntary surrender is singled out as a statutory factor in terminating parental rights." Id. at 213. Sees established that without proof that parental obligations had been forsaken, there would be no termination in a private placement setting.

As the trial court recognized, without a valid termination there can be no adoption. In re Adoption of Children by D., supra, 61 N.J. at 95. This requirement applies to all adoptions, whether they be private placements, ibid., or agency adoptions, N.J.S.A. 9:3–46a, –47c.

Our statutes, and the cases interpreting them, leave no doubt that where there has been no written surrender to an approved agency or to DYFS, termination of parental rights will not be granted in this state absent a very strong showing of abandonment or neglect. See, e.g., Sorentino v. Family & Children's Soc'y of Elizabeth, 74 N.J. 313 (1977) (Sorentino II); Sees v. Baber, 74 N.J. 201 (1977); Sorentino v. Family & Children's Soc'y of Elizabeth, 72 N.J. 127 (1976) (Sorentino I); In re Adoption of Children by D., supra, 61 N.J. 89. That showing is required in every context in which termination of parental rights is sought, be it an action by an approved agency, an action by DYFS, or a private placement adoption proceeding, even where the petitioning adoptive parent is, as here, a stepparent. While the statutes make certain procedural allowances when stepparents are involved, N.J.S.A. 9:3–48a(2), –48a(4), –48c(4), the substantive requirement for terminating the natural parents' rights is not related one iota. N.J.S.A. 9:3–48c(1); In re Adoption of Children by D., supra, 61 N.J. at 94–95; In re Adoption by J.J.P., supra, 175 N.J. Super. at 426–28; In re N., 96 N.J. Super. 415, 423–27 (App. Div. 1967). It is clear that a "best interests" determination is never sufficient to terminate parental rights; the statutory criteria must be proved.[6]

In this case a termination of parental rights was obtained not by proving the statutory prerequisites but by claiming the benefit of contractual provisions. From all that has been stated above, it is clear that a contractual agreement to abandon one's parental rights, or not to contest a termination action, will not be enforced in our courts. The Legislature would not have so carefully, so consistently, and so substantially restricted termination of parental rights if it had intended to allow termination to be achieved by one short sentence in a contract.

Since the termination was invalid,[7] it follows, as noted above, that adoption of Melissa by Mrs. Stern could not properly be granted.

(3) The provision in the surrogacy contract stating that Mary Beth Whitehead agrees to "surrender custody. . . and terminate all parental rights" contains no clause giving her a right to rescind. It is intended to be an irrevocable consent to surrender the child for adoption—in other words, an irrevocable commitment by Mrs. Whitehead to turn Baby M over to the Sterns and thereafter to allow termination of her parental rights. The trial court required a "best interests" showing as a condition to granting specific performance of the surrogacy contract. 217 N.J. Super. at 399–400. Having decided the "best interests" issue in favor of the Sterns, that court's order included, among other things, specific performance of this agreement to surrender custody and terminate all parental rights.

Mrs. Whitehead, shortly after the child's birth, had attempted to revoke her consent and surrender by refusing, after the Sterns had allowed her to have the child "just for one week," to return Baby M to them. The trial court's award of specific performance therefore reflects its view that the consent to surrender the child was irrevocable. We accept the trial court's construction of the contract; indeed it appears quite clear that this was the parties' intent. Such a provision, however, making irrevocable the natural mother's consent to surrender custody of her child in a private placement adoption, clearly conflicts with New Jersey law.

Our analysis commences with the statute providing for surrender of custody to an approved agency and termination of parental rights on the suit of that agency. The two basic provisions of the statute are N.J.S.A. 9:2–14 and 9:2–16. The former provides explicitly that [e]xcept as otherwise provided by law or by order or judgment of a court of competent jurisdiction or by testamentary disposition, no surrender of the custody of a child shall be valid in this state unless made to an approved agency pursuant to the provisions of this act. . .

There is no exception "provided by law," and it is not clear that there could be any "order or judgment of a court of competent jurisdiction" validating a surrender of custody as a basis for adoption when that surrender was not in conformance with the statute. Requirements for a voluntary surrender to an approved agency are set forth in N.J.S.A. 9:2–16. This section allows an approved agency to take a voluntary surrender of custody from the parent of a child but provides stringent requirements as a condition to its validity. The surrender must be in writing, must be in such form as is required for the recording of a deed, and, pursuant to N.J.S.A. 9:2–17, must be such as to declare that the person executing the same desires to relinquish the custody of the child, acknowledge the termination of parental rights as to such custody in favor of the approved agency, and acknowledge full understanding of the effect of such surrender as provided by this act.

If the foregoing requirements are met, the consent, the voluntary surrender of custody shall be valid whether or not the person giving same is a minor and shall be irrevocable except at the discretion of the approved agency taking such surrender or upon order or judgment of a court of competent jurisdiction, setting aside such surrender upon proof of fraud, duress, or misrepresentation. [N.J.S.A. 9:2–16.] The importance of that irrevocability is that the surrender itself gives the agency the power to obtain termination of parental rights—in other words, permanent separation of the parent from the child, leading in the ordinary case to an adoption. N.J.S.A. 9:2–18 to –20.

This statutory pattern, providing for a surrender in writing and for termination of parental rights by an approved agency, is generally followed in connection with adoption proceedings and proceedings by DYFS to obtain permanent custody of a child. Our adoption statute repeats the requirements necessary to accomplish an irrevocable surrender to an approved agency in both form and substance. N.J.S.A. 9:3–41a. It provides that the surrender "shall be valid and binding without regard to the age of the person executing the surrender," ibid.; and although the word "irrevocable" is not used, that seems clearly to be the intent of the provision. The statute speaks of such surrender as constituting "relinquishment of such person's parental rights in or guardianship or custody of the child named therein and consent by such person to adoption of the child." Ibid. We emphasize "named therein," for we construe the statute to allow a surrender only after the birth of the child. The formal consent to surrender enables the approved agency to terminate parental rights.

Similarly, DYFS is empowered to "take voluntary surrenders and releases of custody and consents to adoption[s]" from parents, which surrenders, releases, or consents "when properly acknowledged. . . shall be valid and binding irrespective of the age of the person giving the same, and shall be irrevocable except at the discretion of the Bureau of Childrens Services [currently DYFS] or upon order of a court of competent jurisdiction." N.J.S.A. 30:4C–23. Such consent to surrender of the custody of the child would presumably lead to an adoption placement by DYFS. See N.J.S.A. 30:4C–20.

It is clear that the Legislature so carefully circumscribed all aspects of a consent to surrender custody—its form and substance, its manner of execution, and the agency or agencies to which it may be made—in order to provide the basis for irrevocability. It seems most unlikely that the Legislature intended that a consent not complying with these requirements would also be irrevocable, especially where, as here, that consent falls radically short of compliance. Not only do the form and substance of the consent in the surrogacy contract fail to meet statutory requirements, but the surrender of custody is made to a private party. It is not made, as the statute requires, either to an approved agency or to DYFS.

These strict prerequisites to irrevocability constitute a recognition of the most serious consequences that flow from such consents: termination of parental rights, the permanent separation of parent from child, and the ultimate adoption of the child. See Sees v. Baber, supra, 74 N.J. at 217. Because of those consequences, the Legislature severely limited the circumstances under which such consent would be irrevocable. The legislative goal is furthered by regulations requiring approved agencies, prior to accepting irrevocable consents, to provide advice and counseling to women, making it more likely that they fully understand and appreciate the consequences of their acts. N.J.A.C. 10:121A–5.4(c).

Contractual surrender of parental rights is not provided for in our statutes as now written. Indeed, in the Parentage Act, N.J.S.A. 9:17–38 to –59, there is a specific provision invalidating any agreement "between an alleged or presumed father and the mother of the child" to bar an action brought for the purpose of determining paternity "[r]egardless of [the contract's] terms." N.J.S.A. 9:17–45. Even a settlement agreement concerning parentage reached in a judicially-mandated consent conference is not valid unless the proposed settlement is approved before-hand by the court. N.J.S.A. 9:17–48c and d. There is no doubt that a contractual provision purporting to constitute an irrevocable agreement to surrender custody of a child for adoption is invalid.

In Sees v. Baber, supra, 74 N.J. 201, we noted that a natural mother's consent to surrender her child and to its subsequent adoption was no longer required by the statute in private placement adoptions. After tracing the statutory history from the time when such a consent had been an essential prerequisite to adoption, we concluded that such a consent was now neither necessary nor sufficient for the purpose of terminating parental rights. Id. at 213. The consent to surrender custody in that case was in writing, had been executed prior to physical surrender of the infant, and had been explained to the mother by an attorney. The trial court found that the consent to surrender of custody in that private placement adoption was knowing, voluntary, and deliberate. Id. at 216. The physical surrender of the child took place four days after its birth. Two days thereafter the natural mother changed her mind, and asked that the adoptive couple give her baby back to her. We held that she was entitled to the baby's return. The effect of our holding in that case necessarily encompassed our conclusion that "in an unsupervised private placement, since there is no statutory obligation to consent, there can be no legal barrier to its retraction." Id. at 215. The only possible relevance of consent in these matters, we noted, was that it might bear on whether there had been an abandonment of the child, or a forsaking of parental obligations. Id. at 216. Otherwise, consent in a private placement adoption is not only revocable but, when revoked early enough, irrelevant. Id. at 213–15.

The provision in the surrogacy contract whereby the mother irrevocably agrees to surrender custody of her child and to terminate her parental rights conflicts with the settled interpretation of New Jersey statutory law.[8] There is only one irrevocable consent, and that is the one explicitly provided for by statute: a consent to surrender of custody and a placement with an approved agency or with DYFS. The provision in the surrogacy contract, agreed to before conception, requiring the natural mother to surrender custody of the child without any right of revocation is one more indication of the essential nature of this transaction: the creation of a contractual system of termination and adoption designed to circumvent our statutes.

B. Public Policy Considerations

The surrogacy contract's invalidity, resulting from its direct conflict with the above statutory provisions, is further underlined when its goals and means are measured against New Jersey's public policy. The contract's basic premise, that the natural parents can decide in advance of birth which one is to have custody of the child, bears no relationship to the settled law that the child's best interests shall determine custody. See Fantony v. Fantony, 21 N.J. 525, 536–37 (1956); see also Sheehan v. Sheehan, 38 N.J. Super. 120, 125 (App. Div. 1955) ("Whatever the agreement of the parents, the ultimate determination of custody lies with the court in the exercise of its supervisory jurisdiction as parens patriae."). The fact that the trial court remedied that aspect of the contract through the "best interests" phase does not make the contractual provision any less offensive to the public policy of this State.

The surrogacy contract guarantees permanent separation of the child from one of its natural parents. Our policy, however, has long been that to the extent possible, children should remain with and be brought up by both of their natural parents. That was the first stated purpose of the previous adoption act, L. 1953, c. 264, § 1, codified at N.J.S.A. 9:3–17 (repealed): "it is necessary and desirable (a) to protect the child from unnecessary separation from his natural parents. . . ." While not so stated in the present adoption law, this purpose remains part of the public policy of this State. See, e.g., Wilke v. Culp, 196 N.J. Super. 487, 496 (App. Div. 1984), certif. den., 99 N.J. 243 (1985); In re Adoption by J.J.P., supra, 175 N.J. Super. at 426. This is not simply some theoretical ideal that in practice has no meaning. The impact of failure to follow that policy is nowhere better shown than in the results of this surrogacy contract. A child, instead of starting off its life with as much peace and security as possible, finds itself immediately in a tug-of-war between contending mother and father.[9]

The surrogacy contract violates the policy of this State that the rights of natural parents are equal concerning their child, the father's right no greater than the mother's. "The parent and child relationship extends equally to every child and to every parent, regardless of the marital status of the parents." N.J.S.A. 9:17–40. As the Assembly Judiciary Committee noted in its statement to the bill, this section establishes "the principle that regardless of the marital status of the parents, all children and all parents have equal rights with respect to each other." Statement to Senate No. 888, Assembly Judiciary, Law, Public Safety and Defense Committee (1983). The whole purpose and effect of the surrogacy contract was to give the father the exclusive right to the child by destroying the rights of the mother.

The policies expressed in our comprehensive laws governing consent to the surrender of a child, discussed supra at 429–434, stand in stark contrast to the surrogacy contract and what it implies. Here there is no counseling, independent or otherwise, of the natural mother, no evaluation, no warning.

The only legal advice Mary Beth Whitehead received regarding the surrogacy contract was provided in connection with the contract that she previously entered into with another couple. Mrs. Whitehead's lawyer was referred to her by the Infertility Center, with which he had an agreement to act as counsel for surrogate candidates. His services consisted of spending one hour going through the contract with the Whiteheads, section by section, and answering their questions. Mrs. Whitehead received no further legal advice prior to signing the contract with the Sterns.

Mrs. Whitehead was examined and psychologically evaluated, but if it was for her benefit, the record does not disclose that fact. The Sterns regarded the evaluation as important, particularly in connection with the question of whether she would change her mind. Yet they never asked to see it, and were content with the assumption that the Infertility Center had made an evaluation and had concluded that there was no danger that the surrogate mother would change her mind. From Mrs. Whitehead's point of view, all that she learned from the evaluation was that "she had passed." It is apparent that the profit motive got the better of the Infertility Center. Although the evaluation was made, it was not put to any use, and understandably so, for the psychologist warned that Mrs. Whitehead demonstrated certain traits that might make surrender of the child difficult and that there should be further inquiry into this issue in connection with her surrogacy. To inquire further, however, might have jeopardized the Infertility Center's fee. The record indicates that neither Mrs. Whitehead nor the Sterns were ever told of this fact, a fact that might have ended their surrogacy arrangement.

Under the contract, the natural mother is irrevocably committed before she knows the strength of her bond with her child. She never makes a totally voluntary, informed decision, for quite clearly any decision prior to the baby's birth is, in the most important sense, uninformed, and any decision after that, compelled by a pre-existing contractual commitment, the threat of a lawsuit, and the inducement of a $10,000 payment, is less than totally voluntary. Her interests are of little concern to those who controlled this transaction.

Although the interest of the natural father and adoptive mother is certainly the predominant interest, realistically the only interest served, even they are left with less than what public policy requires. They know little about the natural mother, her genetic makeup, and her psychological and medical history. Moreover, not even a superficial attempt is made to determine their awareness of their responsibilities as parents.

Worst of all, however, is the contract's total disregard of the best interests of the child. There is not the slightest suggestion that any inquiry will be made at any time to determine the fitness of the Sterns as custodial parents, of Mrs. Stern as an adoptive parent, their superiority to Mrs. Whitehead, or the effect on the child of not living with her natural mother.

This is the sale of a child, or, at the very least, the sale of a mother's right to her child, the only mitigating factor being that one of the purchasers is the father. Almost every evil that prompted the prohibition on the payment of money in connection with adoptions exists here.

The differences between an adoption and a surrogacy contract should be noted, since it is asserted that the use of money in connection with surrogacy does not pose the risks found where money buys an adoption. Katz, "Surrogate Motherhood and the Baby-Selling Laws," 20 Colum. J.L. & Soc. Probs. 1 (1986).

First, and perhaps most important, all parties concede that it is unlikely that surrogacy will survive without money. Despite the alleged selfless motivation of surrogate mothers, if there is no payment, there will be no surrogates, or very few. That conclusion contrasts with adoption; for obvious reasons, there remains a steady supply, albeit insufficient, despite the prohibitions against payment. The adoption itself, relieving the natural mother of the financial burden of supporting an infant, is in some sense the equivalent of payment.

Second, the use of money in adoptions does not produce the problem—conception occurs, and usually the birth itself, before illicit funds are offered. With surrogacy, the "problem," if one views it as such, consisting of the purchase of a woman's procreative capacity, at the risk of her life, is caused by and originates with the offer of money.

Third, with the law prohibiting the use of money in connection with adoptions, the built-in financial pressure of the unwanted pregnancy and the consequent support obligation do not lead the mother to the highest paying, ill-suited, adoptive parents. She is just as well-off surrendering the child to an approved agency. In surrogacy, the highest bidders will presumably become the adoptive parents regardless of suitability, so long as payment of money is permitted.

Fourth, the mother's consent to surrender her child in adoptions is revocable, even after surrender of the child, unless it be to an approved agency, where by regulation there are protections against an ill-advised surrender. In surrogacy, consent occurs so early that no amount of advice would satisfy the potential mother's need, yet the consent is irrevocable.

The main difference, that the unwanted pregnancy is unintended while the situation of the surrogate mother is voluntary and intended, is really not significant. Initially, it produces stronger reactions of sympathy for the mother whose pregnancy was unwanted than for the surrogate mother, who "went into this with her eyes wide open." On reflection, however, it appears that the essential evil is the same, taking advantage of a woman's circumstances (the unwanted pregnancy or the need for money) in order to take away her child, the difference being one of degree.

In the scheme contemplated by the surrogacy contract in this case, a middle man, propelled by profit, promotes the sale. Whatever idealism may have motivated any of the participants, the profit motive predominates, permeates, and ultimately governs the transaction. The demand for children is great and the supply small. The availability of contraception, abortion, and the greater willingness of single mothers to bring up their children has led to a shortage of babies offered for adoption. See N. Baker, Baby Selling: The Scandal of Black Market Adoption, supra; Adoption and Foster Care, 1975: Hearings on Baby Selling Before the Subcomm. On Children and Youth of the Senate Comm. on Labor and Public Welfare, 94th Cong. 1st Sess. 6 (1975) (Statement of Joseph H. Reid, Executive Director, Child Welfare League of America, Inc.). The situation is ripe for the entry of the middleman who will bring some equilibrium into the market by increasing the supply through the use of money.

Intimated, but disputed, is the assertion that surrogacy will be used for the benefit of the rich at the expense of the poor. See, e.g., Radin, "Market Inalienability," 100 Harv. L. Rev. 1849, 1930 (1987). In response it is noted that the Sterns are not rich and the Whiteheads not poor. Nevertheless, it is clear to us that it is unlikely that surrogate mothers will be as proportionately numerous among those women in the top twenty percent income bracket as among those in the bottom twenty percent. Ibid. Put differently, we doubt that infertile couples in the low-income bracket will find upper-income surrogates.

In any event, even in this case one should not pretend that disparate wealth does not play a part simply because the contrast is not the dramatic "rich versus poor." At the time of trial, the Whiteheads' net assets were probably negative—Mrs. Whitehead's own sister was foreclosing on a second mortgage. Their income derived from Mr. Whitehead's labors. Mrs. Whitehead is a homemaker, having previously held part-time jobs. The Sterns are both professionals, she a medical doctor, he a biochemist. Their combined income when both were working was about $89,500 a year and their assets sufficient to pay for the surrogacy contract arrangements.

The point is made that Mrs. Whitehead agreed to the surrogacy arrangement, supposedly fully understanding the consequences. Putting aside the issue of how compelling her need for money may have been, and how significant her understanding of the consequences, we suggest that her consent is irrelevant. There are, in a civilized society, some things that money cannot buy. In America, we decided long ago that merely because conduct purchased by money was "voluntary" did not mean that it was good or beyond regulation and prohibition. West Coast Hotel Co. v. Parrish, 300 U.S. 379, 57 S.Ct. 578, 81 L.Ed. 703 (1937). Employers can no longer buy labor at the lowest price they can bargain for, even though that labor is "voluntary," 29 U.S.C. § 206 (1982), or buy women's labor for less money than paid to men for the same job, 29 U.S.C. § 206(d), or purchase the agreement of children to perform oppressive labor, 29 U.S.C. § 212, or purchase the agreement of workers to subject themselves to unsafe or unhealthful working conditions, 29 U.S.C.§ § 651 to 678. (Occupational Safety and Health Act of 1970). There are, in short, values that society deems more important than granting to wealth whatever it can buy, be it labor, love, or life. Whether this principle recommends prohibition of surrogacy, which presumably sometimes results in great satisfaction to all of the parties, is not for us to say. We note here only that, under existing law, the fact that Mrs. Whitehead "agreed" to the arrangement is not dispositive.

The long-term effects of surrogacy contracts are not known, but feared—the impact on the child who learns her life was bought, that she is the offspring of someone who gave birth to her only to obtain money; the impact on the natural mother as the full weight of her isolation is felt along with the full reality of the sale of her body and her child; the impact on the natural father and adoptive mother once they realize the consequences of their conduct. Literature in related areas suggests these are substantial considerations, although, given the newness of surrogacy, there is little information. See N. Baker, Baby Selling: The Scandal of Black Market Adoption, supra; Adoption and Foster Care, 1975: Hearings on Baby Selling Before the Subcomm. on Children and Youth of the Senate Comm. on Labor and Public Welfare, 94th Cong. 1st Sess. (1975).

The surrogacy contract is based on principles that are directly contrary to the objectives of our laws.[10] It guarantees the separation of a child from its mother; it looks to adoption regardless of suitability; it totally ignores the child; it takes the child from the mother regardless of her wishes and her maternal fitness; and it does all of this, it accomplishes all of its goals, through the use of money.

Beyond that is the potential degradation of some women that may result from this arrangement. In many cases, of course, surrogacy may bring satisfaction, not only to the infertile couple, but to the surrogate mother herself. The fact, however, that many women may not perceive surrogacy negatively but rather see it as an opportunity does not diminish its potential for devastation to other women.

In sum, the harmful consequences of this surrogacy arrangement appear to us all too palpable. In New Jersey the surrogate mother's agreement to sell her child is void.[11] Its irrevocability infects the entire contract, as does the money that purports to buy it.

III.   TERMINATION

We have already noted that under our laws termination of parental rights cannot be based on contract, but may be granted only on proof of the statutory requirements. That conclusion was one of the bases for invalidating the surrogacy contract. Although excluding the contract as a basis for parental termination, we did not explicitly deal with the question of whether the statutory bases for termination existed. We do so here.

As noted before, if termination of Mrs. Whitehead's parental rights is justified, Mrs. Whitehead will have no further claim either to custody or to visitation, and adoption by Mrs. Stern may proceed pursuant to the private placement adoption statute, N.J.S.A. 9:3–48. If termination is not justified, Mrs. Whitehead remains the legal mother, and even if not entitled to custody, she would ordinarily be expected to have some rights of visitation. Wilke v. Culp, supra, 196 N.J. Super. at 496.

As was discussed, supra at 425–429, the proper bases for termination are found in the statute relating to proceedings by approved agencies for a termination of parental rights, N.J.S.A. 9:2–18, the statute allowing for termination leading to a private placement adoption, N.J.S.A. 9:3–48c(1), and the statute authorizing a termination pursuant to an action by DYFS, N.J.S.A. 30:4C–20. The statutory descriptions of the conditions required to terminate parental rights differ; their interpretation in case law, however, tends to equate them. Compare New Jersey Div. of Youth and Family Servs. v. A.W., supra, 103 N.J. at 601–11 (attempted termination by DYFS) with In re Adoption by J.J.P., supra, 175 N.J. Super. at 426–28 (attempted termination in connection with private placement adoption).

Nothing in this record justifies a finding that would allow a court to terminate Mary Beth Whitehead's parental rights under the statutory standard. It is not simply that obviously there was no "intentional abandonment or very substantial neglect of parental duties without a reasonable expectation of reversal of that conduct in the future," N.J.S.A. 9:3–48C(1), quite the contrary, but furthermore that the trial court never found Mrs. Whitehead an unfit mother and indeed affirmatively stated that Mary Beth Whitehead had been a good mother to her other children. 217 N.J. Super. at 397.

Although the question of best interests of the child is dispositive of the custody issue in a dispute between natural parents, it does not govern the question of termination. It has long been decided that the mere fact that a child would be better off with one set of parents than with another is an insufficient basis for terminating the natural parent's rights. See New Jersey Div. of Youth and Family Servs. v. A.W., supra, 103 N.J. at 603; In re Adoption of Children by D., supra, 61 N.J. at 97–98; In re Adoption by J.J.P., supra, 175 N.J. Super. at 428. Furthermore, it is equally well settled that surrender of a child and a consent to adoption through private placement do not alone warrant termination. See Sees v. Baber, supra, 74 N.J. 201. It must be noted, despite some language to the contrary, that the interests of the child are not the only interests involved when termination issues are raised. The parent's rights, both constitutional and statutory, have their own independent vitality. See New Jersey Div. of Youth and Family Servs. v. A.W., supra, 103 N.J. at 601.

Although the statutes are clear, they are not applied rigidly on all occasions. The statutory standard, strictly construed, appears harsh where the natural parents, having surrendered their child for adoption through private placement, change their minds and seek the return of their child and where the issue comes before the court with the adoptive parents having had custody for years, and having assumed it quite innocently.

These added dimensions in Sees v. Baber, supra, 74 N.J. 201, failed to persuade this Court to vary the termination requirements. The natural parent in that case changed her mind two days after surrendering the child, sought his return unequivocally, and so advised the adoptive parents. Since she was clearly fit, and clearly had not abandoned the child in the statutory sense, termination was denied, despite the fact that the adoptive parents had had custody of the child for about a year, and the mother had never had custody at all.

A significant variation on these facts, however, occurred in Sorentino II, supra, 74 N.J. 313. The surrender there was not through private placement but through an approved agency. Although the consent to surrender was held invalid due to coercion by the agency, the natural parents failed to initiate the lawsuit to reclaim the child for over a year after relinquishment. By the time this Court reached the issue of whether the natural parents' rights could be terminated, the adoptive parents had had custody for three years. These circumstances ultimately persuaded this Court to permit termination of the natural parents' rights and to allow a subsequent adoption. The unique facts of Sorentino II were found to amount to a forsaking of parental obligations. Id. at 322.

The present case is distinguishable from Sorentino II. Mary Beth Whitehead had custody of Baby M for four months before the child was taken away. Her initial surrender of Baby M was pursuant to a contract that we have declared illegal and unenforceable. The Sterns knew almost from the very day that they took Baby M that their rights were being challenged by the natural mother. In short, the factors that persuaded this Court to terminate the parental rights in Sorentino II are not found here.

There is simply no basis, either in the statute or in the peculiar facts of that limited class of case typified by Sorentino II, to warrant termination of Mrs. Whitehead's parental rights. We therefore conclude that the natural mother is entitled to retain her rights as a mother.

IV. CONSTITUTIONAL ISSUES

Both parties argue that the Constitutions—state and federal—mandate approval of their basic claims. The source of their constitutional arguments is essentially the same: the right of privacy, the right to procreate, the right to the companionship of one's child, those rights flowing either directly from the fourteenth amendment or by its incorporation of the Bill of Rights, or from the ninth amendment, or through the penumbra surrounding all of the Bill of Rights. They are the rights of personal intimacy, of marriage, of sex, of family, of procreation. Whatever their source, it is clear that they are fundamental rights protected by both the federal and state Constitutions. Lehr v. Robertson, 463 U.S. 248, 103 S. Ct. 2985, 77 L. Ed. 2d 614 (1983); Santosky v. Kramer, 455 U.S. 745, 102 S. Ct. 1388, 71 L. Ed. 2d 599 (1982); Zablocki v. Redhail, 434 U.S. 374, 98 S. Ct. 673, 54 L. Ed. 2d 618 (1978); Quilloin v. Walcott, 434 U.S. 246, 98 S. Ct. 549, 54 L. Ed. 2d 511 (1978); Carey v. Population Servs. Int'l, 431 U.S. 678, 97 S. Ct. 2010, 52 L. Ed. 2d 675 (1977); Roe v. Wade, 410 U.S. 113, 93 S. Ct. 705, 35 L. Ed. 2d 147 (1973); Stanley v. Illinois, 405 U.S. 645, 92 S. Ct. 1208, 31 L. Ed. 2d 551 (1972); Griswold v. Connecticut, 381 U.S. 479, 85 S. Ct. 1678, 14 L. Ed. 2d 510 (1965); Skinner v. Oklahoma, 316 U.S. 535, 62 S. Ct. 1110, 86 L. Ed. 1655 (1942); Meyer v. Nebraska, 262 U.S. 390, 43 S. Ct. 625, 67 L. Ed. 1042 (1923). The right asserted by the Sterns is the right of procreation; that asserted by Mary Beth Whitehead is the right to the companionship of her child. We find that the right of procreation does not extend as far as claimed by the Sterns. As for the right asserted by Mrs. Whitehead,[12] since we uphold it on other grounds (i.e., we have restored her as mother and recognized her right, limited by the child's best interests, to her companionship), we need not decide that constitutional issue, and for reasons set forth below, we should not.

The right to procreate, as protected by the Constitution, has been ruled on directly only once by the United States Supreme Court. See Skinner v. Oklahoma, supra, 316 U.S. 535, 62 S. Ct. 1110, 86 L. Ed. 1655 (forced sterilization of habitual criminals violates equal protection clause of fourteenth amendment). Although Griswold v. Connecticut, supra, 381 U.S. 479, 85 S. Ct. 1678, 14 L. Ed. 2d 510, is obviously of a similar class, strictly speaking it involves the right not to procreate. The right to procreate very simply is the right to have natural children, whether through sexual intercourse or artificial insemination. It is no more than that. Mr. Stern has not been deprived of that right. Through artificial insemination of Mrs. Whitehead, Baby M is his child. The custody, care, companionship, and nurturing that follow birth are not parts of the right to procreation; they are rights that may also be constitutionally protected, but that involve many considerations other than the right of procreation. To assert that Mr. Stern's right of procreation gives him the right to the custody of Baby M would be to assert that Mrs. Whitehead's right of procreation does not give her the right to the custody of Baby M; it would be to assert that the constitutional right of procreation includes within it a constitutionally protected contractual right to destroy someone else's right of procreation.

We conclude that the right of procreation is best understood and protected if confined to its essentials, and that when dealing with rights concerning the resulting child, different interests come into play. There is nothing in our culture or society that even begins to suggest a fundamental right on the part of the father to the custody of the child as part of his right to procreate when opposed by the claim of the mother to the same child. We therefore disagree with the trial court: there is no constitutional basis whatsoever requiring that Mr. Stern's claim to the custody of Baby M be sustained. Our conclusion may thus be understood as illustrating that a person's rights of privacy and self-determination are qualified by the effect on innocent third persons of the exercise of those rights.[13]

Mr. Stern also contends that he has been denied equal protection of the laws by the State's statute granting full parental rights to a husband in relation to the child produced, with his consent, by the union of his wife with a sperm donor. N.J.S.A. 9:17–44. The claim really is that of Mrs. Stern. It is that she is in precisely the same position as the husband in the statute: she is presumably infertile, as is the husband in the statute; her spouse by agreement with a third party procreates with the understanding that the child will be the couple's child. The alleged unequal protection is that the understanding is honored in the statute when the husband is the infertile party, but no similar understanding is honored when it is the wife who is infertile.

It is quite obvious that the situations are not parallel. A sperm donor simply cannot be equated with a surrogate mother. The State has more than a sufficient basis to distinguish the two situations—even if the only difference is between the time it takes to provide sperm for artificial insemination and the time invested in a nine-month pregnancy—so as to justify automatically divesting the sperm donor of his parental rights without automatically divesting a surrogate mother. Some basis for an equal protection argument might exist if Mary Beth Whitehead had contributed her egg to be implanted, fertilized or otherwise, in Mrs. Stern, resulting in the latter's pregnancy. That is not the case here, however.

Mrs. Whitehead, on the other hand, asserts a claim that falls within the scope of a recognized fundamental interest protected by the Constitution. As a mother, she claims the right to the companionship of her child. This is a fundamental interest, constitutionally protected. Furthermore, it was taken away from her by the action of the court below. Whether that action under these circumstances would constitute a constitutional deprivation, however, we need not and do not decide. By virtue of our decision Mrs. Whitehead's constitutional complaint—that her parental rights have been unconstitutionally terminated—is moot. We have decided that both the statutes and public policy of this state require that that termination be voided and that her parental rights be restored. It therefore becomes unnecessary to decide whether that same result would be required by virtue of the federal or state Constitutions. See Ashwander v. Tennessee Valley Auth., 297 U.S. 288, 341, 346–48, 56 S. Ct. 466, 482–83, 80 L. Ed. 688, 707, 710–12 (1936) (Brandeis, J., concurring). Refraining from deciding such constitutional issues avoids further complexities involving the full extent of a parent's right of companionship,[14] or questions involving the fourteenth amendment.[15]

Having held the contract invalid and having found no other grounds for the temination of Mrs. Whitehead's parental rights, we find that nothing remains of her constitutional claim. It seems obvious to us that since custody and visitation encompass practically all of what we call "parental rights," a total denial of both would be the equivalent of termination of parental rights. Franz v. United States, 707 F.2d 582, 602 (D. C. Cir. 1983). That, however, as will be seen below, has not occurred here. We express no opinion on whether a prolonged suspension of visitation would constitute a termination of parental rights, or whether, assuming it would, a showing of unfitness would be required.[16]

V.   CUSTODY

Having decided that the surrogacy contract is illegal and unenforceable, we now must decide the custody question without regard to the provisions of the surrogacy contract that would give Mr. Stern sole and permanent custody. (That does not mean that the existence of the contract and the circumstances under which it was entered may not be considered to the extent deemed relevant to the child's best interests.) With the surrogacy contract disposed of, the legal framework becomes a dispute between two couples over the custody of a child produced by the artificial insemination of one couple's wife by the other's husband. Under the Parentage Act the claims of the natural father and the natural mother are entitled to equal weight, i.e., one is not preferred over the other solely because he or she is the father or the mother. N.J.S.A. 9:17–40.[17] The applicable rule given these circumstances is clear: the child's best interests determine custody.

We note again that the trial court's reasons for determining what were the child's best interests were somewhat different from ours. It concluded that the surrogacy contract was valid, but that it could not grant specific performance unless to do so was in the child's best interests. The approach was that of a Chancery judge, unwilling to give extraordinary remedies unless they well served the most important interests, in this case, the interests of the child. While substantively indistinguishable from our approach to the question of best interests, the purpose of the inquiry was not the usual purpose of determining custody, but of determining a contractual remedy.

We are not concerned at this point with the question of termination of parental rights, either those of Mrs. Whitehead or of Mr. Stern. As noted in various places in this opinion, such termination, in the absence of abandonment or a valid surrender, generally depends on a showing that the particular parent is unfit. The question of custody in this case, as in practically all cases, assumes the fitness of both parents, and no serious contention is made in this case that either is unfit. The issue here is which life would be better for Baby M, one with primary custody in the Whiteheads or one with primary custody in the Sterns.

The circumstances of this custody dispute are unusual and they have provoked some unusual contentions. The Whiteheads claim that even if the child's best interests would be served by our awarding custody to the Sterns, we should not do so, since that will encourage surrogacy contracts—contracts claimed by the Whiteheads, and we agree, to be violative of important legislatively-stated public policies. Their position is that in order that surrogacy contracts be deterred, custody should remain in the surrogate mother unless she is unfit, regardless of the best interests of the child. We disagree. Our declaration that this surrogacy contract is unenforceable and illegal is sufficient to deter similar agreements. We need not sacrifice the child's interests in order to make that point sharper. Cf. In re Adoption of Child by I.T. and K.T., 164 N.J. Super. 476, 484–86 (App. Div. 1978) (adoptive parents' participation in illegal placement does not mandate denial of adoption); In the Matter of the Adoption of Child by N.P. and F.P., 165 N.J. Super. 591 (Law Div. 1979) (use of unapproved intermediaries and the payment of money in connection with adoption is insufficient to establish that the would-be adoptive parents are unfit or that adoption would not be in child's best interests).

The Whiteheads also contend that the award of custody to the Sterns pendente lite was erroneous and that the error should not be allowed to affect the final custody decision. As noted above, at the very commencement of this action the court issued an ex parte order requiring Mrs. Whitehead to turn over the baby to the Sterns; Mrs. Whitehead did not comply but rather took the child to Florida. Thereafter, a similar order was enforced by the Florida authorities resulting in the transfer of possession of Baby M to the Sterns. The Sterns retained custody of the child throughout the litigation. The Whiteheads' point, assuming the pendente award of custody was erroneous, is that most of the factors arguing for awarding permanent custody to the Sterns resulted from that initial pendente lite order. Some of Mrs. Whitehead's alleged character failings, as testified to by experts and concurred in by the trial court, were demonstrated by her actions brought on by the custody crisis. For instance, in order to demonstrate her impulsiveness, those experts stressed the Whiteheads' flight to Florida with Baby M; to show her willingness to use her children for her own aims, they noted the telephone threats to kill Baby M and to accuse Mr. Stern of sexual abuse of her daughter; in order to show Mrs. Whitehead's manipulativeness, they pointed to her threat to kill herself; and in order to show her unsettled family life, they noted the innumerable moves from one hotel or motel to another in Florida. Furthermore, the argument continues, one of the most important factors, whether mentioned or not, in favor of custody in the Sterns is their continuing custody during the litigation, now having lasted for one-and-a-half years. The Whiteheads' conclusion is that had the trial court not given initial custody to the Sterns during the litigation, Mrs. Whitehead not only would have demonstrated her perfectly acceptable personality—the general tenor of the opinion of experts was that her personality problems surfaced primarily in crises—but would also have been able to prove better her parental skills along with an even stronger bond than may now exist between her and Baby M. Had she not been limited to custody for four months, she could have proved all of these things much more persuasively through almost two years of custody.

The argument has considerable force. It is of course possible that the trial court was wrong in its initial award of custody. It is also possible that such error, if that is what it was, may have affected the outcome. We disagree with the premise, however, that in determining custody a court should decide what the child's best interests would be if some hypothetical state of facts had existed. Rather, we must look to what those best interests are, today, even if some of the facts may have resulted in part from legal error. The child's interests come first: we will not punish it for judicial errors, assuming any were made. See Wist v. Wist, 101 N.J. 509, 513–14 (1986); see also In re J.R. Guardianship, 174 N.J. Super. 211 (App. Div.), certif. den., 85 N.J. 102 (1980) (although not explicitly mentioned, natural mother's loss of parental rights based substantially on failures of DYFS to arrange visitation with her child). The custody decision must be based on all circumstances, on everything that actually has occurred, on everything that is relevant to the child's best interests. Those circumstances include the trip to Florida, the telephone calls and threats, the substantial period of successful custody with the Sterns, and all other relevant circumstances. We will discuss the question of the correctness of the trial court's initial orders below, but for purposes of determining Baby M's best interests, the correctness of those initial orders has lost relevance.

There were eleven experts who testified concerning the child's best interests, either directly or in connection with matters related to that issue. Our reading of the record persuades us that the trial court's decision awarding custody to the Sterns (technically to Mr. Stern) should be affirmed since "its findings. . . could reasonably have been reached on sufficient credible evidence present in the record." Beck v. Beck, 86 N.J. 480, 496 (1981) (quoting State v. Johnson, 42 N.J. 146, 161 (1964)); see Palermo v. Palermo, 164 N.J. Super. 492, 498 (App. Div. 1978) (noting that family court judge was experienced in dealing with such matters and had opportunity to observe parties and become immersed in details of case). More than that, on this record we find little room for any different conclusion. The trial court's treatment of this issue,

217 N.J. Super. at 391–400, is both comprehensive and, in most respects, perceptive. We agree substantially with its analysis with but few exceptions that, although important, do not change our ultimate views.

Our custody conclusion is based on strongly persuasive testimony contrasting both the family life of the Whiteheads and the Sterns and the personalities and characters of the individuals. The stability of the Whitehead family life was doubtful at the time of trial. Their finances were in serious trouble (foreclosure by Mrs. Whitehead's sister on a second mortgage was in process). Mr. Whitehead's employment, though relatively steady, was always at risk because of his alcoholism, a condition that he seems not to have been able to confront effectively. Mrs. Whitehead had not worked for quite some time, her last two employments having been part-time. One of the Whiteheads' positive attributes was their ability to bring up two children, and apparently well, even in so vulnerable a household. Yet substantial question was raised even about that aspect of their home life. The expert testimony contained criticism of Mrs. Whitehead's handling of her son's educational difficulties. Certain of the experts noted that Mrs. Whitehead perceived herself as omnipotent and omniscient concerning her children. She knew what they were thinking, what they wanted, and she spoke for them. As to Melissa, Mrs. Whitehead expressed the view that she alone knew what that child's cries and sounds meant. Her inconsistent stories about various things engendered grave doubts about her ability to explain honestly and sensitively to Baby M—and at the right time—the nature of her origin. Although faith in professional counseling is not a sine qua non of parenting, several experts believed that Mrs. Whitehead's contempt for professional help, especially professional psychological help, coincided with her feelings of omnipotence in a way that could be devastating to a child who most likely will need such help. In short, while love and affection there would be, Baby M's life with the Whiteheads promised to be too closely controlled by Mrs. Whitehead. The prospects for wholesome, independent psychological growth and development would be at serious risk.

The Sterns have no other children, but all indications are that their household and their personalities promise a much more likely foundation for Melissa to grow and thrive. There is a track record of sorts—during the one-and-a-half years of custody Baby M has done very well, and the relationship between both Mr. and Mrs. Stern and the baby has become very strong. The household is stable, and likely to remain so. Their finances are more than adequate, their circle of friends supportive, and their marriage happy. Most important, they are loving, giving, nurturing, and open-minded people. They have demonstrated the wish and ability to nurture and protect Melissa, yet at the same time to encourage her independence. Their lack of experience is more than made up for by a willingness to learn and to listen, a willingness that is enhanced by their professional training, especially Mrs. Stern's experience as a pediatrician. They are honest; they can recognize error, deal with it, and learn from it. They will try to determine rationally the best way to cope with problems in their relationship with Melissa. When the time comes to tell her about her origins, they will probably have found a means of doing so that accords with the best interests of Baby M. All in all, Melissa's future appears solid, happy, and promising with them.

Based on all of this we have concluded, independent of the trial court's identical conclusion, that Melissa's best interests call for custody in the Sterns. Our above-mentioned disagreements with the trial court do not, as we have noted, in any way diminish our concurrence with its conclusions. We feel, however, that those disagreements are important enough to be stated. They are disagreements about the evaluation of conduct. They also may provide some insight about the potential consequences of surrogacy.

It seems to us that given her predicament, Mrs. Whitehead was rather harshly judged—both by the trial court and by some of the experts. She was guilty of a breach of contract, and indeed, she did break a very important promise, but we think it is expecting something well beyond normal human capabilities to suggest that this mother should have parted with her newly born infant without a struggle. Other than survival, what stronger force is there? We do not know of, and cannot conceive of, any other case where a perfectly fit mother was expected to surrender her newly born infant, perhaps forever, and was then told she was a bad mother because she did not. We know of no authority suggesting that the moral quality of her act in those circumstances should be judged by referring to a contract made before she became pregnant. We do not countenance, and would never countenance, violating a court order as Mrs. Whitehead did, even a court order that is wrong; but her resistance to an order that she surrender her infant, possibly forever, merits a measure of understanding. We do not find it so clear that her efforts to keep her infant, when measured against the Sterns' efforts to take her away, make one, rather than the other, the wrongdoer. The Sterns suffered, but so did she. And if we go beyond suffering to an evaluation of the human stakes involved in the struggle, how much weight should be given to her nine months of pregnancy, the labor of childbirth, the risk to her life, compared to the payment of money, the anticipation of a child and the donation of sperm?

There has emerged a portrait of Mrs. Whitehead, exposing her children to the media, engaging in negotiations to sell a book, granting interviews that seemed helpful to her, whether hurtful to Baby M or not, that suggests a selfish, grasping woman ready to sacrifice the interests of Baby M and her other children for fame and wealth. That portrait is a half-truth, for while it may accurately reflect what ultimately occurred, its implication, that this is what Mary Beth Whitehead wanted, is totally inaccurate, at least insofar as the record before us is concerned. There is not one word in that record to support a claim that had she been allowed to continue her possession of her newly born infant, Mrs. Whitehead would have ever been heard of again; not one word in the record suggests that her change of mind and her subsequent fight for her child was motivated by anything other than love—whatever complex underlying psychological motivations may have existed.

We have a further concern regarding the trial court's emphasis on the Sterns' interest in Melissa's education as compared to the Whiteheads'. That this difference is a legitimate factor to be considered we have no doubt. But it should not be overlooked that a best-interests test is designed to create not a new member of the intelligentsia but rather a well-integrated person who might reasonably be expected to be happy with life. "Best interests" does not contain within it any idealized lifestyle; the question boils down to a judgment, consisting of many factors, about the likely future happiness of a human being. Fantony v. Fantony, supra, 21 N.J. at 536. Stability, love, family happiness, tolerance, and, ultimately, support of independence—all rank much higher in predicting future happiness than the likelihood of a college education. We do not mean to suggest that the trial court would disagree. We simply want to dispel any possible misunderstanding on the issue.

Even allowing for these differences, the facts, the experts' opinions, and the trial court's analysis of both argue strongly in favor of custody in the Sterns. Mary Beth Whitehead's family life, into which Baby M would be placed, was anything but secure—the quality Melissa needs most. And today it may be even less so.[18] Furthermore, the evidence and expert opinion based on it reveal personality characteristics, mentioned above, that might threaten the child's best development. The Sterns promise a secure home, with an understanding relationship that allows nurturing and independent growth to develop together. Although there is no substitute for reading the entire record, including the review of every word of each experts' testimony and reports, a summary of their conclusions is revealing. Six experts testified for Mrs. Whitehead: one favored joint custody, clearly unwarranted in this case; one simply rebutted an opposing expert's claim that Mary Beth Whitehead had a recognized personality disorder; one testified to the adverse impact of separation on Mrs. Whitehead; one testified about the evils of adoption and, to him, the probably analogous evils of surrogacy; one spoke only on the question of whether Mrs. Whitehead's consent in the surrogacy agreement was "informed consent"; an opinion that custody in the Whiteheads was in the best interests of Melissa—the ultimate issue. The Sterns' experts, both well qualified—as were the Whiteheads'—concluded that the best interests of Melissa required custody in Mr. Stern. Most convincingly, the three experts chosen by the court-appointed guardian ad litem of Baby M, each clearly free of all bias and interest, unanimously and persuasively recommended custody in the Sterns.

Some comment is required on the initial ex parte order awarding custody pendente lite to the Sterns (and the continuation of that order after a plenary hearing). The issue, although irrelevant to our disposition of this case, may recur; and when it does, it can be of crucial importance. When father and mother are separated and disagree, at birth, on custody, only in an extreme, truly rare, case should the child be taken from its mother pendente lite, i.e., only in the most unusual case should the child be taken from its mother before the dispute is finally determined by the court on its merits. The probable bond between mother and child, and the child's need, not just the mother's, to strengthen that bond, along with the likelihood, in most cases, of a significantly lesser, if any, bond with the father—all counsel against temporary custody in the father. A substantial showing that the mother's continued custody would threaten the child's health or welfare would seem to be required.

In this case, the trial court, believing that the surrogacy contract might be valid, and faced with the probable flight from the jurisdiction by Mrs. Whitehead and the baby if any notice were served, ordered, ex parte, an immediate transfer of possession of the child, i.e., it ordered that custody be transferred immediately to Mr. Stern, rather than order Mrs. Whitehead not to leave the

State. We have ruled, however, that the surrogacy contract is unenforceable and illegal. It provides no basis for either an ex parte, a plenary, an interlocutory, or a final order requiring a mother to surrender custody to a father. Any application by the natural father in a surrogacy dispute for custody pending the outcome of the litigation will henceforth require proof of unfitness, of danger to the child, or the like, of so high a quality and persuasiveness as to make it unlikely that such application will succeed. Absent the required showing, all that a court should do is list the matter for argument on notice to the mother. Even her threats to flee should not suffice to warrant any other relief unless her unfitness is clearly shown. At most, it should result in an order enjoining such flight. The erroneous transfer of custody, as we view it, represents a greater risk to the child than removal to a foreign jurisdiction, unless parental unfitness is clearly proved. Furthermore, [*93] we deem it likely that, advised of the law and knowing that her custody cannot seriously be challenged at this stage of the litigation, surrogate mothers will obey any court order to remain in the jurisdiction.

VI.   VISITATION

The trial court's decision to terminate Mrs. Whitehead's parental rights precluded it from making any determination on visitation. 217 N.J. Super. at 399, 408. Our reversal of the trial court's order, however, requires delineation of Mrs. Whitehead's rights to visitation. It is apparent to us that this factually sensitive issue, which was never addressed below, should not be determined de novo by this Court. We therefore remand the visitation issue to the trial court for an abbreviated hearing and determination as set forth below.[19]

For the benefit of all concerned, especially the child, we would prefer to end these proceedings now, once and for all. It is clear to us, however, that it would be unjust to do so and contrary to precedent.

The fact that the trial court did not address visitation is only one reason for remand. The ultimate question is whether, despite the absence of the trial court's guidance, the record before us is sufficient to allow an appellate court to make this essentially factual determination. We can think of no issue that is more dependent on a trial court's factual findings and evaluation than visitation.

When we examine the record on visitation, the only testimony explicitly dealing with the issue came from the guardian ad litem's experts. Examination of this testimony in light of the complete record, however, reveals that it was an insignificant part of their opinions. The parties, those with a real stake in the dispute, offered no testimony on the issue. The cause for this insufficiency of guidance on the visitation issue was unquestionably the parties' concentration on other, then seemingly much more important, questions: custody, termination of parental rights, and the validity of the surrogacy contract.

Even if we were willing to rely solely on the opinions of the guardian ad litem's experts, their testimony was not fully developed because the issue was not the focus of the litigation. Moreover, the guardian's experts concentrated on determining "best interests" as it related to custody and to termination of parental rights. Their observations about visitation, both in quality and quantity, were really derivative of their views about custody and termination. The guardian's experts were concerned that given Mrs. Whitehead's determination to have custody, visitation might be used to undermine the Sterns' parental authority and thereby jeopardize the stability and security so badly needed by this child. Two of the experts recommended suspension of visitation for five years and the other suspension for an undefined period. None of them fully considered the factors that have led our courts ordinarily to grant visitation in other contexts, with no suspension, even where the non-custodial parent was less than a paragon of virtue. See, e.g., Wilke v. Culp, supra, 196 N.J. Super. at 496; In re Adoption by J.J.P., supra, 175 N.J. Super. at 430. Based on the opinions of her experts, the guardian ad litem recommended suspension of Mrs. Whitehead's visitation rights for five years, with a reevaluation at that time. The basis for that recommendation, whether one regards it as the right or the wrong conclusion, was apparently bolstered when it was learned that Mrs. Whitehead had become pregnant, divorced Richard Whitehead, and then married the father of her new child-to-be. Without any further expert testimony, the guardian ad litem revised her position. She now argues that instead of five years, visitation should be suspended until Melissa reaches majority. This radical change in the guardian ad litem's position reinforces our belief that further consideration must be given to this issue.

The foregoing does not fully describe the extent to which this record leaves us uninformed on the visitation issue. No one, with one exception, included a word about visitation in the final briefs before the trial court. The exception was Mrs. Whitehead's parents who argued for their own visitation. This claim was denied by the trial court and is not now before us. The oral summations of counsel before the trial court were almost equally bereft of even a reference to the visitation issue. Mrs. Whitehead's counsel did not mention visitation. The Sterns' counsel referred to the guardian ad litem's expert testimony about visitation, not to argue for or against visitation but only to support his argument in favor of termination of Mrs. Whitehead's parental rights. The guardian ad litem did argue the visitation issue, devoting a minimal portion of her summation to it. Only the grandparents dealt with visitation, but with their visitation, not with the issue of Mrs. Whitehead's visitation. Finally, on appeal before this Court the record on visitation is inadequate—especially when compared to the treatment of other issues.

We join those who want this litigation to end for the benefit of this child. To spare this two-year-old another sixty to ninety days of litigation, however, at the risk of wrongly deciding this matter, which has life-long consequences for the child and the parties, would be unwise.

We also note the following for the trial court's consideration: First, this is not a divorce case where visitation is almost invariably granted to the non-custodial spouse. To some extent the facts here resemble cases where the non-custodial spouse has had practically no relationship with the child, see Wilke v. Culp, supra, 196 N.J. Super. 487; but it only "resembles" those cases. In the instant case, Mrs. Whitehead spent the first four months of this child's life as her mother and has regularly visited the child since then. Second, she is not only the natural mother, but also the legal mother, and is not to be penalized one iota because of the surrogacy contract. Mrs. Whitehead, as the mother (indeed, as a mother who nurtured her child for its first four months—unquestionably a relevant consideration), is entitled to have her own interest in visitation considered. Visitation cannot be determined without considering the parents' interests along with those of the child.

In all of this, the trial court should recall the touchstones of visitation: that it is desirable for the child to have contact with both parents; that besides the child's interests, the parents' interests also must be considered; but that when all is said and done, the best interests of the child are paramount.

We have decided that Mrs. Whitehead is entitled to visitation at some point, and that question is not open to the trial court on this remand. The trial court will determine what kind of visitation shall be granted to her, with or without conditions, and when and under what circumstances it should commence. It also should be noted that the guardian's recommendation of a five-year delay is most unusual—one might argue that it begins to border on termination. Nevertheless, if the circumstances as further developed by appropriate proofs or as reconsidered on remand clearly call for that suspension under applicable legal principles of visitation, it should be so ordered.

In order that the matter be determined as expeditiously as possible, we grant to the trial court the broadest powers to reach its determination. A decision shall be rendered in no more than ninety days from the date of this opinion.

The trial court shall, after reviewing the transcripts and other material, determine in its discretion whether further evidence is needed and through what witnesses it shall be presented. The trial court should consider limiting the witnesses to the experts who testified and to Mr. and Mrs. Stern and Mr. and Mrs. Whitehead, using its own judgment in deciding which of them, if any, shall be called on to give further evidence. The trial court, in its discretion, may either hear testimony or receive verified written submissions, relaxing the Rules of Evidence to the extent compatible with reliable fact finding and desirable for an expeditious decision.[20] Many significant facts bearing on visitation have already been adduced. Although additional evidence may be important, we believe that fairness does not necessarily require that it be produced with all of the procedural safeguards implicit in the Evidence Rules. When it comes to custody matters, application of rules, including those concerning evidence, must on some occasions be flexible, New Jersey Div. of Youth & Family Servs. v. S.S., 185 N.J. Super. 3 (App. Div.), certif. den., 91 N.J. 572 (1982), especially in view of the child's interests in this unique situation.

Any party wishing to appeal from the trial court's judgment on visitation shall file a notice of appeal within ten days thereafter, the Court hereby reducing the ordinary time to appeal pursuant to Rule 2:12–2. Any such appeal is hereby certified to this Court.

Any further proceedings in this matter, or related thereto, if made by application to the trial court shall be made to the judge to whom the matter is assigned on remand. That direction applies to applications related to this matter in any way: whether made before, during, or after proceedings on remand, and regardless of the nature of the application. Any applications for appellate review shall be made directly to this Court.

We would expect that after the visitation issue is determined the trial court, in connection with any other applications in the future, will attempt to assure that this case is treated like any other so that this child may be spared any further damaging publicity.

While probably unlikely, we do not deem it unthinkable that, the major issues having been resolved, the parties' undoubted love for this child might result in a good faith attempt to work out the visitation themselves, in the best interests of their child.

CONCLUSION

This case affords some insight into a new reproductive arrangement: the artificial insemination of a surrogate mother. The unfortunate events that have unfolded illustrate that its unregulated use can bring suffering to all involved. Potential victims include the surrogate mother and her family, the natural father and his wife, and most importantly, the child. Although surrogacy has apparently provided positive results for some infertile couples, it can also, as this case demonstrates, cause suffering to participants, here essentially innocent and well-intended.

We have found that our present laws do not permit the surrogacy contract used in this case. Nowhere, however, do we find any legal prohibition against surrogacy when the surrogate mother volunteers, without any payment, to act as a surrogate and is given the right to change her mind and to assert her parental rights. Moreover, the Legislature remains free to deal with this most sensitive issue as it sees fit, subject only to constitutional constraints.

If the Legislature decides to address surrogacy, consideration of this case will highlight many of its potential harms. We do not underestimate the difficulties of legislating on this subject. In addition to the inevitable confrontation with the ethical and moral issues involved, there is the question of the wisdom and effectiveness of regulating a matter so private, yet of such public interest. Legislative consideration of surrogacy may also provide the opportunity to begin to focus on the overall implications of the new reproductive biotechnology—in vitro fertilization, preservation of sperm and eggs, embryo implantation and the like. The problem is how to enjoy the benefits of the technology—especially for infertile couples—while minimizing the risk of abuse. The problem can be addressed only when society decides what its values and objectives are in this troubling, yet promising, area.

The judgment is affirmed in part, reversed in part, and remanded for further proceedings consistent with this opinion.

Questions for Case Study 2–1
1. What are the basic facts of this case?
2. What is the most important issue of this case?
3. What is the court's decision?
4. What are the main reasons given by the court in support of its decision?
5. Do you agree with this case? Why?
6. What effect is this case likely to have on future surrogate mother arrangements?
7. Would the highest court in another state be bound by the New Jersey Supreme Court's decision in a similar case? Why?

For Further Study

Assume that the Supreme Court of the State of Moot will hear a case with similar facts. Prepare a brief that argues either for or against the legality of a similar surrogate parenting arrangement.

Footnotes

1. Subsequent to the trial court proceedings, Mr. and Mrs. Whitehead were divorced, and soon thereafter Mrs. Whitehead remarried. Nevertheless, in the course of this opinion we will make reference almost exclusively to the facts as they existed at the time of trial, the facts on which the decision we now review was reached. We note moreover that Mr. Whitehead remains a party to this dispute. For these reasons, we continue to refer to appellants as Mr. and Mrs. Whitehead.

2. The Stern-Whitehead contract (the "surrogacy contract") and the Stern-ICNY contract are reproduced below as Appendices A and B respectively [not included]. Other ancillary agreements and their attachments are omitted.

3. Another argument advanced by Mrs. Whitehead is that the surrogacy agreement violates state wage regulations, N.J.S.A. 34:11–4.7, and the Minimum Wage Standard Act, N.J.S.A. 34:11–56a to –56a30. Given our disposition of the matter, we need not reach those issues.

4. N.J.S.A. 9:3–54 reads as follows:

   a. No person, firm, partnership, corporation, association or agency shall make, offer to make or assist or participate in any placement for adoption and in connection therewith (1) Pay, give or agree to give any money or any valuable consideration, or assume or discharge any financial obligation; or (2) Take, receive, accept or agree to accept any money or any valuable consideration.

   b. The prohibition of subsection *a* shall not apply to the fees or services of any approved agency in connection with a placement for adoption, nor shall such prohibition apply to the payment or reimbursement of medical, hospital or other similar expenses incurred in connection with the birth or any illness of the child, or to the acceptance of such reimbursement by a parent of the child.

   c. Any person, firm, partnership, corporation, association or agency violating this section shall be guilty of a high misdemeanor.

5. Of course, here there are no "adoptive parents," but rather the natural father and his wife, the only adoptive parent. As noted, however, many of the dangers of using money in connection with adoption may exist in surrogacy situations.

6. Counsel for the Sterns argues that the Parentage Act empowers the court to terminate parental rights solely on the basis of the child's best interests. He cites N.J.S.A. 9:17–53c, which reads, in pertinent part, as follows:

   The judgment or order may contain any other provision directed against the appropriate party to the proceeding concerning the duty of support, the custody and guardianship of the child, visitation privileges with the child, the furnishing of bond or other security for the payment of the judgment, the repayment of any public assistance grant, or any other matter in the best interests of the child.

   We do not interpret this section as in any way altering or diluting the statutory prerequisites to termination discussed above. Termination of parental rights differs qualitatively from the matters to which this section is expressly directed, and, in any event, we have no doubt that if the Legislature had intended a substantive change in the standards governing an area of such gravity, it would have said so explicitly.

7. We conclude not only that the surrogacy contract is an insufficient basis for termination, but that no statutory or other basis for termination existed. See infra at 444–447.

8. The surrogacy situation, of course, differs from the situation in Sees, in that here there is no "adoptive couple," but rather the natural father and the stepmother, who is the would-be adoptive mother. This difference, however, does not go to the basis of the Sees holding. In both cases, the determinative aspect is the vulnerability of the natural mother who decides to surrender her child in the absence of institutional safeguards.

9. And the impact on the natural parents, Mr. Stern and Mrs. Whitehead, is severe and dramatic. The depth of their conflict about Baby M, about custody, visitation, about the goodness or badness of each of them, comes through in their telephone conversations, in which each tried to persuade the other to give up the child. The potential adverse consequences of surrogacy are poignantly captured here—Mrs. Whitehead threatening to kill herself and the baby, Mr. Stern begging her not to, each blaming the other. The dashed hopes of the Sterns, the agony of Mrs. Whitehead, their suffering, their hatred—all were caused by the unraveling of this arrangement.

10. We note the argument of the Sterns that the sperm donor section of our Parentage Act, N.J.S.A. 9:17–38 to –59, implies a legislative policy that would lead to approval of this surrogacy contract. Where a married woman is artifically inseminated by another with her husband's consent, the Parentage Act creates a parent-child relationship between the husband and the resulting child. N.J.S.A. 9:17–44. The Parentage Act's silence, however, with respect to surrogacy, rather than supporting, defeats any contention that surrogacy should receive treatment parallel to the sperm donor artificial insemination situation. In the latter case the statute expressly transfers parental rights from the biological father, i.e., the sperm donor, to the mother's husband. Ibid. Our Legislature could not possibly have intended any other arrangement to have the consequence of transferring parental rights without legislative authorization when it had concluded that legislation was necessary to accomplish that result in the sperm donor artificial insemination context.

    This sperm donor provision suggests an argument not raised by the parties, namely, that the attempted creation of a parent-child relationship through the surrogacy contract has been preempted by the Legislature. The Legislature has explicitly recognized the parent-child relationship between a child and its natural parents, married and unmarried, N.J.S.A. 9:17–38 to –59, between adoptive parents and their adopted child, N.J.S.A. 9:3–37 to –56, and between a husband and his wife's child pursuant to the sperm donor provision, N.J.S.A. 9:17–44. It has not recognized any others—specifically, it has never legally equated the stepparent-stepchild relationship with the parent-child relationship, and certainly it has never recognized any concept of adoption by contract. It can be contended with some force that the Legislature's statutory coverage of the creation of the parent-child relationship evinces an intent to reserve to itself the power to define what is and is not a parent-child relationship. We need not, and do not, decide this question, however.

11. Michigan courts have also found that these arrangements conflict with various aspects of their law. See Doe v. Kelley, 106 Mich. App. 169, 307 N.W. 2d 438 (1981), cert. den., 459 U.S. 1183, 103 S. Ct. 834, 74 L. Ed. 2d 1027 (1983) (application of sections of Michigan Adoption Law prohibiting the exchange of money to surrogacy is constitutional); Syrkowski v. Appleyard, 122 Mich. App. 506, 333 N.W. 2d 90 (1983) (court held it lacked jurisdiction to issue an "order of

filiation" because surrogacy arrangements were not governed by Michigan's Paternity Act), rev'd, 420 Mich. 367, 362 N.W. 2d 211 (1985) (court decided Paternity Act should be applied but did not reach the merits of the claim).

Most recently, a Michigan trial court in a matter similar to the case at bar held that surrogacy contracts are void as contrary to public policy and therefore are unenforceable. The court expressed concern for the potential exploitation of children resulting from surrogacy arrangements that involve the payment of money. The court also concluded that insofar as the surrogacy contract may be characterized as one for personal services, the thirteenth amendment should bar specific performance. Yates v. Keane, Nos. 9758, 9772, slip op. (Mich. Cir. Ct. Jan. 21, 1988).

The Supreme Court of Kentucky has taken a somewhat different approach to surrogate arrangements. In Surrogate Parenting Assocs. v. Commonwealth ex. rel. Armstrong, 704 S.W. 2d 209 (Ky. 1986), the court held that the "fundamental differences" between surrogate arrangements and baby-selling placed the surrogate parenting agreement beyond the reach of Kentucky's baby-selling statute. Id. at 211. The rationale for this determination was that unlike the normal adoption situation, the surrogacy agreement is entered into before conception and is not directed at avoiding the consequences of an unwanted pregnancy. Id. at 211–12.

Concomitant with this pro-surrogacy conclusion, however, the court held that a "surrogate" mother has the right to void the contract if she changes her mind during pregnancy or immediately after birth. Id. at 212–13. The court relied on statutes providing that consent to adoption or to the termination of parental rights prior to five days after the birth of the child is invalid, and concluded that consent before conception must also be unenforceable. Id. at 212–13.

The adoption phase of an uncontested surrogacy arrangement was analyzed in Matter of Adoption of Baby Girl, L.J., 132 Misc. 2d 972, 505 N.Y.S. 2d 813 (Sur. 1986). Although the court expressed strong moral and ethical reservations about surrogacy arrangements, it approved the adoption because it was in the best interests of the child. Id. at 815. The court went on to find that surrogate parenting agreements are not void, but are voidable if they are not in accordance with the state's adoption statutes. Id. at 817. The court then upheld the payment of money in connection with the surrogacy arrangement on the ground that the New York Legislature did not contemplate surrogacy when the baby-selling statute was passed. Id. at 818. Despite the court's ethical and moral problems with surrogate arrangements, it concluded that the Legislature was the appropriate forum to address the legality of surrogacy arrangements. Ibid.

In contrast to the law in the United States, the law in the United Kingdom concerning surrogate parenting is fairly well-settled. Parliament passed the Surrogacy Arrangements Act, 1985, ch. 49, which made initiating or taking part in any negotiations with a view to making or arranging a surrogacy contract a criminal offense. The criminal sanction, however, does not apply to the "surrogate" mother or to the natural father, but rather applies to other persons engaged in arranging surrogacy contracts on a commercial basis. Since 1978, English courts have held surrogacy agreements unenforceable as against public policy, such agreements being deemed arrangements for the purchase and sale of children. A. v. C., [1985] F.L.R. 445, 449 (Fam. & C.A. 1978). It should be noted, however, that certain surrogacy arrangements, i.e., those arranged without brokers and revocable by the natural mother, are not prohibited under current law in the United Kingdom.

12. Opponents of surrogacy have also put forth arguments based on the thirteenth amendment, as well as the Peonage Act, 42 U.S.C. § 1994 (1982). We need not address these arguments because we have already held the contract unenforceable on the basis of state law.

13. As a general rule, a person should be accorded the right to make decisions affecting his or her own body, health, and life, unless that choice adversely affects others. Thus, the United States Supreme Court, while recognizing the right of women to control their own bodies, has rejected the view that the federal constitution vests a pregnant woman with an absolute right to terminate her pregnancy. Instead, the Court declared that the right was "not absolute" so that "at some point the state interests as to protection of health, medical standards, and prenatal life, become dominant." Roe v. Wade, supra, 410 U.S. at 155, 93 S.Ct. at 728, 35 L.Ed.2d at 178. The balance struck in Roe v. Wade recognizes increasing rights in the fetus and correlative restrictions on the mother as the pregnancy progresses. Similarly, in the termination-of-treatment cases, courts generally have viewed a patient's right to terminate or refuse life-sustaining treatment as constrained by other considerations including the rights of innocent third parties, such as the patient's children. Matter of Farrell, 108 N.J. 335, 352 (1987); Matter of Conroy, 98 N.J. 321, 353 (1985). Consistent with that approach, this Court has directed a mother to submit to a life-saving blood transfusion to protect the interests of her unborn infant, even though the mother's religious scruples led her to oppose the transfusion. Raleigh-Fitkin Paul Morgan Hosp. v. Anderson, 42 N.J. 421, 423 (1964); see also Application of President & Directors of Georgetown College, 331 F. 2d 1000, 1008 (D.C. Cir.), cert. den., 377 U.S. 978, 84 S.Ct. 1883, 12 L. Ed. 2d 746 (1964) (ordering blood transfusion because of mother's "responsibility to the community to care for her infant").

    In the present case, the parties' right to procreate by methods of their own choosing cannot be enforced without consideration of the state's interest in protecting the resulting child, just as the right to the companionship of one's child cannot be enforced without consideration of that crucial state interest.

14. This fundamental right is not absolute. The parent-child biological relationship, by itself, does not create a protected interest in the absence of a demonstrated commitment to the responsibilities of parenthood; a natural parent who does not come forward and seek a role in the child's life has no constitutionally protected relationship. Lehr v. Robertson, supra, 463 U.S. at 258–62, 103 S. Ct. at 2991–93, 77 L. Ed. 2d at 624–27; Quilloin v. Walcott, supra, 434 U.S. at 254–55, 98 S. Ct. at 554, 54 L. Ed. 2d at 519–20. The right is not absolute in another sense, for it is also well settled that if the state's interest is sufficient the right may be regulated, restricted, and on occasion terminated. See Santosky v. Kramer, supra, 455 U.S. 745, 102 S. Ct. 1388, 71 L. Ed. 2d 599.

15. Were to find such a constitutional determination necessary, we would be faced with the question of whether it was state action—essential in triggering the fourteenth amendment—that deprived her of that right, i.e., whether the judicial decision enforcing the surrogacy contract should be considered "state action" within the scope of the fourteenth amendment. See Shelley v. Kraemer, 334 U.S. 1, 68 S. Ct. 836, 92 L. Ed. 1161 (1948); Cherminsky, "Rethinking State Action," 80 Nw. U. L. Rev. 503 (1985).

16. If the Legislature were to enact a statute providing for enforcement of surrogacy agreements, the validity of such a statute might depend on the strength of the state interest in making it more likely that infertile couples will be able to adopt children. As a value, it is obvious that the interest is strong; but if, as plaintiffs assert, ten to fifteen percent of all couples are infertile, the interest is of

enormous strength. This figure is given both by counsel for the Sterns and by the trial court, 217 N.J. Super. at 331. We have been unable to find reliable confirmation of this statistic, however, and we are not confident of its accuracy. We note that at least one source asserts that in 1982, the rate of married couples who were both childless and infertile was only 5.8%. B. Wattenberg, The Birth Dearth 125 (1987).

On such quantitative differences, constitutional validity can depend, where the statute in question is justified as serving a compelling state interest. The quality of the interference with the parents' right of companionship bears on these issues: if a statute, like the surrogacy contract before us, made the consent given prior to conception irrevocable, it might be regarded as a greater interference with the fundamental right than a statute that gave that effect only to a consent executed, for instance, more than six months after the child's birth. There is an entire spectrum of circumstances that strengthen and weaken the fundamental right involved, and a similar spectrum of state interests that justify or do not justify particular restrictions on that right. We do not believe it would be wise for this Court to attempt to identify various combinations of circumstances and interests, and attempt to indicate which combinations might and which might not constitutionally permit termination of parental rights.

We will say this much, however: a parent's fundamental right to the companionship of one's child can be significantly eroded by that parent's consent to the surrender of that child. That surrender, if voluntarily and knowingly made, may reduce the strength of that fundamental right to the point where a statute awarding custody and all parental rights to an adoptive couple, especially one that includes a parent of the child, would be valid.

17. At common law the rights of women were so fragile that the husband generally had the paramount right to the custody of children upon separation or divorce. State v. Baird, 21 N.J. Eq. 384, 388 (E. & A. 1869). In 1860 a statute concerning separation provided that children "within the age of seven years" be placed with the mother "unless said mother shall be of such character and habits as to render her an improper guardian." L. 1860, c. 167. The inequities of the common-law rule and the 1860 statute were redressed by an 1871 statute, providing that "the rights of both parents, in the absence of misconduct, shall be held to be equal." L. 1871, c. 48, § 6 (currently codified at N.J.S.A. 9:2–4). Under this statute the father's superior right to the children was abolished and the mother's right to custody of children of tender years was also eliminated. Under the 1871 statute, "the happiness and welfare of the children" were to determine custody, L. 1871, c. 48, § 6, a rule that remains law to this day. N.J.S.A. 9:2–4.

Despite this statute, however, the "tender years" doctrine persisted. See, e.g., Esposito v. Esposito, 41 N.J. 143, 145 (1963); Dixon v. Dixon, 71 N.J. Eq. 281, 282 (E. & A. 1906); M.P. v. S.P., 169 N.J. Super. 425, 435 (App. Div. 1979). This presumption persisted primarily because of the prevailing view that a young child's best interests necessitated a mother's care. Both the development of case law and the Parentage Act, N.J.S.A. 9:17–40, however, provide for equality in custody claims. In Beck v. Beck, 86 N.J. 480, 488 (1981), we stated that it would be inappropriate "to establish a presumption. . . in favor of any particular custody determination," as any such presumption may "serve as a disincentive for the meticulous fact-finding required in custody cases." This does not mean that a mother who has had custody of her child for three, four, or five months does not have a particularly strong claim arising out of the unquestionable bond that exists at that point between the child and its mother; in other words, equality does not mean that all of the considerations underlying the "tender years" doctrine have been abolished.

18. Subsequent to trial, and by the time of oral argument, Mr. and Mrs. Whitehead had separated, and the representation was that there was no likelihood of change. Thereafter Mrs. Whitehead became pregnant by another man, divorced Mr. Whitehead, and remarried the other man. Both children are living with Mrs. Whitehead and her new husband. Both the former and present husband continue to assert the desire to have whatever parental relationship with Melissa that the law allows, Mrs. Whitehead continuing to maintain her claim for custody.

    We refer to this development only because it suggests less stability in the Whiteheads' lives. It does not necessarily suggest that Mrs. Whitehead's conduct renders her any less a fit parent. In any event, this new development has not affected our decision.

19. As we have done in similar situations, we order that this matter be referred on remand to a different trial judge by the vicinage assignment judge. The original trial judge's potential "commitment to its findings," New Jersey Div. of Youth & Family Servs. v. A.W., supra, 103 N.J. at 617, and the extent to which a judge "has already engaged in weighing the evidence," In re Guardianship of R., 155 N.J. Super. 186, 195 (App. Div. 1977), persuade us to make that change. On remand the trial court will consider developments subsequent to the original trial court's opinion, including Mrs. Whitehead's divorce, pregnancy, and remarriage.

20. Ordinarily relaxation of the Rules of Evidence depends on specific authority, either within the Rules or in statutes. See N.J. Rules of Evidence, Comment 2 to Evid. R.2(2), 72–76 (1987). There are numerous examples, however, of relaxation of these Rules in judicial proceedings for reasons peculiar to the case at hand. We regard the circumstances of the visitation aspect of this case as most unusual. In addition to the ordinary risks to the stability of an infant caused by prolonging this type of litigation, here there are risks from publicity that we simply cannot quantify. We have no doubt that these circumstances justify any sensible means of abbreviating the remand hearing.

JENNINGS et al. v. GIBSON

No. 31959

Court of Appeals of Georgia

77 Ga. App. 28

May 6, 1948, Decided

COUNSEL: Harris, Chance & McCracken, for plaintiffs in error. Charles Donald Dimmock, contra.

JUDGES: GARDNER, J. MacIntyre, P.J., and Townsend, J., concur.

OPINION: 1. This case is here on an assignment of error on the overruling of a motion for new trial, filed by Mary B. Jennings and others, defendants in the court below. The plaintiff in the court below was T. Y. Gibson Jr. The facts are substantially that the plaintiff sold to Mary B. Jennings and her son, James Jennings, a musical instrument generally known as a juke box. The sale was made on November 13, 1946, for $185.50. In August, 1946, prior to the sale, James Jennings had an agreement whereby the "juke box" was to be placed in the "juke joint" operated by him on a commission basis of 50 percent of the proceeds taken in by the "juke box." James Jennings was approximately 17 years old at the time of the transaction. After the note was executed he paid one installment of $15.45 which was due on December 13, 1946, and part of another installment in January 1947. The installment payments were due each month during a period of 12 months from the date of the note, November 13, 1946. During the period from the time the "juke box" was placed on a commission basis until the time of the sale of the "juke box" there arose a disagreement concerning the proceeds from the box, the plaintiff contending that James Jennings tripped the mechanism in such a way that it would play without the insertion of a coin. At this point the machine was sold, as above stated, to James Jennings and his mother, Mary B. Jennings, both of whom signed the note. The action was instituted for the difference between the amount of the note, less the payments made by James Jennings after the note for the box was executed. To the suit on the note the defendants entered two defenses, first, the plea of infancy as to James Jennings, and second, a plea of failure of consideration. The jury returned a verdict in favor of the plaintiff. Insofar as the plea of infancy is concerned, after having studied the evidence carefully on this issue, we are convinced that the evidence demanded a finding in favor of the plaintiff and against the defendants. We will not go into all of the evidence, but James Jennings, with reference to this issue testified "they were pretty nice to me. I ran the property. I was the proprietor." He had already testified that his father had died sometime in September, 1946. All the evidence shows that no one other than James Jennings had anything to do with the installation and the the evidence which we have quoted and other evidence demanded a finding against the defendants on the plea of infancy.

With reference to the plea of failure of consideration, James Jennings testified "I did have the machine from October to November before I purchased it. Mrs. Gibson didn't force me to purchase it. The note I signed was of my own free will." The other evidence shows that he had the "juke box" from August, 1946, to November, 1946. There is other evidence to the effect that no complaint was made whatsoever as to the suitableness of the "juke box" until some months into 1947, except on one occasion when James Jennings reported the box out of order and the wife of the plaintiff fixed it. James Jennings testified "she fixed it." The evidence reveals that this was a minor adjustment. The evidence for the plaintiff shows that the mechanism of the machine, if damaged, was damaged by reason of James Jennings tampering with it or tripping it. Mary B. Jennings did not testify. Under all the record in this case, the evidence overwhelmingly authorized the jury to find, indeed if it did not demand a finding, against the plea of failure of consideration. The general grounds are without merit. We will now consider the assignments of error in the special grounds.

2. Special ground 1 assigns error because the court, over objections, allowed the plaintiff while on the stand, to read from a purported copy of a letter which he had purportedly written to Mary B. Jennings on April 15, 1947. The effect of this letter was to demand from her payment of the note and to advise her that he had received the message to come out to her residence or that of her son, James Jennings, concerning the "juke box." The letter further stated that the plaintiff was then living in Macon, that he was in town for only a day, and that it would be impossible for him to confer with them, that he had consulted with his attorney and that he had authorized his attorney to see them in his stead. The purported letter as read, further stated that unless the arrear installments were paid, some action would have to be taken, and that he wrote the letter in the hope that she would settle the matter with the attorney by bringing the past-due payments up to date and continuing the future payments as they became due, but that if she did not do so, suit would be instituted. Under the facts of this case, conceding but not deciding, that the objection was well taken, we see no possible harm that could have resulted from reading the letter.

3. Special ground 2 assigns error because in the colloquy concerning the reading of the letter, the court remarked, "is it a copy of the letter he wrote the defendant?" It is claimed that this query of the court amounted to an expression of an opinion. There is nothing further concerning it. If error at all, it was harmless.

4. Special ground 3 assigns error because the court excluded a question propounded to the plaintiff on cross-examination to the effect "when you sold the juke box to the defendant you did not know whether it would stand up under commercial use or not?" While the court perhaps should have allowed this question to be answered, under all the facts of the record we do not see how it could be reversible error. The defendant had months to determine the serviceability of the box.

5. Special grounds 4 and 5 assign error because the court in charging Code § 20–203, titled "Infants Doing Business by Permission Bound" committed reversible error. That section reads: "If an infant, by permission of his parent or guardian, or by permission of law, practices any profession or trade, or engages in any business as an adult, he shall be bound for all contracts connected with such profession, trade, or business." The complaint here is that the court in the phrase set out in the statute "or engages in any business as an adult" used the word "of" an adult instead of "as" an adult. We can not see any reversible error in this slip of the tongue. As we have already observed, the jury were authorized to find that the evidence overwhelmingly sustained the proposition that James Jennings was engaged in the business as an adult.

6. Special ground 6 complains of the following excerpt from the charge of the court: "Mere inadequacy of consideration alone will not void a contract. If the inadequacy be great, it is a strong circumstance to evidence fraud; and in a suit for damages for breach of contract, the inadequacy of consideration will always enter as an element in estimating the damages." It is conceded that this is a correct abstract principle of law, but it is contended that it is inapplicable to the facts of this case. Even so, we fail to discern any harmful error which resulted to the defendants, under the record of this case.

In conclusion, so far as the special grounds are concerned, we might state that from experience and observation, we have never seen or read of a perfect trial. This court is committed to the proposition that it will not reverse the judgment of a lower court for minor and trivial errors when it is clear that substantial justice has been done. Rosenbusch v. Lester Book & Stationery Co., 16 Ga. App. 539 (85 S.E. 675).

We are asked by the plaintiff to assess attorney's fees under the record in this case. We decline to do so.

None of the grounds shows cause for reversal.

Questions for Case Study 2–2
1. What are the basic facts of the case?
2. What is the legal issue involved in this case?
3. What is the court's decision in this case?
4. What is the court's reasoning in reaching its decision?
5. Would the court have reached the same decision if the minor, James Jennings, had bought the jukebox for his personal use? Explain.

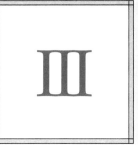

PART III

CONTRACTS FOR THE SALE OF GOODS AND COMMERCIAL PAPER

One of the drawbacks of our federalist system of government is that there can be significant differences in the law from state to state and between the states and the federal government. In general, differences in state laws present only minor inconveniences to individuals and businesses conducting business across state lines. However, some areas in the law are of particular importance to business, and even small variations in the law from one state to another can have a negative effect. Because of this, the National Conference of Commissioners on Uniform State Laws drafted the Uniform Commercial Code (UCC) in an attempt to unify state laws affecting commerce into a single code that all states could adopt, thereby doing away with conflicting laws affecting commerce in the various states. As a result of this concerted effort by some of this country's leading experts, the UCC was enacted with only small changes by the legislatures of all states except for Louisiana by 1967. (Louisiana has not adopted Article 2 [Sales] or Article 9 [Secured Transactions] but has adopted Articles 1, 3, 4, 5, 7, and 8.)

The articles of the UCC are as follows:

Article 1. General Provisions
Article 2. Sales
Article 3. Commercial Paper

Article 4. Bank Deposits and Collections

Article 5. Letters of Credit

Article 6. Bulk Transfers

Article 7. Warehouse Receipts, Bills of Lading, and Other Documents of Title

Article 8. Investment Securities

Article 9. Secured Transactions; Sale of Accounts and Chatter Paper

Article 10. Effective Date and Repealer

Article 11. Effective Date and Transition Provisions

A full treatment of the UCC is not possible in this or any other business law text. The complete text of the code is nearly 1,000 pages, and at least an entire semester could be devoted to a thorough examination of any one of its most significant articles. In the following chapters, we will explore the most salient provisions of Articles 2 and 3 (Sales and Commercial Paper) in what is the single most important statute in the field of business law.

In Chapters 4 through 10, we've examined the basic elements of the law of contracts and explored its application in a wide variety of business contexts. In the first three chapters of this unit, we will examine significant statutory modifications to the common law of contracts brought about by Article 2 of the UCC with respect to contracts for the sale of goods. In Chapter 14, we will explore the law of commercial paper under the UCC.

11

FORMATION AND MODIFICATION OF THE SALES CONTRACT

Learning Objectives

After studying this chapter, you will be able to:

1. Define the concept of goods and be able to give examples of goods and nongoods.
2. Distinguish the common law rule on firm offers and the UCC rule with regard to merchants.
3. Explain how the UCC treats additional terms in an acceptance and distinguish the effect of such terms under the code and under common law.
4. List and define the major defenses to contract formation.
5. Identify three circumstances under which a sales contract can be modified by operation of law.
6. Identify the three types of parol evidence that can be introduced to explain a written contract.

Introduction

Article 2 of the UCC applies to contracts involving the sale of goods. Contracts covering matters other than sale of goods are not covered by the code and are, therefore, still subject to common law rules of contracts in every jurisdiction. *Goods* are tangible movable objects that can be owned. This definition excludes many types of subject matter that can be personally owned such as real estate, fixtures (things permanently attached to land), and intangible property, such as patents, copyrights, and commercial paper (notes, drafts, and certificates of deposit).

The following items are common examples of goods:

Pens	Computers
Shirts	Microwave ovens
Bags of potato chips	Throw rugs
Automobiles	Chairs
Shoes	Music CDs
Boats	Growing crops
Jewelry	Cows, horses, or dogs
Paintings or sculptures	

In a word, any object that has a physical existence of its own, is personal property, and can be moved is considered goods for purposes of the UCC. A mobile home that rests on wheels or a temporary foundation, for example, is goods, since it is personal property and movable, but not if it is attached to real estate on a permanent foundation, since it then becomes real estate and is no longer considered movable. Likewise, a wild deer standing on a person's land is not goods, but it becomes so once it is shot or trapped (wild animals are not owned by anyone until they are either captured or killed).

Offer and Acceptance of the Sales Contract

Article 2 makes minor modifications to the common law rules affecting contract formation in the areas of firm offers made by merchants, the valid methods for accepting an offer, and the effect of some acceptances that contain additional terms.

Merchant's Firm Offers

The common law regards firm offers as revocable unless supported by consideration (anything of legal value given and received in exchange for entering into a contract). The UCC changes this rule when firm offers are made by merchants. Section 2–205 of the UCC makes a merchant's promise to hold an offer open for a stated period of time irrevocable for that period or, if no specific period is stated, for a reasonable time. To hold a merchant responsible for a firm offer not supported by consideration, the UCC requires that the offer be written and signed by the merchant. The maximum duration for a firm offer not supported by consideration is three months.

For purposes of the UCC, a *merchant* is one who regularly deals in goods of the kind involved in the contract.

➤ Ahmed, a used car salesman, offers to sell Dana a 1984 Fiat X 1/9 automobile for $1,500. Dana tells Ahmed that she is interested in the car but needs some time to think about it. Ahmed then orally promises her that he will keep the offer open for 48 hours at the stated price. The following day, Sally offers Ahmed $2,000 for the car. If Ahmed sells the car to Sally, will Dana have any legal recourse?

Ahmed's promise to hold the offer open is not binding, even though he is a merchant with regard to the car (he regularly sells automobiles), because it was not contained in a signed writing and was not otherwise supported by consideration. If Ahmed had written down the promise to sell Dana the car within 48 hours for $1,500 and then signed or initialed the document, he would have been bound to honor the terms of the promise and Dana could have sued him for breach of contract. Keep in mind, however, that signed firm offers not made by merchants are still not binding under the UCC unless supported by additional consideration.

Method of Acceptance (§2–206)

In general, an offer may be accepted by any reasonable means unless the method of acceptance is specifically stated in the offer or the circumstances dictate acceptance in a specific manner. If an offer is for the prompt shipment of goods, it can be accepted either through the shipment of *conforming* (acceptable) or *nonconforming* (unacceptable) goods, or through a promise to ship the goods. By shipping nonconforming goods, the seller both accepts and breaches the sales contract. If the seller ships nonconforming goods as an accommodation to the buyer, however, the shipment is not deemed an acceptance or breach but viewed as a traditional counteroffer by the seller that the buyer is free to accept or reject. For a shipment of nonconforming goods to be deemed an accommodation and not acceptance of the original offer, the seller must make it clear to the buyer that he is sending nonconforming goods as an accommodation.

For example, assume a buyer orders 100 bushels of apples to sell in her farm stand. The seller can accept the buyer's offer and form a binding contract in any of the following ways:

1. By informing the buyer through any reasonable means that he will ship the goods (e.g., phoning his acceptance, mailing a letter of acceptance, telegraphing his acceptance, etc.).
2. By promptly shipping conforming goods. Conforming goods are simply goods that live up to the requirements of the contract (e.g., shipping the right type and quantity of goods in marketable condition).
3. By shipping nonconforming goods. A nonconforming shipment would be one that contains the wrong type of goods, the wrong quantity of goods, or goods not commercially

acceptable (e.g., shipping 100 bushels of rotting oranges, 50 bushels of good oranges, or 100 bushels of apples would constitute nonconforming goods if 100 bushels of oranges had been ordered). When nonconforming goods are shipped, the shipment constitutes both an acceptance of the contract and a breach, so that the seller is immediately guilty of breaching the contract as soon as he accepts it and is liable for damages to the buyer.

Additional Terms in Acceptance (§2–207)

At common law, an acceptance containing additional terms beyond those of the offer is deemed to be a counteroffer that effectively revokes the original offer. The UCC changes the common law with regard to sales contracts, effectively doing away with the requirement that the acceptance must mirror the offer. Under the UCC, an acceptance containing additional terms is valid unless it is made conditional on the seller accepting the new terms. In general, the new terms are simply ignored and do not become a part of the contract.

➤ 1. Jill offers to sell her boat to Felix for $5,000. Felix replies, "I accept and want you to include a boat trailer." The contract is binding, and Felix must pay $5,000 for the boat. The additional terms as to the boat trailer are ignored.
2. In the above example, if Felix replies, "I accept, provided you include a boat trailer," there is no contract, since the acceptance was conditioned on Jill including a boat trailer as part of the deal.

The last example points to the need for great care in the language used in contracts. Felix in the first example might well have intended to make his acceptance conditional on Jill throwing in the boat trailer, but that is not what he said, and the courts will construe the language in a contract in accordance to its strict meaning. Hence, the difference between "I want you to" and "I expect you to" is crucial; the latter clearly conditions the acceptance on the seller consenting to the additional contract term, while the former merely states the buyer's desire that the seller accept the new contract term.

When merchants are involved in sales contracts, additional terms become part of the contract unless they (1) materially change the contract, (2) the acceptance is conditioned on the new terms being acceptable to the seller, or (3) the seller objects within a reasonable time after receiving the acceptance containing the new terms.

➤ 1. Peter offers to sell Gus 1,000 widgets at $2 each. Gus mails a letter of confirmation stating that he accepts the offer and expects the price to include free shipment via UPS. Unless Peter objects within a reasonable time after receiving the letter of confirmation, the term relating to free UPS shipping will become a part of the contract, assuming that the cost is not so large as to materially affect the terms of the contract. (For example, if the cost of shipping the widgets is $50, it would likely be held not to materially alter the terms of the contract, since it represents a small percentage of the total cost of the contract. But if the UPS shipping is $500, or 25 percent of the cost of the contract, the additional term would be deemed a material alteration to the contract and would not become a part of it if Peter fails to object to the term.)

2. In the above example, if Gus accepts "provided you include the price of shipping via UPS as part of the contract," the acceptance would be deemed a counteroffer, not an acceptance, since the acceptance is specifically conditioned on Peter acceding to the new term.

3. In example 1, if Peter receives the letter of confirmation and objects to the free shipping term, it will not become a part of the contract and Gus must pay for the shipping himself.

Keep in mind that both the buyer and seller must be merchants for new terms to become a part of the contract if they are not objected to within a reasonable time. If neither party, or only one, is a merchant, the additional or different terms are simply ignored.

Auction Sales (§2–328)

Article 2 of the UCC also modifies the common law regarding acceptance in auction sales, which are completed when the auctioneer's hammer falls. In an auction contract, a bidder makes the offer, which the auctioneer accepts when he announces the item sold. Sales at auction are considered to be *with reserve,* which is to say that the auctioneer reserves the right to withdraw any item offered for sale at auction at any time before accepting a bid. An auction *without reserve* is one in which the auctioneer agrees to take the highest bid, giving up the right to withdraw an item if he believes the bidding to be too low.

Defenses to Contract Formation

The normal defenses to a breach of contract action available under the common law of contracts are also available when a sales contract is involved, unless the UCC specifically modifies them. Therefore, if a contract for the sale of goods fails because of lack of a valid offer, acceptance, consideration, legality, and genuine assent, the failure may be raised as a defense if one party sues the other to enforce the agreement. In addition to the common law defenses to a breach of contract, the code details what sales contracts need to be in writing and precludes the enforcement of unconscionable contracts.

Statute of Frauds (§2–201)

Contracts for the sale of goods for $500 or more are not enforceable unless they are evidenced by a signed writing. For purposes of the statute of frauds, the writing must make it clear that a contract existed; it need not contain all of the terms of the agreement; these can be provided through parol evidence (e.g., written or oral evidence outside of the writing itself). A writing that states the quantity and description of goods will be sufficient, even though it leaves out important terms such as price, shipment, and quality of the goods to be sold.

There are three situations in which oral contracts for the sale of goods for $500 or more will be enforceable despite the statute of frauds. The exceptions to the statute of frauds requirement of a writing involve specially manufactured goods, admissions in pleadings as to the existence of a verbal contract, and partially performed contracts.

1. *Specially manufactured goods:* An oral contract for specially manufactured goods that are not suitable for sale to others in the normal course of business is enforceable once the seller has taken substantial steps towards performance of the contract.

> Issa Famous orders a tuxedo to be tailored for her pet orangutan. After the ape has been measured and the tailor has cut the material to begin making the tuxedo, Issa changes her mind and cancels the order. The contract is enforceable even without a signed writing, since it involves specially manufactured goods without a readily available resale market. If Issa cancels the order before the tailor has cut the material for the tux, however, the tailor could not sue for the breach unless the contract had been evidenced by a signed writing.

2. *Admissions in pleadings:* If a party to an oral contract for goods worth $500 or more admits to the contract in pleadings or in testimony in open court, the contract will be enforceable to the extent that it is admitted.

> Doyle orally agrees to buy 10 paintings from Ann at $10,000 each, but subsequently changes his mind. When Ann sues Doyle for breach of contract, he testifies in open court that he had agreed to buy two of the paintings for $10,000 but that he doesn't have to because the contract was oral. Doyle is now obligated to buy the paintings, because of his admission, but only the two that he has admitted buying in his testimony.

3. *Partially performed contracts:* A buyer's acceptance of goods ordered under a verbal contract is binding, but only to the extent of goods actually accepted by the buyer.

> Charles orders by telephone from Alison ten oriental rugs at a price of $2,000 each. When the first rug arrives, he accepts it and informs Alison that he will be sending her a check for $2,000 but that he does not wish to receive the remaining nine rugs. With respect to the rug that he accepted,

he must pay the contract price of $2,000. But with regard to the remaining nine rugs in the oral contract, he need not accept their delivery unless the contract was evidenced by a signed writing.

Unconscionable Contracts (§2–302)

If a court finds any provision in a contract to be unconscionable as of the time the contract was entered into, it can refuse to enforce the contract, strike out the unconscionable clause, or reform the contract by modifying the clause so as to prevent an unconscionable result from its application. Although at common law unconscionability is also a defense to a breach of contract, the courts have generally interpreted the UCC liberally in defining what constitutes an unconscionable contract. As a result, it is likelier for a court to find an inherently unfair contract for the sale of goods to be unconscionable than an equally unfair contract not involving the sale of goods.

> Cathy Consumer purchases a video camcorder from Fleece-M-Good Appliance Company. The camcorder has a retail value of $1,000 and is sold at competing stores in the area for $750. Cathy purchases the camcorder for $1,200 and pays an additional $500 for a battery pack, a blank tape, and a carrying case—all of which are included by competing merchants for the $800 price. The machine fails within the first week and Fleece-M-Good refuses to repair or replace it. Cathy could sue to have the contract declared unconscionable and many courts would find in her favor based on the 100 percent difference in the price and its unexpectedly quick breakdown. In contrast, if Cathy paid $200,000 for a house with a value of $100,000, and it required repairs shortly after her moving in, most courts would not grant her relief merely on the basis of her bad bargain. (Note that we are assuming no fraud, duress, or other irregularity here.)

Modification of the Sales Contract

Another important change to the common law of contracts made by the UCC is in the area of contract modifications. At common law, such modifications are generally unenforceable unless supported by consideration. The UCC, however, liberalizes the validity of voluntary modifications of sales contracts.

Voluntary Modification (§2–209)

Under the UCC, voluntary modifications to a sales contract are valid and binding, as long as they are sought and given in good faith, even absent additional consideration. This represents another departure from the common law of contracts, under which agreed-upon modifications to an existing contract are only valid and binding if supported by additional consideration.

➤ Chris agrees to buy all the gasoline she needs for her fleet of taxicabs from Russ for $1.10 per gallon for a period of five years. After the first year of the contract, a regional conflict breaks out in the Middle East and the price of gasoline jumps by 30 percent. Russ then asks Chris to pay $1.50 per gallon of gas until the situation stabilizes, and she agrees. Chris is not obligated to pay the increase under the contract, but once she agrees to do so, she will be bound by the new terms of their modified agreement, even though under the common law of contracts the agreement to pay the 40 cents per gallon increase would not have been binding, since it is not supported by consideration.

Keep in mind that Chris, the buyer in the last example, is under no obligation to agree to the modification of the sales contract suggested by Russ, the seller; she can demand that Russ live up to their original contract. Russ will have to honor the contract unless he can claim *commercial impracticability* or *impossibility of performance* (see the separate discussion in Chapter 10 on discharge and remedies for breach), neither of which would be applicable here since the loss to Russ was foreseeable at the time the contract was formed and gasoline is still available for delivery under the facts given. If Chris does agree to the new terms, however, she will be bound by them.

If a modification is made to a contract that needs to be in writing to be enforceable under the statute of frauds, then the modification must also be in writing. If the sales contract need not be in writing to be enforceable (e.g., in a contract for the sale of goods for $499.99 or less), then an oral modification would be binding.

Operation of Law

In addition to the ability of parties to voluntarily modify sales contracts without additional consideration, there are some circumstances under which operation of law modifies a sales contract.

Casualty to Identified Goods (§2–613)

If the destruction to identified goods is total, the contract is voided. If the destruction or damage is only partial, the buyer has the option of treating the contract as voided or accepting the goods with a reduction in price to allow for the damage. The price reduction that the buyer can take would be measured by the market price of the damaged goods. If the buyer elects to accept the damaged goods at a reduced price, he will not be able to seek any additional damages from the seller.

➤ Bob agrees to buy Phyllis's computer for $1,000. Before she can ship it to him, it is damaged in a fire when her house is struck by lighting. If the computer is destroyed, the contract is voided and performance by both parties is excused. If the computer suffers some smoke damage but is still functional, Bob will have the option of avoiding the contract or buying the computer at a reduced price (the market price of the damaged computer).

Substituted Performance (§2–614)

When the agreed-upon method of delivery becomes either commercially impracticable or impossible, the seller must offer and the buyer must accept a commercially reasonable substitute, if one is available. In other words, the mere unavailability of the carrier that both parties agreed would be used will not void a contract or give rise to a breach of contract action if an alternative carrier is available; the contract will be modified as a matter of law to allow for the alternate carrier to be used.

> ➤ Henry orders a laser printer for $699 from Acme Mail Order Company and asks that it be shipped UPS second-day air. If UPS is unavailable at the time delivery is due through no fault of Acme (e.g., a labor dispute, etc.), then Acme must use a commercially reasonable alternative, such as next-day service from the U.S. Postal Service. As long as the price is reasonably similar, Henry will not be able to object.

Unforeseen Circumstances (§2–615)

If a seller is unable to deliver in whole or in part as promised due to unforeseen circumstances beyond his control, he is excused from performing, as long as he renders whatever performance is practicable under the circumstances, including part performance. If part performance is possible, the seller must allocate his production and delivery among his customers in a fair and reasonable manner. Where delayed delivery, nondelivery, or partial delivery occur because of unforeseen circumstances beyond the seller's control, the seller must notify all affected customers in a timely fashion.

> ➤ Hector, the owner of a factory that produces alligator skin shoes, handbags, and accessories, agrees to purchase 1,000 alligator skins per year for the next five years from Mel, who owns and operates an alligator farm in Australia. After the first year of the contract, Mel's alligator farm becomes infected with a rare, previously unknown disease that kills half of his reptilian crop. As a result, he can't ship the full 1,000 skins to Hector. Mel's obligation will be discharged if he ships as many skins as he can produce to all of his customers on a fair, prorated basis.

The Parol Evidence Rule

Parol evidence is oral or verbal evidence. The parol evidence rule states that once parties set down the terms of their agreement in writing, no parol evidence may be used to modify or change the terms of the written agreement unless fraud, duress, or mistake are alleged. To put it another way, the rule prevents oral evidence from contradicting the terms of a written agreement, although it allows parol evidence to be used to show that the agreement was induced by fraud or duress or that there is a material mistake in the written agreement. The basic purpose of the rule is to protect the integrity of written contracts and to prevent fraud by making it difficult to attack the validity of written terms through extraneous parol evidence that is not a part of the written contract.

The parol evidence rule also applies to contracts for the sale of goods under Section 2–202 of the UCC with, as is often the case under the code, some modification of the common law rule. Under Section 2–202, terms included in a confirmatory memoranda of the contract or otherwise set down in writing as a final expression of their agreement "cannot be contradicted by evidence of any prior agreement or of a contemporaneous oral agreement." In this regard, the code agrees exactly with the common law parol evidence rule. However, Section 2–202 goes on to state that a written agreement may be "explained or supplemented" by parol evidence in regard to:

1. Course of dealing.
2. Usage of trade.
3. Course of performance.
4. Consistent additional terms (unless the court finds the writing to have been intended as an exclusive statement of the terms of the agreement).

Course of Dealing (§1–205 [1]).   Previous conduct by the parties establishes a common basis of understanding for interpreting specific contract provisions and the conduct of the parties. When parties do business over a period of time, a mutual understanding can develop as to interpreting contractual provisions that may not be specifically stated in a contract. The UCC recognizes the importance of past conduct in interpreting the intent of the parties expressed in a written contract. Consider the following example:

➤ Phil places an order for 50 19-inch color television sets from Chan. Nothing is stated as to method of payment or delivery. Normally, this would entitle Chan to cash payment on delivery and would allow her to ship via any commercially reasonable means. But if Phil and Chan have been doing business for years and Chan has always shipped via UPS second-day air and accepted payment from Phil 30 days from delivery, Phil could present parol evidence as to the course of dealing between the parties to help interpret the contract (e.g., to show that Chan was expected to ship via UPS second-day air and to be paid on a net-30 basis).

Usage of Trade (§1–205 [2]).   The UCC defines usage of trade as "any practice or method of dealing having such regularity of observance in a place, vocation, or trade as to justify and expectation that it will be observed with respect to the transaction in question." Evidence as to usage of trade can be introduced to show that there was a reasonable expectation that performance under a given agreement would conform to the expected norm.

Course of Performance (Practical Construction) (§2–208). In a contract for the sale of goods that requires repeated performance over a period of time, the actual performance tendered and accepted is relevant to explaining the terms of a contract.

➤ Noxxe Oil agrees to supply Dana's Gas Station with 1,000 gallons of gasoline per week for one year at the current market price. For the first 10 months, Noxxe ships 400 gallons of 87 octane unleaded regular gas, 400 gallons of 89 octane regular-plus gas, and 200 gallons of 92 octane premium gas per week. Dana accepts the gas and promptly pays for it without complaint. In the 11th month of the contract, Dana informs Noxxe that she wants it to ship 800 gallons per week of 87 octane regular and 200 gallons of 92 octane premium gas, since her customers are not buying the 89 octane regular-plus gasoline. Even though the agreement between Noxxe and Dana does not state the grades of gas to be purchased or the percentages of each grade, the course of performance between Noxxe and Dana would be relevant to show that gas was to be shipped in the same grades and quantities of each grade throughout the contract term.

Section 2–208(2) states that course of dealing, usage of trade, course of performance, and express terms of a contract should be construed as consistent with each other whenever it is reasonable to do so. When a clear conflict occurs, express terms in a contract control course of performance, course of performance controls course of dealing, and course of dealing controls usage of trade. This sets up the following hierarchy of contract construction with regard to determining the agreement between the parties:

1. Written contract provisions, are important always controlling, absent a clear conflict in the contract.
2. Course of performance of the parties with regard to the contract in question.
3. Course of dealing between the parties with regard to previous contracts.
4. Usage of trade.

The previous example of Noxxe Oil and Dana's Gas Station contains ambiguity in the contract, and hence a conflict, since there is no express provision as to what grades of gasoline are to be purchased in what amounts. The course of performance of this contract has Dana accepting Noxxe's shipments for 10 months, including 400 gallons of 89 octane gasoline. In construing the intent of the parties, this will be the most significant fact. Previous contracts between the parties (course of dealing) or the usage of trade would be of secondary importance. If, for example, Dana could show that usage of trade in the gasoline retailing business allows a gas station to order whatever grades of gas it wants, Dana might still be bound to Noxxe's interpretation of the contract as requiring her to accept all three grades of gasoline under the course of performance of this contract over the previous 10 months.

Judge for Yourself

Case 1.   Ron mails an order for 20 pounds of jellybeans from Candy World at $3 per pound. Upon receipt of the order, Candy World ships the jellybeans.

   a. Is this a contract for the sale of goods?
   b. If Candy World ships 10 pounds of jellybeans at $3 per pound, what will Ron's rights be under the contract?
   c. If Candy World ships 20 pounds of gummy bears instead of jellybeans, will it be in breach of contract?
   d. If Candy World ships 20 pounds of gummy bears as an accommodation to Ron, clearly informing him of this fact, will it have breached the contract?

Case 2.   Frank offers to sell his car to Carmen for $4,000 in a letter he sends her. She replies with a letter of her own which states, "I accept and want you to paint the car before you deliver it."

   a. Will a valid contract be formed?
   b. Will Frank have to paint the car before delivering it?
   c. If Carmen replied in her letter, "I accept, provided you paint the car before delivering it," would a contract be formed? Explain.

Case 3.   Hank, a seven-foot, two-inch basketball player, asks Xena, a seamstress, to make him a tuxedo. She agrees and tells him that it will cost $850. She takes his measurements and tells him that the tux will be ready in 10 days.

   a. If Hank changes his mind the following day and calls Xena to cancel the contract, will he be in breach of contract if Xena has not yet begun work on the project? Explain.
   b. If Hank calls to cancel after Xena has already ordered the material from her supplier but has done nothing else to complete the contract, can he cancel without penalty? Why?
   c. If Hank cancels after the material is ordered and Xena has cut it into the required pattern to create the suit, will Hank be able to cancel the contract without penalty?

Case 4.   Noxxe Oil enters into a binding agreement to provide 10,000 gallons of regular gas to Norma's Gas City for a year at a fixed price of $1 per gallon. A month into the contract, conflict breaks out in the Persian Gulf and the price of crude oil increases by 50 percent overnight. Noxxe Oil, who can still find all the oil it needs on the spot market, but at a much higher price than anticipated, asks Norma if she would be willing to agree to a temporary 20 cents per gallon increase. Norma agrees to the temporary increase and begins paying the higher price immediately.

    a. If Norma changes her mind a month later, can she enforce the original agreement?

    b. Would your answer be the same if this were not a contract for the sale of goods (e.g., a service contract or a contract to purchase real estate)? Why?

    c. If Norma refuses to accept the higher price, will Noxxe be able to force her to do so?

Case 5.   Joan agrees to sell her business to Kari for $250,000. When the parties set down the terms of the agreement in a signed writing, the amount is mistakenly written as $25,000. Neither party notices the mistake at the time that the contract is signed.

    a. If Kari wants to enforce the contract as written, will Joan be able to present parol evidence to explain that a mistake was made?

    b. If Joan purposely writes down $350,000 as the consideration to be paid for her business on the written agreement and gets Kari to sign it, can Kari present parol evidence to prove the price agreed to was $250,000? Why?

    c. Would your answer be the same if Joan held a gun to Kari's head as she signed the contract?

    d. If Kari claims that at the time the contract was signed, Joan orally agreed that she would have the storefront painted before the business was transferred, can Kari present witnesses' testimony to this effect?

12

PERFORMANCE OF THE SALES CONTRACT AND RISK OF LOSS

Learning Objectives

After studying this chapter, you will be able to:

1. Describe and give examples of the seller's rights and obligations under the sales contract.
2. Describe and give examples of the buyer's rights and obligations under the sales contract.
3. Explain the difference between shipping and destination contracts.
4. Describe the concepts of risk of loss and insurable interest.

Introduction

Once a contract for the sale of goods comes into existence, it is important to determine the duties of the buyer and seller with respect to the goods and establish when those duties are fully discharged. In addition, it is necessary to determine precisely when title to purchased goods passes from the seller to the buyer and when the buyer acquires enough of an interest in the goods so that he may purchase insurance to protect himself against their loss while in transit and at other times prior to his obtaining possession of the goods. As is usually the case under the Uniform Commercial Code, the buyer and seller are free to control most of these matters by specific contract provisions. For example, the buyer and seller may agree that the buyer will bear the risk of loss if goods are damaged in transit. But when the buyer and seller do not specifically agree in their contract as to who should bear the risk of loss for goods damaged in transit, or when or by what method the buyer must pay for goods the seller shipped to her, the UCC steps in and provides the answer by default. It is imperative that both the buyer and seller be aware of the UCC provisions relating to risk of loss and passage of title to avoid potential economic loss.

Seller's Obligations

The obligations the seller incurs under a contract for the sale of goods differ slightly depending on whether the buyer is to pick up the goods at the seller's place of business, whether the seller must deliver the goods to the buyer himself, or whether the seller must ship the goods through a third-party carrier such as UPS or the U.S. Postal Service.

Goods Not Shipped by a Carrier

When a contract for the sale of goods does not require the seller to ship goods to the buyer via carrier, Section 2–503 of the UCC requires that a seller tender delivery of conforming goods at the buyer's disposition and give her sufficient notice to enable her to take delivery. The seller must tender delivery at a reasonable hour and make the goods available for the buyer to take possession of them. This is true whether the buyer is to pick up the goods at the seller's place of business or another designated location, the seller is to deliver the goods himself, or the seller's employees are to deliver the goods. Consider the following examples:

1. Julie buys a lawn tractor from Acme Lawn Care. Acme promises to notify her when the tractor arrives at its warehouse from the factory, and she agrees to pick it up at the warehouse. A week later the tractor arrives and Acme calls Julie at 2:00 P.M. on a Sunday for her to pick it up. She is not home at that time, and Acme does not call back again. The next day, Acme sells the tractor to another buyer. Has Acme discharged its obligation of tendering delivery? Clearly not, since making a single attempt to call Julie during the weekend is not enough of an effort to tender the goods.

2. Under the above facts, assume that Acme calls Julie on Sunday, as well as during regular business hours each day for the next week, and then sells the tractor to another customer. Will that suffice to discharge the obligation of tendering delivery? In this situation, Acme has made a good faith effort to tender the tractor to Julie and has discharged its duties under the contract. Acme would have a good chance of recovering lost profits from the sale from Julie, since she did not meet her obligation of accepting the goods when validly tendered.

3. Assume the same facts, except that Acme sent Julie a postcard telling her that the tractor had arrived and could be picked up at any time within the next week; Acme also left a telephone message to the same effect on Julie's answering machine. If Julie was away

on vacation and did not get either message in time and Acme sold the tractor to another customer eight days from the date of the original notification, has Acme discharged its duty to tender delivery? Unless Acme had reason to know that Julie would be away on vacation (e.g., if she specifically had told Acme this), Acme's notice to Julie and its keeping the tractor available for delivery to her for seven days would suffice as a valid tender of delivery. Once again, Julie would be in breach of contract and liable for Acme's lost profits on the sale.

Section 2–308 requires that unless the sales contract states otherwise, the seller must tender delivery at his normal place of business or, if he lacks a regular place of business, at his home. If a buyer wants goods to be delivered to her home or elsewhere, she must specifically make this a provision in the contract for the sale of goods.

Goods Shipped by a Carrier

If the seller must ship goods to a buyer through a carrier, the UCC specifies when the goods must be delivered, who must pay for the delivery, and when the seller's responsibilities are discharged. Keep in mind that the following provisions only come into effect if the parties do not agree otherwise.

Delivery by Seller to Specific Destination.   If the seller agrees to deliver the goods to the buyer as part of the sales contract, Section 2–503 requires him to tender delivery at the agreed-upon location at a reasonable hour after giving the buyer reasonable notice of the delivery.

➤ Harry orders a television set from BCA Electronics, which offers free home delivery and installation. BCA tells him it will deliver the set within the next week or so. Three days later, BCA attempts delivery of the set at 2:00 P.M. on a Sunday. Not finding Harry at home, BCA's delivery person returns the set to the store, and it is subsequently resold. When Harry complains a week later that his set has not been delivered, BCA's manager tells him that a delivery was attempted and, since he was not home to receive it, the sales contract was canceled. He also tells Harry that he'll be happy to ship him another set, but at a higher price, since the sale under which he had bought the original set has passed. Harry, who is not amused, sues.

In the above case, BCA will argue that it discharged its obligation by tendering delivery of the set and that if anyone is in breach it is Harry for not having been home to receive it. Harry will counter that BCA's tender of delivery was not reasonable in terms of time or notice. Harry, of course, is correct. Attempting a single delivery in and of itself is never reasonable notice, nor is tendering delivery at 2:00 P.M. on a Sunday. Previous notification of the date and time of delivery or attempts at delivering the goods at different times of the day would suffice in most instances to discharge the seller's obligations, as long as these attempts are reasonable.

Shipment by Seller through Carrier.   The seller may agree to ship goods to the buyer, as opposed to delivering them himself. If so, the seller's duties under the contract are discharged under Section 2–504 of the UCC when he entrusts the goods to a carrier; obtains and ships to the buyer any documents, such as a bill of lading, that are necessary for her to obtain the goods from the carrier once they arrive at their destination; and promptly informs the buyer that the goods have been shipped.

FOB and FAS Shipping Contracts

Section 2–319 of the U.C.C. defines the seller's duties under FOB and FAS contracts. FOB stands for *free on board*. When goods are shipped FOB, a seller is obligated to place the goods in the hands of a carrier without additional cost to the buyer, but the buyer then pays the freight charges. FAS, on the other hand, means *free along side* a vessel. When a seller is bound to ship FAS, he must place the goods along side a ship, with the buyer bearing the cost for the actual loading and transportation of the goods by the vessel.

FOB generally refers to the seller's plant or other place of business. Many, but not all, goods purchased by consumers by mail are shipped FOB seller's plant; this simply means the seller will place the goods in the hands of a carrier such as UPS, the U.S. Postal Service, or some other shipping company at his plant, then charge the buyer for the shipping cost. When a buyer pays for goods plus an additional shipping and handling fee, she is generally not getting the goods FOB, since she is charged for the actual shipping charges plus a packaging and handling charge before the goods are turned over to the carrier.

Although FOB seller's plant is the standard shipping arrangement for most businesses, it is possible to ship FOB buyer's plant or any other location. If a seller ships FOB buyer's plant, he will bear the risk and the cost of getting the goods to the buyer's plant but not of unloading or specifically delivering them *inside* the buyer's plant. Likewise, even though FAS contracts generally specify the closest port to the seller's plant, it is possible to ship to any other location as well. A seller who ships FAS SS *Lovely Lady*, New York City, agrees to place the goods along side the ship *Lovely Lady* in New York City without charge to the buyer; the buyer must then bear the costs of loading the goods onto the ship and their transportation to their ultimate destination. The same seller could agree to ship the goods FAS Miami, in which case he would be obligated to ship the goods free of charge to Miami and unload them there.

When a sales contract is silent about the method of shipment, FOB seller's plant is presumed, and the seller discharges his contractual obligation by placing in the hands of a carrier the goods to be shipped to the buyer. For the seller's obligation to be discharged, he must naturally ship *conforming goods*—or goods that are of the type, quality, and condition deemed acceptable under the contract. If a seller under a contract to ship a crate of Florida oranges ships Florida grapefruits or rotten Florida oranges, he does not discharge his contractual obligation; rather, he is guilty of a breach of contract.

Buyer's Obligations

Like the seller, the buyer has certain obligations imposed by the UCC in every sales contract, including the duty to pay for the goods and the right and obligation to inspect them under certain circumstances. The code also determines at what point the buyer acquires a sufficient insurable interest in goods that he has ordered but not yet received.

Duty to Pay

When a sales contract does not require shipment by carrier, the sale price of the contract is payable in cash at the time the seller tenders delivery, unless the contract itself specifies otherwise. When goods are shipped by carrier, payment is due in cash when the goods are delivered to the buyer. In FOB or FAS shipping situations, even though the seller's duties under the contract are discharged as soon as he places conforming goods in the hands of a carrier, payment will not be due from the buyer until she actually receives the goods.

Payment by check is allowed unless the contract states otherwise; but the seller or his agent (e.g., the carrier) can demand payment in cash if a check is tendered. If cash is demanded, the seller must give the buyer sufficient time to get the cash. If payment by check is accepted, the buyer's obligation under the contract is not discharged until the check is actually paid; if the check bounces, the buyer is in breach of contract.

> Shawn orders a giant-screen television set to watch the upcoming World Series. When it arrives, he pays for it with a check. After the World Series, his check bounces. Aside from the potential criminal liability for passing a bad check, Shawn is also guilty of breach of contract and must pay for the price of the set and any incidental and consequential damages, such as bounced check fees paid by the seller.

In the above example, the seller could have refused the check at the time of the delivery; he would then have had to give Shawn reasonable time to get either cash or a certified check from his bank.

Right of Inspection

Under Section 2–513 of the UCC, the buyer has the right to inspect goods before paying for them. However, if goods are shipped COD (cash on delivery) or when payment is made against a *document of title*—a negotiable instrument that gives its holder the right to receive goods in the hands of a carrier or other third party—the buyer does not have the right to inspect the goods prior to payment. When the buyer receives goods COD or through a document of title—such as a warehouse receipt giving her the right to pick up goods at the location where they are being held, or warehoused—the buyer must pay for the goods before inspecting them. If the goods turn out to be nonconforming because of some defect, she can return them or otherwise recover damages from the seller; but she must initially accept the goods whether or not they are conforming. If this seems unfair to the buyer, keep in mind that she always has the option of requiring the seller to ship goods other than COD; or she can require that the seller ship the goods themselves rather than a document of title, if she wants to retain the right of inspection prior to accepting them.

The buyer must bear the cost of the inspection if she desires one. But if the goods are found to be nonconforming, she can recover the cost of the inspection from the seller.

Section 2–512 states that whenever payment is required without inspection (e.g., COD shipment as per Section 2–513), the buyer may nevertheless refuse to accept the goods if their nonconformity to the contract appears without an inspection. In other words, if the goods are obviously nonconforming, the buyer need not accept them even when he does not have the right of inspection. Consider the following examples:

➤ 1. NSG Company ships a computer system to Mary COD through the U.S. Postal Service. The boxes arrive in perfect condition and appear to contain what Mary ordered. She must pay for the system without inspecting the contents of each box. If she refuses to pay for the delivery unless she can open and test the computer system, she will be in breach of contract and liable for damages, including the shipping costs, the COD charges, and NSG's lost profits.

2. Joan orders an Apple Macintosh system COD. When delivery is tendered to her, she notices that the boxes the system comes in are

clearly labeled "IBM, Inc." She need not accept the system, since it is clear without an inspection that the delivery is of nonconforming goods (e.g., an IBM computer instead of an Apple).

3. Harriet orders a computer system COD. When it arrives, the boxes are seriously damaged and waterlogged. She can refuse delivery without inspection, since it is obvious without inspection that the goods will be nonconforming (e.g., damaged).

Insurable Interest

Once goods to a contract are identified, a buyer acquires an insurable interest in them, entitling him to insure against the goods being damaged, destroyed, lost, or stolen. It is important to note that the buyer often has an insurable interest before he acquires legal title to the goods. In other words, the law acknowledges that once goods under a contract are identified, the buyer has enough of an interest in them to purchase insurance guaranteeing their safe arrival, even though at that point he usually does not own the goods and would not be responsible for their loss or damage. Goods become identified to a contract as soon as the seller marks them in preparation for shipment or otherwise segregates them from the remainder of her stock by clearly identifying them as goods that are to be shipped or picked up by the buyer. The following are examples of identifying goods of a contract sufficiently to give the buyer an insurable interest in them:

- Roping off a section of the seller's warehouse containing goods that are to be shipped to the buyer.
- Tagging goods in a warehouse for future shipment to the buyer.
- Packaging goods for shipment to the buyer in boxes clearly marked with her name and address.
- Placing all goods to be shipped to the buyer on board a ship in a shipping container labeled as belonging to buyer.

In short, any action by seller that marks specific goods from his stock for eventual shipment to buyer will suffice as identifying the goods to the contract.

Risk of Loss

As we have previously seen, a valid contract for the sale of goods comes into existence as soon as the seller either formally acknowledges the buyer's order in writing or ships the goods, whichever comes first. Problems can occur between the time the contract arises to the time the seller tenders conforming goods to the buyer; goods are destroyed, damaged, or stolen without the fault of either party, for example. The question then becomes, Who must bear the risk for the loss? Consider the following situations:

➤   1. The buyer orders goods. The seller acknowledges the order and agrees to ship the goods via carrier within 48 hours. After packaging the goods and addressing them to the buyer, but before the seller turns them over to a carrier for shipment, the goods are destroyed in a fire at the seller's warehouse.
   2. The buyer orders goods, and the seller ships them via carrier. While the goods are in transit, the carrier gets into an accident that destroys or damages the goods.
   3. The buyer orders goods and the seller ships goods via carrier. While they are in transit, the goods are stolen from the carrier.

In each of the above examples, neither the seller nor the buyer are at fault with regard to the damage or theft of the goods. Clearly, if the carrier was negligent (e.g., allowing the goods to be stolen or damaging the goods through an accident while the goods were in its control) it will ultimately be responsible to either the buyer or the seller for the loss or damage to the goods. But, assuming that the carrier is unwilling to pay for the damage or contests its liability, or in situations where the carrier can't pay (e.g., bankruptcy), it is necessary to determine which of the two innocent parties—the buyer or the seller—is responsible for the ensuing damage.

The UCC allows parties to determine who is to bear the risk of loss for goods damaged in the interim between when a contract arises and when the seller delivers the goods and the buyer accepts them. But if the parties fail to make specific provisions in this area, the code provides who must bear the risk of loss under a variety of situations.

Noncarrier Contracts

When goods under a sales contract are not to be delivered by carrier (e.g., when the buyer is to pick them up or the seller is to deliver them), the risk of loss passes from the seller to the buyer upon the buyer's physically taking possession of the goods if the seller is a merchant, or upon the seller tendering delivery of the goods to the buyer if the seller is not a merchant. The following example should help to clarify this point:

➤   Gladys offers to sell her television set to Michael for $300. Michael agrees and pays her $300 for the set and is told by Gladys that he can pick it up at 6:00 P.M. that day. At 6:30 P.M., a thief breaks in to Gladys' home and steals several items, including the television set Michael had purchased.

Michael arrives at 7:00 P.M. and demands the television. When she explains that *his* set was stolen a half an hour *after* he was supposed to pick it up, he is not amused and demands that she return his $300.

The answer to "whose TV is it, anyway?" depends on whether Gladys is a merchant (one who deals in the buying and selling of goods of that kind during the regular course of business). Assuming that Gladys is not in the business of selling televisions, the set that was stolen at 6:30 P.M. belonged to Michael. Since Gladys tendered the television set at 6:00 P.M., the risk of its loss (provided the set was available for Michael to pick up at the appointed time) shifted to him as of that time. If the set was stolen or otherwise damaged or destroyed without the fault of Gladys at any time after 6:00 P.M., Michael must bear the loss. If the set had been stolen at 5:30 P.M., Gladys would bear the loss, since she did not tender it to Michael until 6:00 P.M. under their agreement. On the other hand, if Gladys is a merchant who sells television sets in the regular course of business, she would bear the risk of loss until Michael actually took delivery of the set.

The UCC often holds merchants to a different (usually higher) standard than nonmerchants—which may at first glance seem arbitrary and unfair. It is important to note that the code is rather pragmatic and merely recognizes the economic realities of business dealings. While merchants are responsible for goods in their possession even though they belong to another (e.g., goods a customer has purchased but not yet picked up), most are protected by insurance to cover such losses as a matter of course; whereas consumers who occasionally sell goods are not nearly as likely to be protected by insurance if they suffer a similar loss.

Destination Contracts

When the seller agrees to deliver goods to the buyer as part of the sales contract, the risk of loss passes to the buyer when the goods are tendered to her at their final destination.

> Rest Rite Mattresses sells a mattress and box spring set to Mateo under a contract that includes delivery and setup of the mattress in Mateo's home. On the way to his home, the delivery van is struck from behind while waiting at a red light by a drunken driver, and the mattress is damaged. Rest Rite must bear the loss (it can, of course, sue the drunken driver who is ultimately at fault for the accident) since delivery had not yet been tendered to Mateo. If, on the other hand, the delivery was attempted after duly notifying Mateo and he was not at home, Mateo would be responsible for the loss if the van were struck by the drunken driver *on the way back to the factory*, since the risk of loss would pass to Mateo as soon as the delivery was tendered.

Carrier Contracts

Whenever a sales contract requires a seller to turn over the goods for shipment to a carrier but does not obligate him to deliver the goods to a specific location (e.g., FOB and FAS delivery contracts), the risk of loss passes to the buyer as soon as the seller places the goods in the hands of the carrier. If the goods are damaged while they are in the hands of the carrier, the buyer will bear the risk of loss. The buyer can, of course, sue the carrier if the goods are damaged, lost, or stolen due to its negligence.

➤ Sam orders a microwave oven from Nuke-M-Good Company and agrees to pay $250 FOB seller's plant. Nuke-M-Good arranges delivery through SPD Delivery Service, who is to collect the freight charges from Sam upon delivery. After SPD's driver picks up the package at the seller's plant, he drops it on the way to his truck. Sam must pay Nuke-M-Good for what will be a damaged, and dangerous, microwave oven on delivery. His only recourse will be to sue SPD for its driver's negligence.

Judge for Yourself

Case 1.   Luther orders a stereo system from Audio World. He asks Audio World to deliver it COD via its delivery department.

   a. When the stereo arrives, Luther wishes to pay by credit card. Can he if the delivery person objects? Explain.
   b. If Luther offers to pay by check and the delivery person demands cash, what can Luther do?
   c. If Luther pays by check, when will the contract be fully discharged?
   d. When will the contract be discharged if Luther pays cash?
   e. If the shipping carton is intact upon delivery and is marked as containing the stereo system that Luther purchased, may he nonetheless demand to inspect it before paying for it?

Case 2.   Nowanda Hardtosay, a seller of gourmet popping corn, orders a metric ton of popping corn from a local farmers' cooperative.

   a. Before the corn can be shipped to Ms. Hardtosay, lightning strikes the grain elevator containing corn. Who will bear the risk of loss? Explain.
   b. If the farmer's cooperative had placed the corn in a shipping container marked "for shipment to Nowanda Hardtosay" and lightning then struck the container, destroying the corn, would your answer to the above question be the same? Why?

    c. Would Ms. Hardtosay have had an insurable interest in the corn under question *a* above? What about in question *b?* Explain.

    d. If the farmers' cooperative had placed the container with the corn in the hands of a carrier under an FOB shipping contract and the luckless container was then struck by lightning, who would bear the loss? Explain.

Case 3.   Sonja, the owner of a grocery store, offers to sell her motorcycle to Jamie for $1,000. Jamie accepts, pays the $1,000 price and agrees to pick up the bike at 9:00 A.M. the next morning.

    a. If the bike is stolen overnight, who will bear the risk of loss?

    b. If the bike is stolen at 9:15 A.M., before Jamie picked it up, whose loss would it be?

    c. For purposes of the UCC, is Sonja a merchant with regard to this transaction? Explain.

    d. If Sonja regularly bought and sold motorcycles, as well as groceries, and the motorcycle in question was stolen at 9:15 A.M., before Jamie could pick it up, whose loss would it be?

Case 4.   Burper Pop, a soft drink manufacturer, agrees to ship 10,000 cases of its soda pop from New York to Los Angeles under a contract calling for delivery FOB buyer's plant. When Burper Pop places the goods in the hands of a carrier in New York, the soda is in perfect condition. However, by the time it arrives at the buyer's plant in California, much of the soft drink has been ruined in transit, which was neither the fault of Burper Pop nor the buyer.

    a. Who must bear the loss? Explain.

    b. Would your answer be the same if the shipping contract specified delivery to be made FOB seller's plant? Why?

13

REMEDIES FOR BREACH OF THE SALES CONTRACT AND WARRANTIES

Learning Objectives

After studying this chapter, you will be able to:

1. List three examples of buyer's remedies for breach of the sales contract.
2. List three examples of seller's remedies for breach of the sales contract.
3. Explain the concept of implied warranties and distinguish it from express warranties.
4. Discuss the requirements for disclaiming warranties under the UCC.

Introduction

Sales contracts are as susceptible to breach as any other contract. The common law of contracts provides a variety of remedies to parties who suffer a breach of contract, as we've previously seen in Chapter 10. Under the Uniform Commercial Code, specific provisions are made for remedies available to both buyers and sellers who suffer a breach of contract. As usual, the UCC makes some modifications to the common law of contracts in order that the remedies allowed to buyers and sellers reflect the economic realities of doing business and foster commerce.

The UCC also provides four specific types of warranties covering goods under sales contracts: warranty of title, implied warranty of merchantability, warranty of fitness for a particular purpose, and express warranties. These warranties offer protection for purchases of goods and are of great importance to both merchant buyers and the average consumer.

Buyer's Remedies for Breach

When a seller breaches the sales contract, the buyer can pursue a number of remedies to compensate himself for the breach. These include the right to reject nonconforming goods, the right to sue for damages, and under certain circumstances, the right to sue for specific performance.

Right to Reject Nonconforming Goods (§2–601)

When a seller tenders delivery of nonconforming goods, the buyer may keep them and sue for damages under the contract or, in certain cases, reject the goods and either sue for damages or cancel the contract at his option. The options available to the buyer depend in part on whether the contract is for a single delivery or one requiring the seller to ship the goods in separate installments. When the contract requires only a single delivery by seller and the seller tenders nonconforming goods, the buyer may reject the whole shipment, accept the whole shipment, or accept any separate part of the shipment and reject the rest.

> Janet orders an entertainment system from Acme Electronics that consists of a 19-inch color television set, VCR, stereo system, and integral wood-grained cabinet. The entire system is sold as a unit for $2,000. When the entertainment system arrives, all parts function properly except for the stereo speakers. Janet may, at her option, accept the system and sue for damages (e.g., the price of fixing the speakers) or reject the system, since it is clearly nonconforming goods in that it is defective. She may not, however, accept the television, VCR, and cabinet and return the stereo system with the defective speakers, since the item was sold as a unit and is not divisible into its several parts.

When the nonconforming goods are shipped as part of an installment contract that requires or allows goods to be tendered in a series of separate shipments, the buyer's right to reject the contract is more limited. A buyer can reject a nonconforming delivery if the nonconformity materially impairs the value of that installment and cannot be cured. In other words, a buyer who allows a seller to ship goods in installments will not be able to refuse the shipment unless he first informs the buyer that the goods are nonconforming, gives him the opportunity to cure the defect within a reasonable time, and can show that the nonconformity lessens the value of the goods. This may at first seem to give an unfair advantage to the seller, but it is yet another example of the UCC's pragmatism in recognizing the practical realities of doing business. Minor nonconformities in sales contracts, particularly between merchants dealing in high volumes and repeat sales, are inevitable. The code seeks to encourage commerce and prevent waste by ensuring that parties who work with one another on an ongoing basis can't reject shipments for inconsequential nonconformities without first giving the breaching party the opportunity to cure the breach.

➤ Jerry's Restaurant orders 1,000 one-pound cans of coffee from Wakem Coffee to be delivered in installments of 100 cans per month for 10 months. During the third month of the contract, Wakem ships 90 cans of coffee. Jerry cannot reject the shipment, since this is an installment sale, without first giving Wakem the opportunity to cure the defect within a commercially reasonable time (e.g., by sending the missing 10 cans of coffee within a few days of being notified that the shipment was nonconforming).

Right to Sue for Damages

As with the common law of contracts, buyers who suffer a breach of contract may sue for compensatory damages that will place them in the same position they would have been in had the breach not occurred.

➤ Funville orders 1,000 "Ugly Dudes from the Galactic Core" dolls in August for shipment by October 1, in time for the Christmas rush. Due to the popularity of these horribly ugly new toys, Joy Distributors, the seller, fails to ship until December 26. When the toys finally arrive, Funville can reject the shipment because Joy failed to ship them on time and can sue for lost profits.

Right to Specific Performance (§2–716)

A court has the power to grant specific performance to the buyer under the UCC where the goods in question are unique or "in other proper circumstances" and where mere money damages would not properly compensate the buyer for his loss.

➤ Troy agrees to buy a painting by an up-and-coming artist from Fine Gallery for $500. After Troy paid for the painting but before Fine shipped it, the artist dies. If Fine refuses to deliver the painting because its value has increased to $5,000, Troy may sue for specific performance of the sales contract. In the alternative, Troy may choose to allow Fine to keep the painting and sue for compensatory damages of $9,500—the difference between the contract price and the market value of the painting at the time of Fine's breach.

Buyer's Damages (§2–712 through §2–715)

When the seller fails to deliver goods as promised under a valid sales contract, the buyer may sue for the difference between the contract price of the goods and the market price, or he may recover the difference between the contract price and the actual price of purchasing the goods from another seller. The damages (cost of replacement or the difference between the contract and market prices) are measured as of the time the buyer learns of the seller's breach.

The buyer is also entitled to recover incidental and consequential damages incurred as a result of seller's breach. Incidental damages for the buyer would include the reasonable cost of inspecting the nonconforming goods, temporary storage of the goods, and shipment of them back to the seller. Consequential damages include those stemming from the buyer's particular situation that the seller could have reasonably foreseen at the time the contract was entered into.

➤ Sam the Grocer orders 1,000 bushels of oranges from Fresh Farms. Fresh ships 1,000 bushels of apples. When the goods arrive, Sam has them inspected at a cost to him of $250. When the contents of the shipment are reported to him by his inspectors, he notifies Fresh of his rejection of the goods by telegram and asks for instructions for disposing of them. In the meantime, he arranges for storage of the goods at a cost of $100 per day. When Fresh receives the notice of rejection for the nonconforming goods, it asks Sam to ship them back by any reasonable method. Sam arranges to have the goods shipped back at a cost of $500. Sam may sue Fresh to recover his compensatory damages (lost profits) and all the reasonable incidental expenses incurred in handling the nonconforming goods (the cost of the inspection, the cost of the telegram notifying Fresh of the breach, the cost of storing the goods while awaiting instructions, and the cost of shipping the goods back to Fresh).

Seller's Remedies for Breach

When the buyer breaches the sales contract, the seller has a number of remedies available to her in seeking compensation for her loss. These include the right to withhold goods, the right to recover shipped goods, and the right to force the buyer to accept shipped goods under certain circumstances.

Right to Withhold Goods

When payment for the sale of goods is due under the terms of the contract on or before delivery is made, the seller can withhold delivery until payment is made.

➤ Floyd orders 100 widgets and agrees to wire payment to BCD Inc., the seller, immediately. If BCD has not received payment when the goods arrive at their destination, it can order the carrier not to deliver the goods to Floyd until payment has been made.

Right to Recover Goods

Under Section 2–702 of the UCC, a seller who delivers goods under a credit arrangement to a buyer can reclaim the goods within 10 days of the buyer's receipt of the goods if she learns that the buyer is insolvent. If delivery was made on credit after the buyer misrepresented in writing that he was solvent within three months of the delivery, the seller may reclaim the goods at any time after learning of the buyer's insolvency. For the seller to reclaim the goods, however, the buyer must not yet have resold them in the normal course of business. If an insolvent buyer transfers goods in the normal course of business to a good faith purchaser before the seller reclaims the goods, the seller cannot reclaim the goods from the innocent purchaser.

If the goods are in the hands of a third-party bailee on their way to the buyer when the seller learns of the buyer's insolvency or breach of contract, Section 2–705 of the UCC gives the seller the right to recover the goods from the third party prior to their delivery (e.g., from a carrier or warehouse entrusted with turning over the goods to the buyer).

Right to Force Buyer to Accept Goods

In general, a buyer who wrongfully refuses to accept goods purchased under a valid sales contract is liable to the seller for the seller's lost profits and incidental or consequential damages that flow from the buyer's breach. However, if the seller is not able to sell the goods to another buyer in the regular course of business, of if the goods have been lost or damaged in transit after the risk of loss has passed to the buyer, Section 2–709 gives the seller the right to force buyer to accept the goods. This is, in essence, specific performance allowed to the seller when another remedy would not put him in the position he would have been in had the buyer not breached the contract.

> Art in New York buys goods from Paula in California and agrees to have them delivered to a warehouse in New Jersey, where he will have them picked up. If after the goods arrive in New Jersey, but before Art has picked them up, Paula learns that Art is insolvent, she can recover the goods from the warehouse and not be in breach of contract.

Seller's Damages for Breach

When a buyer breaches the sales contract, the seller can recover his lost profits from the buyer or, alternatively, the difference between the contract price and the market price, or the contract price and the resale price (the latter is the price at which the seller is able to resell the goods to another buyer after a good faith effort). The seller is also entitled to recover incidental damages from the buyer, such as the cost of shipment, storage, and restocking charges.

> CBN Company ships to Tim 100 widgets pursuant to a valid sales contract. When the goods arrive, Tim wrongfully refuses to accept them. CBN can sue Tim for lost profits under the contract and the incidental costs of storing the goods, shipping them back, and restocking them once they arrive at CBN's plant.

Warranties

There are four types of warranties made by sellers to buyers under the UCC: warranty of title and against infringements, the implied warranty of merchantability, the implied warranty of fitness, and express warranties.

Warranty of Title and Against Infringements (§2–312)

In every sales contract, there are a number of implied and express warranties a seller can make to a buyer. Every seller warrants to every buyer that his title to the goods being sold is good, that the transfer is rightful, and that there are no liens or encumbrances against the title to the goods being sold that the buyer is unaware of as of the time of entering into the sales contract. If the seller does not have proper title to the goods being sold, or if there is a lien or other encumbrance on the goods being sold, the seller is in breach of the warranty of title and must pay damages to the buyer.

If the seller is a merchant who regularly deals in goods of the kind being sold, she also makes a warranty against infringement to the buyer. Through this she warrants that the goods are delivered free of any copyright, patent, or trademark infringement.

The warranty of title is an implied warranty automatically attached to every sale made. The seller can, however, disclaim this warranty through specific language notifying the buyer that he does not claim title to the goods sold or that he is only transferring whatever ownership right he has in the property.

> Susan, after breaking up with her boyfriend, wants to sell a ring he gave her as a gift. Margaret agrees to buy the ring for $100. Susan believes that her ex-boyfriend purchased the ring from a jeweler, but she also knows that he'd purchased items from street peddlers of questionable repute in the past. To cover herself against a possible future suit for breach of warranty of title from Margaret, she draws up a sales contract that reads, "In consideration of $100, I hereby sell all of my interest, if any, in a gold ring with a small opal to Margaret Smith. **I sell the ring AS IS, and make no express or implied warranties of any kind or warranty of title to the buyer.**"

As long as Susan sells the ring to Margaret in good faith, Margaret will not be able to sue her in the future for breach of warranty if the ring turns out to be worthless or stolen. The language waiving a warranty must be conspicuous—it must stand out from the written contract by being larger, darker, or of different color. A waiver of warranty that does not stand out from the text of a contract will not be enforced.

Implied Warranty of Merchantability (§2–314)

Every sale made by a merchant who deals in goods of the type sold carries with it an implied warranty that the goods are *merchantable*. For goods to be merchantable, they must meet the following test:

1. They must pass without objection in the trade under the contract description.
2. If they are fungible goods (goods such as gasoline or grain or fruit that by their very nature any unit of the same grade is like any other unit), they must be at least of fair or average quality.
3. They must be fit for the ordinary purposes for which they are intended.
4. They must be properly labeled and packaged in accord with the contract.
5. They must conform to factual descriptions in the label.

The most important test in determining whether the warranty of merchantability has been breached is whether or not goods are fit for the ordinary purposes for which they are intended. If goods sold fail this test, the merchant seller is liable to the buyer for damages. Consider the following example:

➤ Randy purchases $20 of premium unleaded gasoline from Hank's Gas Station. The gas pump from which Randy pumps the gasoline is labeled as containing 93 octane premium unleaded gas. In fact, the gas is 86 octane economy regular gas that is contaminated with water. Hank has breached the warranty of merchantability to Randy under every one of the five tests, since the gasoline will not pass without objection in the trade, is not of average quality, is unfit for the purposes for which it is intended (because of the water contamination), is improperly labeled, and does not conform to the factual description in the label.

Keep in mind that if any one test is not met, the warranty is breached.

It is not necessary for the buyer to show that the seller knowingly sold faulty, mislabeled, or otherwise nonconforming goods to sue for breach of the warranty of merchantability. Merchants are strictly liable for breach of the warranty whether or not they were aware that the goods were not merchantable at the time they sold them. The buyer need not show the merchant seller's negligence to successfully assert a breach of this warranty.

Implied Warranty of Fitness for a Particular Purpose (§2–315)

The warranty of fitness for a particular purpose arises any time a merchant or nonmerchant sells goods to a buyer with the knowledge that the buyer intends them for a particular use and is relying on the seller's superior skill and judgment to select goods suitable to that use. For the warranty to arise, two tests must be met:

1. The seller must be aware that the buyer is purchasing the goods with a particular use in mind.
2. The buyer must rely on the seller's judgment in selecting goods appropriate to his specific intended use.

Consider whether a breach of warranty of fitness for a particular purpose has occurred in each of the following examples:

➤ 1. Bud, a novice fisherman, tells Bertha, the owner of a sporting goods store, that he needs a rod and reel for fly fishing, and asks her to recommend a good model. Bertha, who is new to the trade and unfamiliar with fly fishing, recommends an excellent deep-sea fishing rod and reel set that is inappropriate for fly fishing.

2. John, a freshman college student, offers to buy from Lynn, a second year law student, her contracts, torts, and civil procedure casebooks in the hope that they will assist him in his Business Law I course at State University. John does not ask Lynn if the books will help him, and she does not offer an opinion as to whether or not they will. In fact, the casebooks are worse than useless to John, who spends the rest of the semester trying to make sense of the seemingly incongruous collection of cases in the law books and ultimately fails the course.

3. Ahmad, the owner of a video rental store, asks Dean, a computer science instructor at State University, to recommend a computer system that would allow him to keep the books for his business and maintain a data base of client information and video rentals. Dean offers to sell Ahmad his 8088-based IBM PC computer with two floppy disks and limited memory for $200. The computer, which works flawlessly, needs several minutes to process every customer order update because of the size of the data base, and its lack of a hard disk and limited memory make it impossible for Ahmad to run much of the software he needs for his business.

In the first and third examples above, the sellers have breached the implied warranty of fitness for a particular purpose. In both cases, they were aware of the buyers' intended needs, and in both cases the buyers relied on the sellers' skill and judgment in making the purchase, thereby meeting both tests for breach of the warranty. In the second example, however, there is no breach of warranty, since Lynn, the law student, was not asked her opinion as to the usefulness of the books and did not offer such advice on her own. John, who made the purchase based on his own wrong assumption, must bear the loss caused by his misinformation.

Express Warranties (§2–313)

Any express statement of fact made by the seller to the buyer, any description of the goods, and any showing of a model or sample that the buyer has relied on in agreeing to enter into the contract creates an express warranty; the goods must conform to the statement, description, or sample. The representations about the goods are binding if they are made orally, in writing, or by showing a sample before the buyer agrees to purchase the goods.

While a salesperson's representations about goods can give rise to express warranties, her opinions about the quality of the goods do not. Generalizations and opinions about the quality or value of a product being sold are generally held to be mere sales puffery, or sales talk; a buyer cannot rely on such opinions or generalizations. The following examples of statements by a seller (or her agent, such as a salesperson) would not give rise to an express warranty:

- · This is the best car on the market.
- · If you purchase this blender, you will never regret it.
- · Our products are extremely reliable.
- · You won't find a better buy anywhere.
- · Acme products are the best in the world.
- · This car gives great gas mileage.
- · This widget not only purees asparagus, it also looks marvelous on your coffee table.

The following statements by the same seller would constitute express warranties, as long as they were made before the buyer agreed to purchase the item in question:

- · This car gets an average of 35 miles per gallon.
- · This widget will puree a bushel of asparagus in five minutes.
- · If you find a lower priced import car, we'll give you $1,000.
- · If this blender breaks down within the next year, we'll fix it free.

Disclaimer of Warranties (§2–316)

A seller can disclaim implied warranties of fitness and merchantability by making a clear statement to that effect. Selling goods *as is* or *with all faults* generally disclaims all implied warrants. Note, however, that the requirements for waiving implied warranties vary among states.

Judge for Yourself

Case 1. Keesha orders an AM/FM stereo receiver, amplifier, record player, CD player, dual cassette player/recorder, and speakers from Sounds Good Inc. The system is not sold as a set and the components are listed separately on the bill. When they are delivered, Keesha notices that the system works perfectly, but the CD player is a different brand than that which she had ordered.

- *a.* Can Keesha demand to exchange the CD player but keep the rest of the system after paying for it? Why?
- *b.* Can she reject the shipment and cancel the contract?

    c. If she returns the CD player and Sounds Good informs her that they no longer sell the one she had ordered, what legal remedies are available to her?

    d. Is Keesha entitled to reimbursement for the incidental expense of shipping the nonconforming CD player back to Sounds Good?

Case 2. In describing a new sculpture by a new artist, Pierre, the owner of an art gallery makes the following statement to Rudolph, a prospective buyer:

> This wonderful sculpture by Jeff Oops, *Brass Bedpan over City Landscape,* the most poignant example of humanity's struggle to triumph over existentialist despair ever to have been conceived by a brilliant young artist, is a bargain at $25,000.

    a. Assume that Rudolph purchases the sculpture in question for the asking price. Does Pierre's statement constitute an express warranty as to the sculpture's value? Why?

    b. If most art critics would consider the work a worthless piece of junk, is Pierre guilty of breach of an express or implied warranty based on the above statement?

    c. Which of the following statements made by Pierre would constitute express warranties?
       1. If you purchase the sculpture and are displeased by it after 90 days, you may return it to us for a full refund.
       2. This sculpture is not only art, but a valuable antique as well, since the bedpan used by the artist once belonged to Napoleon.
       3. This sculpture will appreciate at a minimum of 10 percent per year over the next 10 years.

    d. If the sculpture had been stolen from a college fraternity house, where it had been used as a punch bowl, and then sold to the unsuspecting art gallery owner as an original work, will Pierre be in breach of an implied warranty if he sells it in good faith to a buyer? Explain.

Case 3. Lester orders a truckload of Florida oranges from Juan, the owner of a Florida orange grove. Under the terms of the agreement, Juan is to ship the oranges to Lester FOB seller's plant, with payment due on delivery. After the goods are placed in the hands of the carrier, but before they are delivered to Lester, Juan learns that Lester has filed for bankruptcy and will be unable to pay for the shipment if it is delivered.

    a. What can Juan do under the circumstances to protect his rights?

   b. If the goods had been shipped on credit and actually delivered to the insolvent Lester, what would Juan's remedies be under the contract?

   c. If Lester is solvent but refuses to accept the goods upon delivery claiming to have found a cheaper supplier, what can Juan do?

Case 4.   Joyce, wishing to buy a Christmas gift for her husband, visits a computer store and asks the salesperson to recommend a laser printer. She tells the salesperson that the printer must emulate the Hewlett-Packard Laser printer, print at a minimum of eight pages per minute, and be capable of printing 10,000 copies per month. The salesperson recommends the Hewlett-Packard Personal Laser printer, telling her it's a terrific buy but failing to mention that it prints at a speed of only four pages per minute and is not meant for heavy office use.

   a. Has the salesperson breached any express warranties?

   b. Has the salesperson breached any implied warranties? Explain.

   c. If the salesperson demonstrates the Hewlett-Packard Laser Jet III printer to Joyce and sells her the Laser Jet II instead, will he have breached any warranties? (Assume that both printers meet the required duty cycle and print speeds.)

COMMERCIAL PAPER

Learning Objectives

After studying this chapter, you will be able to:

1. Name four of the six necessary criteria for defining commercial paper.
2. Define and distinguish between notes, drafts, checks, and certificates of deposit.
3. Define the term *holder in due course* and explain the significance of this status.
4. Explain the difference between blank, special, and restrictive indorsements.

Introduction

Although it may be difficult to pinpoint the origin of money as a medium of exchange, its importance to the economy is readily apparent. The exchange of hard currency for goods and services facilitates commerce, but there are many circumstances in which doing business on a cash basis is inconvenient or impossible. Consider the sale of an office building for $50 million. Is it likely the seller will offer to pay in cash or the buyer will demand cash as payment? Transportation and storage of such an amount would present significant problems to the buyer and seller alike, not to mention the banks who must physically count the money when the buyer withdraws it from her account and the seller deposits it into his. One way to avoid the problems of transferring large sums of money is to deal on a credit basis: the buyer could give the seller an IOU that the seller could collect on at her convenience. While much business is carried out on a credit basis, most sellers prefer something more substantial than a simple IOU that may or may not be paid upon demand. Fortunately, there are a variety of noncash methods to pay debts in business transactions. Some of these instruments, such as checks, drafts, notes, and certificates of deposit, are readily accepted in business as substitutes for cash because they can be easily negotiated (tranferred from one person to another for value) and they offer protection in the regular course of business. Such instruments are called *commercial paper* and are the subject of Article 3 of the Uniform Commercial Code.

The special protection they give to parties who accept them is what distinguishes negotiable instruments from other valid instruments that evidence debt, such as a simple IOU. Negotiated instruments have certain legal protections, which we will examine shortly, making them readily acceptable as the substitutes for cash in business transactions. Persons who receive such instruments can expect them to be honored when presented for payment.

Criteria for Defining Commercial Paper

Commercial paper consists of four types of written instruments: notes, drafts, checks, and certificates of deposit. Section 3–104 of the UCC sets up the criteria that commercial paper must meet:

1. The instrument must be in writing;
2. signed by the maker or drawer;
3. contain an unconditional promise to pay a sum certain in money;
4. contain no other promise, order obligation, or power not specifically authorized by the code;
5. be payable on demand or at a specific time; and
6. be payable to order or bearer.

If an instrument (a written, signed document containing a promise to pay money or an order for money to be paid) does not meet each of the above criteria, it is not a negotiable instrument. An instrument may fail to meet the requirements for a negotiable instrument and still be legally binding; it simply will not protect parties to whom it is transferred as a negotiable instrument would. Consider the following instruments. Do they meet the requirements for negotiable instruments?

All of the sample instruments on the following page are valid and enforceable, provided the sums in question are owed under valid contracts (and further providing that sample 3 is not an illegal gambling contract). None of the samples, however, meets the requirements for a negotiable instrument. Sample 1 is a simple IOU that does not contain an unconditional promise to pay (it purports to owe the money but makes no specific promise as to its repayment); furthermore, it is not

July 20, 1991

To Rhoda Sirlin

I. O. U. $50 (fifty dollars)

Nowana Pay

Sample 1

July 20, 1991

Pay to the order
of Kenneth J. Ansley
3 (three) ounces of gold

Vic López

Sample 2

July 20, 1991

Pay to the order of Frank Barral $100
(One hundred dollars) if the New York
Yankees win the World Series in 1996

Vic López

Sample 3

payable to the *order of* Rhoda Sirlin or to *bearer.* Sample 2 is not *payable in money,* which it must be. It need not necessarily be in dollars, but it must be in legal tender of some country (e.g., a note payable in yen, lira, marks, or pesetas is negotiable, but one payable in gold, silver, or any other commodity is not). Sample 3 is not negotiable because it contains a *conditional* promise to pay. Each of the above instruments is valid but will not give any special protection to parties who accept them under assignment in the regular course of business.

Parties to Commercial Paper

Before describing the types of commercial paper, we must define some important terminology:

Maker: The person (or company) who makes or executes a note.

Drawer: The person (or company) who makes or executes a draft.

Drawee: The person (or company) who is directed to pay a draft or check. (If the draft is a check, the drawee is the bank in which the drawer has the checking account on which the check is drawn.)

Payee: The person (or company) to whom a note or draft is made payable.

Bearer: The person (or company) in possession of a note or draft made out to him as payee or made out to bearer.

Guarantor: A person who signs a note or draft on its face guaranteeing payment in case it is dishonored when presented for payment. The guarantor is liable to the payee of a note or draft for its face value if the maker or drawee fails to pay the note when the payee properly demands payment. The guarantor's liability is primary to that of indorsers or accommodation parties.

Accommodation party: A person who indorses a note or draft that is not made payable to him to guarantee payment if it is dishonored when presented for payment. An accommodation party has secondary liability and cannot be made to pay on the note unless the principal parties (maker, drawer, and drawee) have all refused payment.

Acceptor: A drawee of a draft who binds himself to pay payee the face value of the draft when it is presented for payment by signing as acceptor on the face of the draft. A payee who obtains good faith acceptance of the draft by the drawee receives a guarantee from him that the draft will be paid when it is properly presented for payment.

Indorser: The person who signs her name at the back of a note or draft naming her as payee to obtain payment on it or negotiate it to a third party.

Indorsee: The person to whom a negotiable instrument is indorsed as the new payee.

Characteristics of Commercial Paper

Commercial paper, or negotiable instruments, can be characterized as either bearer or order paper. *Order paper* is a negotiable instrument that is payable to the order of a specific person or company. A check that reads "Pay to the order of Alice Z. López" is an order instrument, since the drawer is ordering the bank to pay Alice the sum named in the check. "Pay to the order of Internal Revenue Service" is likewise an order instrument: the bank is ordered to pay whatever amount is named in the check to a specific payee—in the latter case, a government agency.

Bearer paper, on the other hand, is not made out to a specific person or agency. The most common example of this is a check made out to cash: "Pay to the order of cash" means pay to anyone who is in possession of the instrument. "Pay to the order of bearer" is another example of a bearer instrument. Any time a specific payee cannot be determined from the words the drawer or maker used to identify the payee, it is assumed that bearer paper is intended, and the instrument is, in fact, bearer paper. Thus, making out a check "Pay to the order of 100 rabid raccoons" is bearer paper, since no specific payee can be identified. Despite what a shocked bank teller might think if such a check were presented for collection, it is very much valid bearer paper, payable to anyone who has it in her possession.

An instrument that sufficiently identifies a specific person or group as payees is deemed order paper, even if it does not name them. A check made out as follows would be order paper: "Pay to the order of the owner of a black Nissan 240 SX, N.Y. license plate 123ABC." Once the instrument is executed, it is payable only to the owner of the automobile in question, who will be entitled to demand payment after proving that he owns such a car. It is possible to trace the payee of such an instrument to only one person, since there could not be two black Nissan 240 SX automobiles in New York with the same license. If the car is registered to two people (e.g., husband and wife as joint owners), the check would be payable to both of them jointly.

While there is some room for creativity in the identification of payees when drafting negotiable instruments, it is never a good idea to express it. At the very least, drafting a negotiable instrument in an unusual manner or, for that matter, on an unusual object will cause problems for the payee when she tries to cash or further negotiate the check. At worst, litigation may be necessary to enforce the validity of the negotiable instrument. Also, keep in mind that parties are not generally obligated to accept checks or other negotiable instruments; they are free to demand cash, if they wish. Therefore, while your corner grocer may willingly accept your check that states "Pay to the order of cash," "Pay to the order of bearer," or perhaps even "Pay to the order of anybody," she is unlikely to accept a check that reads "Pay to the order of life, the universe, and everything," no matter how much you argue (and rightfully so) that it is a perfectly valid bearer instrument.

Types of Commercial Paper

As mentioned earlier, negotiable instruments consist of four basic types: notes, drafts, checks, and certificates of deposit.

Notes

A note is an unconditional promise to pay a sum certain (a specific amount) in money to a named payee or to bearer that is payable on a specific date or on demand. The person or company who drafts a note is the maker, and the person to whom the note is payable is the payee. Notes are a primary means of securing credit, with the debtor executing a note in favor of the creditor. The following example is typical:

➤ Robert wants to buy Aretha's car for $5,000 but only has $1,000 available in cash. He asks her if she'd be willing to accept a note for the balance payable over three years at 10 percent interest. Aretha agrees and turns over the car in exchange for $1,000 in cash and the following negotiable instrument:

PROMISSORY NOTE

NOVEMBER 1, 1993

For good and valuable consideration received, the undersigned promises to pay to the order of Aretha Jones the sum of $4,000.00 (four thousand) dollars with interest at a rate of 10% payable in equal, consecutive monthly payments of $129.07 (One hundred and twenty nine and 07/100 dollars) over the next 36 months with the first payment due on December 1, 1993. In the event that the undersigned fails to make any payment within 10 days of the date that it is due, the entire balance will be due at the option of any holder of this instrument.

Upon default, the maker will pay all reasonable costs of collection, including court costs and attorneys' fees.

Loan principal: $4,000.00
Interest charges: 646.52

Total payments: $4,646.52

Annual interest rate: 10%

Robert Nussbaum

In the above example, Aretha is the payee of the note, while Robert is the maker. Once Robert signs the note, Aretha will be able to negotiate it by indorsing it to a third party. Once the note is indorsed and delivered to the third party, that party becomes the note's holder and can in turn negotiate it to yet another person or keep it and be entitled to payment from Robert under the note's original terms. Aretha can, of course, choose to keep the note and collect the payments from Robert for the entire term. The point is that should she choose to sell the note and get her money immediately from a third party, she will be readily able to do so (assuming that Robert has a good credit history and will make a good risk for any prospective purchaser of the note). What a prospective holder will actually pay Aretha for the note depends on such factors as Robert's creditworthiness and the going rate of interest at the time the note is negotiated. If Robert is a poor credit risk and the prime rate is at 11 percent when Aretha tries to negotiate the note, she will get much less than the face value (i.e., the note will be discounted to reflect the risk involved and the rate of return it offers on the principal loan amount). On the other hand, if Robert has an excellent credit history and the prime rate is at 8 percent when Aretha wants to negotiate the loan, she may well get more than the note's face value from the indorsee.

Drafts

A draft is an unconditional written, signed order by a drawer for a drawee to pay a sum certain in money to the order of a named payee or to bearer. Unlike the maker of a note who promises to pay the payee or her assigns (anyone to whom the payee might negotiate the note) a sum of money himself, the drawer of a draft orders a third party—the drawee—to make the payment to the payee or her assigns. If the drawee does not honor the draft for any reason, the drawer is liable to the payee or her assigns for its payment. Naturally, there must be a contractual obligation between the drawee and the drawer if the drawee is to pay the draft when it is presented. A payee wishing to determine whether the drawee will in fact pay the draft when presented can seek acceptance from the drawee.

The following example illustrates a simple draft. Note that none of the parties is a bank or large company, although they could be:

May 18, 1993

TO: Felipe López
Pay to the order of Jane Doe $100.00
(One hundred dollars.)

Vic López

In the last example, Felipe is the drawee (the person ordered to pay), Vic is the drawer (the person who drafts the note and orders the drawee to pay), and Jane Doe is the payee. The draft meets all of the requirements for negotiability: it is in writing, signed by the drawer, contains an unconditional order to pay a sum certain in money, contains no other promises, is payable to order and is payable on demand, since no specific date for payment is specified. If Jane Doe takes this draft from Vic, she will be able to freely negotiate it. Naturally, both Jane and anyone else to whom she negotiates the draft are likely to want some assurance that the drawee will honor the draft when it is presented for payment. She can get such an assurance by taking the note to Felipe and asking him to accept it. If he agrees, he would simply sign as acceptor on its face as follows:

> May 18, 1993
>
> TO: Felipe López
> Pay to the order of Jane Doe $100.00
> (One hundred dollars.)
>
> *Vic López*
>
> Accepted ___ *J. López* ___

Even if Felipe is under no obligation to Victor to accept the draft, once he signs as acceptor, his obligation to pay the draft when it is presented to him will be absolute.

Checks

A check is simply a draft in which the drawee is a bank. The drawer of a check is a person or company who has an account in a bank against which they are authorized to draw checks. If a payee of a check wants to ensure that there will be enough funds in the account on which the check is drawn to guarantee its payment, she can demand that the drawer have the check certified by the bank. A certified check is the equivalent of a draft that has been accepted by the drawee. Section 3–411 specifically refers to certification of a check by a bank as acceptance of the check; when a bank certifies a check, it guarantees that there will be sufficient funds in the drawer's account for the check to be honored when presented for payment.

May 18, 1993

Pay to the order of   *Veronica Schmidt*

Twenty five and xx/100 dollars | $25.00 |

To: STATE BANK
123 Main Street
Anytown, NY 11111

Lisa Yin

Acct: 1-234567-8

The above sample contains all necessary information for the bank to pay the payee $25 from Lisa Yin's account. Assume the check is not in the standard preprinted form. As long as the instrument contains all the necessary elements to make it negotiable, which the above does, a commercial bank would be obligated to honor the check, provided there are sufficient funds in the named account to cover it.

Most of the checks we come across look pretty much the same, but there is no requirement that one be written on a preprinted, bank-provided form to be negotiable. As long as it meets the familiar requirements—in writing, signed by the drawer, contains an unconditional order to pay a sum certain in money, contains no other promises, is payable to order, and is payable on demand or at a specific date—the type of paper on which the check is written and the format are irrelevant. It is perfectly legal to write a check on a coconut by carving the relevant information with a sharp knife, or, as some whimsical taxpayers have done in the past, write out a check on a shirt to send to the IRS. In both instances, the checks would be legal (although it will probably take some time to convince a bank teller of that fact when the check is deposited for collection).

Certificates of Deposit

Certificates of deposit, or CDs, are notes issued by both commercial banks and savings and loan associations. The only significant difference between a CD and a note is that only banks may issue CDs, whereas any company or individual can issue notes.

Holder in Due Course

Section 3–302 of the UCC lists the requirements for a person to become a holder in due course. To qualify for the special status of *holder in due course*, a person must take a negotiable instrument:

1. For value.
2. In good faith.
3. Without notice that it is overdue, has been dishonored, or has any defense against or claim to it on the part of any person.

A *holder* of an instrument—a person possessing an order instrument that names her as payee, or one possessing a bearer instrument—gains the special protection of holder in due course status whenever she meets the test set out above. Taking the instrument for value means that the holder gave some consideration to receive the instrument; the requirement of good faith is met as long as the holder acted in a just and ethical manner in obtaining the instrument (e.g., if the holder takes an instrument under circumstances that should make her suspicious as to the validity of the instrument, the good faith requirement will not be met); finally, the requirement that the instrument be taken without the knowledge that it has been dishonored, is overdue, or has claims against it by third parties is an extension of the good faith requirement.

The UCC gives special protection to parties who qualify for holder in due course status. They are in a very strong position when accepting a negotiable instrument in that they take it free from all personal defenses that any party might have to payment of it. In many circumstances, a holder in due course receives greater rights and protection in taking negotiable instruments than the original holder of the instrument possessed. In most instances, a holder in due course is absolutely entitled to payment of negotiable instruments in his possession, regardless of defects these may possess.

Section 3–305 outlines the rights of a holder in due course. In essence, a holder in due course takes a negotiable instrument free of all claims to it by parties with whom he has not dealt. The only defenses that can successfully be asserted against a holder in due course are the real defenses of incapacity, duress, illegality of the transaction, forgery of the instrument, and misrepresentation inducing the drawer or maker of the instrument to execute the same without knowledge that she was executing a negotiable instrument. With these exceptions—all of which are real defenses that void the original execution of the instrument—no other defense may be asserted against a holder in due course. Consider the following circumstances:

➤ 1. Mr. Cheatham, a jeweler, sells Earl a counterfeit Rolex watch for $10,000 (the watch is a Korean import worth $19.95). Earl pays by check, and Cheatham negotiates the check to his bank.

2. Terry finds her law professor's paycheck on his lectern after class, where the duly absent-minded professor left it, after indorsing it in blank. The student takes the check and asks a friend to cash it for her, telling him the truth as to how she came to possess the instrument. Terry's friend then negotiates the check to his local grocer, who is unaware that the paycheck was acquired through larceny.

3. An armed robber forces Jeanrette to execute a check at gunpoint.

4. Charlene tricks William into signing a note for $250,000 telling him it's an application to join a new CD music club. William, who trusts Charlene implicitly, signs the note where she indicates. Charlene then negotiates the note to a group of innocent investors and leaves the country.

5. Slick, an upscale day-care center operator, dreams up the brilliant idea of having the children in his care sign notes for $250,000 each, payable in 20 years. (Slick figures chances are good that some of his kids will be independently wealthy in their mid-20s and would like to assure himself a cozy retirement at their expense.) Several of the children who signed the notes in fact become quite wealthy and Slick negotiates those notes 19 years later to innocent third parties.

In the first two examples above, the bank and the grocer are holders in due course, since they acquired the instrument for value, in good faith, and without knowledge that there were any defenses or claims against it by any person. As such, both the grocer and the bank are entitled to payment under the instrument, while Earl (the buyer of the counterfeit Rolex) and the law professor will have to bear the loss. The latter two can, of course, sue Mr. Cheatham, jewelry store owner, for fraud and Terry, the law student, for conversion, respectively, assuming these can be found. In examples 3, 4 and 5, however, Jeanrette, William, and the persons who executed the notes as children will all have valid defenses, even against holders in due course. A check or note issued under duress is void and of no legal effect; since such an instrument is invalid at its inception, even a holder in due course cannot obtain good title to it. Likewise, if a maker or drawer is tricked into executing a negotiable instrument without his knowledge or consent, the instrument is void and can never have any effect, even in the hands of a holder in due course. The same is true of an instrument executed by a child, which is voidable at her option until she reaches the age of consent. The notes in example 5, executed by children of tender years, are void at the inception and will likewise be unenforceable even in the hands of a holder in due course.

Negotiation and Indorsers' Liability

Negotiable instruments are by their nature freely transferable. Although the vast majority of checks, drafts, notes, and certificates of deposit are paid when properly presented to the drawee or maker, some invariably are not. At such times, it is important to determine the liability of parties to the commercial paper. The principal parties to the negotiable instrument (maker, drawer, drawee, acceptor, or guarantor) are primarily liable for its payment. If, however, they are unable or unwilling to pay it when the payee properly presents it, indorsers of the instrument can be called upon to pay it themselves under certain circumstances.

The holder of a negotiable instrument can transfer its ownership to another person or company by indorsing the back of the instrument and delivering it to the person to whom it is indorsed. (*Indorsement* and *endorsement* are synonymous. *Indorsement* is used here because it is the preferred legal term and the UCC uses it.) The indorsement of a negotiable instrument followed by its delivery to the person to whom it is indorsed is termed *negotiation*—the formal name given to the legal transfer of ownership from one holder to another. For an order instrument to be duly negotiated, indorsement followed by delivery to the indorsee is necessary. A bearer instrument (one which is payable to cash, to the order of cash, to bearer, or otherwise fails to mention a specific person to whom it is payable) is negotiated simply by delivery to anyone. Anyone in possession of a bearer instrument is a holder.

Types of Indorsements: (§3–204 to §3–205)

Indorsements may be blank, special, or restrictive. A *blank indorsement* specifies no specific indorsee and can consist of a simple signature on the back of the negotiable instrument. A *special indorsement* is one that specifies to whose order an instrument is payable. A *restrictive indorsement* is one that is conditional, purports to prohibit further transfer of the instrument, and includes the words "for collection," "pay any bank," "for deposit," or any similar term that states the instrument is negotiated to a bank for the purpose of deposit or collection.

Section 3–206 clearly states that restrictive indorsements do not prevent an instrument from being further negotiated. However, a person to whom an instrument is negotiated under a restrictive indorsement must comply with the indorsement if he is to qualify for holder in due course status. If the bank or individual to whom a negotiable instrument is restrictively indorsed does not treat the instrument consistently with the indorsement, it will be liable to the indorser for any damages that result. Example:

▶ Dan restrictively indorses his paycheck as follows: For deposit only into State Bank A/C 1234567. He then signs his name. On the way to the bank, he is mugged and the thief takes the check. She then takes the check and cashes it at her bank—First Bank of Erehwon. Despite the restrictive indorsement, the bank teller pays the thief the face value of the check. Assuming that the thief then leaves the state and cannot be found, First Bank of Erehwon will have to reimburse Dan the full amount of the check, because it failed to honor the restrictive indorsement.

The following examples illustrate blank, special, and restrictive indorsements made on a check originally payable to Lisa Wong:

Blank Indorsement	*Special Indorsement*	*Restrictive Indorsement*
Lisa Wong	*Pay to the order of Henry Marconi* *Lisa Wong*	*For deposit only into First Bank of Erehwon* *A/c 123456* *Lisa Wong*

Liability of Indorsers

Indorsers of negotiable instruments are secondarily liable for payment of the instrument if it is dishonored by the drawee or maker. Indorsers of negotiable instruments guarantee to every other indorser that the instrument will be paid as drafted. If the instrument is dishonored, its holder can force any previous indorser to pay its face value. All that is necessary to preserve this right is giving timely notice that the negotiable instrument has been dishonored. Section 3–501 provides that drawers and indorsers are not liable for payment of an instrument that the drawee has dishonored upon presentment until they are notified of the dishonor. If a bank refuses to pay a check presented for payment, the payee must notify the drawer and all indorsers before she can demand payment of the instrument from them. A bank must notify its customer of dishonor by midnight of the day on which the dishonor occurs; all other persons must give notice of dishonor by midnight of the third day following the dishonor (Section 3–508). Under Section 3–508, a bank or other individual may give notice of dishonor in any reasonable format, including orally or in writing. If notification is made by mail, the notice is deemed effective as of the time the letter is mailed.

Warranties of Presentment and Transfer (§3–417)

The following warranties are made by every transferor of negotiable instruments to the transferee upon negotiation of the instrument under Section 3–417(1):

1. That he has good title to the instrument or is authorized to transfer the instrument on behalf of one who has good title to it.
2. That he has no knowledge that the signatures of the maker or drawer are unauthorized (a holder in due course does not make this warrantee to a maker, drawee, or acceptor of a draft).
3. That the instrument has not been materially altered (a holder in due course does not make this warrantee to the maker of a note or drawer of a draft, to a drawee, or to an acceptor of a draft).

In addition to the above warranties by all transferors, any person who transfers a negotiable instrument and receives consideration for the transfer also warrants the following under Section 3–417(2):

1. That she has good title to the instrument or is authorized to obtain payment or acceptance on behalf of one who has good title.
2. That all signatures are genuine or authorized.
3. That the instrument has not been materially altered.
4. That there is no valid defense from any party against her.
5. That she has no knowledge of any insolvency proceeding instituted with respect to the maker, the acceptor, or the drawer of an unaccepted instrument.

Section 3–417(3) provides that a transferor may limit the warranty liability specified under Section 3–417(2) by transferring the instrument "without recourse." If the instrument is transferred with the restrictive indorsement "without recourse" above the transferor's signature, only the warranties under Section 3–417(1) and the warranty in Section 3–417(2) relating to her lack of knowledge of any insolvency proceedings against the maker, acceptor, or drawer will be made. (In other words, by transferring an instrument "without recourse," the transferor makes no warranties as to his title, the genuineness of signatures, material alterations, or defenses by third parties affecting the instrument.)

The warranties of presentment and transfer are implied warranties made by all transferor's of negotiable instruments. Dishonor of an instrument when it is presented for payment to a maker or drawee can give rise to an action for breach of one of the above warranties.

Judge for Yourself

Case 1.   Robben offers a used car to Mark, telling him that it is three years old, has 12,000 miles on the odometer, and is in perfect mechanical condition. In fact, the car is eight years old, has over 100,000 miles, and has several cracks in its engine block. Mark buys the car based on Robben's fraudulent misrepresentations and issues a check for $10,000. Robben then indorses Mark's check over to a car wholesaler in return for 10 used cars. The wholesaler, unaware of Robben's shady business practices, further indorses and negotiates the check to his bank.

a. Is Robben a holder of the check?

b. Is Robben a holder in due course of the check?

c. Is the wholesaler to whom Robben negotiates the check a holder in due course of the instrument?

d. Is the wholesaler's bank a holder in due course of the instrument?

e. If Mark stops payment on the check after Robben has transferred the instrument to the wholesaler, will he have a valid defense against the wholesaler to refuse payment of the check?

f. Would Mark have a valid defense to refuse payment to Robben, the original seller?

Case 2.   The following instrument is presented for payment at State Bank, where Mr. Tai Chung Chang has a checking account (#1–234567). The instrument is drafted on what appears to be a yellow legal pad. The signature is genuine. All items are handwritten or typewritten.

May 18, 1993

Pay to the order of *Alejandra Patiño* $200.00

Two hundred and xx/100 —— dollars

To: STATE BANK
123 Main Street
Anytown, NY 11111

Tai C. Chang

Acct: 1-234567

---

a. Is the instrument valid?

b. What is the nature of the instrument?

c. If the instrument had been written on balsa wood, would it still be valid?

d. Assuming the instrument is valid, is it order or bearer paper? Explain.

e. Assume Alejandra indorses the instrument by signing her name on its back, without adding any additional language. What type of indorsement would that be? Would the instrument now be order or bearer paper?

Case 3. Examine the following instrument and answer the questions that follow:

May 18, 1993

Two (2) years from today, the undersigned
promises to pay Ranji Singh $10,000 (ten thousand
dollars) with interest thereon at a rate
of 9.75% per year.

Elliott Lincger

Payment Guaranteed: *Robert Nussbaum*

---

a. Is the instrument involved negotiable? Why?

b. What type of instrument is it?

c. Who are the various parties to the instrument?

Case 4. A thief enters Christine's home and steals her checkbook. She then proceeds to a local electronics store and, posing as Christine, purchases $3,000 in electronics equipment, writing out one of Christine's checks as payment and skillfully forging Christine's signature. When Christine learns of the robbery, she immediately notifies her bank and places a stop payment order on all checks. When the electronic store's check is not honored by the bank, the store owner sues Christine for $3,000, claiming that she is a holder in due course with regard to her check and demanding payment.

    a. Is the store owner a holder in due course? Explain.

    b. Is the store owner entitled to payment from Christine? Explain.

    c. If the thief forced Christine at gunpoint to sign all of her checks in blank and then went on a shopping spree, paying for all items with checks containing Christine's real signature, would subsequent holders in due course of the checks be entitled to demand payment from Christine? Explain.

TRANS-AIRE INTERNATIONAL, INC., Plaintiff-Appellant, v.
NORTHERN ADHESIVE COMPANY, INC., Defendant-Appellee

No. 88–1325

UNITED STATES COURT OF APPEALS FOR THE SEVENTH CIRCUIT

882 F.2d 1254; 1989 U.S. App. LEXIS 12593

November 10, 1988, Argued August 21, 1989, Decided

JUDGES: Coffey, Ripple, and Kanne, Circuit Judges.

OPINION:

KANNE, Circuit Judge.

Trans-Aire International, Inc. purchased a contact adhesive from Northern Adhesive Company, Inc. to laminate various materials during the process of converting standard automotive vans to recreational vehicles. The adhesive failed to perform during the summer months as Trans-Aire had hoped, and it sued Northern under a wide variety of legal theories. The district court entered summary judgment in favor of Northern, and Trans-Aire appeals. We affirm.

I. BACKGROUND

Trans-Aire International, Inc. converts ordinary automotive vans into recreational vehicles. Prior to October of 1982, Trans-Aire installed interior carpet and ceiling fabrics with an adhesive product, "3M 4500," manufactured by 3M Company. However, Trans-Aire experienced problems with that adhesive. Apparently, when the temperature rose inside a van, the adhesive often would fail to hold the fabrics in place.

Trans-Aire contacted Northern Adhesive Company, Inc., a manufacturer of a wide range of adhesive products, to find a replacement for the 3M product. Trans-Aire never requested a specific adhesive by name and instead merely informed Northern of the purposes for which Trans-Aire needed an adhesive. In response, Northern sent several adhesive samples to Trans-Aire for experimentation purposes. Allegedly, Northern told Trans-Aire that one of their adhesives, Adhesive 7448, was a "match" for the 3M product which had failed previously.

Trans-Aire tested the sample adhesives by putting them into its application equipment and applying them in the same manner in which Trans-Aire had been applying the 3M adhesive. The tests were conducted in a cool plant, rather than under the warmer weather conditions which had caused the 3M product to fail. Nevertheless, Trans-Aire's chief engineer, Stephen Fribley, determined that Northern's Adhesive 7448 was better than the 3M product.

Fribley summarized the results of the various test applications to Robert Higgins, Trans-Aire's president. Fribley suggested to Higgins that they test Northern's adhesive under summer-like conditions. However, Higgins stated that he was satisfied that Adhesive 7448 was better than the 3M product.

When Higgins asked, Fribley told Higgins that to his knowledge Adhesive 7448 had no warranty. A Northern representative confirmed Fribley's belief, stating that "there was no warranty on [Adhesive 7448] other than that— what they would ship would be like the sample. It would be the same chemistry." Fribley informed Higgins of this conversation.

Between November of 1982 and May of 1983, Trans-Aire ordered several shipments of Adhesive 7448. Trans-Aire placed each order by telephone and subsequently confirmed its request by sending a written purchase order.

Trans-Aire began to use Adhesive 7448 in late 1982 after placing its initial order. Beginning sometime in the spring of 1983, Trans-Aire learned of numerous delamination problems in the interiors of the RVs in which Adhesive 7448 had been used—the same problems experienced previously with the 3M product. As a result, Trans-Aire was forced to repair well over 500 vans.

Trans-Aire filed a nine-count complaint against Northern. The district court initially dismissed portions of the complaint and later granted Northern's motion for summary judgment upon the remaining claims.

II. DISCUSSION

Trans-Aire appeals the district court's decision to grant Northern's motion for summary judgment upon Trans-Aire's various breach of warranty and contract claims. At oral argument, counsel for Trans-Aire admitted that no material factual dispute exists and asserted that Trans-Aire instead intended to challenge the district court's legal conclusions. Nevertheless, counsel also stated that Trans-Aire disputed the inferences to be drawn from the established facts. Apparently, counsel was commenting upon Trans-Aire's briefs in which it devotes substantial time to insuring that we are aware that Northern's summary judgment motion largely was based upon the deposition of Trans-Aire's former employee and chief engineer, Stephen Fribley.

Trans-Aire evidently hopes to convey the impression that perhaps Fribley's testimony is not credible. However, we have held in the past that "[a] motion for summary judgment cannot be defeated merely by an opposing party's incantation of lack of credibility over a movant's supporting affidavit. . . . ." Walter v. Fiorenzo, 840 F.2d 427, 434 (7th Cir. 1988). Thus, because counsel admitted that it cannot offer any evidence which conflicts with that offered in support of Northern's motion for summary judgment, we will focus solely upon Trans-Aire's ability to demonstrate that the district court's legal conclusions are erroneous.

A. Implied Warranties of Fitness for a Particular Purpose and of Merchantability

Section 2–314 of the Illinois Commercial Code[1] provides that every sale of goods by a merchant includes an implied warranty that the goods are fit for the ordinary purposes for which they are used unless the warranty is modified or excluded.[2] Section 2–315 of the code states that a sale of goods also includes an implied warranty of fitness for a particular purpose if a seller knows of the buyer's particular purpose for the goods and the buyer relies upon the seller's skill or judgment to select suitable goods.[3] However, Section 2–316 of the code states that no implied warranties apply when a buyer examines the goods or a sample as fully as he desires, or refuses to examine the goods, prior to the purchase.[4]

The district court first held that no warranty of fitness for a particular purpose arose under the facts and circumstances of this case because Trans-Aire did not rely upon Northern's skill or judgment to select an adhesive. Nevertheless, the court also held that even if such a warranty existed, it and any implied warranty of merchantability were excluded or waived under Section 2–316, as a matter of law, when Trans-Aire examined Adhesive 7448 "as fully as it desired" prior to placing its purchase orders. Trans-Aire challenges the court's legal conclusions under Section 2–316 as well as the court's holding that no implied warranty of fitness for a particular purpose arose.

Initially, we hold that the district court correctly concluded that no warranty of fitness for a particular purpose existed. We agree with the district court that Trans-Aire cannot demonstrate that it relied upon Northern's skill or judgment in deciding to purchase Adhesive 7448, even assuming that Northern knew of the purpose for which Trans-Aire needed the adhesive.

Trans-Aire's chief engineer, Fribley, expressly stated in a deposition that he did not rely upon Northern's skill or judgment when Trans-Aire decided to purchase Adhesive 7448. Trans-Aire asserts that Fribley was not authorized to and did not negotiate the purchase of Adhesive 7448 and therefore his testimony is not dispositive of the issue whether Trans-Aire relied upon Northern's judgment. However, Trans-Aire's president, Higgins, clearly did make the final purchase decision and the record supports Northern's assertion that Higgins relied upon Fribley's recommendation. Furthermore, it is undisputed that Fribley's recommendation and Higgins' final decision were based upon the tests which Fribley conducted, not any express or implied representations made by Northern.[5] We therefore must agree with the district court that Trans-Aire cannot demonstrate that an implied warranty of fitness for a particular purpose existed.

However, we need not dwell upon this issue because we agree with the district court that Trans-Aire excluded all implied warranties by its actions. Under Section 2–316 of the Illinois Commercial Code, implied warranties are excluded when a party examines a product or sample "as fully as it desires" or "refuses to examine" the product or sample in a reasonable manner given the circumstances of the case. The undisputed facts and circumstances of this case preclude Trans-Aire's attempts to maintain an action based upon breaches of any existing implied warranties of fitness for a particular purpose or of merchantability.

As we indicated earlier, Northern offered the deposition testimony of Trans-Aire's former chief engineer, Fribley, to support its defense that Trans-Aire in fact tested samples of Adhesive 7448 "as fully as it desired." Fribley's undisputed testimony establishes that while he was Trans-Aire's chief engineer, Trans-Aire experienced problems with a 3M adhesive which it was using in its van conversion process and that he had contacted Northern to find a replacement. Northern sent a sample of Adhesive 7448 to Trans-Aire which Fribley tested in the usual laminating equipment. However, rather than testing the adhesive under summer-like conditions, the same conditions under which the 3M product had failed, Fribley stated that he performed the tests under "cool" conditions in the plant. He found the adhesive to be satisfactory under these conditions and reported the results to Trans-Aire's president, Higgins.

Fribley apparently realized that the cool conditions were inadequate to test the adhesive's performance characteristics during warmer weather. According to his undisputed testimony, he suggested to Higgins that the adhesive undergo heat testing because he knew that the inherent nature of contact adhesives is to soften with heat.[6] Nevertheless, Trans-Aire's president believed that "the testing we had done proved the product satisfactory for our application."

Upon these facts, we must agree with the district court's finding that Trans-Aire clearly tested the samples as fully as it desired and refused to conduct further tests which would have confirmed a characteristic of contact adhesives which they already knew to be true, that they soften with heat. Trans-Aire attempts to argue that it did not have the means to discover the "latent defects" of the adhesive, because of the cool plant conditions at the time the tests were performed, and that Section 2–316 does not exclude the implied warranties under these circumstances. See Ill. Ann. Stat. ch. 26, para. 2–316 Comment 8 (Smith-Hurd 1963 & Supp. 1989) ("an examination under circumstances which do not permit chemical or other testing of the goods would not exclude defects which could be ascertained only by such testing"). We agree with the district court that this argument is without merit.

As Judge Williams noted, the portion of Fribley's deposition which discusses the conditions under which the tests were performed states nothing directly regarding the feasibility of heat testing. Instead, Fribley merely discussed the difficulty of applying the adhesive at a cold temperature and stated that the plant's temperature could not be adjusted "to meet different factors." No evidence exists to indicate what factors he meant. Trans-Aire itself offered no evidence of its own which indicates why the tests could not be performed.[7] The only concrete evidence of record as to why the heat tests were not performed is that Trans-Aire's president did not feel that they were necessary. Thus, the feasibility of the testing actually cannot be found to be in issue.

"A professional buyer examining a product in his field will be held to have assumed the risk as to all defects which a professional in the field ought to observe." Ill. Ann. Stat. ch. 26, para. 2–316 Comment 8 (Smith-Hurd 1963 & Supp. 1988); see also Blockhead, Inc. v. Plastic Forming Co., 402 F. Supp. 1017, 1025 (D. Conn. 1975) ("The scope of the exclusion obtained through a buyer's examination depends not only on the examination made, but on the examination that should have been made by the particular buyer"). Trans-Aire clearly knew that contact adhesives generally soften with heat; in addition to Fribley's general observations, it is undisputed that "Trans-Aire had experienced problems with another adhesive which it admits (and even argues in its favor) was a "match" for Adhesive 7448. We may only conclude that Trans-Aire's actions and statements evidence a clear intent to waive any reliance upon the implied warranties. We therefore hold that Trans-Aire cannot now maintain claims for breach of any existing implied warranties of fitness for a particular purpose or of merchantability and that summary judgment was appropriate.

B. Express Warranty

Trans-Aire next argues that the district court erroneously concluded that an express warranty was not created in this case. Trans-Aire contends that by sending specific adhesive samples to Trans-Aire in response to a general statement of need to find a new adhesive for the inadequate 3M product Northern expressly warranted that those samples would meet Trans-Aire's production needs. "Trans-Aire apparently did not make this specific argument below, but it certainly would not have fared any better than it does here.

The record indicates that Trans-Aire requested product information from Northern and stated that it wished to purchase a "suitable" product. According to Fribley's undisputed testimony, a Northern representative did not state that any of its adhesives were "suitable" for Trans-Aire's purposes and instead merely commented that Northern manufactured various adhesives, one or more of which "might be applicable." At best (or perhaps worst), Northern stated that its Adhesive 7448 product was a "match" for the 3M product with which Trans-Aire had experienced lamination failures in warmer settings. Thereafter, Northern sent several adhesive samples to Trans-Aire for testing purposes in hopes that Trans-Aire would find an adhesive which it could use. With these facts, Trans-Aire cannot now claim that Northern provided a specific product in response to its needs which amounted to an "affirmation of fact" that the adhesive would meet Trans-Aire's manufacturing needs. See Ill. Ann. Stat. ch. 26, para. 2–313(1)(a) (Smith-Hurd 1963).

As for "Trans-Aire's remaining arguments, we need only reiterate the points made by the district court. Without any doubt whatsoever, Trans-Aire knew that Adhesive 7448 included no express warranties. Fribley told Trans-

Aire's president, Higgins, that he "didn't know of any adhesive that had a warranty on it due to the many variables of temperature and materials and application methods." More importantly, Northern confirmed Fribley's belief when it stated "that there was no warranty on [Adhesive 7448] other than that—what they would ship would be like the sample. It would be the same chemistry." Fribley relayed this information directly to Higgins. We therefore hold that the district court correctly granted summary judgment in favor of Northern on the express warranty count.

C. Breach of Purchase Order Contract

Finally, Trans-Aire argues that the district court improperly granted summary judgment in favor of Northern on the breach of purchase order contract claim. In its complaint, Trans-Aire alleged that it confirmed each of twelve separate telephone orders for Adhesive 7448 by mailing a purchase order to Northern. Each purchase order provided that Northern would "protect, defend or save harmless" Trans-Aire from all damages and claims for liability for property damage resulting from the sale or use of Adhesive 7448.[8] The district court found that the additional terms contained in the written purchase orders "materially altered" the parties' agreement and could not be considered part of the contract. Trans-Aire challenges the validity of this legal conclusion.

The parties do not challenge the district court's reliance upon our earlier statements that "once the existence and terms of an alleged oral agreement have been established, it is necessary to refer to Section 2–207. . . to ascertain whether a term in a written confirmation but not in the parties' oral agreement is binding on the recipient of the written confirmation." C. Itoh & Co. (Am.) v. Jordan Int'l Co., 552 F.2d 1228, 1233 (7th Cir. 1977). Instead, they argue over the district court's interpretation of the indemnification clause under that section.

Section 2–207 of the Illinois Commercial Code provides that additional terms included in a written confirmation "are to be construed as proposals for addition to the contract" and will not become part of the contract if "they materially alter it." See Ill. Ann. Stat. ch. 26, para. 2–207(2) (Smith-Hurd 1963); McCarty v. Verson Allsteel Press Co., 89 Ill. App. 3d 498, 411 N.E.2d 936, 44 Ill. Dec. 570 (1980). A term is considered to be a material alteration if its inclusion would "result in surprise or hardship if incorporated without express awareness by the other party." Ill. Ann. Stat. ch. 26, para. 2-207 Comment 4 (Smith-Hurd 1963); Clifford-Jacobs Forging Co. v. Capital Eng'g & Mfg. Co., 107 Ill. App. 3d 29, 32, 437 N.E.2d 22, 24, 62 Ill. Dec. 785, 787 (1982); see also Chicago Litho Plate Graining Co. v. Allstate Can Co., 838 F.2d 927, 931 (7th Cir. 1988). Generally, whether an additional term "materially alters" a contract should not be determined upon a summary judgment motion because the inquiry is merely part of a process to ascertain the parties' bargaining intent. Clifford-Jacobs Forging Co., 107 Ill. App. 3d at 33, 437 N.E.2d at 25, 62 Ill. Dec. at 788. However, summary judgment may be appropriate when the parties cannot honestly dispute that a term would result in surprise or undue hardship unless both parties agree to its inclusion. Id.; see also Ill. Ann. Stat. ch. 26, para. 2-207 Comment 4 (Smith-Hurd 1963).

The district court found that, as a matter of law, an indemnification clause constitutes a material alteration of the parties' agreement. Trans-Aire contests this conclusion, noting that between November, 1982 and May, 1983 it sent purchase orders containing the indemnification clause to Northern on twelve different occasions. On these facts, it contends that inclusion of the term, although not expressly agreed upon, could not have been a "surprise" to Northern. Relying upon our decision in Schulze & Burch Biscuit Co. v. Tree Top, Inc., 831 F.2d 709 (7th Cir. 1987), Trans-Aire concludes that the indemnification clause cannot be characterized as a material alteration.

In Schulze, we considered a nonassenting party's claim that an arbitration clause in a preprinted confirmation form should be deemed a material alteration of the parties' agreement and thus unenforceable without both parties' assent. There, the party sending the confirmation form and seeking to enforce the arbitration clause offered evidence which showed that it had sent nine of these forms over an unspecified period of time before sending an identical form containing the identical clause which it now sought to enforce. Id. at 715. We stated that this "course of dealing" between the parties, see Ill. Ann. Stat. ch. 26, para. 1–205 (Smith-Hurd 1963), foreclosed any claim of "unfair surprise" by the party seeking to avoid enforcement of the arbitration clause. We therefore held that the clause could not be characterized as a material alteration of the parties' agreement. Id. We noted that the party which received each of these forms needed only to object to the arbitration clause within a reasonable amount of time under Section 2–207(2)(c) if it wished to exclude the term from the governing agreement. Ill. Ann. Stat. ch. 26, para. 2–207(2)(c) (Smith-Hurd 1963).

We agree with Trans-Aire that at first blush our decision in Schulze appears to support its contention that a "course of dealing" existed between Trans-Aire and Northern which arguably would preclude a finding that inclusion of the indemnification clause constitutes a material alteration of the parties' agreement. Nevertheless, we believe that we are presented with a different situation than we faced in Schulze.

As we stated above, Comment 4 to Section 2–207 defines a material alteration as one which would "result in surprise or hardship if incorporated without the express awareness of the nonassenting party." Ill. Ann. Stat. ch. 26, para. 2–207 Comment 4 (Smith-Hurd 1963) see Maxon Corp. v. Tyler Pipe Indus., 497 N.E.2d 570, 576 (Ind. App. 1986) (an Indiana court interpreting the identical section of the Uniform Commercial Code and considering a similar indemnification clause); Dohm & Nelke v. Wilson Foods Corp., 531 N.E.2d 512, 514 (Ind. App. 1988) (agreeing with Maxon that indemnification clauses require the express consent of both parties). Under this language, an additional term may be characterized as a material alteration if it either "surprises" the nonassenting party or if its inclusion, without an express meeting of the minds, would impose an unreasonable "hardship" upon the nonassenting party. With this overlooked distinction made, we believe that Schulze, as well as Barliant v. Follett Corp., 138 Ill. App. 3d 756, 483 N.E.2d 1312, 1316, 91 Ill. Dec. 677, 681 (1985), the other decision which Trans-Aire relies upon at length, are distinguishable.

In Schulze and Barliant, the additional term in issue could not be characterized as imposing a significant hardship upon the nonassenting party. In Schulze, we considered an arbitration clause which stated that all disputes arising out of a sale would be "arbitrated in the usual manner." 831 F.2d at 711. No Illinois court had considered the issue whether such a term was a material alteration per se. Id. at 713–14. However, it is clear that the term would impose no substantial hardship upon the nonassenting party. True, the term deprived the party of certain rights. However, for all practical purposes, the term had little effect upon the nonassenting party's economic welfare. That is, the nonassenting party still had an opportunity to prosecute or defend its interests albeit in a different forum. We thus did not discuss the hardship aspect of the term and focused solely upon whether the additional term resulted in surprise to the nonassenting party, ultimately finding that the parties' course of dealing precluded any claim of surprise.

Similarly, in Barliant, 483 N.E.2d at 1314–15, 91 Ill. Dec. at 681–82, the court recognized at the outset that a term dealing with the costs of transporting certain goods was not unreasonable in itself because of the recognized industry custom. Thus, that court likewise focused solely upon the surprise, or lack thereof, to the nonassenting party and determined that the nonassenting party had implicitly accepted the term through an established course of dealing and the existing usage of trade. As a result, both Schulze and Barliant turned almost exclusively, if not entirely, upon the element of surprise.

We are not convinced that the additional indemnification term should not be characterized as a material alteration of the parties' agreement even if we focus solely upon the element of surprise.[9] However, the indemnification clause clearly imposes an unreasonable hardship upon Northern which should not be enforced without evidence of mutual assent to that term.

Admittedly, we face a situation where the Illinois courts apparently have not addressed the issue whether an indemnification clause is a material alteration per se, although at least one court in Illinois has suggested that an indemnification clause might be unreasonable. See McCarty, 89 Ill. App. 3d 498, 44 Ill. Dec. 570, 411 N.E.2d 936. Nevertheless, under the facts and circumstances of this case, it is unmistakable that the additional term must be deemed a material alteration of the parties' agreement.

Unlike the enforcement of the arbitration clause in Schulze or the transportation clause in Barliant, we create the very real possibility that Northern will incur substantial economic hardship, which it never expressly contemplated, if we enforce the indemnification clause in issue. The indemnification clause has the same effect as a provision which disclaims or excludes various warranties ordinarily included in the sale of goods. The latter is regularly characterized as a material alteration as a matter of law, see Ill. Ann. Stat. ch. 26, para. 2–207 Comment 4 (Smith-Hurd 1963); see also Album Graphics, Inc. v. Beatrice Foods Co., 87 Ill. App. 3d 338, 347, 408 N.E.2d 1041, 1048, 42 Ill. Dec. 332, 339 (1980), and we see no reason why an indemnification clause should not be characterized likewise. See, e.g., Maxon, 497 N.E.2d at 575–80.

An indemnification clause, like a warranty disclaimer, relieves a party of otherwise well-established legal duties and obligations. Clearly, a shift in legal liability which has the effect of relieving one party of the potential for significant economic hardship and placing this burden upon another party is an important term in any contract. Thus, it is not surprising that such a term, if it is to be included in a contract, is ordinarily the subject of active negotiation between parties. We therefore do not believe that a party charged with legal duties and obligations may reasonably rely upon a boilerplate clause in a boilerplate form and a corresponding operation of law to shift substantial economic burdens from itself to a nonassenting party when it had every opportunity to negotiate such a term if it desired.

By including the indemnification clause in very small print on the back of a preprinted form, Trans-Aire in effect sought a guarantee, or warranty, that the adhesive would serve its production needs even though Northern affirmatively stated that the sale included no express warranties and actively encouraged Trans-Aire to test various samples prior to purchase to determine their usefulness, thereby negating any implied warranties. Furthermore, Trans-Aire attempted to include this term as part of the parties' bargain, without Northern's assent, even though Trans-Aire knew that some significant possibility existed that the adhesive would fail under warm weather conditions just like its functional equivalent had done. Under these circumstances, we do not believe that Trans-Aire can prevail. We therefore hold that the indemnification clause constituted a material alteration of the parties' original agreement and did not become a part of that agreement.

III. CONCLUSION

We hold that the district court correctly entered summary judgment in favor of Northern Adhesive Company, Inc. upon Trans-Aire International, Inc.'s claims for breaches of any existing implied and express warranties and for breach of contract. Trans-Aire wholly failed to offer evidence to contradict the evidence of record and the district court's legal conclusions are without error.

Trans-Aire waived any existing warranties of merchantability and of fitness for a particular purpose. Further, the record reveals that no express warranties existed. Finally, we hold that the purchase order indemnification clause materially altered the terms of the parties' agreement and failed to become a part of that contract.

The district court's decision is AFFIRMED.

Questions for Case Study 3–1
1. What are the basic facts of the case?
2. What are the most important issues in this case?
3. What is the court's decision with regard to each of the plaintiff's claims?
4. Do you agree with the court's reasoning?

Footnotes

1. Even though Illinois has amended the Illinois Commercial Code and now refers to each provision as a "paragraph" rather than as a "section," as found in the current version of the Smith-Hurd Illinois Annotated Statutes (1963), we will continue to refer to the relevant provisions as sections to facilitate ease of research and to maintain consistency with the Uniform Commercial Code.

2. Section 2–314 states:
   (1) Unless excluded or modified (Section 2–316), a warranty that the goods shall be merchantable is implied in a contract for their sale if the seller is a merchant with respect to goods of that kind. . . .
   (2) Goods to be merchantable must be at least such as. . . .
   (c) are fit for the ordinary purposes for which such goods are used; . . . . Ill. Ann. Stat. ch. 26, para. 2–314 (Smith-Hurd 1963).

3. Section 2–315 provides:
   Where the seller at the time of contracting has reason to know any particular purpose for which the goods are required and that the buyer is relying on the seller's skill or judgment to select or furnish suitable goods, there is unless excluded or modified under the next section an implied warranty that the goods shall be fit for such purpose.

4. Section 2–316(3)(b) states that:
   When the buyer before entering into the contract has examined the goods or the sample or model as fully as he desired or has refused to examine the goods there is no implied warranty with regard to defects which an examination ought in the circumstances to have revealed to him. . . . Ill. Ann. Stat. ch. 26, para. 2–316(3)(b) (Smith-Hurd 1963 & Supp. 1989).

5. The purchase of Adhesive 7448 began when Trans-Aire stated to Northern that it was experiencing problems with the 3M product which it currently was using in its van conversion process. In response, Northern supplied Trans-Aire with several different adhesive samples and "suggested that [Adhesive 7448] was the best they felt they had to offer . . . ." Trans-Aire offers no evidence to support its contention that its ultimate decision to purchase Adhesive 7448 was based upon Northern's submission of particular test samples rather than upon the results of the tests which Fribley performed and reported to Higgins.

6. Fribley's deposition testimony states: I suggested that the application that we were putting it in, that a lot of times vehicles in the south and southwest, in the summertime, Arizona, Florida, some places such as that, that when they get closed up, it gets very hot in there, particularly like dark vehicles, that—and its—in the nature of contacted [sic]—contact adhesives that they're—they will also soften with heat, and I didn't know what temperature that would occur.

7. Northern suggests that Trans-Aire could have tested the adhesive's effectiveness under warm weather conditions by placing electric heaters inside of a van, by testing a small sample of the applied adhesive in a conventional oven, or by sending samples out to an independent laboratory for testing. The ease with which at least the two former tests could have been conducted appears to undercut Trans-Aire's assertions that testing sufficient to establish the characteristics which Fribley already suspected was impossible or at least highly impractical.

8. The indemnity clause provides in part: By accepting this order, [Northern] agrees to defend, protect, and save harmless [Trans-Aire] and its vendees from all damages, claims and costs, including attorney fees, arising out of . . . (2) liability for personal injuries, death or sickness or damages to personal property which

may be sustained by or claimed by person or persons in connection with the sale or use of the products hereby purchased, based upon improper or negligent manufacturing thereof or defects in the design thereof.

9. While it is significant that the parties exchanged twelve forms containing the identical clause, it is also noteworthy that all twelve transactions occurred in a span of approximately six months. Although the record is silent as to the temporal spacing of the orders, we must acknowledge the possibility that the orders were placed in such a manner that Northern had little opportunity to recognize that Trans-Aire wished to modify their earlier understanding. Thus, the number of forms exchanged in itself may be insufficient to establish a "course of dealing." Unfortunately, Schulze offers little guidance on this particular point. However, in Barliant, the court stressed that no "surprise" occurred because the nonassenting party received "clearly marked" invoices which it paid "in full on 24 consecutive occasions over an 18-month period."

Furthermore, a course of dealing analysis is not as easily performed here as in Schulze. As discussed above, in Schulze a party attempted to enforce an arbitration clause following the delivery of unsatisfactory goods. In each of nine separate prior purchases, the goods had been satisfactory. In contrast, Trans-Aire here apparently seeks to impose liability for damages resulting from its use of adhesive received following the very first order as well as from adhesive received following its twelfth order. On these facts, it is more difficult to find that a course of dealing existed to justify enforcing the indemnification clause for the early purchases, even if we were to assume that Trans-Aire could demonstrate that such a course developed later. Fortunately, we need not decide this issue definitively for purposes of resolving this appeal.

IV

PROPERTY

The concept of property has been the subject of much discussion and debate for philosophers, writers, politicians, and other intellectuals throughout history. James Fenimore Cooper, the popular American writer, saw property as "the groundwork of moral independence"; Abraham Lincoln described it as "the fruit of labor" and "a positive good in the world"; for John Locke, the English philosopher and political theorist, it was "the reason why men enter into society"; Walter Lippmann, the highly respected American journalist, described it as "the only dependable foundation of personal liberty"; while Pierre J. Proudhon, the noted French anarchist, saw it as "theft," saying it represented the exploitation of the worker.

Philosophical and political definitions aside, property is a relatively simple concept in the eyes of the law: the right of an individual to exclusively possess, use, and dispose of anything that can be owned. Broadly speaking, there are two separate types of property: personal and real. Personal property is characterized by its portable nature; it can be carried from place to place. Furthermore, personal property can be either tangible or intangible. Tangible personal property encompasses ownership interest in things that have a physical existence and are able to be moved, or carried, from place to place. Most property falls into this category; a car, wallet, photograph, textbook, shirt, pen, and watch are all common examples of tangible personal property. Intangible personal property, on the other hand, by its very nature does not have a physical existence, but is merely a *right* that can be owned, as opposed to a real, tangible object. Common examples of intangible property include copyrights, patents, trademarks, stocks, and bonds. A person who owns 100 shares of IBM, for example, owns intangible property; her stock certificates physically exist (she can hold them in her hand), but what she really owns is a tiny percentage of IBM Corporation that the certificates merely represent—and that ownership right is intangible, since it does not have a physical existence. The same holds true for a copyright, patent, or bond; a patent, copyright, or bond certificate may be a tangible piece of paper, but the thing owned—an idea, the rights to a song or book, and the right to be repaid a certain amount of money lent to a company or municipality—has no physical existence and constitutes intangible property. Finally, real property constitutes land and all things permanently attached to it. What distinguishes real from tangible personal property is that it is by nature fixed and cannot be easily moved from one place to another. Land, buildings, and living trees are all considered real property, as are the air above land and the minerals, water, and anything contained below ground level.

The next three chapters present an overview of the law relating to personal, intangible, and real property, beginning with the most common type—personal tangible property.

15

PERSONAL PROPERTY AND BAILMENTS

Learning Objectives

After studying this chapter, you will be able to:

1. Explain the legal ramifications of buying illegally owned property.
2. List the various ways in which one can come to own personal property.
3. Describe the difference between a patent and a copyright.
4. Define lost, mislaid, and abandoned property, and explain the rights of finders of such property.
5. List the rights and obligations of bailors and bailees under a bailment contract.

Introduction

Personal property, as discussed in the introduction to Unit IV, is any object subject to ownership other than real estate or anything permanently attached to real estate. Personal property can be tangible or intangible and includes crops that have been harvested, domestic animals, and livestock. While some of the best things in life may be free, there are precious few things in life that cannot be owned. The wind, the rushing waters of a river, and the sun belong to no one since no individual or group can possess and control them; yet they can be harnessed and the energy they produce owned. For example, wind farms, hydroelectric plants, and solar energy generating stations use windmills, water-driven turbines, and huge mirrors to harness the energy from the wind, river currents, and the sun, respectively. Likewise, butterflies and lions may be born free, but they are owned if captured or killed. In this chapter, we will examine the laws relating to the acquisition and transfer of personal property, as well as the law of bailments.

Acquiring Title to Personal Property

Despite the often-repeated phrase that *possession is nine tenths of the law,* possession of personal property alone is almost never enough to give to the possessor good title, or ownership rights, to the thing possessed. The only exception is wild animals. Like the sun and the wind, wild animals are owned by no one while they are unharnessed; but merely capturing or killing a wild animal does convey an ownership interest over the animal or its carcass. A deer belongs to a hunter the moment he kills it, and a butterfly belongs to a child the moment she captures it. The only exceptions are wild animals taken without a proper license where one is required or by a poacher on another's land. In the former instance (e.g., a hunter who kills a deer out of season or without first obtaining the proper hunting license), the animal taken belongs to the state; in the latter instance, the animal belongs to the owner of the real property where it was killed if the killing was lawful or to the state if it was not. Merely being in pursuit of a wild animal does not give the pursuer a property interest in the animal until it is actually captured or killed. If a captured animal escapes its capturer, the animal regains its status as a wild animal and is not considered personal property until it is again captured or killed.

Purchase or Manufacturing

The most common means of obtaining a property interest, or title, in personal property is through its purchase. The giving of consideration, or payment, for personal property pursuant to a valid contract transfers all ownership interests from the seller to the buyer. Figure 15–1 is an example of a bill of sale for personal property. When personal property is transferred in exchange for valid consideration, the buyer obtains the same title to the property that the seller had to give. Generally, a buyer who in good faith purchases personal property that the seller has no right to dispose of obtains no ownership interest in the property.

> Steve, a thief, sells Sandra a VCR for $200. Unaware that Steve is a thief, Sandra purchases the VCR in good faith. Sandra does not obtain good title to the VCR, since she can only obtain from Steve whatever property interest was his to sell. Since Steve is a thief with no legal title to the VCR, Sandra obtains no title to it from him.

Ownership of stolen property remains with its true owner, regardless of how many times it is illegally transferred after it is stolen. The good faith of the subsequent purchasers is immaterial. In the last example, if the true owner of the VCR turns up two years after it was stolen, he would be entitled to have it returned to him. Sandra's only remedy is to sue Steve, the thief, for a refund of her purchase price.

FIGURE 15–1 **Bill of Sale for Personal Property**

BILL OF SALE PERSONAL PROPERTY 308

Know all Men by these presents

that

in consideration of

paid by

the receipt whereof is hereby acknowledged, do hereby grant, sell, transfer, and deliver unto the said

the following goods and chattels, namely:

To have and to hold all and singular the said goods and chattels to the said

and

executors, administrators, and assigns to their own use and behoof forever.

And   hereby covenant with the grantee   that   the lawful owner   of the said goods and chattels; that they are free from all encumbrances,

that   have good right to sell the same as aforesaid; and that   will warrant and defend the same against the lawful claims and demands of all persons,

In witness whereof   the said

hereunto set   hand   and seal   this   day of

in the year one thousand nine hundred and

Signed and sealed in the presence of

_____

_____   }   _____

_____   _____

There is another way to obtain title to personal property other than through its legal purchase. A person who creates or manufactures personal property has an interest in that particular property. A writer owns his work as soon as she sets it down on paper or otherwise permanently stores it (e.g., saves it onto a hard disk or a floppy disk using her word processor), and a sculptor owns his sculpture as soon as he creates it. The very act of creation transfers a property interest in the thing created to its creator, who may then dispose of it at will.

Patents, Copyrights, and Trademarks

A *patent* gives an inventor the exclusive right to profit from her invention for 17 years. An inventor wishing to reserve the right to exclusively use his invention needs to apply for a patent to the Patent and Trademark Office. To be issued a patent, the inventor needs to show that the invention is novel, useful, and substantially different from any other existing patented invention. Although most inventions concern some type of physical object or new machine (such as the proverbial "better mousetrap"), it is also possible to patent new chemical compositions of matter (e.g., a better dish-washing detergent), new plants, and even genetically engineered organisms, such as oil-eating bacteria. After the 17-year period, the inventor's right to exclusively use, license, sell, or give away the right to use his invention ends; the invention then becomes part of the *public domain,* and anyone may use it without the inventor's permission or having to pay her royalties. To extend a patent beyond the 17 years, an inventor must reapply for a new patent, which the patent office will issue only if significant improvements to the invention warrant it.

A *copyright,* like a patent, gives its holder the exclusive right to use the copyrighted material throughout the author's life and continues for 50 years after her death. Under the U.S. Copyright Act of 1976, an author automatically obtains a copyright to work as soon as it is produced, whether or not he formally submits it to the U.S. Copyright Office for copyright protection. To come under copyright protection, new work must contain the word *copyright* or the letter *c,* followed by the year the work was first produced and the author's name. Artistic, literary, and musical works are all copyrightable, along with other works that involve artistic expression and effort. Songs, music, books, poems, magazine articles, paintings, movies, photographs, and computer software are some of the works that may be copyrighted. Upon the expiration of the copyright period, the work is considered to be in the public domain and may be used by anyone without the permission of the author or her heirs.

Modern technology such as photocopy machines, audio and video tape recorders, computer scanners, cameras, and computers make it easy to copy and use copyrighted material. In part as recognition of the realities of the new technology, the 1976 Copyright Act allows a limited right to use copyrighted material without the owner's consent under certain circumstances: under the *Fair Use Doctrine*, individuals may for their own use copy parts of copyrighted materials that they own, as long as these are not sold or given to others. Thus, an individual may copy a record he owns onto a cassette tape, as long he uses the tape himself. But copying a record, CD, or tape onto another tape to sell or give it as a gift to another clearly violates copyright laws, and anyone doing so is liable for both criminal and civil penalties. The Fair Use Doctrine does, however, allow copying limited parts of a copyrighted work for nonprofit educational or research purposes. Therefore, a college professor may copy several pages from a textbook to distribute to his class as a learning tool; but he may not copy a substantial portion of the book and likewise distribute it. In weighing whether a specific use of copyrighted material is permissible, courts look at the purpose of the use, the extent of unauthorized use, and the potential for harm to the copyright holder. Thus, copying a poem from a book of copyrighted poetry for classroom use is allowed, but copying an entire chapter is probably not; while copying the entire book definitely constitutes copyright infringement that would subject the professor to civil and criminal penalties, notwithstanding the educational and nonprofit use involved.

A *trademark* is any symbol, graphic image, word, or name attached to a manufacturer's product to distinguish it from other similar products on the market. The most common trademark is a product's name. Thus, Coca-Cola and Coke are trademarks of the Coca-Cola Company. To protect a name, slogan, or other distinctive mark attached to a product, the company must register it with the U.S. Patent and Trademark Office. To obtain trademark protection, the name or symbol must be unique and not a generic term. Thus, while *Coke* is a registered trademark, the word *cola* cannot be registered as a trademark, since it is a generic name. A company can protect its trademark from infringement by any other company; and infringement can occur even when the actual name is not used, if the name or style of presentation is too close to the protected trademark. A soft drink called *Koke*, for example, was deemed to violate the Coca-Cola Company's trademark, and you can bet that *Cola-Coca* would also be deemed a violation—especially if the distinctive script of the Coca-Cola Company's trademark were also used. But *Caren's Cola* would not be an infringement (unless she also referred to it as *The Real Thing* or closely matched the script of the Coca-Cola Company's trademark.)

Gifts

The giving of a *gift* effectively transfers the ownership interest from the giver to the receiver. As with any transfer of interest, the receiver of the gift will only get whatever ownership interest the giver actually has in the gift. Thus, a thief can no more transfer good title by a gift than she could by the sale of the stolen property.

A gift is characterized as a transfer of property made out of "detached, disinterested generosity," and the receiver need not give consideration for the transfer to be valid. (If consideration is given, the transfer is a sale, not a gift.) For a gift to be effective, three elements must be present:

1. Donative intent by the giver.
2. Delivery to the receiver.
3. Acceptance by the receiver.

Donative Intent.   The requirement of donative intent mandates that the giver (otherwise known as donor) intended to make a gift and was motivated by detached, disinterested generosity. A gift made with the purpose of obtaining something in return does not meet the donative intent requirement. Also, a donor must have the mental capacity to formulate the donative intent; a gift made by a mentally incompetent person, for example, is invalid.

▶   Martha Schmidt, vice president of sales for ABC Corporation, is given a
$100,000 bonus at the end of the year by the company. The bonus is accompanied by a letter that reads in part, "The board of directors of ABC Corporation has voted to give you a gift of $100,000 to reward you for an exceptional year in which you've managed to break all of our previous sales records." Martha accepts the gift and fails to report it as income for tax purposes, claiming that it was a gift by ABC Company to her and, as such, is not taxable. (True gifts are not taxable by the federal, state, and local governments to the recipient, because they are not deemed to be income. Gift taxes are currently payable by the donor of the gift if it is for more than $10,000 per year to a single person, but the proceeds of the gift are not taxable to the donee regardless of the amount.) Does the $100,000 payment constitute a gift? In cases such as this, the Internal Revenue Service has always held that the donor lacked the donative intent to make a valid gift, since it was not made out of detached, disinterested generosity, but rather for business reasons (e.g., hoping that the donee would work just as hard in the future or stay with the company). Federal courts have always upheld such rulings by the IRS.

Delivery.   For a gift to be valid, the donor must deliver it to the donee. For the delivery to be effective, the donor must give up complete dominion and control over the subject matter of the gift. As long as the donor retains either the items themselves or the right to regain possession of the items given away, the gift is invalid. If the goods are not in the possession of the donor, any act that makes it clear that the donor is relinquishing all possession over the goods to the donee will suffice as a delivery. If, for example, the donor gives a safety deposit box to the donee and instructs her to take the gift from it, the delivery of the key itself will be deemed as a constructive delivery of the item in the safety deposit box.

Acceptance.   Finally, the donee must accept a gift before it becomes effective. One cannot be forced to accept a gift; he must indicate his willingness to accept it either through words or actions before it is effective. Assuming that the donative intent and delivery requirements are met, as soon as the donee indicates acceptance, the property interest of the donor in the gift are transferred to him. The donor is free to change her mind at any time until the donee accepts the gift; once acceptance is effective, the gift becomes irrevocable and the donee's property interest in it absolute (assuming, once again, that the donor had a valid interest to transfer).

Gifts Made in Contemplation of Death.   A gift made in contemplation of death, otherwise known as a *gift causa mortis,* is one in which the donor makes the gift while under an immediate and present fear of death. While such a gift is valid, the donor may revoke it if she does not die of the expected cause of death at the time the gift was made. When gifts causa mortis are involved, the same requirements as for regular *inter vivos* gifts, or gifts between the living, apply: donative intent, delivery, and acceptance must be present, and delivery must be made directly to the donee.

➤   1. Helen, on the eve of her departure for the Persian Gulf, gives her entertainment system to her sister, Clara, telling her, "I want you to have this, since I'm sure Operation Desert Shield is going to turn into a long, ugly war, and I don't think I'll come back home alive." Fortunately, Operation Desert Storm turns out to be a relatively brief conflict with fortuitously few Allied casualties. As soon as Helen returns home, she is entitled to have her entertainment system returned to her, since she has survived the event she feared would cause her death, and the gift is thus revoked.

   2. Harvey is diagnosed as having incurable stomach cancer and is told he has only days to live. He calls all of his friends and loved ones to his bedside and gives each one a gift of personal property. The next day, his doctor informs him that there was a mixup in X-rays and that he is fine. All gifts are automatically revoked and Harvey is entitled to their return.

   3. In the above example, assume that Harvey is so angered by his doctor's incompetence that he suffers a massive stroke and dies. The gifts would still be automatically revoked, because Harvey's death, although right on schedule, was not caused by the reason

he feared at the time he made the gifts; he did not die of that which he dreaded—stomach cancer—but something he was completely oblivious to—the incompetence of his physician.

Lost, Mislaid, and Abandoned Property

It is a popular misconception that the finder of lost or mislaid property acquires title to it, as if title to property were somehow forfeited through a person's carelessness in losing an object or inadvertently leaving it behind. In fact, the title to lost or *mislaid* property (property intentionally placed somewhere by its owner and then inadvertently forgotten) remains with the owner, who may claim it at any time, subject to some limitations outlined below. If an owner abandons his property, anyone may acquire title to it by merely taking possession of it. For property to be abandoned, its true owner must have intentionally relinquished all claim to it. Placing an old television set at the curbside next to full garbage pails would constitute abandonment of the set, and any passerby who took possession of it would become its new owner.

Many jurisdictions have enacted legislation dealing with how one acquires title to lost or mislaid property. In New York State, the issue is dealt with in Article 7–B of the Personal Property Law. Under the statute, the finder of lost or mislaid property must take the following steps, depending on its value:

1. Property worth less than $10: The finder must make a reasonable effort to find the owner of the property and restore it to him. If unsuccessful in finding the owner, title vests in the finder one year from the date the property was found.
2. Property worth $10 or more and commercial paper: The finder must find the owner within 10 days or turn over the property to the local police. The police are then charged with making reasonable efforts to find the property's true owner. If they cannot find the owner and if the property is not claimed within the following statutory periods, title will vest in the finder:
   a. For property worth less than $100, in three months.
   b. For property worth $100 to $500, six months.
   c. For property worth $500 to $5,000, one year.
   d. For property worth more than $5,000, three years.

Finally, title to any personal property—regardless of how acquired—will rest with the person who has it in her possession after the statute of limitations for bringing an action to recover the property has run out. (The only way to know the applicable statute of limitations in a given jurisdiction is to consult the applicable statute, such as the New York example just quoted.) Consider the following example:

> Harry notices that Martha has inadvertently dropped an expensive camera as she attempted to cross a busy intersection. He takes possession of the camera but does not return it to Martha. His state requires that found goods be turned over to the police 10 days from the time they are found if they have a value in excess of $10. Harry is aware of the law but chooses to ignore it and wait, since he also knows that the statute of limitations for bringing an action for conversion in his state is four years and that Martha will not be able to sue him to return her camera after that time. If Martha does not demand that Harry return her camera within the four-year period that her state's statute of limitations allows, title in the camera will vest in Harry through adverse possession, after which time neither Martha nor anyone else will be able to claim the camera from him. (Harry may, however, be tried for larceny if the statute of limitations has not run for that crime.)

The above result may seem unfair, but the law requires that parties take some affirmative steps to protect their own rights and that legal actions be brought in a timely fashion to weed out stale claims from an already overtaxed legal system. (For a further discussion of adverse possession relating to real property, see Chapter 17.)

Accession

Another circumstance that affects ownership of title is accession. *Accession* is the increasing of the value of property by the addition of new material or by expending labor in its improvement. When accession occurs to property not owned by the person who adds value to it, a problem arises as to who should have title. In most jurisdictions, who will benefit from accession depends on the circumstances. In every jurisdiction, accession by a willful trespasser gives the trespasser no property interest in or claim to the property, regardless of the amount of money, time, or labor expended in improving it. If a thief steals an automobile and then spends thousands of dollars to bring it up to perfect operating condition, the automobile will still belong to its true owner. It will make no difference whatsoever if the thief stole a junk heap and turned it into a terrific cream puff. The owner will be entitled to have his car returned to him and benefit from all improvements made on it without having to reimburse the thief for any of his expenses.

A more difficult problem arises when accession is made by an innocent trespasser (one who took the property in good faith, not realizing it belonged to another). In such circumstances, the courts will weigh the reasonableness of the trespasser's conduct and the value added to the personal property through her efforts in determining what remedy to award the true owner. If the innocent trespasses completely transformed the property, courts will generally allow her to keep the property but require her to compensate the true owner for its original, unimproved value. If the innocent trespasser's improvements are minor and have not transformed the property, the true owner is entitled to its return and need not compensate the trespasser for her efforts. The true owner is also entitled to sue for incidental and consequential damages caused by the trespass. Consider the following example:

> Charles, while walking home from work, notices an old bicycle lying by the side of the road, near some garbage cans. He thinks the bicycle has been abandoned by its owner and happily takes it home with him. During the next two months, he painstakingly restores it to better than new condition after expending considerable time and some money to replace worn parts. Through his work, the bicycle is transformed from an old, nearly worthless clunker to a wonderful, customized bicycle worth several hundred dollars. The first time he takes it for a ride, its true owner recognizes it and demands that Charles return it to him. Assuming the owner can convince the trier of facts that he never intended to abandon the bicycle but merely set it down for a minute near the curb, will he be entitled to its return? Most courts would hold that he is not. Charles is not a wrongdoer (e.g., willful trespasser), but rather an innocent trespasser who acted in a reasonable manner under the circumstances in taking the seemingly abandoned, worthless bike. His efforts have greatly increased the bike's value, and it would be inequitable to allow the owner, who contributed to Charles's mistake, to profit from his efforts. What the owner is entitled to is the reasonable value of the bicycle before Charles's improvements.

Bailments

Until now, we've been discussing the various means through which title, or ownership, to personal property can be acquired. There are many instances, however, when we find ourselves temporarily entrusted with the property of another. If your friend asks you to take care of her dog for the weekend, or if you borrow her binoculars to go to the ball game, you are temporarily entrusted with her property (the dog and binoculars), even though you clearly do not own it, and your rights and responsibilities with regard to that personal property will be determined by the law of bailments. A *bailment* is a legal relationship that arises out of the temporary transfer of the possession of personal property by one person to another for a specific purpose, with the understanding that the property is to be returned at some future time or otherwise disposed of. The person who entrusts his property into the care of another is called the *bailor,* and the person entrusted with the property of another is called the *bailee.* We all enter into bailments all the time, whether we are aware of it or not. The following are all common examples of bailments:

> 1. Susan leaves her car in a parking garage, agreeing to pick it up two hours later and pay the parking attendant $10.95. (Susan is the bailor and the parking garage is the bailee.)

2. Cathy asks Jane to hold her pocketbook and coat for her while she goes to the restroom. (Cathy is the bailor and Jane the bailee.)

3. Sam borrows a camcorder from Sandra and agrees to return it unharmed in two days. (Sam is the bailee and Sandra the bailor.)

Types of Bailments

There are basically three types of bailments: bailment for the sole benefit of the bailor, bailment for the sole benefit of the bailee, and mutual benefit bailment.

Bailment for the Sole Benefit of the Bailor.   This is a gratuitous bailment in which the bailor entrusts her property with the bailee solely for her benefit without compensation. Example 2 above, where Cathy asks Jane to hold her pocketbook and coat while she goes to the restroom, is an example of a bailment for the sole benefit of the bailor. The only person who receives a benefit under the arrangement is Cathy, the bailor.

Bailment for the Sole Benefit of the Bailee.   This is a bailment in which the person entrusted with the bailor's property is the only one to reap a benefit from the arrangement. Example 3 above illustrates this type of bailment: Sam, the bailee, is the only one to benefit from borrowing Sandra's camcorder.

Mutual Benefit Bailment.   This is a bailment where both the bailor and bailee receive some tangible benefit. Example 1 above illustrates this type of arrangement: Susan receives the benefit of being able to park her car, and the garage gets $10.95 from Susan for accepting the bailment of her car.

Bailor's and Bailee's Rights and Duties

Bailee's Rights.   The bailee has the exclusive right to possession of the bailed goods in accordance with the provisions of the bailment contract, along with the right to use the goods if that right is part of the bailment agreement. Unauthorized use of bailed goods can lead to liability for the tort of conversion if the goods are injured in any way because of the unauthorized use.

> Mark asks Sandra to take care of his motorcycle while he goes on a trip. He does not allow her the right to ride it or otherwise use it. She agrees to look after it. If Sandra sells the bike while Mark is gone, she is clearly guilty of conversion, but she is also liable to him for any unauthorized use. Thus, if she rides it without his permission, rents it out to others, or

allows harm to come to it by her direct action or negligence, she will be liable to him for damages in tort (negligence, trespass to personal property, or conversion).

Bailee's Duties.   The bailee has the duty to exercise due care with regard to the bailed goods. At common law, the duty of care owed by the bailee depended on the type of bailment, with slight care being owed for gratuitous bailments for the sole benefit of the bailor, moderate care for mutual benefit bailments, and great care for bailments for the sole benefit of the bailee. The modern rule is to simply apply a standard of reasonable care and to take into account the relative benefit to the parties in determining what care is appropriate under the circumstances.

Bailor's Rights.   The bailor has the right to expect the bailee to faithfully discharge her duties under the bailment contract; he can sue the bailee under a theory breach of contract or torts if the bailee fails to observe her responsibilities. Tort theories under which the bailor can bring suit include conversion, negligence, and replevin to recover the bailed goods. Consider the following brief examples:

1. Jane asks Bill to look after her pet turtle while she goes on vacation for a week. When Jane returns, she learns Bill has made turtle soup of her turtle. She can sue for conversion.
2. If, upon her return, Jane learns the turtle was injured by Bill's dog and requires extensive medical care, she can sue for negligence (assuming she can show Bill failed to exercise due care in keeping the dog away from the turtle).
3. If, upon her return, Jane finds Bill has fallen in love with the turtle and refuses to return it, she can sue for conversion (for its price) or replevin (to have it returned to her).

Bailor's Duties.   The bailor has the duty to compensate the bailee in all but gratuitous bailments and must reimburse him for all expenses reasonably necessary to carry out the bailment. If, for example, Jane's turtle in the last example falls ill while in Bill's care through no fault of his, she must reimburse him for any reasonable medical expenses he has incurred in caring for the animal. Likewise, she must reimburse him for the reasonable cost of feeding the turtle if he demands it.

Constructive Bailments

There are situations in which the law implies a bailment, even when one does not exist by the consent of the parties. A common example is that of the finder of lost or mislaid property. Even though no actual bailment exists, since the bailor did not entrust the property to the bailee or deliver it into his care, the law treats the finder of such property as an involuntary bailee. As such, the finder of mislaid or lost property must take reasonable care of the property until the true owner is found, he turns it over to the police, or the statute of limitations runs out, whichever comes first.

Disclaimers of Responsibility

In general, bailees may exempt themselves of all liability from harm that may come to bailed property, as long as they give proper notice to bailors. Conspicuously posted signs to the effect that bailees are not responsible for theft or damage to bailed property in their care, as well as standard form liability waivers printed on the back of parking receipts, have generally been upheld by the courts as valid. There are exceptions, however; courts generally do not like exculpatory clauses—particularly in adhesion contracts (preprinted, fine-print form contracts that a consumer must either accept or reject in its entirety and that are not framed as a result of bargaining between the offeror and offeree). Courts will weigh factors such as the consideration charged by the bailee for the bailment and the extent of its negligence in determining the reasonableness of such exculpatory clauses. In addition, most jurisdictions will not allow liability waivers that seek to exculpate a bailee from the negligence of its own employees.

Judge for Yourself

Case 1. Tom, Dick, and Harriet go big-game hunting for bear in the Adirondacks. Tom spots a bear first and yells, "He's mine!" Dick begins chasing the bear, hoping to capture it alive (doubtless being the dumbest of the three), and Harriet shoots the bear, killing it just as Dick was about to jump it from behind.

  a. To whom does the bear belong?
  b. If Dick had reached the bear just before Harriet shoots it and been torn to shreds trying to convince it to "come along peacefully," to whom does the bear belong (assume Dick's executor claims the bear should be part of Dick's estate)?
  c. Assume that Dick shoots the bear and takes possession of the carcass, and further assume that the bear was taken on land belonging to farmer Jones, without Jones's permission. Who owns the bear?
  d. Assume that Dick shoots the bear and takes possession of it but only has a small-game license that does not legally allow him to hunt bears in New York State. Who owns the bear?
  e. Assume that noone shoots a bear and that in anger all three decide to go by the Bronx Zoo on their way home and bag a real trophy. If the three shoot a lion, a tiger, and an elephant, respectively, at the zoo, who owns the animals?

Case 2. Cindy finds a block of wood near the entrance to an apartment house. She believes one of the residents must have abandoned it there. She takes the wood and sculpts a masterful Don Quixote astride his tired steed, charging at a windmill. As soon as she finished the final touches on her sculpture, the owner of the wood comes knocking at her door demanding to know why she took his firewood. When he sees what she has transformed it into, he demands that she turn over the sculpture.

   a. Assuming that Cindy is an innocent trespasser, will she have to turn over the sculpture? Why?

   b. What remedy is the owner of the wood entitled to?

   c. Assume that Cindy, an unemployed artist, took the wood knowing it belonged to somebody else and hoping to be able to pay for it later if she sold the sculpture she would make from it. Is the original owner entitled to have the sculpture? Why?

Case 3. Rodney borrows Sue Ellen's business law notes to study for a quiz.

   a. What type of bailment is involved?

   b. At common law, what duty of care does Rodney have with regard to the notes?

   c. What duty of care must Rodney exercise under the modern rule?

Case 4. Marge rents a car from the ZYX Rental Co. The rental agreement states that Marge may use the automobile for 24 hours anywhere within the state of New York but that she cannot take the car out of the state due to insurance regulations.

   a. What type of bailment is this?

   b. If Marge drives to Connecticut and gets into an accident with a hit-and-run driver, will she be liable for the damages to the rental company? If so, under what theory or theories may the rental company sue her?

   c. Marge parks in a New York City garage and is given a ticket that has a liability waiver printed on its back in small but legible type. Is the waiver effective to protect the garage against vandalism to her car performed by third parties not connected with the garage?

   d. Will the liability waiver insulate the garage from having to pay damages for vandalism performed by its own employees?

16

REAL PROPERTY

Learning Objectives

After studying this chapter, you will be able to:

1. List the types of concurrent ownership and describe how they differ.
2. Describe the major differences between the traditional fee simple ownership and owning a cooperative, condominium, or time-share.
3. List and define the major types of easements.
4. Define and distinguish between easements, licenses, and profits.
5. Define adverse possession and explain how it can be used to obtain title to real estate and easements by prescription.

Introduction

Real property, or real estate, consists of land, everything permanently attached to the land (such as buildings, trees, and fixtures), and the air space above and the contents of the soil beneath it. What distinguishes real property from personal property is that the former is fixed and unmovable, while the latter is portable, or capable of being moved.

At common law, the owner of real estate was deemed to own not just the land and everything permanently attached to it (including buildings, timber, and growing crops), but also the air rights above the land all the way to the heavens and the mineral rights below to the center of the earth. A problem arose as to air rights with the advent of air travel: if a person owns the space above his land all the way to the heavens, then a dirigible flying hundreds of feet above it is trespassing, as is a jet flying at 30,000 feet or a satellite in orbit several miles above the land. Fortunately, the law is ever flexible, and the traditional common law definition of air rights was adjusted to conform with the modern realities of air travel. Today, local land-use ordinances determine how far above one's land a structure may be built. Therefore, if a jurisdiction states that air rights extend 30 feet above the surface of the land, a plane flying 1,000 feet above it is not trespassing; but a person throwing a stone or firing a bullet 29 feet over the land would be guilty of trespass.

Subsurface rights have not been modified from the traditional common law definition, and landowners today still technically own the space below their land to the center of the earth. What about underground travel? Does an urban subway system trespass on property owners' subsurface rights? Yes; but the government can, by its power of *eminent domain,* condemn any property for public use and pay its owner the reasonable value of such property. If a municipality wishes to build a subway system that passes below private property, it can condemn the subsurface rights to such property and compensate its owner appropriately.

Possessory Interests in Land

Estates in land give the owner varying degrees of possessory interests in the land she owns. These range from the total ownership right of *fee simple absolute,* which gives the owner the complete right to use and dispose of the land as she sees fit forever, to a variety of qualified interests in land that represent less than complete, perpetual ownership. The more common estates in land, also known as *freehold estates,* are briefly discussed below.

Fee Simple

Fee simple ownership is the most complete ownership right recognized by law. The owner of a fee simple interest in realty has the absolute right to dispose of the property forever; he may use the property, destroy it, give it away, sell it, or otherwise dispose of it in any way he wishes during his lifetime, or, upon his death, bequeath it to his heirs who will likewise inherit the absolute right to use or transfer the property at will forever.

Life Estate

A life estate is an ownership interest in realty that lasts only for a person's lifetime. The owner of a life estate, called a *life tenant,* has many, but not all, of the rights of a fee simple owner during her lifetime. Since the life estate is necessarily temporary, the owner may not sell the property outright, but she may sell what possessory interest she has in it; she can transfer to any third party the right to use and occupy the land during her lifetime. Likewise, because the estate is temporary, she must take steps not to destroy its value for the person or persons who will receive the land after her death. The life tenant has the right to enjoy the ordinary uses of the land and to receive ordinary profits from the land during her lifetime. But if she does anything that injures the interest of persons who will receive the land after her death, she will be guilty of *waste* and be liable for damages to the person or persons who own the future interest in the land. For example, a life tenant may cut down trees in the land to make firewood for his own use or to use as timber for improvements to the land, but he may not sell all the trees to a mill for a profit. Likewise, he may use water and minerals contained on or below the surface of the land, but he may not remove the same in such large quantities so that it infringes on the rights of the future owners of the land. Consider the following example:

> ➤ Harry owns both an oil field and a gold mine. He deeds to his two children, Charlie and Sally, the oil field and gold mine, respectively, for their lives, with the remainder of the property to go to UNICEF, his favorite charity. Throughout the past 10 years, the oil field has produced 1,000 barrels of oil per day, and the gold mine has produced approximately 1,000 ounces of gold per year. Charlie and Sally may continue to extract 1,000 barrels of oil per day and 1,000 ounces of gold per year for their own use. If they decide to greatly increase the output during their lifetime by, for example, strip mining and sinking new wells, they will be guilty of waste and will be liable for damages to the future owner of the land—UNICEF. UNICEF will also be able to seek an injunction to stop Charlie and Sally from committing waste if it learns of their plans in time; otherwise, it can sue them for damages.

In addition to refraining from committing waste on the property, the life tenant must pay taxes on it during his lifetime. He must also make repairs to structures on the land to the extent of any income he receives from it or, if none is received, to the extent of the reasonable rental value of the land.

Concurrent Ownership

Property—both real and personal—may be owned by a single person or by two or more people. When it is owned by more than one person, it is said to be owned concurrently. Fee simple and life estates are subject to three types of concurrent ownership: tenancy in common, joint tenancy, and tenancy by the entirety.

Tenancy in Common

In tenancy in common, each tenant owns a proportionate interest in the land. Each tenant in common shares the right to possess and use the land equally with every other tenant in common of the same land; in addition, each can transfer his right in the land to anyone else during his lifetime or by will upon his death.

➤ Tom, Dick, and Harriet decide to pool their resources to purchase a home. Tom provides 80 percent of the financing, Harriet 19 percent, and Dick 1 percent. The deed lists Tom as owning an 80 percent interest in the property, Harriet a 19 percent interest, and Dick a 1 percent interest. Despite their unequal ownership rights, each one has an equal right to possess the entire property as long as the tenancy in common is maintained and to transfer their interest to any third party, who would have the same right.

The above example illustrates two potential problems with all types of joint ownership. First, even though the ownership interest of each party may be unequal, each enjoys an equal right to use and occupy the land. This means that Dick, with his 1 percent ownership interest, has the same privileges with respect to occupying all of the property as do Tom and Harriet. Even more problematic is each owner's right to freely transfer his or her share to any third party. If Dick falls out with Tom and Harriet, he would be able to give away his 1 percent interest in the property to Charles Manson, should he be paroled at some point in the next century. This would leave Tom and Harriet, who together own 99 percent of the house, having to share the same equally with good old Charlie! For this reason, most purchasers of real estate under some type of concurrent ownership arrangement execute a separate contract specifying what portions of the property each will be entitled to use, limiting the transfer of the property to third parties without the approval of the other tenants, and giving these the right of first refusal with regard to purchasing any tenant's share in the property for the same price offered by an outside party.

Joint Tenancy

Joint tenancy is the same as tenancy in common with one important addition: the right of survivorship. Joint tenants own property under the same conditions as tenants in common, but when one dies, the survivors automatically absorb his ownership interest. The deceased joint tenant's share automatically passes to the surviving joint tenant(s) and cannot be disposed of through a provision in the decedent's will.

➤ Darren and Darlene own property as joint tenants, with each holding a 50 percent interest. Darlene dies, leaving a provision in her will that her share of the property is to pass to Patty, her daughter. Darren will automatically become the owner of the entire property upon Darlene's death, and the testamentary provision will have no effect, since the realty will not be part of Darlene's estate.

Tenancy by the Entirety

Tenancy by the entirety is a form of joint tenancy reserved for property owned by husbands and wives. Fewer than half the states recognize this form of tenancy. The main difference between tenancy by the entirety and joint tenancy is that property owned by a husband and wife cannot be transferred without both spouses' consent. As with joint tenancy, the survivor automatically becomes the sole owner of the whole property upon the spouse's death. In states that recognize tenancy by the entirety, such as New York, when a husband and wife purchase real estate jointly, it is presumed to be as tenants by the entirety unless the deed specifically states otherwise.

Owners of property as tenants in common or joint tenants each have the right to petition a court to partition the land at any time. If the land in question is unimproved, a court can partition it by dividing it into separate parcels in an equitable manner, with each parcel reflecting the ownership interest of each tenant in the whole land. For example, if two joint tenants own equal shares in 10 acres, a court can divide the land into two equal parcels of 5 acres and give each owner a deed to his own parcel. When it is impractical to subdivide the land (e.g., a one-family home owned by three people), a court can order the sale of the property and the equitable division of the proceeds among the tenants. The partitioning can be voluntary when all owners agree to it, or involuntary when one or more of them do not want the partition to be made. Any individual owner has the right to have the land partitioned at any time, regardless of the wishes of her co-tenants.

Nonpossessory Interests in Land

There are essentially four nonpossessory, or nonfreehold, interests in land that give its holder the right to use and occupy land but no ownership interest in it. These are term tenancy, periodic tenancy, tenancy at will, and tenancy at suffrance.

Term Tenancy

An estate for years, also known as a tenancy for years, arises out of a contractual agreement in which the landowner gives the tenant the right to occupy and use the realty for a set period, or *term,* in exchange for a given consideration such as rent. The term of the tenancy can last for any given period, usually one or more years. The most common example of a term tenancy is a one- or two-year apartment lease. An agreement to lease real property does not transfer an interest in property within the meaning of the statute of frauds; a lease, therefore, need not be in writing to be binding if it is to last for less than one year. A lease of real estate for one year or more needs to be in writing to satisfy the statute of frauds since it is a contract that cannot be performed within one year.

Periodic Tenancy

A periodic tenancy, also known as a tenancy from term to term, continues for a specified period, at the end of which it is automatically renewed unless either the owner or tenant gives proper notice of his wish to terminate the tenancy. The most common example of this type of tenancy is a month-to-month tenancy of an apartment or a home. A tenant agrees to pay $550 rent the first of each month. At the end of the month, the tenancy is automatically extended unless either the landlord or the tenant has given the other party one month's notice to discontinue it. A term tenancy can become a periodic tenancy if the tenant pays and the landlord accepts the regular monthly rent at the expiration of the term stated in the lease. For example:

> Beth signs a two-year lease running from January 1992 through December 1993. In January 1994, her lease has expired, but she stays on and tenders to the landlord the usual monthly rent. At that time, she has entered into a periodic tenancy—one that will run from month to month until either she or the landlord give one another one month's notice that they wish to end the arrangement.

Tenancy at Will

A tenancy at will is one that either the landlord or tenant can terminate at any time without previous notice. Unless there is a specific understanding between the parties that they intend to enter into a tenancy at will, a periodic tenancy is assumed to exist. Therefore, if a tenant moves into an apartment and begins paying rent on a monthly basis, a month-to-month periodic tenancy will be presumed unless there is a specific agreement between the parties for a tenancy at will.

Tenancy at Suffrance

A tenancy at suffrance comes into existence when a tenant lawfully in possession of rented property under a tenancy at will, periodic tenancy, or term tenancy remains in possession of the property without the landlord's consent at the expiration of the tenancy. Such a tenant is, in fact, a trespasser and becomes liable to the landlord for the market value of the rental property over the period that he occupies it pending eviction proceedings.

Rights and Responsibilities of Landlords and Tenants

Tenant's Rights

During his tenancy, a tenant is entitled to occupy property that is habitable and free from unreasonable dangerous defects. Most states, either through legislation or court decision, provide some measure of protection to tenants who are denied essential services by landlords or whose rental property has become uninhabitable due to the landlord's unwillingness to make necessary repairs. In addition, all landlords make an implied *covenant of quiet enjoyment* to tenants, through which they warrant that the tenant will be allowed to enjoy the rented property free from outside interference preventable by the landlord. A tenant can treat a landlord's unwillingness to provide essential services or make necessary repairs, or any other condition within the landlord's power that prevents her from peacefully enjoying the rented property, as *constructive eviction* and a breach of the lease. To sue the landlord for damages, the tenant must give the landlord timely notification of the defect and a reasonable opportunity to cure it; if the landlord does not cure the defect within a reasonable time after being notified of its existence, the tenant is entitled to leave the premises and sue for constructive eviction. If the tenant does not leave the premises, however, he is deemed to have waived his right to do so and will not be able to sue the landlord for damages. In addition, the acts that the tenant claims constitute constructive eviction by making the premises uninhabitable must be caused by the landlord, not by third parties over which the latter has no control. If, for example, a landlord refuses to fix a badly leaking roof or fails to provide heat or hot water after being duly notified, he is guilty of constructive eviction. But if a water main break in the street causes the rental premises to be without heat or hot water until the city fixes the problem, the landlord is not responsible for the condition and the lack of heat or hot water will not constitute a constructive eviction.

The tenant, if he doesn't agree to the contrary, has the right to assign or sublease the leased premises. An *assignment* of the premises occurs when a tenant transfers all of her rights and responsibilities in the rental property to a third party; a *sublease* occurs when a tenant leases only a part of the rental property to a third party, or the entire rental property but for only a part of the lease period:

➤ 1. Alejandro assigns the remaining year of his two-year lease to Alissa, who will take over the property and inhabit it until the end of the lease period and make the monthly payments directly to the landlord. This is an assignment.

2. Alejandro agrees to allow Alissa to inhabit his apartment for two months, while he is on vacation, in return for her paying him $1,000. This is a sublease.

Most landlords are understandably leery of assignments and subleases, since they have no control over the tenant's selection of the assignees or sublessees. For this reason, most written leases contain clauses specifically prohibiting assignment or subleasing without the landlord's express consent.

Tenant's Responsibilities

A tenant is responsible for payment of rent when due, and a failure to do so is a breach of the lease and grounds for eviction. A tenant is also responsible for making minor repairs to the rental property, including unstopping clogged sinks or changing a leaky washer. Major structural repairs are, of course, the landlord's responsibility. Major repairs, such as fixing broken plumbing inside a wall, repairing a leaky roof, or waterproofing a leaky basement, would all be the landlord's responsibility. Where additional restrictions on the tenant's conduct are specified in a lease, the tenant must abide by them.

Landlord's Rights

The landlord's principal right under a rental agreement is the collection of the agreed-upon rent on a periodic basis. A tenant who fails to pay his rent on time is in breach of the tenancy agreement and can be evicted by the landlord. In addition, the landlord can expect the tenant to return the leased property in the same condition that she occupied it, minus acceptable wear and tear. The landlord also has the right to expect the tenant to make minor repairs to the rental property as necessary and can sue for waste if the tenant's neglect to do so results in damage to the rented property. Finally, the landlord has the right to expect the tenant to notify her of any major damage to the property requiring her attention, when she would not otherwise discover the damage herself. If the roof leaks, for example, the tenant must notify the landlord immediately so she can get it fixed. If the tenant fails to notify the landlord and greater damage ensues, the tenant will be liable for the damage to the extent that a timely notification would have avoided it. The landlord can reserve to herself additional rights or place on the tenant additional duties pursuant to specific provisions in a lease.

Landlord's Responsibilities

At common law, *caveat emptor* (let the buyer beware) was a term that very much applied to tenants of rental property, since the landlord was under no obligation to provide safe or even habitable premises to the tenant. Today, however, there is a growing trend to hold landlords accountable for providing safe, habitable premises for tenants. In most jurisdictions, a landlord has a duty to exercise reasonable care with respect to residential tenants. Injuries suffered by tenants as a result of a landlord's negligence in correcting any dangerous condition can lead to liability. Landlords can be held responsible for tenants' injuries even arising from the criminal acts of others, such as muggings and rapes, that might have been prevented had some rudimentary protective measures (e.g., working locks on doors) been in place. In addition, the landlord has the duty to provide necessary services to his tenants and to maintain the premises in a habitable condition; failure to live up to this duty is a breach of the implied covenant of quiet enjoyment and results in a constructive eviction of the tenant.

Easements, Licenses, Profits, and Future Interests

Easements, licenses, and profits are additional nonpossessory interests in land that, while not providing an ownership interest in property, allow the property of one person to be used for limited specific purposes for the benefit of another.

Easements

An easement is the right to use the land of another for a specific, limited purpose, such as getting in and out of one's own land.

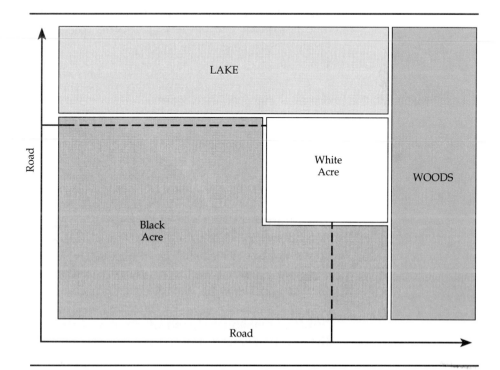

In the situation illustrated above, an easement of Black Acre in favor of White Acre would be necessary. The owner of White Acre has no right of access to the road. To gain such access, he can negotiate an easement with the owner of Black Acre allowing him to cross the latter's land over one of the two spots noted by the dashes. Once he obtains the easement, the owner of White Acre will be able to cross Black Acre to enter and leave his land without being guilty of trespass. The owner of Black Acre would continue to have complete use of all of his land, including the tract of land over which the owner of White Acre is given the easement, as long as he does not interfere with the easement (i.e., as long as he allows the owner of White Acre to freely pass over the land to enter and leave his property).

Easements Appurtenant and Easements in Gross.   Two basic types of easements can be created: *easements appurtenant* and *easements in gross.* In an easement appurtenant, the special use of one piece of land over which the easement is granted benefits another piece of land. The land benefited by the easement is called the *dominant tenement,* and the land burdened by the easement is called the *servient tenement.* The example diagramed above represents an easement appurtenant, since it benefits the owner of White Acre in the use or enjoyment of his land; Black Acre is the dominant tenement, and White Acre the servient tenement. An easement in gross is one that does not benefit a specific tract of land owned by the holder of the easement. The holder is given the right to use part or all of the land for a specific purpose, but such use is not for the benefit of another piece of land. The following are examples of easements in gross:

➤   1. John, a hunter, negotiates an easement with the owner of Black Acre giving him the right to use the land for target practice during the hunting season.
   2. Jane, an archaeologist, negotiates an easement from the owner of White Acre allowing her to conduct a dig in a particular area for Indian artifacts.
   3. Limbo Oil negotiates with the owner of Blighted Acre to cart shale over Blighted Acre for the next 10 years.

Affirmative and Negative Easements.   An easement can be classified as either *affirmative* or *negative* depending on the type of right it grants to its holder. An easement is affirmative when it allows its holder to physically enter into the property it covers (the servient tenement) to conduct the activity permitted under the easement. The last three examples of easements in gross cover affirmative easements, since the hunter, archaeologist, and oil company are given the right to enter into the servient tenements to perform the permitted acts of target shooting, digging, and carting shale, respectively. A negative easement, on the other hand, prevents the owner of the servient tenement from making a particular use of the land which, absent the easement, she would be free to engage in. Consider the following example:

> Hilda, a wealthy socialite from New York City, decides to purchase a summer estate in Otsego county, 200 miles northwest of New York City. After building a duly ostentatious home in her new property, she is horrified to learn that her neighbors are farmers who freely utilize organic manure to fertilize their crops in the spring, summer, and fall. Unwilling to put up with what is to her an offensive odor throughout her summer vacations, she offers her neighbors $100,000 in return for a negative easement preventing them from farming their land during the summer months.

Hilda's easement does not give her the right to go into her neighbors' land for any specific purpose; rather, it prevents her neighbors from using their land in a way that, were it not for the negative easement, they would be free to use it.

Creating Easements.   There are four separate ways of creating an easement: express grant, reservation, implication, and prescription.

Express Grant.   This creates an easement in an interest in land in much the same way as any land conveyance—by executing, conveying, and recording a deed. Unless the deed conveying the easement states otherwise, an easement will be deemed to last perpetually in most jurisdictions. It is possible, however, to create an easement that lasts only for the life of a person or for a set number of years. Because easements convey interests in real estate, albeit not ownership interests, they must be evidenced by a signed writing to satisfy the statute of frauds.

Reservation.   An owner of land can convey it while reserving to himself the right to use that land for a given purpose after the conveyance. For example, Farmer Jones wishes to sell his land but wants to continue farming it for another five years, until he retires. He finds a buyer who is interested in the long-term investment potential of the land and does not mind if Jones continues to use the land for the next five years. When Jones conveys the land with the specific provision in the deed that he may continue farming for five years, he will retain an easement by reservation.

Implication.   An easement by implication arises when parties convey land but neglect to specifically mention that an easement will be necessary for the land to be used. Look at the following example:

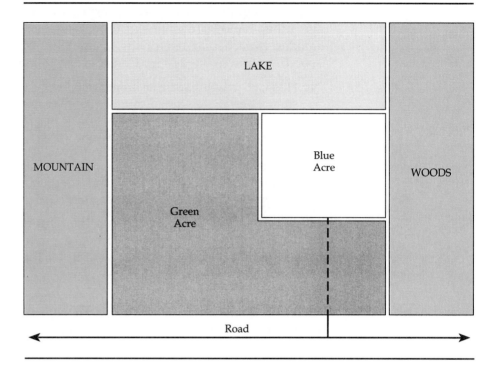

Assume that Mr. Wong owned both Blue Acre and Green Acre and conveyed Blue Acre to Mr. Washington. Neither Wong nor Washington realized that Blue Acre lacked direct access to a road when the conveyance was made. A court would hold that, under the circumstances, an easement by implication arose by the conveyance of Blue Acre, since such an easement is a necessity for Blue Acre to be of any use. An easement by implication can also arise when, prior to the conveyance, the land of another had been in previous use for a specific purpose. In the above diagram, assume that a home on Blue Acre is set up to discharge waste onto a cesspool in Green Acre. If this previous use was in existence when the land was conveyed and no mention of it is made in the deed, an easement by implication will exist, allowing the owner of Blue Acre to continue using the cesspool in Green Acre.

Prescription.   If land is used for a specific purpose for a long enough period, an easement by prescription will arise, regardless that no actual permission was ever given for such use. As with adverse possession (discussed below), if a person openly, exclusively, and continuously uses a piece of land for a particular purpose for a set period (usually 20 years), an easement by prescription will come into effect that no one can challenge.

➤ Over a period of 20 years, Harold allows his cows to graze in a one-acre tract of land he does not own. His use of the land is continuous, open, and notorious. At the end of 20 years, he has an easement by prescription that neither the original owner of the land nor any of her assigns will be able to challenge.

Licenses

Unlike an easement that actually grants its holder limited rights to real estate, a license merely gives one person the right to temporarily enter another's land. A license is a revocable privilege given by the owner of realty for a licensee (the person to whom the license is given) to enter into his land for a specific purpose. Since a license does not create an interest in realty within the meaning of the statute of frauds, it can be spoken rather than written. The grantor of the license can revoke it at any time, and it is automatically revoked by his death. When the grantor revokes the license, the licensee must immediately leave the grantor's premises; this is true even if the licensee paid a fee for the license. If a licensee fails to immediately leave the premises upon demand (i.e., upon revocation of the license), he is guilty of trespass and subject to criminal prosecution and civil penalties. The following are examples of licenses granted by the owner of real property to a licensee:

➤ 1. Chuck allows Victor to enter his land to practice skeet and target shooting.
2. Aretha purchases a ticket to a movie and is allowed into the theater.
3. Francisco purchases a ticket and is allowed into Disney World.
4. Ken knocks on Dan's door, and the latter invites him into his home.

Note that in examples 2 and 3 above, Aretha and Francisco pay for the privilege of being given a license to enter the theater and Disney World, respectively. Nevertheless, the management of each establishment may revoke either's license at any time, *with or without cause*. If the license is revoked without cause, the licensee is free to sue for breach of contract; but he must still leave the premises.

Profits and Future Interests

A *profit* is a nonpossessory right in real estate giving the holder the privilege to go into another's land to remove something from it (e.g., soil, precious metals, minerals, water, etc.). Profits are created in the same way as easements but function slightly differently: an easement allows one the privilege to enter into another's land for a specific use, while a profit permits one to *remove* a given substance from the land.

Future interests are nonpossessory interests in real property that can turn into possessory interests in the future upon a given event. Whenever property is transferred other than by a fee simple conveyance, a future interest is retained to the property either for the benefit of the grantor or some other third party. If the future interest, otherwise known as a *residuary interest,* is for the benefit of the original grantor or her estate, it is called a *reversion;* if it is for the benefit of some other third party it called a *remainder.* If a reversion or remainder interest is given contingent upon an event that is not certain to occur, the residuary interests are termed *possibility of a reverter* and *contingent remainder,* respectively. The following examples will illustrate:

> 1. Harold conveys White Acre *to Jane for life.* He has retained a reversionary interest in the land, since its title will revert to him or to his estate upon Jane's death.
> 2. Harold conveys White Acre *to Jane for life, remainder to Joan.* Joan's residuary interest in White Acre is a remainder, since she is the third party in whose favor title to White Acre will accrue upon Jane's death. If Joan dies before Jane, the remainder interest in White Acre will pass to her heirs.
> 3. Harold conveys White Acre *to Jane provided she remains single, and to Joan if Jane should marry.* Joan is given a contingent remainder interest in White Acre that may or may not accrue to her or her heirs depending upon whether Jane marries.
> 4. Harold conveys White Acre *to Joan for as long as the St. John's Redmen have a winning season.* Harold retains the possibility of a reverter, since title to the property will vest in him or his heirs if the Redmen ever have a losing season.

Acquiring Title to Real Property

Like personal property, real estate can be acquired in a number of ways, including by purchase, gift, or inheritance; by condemnation by the state; and even by simply holding on to it long enough under certain circumstances (adverse possession).

Deed

The most common method of transferring title to real property is through conveyance of a deed by a grantor (the person transferring the property) to a grantee (the person to whom the property is being transferred). A deed is a signed writing by the owner (the grantor) of real property that transfers ownership to another (the grantee). To be valid, a deed must contain the following information:

1. The names of the grantor(s) and grantee(s).
2. Words that clearly show an intent to transfer the land.

3. A clear description of the land being transferred.

4. The signature of the grantor(s).

Once a valid deed is executed, the grantor must deliver it to the grantee. Title to the property passes upon delivery of the deed.

Eminent Domain

At common law, all land in the realm belonged to the crown, with the king or queen free to dispose of it at will. What the king gave by way of grants to favored subjects, he was free to take back under his power of eminent domain—the predominant right of the king to dispose of all property. Our present government still preserves the right of eminent domain. With regard to real property, the government retains a right that is superior even to holders of a fee simple absolute interest in realty; if the government decides it needs a tract of land for public use, it can condemn the land and take it from its owner, provided the latter receives the reasonable value of the land. When either the local, state, or federal government condemns land for public use, the landowner can first bargain with the government for a fair price and, if agreement is reached, willingly transfer the land for the offered consideration. If they cannot reach agreement, the landowner can ask a court to determine the market price of the land.

> ➤ Sally Homeowner lives in a house where she and five generations of Homeowners before her have lived all their lives. Sally's state decides to build a new six-lane highway, but Sally's house is in the way. The state condemns Sally's house and offers her its reasonable market price. Sally vows to fight for her rights. Will she win? No. Her only right is to be paid a fair price for the house. What of her emotional attachment to the house or its personal value? Alas, such considerations will not daunt the march of progress.

Inheritance

Real property, as well as personal property, can be disposed of by will or through the provisions of intestacy statutes that determine how the property of a decedent is to be divided when a valid will is not available. (For a full treatment of wills and intestacy, see Chapter 17.)

Adverse Possession

Mere possession of real property gives rise to an inference that the possession is lawful. The longer the possession, the stronger the inference becomes, until it reaches a point when the presumption of lawful possession becomes irrefutable. Such is the nature of ownership of real property by adverse possession. If a person remains in continuous possession of real property for a set period under certain circumstances, mere possession will be transformed into legal title. For title to be acquired through adverse possession, all of the following conditions must be met:

1. *The possession must be open and notorious.* This requirement is met when the possessor of the property openly treats it as his own.

2. *The possession must be continuous for the statutorily mandated period, usually 20 years.* Intermittent use of the property will not suffice—the adverse possessor must treat the property as his own in an open and notorious manner throughout the required time.

3. *The possession must be adverse and exclusive.* If the possession is accomplished with the owner's permission, or if the owner and the adverse possessor both use the land at the same time, no claim for adverse possession will exist.

4. *The possession must be with claim of right.* It is enough in this regard for the adverse possessor to announce to others that he is the owner. Most states do not require the claim to be made in good faith—it is enough if the adverse possessor tells others he is the owner, even if he knows he has no claim to the property.

Consider the following example:

➤ William and Wendy move into town and clear a half-acre lot in a 200-acre tract owned by John Doe, an absentee landowner who lives in another state. They build a house, plant a few crops, and live in the land for 20 years, telling people that they are the owners. Twenty-one years later, John Doe learns of William and Wendy's adverse possession and tries to oust them from his land. He is too late; the adverse possession had been open and notorious, continuous for 20 years, adverse, exclusive, and with claim of right (Wendy and William claimed to others that they owned the land, meeting the claim of right requirement.)

In the above example, the half-acre tract that William and Wendy used belongs to them by virtue of their adverse possession. Notice, however, that the remaining 199.5 acres still belong to John Doe, since the couple never treated them as their own.

If William and Wendy lived on the land for 19 years, abandoned it for a year, and then returned for an additional 2 years, they would not have a valid claim of adverse possession; the 20-year time span must be uninterrupted. If they stay on for an additional 18 years, however, they would then meet the 20-year uninterrupted possession requirement.

Recording Statutes

A problem existed at common law when an unscrupulous grantor transferred an interest in real property to more than one grantee. Whenever this happened, the courts would follow the *first in time, first in right* rule, making the first grantee of the land its true owner. But it is not always easy to prove who was first in time when a grantor made multiple conveyances. Governments resolved the problem by enacting recording statutes that provided a simple way for grantees to prove when they acquired title and to give notice to others that a transfer in title had taken place. Every state today has a recording act that protects a grantee's interest in land and provides a permanent record of all land transfers.

> ➤ Terry, the owner of Black Acre, executes a deed transferring the property to Debbie at noon, a second deed transferring the land to Jack at 1:00 P.M., and yet another transferring the land to Sylvia at 2:00 P.M., all on the same day. After taking the money from each grantee, Terry leaves the country and cannot be found. Sylvia, the last grantee, records the deed at 3:00 P.M. An hour later, Debbie and Jack show up in the recording office to try and record their deeds. Who owns the land?

At common law, Debbie would own the land, presuming she could prove that the conveyance to her came before that of the other two parties. Under recording statutes, however, Sylvia would prevail. Even though she was the last to receive a conveyance from Terry to Black Acre, she was the first to record her deed, thus perfecting her interest in the property.

Property Ownership through Cooperatives, Condominiums, and Time-Shares	The rise in population density in urban areas coupled with the increase in value of traditional one- and two-family homes gave rise to the popularity of two new types of property ownership in the United States starting in the 1950s. Both cooperative and condominium property ownership differ radically from traditional fee simple ownership. Cooperative ownership is, in fact, not ownership of realty at all, but rather of shares in a cooperative corporation that give their holder the right to occupy an apartment. Condominium ownership, on the other hand, does represent fee ownership of realty, but in a radically different form: the condo owner does not own the traditional land, mineral, and air rights to property, but rather the space within the walls of his condominium unit. He is a co-tenant of all other parts of the building and its grounds with the owners of the complex's other condominiums. Finally, time-share ownership further subdivides a condominium or cooperative unit into slices of time, with each owner holding title to,

or the right to occupy, a condo or co-op for a given length of time each year. We will analyze each form of ownership in greater detail in the following discussion.

Cooperatives

In cooperative property ownership, a corporation purchases a multi-family dwelling—either existing or new construction—and in turn sells shares in the building to individuals who, by purchasing the shares, are entitled to occupy an apartment in the co-op. The owner of a share in a cooperative does not own realty as such, but rather owns intangible personal property—the shares in the cooperative that give her the right to occupy an apartment in it. The actual property is owned by the cooperative—the corporation that purchased the building and runs it on behalf of the shareholder/tenants. The corporation itself holds the deed to the building in its own name, pays taxes, and expends all necessary capital to manage the building and provide needed services, such as heat, hot water, and grounds maintenance. The shareholder/tenants in turn pay a monthly maintenance fee that represents a portion of all management expenses for the building, including real estate taxes and maintenance charges. The amount of a shareholder/tenant's maintenance fee is proportionate to the value of his shares, which is in turn relative to the value of the apartment he occupies. The actual price of the co-op share and its attendant maintenance fee depend on such matters as the size of the apartment and its distance from the ground floor; in general, the larger the apartment and the further away it is from the noise of the ground floor, the more it costs. The portion of the co-op monthly maintenance fee earmarked for payment of real estate and other taxes (e.g., school taxes) is tax deductible by the shareholder/tenant. (Typically, 50-60 percent of monthly maintenance fees are tax deductible, but this can vary widely.)

Because the owner of a co-op does not own real property, but merely owns shares in the corporation that actually owns the realty, there are substantial restrictions on his ability to transfer his shares; cooperative boards usually set up guidelines for transfer of shareholders' shares to new owners and typically reserve the right to interview and approve would-be buyers.

Condominiums

Condominium property ownership is not indigenous to the United States but was imported from Europe and Latin America, where it has been popular for a great many years. Condominiums are considered real property, and their owners are far freer to transfer condos than are co-op owners. In condominium property ownership, a multiple dwelling is purchased and subdivided by the developer, with each unit maintaining a separate deed. Because condos are considered realty, owners pay real estate and school taxes directly to the state government, rather than indirectly through their monthly maintenance fees.

The owner of a condominium literally owns the space within his unit—*from the paint in*—individually, and all other structures, including the walls, floors, ceilings, and common areas such as hallways, stairwells, and elevators as a tenant in common. Like the co-op shareholder/tenant, the condo owner pays a monthly maintenance fee that represents a portion of the total expense of running the building equal to the relative value of his condominium unit. Like with a co-op, the value of an individual condo unit is based mainly on its size and distance from the ground floor. The monthly maintenance fees cover such operational expenses as building maintenance, the provision of heat and hot water, and other building services (like security, grounds maintenance, snow removal, and so forth.) In addition to the monthly maintenance charges, members of a condominium association from time to time levy special charges for extraordinary repairs or improvements to the building. If, for example, 80 percent of the residents want to install central air conditioning or a heated pool, such improvements would be undertaken and all condo owners would be billed for a total share of the expense in accordance with the relative value of their unit.

Even though condominiums are typically new, high-rise structures, they need not be. It is perfectly possible (if not economically practical) to turn a two- or three-family house into a condominium. Indeed, one could conceivably turn a four-bedroom single-family home into a four-unit condominium, issuing a deed for each bedroom and keeping the dining room, kitchen, living room, bathrooms, and backyard as common areas.

Time Shares

Time-share property ownership takes the co-op and condominium forms one step further and divides each unit into slices of *time*, typically one-week blocks. Individuals then purchase the right to occupy the particular unit for the time involved every year. Time-share schemes vary, as do the underlying property they cover. It is possible to sell time-shares to a private home, a co-op, or a condominium complex. And time-shares can be true forms of property ownership (e.g., a 1/25th fee simple interest in a condominium unit, giving its owner the right to occupy the unit for a two-week period forever) or a mere license to occupy premises for the time they cover (e.g., the right to occupy a cooperative apartment for two weeks per year for the next 10 years). Time-shares are particularly popular in areas with great tourist appeal, although they have been popping up in recent years in unexpected, out-of-the-way places.

Owners of fee simple time-share interests, as well as non–fee simple license interests, pay a yearly maintenance fee similar to the monthly maintenance fees paid by co-op and condo owners; this fee typically includes a portion of the real estate taxes due on the unit and various maintenance and management expenses. There is great appeal to promoters of time-shares in that a single unit can be sold piecemeal for many times its price. Consider the following example:

> ABC Corporation owns a condominium complex of 25 units in Hawaii. The average market price of each unit is $100,000. It decides to turn the complex into time-shares and sell each unit in one-week chunks, giving each buyer a 1/52nd fee simple interest in each unit, along with the right to occupy it during a stated one-week period during the year. On average, the one-week time-shares sell for $2,500 each. The total price at which each unit is sold, then, will be $4,000 × 52, or $208,000—more than twice the price per unit ABC would have been able to realize by selling each unit as a traditional condominium.

The appeal of individual time-shares is the possibility of purchasing the right to vacation yearly in a popular vacation spot for a fraction of what a traditional vacation home would cost. Unfortunately, over the last decade some unscrupulous operators have offered overpriced time-shares through high-pressure sales tactics. As with any major purchase, *caveat emptor* is the operative phrase. The overwhelming number of time-share offerings are legitimate, and some can offer exceptional vacation values to consumers who shop wisely.

Judge for Yourself

Case 1. Mary agrees to rent an apartment to Joshua for $500 per month. They do not enter into a formal lease and make no other agreement.

    a. What type of tenancy is involved?

    b. If either party wishes to terminate the agreement, what will they need to do?

    c. If the roof of the apartment develops a leak, what must Joshua do?

    d. If the washer in Joshua's sink leaks, whose responsibility is it to fix it? Why?

Case 2. Fred and Barney own homes on adjacent lots. Over a period of 20 years, Fred, with Barney's permission, parks his car on Barney's land. After 20 years of putting up with Fred's car on his property, Barney tires of the arrangement and informs Fred that he may no longer park the car there.

    a. How would you classify Fred's use of Barney's land for 20 years?

    b. If Fred refuses to stop parking his car on Barney's land, what remedies, if any, are open to Barney?

    c. Can Fred claim an absolute right to Barney's land through adverse possession? Explain.

    d. Would Fred have a valid claim of adverse possession if he continues to use Barney's land for an additional 20 years after Barney tells him not to?

Case 3.   Sally and Jane buy two tickets to see a movie at their local theater. Halfway through the movie, they are bored by it and decide to strike up a conversation. Other patrons, annoyed by their conduct, ask them to quiet down, and loud words are exchanged. The manager finally steps in and asks the young ladies to leave. They refuse, becoming even more boisterous and loudly proclaiming that they paid for the right to be in the theater and need not leave until the movie is over. The manager then has them physically removed from the theater and forces them to wait in the lobby—very much against their wishes—until police arrive to arrest them for criminal trespass.

    a. Will the manager be able to prove a case of trespass against the two young women?

    b. Will the women have a valid case of false arrest against the theater and/or its manager?

    c. If the manager refuses to return the price of admission to the women, can they sue him for it? If so, under what legal theory? Will they recover?

Case 4.   Emily Harrison transfers a deed to her son, Ricky, that reads, "To Ricky Henderson, provided he graduates from college by 1997, otherwise to Jamie Henderson."

    a. Assuming that Ricky graduates from college by the stated date, what type of interest will he have in the property?

    b. What type of interest does Jamie have in the property when the deed is issued?

    c. Emily, who has a terrible memory, conveys the same land to Oscar a week later for $100,000. Oscar immediately records the deed, something that neither Ricky nor Jamie had yet done. What are the rights of the parties?

17

Wills, Trusts, and Insurance

Learning Objectives

After studying this chapter, you will be able to:

1. Explain why most people, even those without large estates, need a will.
2. Define noncupative and holographic wills.
3. Explain the consequences of having an interested party sign a will as a witness.
4. Define intestacy and explain the consequences of dying intestate.
5. List the four necessary components of a legal trust.

Introduction

As we've seen in the last two chapters, a person can transfer title to personal and real property to another person through a variety of means throughout his life: he can rent, sell, or give it away at his whim. One of the most fundamental rights of property ownership is the prerogative to dispose of it freely according to one's wishes. A property owner enjoys this right throughout her lifetime and can extend it even after death by executing a valid will that provides how her property is to be disposed of. When a person dies without having executed a valid will, the state, in accordance with its intestacy statute, will step in and draft one in an attempt to dispose of the decedent's property to the surviving family. The state will follow what it believes to be the wishes of most citizens. In this chapter, we will examine the basic requirements for drafting a valid will in most states and how the state is likely to distribute the property of a person who dies without a will. We will also see how an owner can transfer property through a trust, placing real or personal property in the care of one or more persons [the trustee(s)] for the benefit of another (the beneficiary).

Purposes of a Will

Although the primary use for a will is to dispose of property after death, that is by no means its only use. In fact, it is possible to have a valid will that makes no testamentary disposition of property, or simply states *who is not* to receive any property from the decendent's estate. A valid will can be used to accomplish any or all of the following objectives:

1. Disposing of one's personal and real property.
2. Directing how personal or real property is not to be disposed.
3. Disposing of one's body or any body parts.
4. Appointing an executor.
5. Appointing a guardian for one's dependent children.

It is a common misconception that a will is only useful to a person of considerable means. In fact, having a will can be extremely valuable, even for a poor person, since the distribution of property is only one of a will's many functions. Also, a person of modest means may still own property with a high sentimental, if not material, value; a will can ensure that the property is distributed to someone who values it. In addition, regardless of a person's economic status, he may want to choose who cares for his most cherished resource—his children— rather than leaving the choice of guardian to a court. Likewise, a will can name an executor or executrix to handle the decedent's affairs after death—otherwise, a court is likely to appoint the closest living family member to that task, whether or not the person is competent and emotionally prepared for the undertaking. Furthermore, a will can specify a testator's wishes as to the disposition of her body or its parts. Finally, a valid will avoids the time and trouble required to appoint an executor and distribute a decedent's property through intestacy, greatly simplifying proceedings after death. Any one of these reasons in itself justifies the relatively small price of having an attorney prepare a will. For those who cannot afford an attorney, a variety of form books are available in most public libraries that can help one in preparing a will. Although there is no substitute for the advice and guidance of a competent attorney in drafting a will, a lay person can do it himself by carefully using one of these generic self-help guides.

Types of Wills

A will is an oral statement or formal written document that determines how a person's property is to be distributed after death. To be valid and therefore legally enforceable, a will must conform to the specific requirements of the jurisdiction in which it was made. While the formalities of executing a will vary somewhat from state to state, in general a will must meet the following requirements to be valid:

1. It must be executed by a person of legal age who possesses the mental capacity to dispose of property.
2. It must be in writing.
3. It must be signed.
4. It must be witnessed by at least two or three people, depending on the state.

These qualifications will be discussed in detail in this chapter.

Persons who have not reached the age of consent (18 in most states) cannot draft a valid will. Unlike a minor's contract, which is deemed ratified unless the minor disaffirms it prior to reaching the age of consent or within a reasonable time thereafter, a will executed by a minor is null and void and as such, not deemed ratified when the minor reaches the age of consent.

To understand the language of wills and trusts, you must be familiar with the following terms:

- *Decedent:* One who has died, whether or not leaving a valid will.
- *Devisee:* One who takes real property (a *devise* or *bequest*) under a will.
- *Distributee:* A person entitled to share in the distribution of a decedent's estate under a will or the laws of intestacy.
- *Executor:* A man appointed by a testator or testatrix to carry out the provisions of his/her will.
- *Executrix:* A woman appointed by a testator or testatrix to carry out the provisions of his/her will.
- *Issue:* All offspring who descended from a common ancestor.
- *Legatee:* One who takes personal property (a *legacy*) under a will.
- *Testator:* A man who creates a will.
- *Testatrix:* A woman who creates a will.
- *Witness:* One who signs his or her name to a will for the purpose of attesting to its authenticity.

Noncupative Wills

A noncupative will is an oral will. Although most states require wills to be in writing, many states recognize noncupative wills, at least in certain circumstances. The most common acceptance of noncupative wills is in cases of armed forces personnel during a time of armed conflict (declared war or military action) or mariners at sea. For this reason, noncupative wills are often referred to as *soldiers'* and *sailors' wills.* Typically, a valid noncupative will automatically expires after a set time if the testator does not first revoke it. In New York, for example, a noncupative will made by a soldier engaged in armed conflict expires within one year after the soldier leaves the service or one year from the date that the hostilities cease, whichever comes first. In the case of seamen, the noncupative will automatically expires three years after it is made in New York. (Seamen need not be engaged in armed conflict for their noncupative wills to be valid; indeed, noncupative wills by members of the merchant marine are perfectly binding whenever they are made, as long as they are made by a mariner while at sea.) Noncupative wills still need at least two, and often three, witnesses to be binding; witnesses, of course, cannot sign a noncupative will, but they can testify that the will was orally spoken in their presence and state what its specific provisions were.

Holographic Wills

A holographic will is one that is entirely written out in the testator's hand. Such wills are subject to the same requirements as all written wills, but many jurisdictions dispense with the requirement that it be witnessed if it is entirely in the testator's handwriting. The requiring of witnesses is to prevent fraud, such as forgery of the testatrix's signature. It is much harder to forge an entire document when it is written longhand, thus such wills are typically enforceable even if not witnessed.

Validity of a Will

For wills to be enforceable, they need to be signed, witnessed, and published. For purposes of a will, a *signature* is any mark made by a testatrix or testator intended to be her or his signature. Thus, an X placed by an illiterate testator will suffice as a valid signature, as will a typewritten name placed on the will be the testator or the signing by means of initials. This is the same rule we've previously encountered during the discussion of contracts and commercial paper. Although any mark can satisfy the signature requirement, it is always best to use one's full signature, since the validity of the signature must be proven in probate court if it is challenged.

Most jurisdictions require that the signature appear at the end of the will, just above the witnesses' signatures. Generally, if a testator signs before the end of the will, the will is valid, but any matter following the signature is ignored. Consider the following example:

Article II
I leave to my niece, Harriet, the sum of $10,000.

Article III
I leave to my daughter, Wendy, the sum of $25,000.

Article IV
I leave all other property to my husband, Harold.

Emma Testator

Article V
I leave my summer house in Florida to my parents,
Ron and Edna Outaluck.

Witness #1 _____

Witness #2 _____

Witness #3 _____

The above will is valid, even though Emma signed it in the wrong spot. But the last provision (Article V) will be ignored in most states, since it appears after the signature. In a minority of states, a will not signed at the end will be void.

At common law, witnesses had to be disinterested parties for their attestations to be valid. This means that any legatee (one who receives personal property) or devisee (one who receives real property) under the will was incompetent to serve as a witness, and any will witnessed by a legatee or devisee was deemed void and could not be probated. The more modern view, however, allows a will witnessed by a legatee or devisee to be probated in many jurisdictions, but that witness is prevented from taking his devise or bequest under the will. In cases where an interested witness signs as an extra, unnecessary witness to the will (known as a *supernumerary*), she may typically receive her legacy or devise. An attesting witness can also take under a will if she would be entitled to a bequest or devise under the laws of intestacy (covered later in this chapter); under such circumstances, the interested witness is allowed the lesser of her bequest or devise or the share allowed her by the intestacy statute. Consider the following example:

> John Smith dies leaving a will and is survived by three children: Tom, Dick, and Harriet. In his will, John leaves Dick $10 with the instruction that he buy a copy of the *National Business Employment Weekly*, get a haircut, and find a job. To Harriet, he leaves his prized butterfly collection,

worth $2.95. To Tom, he leaves the rest of his estate, worth $1 million. The state involved required that a will have two witnesses. John has Sally, Ralph, and Tom witness the will. Will Tom get his million dollars? Yes, because he signed as a supernumerary—his signature is one of three in the will when only two are required. Tom's signature will simply be ignored. If, on the other hand, only Sally and Tom had witnessed the will, Tom would have a problem. The will would be valid, but he would be barred from collecting under it. (In most states, however, he could take the lesser of his intestacy share or the actual bequest, if he is entitled to take under the state's intestacy statute had John died without a will.)

Some states require that a will be *published*, which simply means that the testator or testatrix must present the will to the witnesses to sign while declaring to them that "this is my will." In many states, however, the act of physically giving a will to a witness to sign, even if no words are spoken, will satisfy the requirement of publication.

Intestacy

Every state has an intestacy statute that determines how a decedent's property will be distributed when the decedent dies without a will or dies leaving an invalid will that cannot be probated. These statutes are similar in all states, even though the specific distributions to a decedent's issue can vary. (For a detailed analysis of a typical intestacy statute, you can examine New York's fairly typical intestacy statute in Case Study 4–3 at the end of this unit.)

Most states permit any relative to be disinherited simply by making no provision for her/him in a will. The only exception is a spouse, who can never be disinherited. A spouse is always entitled to a minimum of the intestacy share provided by statute. Hence, if a wife tries to disinherit her husband and leave her entire estate to her children, the husband will be able to challenge the will and claim his intestate share. Children can be disinherited in every state (some states require a specific provision in a will disinheriting a child, while in others, such as New York, the mere omission of a devise or bequest to a child effectively disinherits him or her.)

For many people, the intestacy statute provides precisely the kind of distribution of their estate that they would have made had they drafted a will. But for many others, it does not. A person must be aware of the provisions of the intestacy laws in the jurisdiction where she lives, since the only way to circumvent them is by leaving a valid will.

Figure 17–1 presents an example of a simple will.

FIGURE 17-1 **A simple will**

MASSACHUSETTS WILL

Be it Remembered that I,

of

in the Commonwealth of Massachusetts, being of sound mind and

memory, but knowing the uncertainty of this life, do make this my

last will and testament, hereby revoking all former wills by me

at any time heretofore made.

After the payment of my just debts and funeral charges, I

bequeath and devise as follows:

In testimony whereof I hereunto set my hand and in the presence

of two three witnesses declare this to be my last will this

day of   in the year one thousand nine hundred

....

On this   day of   A. D. 19

of   Massachusetts,

signed the foregoing instrument in our presence, declaring it to

be h   presence, and in the presence of each

other, hereto subscribe our names.

....

....

....

Commonwealth of Massachusetts, county of   , before me, the under-

signed authority on this day personally appeared _____

and _____

known to me to be testator and the witnesses, respectively

whose name are signed to the attached or foregoing instrument,

and, all of these persons being by me duly sworn

the testator declared to me and to the witnesses in my presence that

the instrument is h   last will and that he had willingly signed or

directed another to sign for h   , and that he executed it as h

free and voluntary act of the purposes therein expressed: and

each of the witnesses stated to me, in the presence of the testator,

that h   signed the will as witness and that to the best of h

knowledge the testator was eighteen years of age or over, of sound

mind and under no constraint or undue influence.

....
                                          Testator
....
                                          Witness
....
                                          Witness

Subscribed and sworn before me by the said
Testator and the said witnesses, this   day of

"Self-Proving Affidavit" (removes the necessity for proving the Will when it is offered for probate).

No person who is to receive anything under a will, and no husband or wife of any such person, should be a witness to such will. But a person is not rendered incompetent as a witness to a will by the fact that he is named therein as executor. If the testator is too feeble to sign the will, his signature may be written for him by some other person "in his presence and by his express direction." The testator should sign first, and the witnesses thereafter.

Trusts

A trust is a form of property ownership whereby one person holds and manages personal or real property for the benefit of another. The person who holds the property is called the *trustee,* and the person for whose benefit the property is held is called the *beneficiary.* The trustee is the legal owner of the property, and the beneficiary, who is entitled to enjoy the benefits that flow from the trustee's management of the property, cannot tell him how to manage it.

The trustee is bound to the beneficiary by a fiduciary relationship; as such, the trustee is bound by law to act in the best interest of the beneficiary to the best of her abilities. A trustee who violates the fiduciary relationship by acting in a manner inconsistent with furthering the best interests of the beneficiary can be removed by means of a legal suit.

The reasons why trusts are created range from tax avoidance to making gifts to minors or others whom the benefactor does not trust to manage the gift. Consider the following situation:

> Ernest, a doting father, wishes to provide for the future of his daughter, Ellen. He knows, however, that Ellen is a spendthrift who, if given a large, lump sum of money, would squander it in a matter of a few months. So he sets up a trust for Ellen's benefit by placing $200,000 in the hands of his trusted financial advisor, Paula. Paula, as trustee, will have complete control over the *corpus* (literally, *the body,* or underlying property) of the trust; she will invest the money as she sees fit, being answerable to no one for her actions, as long as they are performed in good faith. Ellen, the beneficiary of the trust, will be entitled to the fruits of Paula's efforts—the profits realized from the trust—in a manner outlined in the trust agreement. Paula, on the other hand, will be entitled to a fee for her services.

The last example is commonly known as a *spendthrift trust*—a trust set up to provide an income for persons whom the grantor feels cannot be trusted to responsibly manage their own affairs.

Types of Trusts

There are essentially two types of trusts: *inter vivos* and *testamentary* trusts. Inter vivos trusts (literally, *trusts between the living*) are set up during the lifetime of the *grantor* (the owner of the property given over to the trust for another's benefit, also known as the *creator* or the *settlor* of the trust). Testamentary trusts, as the name implies, are set up after the grantor's death through provisions made in a will. Whether a trust is classified as inter vivos or testamentary, it will have the following four necessary elements:

1. A designated beneficiary or beneficiaries.
2. One or more designated trustees.

3. A fund (or trust corpus) that is sufficiently identified so as to enable title to pass to the trustee(s).
4. Actual delivery of the trust fund to the trustee(s) by the grantor with the intention of passing title to her (them).

Any grantor who has the capacity to enter into a contract can set up a trust for any legal purpose. Trusts can be set up to run for any period of time or, in certain circumstances (such as charitable trusts), to have perpetual existence. If the trust is to have only a temporary existence, such as a set duration in years or the lifetime of a given person, it automatically terminates at the appointed time or upon a given event, such as the death of the beneficiary. In such cases, the trust corpus may revert to the grantor or may be given over to any other third person in accordance with the trust agreement.

The grantor can make a trust either revocable or irrevocable once it comes into existence. The simplest and most common type of revocable trust is a *Totten trust*. A Totten trust is set up by a depositor who deposits a sum of money into a bank account in his own name as trustee for a third-party beneficiary. During her lifetime, the grantor of a Totten trust can revoke it at any time simply by withdrawing the funds from the account. If the grantor does not revoke the trust during her lifetime, it becomes irrevocable at her death, and the beneficiary is then entitled to the trust corpus. The grantor can also make a Totten trust irrevocable during her lifetime by unequivocally conveying that intention, such as turning over the passbook to the beneficiary.

Insurance

Running a business is a risky proposition. Regardless of the nature of the business, there is always the danger of losses stemming from such circumstances as the negligence of one's employees, the death of a key person in the company, and the loss of property through fire, theft or vandalism. For this reason, risk management plays a crucial part in assuring the success of any business. While no strategy can completely insulate a businessperson from the daily risks inherent in running a business, careful planning and purchasing adequate insurance to cover potential losses can often mean the difference between a successful business and one that fails.

One can purchase insurance to cover nearly any risk of loss to life, health, or property. The principle underlying insurance is a simple one: the distribution of risk. If there is a chance that something bad can happen to a given group of people, you can bet it will happen to some of them. Insurance allows a group of people at risk to protect themselves by making small payments through their insurance premiums that will cover the losses that will inevitably be suffered by some of them.

Insurable Interest

Before a person can purchase insurance on a person or thing, the law requires that he have an insurable interest in the person or thing being insured. A person cannot insure against harm to personal or real property she does not own or otherwise have the legal right to use. Likewise, a person cannot insure the life of another human being unless he has a legally sufficient interest in the person's well-being to justify purchasing a policy on the person's life. With regard to life insurance, an insurable interest can exist when the person purchasing the policy either has a financial interest in the person being insured or is a close family member. Thus, an employer may insure the life of any employee, since it has a financial interest in the employee's life that stems from the employer/employee relationship. Likewise, parents may insure the lives of their children, children that of their parents, and spouses may insure one another's lives. But one cannot insure a neighbor's life or even a close friend, let alone that of a perfect stranger.

There are strong public policy grounds for requiring an insurable interest as a prerequisite to the procurement of insurance. Without it, an insurance contract is nothing more than gambling.

The Insurance Contract

An insurance contract, called a policy, is a binding agreement between an insurance company (the insurer) and a policy holder (the insured), whereby the insured agrees to make periodic payments, called premiums, in exchange for a promise that the insurer will indemnify him if he suffers a type of loss covered under the policy. Since it is a contract, an insurance policy must meet the normal criteria for any valid contract: there must be an offer, an acceptance, consideration, legality, and genuine assent. In addition, insurance contracts must be in writing and signed by both the insured and an agent of the insurer. When the insured signs an insurance contract with an agent of the insurer and pays his first premium, the policy goes into effect immediately and the insured is protected from any loss covered under the policy. If a person purchases insurance from a broker, however, the policy does not go into effect until the insurance company accepts it, since a broker is not acting as an agent for the insurance company, but rather for the insured, as the following example illustrates:

> Roberta signs an agreement with John Doe, an insurance broker, to purchase a $50,000 life insurance policy from the Bigco Insurance Company and names her husband as the beneficiary. She writes a check for $100 representing the first year's premium and gives it to the broker. On her way home from the broker's office, she is struck by lightning and dies. Despite the fact that she has paid for the policy, her husband will not receive any benefit under the policy because it had not been accepted by

Bigco at the time of Roberta's death. Her completed application and check were merely an offer for Bigco to issue the requested policy. If Roberta had dealt directly with an agent of Bigco, rather than going through a broker, she would have been immediately insured, since the agent, unlike the broker, would have had the power to immediately bind Bigco to the insurance contract.

With some types of insurance contracts, such as car insurance, brokers can issue binders that will bind the insurance company as soon as the contract is signed and the premium paid. In any case, it is not fair to infer from the above example that it is always better to deal with an agent than it is with a broker; there are benefits and liabilities to dealing with each. The primary benefit of dealing with a broker is that, because she does not represent any one company, one can often find more flexible coverage and a lower price. The chief benefit of dealing with an agent is that coverage generally takes effect immediately, regardless of the type of policy involved.

Types of Insurance

Although one can insure nearly anything from the risk of loss, the type of insurance of primary interest to business falls into three main types: liability, health, property and life.

Liability insurance, as the name implies, can insure a business from liability from a variety of possible sources, including injuries suffered by employees or customers on business premises, injuries caused by employees and, in the case of professional corporations or individuals in private practice, negligence or malpractice. Health insurance is often provided by employers as a benefit for their employees and management. Property insurance can be purchased to protect a company from the intentional, criminal or negligent destruction of personal or real property by such circumstances as fire, theft, vandalism, flood and other natural disasters. Finally, life insurance is often obtained by businesses as part of the benefit package they offer employees and management, but it can also be purchased to protect the business itself from the death of key employees, such as officers and directors of a corporation, whose death could cause the company financial loss.

Cancellation of the Insurance Policy

An insurance policy can be canceled by the insurance company that issues it under certain circumstances. These include the nonpayment of premiums, the filing of an excessive number of claims and material misrepresentations in the insurance application. With regard to misrepresentations, they make the insurance policy voidable at the option of the insurer if they materially affect the risk undertaken by the insurer and if the insurer would not have issued the policy had the misrepresentation been made. If the misrepresentation merely affects the price of the policy, then the amount of coverage is generally reduced to conform to what the actual premium would have purchased had the misrepresentation not been made. The following examples will illustrate:

1. Lenny, who has been told that he is suffering from inoperable liver cancer, purchases a $100,000 life insurance policy naming his wife as beneficiary. He does not disclose his health condition in the application. Three years later, he dies. If the insurance company learns of the misrepresentation in the application, it will not have to pay on the policy, but will merely return Lenny's premiums to his estate. The misrepresentation clearly increased the company's risk, and it would not have issued the policy had it known the truth.

2. Rhonda, a smoker, states in her life insurance application for a $100,000 life insurance policy that she is a nonsmoker. Three years later, she dies. Her beneficiary will be entitled to payment on the policy, even though the fact that she was a smoker increased the insurer's risk, because the insurer would still have insured her had it known the truth. However, the amount that will be paid under the policy is not $100,000, but rather a lesser amount representing the coverage that her premiums would have bought for a smoker's policy. (If, for example, a smoker's policy is 25 percent more expensive than a nonsmoker's policy, the face value of the policy would be reduced by 25 percent.)

Judge for Yourself

Case 1.   Fausto drafts a will that contains the following clauses:

1. To my wife, Sandra, whose guts I've hated for the past 25 years, I leave nothing but my undying hatred.
2. To my son, Harold, I leave my old pair of sneakers and a copy of the latest Sunday edition of *The New York Times,* so that he can hit the pavement and get a job.
3. To my daughter, Darlene, I leave $1 million and my home in the Hamptons.
4. To my secretary, Lina Lovely, I leave the balance of my estate.
5. I appoint my daughter, Darlene, to be executrix of my estate.
6. I leave my body to State Hospital, which may utilize it for any purpose consistent with medical research, including adding my organs to its organ bank. In so doing, I hope that my death may contribute to the furtherance of medical knowledge and perhaps even save a life.

Assume that the will was duly witnessed and executed while the testator was of sound mind and that he dies leaving a $10 million estate.

    a. Does the will effectively disinherit Fausto's wife? Why?

    b. Does the will effectively disinherit the son, Harold?

    c. Is it proper to include in a will a gift of the testator's body for scientific purposes?

    d. Assume that the state in which the will was executed requires the signatures of three witnesses for it to be valid, and further assume that the daughter, Darlene, signed as one of the three witnesses. What effect will this have on the validity of the will? On Darlene's devise? Explain fully.

Case 2. Assume that the will in Case 1 is challenged and held to be invalid due to the testator's mental incapacity at the time the will was drafted. Further assume that all other facts are the same and that the wife Sandra, the daughter Darlene, and the son Harold were alive when the testator died, along with the testator's parents, grandparents, and a plethora of brothers, sisters, nieces, nephews, and first cousins.

    a. If the intestacy statute in the testator's state is patterned after New York's, who will be entitled to receive part of the testator's estate, and in what amounts? (Remember, the total estate is $10 million.) See case study 4–3 for the text of the New York intestacy statute.

    b. If Harold predeceased his father, leaving three children of his own, what, if anything, would each of them be entitled to receive under the intestacy statute?

Case 3. Irving, a blue-collar worker of modest means, dies intestate. His wife, Martha, survives him, as do his children, Thomas and Gwendolyn. Irving and Martha owned their own home as tenants by the entirety; the equity in the home is $150,000. Other than the home, the total value of Irving's estate after paying off his debts is $4,000.

    a. Assuming an intestacy statute similar to New York's, what are the wife and children entitled to receive from the estate under the intestacy statute? See case study 4–3 for the text of the New York intestacy statute.

    b. What will happen to the house?

    c. Irving had always maintained that wills are for the rich and that the only purpose they have for common folks is to line the pockets of all the lawyers out there. Was he right? Explain.

Case 4. Loretta, a politician, decides to place all her property into a blind trust to avoid possible conflict of interest problems while she is in office. She asks her attorney to set up the trust and be its sole trustee. The attorney sets up the trust to remain in existence as long as Loretta is in office and to automatically terminate, with the corpus of the trust reverting to Loretta, upon her leaving public office.

a. What can Loretta do if she finds out that the trustee is embezzling money from her fund?

b. If Loretta finds that the lawyer, while acting in good faith, is not as aggressive as she'd like him to be in his investment strategy, can she take over the management of the trust?

c. Does the fact that the trust has limited duration bring into question its validity?

CASE STUDY 4–1
BAILMENTS

MILTON BLAKEMORE, ET AL. v. JOHN B. COLEMAN, d/b/a THE
FAIRFAX and THE JOCKEY CLUB, APPELLANT
No. 82–1187
UNITED STATES COURT OF APPEALS FOR THE DISTRICT OF
COLUMBIA
CIRCUIT

701 F.2d 967
Argued November 1, 1982
March 4, 1983

PRIOR HISTORY: Appeal from the United States District Court for the District of Columbia

COUNSEL: M. Michael Cramer, for Appellant. Michael J. Connelly, for Appellees. Robert J. Woody and E. Payson Fitts were on the brief, for Appellees.

OPINION:

Before: MACKINNON, MIKVA and SCALIA, Circuit Judges.

MIKVA, Circuit Judge: This case, premised on diversity jurisdiction, requires that the court apply the law of bailment for the District of Columbia. Eleanor and Milton Blakemore initiated this suit in federal district court to obtain damages for jewelry that disappeared while they ate lunch in The Jockey Club restaurant, owned by John B. Coleman and located in The Fairfax Hotel (collectively referred to as defendants). The case proceeded through a full trial, after which a jury awarded the Blakemores $35,680 in compensatory damages. We reverse the judgment on that verdict, however, because a central issue was erroneously removed from the jury's deliberations: whether the defendants had constructive knowledge that valuable jewelry was stored in the Blakemore's luggage. We therefore remand this case to the district court for a new trial.

I. BACKGROUND

The decision in this case turns uniquely on the facts. The Blakemores were in Washington, D.C. to celebrate President Reagan's inauguration, staying as overnight guests at a hotel in Georgetown. Before returning home, they decided to have lunch at The Jockey Club, a restaurant with a reputation for elegance. Upon arriving at the restaurant, which was then part of The Fairfax Hotel, the Blakemores checked their car and three large suitcases with the hotel doorman. At the same time, they carried two pieces of hand luggage—a briefcase and a small, carry-on bag—into the hotel themselves. It was the carry-on bag that contained the jewelry that eventually disappeared; specifically, the missing jewelry was in one of two small jewelry pouches that the Blakcmores had stored in the bag. The bag itself was made of leather, was two-feet long by nine-and-one-inches wide, and was closed only by means of a zipper. No other locks or safety devices secured the main compartment of the bag.

When the Blakemores entered the hotel, they checked their two bags with the hotel bellman, who proceeded to place the bags in a small holding room or checkroom adjacent to the lobby. That room had neither a door separating it from the lobby nor any posted sign that would limit the defendants' liability under D.C. CODE ANN. § 34–101 (1981) (allowing hotels to limit liability if, inter alia, they conspicuously post such notice). The Blakemores did not inform the bellamn [sic] of the valuable jewelry contained in their bags or ask about locked storage area; neither did the bellman inquire whether such valuables existed or inform the Blakemores that safety deposit boxes or other locked storage compartments were available for their use.

Following their lunch in the restaurant, the Blakemores returned to the hotel lobby to retrieve their belongings. Having done so, Mrs. Blakemore immediately opened the carry-on bag only to discover that one of the jewelry pouches was missing. It was at this point that the defendants actually were notified of the jewelry's existence and apparent disappearance. A search of the hotel by employees of The Fairfax and the police was unsuccessful in locating the missing pouch or any of the jewelry that it contained.

Four months later, the Blakemores filed this action in district court seeking compensation for the missing jewelry. At a pretrial conference, counsel for the Blakemores requested jury instructions that incorporated a theory of innkeeper's liability, or alternatively, that charged the defendants with responsibility under the law of bailment. The trial judge ruled against the Blackmores on the issue of innkeeper's liability, but allowed the case to go to jury on an ordinary bailee-for-hire theory. Specifically, the jury was instructed in relevant part as follows:

If you find by a preponderance of the evidence that the defendant's employees accepted the custody of the plaintiffs' luggage, and that the plaintiffs' jewelry was contained in such luggage when checked with the defendant's employee, but was missing [when] that luggage was returned to the plaintiffs, you must find defendant liable for the loss of the jewelry.

Trial Transcript (Tr.) 438. Based on this instruction, the jury returned its verdict in favor of the Blakemores. The defendants then moved for judgment notwithstanding the verdict or, in the alternative, for a new trial, claiming that the court erred when it failed to instruct the jury that the defendants could be held liable as bailee of the jewelry only if they had knowledge, either actual or constructive, of the jewelry's existence. See Record EXCERPTS (RE) 10. These motions were denied by the district court in a written order, RE 6–9, and this appeal followed.

II. INNKEEPER'S LIABILITY

Before discussing the issue of constructive knowledge that is central to this appeal, we must consider an alternative basis urged by the Blakemores for upholding the judgment of the district court. Specifically, the Blakemores argue that the trial judge should have found the defendants subject to innkeeper's liability, making them responsible for the contents of luggage belonging to their guests regardless of their knowledge about those contents.[1]

See, e.g., Governor House v. Schmidt, 284 A. 2d 660 (D.C. 1971). It is true that application of the strict liability imposed on innkeepers would require affirmance of the district court's judgment; but the Blakemores misconstrue the basis on which D.C. law premises an innkeeper-guest relationship. Indeed, in the latest case to define the scope of that relationship, Wallace v. Shoreham Hotel Corp, 49 A. 2d 81 (D.C. 1946), the D.C. Municipal Court of Appeals explicitly held that "[o]ne who is merely a customer at a bar, a restaurant, a barber shop or [a] newsstand operated by a hotel does not thereby establish the relationship of innkeeper and guest." Id. at 82; cf. Governor House, 284 A. 2d at 661–62 (applying innkeeper's liability in action brought by overnight guests of hotel); Hotel Corp. of America v. Travelers Indemnity Co., 229 A. 2d 158 (D.C. 1867) (same). Absent any indication that the D.C. courts have subsequently modified that definition, the federal courts are bound to follow that holding when applying D.C. law.

Nor is there any sound justification for distinguishing between the Blakemores and other restaurant patrons simply because the restaurant they happened to visit is located within a hotel. Cake v. District of Columbia, 33 App. D.C. 272 (D.C. Cir. 1909), heavily relied on by the Blakemores, is not to the contrary. In that case, the court defined "bona fide registered guests" to include customers partaking of a hotel's food or lodging. Id. at 277. That court, however, was interpreting language included in a criminal statute, and was not delineating the scope of the innkeeper-guest relationship created by the common law. Thus, the district court was correct to conclude that the Blakemores could not premise their action on the strict liability imposed on innkeepers.

III. CONSTRUCTIVE KNOWLEDGE

The Blakemores can sustain their damages award, therefore, only under a bailee-for-hire theory. The law of bailment for the District of Columbia, which the defendants admit is applicable to this case, requires that the subject matter of the bailment be delivered to, and accepted by, the bailee. It is not required, however, that the bailee have actual knowledge of the property in its custody in order to be liable for the property's eventual loss. Rather, when the property that is subject to the bailment is enclosed within a container, responsibility for its disappearance may rest with the bailee even though the bailee has only constructive or imputed knowledge of its existence. See Dumlao v. Atlantic Garage, Inc., 259 A. 2d 360 (D.C. 1969) (contents of an automobile); Hallman v. Federal Parking Services, 134 A. 2d 382 (D.C. 1957) (same). Such constructive knowledge about the contents of a container has been defined to include those items that are in plain view, see Dumlae, 259 A. 2d at 362, or that could be expected, given "common knowledge and experience," to be in a container under the specific facts and circumstances of a particular case, see Hallman, 134 A. 2d at 385.

The mere articulation of this legal standard inescapably leads to the conclusion that a finding of constructive knowledge is a mixed question of law and fact. As with a finding of negligence, the specific facts underlying a given situation must be determined by the trier of fact before the legal standard can be properly applied. In the usual trial setting, the trial judge will explain the legal standard in his or her instructions, but the jury, uniquely qualified to make factual determinations, will apply that standard to the particular facts at issue. See generally W. PROSSER, HANDBOOK OF THE LAW OR TORTS § 37 (4th ed. 1971) (discussing respective functions of court and jury in finding of negligence). In the present case, therefore, whether the defendants had constructive knowledge that the Blakemores' carry-on bag might contain valuable jewelry should have been left to the jury.

The district court ruled first that "[t]he evidence mandated a finding of constructive notice, leaving no question of fact for the injury in this regard," RE 8, and then that "[a]rticles of jewelry are, as a matter of law, commonly and appropriately carried in hand luggage," id. Both rulings, which had the effect of conclusively removing this issue from the jury's deliberations, were erroneous.[2]

The first ruling quoted above—that the evidence "mandated a finding" of constructive knowledge—effectively concluded that every reasonable juror necessarily would have found that the defendants had implied notice of the valuable jewelry contained in the Blakemores' carry-on bag. Although such a finding would not be clearly erroneous if the trial judge were serving as the trier of fact, the trial court committed reversible error when it removed the issue from the jury. The only fact that was conclusively established at trial was that the bag had some tangible contents. Whether those contents were valuable jewelry or just dirty laundry, however, could not be considered a foreclosed issue. Indeed, facts clearly existed from which conflicting inferences could be drawn. For example, it is conceded that the Blakemores arrived at the hotel only to have lunch, that they neither mentioned the valuables stored inside the bag or complained when the bag was placed in an unlocked holding room, and that the bag itself was unlocked. By themselves, these facts would seem to require submission of the case to the jury. Cf. Dumlao, 259 A. 2d at 362 (upholding a directed verdict in a bailment case when there was "no evidence to show knowledge"). Compare Wilkerson v. McCarthy, 336 U.S. 53, 57 (1949) ("It is the established rule that in passing upon whether there is sufficient evidence to submit an issue to the jury we need look only to the evidence and reasonable inferences which tend to support the case of a litigant against whom a peremptory instruction has been given") with Drapaniotis v. Franklin, 504 F. 2d 236, 237 (D.C. Cir. 1974) (per curiam) ("[i]n resolving [whether the trial court erred in directing a verdict for appellee] we must, of course, view the evidence, and the permissible inference therefrom, in the light most favorable to appellant") (citing Brady v. Southern Railway, 320 U.S. 476, 479 (1943) and Muldrow v. Daly, 329 F. 2d 886, 888 (D.C. Cir. 1964)). See generally Vander Zee v. Karabatsos, 589 F. 2d 723, 726–28 (D.C. Cir. 1978) (discussing standard for entering a directed verdict or j.n.o.v.) cert. denied, 441 U.S. 962 (1979). This is especially true when, as in this case, the trial judge takes an issue from the jury by ruling in favor of the party that bears the burden of persuasion. Cf. Lucas v. Auto Parking, 62 A. 2d 557, 559 (D.C. 1941) (burden on plaintiff to prove bailment).

Nor can we approve of the district court's ruling that valuable jewelry is, "as a matter of law, commonly and appropriately carried in hand luggage." To support that ruling, the trial judge relied on Hasbrouck v. New York Cent. & H.R.R., 95 N.E. 808 (N.Y. 1911), and the Blakemores cite Sherman v. Pullman Co., 139 N.Y.S. 51 (App. Div. 1013). Even if these New York cases are somehow controlling in a diversity case applying D.C. law, they do not stand for the proposition stated. In Hasbrouck, for example, the specific paragraph relied on, 95 N.E. at 813, was an appellate court conclusion that there was sufficient evidence to support the trial judge's findings of fact; no conclusion of law about jewelry was made at the trial level. Similarly, in Sherman, the appellate court simply held that the lower court's conclusion that the term "baggage" included jewelry found inside was not "against the weight of the evidence." 139 N.Y.S. at 52. Thus, in both cases the courts were affirming findings of fact made by trial judges serving as triers of fact; neither opinion is appropriate precedent for the lower court's action in the present case.

In sum, a straightforward application of the law of bailment for the District of Columbia requires that the jury determine whether the defendants in this case had constructive knowledge of the existence of valuable jewelry in the Blakemores' carry-on bag. To this extent, the district court's judgment must be reversed, and the case remanded for a new trial.

IV. PROCEEDINGS ON REMAND

Our holding requires that a retrial on all issues be held. Any decision concerning the defendant's constructive knowledge of valuable jewelry is too enmeshed with the other issues presented to allow for separate consideration.

Even assuming the jury concludes that the defendants had constructive knowledge that valuable jewelry was contained in the Blakemores' carry-on bag, it does not follow that the defendants would be liable for unlimited amount or value of jewelry. The defendants had a right to assume that patrons of the restaurant would not check articles having an unreasonably high value without informing the bellman. Thus, the trial judge should further instruct the jury to limit its potential damage award to the maximum value of goods which the defendants reasonably could expect to be left in baggage checked under the particular circumstances of the present case. Only in this way can the necessary and appropriate limits be set on the liability that might be imposed on the defendants.

It is so ordered.

Questions for Case Study 4–1
1. What are the basic facts of this case?
2. What are the legal issues involved?
3. What is the decision of the court?
4. What is the legal rationale for the court's decision?
5. What does this case teach you about the liability of hotels to their guests?

6. Why does the strict liability of innkeepers not apply to the hotel in this case?

Footnotes

1. The defendants argue, without citation, that the Blakemores have not properly raised the issue of innkeeper's liability because they did not formally file a cross-appeal in this court. Such a contention, however, fails to comprehend the ordinary practice of federal appellate courts. Although an appellee may not attack a district court order "with a view either to enlarging his own rights thereunder or of lessening the right of his adversary," it is "settled that the appellee may, without taking a cross-appeal urge in support of a decree any matter appearing in the record, although his argument may involve an attack upon the reasoning of the lower court or an insistence upon matter overlooked or ignored by it." United States v. American Ry. Express, 265 U.S. 425, 435 (1924) (Brandeis, J.) (footnote omitted); see also Colautti v. Franklin, 439 U.S. 379, 397 N. 16 (1979); Koniag, Inc. v. Andrus, 580 F. 2d; 601, 605 n. 3 (D.C. Cir.), cert. denied, 439 U.S. 1052 (1978).

2. The Blakemores maintain that the defendants did not timely object to the trial judge's rulings on the issue of constructive knowledge. Specifically, they argue that the jury instructions originally proposed by counsel for the defendants and the objections raised immediately before the court recited its chosen instructions to the jury concerned only actual knowledge. The proposed jury instructions, however, referred to the "knowledge" of the defendants, see RE 18, and therefore could be read to include either actual or constructive knowledge. Indeed, the defendants' pretrial brief expressly cited the "express or imputed knowledge" standard. See Defendant's Pretrial Brief at 4, reprinted in Appendix to Reply Brief of Appellant. As for the sufficiency of objections raised prior to the court's instructions to the jury, the trial transcript only indicates an objection to "complete knowledge" instructions. Tr. 425–46. Those words, however, apparently were intended to be a brief reference to extended discussions that had already occurred in the judge's chambers. Thus, "complete knowledge" is properly read to include actual or constructive knowledge, and the defendants have satisfied Federal Rule of Civil Procedure 51.

CASE STUDY 4–2
COPYRIGHT INFRINGEMENT

TIN PAN APPLE, INC., SUTRA RECORDS, INC., FOOLS PRAYER
MUSIC, INC., and MAR MORALES, DARREN ROBINSON, and DAMON
WIMBLEY (together p/k/a the "FAT BOYS"), Plaintiffs, v.
MILLER BREWING CO., INC., BACKER & SPIELVOGEL, INC. and JOE
PISCOPO, Defendants

Case No. 88 Civ. 4085 (CSH)

UNITED STATES DISTRICT COURT FOR THE SOUTHERN DISTRICT OF
NEW YORK

737 F. Supp. 826; 1990 U.S. Dist. LEXIS 5747; 15 U.S.P.Q.2D
(BNA) 1412; Copy. L. Rep. (CCH) P26,577

May 14, 1990, Decided

COUNSEL: RICHARDS & O'NEIL, New York, New York, Attorneys for
Plaintiffs, Of Counsel: Jonathan Zavin, Esq.

DAVIS & GILBERT, New York City, New York, Attorneys for Defendants. Howard J. Schwartz, Esq., Maribel Figueredo, Esq.,
Bruce Ginsberg, Esq., of counsel.

JUDGES: Charles S. Haight, Jr., United States District Judge.

OPINION: MEMORANDUM OPINION AND ORDER

CHARLES S. HAIGHT, JR., UNITED STATES DISTRICT JUDGE.

Background

This action arises out of the professional activities of the three individual
plaintiffs, Mark Morales, Darren Robinson, and Damon Wimbley, profession-
ally known as the "Fat Boys." The amended complaint alleges that by 1983,
these plaintiffs were singing together and performing in a distinctive singing
style known as "rapping." Rapping is generally alleged to be "spoken or
semi-sung rhyming verse recited over a powerful rhythm track created by
drums and drum sounds; it is lyrics over an almost exclusively percussion-
based melody." Amended complaint at para. 11.

Plaintiff Tin Pan Apple, Inc. is alleged to be the owner of the registered service mark FAT BOYS for performing services and a copyright owner of various FAT BOYS sound recordings. Plaintiff Sutra Records, Inc. is the copyright

owner of various FAT BOYS sound recordings, including specific recordings
listed in para. 16 of the amended complaint. Plaintiff Fools Prayer Music, Inc.
is one of the copyright owners of and the administrator of various compositions the FAT BOYS perform, including all but one of the compositions listed
in para. 16. Id. at paras. 2–4.

Defendant Miller Brewing Co., Inc., manufactures and distributes beer. Defendant Backer & Spielvogel, Inc., is an advertising agency that creates commercials and advertising campaigns for Miller. Defendant Joe Piscopo is a comedian who appeared in the television commercial forming the subject
matter of this suit.

The amended complaint alleges at para. 29:

In 1987, defendants created, manufactured and arranged for the repeated
broadcast of a 30-second commercial on prime-time television for Miller Beer
featuring three FAT BOYS look-alikes performing in the distinctly FAT BOYS
style described above (the "Commercial"). Miller and/or Backer & Spielvogel
had contacted Morales, Wimbley and Robinson to appear in such a commercial as FAT BOYS, but the boys had declined. The Commercial has appeared
repeatedly on national television, including in the State of New York, and in
other media and continues to appear there.

The pleading contains detailed descriptions of the individual plaintiffs'
physical appearance and dress while performing; the manner in which they
perform; their youth; and the messages they seek by the lyrics of their songs
to convey to youth: "to stay in school, to avoid all use of drugs or alcohol,
and to abstain from sexual activity or to use contraceptive protection." P. 27;
see also P. 22–26, 28.

In these circumstances, plaintiffs' amended complaint asserts nine claims
against defendants. The first two allege copyright infringement, of musical
compositions and sound recordings respectively, and are founded upon the
federal Copyright Act. . . .

The Copyright Claims

Given these considerations, it is idle for defendants to argue on this motion
that they have never "copied any of the copyrighted works in question."
Reply Brief at 2. Plaintiffs allege that defendants copied parts of one or
more of their copyrighted sound recordings, and composed and broadcast
a melody substantially similar to one or more of plaintiff's compositions.
The precise meaning of "one or more" may be explored on discovery, and
plaintiff's [sic] have the burden of proof; but for purposes of the present motion, defendants concede copying the Fat Boys' particular expression of rap
music.

This does not end the inquiry. Defendants submit a copy of the television
commercial in suit which the Court has examined. Defendants' main defense
to the copyright claims characterizes the commercials as a[n] "obvious parody
of rap", constituting a "fair use which prevents a claim of copyright infringement." Main Brief at 6.

Whatever legal meaning "parody" may have in other contexts, cf. Hustler Magazine v. Falwell, 485 U.S. 46, 99 L. Ed. 2d 41, 108 S. Ct. 876 (1988) (application of First Amendment to magazine publisher's caricature of a public figure), in copyright law parody forms a part of the broader concept of fair use. Section 101 of the 1976 Copyright Act Revisions, 17 U.S.C. § 107, intended to be a codification of preexisting law, MCA, Inc. v. Wilson, 677 F. 2d 180 (2d Cir. 1981), provides in part that "the fair use of a copyrighted work. . . for purposes such as criticism, comment, . . . is not an infringement of copyright." The House Committee on the Judiciary reporting on the statute in H.Rep. No. 94–1476 (reprinted in West's U.S.C.A. 1977 at 111–117), observes that the act gives "express statutory recognition for the first time" to the "judicial doctrine of fair use, one of the most important and well-established limitations on the exclusive right of copyright owners. . . ." A list of examples of fair use which the Committee derived from the Register's 1961 Report includes "use in a parody of some of the content of the work parodied. . . ."

In Warner Bros., Inc. v. American Broadcasting, Inc., 720 F. 2d 231, 242 (2d Cir. 1983), the Second Circuit said:

under the "fair use" doctrine, codified in 17 U.S.C. § 107(2) (Supp. V 1981), courts have allowed the taking of words or phrases when adapted for use as commentary or parody, see, e.g., Elsmere Music, Inc. v. National Broadcasting Co., 623 F. 2d 252 (2d Cir. 1980) (per curiam); Berlin v. E.C. Publications, Inc., 329 F. 2d 541 (2d Cir.), cert. denied, 379 U.S. 822, 85 S. Ct. 46, 13 L. Ed. 2d 33, 144 U.S.P.Q. (BNA) 464 (1964).

The "parody" branch of the "fair use" doctrine is itself a means of fostering the creativity protected by the copyright law. It also balances the public interest in the free flow of ideas with the copyright holder's interest in the exclusive use of his work.

Parody, then, qualifies generally as fair use in copyright law. Whether a particular work qualifies as fair use requires consideration of the four elements § 107 goes on to recite:

In determining whether the use made of a work in any particular case is a fair use the factors to be considered shall include:

(1) the purpose and character of the use, including whether such use is of a commercial nature or is for nonprofit education purposes;

(2) the nature of the copyrighted work;

(3) the amount and substantiality of the portion used in relation to the copyrighted work as a whole; and

(4) the effect of the use upon the potential market for or value of the copyrighted work.

In the area of parody as copyright infringement, Second Circuit case law focuses first upon the general question—is the defendant's work truly a parody?—and then considers the four particular factors set forth in § 107(1)–(4).

Thus in Elsmere Music, Inc. v. National Broadcasting Co., 482 F. Supp. 741 (S.D.N.Y.), affirmed 623 F. 2d 252 (2d Cir. 1989), upon which the present defendants rely, the alleged infringement arose out of a skit on the television program "Saturday Night Live" which, in the court of appeals' phrase, "poked fun at New York City's public relations campaign and its theme song." 623 F. 2d at 253. That fun was poked by a parody of the copyrighted song "I Love New York" called "I Love Sodom." The district court summarized the nature and thrust of the parody:

The song "I Love Sodom," as well as the sketch of which it was a part, was clearly an attempt by the writers and cast of SNL to satirize the way in which New York City has attempted to improve its somewhat tarnished image through the use of a slick advertising campaign. 482 F. Supp. at 745.

District Judge Goettel rejected the plaintiff's argument that the song "I Love Sodom" and the sketch of which it was a part "did not constitute a valid parody of the 'I Love New York' advertising campaign." Id. at 746. Judge Goettel then said:

Having found that SNL sketch and song validly parodied the plaintiff's jingle and the "I Love New York" advertising campaign in general, the Court next turns to the important question of whether such use has tended to interfere with the marketability of the copyrighted work. Id. at 747.

Judge Goettel answered that question in the negative and dismissed plaintiff's infringement action.

The Second Circuit affirmed per curiam "On Judge Goettel's thorough opinion," 623 F. 2d at 253; but notwithstanding that thoroughness, was moved to append a footnote which reads as follows:

The District Court concluded, among other things, that the parody did not make more extensive use of appellant's song than was necessary to "conjure up" the original. 482 F. Supp. at 747. While we agree with this conclusion, we note that the concept of "conjuring up" an original came into the copyright law not as a limitation on how much of an original may be used, but as a recognition that a parody frequently needs to be more than a fleeting evocation of an original in order to make its humorous point. Columbia Pictures Corp., v. National Broadcasting Co., 137 F. Supp. 348, 354 (S.D. Cal. 1955). A parody is entitled at least to "conjure up" the original. Even more extensive use would still be fair use, provided the parody builds upon the original, using the original as a known element of modern culture and contributing something new for humorous effect or commentary.

I perceive in that footnote a Second Circuit articulation of what a "valid parody" is. And I conclude that a work, clearly copied from a protected work (as I am bound to regard the defendants' work at bar) must be a valid parody if it is to qualify even for consideration as an example of fair use under § 107.

That conclusion is not inconsistent with Berlin v. E.C. Publications, 329 F. 2d 541 (2d Cir. 1964), the second case upon which present defendants rely. In Berlin the publishers of "Mad Magazine" put together a "collection of parody lyrics to 57 Old Standards which reflect the idiotic world we live in today." 329 F. 2d at 543. So that the parody lyrics could be sung, they were written in the same meter as the original lyrics, as illustrated by the parody of "A Pretty Girl is Like a Melody": "Louella Schwartz Describes her Malady." The court of appeals affirmed dismissal of the original song publisher's claims of infringement. Judge Kaufman wrote:

The disparities in theme, content and style between the original lyrics and the alleged infringements could hardly be greater. In the vast majority of cases, the rhyme scheme of the parodies bears no relationship to the originals. While brief phrases of the original lyrics were occasionally injected into the parodies, this practice would seem necessary if the defendants' efforts were to "recall or conjure up" the originals; the humorous effect achieved when a familiar line interposed in a totally incongruous setting, traditionally a tool of parodists, scarcely amounts to a "substantial" taking, if that standard is not to be woodenly applied. Similarly, the fact that defendants' parodies were written in the same meter as plaintiffs' compositions would seem inevitable if the original was to be recognized, but such a justification is not even necessary; we doubt that even so eminent a composer as plaintiff Irving Berlin should be permitted to claim a property interest in iambic pentameter. Id. at 545.

The Second Circuit concluded its opinion in Berlin with these words:

At the very least, where, as here, it is clear that the parody has neither the intent nor the effect of fulfilling the demand for the original, and where the parodist does not appropriate a greater amount of the original work than is necessary to "recall or conjure up" the object of his satire, a finding of infringement would be improper. Ibid.

The alleged copyright infringers in Elsmere and Berlin were a comedy television program and a comic magazine: both vehicles for the expression of that creative flow of ideas which the Second Circuit identified in Warner Bros as the justification for the parody branch of the fair use doctrine. But there is ample authority for the proposition that appropriation of copyrighted material solely for personal profit, unrelieved by any creative purpose, cannot constitute parody as matter of law. Judge Leval reached that conclusion for this Court in D.C. Comics v. Crazy Eddie, 205 U.S.P.Q. (BNA) 1177 (S.D.N.Y. 1979). The defendant produced and broadcast on local television channels a filmed commercial for his consumer electronic equipment which represented a "detailed copying" of plaintiff's copyrighted televised "trailers" for "Superman" television programs. Defendant argued that his commercial was a parody of the protected "Superman" work, relying as do defendants at bar upon Berlin. Judge Leval rejected the defense of a parody as fair use:

Recognizing the validity of the proposition that parody is entitled to greater freedom than other uses, see Berlin v. E.C. Publications, Inc., 329 F. 2d 541, 141 U.S.P.Q. (BNA) 1 (2d Cir. 1964), I find that defendant's commercial is not parody. This is not a case of fair use, but one of unjustifiable appropriation of copyrighted material for personal profit. 205 USPQ at 1178.

In Warner Bros. v. American Broadcasting Companies, supra, the Second Circuit expressly approved D.C. Comics, Inc. v. Crazy Eddie, Inc., in an analysis which it is useful to quote at length:

No matter how well known a copyrighted phrase becomes, its author is entitled to guard against its appropriation to promote the sale of commercial products. That doctrine enabled the proprietors of the Superman copyright to prevent a discount chain from using a television commercial that parodied well-known lines associated with Superman. D.C. Comics, Inc. v. Crazy Eddie, Inc., 205 U.S.P.Q. (BNA) 1177 (S.D.N.Y. 1979) ("Look! . . . It's a bird! . . . It's a plane! . . . It's . . . Crazy Eddie!"). But an original work of authorship with elements of parody, though undoubtedly created in the hope of commercial success, stands on a different footing from the products of a discount chain. Whatever aesthetic appeal such a work may have results from the creativity that the copyright law is designed to promote. It is decidedly in the interests of creativity, not privacy, to permit authors to take well-known phrases and fragments from copyrighted works and add their own contributions of commentary or humor. 720 F. 2d at 242 (footnote omitted).

It is worth noting that D.C. Comics, as interpreted by the Second Circuit in Warner Bros., did not involve the sale by defendant of products which competed with plaintiff's product. The Crazy Eddie electronics discount chain did not compete in any fashion with the plaintiff's Superman comic books and filmed television productions. No matter: the parody as fair use defense failed because defendant's use of appropriated copyrighted material "to promote the sale of commercial products" simply did not qualify as parody.

Original Appalachian Artworks v. Topps Chewing Gum, 642 F. Supp. 1031 (N.D.Ga 1986), reaches the same result, although within the context of the first element specified in § 107, namely, "the purpose and character of the use, including whether such use is of a commercial nature or is for nonprofit educational purposes. . . ." In Topps the defendant, a chewing gum manufacturer, began distributing "Garbage Pail Kids" stickers and chewing gum cards. Plaintiff, a marketer of dolls under the copyright and trademark "Cabbage Patch Kids," brought an action for copyright and trademark infringement. The defendant argued fair use under the Copyright Act on the basis of parody. The District Court rejected the parody defense because "the primary purpose behind defendant's parody is not an effort to make a social comment but is an attempt to make money." The court continued:

Neither are the Garbage Pail Kid stickers merely one of a series of spoofs of various different products, as defendant has produced in the past, nor a single cartoon or editorial in a broader satirical product such as Mad Magazine. The basic concept behind the defendant's stickers is aimed at capitalizing on the Cabbage Patch craze. 642 F. Supp. at 1034.

In a case where plaintiff and defendant competed in the entertainment field, the Second Circuit stressed defendants' commercial purposes in rejecting a fair use defense based on parody:

The district court held that defendants' song was neither a parody or burlesque of Bugle Boy nor a humorous comment on the music of the '40's. [MCA, Inc. v. Wilson] 425 F. Supp. [443] 453. We are not prepared to hold that a commercial composer can plagiarize a competitor's copyrighted song, substitute dirty lyrics of his own, perform it for commercial gain, and then escape liability by calling the end result a parody or satire on the mores of society. Such a holding would be an openended invitation to musical plagiarism. We conclude that defendants did not make fair use of plaintiff's song. MCA, Inc. v. Wilson, 677 F. 2d 180, 185 (2d Cir. 1981).

The Supreme Court in two recent cases has emphasized commercial purpose as a factor militating against fair use. Sony Corporation of America v. Universal City Studios, Inc., 464 U.S. 417, 451, 78 L. Ed. 2d 574, 104 S. Ct. 774 (1984) (". . . although every commercial use of copyrighted material is presumptively an unfair exploitation of the monopoly privilege that belongs to the owner of a copyright, non-commercial uses are a different matter.") (held, non-commercial home use recording of material broadcast over the public airways was a fair use of copyrighted works and did not constitute copyright infringement); Harper & Row v. Nation Enterprises, 471 U.S. 539, 562, 85 L.

Ed. 2d 588, 105 S. Ct. 2218 (1985) (quoting the above language from Sony and adding: "the crux of the profit/nonprofit distinction is not whether the sole motive of the use is monetary gain but whether the user stands to profit from exploitation of the copyrighted material without paying the customary price.") (article in The Nation using generous verbatim excerpts of President Ford's unpublished expression to lend authenticity to his account of his forthcoming memoirs constituted an arrogation of the right of first publication a.

In D.C. Comics, Judge Leval did not feel it necessary to analyze the four "fair use" factors specified in § 107. He simply concluded that the television commercial could not qualify as a fair use parody because it was nothing more than an unjustifiable appropriation of copyrighted material for personal profit. The other cited cases engage in a more detailed § 107 analysis. I do not think it makes any difference here, since in either event defendants' commercial does not qualify as parody. The commercial's use is entirely for profit: to sell beer. Even if the concept of parody is impermissibly stretched to include this commercial, it does not qualify as fair use, since accepting the pertinent allegations of the complaint as true, the commercial in no manner "builds upon the original," nor does it contain elements "contributing something new for humorous effect or commentary." Elsmere, supra.

An additional factor militating against fair use emerges from plaintiff's pleading. A court may consider "whether the paraphrasing and copying was done in good faith or with evasive motive." MCA, Inc. v. Wilson, supra, at 183. Plaintiffs allege that defendants Miller and its advertising agency had contacted plaintiffs Morales, Wimbley and Robinson to appear in such a commercial but they had declined. Subsequently defendants put together the commercial in suit, using look-alikes of the individual plaintiffs as background performers for Piscopo. Accepting as I must on this motion the truth of all reasonable inferences to be drawn from the complaint's factual allegations, it requires no effort to infer that, having been rebuffed by plaintiffs for such a commercial, defendants Miller and Backer proceeded to copy them. The finders of the fact could equate such conduct with bad faith and evasive motive on defendants' part.

Defendants insist that the complaint does no more than allege violation by the commercial of "the style of rap music as performed by the Fat Boys," and contend that "the copyright laws do not give a registrant exclusive ownership and control over an entire jenre [*sic*] music." Reply Brief at 4. On this motion, however, I must accept as true plaintiffs' allegations that the commercial infringes both copyrighted compositions, para. 36, and copyrighted sound recordings, para. 42.

Defendants' motion to dismiss the copyright claims is denied.

The Trademark Claims

The complaint alleges that plaintiffs Morales, Wimbley and Robinson adopted the name FAT BOYS to identify their musical performing group, and that on application of plaintiff Tin Pan Apple, Inc., that name was registered on the principal register in the United States Patent and Trademark Office. The complaint further alleges that Tin Pan Apple and the individual plaintiffs have entered into license agreements for the use of the name FAT BOYS for products such as clothing and toys; that the group has achieved commercial success and established good will associated with the name of FAT BOYS as a singing group; that the individual plaintiffs' "unique musical and performance style" has caused their name and service mark to become associated in the public mind "with a certain style of performance, type of music and message to be delivered by the music"; and that the public associates the individual plaintiffs "specifically with FAT BOYS in their recognizable personae of overweight, young singers who create a melody for their songs by vocal sounds rather than instruments and who consistently appear before the public wearing square studded eyeglasses, T-shirts, stripped sneakers, satin baseball jackets and large, gold name pendants around their necks." Paras. 45–49. Defendants' commercial is alleged to represent a deliberate attempt to misrepresent, mislead and confuse the public and customers of plaintiff's products and services into falsely believing:

1) that defendants' Commercial for a Miller-brand beer is performed by Morales, Wimbley and Robinson as FAT BOYS; 2) that defendants' Commercial for a Miller-brand beer is performed by Morales, Wimbley and Robinson as FAT BOYS in conjunction with and as back-up musical vocals to defendant Piscopo; 3) that Morales, Wimbley and Robinson, as FAT BOYS, endorse the drinking of beer and, specifically, the Miller product.

The complaint further alleges the particular physical characteristics and performance styles of the individual plaintiffs, and the manners in which the participants in the commercial closely resemble those characteristics and styles. Paras. 22–26, 30–31. Jurisdiction over the trademark claims is predicated on the Lanham Act, 15 U.S.C. §§ 1114, 1125(a).

Defendants argue that there is no substantial similarity between the performance depicted on the commercial and the performance of the Fat Boys, and hence no likelihood of consumer confusion. But I must take the complaint's factual allegations as true, and there is no basis for concluding on the pleadings that plaintiffs do not have a viable claim on this element.

Defendants again rely upon the defense of parody. The Second Circuit recognizes parody as a defense to a Lanham Act claim. Indeed, in Cliffs Notes, Inc. v. Bantam Doubleday Dell Publishing, Inc., 886 F. 2d 490 (2d Cir. 1989), the court upheld that defense and reversed the district court's preliminary injunction. The publisher of a college study guide, "Cliffs Notes," brought an action alleging that a cover of a parody, "Spy Notes," would give consumers the false impression that the parody was the study guide publisher's product. Defendant said that its product was a permissible parody. Judge Feinberg's opinion starts with the proposition "that parody is a form of artistic expression, protected by the First Amendment."[1] 886 F. 2d at 493. At the same time, the court recognized that "trademark protection is not lost simply because the allegedly infringing use is in connection with a work of artistic expression, ibid., citing and quoting Silverman v. CBS, Inc., 870 F. 2d 40, 49 (2d Cir.), cert. denied 106 L. Ed. 2d 568, 109 S. Ct. 3219 (1989). The Second Circuit then said in Cliffs Notes:

Conflict between these two policies is inevitable in the context of parody, because the keystone of parody is imitation. It is hard to imagine, for example, a successful parody of Time magazine that did not reproduce Time's trademarked red border. A parody must convey two simultaneous—and contradictory—messages: that it is the original, but also that it is not the original and is instead a parody. To the extent that it does only the former but not the latter, it is not only a poor parody but also vulnerable under trademark law, since the customer will be confused. Id. at 494.

Relying upon its prior analysis in Rogers v. Grimaldi, 875 F. 2d 994 (2d Cir. 1989), and observing that "the expressive element of parodies requires more protection than the labeling of ordinary commercial products," Id. at 495, the Second Circuit concluded in Cliff's Notes that the public interest in free expression and parody outweighed the slight risk of consumer confusion between the covers of the two publications.

For essentially the same reasons stated in connection with plaintiff's copyright claims, I decline to recognize defendants' commercial as parody. Accordingly that defense fails again.

A copyright claim is made out when defendant copies the protected work without the defense of fair use (such as parody). There is an additional element to a trademark claim. "The heart of a successful claim based upon §§ 32(1) and 43(a) of the Lanham Act, 15 U.S.C. §§ 1114(1) and 1125(a), and common law trademark infringement is the showing of likelihood of confusion as to the source or sponsorship of defendant's products." Standard & Poor's Corp. v. Commodity Exchange, 683 F. 2d 704, 708 (2d Cir. 1982). In this circuit courts consider six primary (although not exclusive) factors in deciding the issue of likelihood of confusion: (1) the strength of plaintiff's marks and name; (2) the similarity of plaintiff's and defendant's marks; (3) the proximity of plaintiff's and defendant's products; (4) evidence of actual confusion as to source or sponsorship; (5) sophistication of the defendant's audience; and (6) defendant's good or bad faith. Standard & Poor's Corp., supra, at 708; Polaroid Corp. v. Polarad Electronic Corp., 287 F.2d 492, 495 (2d Cir), cert. denied, 368 U.S. 820, 82 S. Ct. 36, 7 L. Ed. 2d 25, 131 U.S.P.Q. (BNA) 499 (1961).

On this aspect of the case at bar, Judge Motley's opinion in Allen v. National Video, Inc., 610 F. Supp. 612 (S.D.N.Y. 1985), is instructive. The plaintiff was the celebrity Woody Allen. Defendant National, the owner of a nationally franchised video rental chain, hired defendant Ron Smith Celebrity Look-Alikes to find an individual closely resembling Allen (the defendant Boroff), who defendant then used in a pictorial advertisement. Judge Motley granted plaintiff summary judgment on his trademark claim and a nationwide injunction. In a "look-alike" case, the court in Allen equated the (see court) first factor to "the extent to which plaintiff has developed a favorable association for his mark in the public's mind"; "mark" in this context consisting of the plaintiff's name and likeness. The second element, similarity of the "marks", reflects the similarity of plaintiff to the individual or individuals used by defendant.

As to the third factor, proximity of the products, the court in Allen observed that while plaintiff did not own a video rental chain, he was involved in producing and distributing his own motion pictures, and was "strongly identified with movies in the public mind." Id. at 628. Judge Motley also noted that "there is no requirement under the Act that the plaintiff and the defendant actually be in competition", ibid, citing James Burrough Ltd. v. Sign of the Beefeater, Inc., 540 F. 2d 266 (7th Cir. 1976).

Evidence of actual confusion, the fourth factor, "although highly probative of likelihood of confusion, is not required." Ibid.[2] As to the fifth factor, sophistication of the defendant's audience, the court in Allen reasoned that the average customer of National Video, or reader of the magazine "Video Review" (in which defendants' advertisement appeared) were "likely to be comparatively sophisticated about movies. . . ." Nonetheless, the court concluded, "given the close resemblance between defendant Boroff's photograph and plaintiff, there is no reason to believe that the audience's relative sophistication eliminates all likelihood of confusion; at a cursory glance, many consumers, even sophisticated ones, are likely to be confused." Ibid.

On the final factor, the good or bad faith of defendant, Judge Motley properly observed that where a defendant designs an advertisement intentionally to evoke an association with a plaintiff, they "must therefore at least have been aware of the risk of consumer confusion, which militates against a finding that their motives were completely innocent."

Turning from this useful "look-alike" case to the one at bar, I must first observe that the present motion is not that of plaintiff for summary judgment (which Judge Motley granted in Allen). Rather, defendants move to dismiss the complaint; and the standard is that of Rule 12(b)(6). Under the familiar principles discussed supra, the first and second factors—the strength of the plaintiffs' "marks" and name and the similarity of plaintiffs' and defendants' marks—are sufficiently alleged in the amended complaint and must be taken as true. The third factor, proximity of the products, which necessarily implicates consideration of the relevant market, suggests some differences: presumably not all devotees of rap music also drink beer. But it seems safe to assume that many of them do, and this factor is satisfied if there is a sufficient "intersection" of the audience involved. Allen v. Men's World Outlet Inc., 679 F. Supp. 360, 368 (S.D.N.Y. 1988).

As to actual confusion, the purpose of a Rule 12(b)(6) motion is not to seek out the sufficiency of evidence. In any event such evidence is not required to state a claim.

The fifth factor, sophistication of the defendant's audience, militates in plaintiffs' favor. The populations involved are individuals who watch performances of rap music and individuals who drink beer. Defendants cast wide nets. One cannot assume so great a degree of sophistication as to negate likelihood of confusion.

Given the factual allegations of the complaint, the sixth factor, defendants' bad faith, also militates strongly in favor of plaintiffs' claim. Indeed, the case is stronger for plaintiffs in that regard than Allen v. National Video, Inc. In that case, Judge Motley regarded defendants' motives as dubious when they deliberately procured a Woody Allen look-alike, even though there had been no prior communications with Allen about the advertisement in question. Plaintiffs at bar allege that defendants asked them to participate in a Miller Beer television commercial, they refused, and defendants then procured the look-alikes. That is bad faith raised to a higher power. A comparable course of conduct was characterized in Midler v. Ford Motor Co., 849 F. 2d 460, 462 (9th Cir. 1988), as that "of the average thief."

Plaintiff's trademark claims survive Rule 12(b)(6) challenge. Defendants' motion to dismiss these claims is denied.

The Rights of Privacy and Publicity Claims—"Look-Alikes"

Plaintiffs' sixth claim is based upon §§ 50 and 51 of the New York Civil Rights Law, whose provisions appear in the margin.[3] In essence, the individual plaintiffs claim that after they refused to make a television commercial for Miller and its advertising agency, defendants "publicly advertised for three fat Black males to appear in a commercial," and that the males appearing in the commercial in suit (exclusive of Piscopo) "bear a striking resemblance to and are look-alikes of each of the 'three fat Black males' constituting the Fat Boys." Amended Complaint para. 64.

Sections 50 and 51 of the Civil Rights Law "are penal in part, and should be construed accordingly," Lombardo v. Doyle, Dane & Bernbach, Inc., 58 A.D. 2d 620, 396 N.Y.S. 2d 661, 663 (2nd Dept. 1977). Ordinarily plaintiffs' "names, portraits, or pictures" must be used by a defendant to state a claim under §§ 50 and 51. Wojtowicz v. Delacorte Press, 43 N.Y. 2d 858, 403 N.Y.S. 2d 218, 374 N.E. 2d 129 (1978). The Civil Rights Law "is to be strictly construed and is not to be applied so as to prohibit the portrayal of an individual's personality or style of performance." Lombardo, supra, at 664.

Notwithstanding these general principles, there is also authority for the proposition that a defendant's deliberate seeking out and use of as close a look-alike as possible to the plaintiff falls within the ban of the statute, even if the plaintiff's name is not used. In Onassis v. Christian Dior–New York, Inc., 122 Misc. 2d 603, 472 N.Y.S. 2d 254 N.Y. Sup. Ct. (1984), aff'd., 110 A.D. 2d 1095, 488 N.Y.S. 2d 943 (1st Dept. 1985), defendant manufacturer retained the ubiquitous Ron Smith Celebrity Look-Alikes to find a model closely resembling Mrs. Jacqueline Kennedy Onassis to use in a pictorial advertisement, knowing full well that Mrs. Onassis would not consent to pose herself. While recognizing the requirement that the Civil Rights Law, "being in derogation of common law, receive a strict, if not a literal construction," 472 N.Y.S. 2d at 258, the court went on to say:

However, "since its purpose is remedial . . . 'to grant recognition to the newly expounded right of an individual to be immune from commercial exploitation' Flores v. Mosler Safe Co., 7 N.Y. 2d 276, 280-281 [196 N.Y.S. 2d 975, 164 N.E. 2d 853]; see Lahiri v. Daily Mirror, 162 Misc. 776, 779 [295 N.Y.S. 382]), section 51 of the Civil Rights Law has been liberally construed over the ensuing years." Stephano v. New Group Publications, Inc., 98 A.D. 2d 287, 295, 470 N.Y.S. 2d 377 (First Dept., 1984). Ibid.

The court granted Mrs. Onassis a preliminary injunction against publication of the ad, distinguishing Lombardo, supra, on the ground that the actor impersonating the plaintiff bandleader "did not physically resemble the plaintiff." Id. 472 N.Y.S. 2d at 260. The court stated further:

The essence of what is prohibited, as the statute, the cases, and the dictionary definitions make clear, is the exploitation of one's identity as that is conveyed verbally or graphically. A photograph may be a depiction only of the person before the lens, but a "portrait or picture" gives wider scope, to encompass a representation which conveys the essence and likeness of an individual, not only actuality, but the close and purposeful resemblance to reality. That is how it was defined in Binns v. Vitagraph Co. of America, supra, as any representation, including the picture of another, which was intended to be, and did, in fact, convey the idea that it was the plaintiff. Id. at 261.

Binns v. Vitagraph Co. of America, 210 N.Y. 51, 103 N.E. 1108 (1913), cited by the Onassis court, held that the use of an actor to represent plaintiff, a heroic wireless operator within the public eye in a photoplay violated the statute. The New York Court of Appeals said:

A picture within the meaning of the statute is not necessarily a photograph of the living person, but includes any representation of such person. . . .

In Allen v. National Video, Inc., supra, involving the Woody Allen look-alike, Judge Motley decided the case under § 43(a) of the Lanham Act. However, in the context of § 51 of the Civil Rights Law she cited Onassis for the proposition that "an exact duplication of plaintiff was not necessary to make out a cause of action under the statute, so long as the overall impression created clearly was that plaintiff had herself appeared in the advertisement," and went on to say:

When, as in Onassis, the look-alike seems indistinguishable from the real person and the context of the advertisement clearly implies that he or she is the real celebrity, a court may hold as a matter of law that the look-alike's face is a "portrait or picture" of plaintiff. 610 F. Supp. at 623.

I conclude that for Rule 12(b)(6) purposes the amended complaint states a viable claim under §§ 50 and 51 of the New York Civil Rights Law. Defendants correctly observe that the present record includes no photographs, videos or other depictions of the individual plaintiffs from which an evaluation of physical resemblance may be made. Thus decision at this stage of the case does not preclude a motion by defendants for summary judgment on a more complete record. But the complaint's allegations of physical similarity, which I must accept as true, state a claim, given the cited cases' recognition that close resemblance in certain circumstances may violate the statute.

Defendants' motion to dismiss the §§ 50 and 51 claims based on "look-alikes" is denied.

The Rights of Privacy and Publicity Claims—"Sound-Alikes"

In their seventh claim, plaintiffs invite this Court to "correct" an "oversight" of the New York Legislature and hold that defendants' use of sound-alikes of their voices violates §§ 50 and 51. I decline the invitation.

The statute extends the right of privacy to an individual's "name, portrait or picture. . . ." It is one thing to regard a close physical resemblance as the functional equivalent of a picture; that is the thrust of the cases cited in the preceding section. The same sense, that of vision, is involved. It is quite a different proposition to bring the sense of sound within the statute when the legislature has so far declined to do so. That is not an appropriate judicial function.

In Lahr v. Adell Chemical Co., 300 F. 2d 256 (1st Cir. 1962), the First Circuit construed the New York statute in holding that defendant's copying of the comedian Bert Lahr's distinctive voice in a commercial featuring a cartoon duck did not state a claim. Judge Aldrich observed that the statute covered only commercial use of a party's "name, portrait or picture," adding: "The statute is very specific." Id. at 258. Plaintiffs at bar point out that Lahr did not involve combined use of look-alikes and sound-alikes, but that seems to me a distinction without a difference. It is still a legislative function to decide whether copying a party's voice violates the statute in any circumstance. Plaintiffs cite Midler v. Ford Motor Co., 849 F. 2d 460 (9th Cir. 1988), but the case does not assist them. True enough, Ford and its advertising agent asked the noted popular singer Bette Midler to make a commercial and, upon her refusal, hired a singer who sounded like her: conduct comparable to that alleged against defendants at bar. The commercial did not use Midler's name or picture, but the Ninth Circuit, construing California law, articulated a cause of action for commercial use of a sound-alike. The court of appeals derived from California statutes protecting use of a person's "name, voice, signature, photograph or likeness" comparable common law rights which by analogy also constituted "property rights," id. at 463; defendants were held to have misappropriated Midler's property and thus committed a tort under California law. I do not presume to comment on the Ninth Circuit's exegesis of the law of another state. I hold only that the New York Civil Rights Law does not yet extend to sound-alikes.

It does not follow that resemblances in sound between the Fat Boys' performances and the commercial are not probative of any issues in the case. Similarity of sound in combination with similarity of appearance may militate in favor of plaintiffs' other claims, just as defendants would be assisted if the individuals appearing with Piscopo in the commercial looked like the Fat Boys but sounded like the Vienna Boys' Choir. But plaintiffs' sound-alike claim does not state a separate cause of action under the Civil Rights Law. Accordingly defendants' motion to dismiss that claim under Rule 12(b)(6) is granted.

Conclusion

Defendants' motion to dismiss the complaint for failure to state claims upon which relief can be granted is granted as to the Seventh, Eighth, and Ninth claims. Those claims are dismissed with prejudice.

Defendants' motion is denied in all other respects.

Discovery and preparation for trial will be supervised by a Magistrate in accordance with an Order previously entered.

It is SO ORDERED.

Questions for Case Study 4–2
1. What are the basic facts of this case?
2. What are the legal issues involved?
3. What is the decision of the court?
4. What is the legal rationale for the court's decision?

Footnotes

1. The effect of that proposition in the case at bar is problematical, since "[t]he Constitution. . . accords a lesser protection to commercial speech than to other constitutionally guaranteed expression." Central Hudson Gas & Electric v. Public Service Commission of New York, 447 U.S. 557, 562–63, 65 L. Ed. 2d 341, 100 S. Ct. 2343 (1980). It is easier to characterize the parody involved in Cliff's Notes as "a form of artistic expression" than defendants' beer commercial at bar.

2. That is the rule in respect of a demand for injunctive relief (as in Allen). Plaintiffs at bar seek, inter alia, injunctive relief. A trademark plaintiff must prove actual confusion to recover money damages. PPX Enterprises v. Audiofidelity Enterprises, 818 F. 2d 266, 271 (2d Cir. 1987).

3. § 50 provides:

   A person, firm or corporation that uses for advertising purposes, or for the purposes of trade, the name, portrait or picture of any living person without having first obtained the written consent of such person, or if a minor of his or her parent or guardian, is guilty of a misdemeanor.

   § 51 provides in pertinent part:

   Any person whose name, portrait or picture is used within this state for advertising purposes or for the purpose of trade without the written consent first obtained as above provided may maintain an equitable action in the supreme court of this state against the person, firm or corporation so using his name, portrait or picture, to prevent and restrain the use thereof; and may also sue and recover damages for any injuries sustained by reason of such use and if the defendant shall have knowingly used such person's name, portrait or picture in such manner as is forbidden or declared to be unlawful by the last section, the jury, in its discretion, may award exemplary damages.

CASE STUDY 4–3
INTESTACY

New York State Estates Powers and Trusts Law

Article 4
[Intestacy Statute—As of Aug. 1991]

§4–1.1. Descent and distribution of a decedent's estate

The property of a decedent not disposed of by will, after payment of administration and funeral expenses, debts and taxes, shall be distributed as follows:

A. If a decedent is survived by:

(1) A spouse and children or their issue, money or personal property not exceeding in value four thousand dollars and one-third of the residue to the spouse, and the balance thereof to the children or to their issue per stirpes.

(2) A spouse and only one child, or a spouse and only the issue of one deceased child, money or personal property not exceeding in value four thousand dollars and one-half of the residue to the spouse, and the balance thereof to the child or to his issue per stirpes.

(3) A spouse and both parents, and no issue, twenty-five thousand dollars and one-half of the residue to the spouse, and the balance thereof to the parents. If there is no surviving spouse, the whole to the parents.

(4) A spouse and one parent, and no issue, twenty-five thousand dollars and one-half of the residue to the spouse, and the balance thereof to the parent. If there is no surviving spouse, the whole to the parent.

(5) A spouse, and no issue or parent, the whole to the spouse.

(6) Issue, and no spouse, the whole to the issue per stirpes.

(7) Brothers or sisters or their issue, and no spouse, issue or parent, the whole to the brothers or sisters or to their issue per stirpes.

(8) Grandparents only, the whole to the grandparents. If there are no grandparents, the whole to the issue of the grandparents in the nearest degree of kinship to the decedent per capita.

(9) Great-grandparents only, the whole to the great-grandparents. If there are no great-grandparents, the whole to the issue of great-grandparents in the nearest degree of kinship to the decedent per capita. Provided that in the case of a decedent who is survived by great-grandparents only, or the issue of great-grandparents only, such great-grandparents or the issue of such great-grandparents shall not be entitled to inherit from the decedent unless the decedent was at the time of his death an infant or an adjudged incompetent. Provided, further, that this subparagraph nine shall be applicable only to the estates of persons dying on or after its effective date.

B. If the distributees of the decedent are in equal degree of kinship to him, their shares are equal.

C. There is no distribution per stirpes except in the case of the decedent's issue, brothers or sisters and the issue of brothers or sisters.

D. For all purposes of this section, decedent's relatives of the half blood shall be treated as if they were relatives of the whole blood.

E. Distributees of the decedent, conceived before his death but born alive thereafter, take as if they were born in his lifetime.

F. The right of an adopted child to take a distributive share and the right of succession to the estate of an adopted child continue as provided in the domestic relations law.

G. A distributive share passing to a surviving spouse under this section is in lieu of any right of dower to which such spouse may be entitled.

Analysis for Case Study 4–3

Under the New York intestacy statute, a decedent who dies without a valid will has his property distributed as follows:

1. If he leaves behind a spouse and children or their issue (i.e., blood descendants of deceased children), the spouse receives the first $4,000 plus one third of the residue of the estate, if any, with the remaining two thirds going to the children per stirpes. (Per stirpes means that each child gets an equal portion, and if any child dies before the testator, that child's share passes to his/her direct descendants. When a bequest or devise is made per capita, both named beneficiaries and the issue of deceased beneficiaries share equally.)

   Wife dies intestate leaving two children and a husband, along with an estate worth $40,000. Distribution is made as follows: $4,000 to the husband plus one third of the remaining $36,000 ($4,000 + $12,000 = $16,000). Each child gets an equal share of the remaining $24,000 ($12,000 each).

2. If the decedent leaves a spouse and only one child or the issue of one child: The first $4,000 to the spouse and the balance divided equally between the spouse and child or the child's issue.

   Husband dies leaving a wife and child, along with an estate worth $40,000. The wife receives $4,000 plus one half of the balance of the estate ($4,000 + $18,000) and the child (or its issue, if the child has died) receives the balance ($18,000).

3. If the decedent leaves a spouse and both parents, but no children: $25,000 plus one half of the residue to the spouse, the remainder to the parents equally. (If only the parents survive, they share in the entire estate equally.)

   Wife dies leaving $100,000 estate. The husband receives $25,000 plus half of the residue ($25,000 + ½ of $75,000 = 25,000 + $37,500 or $62,500). The parents each receive an equal share of the balance (½ of $37,500 or $18,750 each).

4. If the decedent leaves a spouse and one parent, but no children: $25,000 plus one half of the residue to the spouse, the balance to the parent. (If there is no surviving spouse, all goes to the surviving parent.)

   Husband dies leaving a wife and father and a $100,000 estate. The first $25,000 goes to the wife, along with one half of the residue ($25,000 + ½ of $75,000, or $62,500). The balance ($37,500) goes to the father.

5. If the decedent leaves a spouse but no children or their issue and no living parents, everything goes to the spouse.

6. If the decedent leaves children or their issue and no spouse, everything goes to the children per stirpes.

   Woman dies leaving a $99,000 estate, no husband, two children, and three grandchildren of a dead child. The two living children each take a one-third share, and the three grandchildren share equally in their dead parent's share. Thus, each living child will get $33,000 and each grandchild $11,000 (an equal share of their parent's $33,000 share). Incidentally, if the distribution were per capita, rather than per stirpes, the living children and grandchildren would all share in the estate equally, with each receiving a one-fifth share of the $99,000 estate, or $19,800 each. (Per capita counts heads, while per stirpes counts lines of descendants.)

7. If the descendant leaves behind brothers and sisters or their issue, but no spouse, children (or their issue), or parents, the brothers and sisters or their issue share equally in the estate per stirpes.

   Decedent leaves a $20,000 estate and a live sister, as well as two children of a dead brother. The sister will receive half of the estate ($10,000), with the other half going to the two nephews ($5,000 each).

8. If the decedent leaves only living grandparents and no spouse, children (or their issue), parents, or brothers and sisters (or their issue), all goes to the grandparents or to the issue of the grandparents' closest in kinship to the decedent per capita.

   Decedent dies leaving only one aunt and two first cousins, the children of a dead uncle. The aunt and the first cousins each share in the estate equally per capita.

9. If only great-grandparents are left, they take all. If only the issue of great-grandparents are left, they take in the closest degree of kinship (e.g., great aunts and uncles, etc.) per capita.

10. If a decedent leaves no relatives closer than great-grandparents or their issue, then the whole of the decedent's estate goes to the state.

For purposes of the statute, adoptive children have the same right as natural children, and relatives of the half-blood have the same rights as whole-blood relatives. Illegitimate children also have the rights of legitimate children if the estate of the mother of the illegitimate child is involved. The illegitimate child of a father enjoys the same rights as legitimate children *only* if the father acknowledged the child during his life, a successful paternity suit was brought against him, or he subsequently married the child's natural mother.

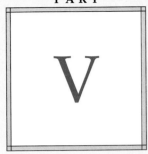

BUSINESS ORGANIZATION

One of the most fundamental decisions all businesspersons face in starting a business is how to organize that business. There are basically three forms that a business can take: the sole proprietorship, the partnership, and the corporation. Each type has both benefits and liabilities that a businessperson should be aware of; much of this unit will be devoted to exploring these in some detail. But first, we will explore the law of agency, since it forms the basic foundation upon which the partnership and corporate forms of business organization rest.

18

AGENCY, EMPLOYMENT, AND ETHICS

Learning Objectives

After studying this chapter, you will be able to:

1. Differentiate agency by agreement, agency by operation of law, and agency by estoppel and provide an example of each.
2. List the agent's duties and the principal's duties under an agency agreement.
3. Describe the legal consequences of an agent acting without authority.
4. Describe common circumstances for agency termination.
5. List the types of discrimination in employment prohibited by the Civil Rights Act of 1964 and its various amendments.
6. Explain the positive and negative aspects of workers' compensation legislation for workers injured in the course of their employment.

Introduction

Agency is a relationship where one party consents to act on another's behalf in entering into contracts with third parties. The person who acts on another's behalf is called the *agent,* and the person on whose behalf the agent acts is called the *principal.*

➤ Henry asks Danielle to go to the corner grocery store and buy a loaf of bread, a pound of ham, and a gallon of milk. He asks her to bring back the goods and have the grocer charge his account. Danielle complies with the request, and the grocer gives her the goods on credit, charging Henry's account.

In the above example, Henry is the principal, who authorizes Danielle to act as his agent to enter into a simple contract on his behalf (the purchase of groceries on credit) with a third party (the grocer). In this chapter, we will explore the law of agency and its impact on business transactions, as well as the rights and responsibilities of parties to agency agreements and the third parties with whom they contract.

The law of agency is of great importance to both individuals and businesses. As individuals, we often need others to act on our behalf when we are unable or unwilling to do so ourselves. The law of agency recognizes the right of one individual to empower another to act in his place. The most common example of this is found in a power of attorney, whereby one person (the principal) can authorize another (the agent, or *attorney in fact*) to conduct any business on his behalf that he himself can legally conduct. For businesses, the law of agency has even greater importance. As we will see in the next two chapters, partnerships and corporations depend heavily on the law of agency to conduct their day-to-day operations. A corporation in particular cannot exist without agents (its corporate officers) to carry out business on its behalf, since the corporation has no physical existence and can only act through its agents. An agency relationship is created to allow one person, the agent, to act on behalf of another, the principal. In essence, the agent acts as a stand-in, or *proxy*, for the principal, carrying out business on his behalf; therefore, any contract that the agent enters into on the principal's behalf binds the principal just as if she had entered into the contract herself.

Creation of an Agency

There are three circumstances under which agency is most commonly created: agency by agreement, agency by operation of law, and agency by estoppel.

Agency by Agreement

Agency is a consensual relationship that comes into existence when an agent agrees to act on behalf of a principal to carry out some act. A valid agency can be formed by an oral or written agreement that clearly gives an agent authority to act on behalf of a principal. If the action that the agent is to undertake on the principal's behalf needs a signed agreement, then the agency agreement must also be evidenced by a signed writing; this is called the *equal dignities rule*. If a principal empowers an agent to purchase real estate on his behalf, the agency agreement must be in writing, since the agent will have to execute a signed writing (the real estate contract) on the principal's behalf to purchase the real estate. An agency can also be implied from the conduct of the parties when a principal clearly authorizes an agent to act on her behalf, even though no express oral or written agency agreement may exist. Consider the following example:

> ➤ Loretta owns a self-serve gas station. Duane, who is not employed by her, regularly helps customers by pumping gas, checking engine oil levels, and washing their windows. Loretta allows Duane to help her customers and provides him with wash cloths and window cleaning fluid. Duane's only payment for his services comes from the tips he earns from customers.

Through her acquiescence and assistance of Duane's efforts, Loretta has very likely made Duane her agent. The significance of the existence of an agency agreement between Duane and Loretta may seem academic, but it can be crucial if Duane is injured in the performance of his duties or if he damages a customer's automobile through his negligence. If he is acting as Loretta's agent, he will be entitled to reimbursement from Loretta for any job-related injuries, and Loretta will be legally liable for any damage Duane causes to customers' cars while he is acting within the scope of his implied authority.

Agency by Operation of Law

Courts sometimes find an agency relationship to exist by operation of law on public policy grounds when there is no agency agreement by the parties, but they have a special relationship that justifies holding one party to be the agent of the other. A common example of an agency by operation of law would include contracts for necessaries (e.g., food, clothing, shelter, or medical care) entered into by a dependent spouse or child. The following examples will illustrate such agencies:

> ➤ 1. The dependent spouse buys $100 worth of groceries and asks the grocer to bill the husband. The husband does not know about the wife's purchase and has not approved it.
>
> 2. The dependent son goes to hospital emergency room for care and asks that the mother be billed for the charges. The mother is unaware of the son's actions and has not approved them.

In both of the above examples, most courts would hold an agency by operation of law to exist, since the spouse and parent have a legal duty to provide for the needs of their dependents. Note that if the wife in example 1 bought $100 worth of liquor or the son in example 2 had the mother billed for nonessential medical services (e.g., plastic surgery), no agency would exist since there is no duty for a spouse or parent to provide liquor or elective surgery for their dependents.

Agency by Estoppel

When a principal causes a third person to reasonably believe that a given person is her agent, the principal will be *estopped* from denying the existence of the agency with regard to any dealings the third person has had with the purported agent acting on the principal's behalf. To put it another way, if a principal misleads a third party into believing that a person is her agent, the principal will not be able to deny the agency.

> ⮞ Stephanie, the CEO of a large corporation, introduces her nephew, Poindexter, to several executives of companies with whom she does business on a regular basis and tells them that he is her new purchasing manager. In fact, Poindexter is not employed by her firm and has no actual authority to conduct any business for the company. The following day, Poindexter mails a purchase order for a $1 million computer system to the sales manager of Abracadabra Systems whom he's met at the cocktail party. Even though Poindexter has no actual authority to make the purchase, Stephanie's company will be bound to honor the sales contract. She can, of course, sue Poindexter personally for any damages the company suffers as a result of his unauthorized act.

Agent's Duties

Agency is a *fiduciary relationship*—a relationship based on trust, in which the agent and principal owe each other a duty to act with absolute good faith and honesty. In addition to the good faith and honesty demanded of all parties to fiduciary relationships, an agent owes his principal the duties of loyalty, obedience, performance, notification, and accounting. Each of these is briefly defined below.

Loyalty

The agent owes his principal an absolute duty of loyalty. This means that in carrying out his duties, the agent must put the interest of his principal above his own or those of third parties. The duty of loyalty extends to, among other things, keeping confidential any sensitive information the agent learns through the agency relationship and refraining from using the relationship for his own advantage or that of third parties—whether or not such use injures the principal. If the agent breaches the duty of loyalty, the principal can sue him for actual damages and to recover any profits that he has made through the abuse of the agency relationship.

> ⮞ Joanna hires Roseanne to act as her agent in buying a house at an auction and authorizes her to bid up to $100,000 on the property. While at the auction, Roseanne is surprised to find that no one bids more than $20,000 on the property and, finding it to be a bargain at that price, buys it for $20,500 for herself. She has violated the duty of loyalty to her principal in bidding on the house herself and can be sued by Joanna for damages.

Obedience

The agent must follow the reasonable, legal instructions of the principal to the letter. If she fails to do so, she is in breach of the agency agreement and can be sued for damages. When the principal's instructions are vague or subject to more than one reasonable interpretation, the agent discharges her duty of obedience by acting in good faith in a manner that is reasonable under the circumstances.

> ➤ If in the last example, Roseanne refuses to bid more than $50,000 for the house on Joanna's behalf, despite her specific instructions to buy it for up to $100,000, she would be guilty of violating her duty of obedience and could be sued for damages by Joanna.

Performance

An agent must use reasonable diligence and skill in performing his duties under an agency agreement. If the agent is a skilled professional, such as an attorney, physician, or accountant, he must demonstrate the basic competence and skill for a practitioner in his profession. If the agent is acting pursuant to a valid agency contract (i.e., if he is being paid for his services), he can be sued for breach of contract if he fails to act as promised. Even if the agent is acting gratuitously, he is still subject to liability in tort for failure to exercise reasonable care in carrying out his duties under the agency (malpractice).

Notification

Under an agency agreement, the principal is held to have *putative* knowledge of all that the agent knows concerning the agency; whatever knowledge the agent has that is relevant to the agency is held to also be known by the principal, whether or not she is actually aware of it. Therefore, the agent has the duty to give timely notification to her principal about any matter concerning the agency that she learns in carrying out her duties.

> ➤ In the last example, if Roseanne finds that the house is infested with termites prior to the bidding but still bids $100,000 on the house without first informing Joanna, she will be liable to Joanna for breaching her duty of notification. She will also be guilty of negligence in carrying out her duties.

Accounting

If there is no specific agreement to the contrary, agents have the duty to keep records of all transactions concerning the agency and to make them available to the principal upon request. The agent must report all income and expenses resulting from the agency agreement for property in the agent's control—even illegal transactions. If, for example, an agent receives a bonus or cash incentive for entering into a contract with a third party on the principal's behalf, he must report that gift to the principal; it legally belongs to the principal. If the agent fails to account for such proceeds and to turn them over to the principal, he is guilty both of breaching his duty to account and his duty of loyalty.

Principal's Duties

Although the agency relationship primarily benefits the principal whom the agent serves, principals also owe certain duties to the agents who serve them. These include the duties of cooperation, compensation, indemnification, and reimbursement.

Cooperation

A principal must assist the agent in the performance of her duties and must refrain from doing anything that impedes her from successfully carrying out her duties under the agency. The duty of cooperation requires a principal to make available to his agent any information she needs to successfully carry out her duties under the agency. This duty prevents the principal from directly or indirectly impeding the agent from faithfully executing the assigned duties.

> Bob asks Barbara, an art expert, to travel to California to an art auction and purchase an impressionist painting of her choosing up to $20,000. He also agrees to pay her $3,000 plus expenses for her services if she succeeds. While Barbara is in transit, Bob learns that he has taken a beating in the stock market and wants to back out of his art deal without having to admit to Barbara that he has fallen on tough economic times. Without informing Barbara, he phones the gallery owner and offers him $1,000 if he refuses to admit Barbara into his gallery. The owner complies. Bob is guilty of breaching his duty of cooperation to Barbara, and she can sue him for damages (the $3,000 she would have earned if not for his interference plus reasonable expenses she has incurred in carrying out his instructions).

Compensation

Unless the agent has made it clear that he is willing to undertake the duties of the agency gratuitously (free of charge), he is entitled to be compensated for his services, and the principal is obligated to compensate him. Usually, the compensation is agreed upon as part of the agency agreement. If no compensation is specified, and if it is not clear from the circumstances that the agent has agreed to render performance gratuitously, the agent is entitled to receive the reasonable value of his services.

➤ Larry asks Cathy, an attorney, to write the XYZ Department Store credit department to demand that they adjust an error in her account. Cathy (Larry's agent for purposes of writing the letter) drafts the letter and bills Larry $75 for her services. Larry refuses to pay, claiming that he believed Cathy would not charge him for the service and that no fee was specified at the time he asked her to draft the letter. Cathy would be entitled to the payment of a reasonable fee for her services, since no fee was specified; assuming $75 is the reasonable value of the service performed by Cathy in the locality where she practices law, Larry is under a duty to pay the fee. (Larry's only defense is to prove that Cathy agreed to draft the letter gratuitously.)

Indemnification

The principal has the duty to *indemnify,* or compensate, the agent for any losses suffered as a result of authorized legal acts that he performs under the agency agreement.

➤ Harry, the president of ZYX Corporation, is personally sued for breach of a contract he had entered into on behalf of his company. If he loses, he is entitled to indemnification from ZYX for any judgment he is forced to pay the plaintiff, as long as his breach of the contract was done in good faith and was in ZYX's interest.

Reimbursement

The principal must reimburse the agent for any expenses incurred as a result of carrying out legal authorized acts under the agency agreement. The agent must, of course, properly document and account for all expenses to the principal. In the above example, if Harry defends himself against the lawsuit, he is also entitled to be reimbursed by ZYX for the cost of his legal defense.

Agent's Authority

When an agent acts within the scope of the authority vested in him by the principal, those acts bind the principal just as if the principal herself had undertaken them. This is true both for contracts entered into by the agent on the principal's behalf and torts committed by him while acting within the scope of his authority. The key in determining whether a principal is bound by her agent's acts is the existence of clear authorization. An agent can possess two types of authority in acting on a principal's behalf: actual authority and apparent authority. If the agent acts pursuant to either actual or apparent authority, the principal will be bound by his actions. On the other hand, the principal is generally not liable for contracts or torts of an agent who acts without the principal's authority.

Actual Authority

Actual authority can be either express or implied. An agent acts with actual express authority when he performs in accordance with his principal's instructions. Express authority can be oral or written, as long as it specifically spells out what the agent is authorized to do. Actual authority can also be implied in one of two ways: conferred by custom for the specific type of agency undertaken or inferred as being reasonably necessary to carry out the agent's express authority. For example, a life insurance salesperson will have the express authority to issue life insurance contracts for the principal company and the implied authority to collect deposits from clients upon the signing of a life insurance contract, even if the authority to collect funds is not expressly mentioned in the agency contract (e.g., life insurance agents traditionally collect funds from new clients, so that the authority is implied from the custom of the trade).

Apparent Authority

Apparent authority comes into existence when the principal through his words or actions causes a third party to reasonably believe that a given person has authority to act as her agent, but the person in fact has no such actual express or implied authority. In such circumstances, the principal will be estopped from denying the existence of actual authority and be bound by the purported agent's actions. The agent's words or actions alone will not create apparent authority; the principal must be the one who caused a third person to justifiably believe that the agent had express authority to act on her behalf. For example, if A (agent) tells T (third party), "I am authorized to act on P's (principal's) behalf," this statement alone does not confer apparent authority on A; but if A makes the same statement to T in P's presence and P says nothing, T can assume that A is in fact authorized to act on P's behalf, since P will have contributed to T's misconception about A's authority. It is likewise the case if P tells T, "A is my agent," when in fact he is not.

▶ Martha tells Jim to travel from New York City to Newark, New Jersey, to purchase an automobile for her at an auction. She instructs Jim to purchase either a Ford Mustang or a Nissan Maxima not more than four years old and with not more than 25,000 miles. She further authorizes him to bid up to $4,000 for the car.

   A. Jim purchases a Ford Mustang that is three years old and has 25,000 miles on the odometer for $3,500. He has clearly acted within his actual authority, and Martha is bound by the contract. Furthermore, if Jim crashes into another automobile along the way, both Martha and Jim can be sued for the damage, since Martha is responsible for the torts (but not the crimes) of Jim while he carries out his duties under the agency agreement.

B. If Jim purchases a 1992 Ferrari for Martha, at a cost of $60,000, she will not be personally liable for that contract, since Jim clearly did not have the authority to enter into it. Likewise, if Jim takes a side trip through Connecticut to visit his girlfriend and gets into an accident, Martha will not be liable for the tort, since Jim was not carrying out his business in Connecticut, and the trip was not for Martha's benefit.

C. Martha calls the auctioneer in New Jersey and tells him that Jim will be bidding on automobiles on her behalf later that day. She then changes her mind and revokes Jim's authority. If Jim travels to New Jersey anyway and bids on a car, Martha will be bound by Jim's apparent authority. Even though Jim's actions were unauthorized, Martha misled the auctioneer into believing that Jim would be bidding on her behalf and will be estopped from denying his authority.

Agent's Unauthorized Actions

A principal is not responsible for his agent's unauthorized acts. If an agent acts without express or implied authority, only he is bound by the contract, regardless of whether the principal is disclosed, partially disclosed, or undisclosed. For this reason, it is essential that parties dealing with agents independently verify the agent's authority to bind the principal. Verification can be made by contacting the principal or requiring written authorization of the principal's authority prior to entering into the contract.

➤ Paul authorizes Sue to purchase a one-acre tract of land for a maximum price of $100,000. Sue finds a two-acre tract for $150,000 and purchases it on Paul's behalf, telling the seller that she is acting on behalf of a principal and disclosing his name. Since the act was unauthorized (i.e., Sue acted beyond the scope of her authority in purchasing the land), Paul is not bound under the contract. If the seller did not verify Sue's authority to bind Paul, he will only be able to sue Sue herself for damages if Paul refuses to purchase the land under the agreed-upon terms.

If a principal agrees to honor a contract entered into by an agent without express or implied authority to bind the principal, the agent's unauthorized action is deemed ratified and the principal becomes primarily liable under the contract. The principal is not, however, under any obligation to ratify the unauthorized acts of his agents and may refuse to do so at will. In the last example, if Paul thinks that the two-acre tract is a good deal at $150,000, he can ratify Sue's unauthorized contract and thereby become liable to the seller, taking the place of Sue, the unauthorized agent, as a principal party to the contract. The following example gives an additional illustration of a principal's ratification of an agent's unauthorized act.

> ➤ Sandy knows that Lenore is interested in purchasing a home for under $100,000. While Lenore is on vacation, her neighbor, John, places his home for sale at $85,000—a very good price for a home in her community. She contracts with John to buy the home as an agent for Lenore. Since Lenore did not authorize Sandy to act on her behalf, she is under no obligation to honor Sandy's contract. But she is free to ratify it, at her choice, if she wishes to. If Lenore does not ratify the contract, Sandy will be personally liable to John for breach of contract unless she purchases the house herself.

Liability for Contracts

As previously noted, when an agent acting under actual authority enters into a contract on behalf of a principal, the principal is bound by the contract as if he had entered into it himself. As long as the third party knows that the agent is acting on a principal's behalf and is aware of the principal's identity, the agent herself is not bound on the contract. In circumstances where a principal is fully disclosed to the third party, the agent acts merely as an intermediary in entering into the contract; the parties to the contract are the principal and the third party. When the third party is not aware that the agent is acting as an agent, however, the agent herself is a party to the contract and responsible for its execution. The liability of the agent on the contract depends on the extent to which her principal is disclosed to the third party, as we will see below.

Disclosed Principal

A principal is disclosed when the third party is aware that the agent is acting as an agent for a named principal. When the third party contracts with an agent acting for a fully disclosed principal, the agent is not a party to the contract and has no liability under it. If the principal breaches the contract, the third party must sue the principal directly and cannot sue the agent.

> ➤ The purchasing agent for Acme Computer Company places an order for 100 hard disk drives from a supplier. The supplier knows that the goods are being purchased for Acme by the agent, its purchasing manager. If Acme wrongfully refuses delivery of the goods, the supplier can sue it for breach of contract but cannot sue the agent personally, since Acme was a fully disclosed principal at the time the contract was entered into.

Partially Disclosed Principal

A principal is partially disclosed when the third party is aware that the agent is acting on behalf of a principal but does not know who the principal is. In contracts involving partially disclosed principals, the agent is a party to the contract and can be sued personally if the principal breaches the contract. In addition, if the third party learns the identity of the partially disclosed principal after entering into the contract, the principal can also be sued for any breach of contract. Note that if the agent is sued for a partially disclosed principal's breach, the agent is entitled to indemnification from the principal for any judgment levied against it.

➤ Very Large Corporation (VLC) wants to purchase a tract of real estate to expand its corporate offices. It knows that if potential sellers learn of its identity, they are likely to greatly increase the asking price for any real estate it shows an interest in. Therefore, VLC contracts with a real estate broker to act as its agent in purchasing an adequate piece of land and instructs the agent not to reveal its identity. The agent approaches several sellers and tells them that she is interested in purchasing their land on behalf of a client that she is not at liberty to disclose. If she purchases a tract of land and the principal later refuses to pay for it, the agent will be personally liable on the sale, since the third-party seller was not aware of the principal's name (the principal was partially disclosed).

Undisclosed Principal

A principal is undisclosed when the third party is unaware that the agent is acting on another's behalf (and, of course, does not know the identity of the principal). When the principal is undisclosed, the agent and the third party are the only parties to the contract and only the agent is liable on it. Even if the third party subsequently learns of the disclosed agency, it cannot sue the principal for any breach, since the principal has no ties to the contract. If the agent is sued for the principal's breach, she will be able to seek indemnification from her principal for any loss under her agency agreement.

Termination of Agency

An agency can be terminated either voluntarily or by operation of law. Once an agency terminates, the agent's power to bind the principal ends. The agent, however, will still retain apparent authority with respect to third parties with whom he has been conducting business on the principal's behalf until such third parties are notified that the agency has ended.

Voluntary Termination

An agency may end voluntarily under the following situations.

Act of Either Party.   Since an agency relationship is consensual in nature, either the agent or the principal can terminate it at any time simply by making it known he no longer wishes to continue it. If the agent ends the agency, it is called a *renunciation of authority;* if the principal does, it is called a *revocation of authority.*

The agent's power to renounce his authority and the principal's power to revoke the agent's authority exist even when the agency agreement itself states that it will last for a set period; in such a case, the party who exercises his right to terminate the agency is in breach of the agency contract and can be sued for damages by the nonbreaching party.

> ➤ Agatha owns a used-car dealership. She enters into an agency agreement with Marvin empowering him to purchase cars at auto auctions on her behalf. The agreement specifically states that it will last for five years and that it cannot be dissolved before that time. After six months, Marvin is offered a better deal from one of Agatha's competitors and decides to terminate his agency with Agatha. He has the absolute right to terminate the agency at will, but Agatha can sue him for breach of contract for any damages she suffers as a direct result of his breach (e.g., if she has to pay another agent of Marvin's skill a higher salary than Marvin earned, Marvin is liable to Agatha for the difference in salaries).

If Agatha wishes to end the agency before the five-year term has expired, she can also do so, but she will be liable for damages to Marvin if he cannot secure a similar agency for another principal at the same or a higher profit.

If both parties agree to terminate the agency, the agency contract is rescinded and neither party may sue the other for its breach.

Lapse of the Time.   An agency agreement can specify that it will expire at the end of a specific period of time. If that is the case, the agency automatically terminates at the end of the specified period. In the last example, if Marvin continues to serve as Agatha's agent for the agreed-upon period, the agency will automatically terminate at the end of the fifth year under their agreement. If no duration for the agency is specified, it will last as long as both parties agree to continue it, and either party can end it at any time without incurring liability for breach of the agency agreement.

Termination by the Occurrence of a Stated Event.   If the parties agree that the agency will terminate upon the happening of a given event, the agency automatically terminates when the stated event comes to pass. If, for example, Tina gives Jerome a general power of attorney authorizing him to conduct all business on her behalf as long as the president of the United States is a Republican, the agency created by the power of attorney will end as soon as a Democrat (or other non-Republican candidate) is elected president.

Achievement of the Agency Objective.   When an agency is created to achieve a particular purpose, it automatically terminates when that purpose is achieved. If, for example, Juan enlists Pedro as his agent for purposes of selling his home, Pedro's authority under the agency ends as soon as the house is sold, and the agency is thereby terminated.

Termination by Operation of Law

Agency will automatically terminate by operation of law under any of the following circumstances.

Death or Insanity.   If either the principal or agent dies or is adjudged to be insane, the agency automatically ends. Any acts that the agent takes on the principal's behalf after the principal's death or insanity do not bind the principal or his estate. This can leave the agent in a precarious position, since she may be personally liable on such contracts (i.e., undisclosed principal or partially disclosed principal) if the principal's representative elects not to honor them. Some states have enacted legislation to protect innocent agents under such circumstances.

Bankruptcy.   As a general rule, the bankruptcy of the principal automatically terminates the agency. The bankruptcy of the agent, however, does not generally terminate the agency, nor does the mere insolvency of the principal until it results in bankruptcy.

Impossibility of Performance.   The loss or destruction of the subject matter of the agency automatically terminates the agency. The same is true if legislation makes the underlying transaction under an agency agreement illegal or if the agent's and principal's respective countries go to war. The following examples will illustrate:

➤   1. Lydia authorizes Ramón to sell her automobile. The car is subsequently stolen (or destroyed in an accident or fire). The agency automatically ends upon the destruction of the underlying subject matter, that is, the car.
2. Bruce authorizes Hans to purchase 100 South African Kruggerands per month at market price for the next year. Before Hans can purchase the first month's order, Congress passes a law that makes it illegal to buy or sell Kruggerands in the United States. The agency terminates by the subsequent illegality of the transaction for which it was formed.

3. Libom Oil, a U.S. company, procures the services of an Iraqi firm to act as its agent in entering into long-term oil exporting contracts in Iraq. A short time thereafter, war breaks out in the Persian Gulf as a U.S.–led coalition attempts to free Kuwait from an Iraqi occupation. The agency is automatically suspended by the ensuing hostilities of Operation Desert Storm. (After the brief war ends and relations between Iraq and the United States are stabilized, the agency can resume.)

Impracticability of Performance.   Whenever circumstances change in such a way that the agent can reasonably infer the principal would no longer wish her to pursue the subject matter of the agency, the agency automatically terminates. Consider the following illustration:

➤ Lenny authorizes Deidre to act as his agent in purchasing a specific tract of land that he intends to later subdivide and sell as 100 building lots. While negotiating the land purchase, Deidre learns that the state has just approved the building of nuclear power plant in an adjoining tract of land. The agency automatically terminates, since the nuclear power plant will make the land unappealing as a future housing development—even though such a development could still conceivably take place.

Notice to Third Parties upon Termination of Agency

When an agency terminates by operation of law, the principal has no duty to notify third parties of the fact. Whenever either party or both voluntarily terminate the agency, however, the principal has a duty to personally notify every third party with whom the agent had past dealings on the principal's behalf. If a principal fails to give such notification, he will be bound by any contracts entered into by the agent on his behalf after the termination, since the third party believes the agent still has apparent authority to bind the principal. Notification to third parties the agent had dealt with for the principal can take any reasonable form: personal contact, letter, telegram, or telephone calls are all effective. With regard to third parties who may have been aware that the agency existed but who had not had prior dealings with the agent, *constructive notice* is sufficient. The most common means of giving constructive notice is to place a *legal notice* in a newspaper of general circulation in the area that the principal does business. Such legal notices, generally tiny articles of very small type grouped together in a newspaper's classified section, are deemed sufficient notices to the public at large that an agency has terminated.

Whenever a principal voluntarily terminates an agency relationship, the agent's authority to bind her continues until the agent is actually notified of the termination or until he learns of it independently.

If an agent happens to read of the termination in a legal notice, his authority to bind the principal ends, even if the principal has not directly communicated his decision to the agent.

Employees as Agents

While some aspects of agency may seem esoteric, most people who work for an employer are agents, since they are authorized to conduct business on behalf of the employer and are subject to the employer's control. This is not to say that all employees can enter into binding contracts with third parties on behalf of their employers. As we have seen, an agent can only bind a principal when she acts within the scope of her actual or apparent authority. Thus, while a corporate president and a maintenance worker for the same corporation are both employees and agents, the former has wide-ranging authority to enter into contracts with third parties on the corporation's behalf, while the latter has no such authority and can, therefore, not enter into binding contracts with third parties on the coporation's behalf.

Independent Contractors

An independent contractor differs from an employee in that he is not deemed to be an agent of the employer. As such, the employer is not liable for the torts committed by an independent contractor while she performs her assigned duties, and the duties that agents and principals owe one another do not apply to an employer and an independent contractor, while they do apply to an employer and an employee. Some of the factors that courts examine in determining whether a particular individual is an employee or an independent contractor are the length of time the person has worked for the employer, the amount of control the employer exercises over the person, the amount of time the person works for an employer every week, whether the person appears on the employer's regular payroll, and whether the person has an exclusive employment relationship with the employer. Thus, a maintenance worker who works exclusively for an employer 40 hours per week is clearly an employee, while a window washer who spends 10 hours per month washing the employer's windows, regularly works for other businesses, and bills the employer for his work on an hourly basis every month is clearly an independent contractor. If the latter drops a bucket of water on the head of an innocent passerby while performing his duties for the employer, the employer is not liable for the damage, whereas he would be if the independent contractor were his employee.

Employment Law

The employer/employee relationship is firmly rooted in agency and contract law. Whenever one person agrees to work under the direction and control of another in return for wages and other benefits, an employment relationship comes into existence. The employer's and employee's rights and duties are rooted in the general common law of contracts and agency. In addition, specific federal and state statutes help to define both the employer's and employee's rights and responsibilities. Some of the important areas affected by employment legislation are union activity, pension plans, compensation for work-related injuries, health and safety standards, and unemployment benefits.

Collective Bargaining

At common law, workers had no right to form labor unions or to engage in collective bargaining. Employees were deemed to serve strictly *at the will* of their employers. While employers had to honor contractual obligations to their employees, such as paying them the agreed-upon price for their services, employees had little protection other than that expressly found in their employment contracts. An employee could be fired for any or no reason, and the mere attempt to join a labor union usually resulted in the worker being fired. In the 1930s, Congress began enacting crucial legislation giving employees the right to unionize and strike.

> *Norris-La Guardia Act of 1932.* This gave employees the right to engage in peaceful strikes and to engage in picketing and boycotts.
>
> *National Labor Relations Act of 1932* (also known as the *Wagner Act*). This established the right of all employees to engage in collective bargaining and to strike. It also established the National Labor Relations Board to oversee union elections and provided the means for preventing unfair labor practices by employers.
>
> *Labor-Management Relations Act of 1947* (also known as the *Taft-Hartley Act*). This amended the National Labor Relations Act to include provisions to protect employers from unions' unfair labor practices. It illegalized *closed shops*—the requirement that new employees be union members as a condition of employment. (*Union shops*, which do not require that hired employees be members of the union at the time they are hired, but require that they join the union after being hired, were not made illegal by the act). The act also gave to the President the right to impose an 80-day cooling-off period in cases of strikes that would create a national emergency. The cooling-off period has been imposed on striking air traffic controllers, coal miners, steel workers, and longshoremen since 1959.

Labor-Management Reporting and Disclosure Act of 1959 (also known as *Landrum-Griffin Act*). This regulated unions' internal procedures, such as elections. For example, it required that regular elections of union officers occur, that such elections be by secret ballot, and that no ex-convicts or communists may serve as union officers. The act also outlawed agreements by employers and unions not to handle, deal in, or use nonunion produced goods.

Pension Plans

Although employers are not required to provide employees with pension plans, those who do must adhere to the *Employees Retirement Income Security Act* of 1974 (ERISA). The act imposes fiduciary duties on pension fund administrators, requiring them to protect employee's interests with the highest duty of care. The act also sets up mandatory reporting standards that require pension fund administrators to make detailed periodic reports to the U.S. Secretary of Labor. Furthermore, ERISA requires that employees' rights to pensions vest in a maximum of 10 years; this means that after 10 years of service, an employee is absolutely entitled to receive a pension benefit upon retirement. The longer an employee works past the minimum 10-year vesting period, the larger her pension will be.

The *Retirement Equity Act* of 1984 permits an employee to leave the work force for up to five consecutive years and still retain eligibility for pension benefits. It also mandates that the spouse of an employee who is eligible to receive pension benefits sign a waiver before the employee can waive the survivor's annuity option that the act requires.

> 1. Henrietta, an employee whose rights to her employer's pension plan have not vested, quits her job to raise a family after working for the employer for nine years. Four years, 364 days later, she decides to rejoin the work force and is rehired by her employer. Henrietta's pension rights will be reinstated and her right to a pension will vest if she continues to work for the same employer for one more year.

2. After working for one more year for the same employer, Henrietta quits. Her pension is now vested. When she is ready to begin collecting her pension, she is offered a choice of receiving $300 per month for life or $200 per month for life with the same amount continuing upon her death for her husband's life if he survives her. If she chooses to take the higher amount, she will need her husband's permission.

Workers' Compensation

Every state has enacted some form of workers' compensation statute that defines and limits the compensation employees are entitled to when they are injured on the job. In addition, civil employees of the federal government are covered by a separate workers' compensation statute, the *Federal Employees' Compensation Act*. In general, workers' compensation statutes guarantee that employees injured in the course of their employment will be compensated for their injuries and severely limit the common law defenses to such recovery, including contributory negligence and assumption of risk. On the other hand, while such statutes guarantee some type of recovery for nearly all injured employees, they limit such coverage to a fairly low amount. In addition, such statutes do away with a worker's common law right to sue the employer for breach of contract or tort for injuries received in the regular course of employment. When a worker is injured on the job, workers' compensation typically pays all medical bills, and the worker may also be entitled to a cash award for any permanent disability suffered as a result of his injury.

➤ Sam, a laborer, works for a contractor who is covered under his state's workers' compensation statute. During the course of his employment, Sam severely injures his thumb when a drill he is using malfunctions. After a workers' compensation hearing and examination, it is determined that Sam will suffer a permanent loss of 20 percent of the normal use of his thumb due to the accident. Under his state's statute, the permanent loss of a thumb is valued at $5,000. Sam will be entitled to a cash award of 20 percent of $5,000, or $1,000 for his injury. In addition, his employer or the employer's insurance carrier will pick up all medical bills incurred by Sam for the treatment of his injury.

The good news for Sam in the previous example is that he will not have to sue anyone to have his medical bills paid for and that he will get some cash for his loss. On the down side, he will not be able to sue his employer if the employer's negligence caused the accident and will not recover for pain and suffering, as he could under the common law. The only hope for Sam to recover a significant judgment under the facts given is to sue the manufacturer of the defective drill for damages under a products liability theory, since the drill manufacturer is not covered by the workers' compensation statute.

Unemployment Insurance

With the exception of some railroad and federal workers who are covered under separate acts, most employees are covered by the unemployment insurance provisions of the *Social Security Act* of 1935. Under the act, the federal and state governments jointly administer unemployment insurance. While there are some differences between the various states' requirements and benefits, unemployment insurance is available to workers in all states. Generally, workers who lose their job through no fault of their own (those who are not fired for cause and who did not voluntarily leave their jobs) are entitled to receive unemployment insurance. To collect benefits, unemployed workers must generally show that they cannot find any job for which they are qualified, that they are making a diligent effort to find work, and that they have worked the required number of weeks in the previous year to qualify for unemployment benefits.

Health and Safety

Congress passed the *Occupational Safety and Health Act* of 1970 (OSHA) to insure employees a safe work environment. The act established health and safety standards and a mechanism for their enforcement. In addition to OSHA, many states have passed separate statutes dealing with safety in the workplace.

Illegal Discrimination

The *Civil Rights Act* of 1964 and its various amendments have outlawed discrimination against employees based on race, color, religion, national origin, and sex in any stage of employment. The act applies to any employer or labor union with 15 or more employees or union members and to all employment agencies. The act also specifically prohibited such discrimination in the federal government. An employer of union coming within the act cannot discriminate on the basis of the protected criteria without showing a good faith reason for doing so. For example, requiring that an applicant for the position of Catholic priest be both male and Catholic is permissible discrimination; both are good faith requirements for the job. But refusing to hire male flight attendants merely because the airline claims that most passengers prefer female flight attendants is not permissible discrimination, even if done for a bona fide business reason.

Keep in mind that under the act, employers who hire 14 or fewer employees *can* discriminate on the basis of race, color, religion, national origin, and sex, unless a state statute prevents it.

Ethics and the Law

Ethics is the branch of philosophy that concerns itself with the study of human character and behavior. The heart of philosophical inquiry in this field revolves around morality and the timeless basic issue of right and wrong and good and evil as they relate to human conduct. Although seldom outwardly acknowledged, ethical considerations have always played a vital role in the forming of legal systems throughout the world, and in their continuing evolution. The very idea of law is rooted in certain immutable moral tenets: that citizens of a state must conform to certain standards of behavior for the good of society, or be punished for their breach. Likewise, many of our most fundamental laws are deeply rooted in time-tested ethical precepts, such as proscriptions on murder, theft, and adultery. Not surprisingly, as in the last three examples, much of the basis for American law can be traced to religious beliefs, in particular the Judeo-Christian ethic. This is not to suggest that religious morality is the sole basis for our law; it is, however, a very important and tangible one.

As a society changes and evolves, the law tends to reflect changes in that society's attitudes. Although the law is seldom proactive in reflecting societal changes, it generally does so in a reactive manner; in other words, laws seldom lead societal change but invariably reflect it slowly over time. It can be argued that the past fifty years have seen a notable shift in American jurisprudence from its traditional Judeo-Christian value system towards ethical relativism—a view that morality is relative to each culture and that there is no one set of values or timeless code of ethics that can be imposed on all societies. Thus, many laws that clearly reflected a religious-based value system have either been overturned or, if they are still on the books, are largely unenforced. Abortion on demand and the abolition of school prayer are two examples of the fundamental shift in values reflected in the law. This shift can also be seen in the overturning of most blue laws—laws that sought to regulate moral behavior by discouraging work or alcohol consumption on the Sabbath, encouraging the attendance of religious services and criminalizing many sexual practices. The modern trend is to allow business to be freely on Sunday. And, although most jurisdictions still prohibit a wide range of sexual practices, even between consenting spouses in the privacy of their bedroom, these laws are seldom enforced.

Professional Ethics

Although one can easily argue that morality cannot be legislated, a number of professional organizations try to regulate the business behavior of their members by promulgating minimum rules of conduct that members must follow. Perhaps the best examples of these can be found in the codes of ethics of the American Bar Association and the American Medical Association. Both organizations impose strict rules of behavior on their members. Adherence to the codes of ethics of these organizations is a prerequisite to exercising the privilege of practicing law or medicine. The basic purpose to these rules is to ensure that members conduct themselves in an ethical manner in their professional and personal lives. The American Bar Association's Code of Professional Responsibility, for example, allows attorneys to be disciplined for the violation of any disciplinary rule of the ABA or of the bar association for the state in which she practices. Attorneys can also be disciplined or disbarred for committing any crime or act of moral turpitude, which is defined as any act of dishonesty, corruption, violence or professional misconduct—whether or not these are related to the practice of law. Thus, a lawyer who cheats a client is subject to censure or disbarment, but so is one who shoplifts or gets into a barroom brawl.

Even in the area of professional ethics, however, there have been some subtle changes in attitudes. Some of the most notable concern advertisement and rate schedules. Again turning to the law as an example, the American Bar Association, along with the bar associations of many states, traditionally published guidelines of reasonable rates to be charged by attorneys and strictly prohibited advertisements. (The same was true of the American Medical Association). Today, publication of rate schedules has been prohibited by the courts, and advertising bans have been lifted. As a result, lawyers and physicians are free to advertise their practices with few constraints in the various media. The consumer is thus arguably better served, as professionals compete with each other like so many used car salesmen.

Business Ethics

While many of the professions are to a large extent self-regulating, this does not apply to business in general. The rules of conduct exacted from individuals in society have been relaxed to some extent in the latter part of this century, while the rules of conduct expected of businesses have been correspondingly tightened in a number of areas, including employment, environmental issues, and even dealings abroad. The free hand enjoyed by businesses at common law in their dealings with customers and employees alike has been severely restricted. Government has imposed social responsibility on businesses by way of administrative regulation and legislation. Some of the most salient areas where this can be observed are as follows:

> **Employment:** Discrimination on the basis of race, color, sex, and religion has been prohibited to most businesses engaged in interstate commerce. Affirmative action plans for correcting previous patterns of discrimination have been encouraged and in some instances mandated. This has raised the related ethical issue of reverse discrimination as members of traditionally under-represented groups are hired or retained under affirmative action plans over nonminority workers. In another area affecting

employment, some legislation has been passed both at the state and federal levels preventing employers from dismissing whistle blowers—employees who expose unethical or illegal practices of their employers.

The Environment: Government regulation has sought to impose fines on companies that pollute or otherwise harm the environment, both by federal and state regulations and through increasingly allowing civil lawsuits against such companies. Recent cases where such issues emerged and thereby sparked continuing debate over corporate responsibility include the *Exxon Valdes* oil spill off the Alaskan coast and the Union Carbide tragedy in Bhopal, India, where a leak of 25 tons of the deadly pesticide methyl isocyanate caused thousands of deaths and injured over 100,000 people.

Bribery of Foreign Officials: While bribery of U.S. officials has always been illegal, until fairly recently, companies doing business abroad were free to bribe foreign officials—a normal means of doing business in many countries. Some highly publicized cases of payoffs to foreign officials by American companies in order to procure lucrative contracts in the 1970s gave rise to The Foreign Corrupt Practices Act of 1977. The act prohibits the giving of bribes by American companies or their officers or directors to foreign government officials where the purpose is to obtain or retain business.

Foreign Trade: The government has sought to extend ethical responsibility to foreign countries with questionable human rights records by restricting trade with such nations. Two examples of this policy in recent times include trade restrictions with South Africa in protest of its apartheid policies and the temporary withdrawal of favorite nation trading status from China after the massacre of hundreds of student demonstrators in June of 1989 at Peking's T'ien-an-Men Square.

It is difficult to speculate on the future integration of ethical issues in the law. In the short term, however, it seems likely that the trend will be to continue liberalizing constraints on personal freedoms, while increasing the moral accountability of businesses. If this assumption is correct, we should see a continued withdrawal by government legislation on personal issues of choice, such as abortion, sexual preference and perhaps even euthanasia, and further restraints on the way business is conducted at home and abroad.

Judge for Yourself

Case 1.   Elena, the purchasing agent for Bigco Inc., contacts five different suppliers to obtain price quotes for office supplies she needs. The price for the identical office supplies ranges from $855 to $500, including shipping and handling charges. As purchasing agent, Elena has complete autonomy in selecting suppliers and placing orders up to $5,000; before placing orders in excess of $5,000, she must get signed authorization from the company's comptroller.

a. If Elena purchases the supplies from the most expensive supplier because she is angry at her employer for turning down her recent request for a raise, what duty of an agent has she breached?

b. If Elena purchases a $20,000 computer system from a dealer she has never ordered from in the past, can the employer refuse to accept the system when it arrives without being liable to breach of contract to the supplier? Explain fully.

c. Can the supplier sue Elena for damages if the employer does not accept the computer system?

d. If the employer learns that Elena ordered the office supplies from the most expensive source and fires Elena, can he refuse acceptance of the order without being guilty of breach of contract with regard to the supplier?

Case 2.   In the above case, assume that Elena purchased the supplies from the most expensive supplier because he offered her a 10 percent kickback of the purchase price.

a. If Elena keeps the bribe without informing the employer, what duties has she breached?

b. If Elena purchased $4,000 in necessary office supplies from the lowest-priced dealer, who then sends her a $300 VCR as a surprise bonus to thank her for her business, can she keep the VCR? Explain.

c. Assume that Elena purchased the supplies from the second-least expensive supplier because she trusted the company, as opposed to purchasing the supplies from the least expensive supplier, with which she was completely unfamiliar. Is she guilty of breaching any duty to the principal? Explain.

Case 3.   Nicholas, an officer of Galaxy Inc., is authorized by Galaxy's board of directors to negotiate the buyout of Local Corporation, a small family-owned company that has gotten into financial difficulty and is trying to stave off bankruptcy. Because Galaxy Inc. is a very large company, its board has instructed Nicholas not to inform Local Corporation that he is acting on its behalf but rather to make it seem as though he is offering to buy the company as an individual.

a. If Nicholas hammers out a deal for the buyout without letting Local Corporation know that he is acting on behalf of a third party, and Galaxy later refuses to honor the deal, is Nicholas personally liable on the contract?

b. If Nicholas tells Galaxy that he is acting on behalf of a third party but does not disclose its identity, will he be a party to the contract and liable for its breach if Galaxy refuses to honor it? Is Galaxy liable on the contract? Explain.

c. If Nicholas discloses that he is acting on Galaxy's behalf, despite his instructions to the contrary, and Local Corporation agrees to the takeover, is Nicholas a party to the contract? What legal consequences, if any, can the unauthorized disclosure of Galaxy's identity have for Nicholas?

Case 4. Farrah signs a five-year contract with XYZ Corporation making her a vice president for sales. After the first year of the contract, ABC corporation offers Farrah a similar corporate position at twice her current salary.

a. Can Farrah unilaterally end her agency relationship with XYZ if the latter is unwilling to allow her to get out of the employment contract? Explain.

b. What can XYZ do if Farrah takes ABC's offer?

c. If XYZ is unhappy with Farrah after one year, can it fire her? If it does so, what can Farrah do?

d. Assume that Farrah is fired after one year and on the same day finds a similar job with another company at a higher salary. Can she sue XYZ for breach of her employment contract? If she does, what damages will she be entitled to receive?

19

PARTNERSHIPS

Learning Objectives

After studying this chapter, you will be able to:

1. Define *partnership* and explain its legal difference from a corporation.
2. Explain the positive and negative aspects of a partnership.
3. Name and describe the ways to dissolve a partnership.
4. Explain the need to notify third parties upon the dissolution of a partnership.

Introduction

A partnership can be defined as an association of two or more competent persons to carry on a business as co-owners for profit. This definition, taken from the Uniform Partnership Act, states the three basic requirements for a valid partnership:

1. Joint ownership,
2. of a business for profit,
3. by two or more competent persons.

As one of the three basic forms of business organizations (the sole proprietorship, the partnership, and the corporation), the partnership offers some attractive benefits as well as some potential pitfalls. On one hand, operating a business as a partnership allows several persons to pool their economic resources and personal skills to further an enterprise for their mutual benefit; also, a partnership requires a minimum of paperwork to get started or to run. The partners directly control the business and have a voice in its management. Once a partnership is formed, other partners may join it only upon the unanimous consent of all partners. A partnership also benefits from preferential tax treatment, since, unlike the corporation, the partnership does not pay state or federal income taxes as a business entity; rather, each partner pays federal and, if applicable, state income taxes on her own income. This avoids the double taxation that shareholders in a corporation are subjected to. (A corporation pays taxes on profits, and the shareholders are then taxed again on the portion of the same profits that they receive as dividends.) On the other hand, each partner is personally subject to unlimited liability for debts incurred by the partnership, not just for the extent of his ownership share in the business.

Unlike the corporation, a partnership is not recognized as having a separate legal existence beyond the partners that make it up. Although a partnership can do business in its own name, it is not seen as a legal entity and, as such, cannot sue or be sued in its own name, nor can it own property or borrow money. Fortunately, its status as a nonentity means that it does not need to pay taxes as a business concern. Rather, each individual partner is taxed on her share of the profits that the partnership earns (and each may write off a share of the operating expenses as well). In most states, partners own both real and personal property used by the partnership as tenants in common without the right of survivorship; each partner is billed for property taxes and other expenses as an individual. In partnerships made up of a large number of people (e.g., many large law firms that have, for a variety of reasons, not been transformed into professional corporations), the bookkeeping can become rather cumbersome, as each partner's relative share in the profits (or losses) of the business is computed.

Sole Proprietorship

Before turning our attention to partnership formation, a few words are in order about the oldest form of business organization: the sole proprietorship. As its name implies, the sole proprietorship consists of a single individual owning and operating a business for profit. Although it is possible for the owner of a sole proprietorship to employ others to assist in the daily operation of the business, what distinguishes the sole proprietorship from its closest sibling, the partnership, is that a single individual owns and manages the business.

The attractiveness of the sole proprietorship is that business decisions are easy to implement; the owner does as he pleases and no third parties or co-owners need to be consulted on business decisions. In every state, this is the simplest form of business to organize, since the paperwork involved is minimal. Unless the business requires special approval of a state agency, such as a liquor license or health department clearance for a restaurant, an individual wishing to start a business under his own name can do so in most states without having to file any paperwork. If the owner decides not to include her name as part of the business, then she must file a brief application, usually with the state's secretary of state, for permission to do business under that name. Unless the chosen name is currently being used by a similar business in the state, or unless it violates an existing business's registered trademark or service mark, such applications are routinely approved upon the filing of the required form with a small application fee.

➤ 1. Harriet Smith wants to open a stationery store in her town. She rents office space and begins doing business immediately under the name *Harriet Smith's Stationery Store.* In most states, she needs no approval before she can begin her business. (She must, of course, maintain valid records of her business profits and losses for tax purposes, and must also collect and remit sales taxes, if applicable in her state.)

2. If Harriet decides to call her shop *Harriet's Stationery* or *Harriet's Cards,* she would also not need to procure approval in many states, since she would be operating under her own name, albeit a partial name only.

3. If Harriet wants to call her stationery store *Gifts 'N Such,* she must apply for permission to do business in the state under that name, since it is not her proper name.

The benefits that a sole proprietorship offers are accompanied by some significant liabilities. Chief among these is that the owner has only his or her skills to count on in running the business, and, while profits need not be shared with partners or shareholders, neither is the liability should the business fail; the owner is personally responsible for all liabilities incurred by the business, be they contractual, financial, or tort related. The owner's personal assets, not merely the assets of the business, are subject to attachment by creditors or to satisfy any judgments against the business, such as a successful lawsuit by a customer who is injured on business property. These drawbacks have made the sole proprietorship a less than ideal form of business organization for most new businesses. The relative safety and options for raising capital available to the limited partnership and corporation (discussed later in this chapter and in Chapter 20) have made those forms of business organization more attractive to both existing and new businesses. Nevertheless, the sole proprietorship is still a viable form of business organization used by many new businesses, particularly in professions such as law, medicine and writing.

Partnership Formation

The partnership form of business organization has its roots in both contract law and the law of agency. Indeed, both under the common law and the modern Uniform Partnership Act adopted by most states today, a partnership is little more than a way for people to do business under the guidelines of the laws of contracts and agency.

Entering into a Partnership

In general there are no specific formalities necessary for entering into a partnership agreement. The same rules that apply to the formation of a valid contract apply to the formation of a partnership agreement. A partnership, like any contract, can be formed by an oral or written agreement, and it can be implied from the conduct of the parties, even when no specific oral or written agreement exists.

> ➤ Fritz, Patrick, and Ellen purchase a grocery store together, with Ellen providing 50 percent of the capital and Fritz and Patrick 25 percent each. All three have a voice in running the business, and all three share profits in accordance to the percentage of the capital that they originally invested. The three, who are good friends, never discussed entering into a partnership as such, nor did they ever set down in writing any agreement to that effect. Fritz, Patrick, and Ellen are partners, since their conduct clearly implies the existence of a partnership.

Like all contracts, the partnership agreement is subject to the statute of frauds. As such, the partnership agreement must be in writing if it is to last for more than one year.

Partnership by Estoppel

If you'll recall from the previous chapter, an agency by estoppel arises when a principal through his words or actions leads a third party to justifiably believe that a given person is his agent. If the third party deals with the purported agent under such circumstances, the principal will be estopped from denying the existence of the agency and bound by any contract that the agent entered into on his behalf. The same holds true for a partnership: if a third party is justifiably misled into believing that a particular person is a partner by the words or actions of one or more of the true partners, the partners will be bound by apparent partner's acts just as if she were a true partner.

> ➤ Michael, who is romantically interested in Lorraine, introduces her as his new law partner to a group of clients at a social function. Lorraine, who is a new member of the bar with no prior litigation experience, later agrees to represent one of these clients in a complicated antitrust action. Because of her lack of expertise in the area and general inexperience, she loses the case, causing the corporate client several million dollars in civil and criminal penalties. When the client sues Lorraine for malpractice, both she and Michael will be liable for any judgment against her if the client can establish that he retained Lorraine in reliance on her being Michael's partner. (Law partners are jointly liable for the malpractice of every partner.)

Membership in a Partnership

As noted previously, a partnership is formed by the consent of two or more people to carry out a business for profit as co-owners.

Limited Partnership

Unlike a general partnership, the limited partnership did not exist at common law. It is a creature of statute in states that specifically allow it as a form of business organization. The main difference between general and limited partnerships is that in the latter, partners retain limited liability for partnership losses to the extent of the amount each has invested. Like a general partnership, a limited partnership requires an agreement by two or more people to enter into a business for profit as joint owners. Some of the salient features of a limited partnership are:

1. They must contain at least one general partner with unlimited liability.
2. They must be entered into pursuant to a written agreement as specified by statute.
3. The agreement must be filed with the appropriate state agency (e.g., secretary of state or county clerk's office).
4. Limited partners cannot be involved in running the business, but must merely be investors who share in its profits and losses to the extent of their investment.

If a limited partner becomes involved in the day-to-day operation of the business or has a voice in its management, he becomes a general partner and loses the protection of the limited liability offered by the limited partner status.

Liability of Partners

Partners are jointly liable for contracts made on behalf of the partnership as well as torts committed by other partners or employees of the partnership in the regular course of business. This is one of the most dangerous aspects of the partnership form of business organization: each partner is personally responsible for all civil damages in tort or contract incurred by the partnership. Consider the following example:

➤ Albert, Betty, and Carlos enter into a partnership agreement to jointly run a bakery business. Albert invests $1,000 in the business, Betty $10,000, and Carlos $100,000. Albert, the baker, negligently bakes a loaf of bread with shards of glass in it. A customer who purchases the bread suffers internal injuries after consuming it and recovers a $1 million products liability judgment. At the time of the judgment, the partnership owed $500,000 to Able Bank on a mortgage. A sale of all partnership proceeds results in $100,000 in capital. The partners are jointly responsible for the remaining $1.4 million. If Albert and Betty declare bankruptcy but Carlos has $1.4 million in assets, including an expensive house, car, and yacht, he will be personally liable for the full amount of the partnership's debt, and creditors can reach his personal assets (including the home, luxury auto, and yacht) to satisfy the partnership's debts.

Liability is joint and several with those of the other partners, which means that partners may be sued together or separately for the full amount of the debt. If creditors collect the entire debt from a single partner, that partner will be able to seek indemnification from his co-partners for their equitable share of the debt. But this serves as little consolation to a partner who, like Carlos in the last example, has deep pockets (substantial assets) and bankrupt co-partners!

Partners are not subject to criminal liability for criminal acts committed by their co-partners in the course of the partnership unless they participated in the illegal activity.

Dissolution of a Partnership

Like an agency, a partnership can be dissolved in a variety of ways ranging from acts of the parties to operation of law.

Act of the Parties

A partnership, like an agency, can be dissolved at any time in accordance with the wishes of any single partner. Any one partner may terminate the whole partnership if he wishes; the remaining partners will, of course, be free to enter into a new partnership agreement amongst themselves. This brings up another common problem with partnerships: their tenuous nature. Because each partner can dissolve the partnership at will, it is impossible to judge a partnership's long-term viability at its start. The specter of dissolution will always hang over the head of each partner.

A partnership agreement can state that the partnership will dissolve at a certain date or upon a given event. If this is the case, the partnership will automatically terminate upon the stated date or event. Even in cases when a partnership is to have a set duration, any partner may force its dissolution by unilaterally declaring his wish to that effect. If that happens, the partner may be liable to her co-partners in an action for breach of contract, but the partnership will be dissolved.

Operation of Law

A partnership, like an agency, may also be dissolved by operation of law in three circumstances: the death or incapacity of any partner, the bankruptcy of any partner, or a finding by a court that the partnership is set up to conduct illegal business.

Notifying Third Parties upon Dissolution

As with an agency, actual notice of dissolution must be given to third parties who have had business dealings with the partnership, and constructive notice (a legal notice in a newspaper of general circulation in the geographic area where the partnership conducted its business) must be given to third parties who may have been aware of the partnership's existence but had not directly dealt with it in the past. Failure to give the required actual or constructive notice continues the apparent authority of every partner to bind the partnership to new contracts. Each partner in the partnership must also receive actual notice of the partnership's dissolution; until then, each partner retains actual authority to continue conducting business on the partnership's behalf.

After a decision is made to dissolve the partnership and all partners have been notified, the partnership can continue to operate only in carrying out transactions designed to wrap up its business. Some of the transactions permitted during this period include selling partnership assets, filling existing orders, and paying off creditors. The partnership can enter into no new business during this period.

Judge for Yourself

Case 1. Ursula and Ramón share a deep interest in and admiration for native American culture and would like to open a store in a college town devoted to selling jewelry and artwork produced by members of the various Indian nations, as well as books, music, and videos that explore the vast richness and diversity of this overlooked American natural resource.

  a. If Ursula and Ramón want to run their business as a not-for-profit partnership, funneling all profits back to the various Indian nations, may they do so?

  b. If Ramón and Ursula rent a small storefront together and begin doing business, sharing in the running of their store and in the profits it generates, are they in a partnership together if no oral or written agreement to that effect exists? Explain.

  c. If Ursula invested $10,000 and Ramón $5,000 in the business, what will be the maximum liability of each for partnership debts?

Case 2. Assume the same facts as in the last case. A customer walks into the shop after reading its name, "Indian Treasures," and tries to sell Ursula a baseball autographed by members of the Cleveland

Indians baseball team and a basketball signed by members of the St. John's University Redmen basketball team. She is so enraged that she cracks a large ceremonial tortoise rattler over the numskull's skull.

a. If the hapless sports fan sues Ursula for the tort of battery, will Ramón be liable to pay any potential judgment?

b. If the battered customer presses criminal charges against Ursula, and she is found guilty of criminal assault and sentenced to two days in the county jail, will Ramón also share her sentence?

Case 3.   Assume the same facts as in the previous two cases.

a. What will be the effect on the partnership if either Ursula or Ramón declares bankruptcy?

b. If Ramón dies, may Ursula continue doing business indefinitely under the partnership if Ramón's heirs do not object?

c. If Ursula feels remorse about having lost her temper with the customer, can she make him a partner if Ramón objects? Does it matter if Ursula owns 80 percent of the business and Ramón only 20 percent?

d. If Ramón does not object, can the customer be made a third partner in the ongoing business?

Case 4.   Assume the same facts as in the last three cases.

a. If Ursula and Ramón wanted to make the battered customer into a limited partner, could they orally enter into a limited partnership agreement?

b. What are the main characteristics of a limited partnership?

c. Assume that Ursula, Ramón, and the customer enter into a limited partnership agreement in accordance with the requirements of the limited partnership statute in their state. What would be the consequences for the limited partner if he gets involved in running the business?

d. If they wanted to, could Ursula, Ramón, and the customer enter into a limited partnership where each of them is a limited partner? Explain.

20

CORPORATIONS

Learning Objectives

After studying this chapter, you will be able to:

1. List the characteristics of a corporation.
2. Explain what is meant by a corporation having the status of an *artificial person*.
3. List the requirements for formation of a corporation.
4. Explain why agency law is crucial to the corporation.
5. List the requirements for qualifying as a *Subchapter S* corporation.

Introduction

Unlike a partnership, the corporation is a legal entity in the eyes of the law—an artificial person with an existence apart from the individuals who own and manage it. As an entity, a corporation enjoys most of the privileges and shares in most of the responsibilities of natural persons: it can avail itself of most constitutional protections offered to natural persons and can own property in its own name, but it must also pay taxes (albeit at a lower rate than natural persons) and is subject to civil and some criminal penalties for acts it performs through its agents.

The corporation did not exist at common law; it is purely a creature of statute. As such, the corporation is governed primarily by the guidelines of the state statute that provides for its creation. The requirements for a corporation's creation and management vary somewhat between states; but as is usually the case, common threads can be found in the corporate statutes of all states, which we will examine here.

Characteristics of a Corporation

Most corporations share five basic elements: limited liability, status as an artificial person, centralized management, the right of perpetual existence, and the right to most constitutional protections.

Limited Liability

As we have seen in the last chapter, one of the greatest disadvantages of a partnership is that individual general partners are subject to unlimited liability for the debts incurred by the partnership. Since a partnership does not enjoy an existence apart from the individual partners who make it up, those individuals directly incur the partnership's debts. A corporation, however, is a special entity by statute, meaning its debts are treated as those of an *individual;* thus, a corporation's shareholders risk only the amount of capital they invest in the shares. If the corporation becomes insolvent, it can avail itself of bankruptcy protection much as an individual and have a court determine how its assets will be distributed to its debtors. The corporate stockholders' personal assets are not considered the corporation's assets. This makes investing in a corporation appealing to investors, who receive the equivalent protection of limited partners, but who can, as owners of the corporation, have a voice in its management by voting at stockholders' meetings and thereby electing or removing corporate directors.

Status as an Artificial Person

The corporation's status as a legal entity—an artificial being in the eyes of the law—allows a corporation to own and transfer property in its own name, enter into contracts, and be subject to civil and criminal penalties for its actions.

Centralized Management

Management of a corporation is centralized in a board of directors elected by stockholders. The board of directors in turn elects corporate officers from the president on down who are responsible for the day-to-day running of the corporation. Those officers in turn hire other employees and manage the corporation's affairs. Officers typically serve at the pleasure of the board of directors, and the board serves at the pleasure of the corporation's stockholders, who can elect or remove board members by voting at stockholders' meetings. Individual stockholders' votes carry the weight of the number of shares they own. Thus, an individual or group of stockholders controlling more than 50 percent of a corporation's shares can dictate who serves on the board of directors and thus indirectly control the corporation. Stockholders can, and often do, serve as corporate directors or officers.

Perpetual Existence

Unlike a partnership or sole proprietorship, a corporation can enjoy perpetual existence until it is dissolved. The incapacity, bankruptcy, or death of individual directors, officers, or stockholders has no effect on the corporation's continued existence. A certificate of incorporation can, however, provide that the corporation will be dissolved after a certain period of time.

Constitutional Protection

A corporation enjoys the constitutional protections of due process and equal protection under the 5th and 14th Amendments. It cannot, however, claim the 5th Amendment's privilege against self-incrimination and is not entitled to the privileges and immunities protection offered to individuals by the 14th Amendment. This means that a corporation sued civilly or criminally cannot shield itself under the 5th Amendment and refuse to present potentially damaging testimony against itself through its officers or directors. The officers or directors can, however, refuse to offer testimony that may tend to incriminate them personally in criminal activity. Also, states have the right to limit the activity of foreign corporations (such as those doing business in one state that are chartered under the corporate statutes of another state) within its borders. Under the privileges and immunities clause of the 14th amendment, every state must treat citizens of other states in the same way that they do their own citizens and cannot apply stricter standards or requirements for them to do business within its borders. The same privilege does not extend to corporations; as a result, states are free to apply stricter licensing criteria for foreign corporations than they do for their own.

Formation of a Corporation

Corporate promoters carry out the necessary groundwork for a corporation, including the legal work involved in forming the new venture and the financial task of attracting investment for it.

Before a corporation comes into existence, the promoter enters into contracts with third parties, such as land or equipment purchases and commercial leases. Once the corporation is formed, these preincorporation contracts are not binding unless the corporate board specifically adopts them or they are adopted by implication when the corporation accepts the benefits they offer.

As a general rule, corporate promoters are personally liable for contracts they enter into on behalf of the proposed but as yet nonexistent corporation. If, for example, a promoter enters into a long-term commercial lease on the proposed corporation's behalf and the corporation's directors refuse to adopt it, the promoter will be liable for its breach. Promoters can protect themselves against such an eventuality by making third-party contracts contingent upon acceptance by the corporation once it comes into existence (a term that is often unacceptable to third parties).

Once a corporation adopts contracts entered into on its behalf by a promoter prior to its incorporation, it becomes solely liable for them to the third parties with whom they were made. Upon adoption, the promoter's personal liability on the contracts ends.

Requirements for Formation

Although requirements for the formation of a corporation vary somewhat from state to state, the following are typical:

1. Incorporators, who must be natural persons of legal age, file a certificate of incorporation with the appropriate state agency (typically, the secretary of state). That certificate must meet all the legal requirements set out in the state's business corporation statute.
2. Once the state processes the certificate of incorporation, it issues the corporate charter, bringing the corporation into existence.
3. Incorporators hold an organizational meeting, adopt the corporate bylaws, and elect the first board of directors.

The Certificate of Incorporation

The certificate of incorporation filed with the appropriate state agency must contain all of the following:

> *Corporate name:* The name that the corporation is to be known by must be stated and must not be the same as that of any other domestic or foreign corporation authorized to do business in the state, nor must it be so similar to the name of an existing corporation so as to confuse the public.
>
> *Indication of corporate nature in name:* A corporation must use words such as *corporation, incorporated,* or *limited* after its name, or an abbreviation of one of these terms (i.e., Inc., Corp., or Ltd.), so that its corporate nature is immediately apparent.

Prohibited words or phrases: Many states' business corporation statutes prohibit the use of enumerated words or phrases that might mislead the public into believing that the corporation has powers it does not have or is in some way connected with the state, local, or federal governments. New York's business corporation law, for example, prohibits the use of the names *doctor, lawyer, finance,* and *bank* (among others) in the corporate name (BCL §301).

Statement of corporate purpose: Corporations can generally be set up to accomplish any lawful purpose, including profit and not-for-profit ventures. States' business corporation laws require that the purpose of the corporation be stated in the certificate of incorporation in varying degrees of specificity. If a state requires that the corporation specifically enumerate the purposes for its formation, it may only engage in the types of business that are noted in its certificate of incorporation. For example, a corporation set up to "deal in the purchase and sale of real estate" may not go into the computer retail business, even though both are perfectly legal ventures. (A real estate business can, however, be modified to allow for the sale of computers if the certificate of incorporation is duly amended.) Some states allow for very broad statements of corporate purposes, such as "to perform all business allowed by law."

Office of the corporation: The certificate of incorporation must include the address of the corporate office for the corporation.

Designation of state official for service of process: A state official, typically the secretary of state, must be designated as agent to accept service of process on the corporation. This provision facilitates third parties' suits against the corporation by making it possible to serve the state official with the legal papers necessary to begin a lawsuit against the corporation.

Description of authorized shares: The certificate of incorporation must state the types and numbers of shares that the corporation is authorized to issue.

Duration of corporation: If the corporation is not to have perpetual existence, the period of duration of the corporation must generally be specified.

Shareholders, Officers, and Directors

Each shareholder of a corporation is a part owner to the extent of the number of outstanding shares she owns. Shareholders do not, however, have a direct voice in the corporation's management unless they are elected to the board of directors or appointed by the board as officers of the corporation. The shareholder's control of the corporation is indirect and exercised only through voting at stockholders' meetings either in person or by *proxy* (written authorization allowing another stockholder to vote her stock on her behalf) for one of three purposes:

1. Election of directors.
2. Approving major organizational changes (e.g., sale of corporate assets and merger or dissolution of the corporation).
3. Amending the certificate of incorporation (e.g., to allow the corporation to engage in business other than originally provided for in the certificate of incorporation).

A corporation can only act through its agents, since it lacks physical existence and cannot therefore act on its own behalf. The *corporate bylaws* (internal rules for the corporation created and adopted by its board) can specify the number of officers a corporation is to have, or the board can name these as the need arises. Typically, the board elects the president, vice president(s), treasurer, and secretary, or the shareholders do directly, if the certificate of incorporation so provides. Both officers and directors are empowered to act on the corporation's behalf and have the power of agents under general agency law; as such, they may bind the corporation to contracts with third parties that they have either express, implied, or apparent authority to make. They owe the corporation the fiduciary duties that any agent owes his principal, including loyalty, obedience, performance, notification, and accounting; the corporation in turn owes them the duties of a principal, including cooperation, compensation, indemnification, and reimbursement.

Subchapter S Corporations

As previously noted, the greatest disadvantage of the corporate form of business organization is the double taxation that corporate profits are subject to: a corporation pays taxes on profits, the after-tax revenue is then distributed in whole or in part to its stockholders as dividends, and the stockholders pay income taxes on the dividends. In contrast, the profits of a partnership or sole proprietorship are only taxed once: as earned income to the owner of the business or its partners. This presents a problem for persons wishing to incorporate a small business, since the protection offered by the corporate form of ownership may be outweighed by the accompanying additional tax burden. Fortunately, the Internal Revenue Code provides a viable solution for most small businesses by allowing them to elect to be taxed as a *Subchapter S* corporation and, in effect, avoid having to pay corporate income taxes if they qualify for the special status.

Subchapter S corporations are defined by Internal Revenue Code sections 1371–1379.

Section 1371 (A) Small Business Corporation—For purposes of this subchapter, the term *small business corporation* means a domestic corporation which is not a member of an affiliated group (as defined in section 1504) and which does not:

1. Have more than 15 shareholders;
2. have as a shareholder a person (other than an estate and other than a trust described in subsection (E)) who is not an individual;
3. have a nonresident alien as a shareholder; and
4. have more than one class of stock.

In addition to the above requirements, a Subchapter S corporation must also meet the following tests:

5. Section 1372(A) requires that all shareholders must consent to the election of Subchapter S status.
6. Section 1372(E) (5) (a) states that the corporation may not derive more than 20 percent of its income from certain types of passive investments enumerated in the statute. (Section 1372(E) (5) (c) defines passive investment income to include, among other things, income derived from rents, royalties, and sale of stocks.)
7. Section 1373 states that undistributed corporate income is taxable as gross income to the shareholders. (Shareholders in a regular corporation are only taxed on the income distributed as dividends, but not on corporate profits that are retained by the corporation or otherwise reinvested.)
8. Section 1374 allows net operating losses of the corporation to be deducted from the stockholder's gross income to the extent of his investment in the corporation. (Shareholders in a regular corporation cannot take such deductions.)

Subchapter S status allows most *closely held corporations* (small, privately held corporations whose shares are not traded in any stock exchange) to receive preferential tax treatment closely related to that received by partnerships—the form of business organization they most closely resemble. Thus, the small business owner can avail herself of the protection of the corporate form of ownership without its attendant tax penalties.

Corporate Entity and Fraud

For a corporation to offer its shareholders the protection of limited liability, it must be run in accordance with the requirements under a state's business corporation law. If the corporation is used to defraud creditors, stockholders will lose the protection of limited liability and will be held personally liable for all the corporation's debts. This is likewise true when people set up a corporation merely to insulate themselves from unlimited liability but run the business as a partnership or sole proprietorship; in such dummy corporations, stockholders are also subject to unlimited personal liability for the corporation's debts. Consider the following example:

> Barney, a contractor, sets up Gorgeous Homes, Inc., a corporation involved in the home remodeling business. Barney is the corporation's sole stockholder and president. He and his wife serve on the board of directors, and his wife is the corporation's secretary. Barney and his wife never hold stockholders' or board of directors' meetings. All profits from the corporation go into Barney's personal bank account, held jointly with his wife. Payment for corporate debts are made from the couple's joint checking account.

Under the above facts, Gorgeous Homes, Inc. would be held to be a dummy corporation. If the corporation is sued for breach of contract or a tort, a court would allow *piercing of the corporate veil*—ignoring the existence of a dummy corporation—and hold Barney personally liable for all corporate debts.

For stockholders to be insulated from personal liability for corporate debt, the corporation must have a *bona fide* (good faith, true) existence. This means that all the formalities required of corporate existence must be adhered to, including regular meetings of stockholders and of the board of directors evidenced by written minutes of business conducted at such meetings; proper accounting of corporate profits and expenses; corporate accounts separate from those of stockholders or directors; and so on. Where a corporation exists only on paper, the courts will ignore its existence and treat it as what it really is: a sole proprietorship or partnership.

The mere fact that only one or two individuals own a corporation will not render it invalid. Most states permit a single individual to own a corporation as long as it has at least two directors, one of whom typically serves as the corporation's secretary. All that is required is that the owner honor the separate existence of the corporation, which at a minimum means keeping corporate assets separate from his personal assets, holding the required regular meetings of stockholders and directors, keeping written minutes of business transacted at these meetings on file, and paying all corporate taxes.

Judge for Yourself

Case 1.   Regina is a seamstress who makes clothing to order for customers. She conducts her business out of a small boutique in Yonkers, New York, under the name of "Regina's Fashions." Business has been good over the past several years, and she would like to expand by opening a second store and hiring additional employees to help her run it. She knows that you are taking a business law course and asks your advice so that she will be better informed as to her options before consulting her attorney to prepare the paperwork.

    a. She wants to know what the main benefit of incorporating will be for her. Tell her.

    b. She also wants to know if there are any potential disadvantages to incorporating her business. Explain at least two possible disadvantages to her.

    c. Regina would like to set up a corporation in which she is the only stockholder. Is this possible?

Case 2.   Assume that Regina in the last example consults with her attorney and agrees to form a corporation. She asks Lawrence to take care of the preincorporation paperwork as an incorporator and to begin negotiating a commercial lease for a new storefront. Lawrence, who has never done this before, asks your advice on several matters. You immediately tell him that you are not qualified to give legal advise and suggest that he see an attorney. Lawrence agrees to do so but asks that you give him some idea of problem areas that might affect him as an incorporator so he can be better prepared to discuss these in detail with his lawyer. Answer the following questions:

    a. Is it possible for Lawrence to be personally liable for any of the contracts he enters into on the corporation's behalf before it is formed?

    b. If Lawrence is subject to any potential liability in his preincorporation dealings with third parties, how can he cover himself?

Case 3.   John Doe, an unscrupulous businessman, sets up a corporation with the intention of defrauding the public. He is careful to observe all of the requirements in his state's business corporation statute. When the state issues the corporate charter, he sells shares in the company to 100 unsuspecting investors, each of whom pays $10,000. At the first stockholder's meeting, the shareholders elect John as the corporation's chief executive officer and appoint him chairman of the board of directors. As CEO, John enters into several contracts on behalf of the corporation, including lending agreements with three local savings banks, borrowing $1 million from and issuing an unsecured note to each bank. He then deposits the $3 million in loan money and the $1 million in investor's capital into his Swiss bank account and leaves the country for one with a warmer climate and no extradition treaty with the United States.

    a. Assume that a court will find that the corporation was set up as a dummy corporation from the start with the sole purpose of defrauding the public. What will be the maximum liability of the stockholders to creditors and other parties with whom the corporation entered into contracts?

    b. Assume that a court will not find that the corporation was set up with the purpose of defrauding the public, but rather that the chairman of the board defrauded the corporation and absconded with the funds after the corporation had been in business for several years. What is the liability of each stockholder?

    c. If John is foolish enough to return to the United States, what civil penalties is he liable for?

Case 4.   A business law class of 25 students decides to form a corporation in which each student will own a 1/25th interest. The purpose of the corporation will be to provide tutorial services to fellow students for a price and to publish old copies of exams for old courses in the college's management division to serve as study aids.

    a. What basic steps must the students follow to form their corporation?

    b. If all 25 students are 17 years old, can they act as incorporators on behalf of their corporation?

    c. What basic information must be contained in the certificate of incorporation?

    d. Can the students elect to set up their business as a Subchapter S corporation? Explain.

CASE STUDY 5–1
PARTNERSHIP

FRED REDMAN, Plaintiff and Appellant, v. WILLIAM WALTERS,
Defendant and Respondent

Civ. No. 42129

Court of Appeals of California, First Appellate District,
Division One

88 Cal. App. 3d 448; 152 Cal. Rptr. 42

January 18, 1979

SUBSEQUENT HISTORY: Respondent's petition for a hearing by the Supreme Court was denied March 14, 1979.

PRIOR HISTORY:
Superior Court of Alameda County, No. 484564–7, William J. Hayes, Judge.

DISPOSITION: The order granting the motion for summary judgment and dismissing plaintiff's complaint is reversed.

COUNSEL: John W. Larson for Plaintiff and Appellant.

> William Walters, in pro per., Ronald E. Mallen, David R. Harrison, David W. Evans and Long & Levit for Defendant and Respondent.

JUDGES: Opinion by Elkington, J., with Racanelli, P. J., and Newsom, J., concurring.

OPINION: The superior court, on defendant William Walters' motion for summary judgment against plaintiff Fred Redman, entered an order that "the motion herein be and it is granted," and that plaintiff's "complaint herein be and it is dismissed and that judgment be entered for defendant [Walters]." We treat the order as an appealable order dismissing plaintiff's action insofar as it relates to defendant Walters. (See Herrscher v. Herrscher, 41 Cal. 2d 300, 303–304 [259 P. 2d 901]; Sylvestre v. King Mfg. Co., 256 Cal. App. 2d 236, 238 [64 Cal. Rptr. 4]; Legg v. Brody, 187 Cal. App. 2d 79, 83 [9 Cal. Rptr. 593] [cert. den., 365 U.S. 889 (6 L. Ed. 2d 198, 81 S. Ct. 1042)].) And we entertain plaintiff Redman's appeal therefrom.

Declarations before the superior court established the following.

In 1969 plaintiff Redman employed legal representation of the "Law Offices," or partnership, or association, or some other arrangement of attorneys, known as "MacDonald, Brunsell & Walters." The purpose was the commencement and maintenance of a lawsuit for Redman, who advanced "the sum of $1,000.00 to cover actual costs." The lawsuit was thereafter filed, with "MacDonald, Brunsell & Walters" as Redman's attorneys of record. William Walters, the instant respondent, was the person designated as "Walters" of "MacDonald, Brunsell & Walters."

In 1970 Walters severed his relationship with the other attorneys of the above described grouping and commenced practicing law elsewhere. He had "never met" Redman, nor was he "aware he existed," nor had he "ever discussed or in any way participated in any review of the [subject] legal services . . . ." Nor had he a "communication of any nature from any party or any attorney on this lawsuit, and to my knowledge I have not participated in nor received any compensation whatsoever for any services purportedly rendered on behalf of Fred Redman." All of Redman's dealings in relation to his lawsuit had been with Attorney Brunsell.

After Walters' departure, the law practice arrangement, or a similar one, continued under the name of "MacDonald & Brunsell" and later, "MacDonald, Brunsell & Caton," which entitlements appeared, without formal substitution, as attorneys of record for Redman in the lawsuit. Redman was never advised of the changed names, or attorneys, except that he may have observed them in a notice of deposition or other communications or information. But he had never consented to any change or substitution of attorneys.

In late 1974, Redman's lawsuit was dismissed, under the provisions of Code of Civil Procedure section 583, subdivision (b), for failure to bring it to trial within five years. Upon learning of this, Redman commenced an action for damages including as defendants therein "MacDonald, Brunsell & Walters, a Partnership," and "William Walters." The cause of action alleged was that "defendants, and each of them, failed to exercise reasonable care and skill in representing the plaintiff in such action, neglected to adequately prepare and prosecute said case to disposition and carelessly and negligently failed to bring the action to trial within five (5) years after the date on which it was filed; and further, defendants permitted that action to be dismissed for want of prosecution pursuant to section 583 of the Code of Civil Procedure, which order of dismissal was made December 18, 1974, and filed December 23, 1974."

It is the latter action from which the appeal before us has emanated.

On Walters' motion for summary judgment the parties' affidavits conclusively established, and the superior court properly concluded as a matter of law, (1) that "MacDonald, Brunsell & Walters" held itself, or themselves, out to the public and to Redman as a partnership consisting of the three named persons, and (2) that Redman reasonably believed that he had engaged such partnership to commence and prosecute his lawsuit.

From this it necessarily followed, and the trial court properly assumed, that in its relations with Redman, "MacDonald, Brunsell & Walters" was a partnership or its equivalent, an ostensible partnership or partnership by estoppel. (See Corp. Code, §§ 15004, 15016; Blackmon v. Hale, 1 Cal. 3d 548, 557 [83 Cal. Rptr. 194, 463 P. 2d 418]; Hansen v. Burford, 212 Cal. 100, 110–111 [297 P. 908]; Westcott v. Gilman, 170 Cal. 562, 568–569 [150 P. 777]; Foote v. Posey, 164 Cal. App. 2d 210, 216 [330 P. 2d 651]; Nels E. Nelson, Inc. v. Tarman, 163 Cal. App. 2d 714, 725 [329 P. 2d 953]; Hayward's v. Nelson, 143 Cal.

App. 2d 807, 814–816 [299 P. 2d 1013]; Asamen v. Thompson, 55 Cal. App. 2d 661, 669 [131 P. 2d 839]; Snavely v. Walls, 13 Cal. App. 2d 600, 601–602 [57 P. 2d 161].) For the purposes of both of Redman's actions "MacDonald, Brunsell & Walters" must and will be deemed by us, a "partnership."

In its "Memorandum Decision" the superior court expressed the following conclusions. Although a "partnership" had existed, because of its "dissolution" in 1970 "defendant Walters was not the attorney of record for the plaintiff [Redman] on October 14, 1974, the date of the alleged negligent act, and the relation of attorney and client not existing defendant Walters had no duty to perform and as such there was no negligence on his part." Further, upon the "dissolution," "MacDonald & Brunsell" (without Walters) became Redman's attorneys and attorneys of record, and thus his agents. As his agents they had knowledge of the "dissolution" and that they alone had become Redman's attorneys. This knowledge, by operation of law, was "imputed" to Redman, the principal. The court reasoned: "It is a general rule of agency that notice to or knowledge possessed by an agent is imputed to the principal which rule applies for certain purposes in the relation of attorney and client. The rule rests on the premise that the agent has acquired knowledge which it is his duty to communicate to his principal and the presumption that he has performed that duty. Under our law the presumption is deemed conclusive for the purposes of civil action."

We disagree with the rationale and conclusions of the superior court. In our opinion the order dismissing Redman's complaint on Walters' motion for summary judgment was erroneous, and must be reversed.

Our analysis follows.

As noted, the "partnership" of "MacDonald, Brunsell & Walters" had accepted employment from Redman to commence and prosecute his lawsuit. Upon its "dissolution" 10 months later the "partnership" was not terminated in respect of its duty to fulfill its contractual obligation to Redman. For: "On dissolution the partnership is not terminated, but continues until the winding up of partnership affairs is completed." (Corp. Code, § 15030; and see Security First Nat. Bk. v. Whittaker, 241 Cal. App. 2d 554, 556–557 [50 Cal. Rptr. 652]; Associated Creditors' Agency v. Wong, 216 Cal. App. 2d 61, 67 [30 Cal. Rptr. 705].)

Among the partnership affairs of "MacDonald, Brunsell & Walters" to be "wound up" was the performance of its agreement with Redman, or that party's consent, express or implied, or perhaps by estoppel, to nonrepresentation by the outgoing partner, Walters. As said in Cotten v. Perishable Air Conditioners, 18 Cal. 2d 575, 577 [116 P. 2d 603, 136 A.L.R. 1068]: "In general a dissolution operates only with respect to future transactions; as to everything past the partnership continues until all pre-existing matters are terminated." (See Corp. Code, § 15030.) And: "The dissolution of the partnership does not of itself discharge the existing liability of any partner." (Corp. Code, §§ 15036, subd. (1); and see Corp. Code, §§ 15013, 15015.) An individual partner's liability in such a case will not be terminated except by performance of an agreement creating the liability, or by express or implied consent of the other contracting party that he need not so perform. (Credit Bureaus of Merced County v. Shipman, 167 Cal. App. 2d 673, 677 [334 P. 2d 1036]; Asbestos etc. Co. v. Lennig-Rapple Co., 26 Cal. App. 177, 182 [146 P. 188].)

It follows that in respect of Redman, unless he had in some manner consented (or was estopped to claim otherwise) to nonrepresentation by Walters, "MacDonald, Brunsell & Walters" continued as a partnership and Walters as a partner. And as such a partner Walters would, of course, be responsible also for the negligent act of the partnership or one or more of his partners. Apposite would be Corporations Code section 15013, as follows: "Where, by any wrongful act or omission of any partner acting in the ordinary course of the business of the partnership or with the authority of his copartners, loss or injury is caused to any person, not being a partner in the partnership, or any penalty is incurred, the partnership is liable therefore to the same extent as the partner so acting or omitting to act." (To the same effect see Roberts v. Craig, 124 Cal. App. 2d 202, 209 [268 P. 2d 500]; Madsen v. Cawthorne, 30 Cal. App. 2d 124, 125–126 [85 P. 2d 909]; Wiggins v. Pacific Indemnity Co., 134 Cal. App. 328, 338 [25 P. 2d 898, 25 P. 2d 902].)

No validity whatever is found in Walters' contention, and the superior court's conclusion, that because of the principal and agent relationship inherent in that of client and attorney, knowledge of the dissolution was imputed to Redman who thereby was conclusively presumed to have consented to substitution of MacDonald & Brunsell as his attorneys in the earlier litigation.

It is settled law that " '[knowledge] of the agent is not knowledge of the principal as to matters not within the scope of the agent's authority' " conferred by the principal. (J. A. Eck Co. v. Coachella Valley O. G. Assn., 102 Cal. App. 1, 9 [282 P. 408]; see also Herdan v. Hanson, 182 Cal. 538, 545 [189 P. 400]; Los Angeles Inv. Co. v. Home Sav. Bank, 180 Cal. 601, 606 [182 P. 293, 5 A.L.R. 1193]; Thompson v. Williams, 190 Cal. App. 2d 56, 60 [12 Cal. Rptr. 9]; Crofoot v. Blair Holdings Corp., 119 Cal. App. 2d 156, 194 [260 P. 2d 156].) "The knowledge of the agent is considered and imputed as the knowledge of the principal only when the former acquires it in the course of his agency. If he does not acquire it while acting within the scope of his authority, the knowledge is no more to be imputed to the principal than to an utter stranger." (Palo Alto etc. Assn. v. First Nat. Bank, 33 Cal. App. 214, 224 [164 P. 1124].) Here, the unilateral decision of the partnership to dissolve, and continue the representation of Redman by two of its members, was patently not within the authority granted it by Redman.

Moreover, such a rule of presumed knowledge of the principal will apply only in respect of a third person dealing with the agent. "Imputation of knowledge is based upon the necessities of general commercial relationships, and where a principal acts through an agent, a third person dealing with such agent is entitled to rely upon his knowledge and notice and it binds the principal . . . the principal through an agent or otherwise." (Hale v. Depaoli, 33 Cal. 2d 228, 232 [201 P. 2d 1, 13 A.L.R. 2d 183].) Here we are unconcerned with such a "third person."

And even were we to presume, arguendo, such notice to Redman, it does not reasonably follow that he had consented, or had as a matter of law waived objection, or been estopped to object, to a change in the partnership's obligation to represent him.

We have not left unconsidered the superior court's further comment that: "The file reflects that the notice of deposition in 1972 in an action involving this plaintiff was noticed by the law firm of 'MacDonald and Brunsell.' Correspondence on the letterhead of MacDonald Brunsell was addressed in that action; letters were addressed by the then defense attorneys to the law firm of MacDonald and Brunsell; the motion to dismiss the action noticed the attorneys for the plaintiff as being MacDonald, Brunsell and Caton. . . . [The] letters sent to a plaintiff's attorney must be treated as having been sent to [him]; knowledge of the attorneys is imputed to the client."

As pointed out, under the circumstances of this case, "knowledge of the attorneys is [not to be] imputed to the client." Otherwise we perceive the court's meaning to be that as a result of such matters, Redman had in some way waived, or been estopped to assert, Walters' continuing liability in respect of the lawsuit after the "dissolution." But assuming arguendo the existence of such evidence, it lends no support to the superior court's order here under attack. The existence or absence of estoppel, or waiver, is ordinarily a question of fact, and is one of law only when the evidence is not in conflict and is susceptible only of one reasonable inference. (Driscoll v. City of Los Angeles, 67 Cal. 2d 297, 305 [61 Cal. Rptr. 661, 431 P. 2d 245]; Albers v. County of Los Angeles, 62 Cal. 2d 250, 266 [42 Cal. Rptr. 89, 398 P. 2d 129]; Hefferan v. Freebairn, 34 Cal. 2d 715, 722 [214 P. 2d 386]; Glendale Fed. Sav. & Loan Assn. v. Marina View Heights Dev. Co., 66 Cal. App. 3d 101, 151 [135 Cal. Rptr. 802]; Los Angeles Fire & Police Protective League v. City of Los Angeles, 23 Cal. App. 3d 67, 75 [99 Cal. Rptr. 908].) At most, if anything, the evidence pointed out raised a triable issue of fact. And of course a summary judgment may not be upheld where the evidence presents such a triable issue of fact. (See Empire West v. Southern California Gas Co., 12 Cal. 3d 805, 808 [117 Cal. Rptr. 423, 528 P. 2d 31]; Corwin v. Los Angeles Newspaper Service Bureau, Inc., 4 Cal. 3d 842, 851 [94 Cal. Rptr. 785, 484 P. 2d 953].)

In situations such as that before us, law firms or related associations would be well advised to heed the rules stated by Corporations Code section 15036, as follows:

"(1) The dissolution of the partnership does not of itself discharge the existing liability of any partner.

"(2) A partner is discharged from any existing liability upon dissolution of the partnership by an agreement to that effect between himself, the partnership creditor and the person or partnership continuing the business; and such agreement may be inferred from the course of dealing between the creditor having knowledge of the dissolution and the person or partnership continuing the business.

"(3) Where a person agrees to assume the existing obligations of a dissolved partnership, the partners whose obligations have been assumed shall be discharged from any liability to any creditor of the partnership who, knowing of the agreement, consents to a material alteration in the nature or time of payment of such obligations. . . ."

The order granting the motion for summary judgment and dismissing plaintiff's complaint is reversed.

Questions for Case Study 5–1

1. What are the basic facts of this case?
2. What are the legal issues involved?
3. What is the decision of the court?
4. What is the legal rationale for the court's decision?

VI

COMPUTERIZED
LEGAL RESEARCH

The work that attorneys do in society has long been misrepresented in popular culture through two-dimensional characterizations in television shows, movies, and novels. Whether a lawyer is depicted as a tireless, brilliant, idealistic litigator tilting at the windmills of an uncaring bureaucracy and an unresponsive legal system, or as a morally decrepit shyster using the system to his own ends at the expense of justice, the setting is usually the same: the courtroom. The dramatization of a succulent courtroom trial generally pits good against evil in an archetypal battle for justice. Who can tell how many men and women have been inspired to pursue legal careers by watching "Perry Mason," "LA Law," or even my personal favorite, "Rumpole of the Bailey"? As is often the case, however, reality is far more sedate and unexciting than fiction, and the practice of law is far better exemplified by tedious research than the verbal thrusts and parries of courtroom drama. Indeed, most practicing attorneys never see the inside of a courtroom in their professional capacities, and even the most experienced litigators spend far more time in the law library than in the courtroom.

In our common law system, legal research is of paramount importance. Before an attorney can give definitive advice to a client on any but the most routine matters, she must consult both statutory law and case law; even if she is familiar with the relevant law, she must verify that meaningful changes in it have not occurred. As we have already seen in the discussion of sources of the law in Chapter 1, change is an important part of the common law. Legislative enactments and court decisions constantly weave minor, and sometimes major, changes into the fabric of the law.

Legal research is perhaps the least glamorous but unquestionably the most essential element of practicing law. Fortunately, today's attorneys have a powerful tool in conducting quick and effective legal research: computer-assisted research—the subject of our final chapter.

21

LEGAL RESEARCH USING LEXIS®

Learning Objectives

After studying this chapter, you will be able to:

1. Differentiate between traditional and computerized legal research.
2. List the advantages of computerized legal research over traditional research.
3. Explain why computerized legal research can be more cost-effective than traditional legal research.
4. Distinguish between primary and secondary sources of legal research and give examples of each.

Introduction

Legal research is absolutely essential to the practice of law. American jurisprudence is neither stagnant nor static; that is both its greatest strength and its major weakness. In civil law jurisdictions, the body of the law is much more stable than it is in our common law system. In civil law jurisdictions, which by far predominate throughout the world, all law is codified in statutes that leave little interpretation to the courts. For this reason, it is fairly simple for the average citizen in a civil law jurisdiction to learn both what the law is and how it applies to a given situation. Indeed, that is the primary purpose for codifying the law: to notify citizens of their rights and obligations in clear and unambiguous terms. As a result, attorneys are neither as numerous nor as necessary in civil law jurisdictions, and many routine legal matters are regularly handled by nonattorneys—licensed paralegals who prepare routine legal documents and give legal advice on uncomplicated legal matters. By contrast, it is illegal in every common law jurisdiction in the United States for anyone other than a licensed attorney to prepare most legal documents on behalf of another or to give legal advice. Even licensed attorneys can only advise clients in the jurisdiction(s) in which they are permitted to practice law. For example, a New York attorney may not advise clients in New Jersey unless he is also a member of the New Jersey bar.

Unlike civil law, which changes very slowly over long periods of time, common law is in a constant state of flux. This is not to suggest that radical changes occur daily in the law; in fact, change generally happens slowly in common law, as it does in civil law. But the *possibility of change* is far greater in common law. Courts have the power to interpret statutes and to reverse precedent. For example, as of this writing, a woman has the right to an abortion on demand through the first trimester of pregnancy in every state; the Supreme Court of the United States has guaranteed that right in *Roe v. Wade*. By the time this text is used in the classroom, however, the Supreme Court may have modified, distinguished, or overturned *Roe v. Wade*, and a woman's right to an abortion may be intact, curtailed, or nonexistent.

Traditional Legal Research

The traditional method of conducting legal research is for an attorney to consult the various sources that publish legal opinions, statutes, and local ordinances. Trial court decisions are not usually published; the clerks of the various courthouses keep records of trials locally, and attorneys can request them directly from the clerks. Appellate decisions, however, are reported in every state. Most states periodically publish such reports in official reporters—hardbound volumes generally published on a yearly basis and updated quarterly by softbound supplements. In addition to the state's official court reporters, there are a variety of private companies that also publish court decisions and legislative enactments in collections that they sell to law libraries and individual practitioners on an ongoing basis. Among the private publishers, West Publishing Company is the best known. It publishes a series of seven regional reporters that cover state appellate court decisions since the late 1800s: *Atlantic Reporter, North Eastern Reporter, North Western Reporter, Pacific Reporter, South Eastern Reporter, South Western Reporter*, and the *Southern Reporter*. The *North Eastern Reporter*, for example, covers Illinois, Indiana, Massachusetts, New York, and Ohio. West Publishing Company also publishes several federal reporters covering every major federal court, from the Supreme Court to the Court of Military Appeals. West's federal reporters include *Federal Reporter, Federal Supplement, Federal Rules Decisions, Supreme Court Reporter, Bankruptcy Reporter*, and the *Military Justice Reporter*.

An attorney conducting legal research has at his disposal both the official state reporters and the West reporters to assist him in finding relevant case law. Statutes are also published in a variety of reporters at the state and local levels, as are administrative regulations and some administrative decisions. These taken together constitute primary sources of the law. Important secondary sources also exist by way of legal encyclopedias, such as *Corpus Juris Secundum,* which comment on the general body of the law and can serve as an important starting point to legal research. Most law schools also publish useful commentaries on the law from noted legal scholars in their law review publications; attorneys sometimes use these to bolster their arguments in legal briefs, although they do not carry the same weight as primary sources.

The problem with printed sources of legal research is twofold: (1) they are expensive—only large law firms and law libraries can afford the cost of maintaining all the primary and secondary sources an attorney needs to carry on a general law practice—and (2) they are cumbersome to use. Even for an attorney experienced in conducting legal research with all available primary and secondary sources, the process is slow, tedious, and time-consuming. In the real world, where an attorney may not be intimately familiar with the available sources for the legal point he is researching, and where such resources may be unavailable because of his research facility's limited space or funds or because another attorney is currently using the particular volume that he needs, the result can be frustration and wasted time. Fortunately, a viable alternative exists that can supplement, or even completely supplant, traditional legal research: computerized legal research. Armed with a computer terminal or home computer, the right legal research software, and an on-line legal research service, any attorney can obtain vital primary and secondary legal research information from anywhere in the world where a telephone line is available—and do so faster, more accurately, and more cost-effectively than by utilizing traditional methods of research.

Computerized Legal Research

At present, two services provide computerized legal research capabilities to attorneys: Mead Data Central's LEXIS[1] and West Publishing Company's WESTLAW®. Although both services operate somewhat differently, each provides legal practitioners easy access to nearly all primary and some important secondary research material necessary for effective practice in any area of the law. Computerized legal research is faster and more accurate than traditional research; new cases and statutes are reported in LEXIS and WESTLAW often months before they can be found in the printed supplements to the traditional case reporters. Their only negative aspect is cost: the fees for LEXIS and WESTLAW are considerable. A single on-line research session

---

[1]Some material in this chapter including screen images is reprinted with permission of Mead Data Central, Inc., provider of the LEXIS®/NEXIS® services. Copyright 1992, Mead Data Central, Inc.

with either service can easily result in charges of several hundred dollars. For attorneys who bill the cost of legal research to their clients, however, these on-line services may actually cost less than traditional research billed at an hourly rate. There is no question that the average attorney or paralegal can greatly increase his or her productivity by using computer-assisted research, and do so cost effectively. After spending three months making extensive use of LEXIS while writing this text, I would no more consider practicing law using traditional research tools than I would turn in my computer's word processing and spreadsheet programs for a pencil and a slide rule.

Computer-Assisted Research Using LEXIS

General Overview of LEXIS

Mead Data Central's LEXIS service is the first of its kind, having been established in the early 1970s. LEXIS is a full-text legal research data base; it provides the complete text of nearly all state and federal courts of record, as well as state and federal statutes and ancillary materials.

When conducting legal research, it is a simple matter to find a particular case when its name is known; someone wishing to find *Roe v. Wade* will have no difficulty using either the official Supreme Court of the United States reporter or the West *Supreme Court Reporter*. But finding all relevant cases on a particular point of law in order to cite them as precedent is not a simple matter when the names of the cases are not known. The task is simplified somewhat by various indexes available for both the official and third-party reporters. Nevertheless, the chore can be onerous. Assume, for example, that a state legislature passes a statute that makes the burning of the U.S. flag a misdemeanor punishable by either a fine not to exceed $5,000 and/or imprisonment not to exceed one year in the state penitentiary. After the statute is passed, Jane Doe publicly burns the flag to protest what she believes to be an unconstitutional law. She is promptly arrested and prosecuted for the crime. Her attorney knows that the Supreme Court of the United States has recently held a similar statute unconstitutional, but he doesn't remember the name of the case or whether it was decided in 1990 or 1991. He could search an index of Supreme Court decisions for recent cases dealing with freedom of speech or the first amendment. After identifying all possible cases by name and the volume and page number where they appear in the official reporter, the attorney could scan the full opinion of each until finding the right one. The attorney could accomplish this relatively simple search in less than 20 minutes using traditional research tools, provided another researcher was not using the necessary indexes and the relevant volumes in the court reporter at the same time. Using a full-text search capabilities of

LEXIS, the attorney could accomplish the same search in less than two minutes, even if many other researchers were accessing the very same case for their own research at the same time. And, more important, an attorney or paralegal could do the complete research from the comfort of his desk in the time it would take the average researcher to walk to the law stacks and consult the first legal index.

Perhaps the strongest feature of LEXIS is that as a full-text data base it allows research to be conducted by specifying case names, words, or phrases of interest appearing within any cases or statutes in a given jurisdiction. It even allows for the case law of more than one state to be researched simultaneously, as well as the case law in the various federal courts. The result is that simple and complicated legal research can be completed far more efficiently than through traditional means.

Legal Data Bases Available through LEXIS

The value of a law library is directly proportional to the breadth of its collection. The ideal law library would contain every existing primary and secondary source of law for both the United States and every foreign country: every statute, every legal decision, and every published commentary on the law. The cost and space required for such a collection make it a practical impossibility for even the largest universities or law firms to attain. In practical terms, the larger a law library's collection is, the greater its value to the legal practitioner. By this yardstick, the electronic law library contained in LEXIS is most impressive in terms of both the quantity and quality of up-to-date primary and secondary research material it contains.

Primary Sources.   LEXIS contains one of the most comprehensive legal libraries of reported cases and statutes available anywhere. Its general-federal library (GENFED) data base provides comprehensive coverage of federal court decisions and federal legislative enactments. The GENFED library contains over 50 individual data bases, including the following:

US—United States Supreme Court decisions.

USAPP—U.S. Courts of Appeals and Court of Appeals for the Federal Circuit decisions.

DIST—District Courts and Court of International Trade decisions.

USCS—United States Code Service (federal statutes).

FEDREG—Federal Register.

USAG—United States attorney general's decisions.

RECORD—Congressional Record files.

In addition to GENFED, LEXIS also provides comprehensive coverage of state court decisions and state and federal statutes in its CODES library, which provides coverage of most state's statutes and the United States Code Service.

Finally, LEXIS provides separate legal data bases for each state and the District of Columbia. The New York library, for example, contains 13 separate data bases covering all appellate courts, the N.Y. attorney general's opinions, Public Service Commission decisions, the N.Y. comptroller's decisions, and selective statutes and tax court decisions.

Specialized Libraries. In addition to the state and federal legal libraries noted, LEXIS offers some 50 specialized legal libraries, including the following:

ADMRTY—Admiralty.

ABA—American Bar Association.

BANKNG—Federal banking.

BKRTCY—Federal bankruptcy.

BNA—Bureau of National Affairs, Inc.

COPR—Corporate law.

EMPLOY—State employment law.

ENVIRN—Environmental law.

HEALTH—Health law.

MILTRY—Military justice.

FEDSEC—Federal securities.

STSEC—State securities.

FEDTAX—Federal tax.

STTAX—State tax.

The specialized libraries include coverage of various French, United Kingdom, and European Community laws.

Secondary Sources. The LEXIS service also provides valuable secondary research material, including the Law Review library (LAWREV), the legal reference library (LEXREF) and the American Law Reports annotation library (ALR). In addition to the LEXIS library, Mead Data Central also offers LEXIS subscribers access to its NEXIS service, which provides a wide variety of useful up-to-date business, financial, and news information through a number of separate library services. The following is only a partial listing of the libraries available through NEXIS:

NEXIS—The NEXIS library, offering a variety of information services on business, finance, and legal matters, as well as general news.

ADPR—Advertising and public relations.

LEXPAT—United States Patent and Trademark Office.

CMPCOM—Computers and communications.

INSURE—Insurance.

TRAN—Transportation news.

ENERGY—Energy.

INTNEW—International news.

APOLIT—Associated Press political service.

NAARS—Accounting information.

In addition to NEXIS, LEXIS subscribers can also access MEDIS, a medical information data base containing a variety of health-related information. The price of accessing the NEXIS and MEDIS libraries varies depending on the specific library to be searched. In general, the price is comparable to that of using LEXIS.

Hands-On Legal Research Using LEXIS

Required Equipment. LEXIS requires rather modest computer equipment to run. Nearly any IBM PC compatible computer with either a monochrome or color monitor can be used to access LEXIS, provided it is equipped with a modem—a device that allows computers to communicate with each other through regular phone lines. The communications software necessary for a personal computer to access LEXIS is simple to set up and use. A novice computer user can install it with little difficulty in only minutes; an excellent, easy-to-use manual provided with the software makes the installation process simple. Once installed, the software automatically dials LEXIS through the chosen access network. A list of available networks and their telephone numbers is also provided; from most large cities, LEXIS can be accessed through a local telephone call, an important benefit since accessing it through a long-distance connecting network can significantly increase the cost, with most research sessions likely to last for at least an hour (not including the time for downloading documents—having documents electronically transmitted to one's computer for later use).

Although the minimum equipment required for use of LEXIS can be purchased for well under $1,000, it is also possible to lease dedicated computer equipment from Mead Data Central as part of the subscription agreement. Terminals, printers, and modems are available; given their cost, however, and the relative ease of accessing LEXIS through nearly any desktop or laptop IBM PC compatible system, equipment rental would not be desirable for the average user.

Figures 21–1 through 21–13 illustrate various menus and options involved in using LEXIS.

FIGURE 21-1   **Opening Screen for the LEXIS®/NEXIS® Services'
Research Software**

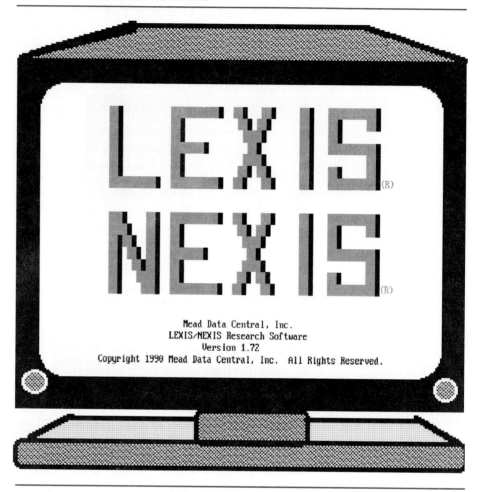

Mead Data Central, Inc.
LEXIS/NEXIS Research Software
Version 1.72
Copyright 1990 Mead Data Central, Inc. All Rights Reserved.

Learning to Use LEXIS

As is true of any software program, learning to use LEXIS requires some patience and time. In general, the program is easy to use. Its user-interface, however, is spartan by today's standards, lacking such modern niceties as pull-down menus, context-sensitive help screens, and mouse support. In addition, some of the program's commands are neither intuitive nor easily learned. LEXIS in part makes up for these shortcomings by including templates for both standard and enhanced computer keyboards that permit accessing most commands through function keys. (The dedicated terminals that can be rented from LEXIS at an additional cost provide dedicated function keys for most functions.)

As previously noted, using LEXIS can be expensive, since users pay for access to the service both for the time they connect to it (through the access network) and for each search made. Fortunately,

FIGURE 21-2   **Installation Menu**

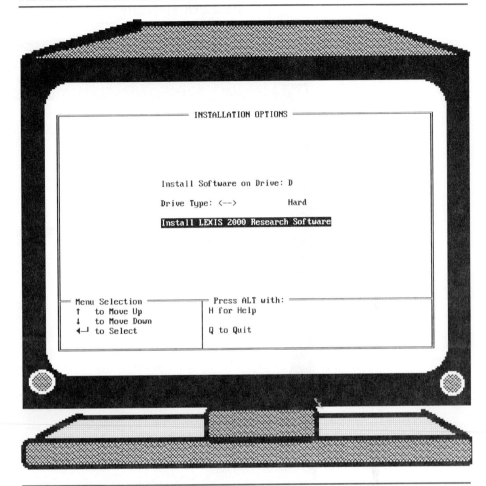

The process of installing the LEXIS 2000® research software is largely automated. Simple menus, on-line help, and thorough printed documentation guide the reader through every step of the initial installation and customization of the software.

LEXIS provides nearly free access to a practice data base through which new users can hone their computer-assisted research skills by researching a dedicated data base containing primarily older cases; while accessing the practice data base, users pay only modest network access charges and, of course, their phone charges.

Sample Searches Using LEXIS

Assume that you needed to find the latest U.S. Supreme Court case dealing with burning the flag. Using LEXIS, you could access the case in only a few minutes, even without knowing its name. The process would be as follows:

FIGURE 21-3   **Opening Menu for the LEXIS®/NEXIS® Services'
Research Software**

The setting-up and running of the research software is so straightforward and intuitive that most users with previous computing experience will not need to refer to the excellent manual. Configuring the software for a user's specific system is simplicity itself, as the next few screens illustrate. First, a user selects the Setup Research Software Menu option from the opening menu by highlighting this option through the cursor control keys and then pressing enter. This done, the screen represented above appears.

1. Access LEXIS by turning the computer on, loading the LEXIS software, and selecting the DIAL LEXIS option.
2. Select the GENFED data base.
3. Select the US file (for U.S. Supreme Court cases).
4. Enter a search command. In this case, the search command is simple: FLAG BURNING. Once the command is issued, LEXIS searches the full text of every U.S. Supreme Court decision for a match to the search criteria and responds with the number of cases in which the words *flag burning* are found. This search

FIGURE 21-4   **Setup Research Software Menu**

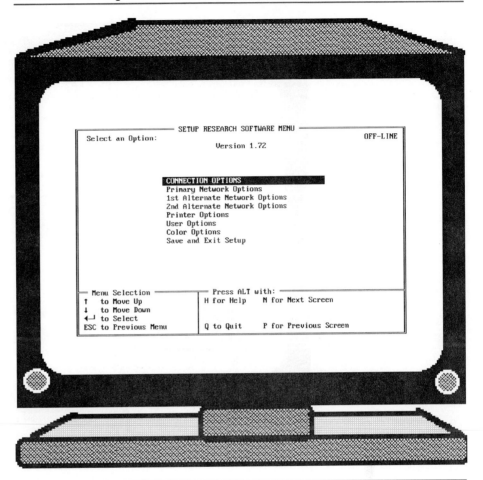

The user has a variety of choices in configuring the LEXIS® service to her computer equipment. Available hardware must be identified to LEXIS® so that it can utilize it. This includes telling the program the type of printer and modem that is available, what drive to store downloaded files in, and even aesthetic preferences, such as what colors to display on a color monitor, if one is available.

finds exactly five cases that contain the words *flag* followed by *burning*. (The actual time it takes LEXIS to conduct the search and return the number of cases that meet the desired criteria is less than 15 seconds!)

5. If the number of cases that match the search criteria is manageable, the researcher can immediately begin browsing through them; otherwise, the search criteria can be further limited to prevent accessing too many cases. By depressing the appropriate function key (*F1* for next page) or executing a dot-command (*.np* for next page), a researcher can go from one page in a reported case to the next, as well moving from one

FIGURE 21-5   **Connection Options Menu**

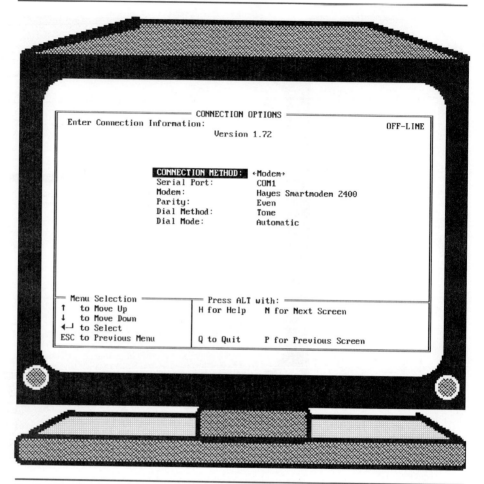

Configuring the research software to reflect a user's specific equipment is a simple matter. The software was tested on three computers (two IBM PC/AT compatible systems and an IBM PC/XT compatible laptop) using three different modems (an internal Hayes-compatible 2400 baud modem, an internal Hayes-compatible 1200 baud modem, and an external Hayes 1200 baud modem). Configuring the software or reconfiguring it to reflect upgrades to the system, such as adding a faster modem, is a simple matter even for an inexperienced user.

case to the next with similar ease. In this search, the first case cited, *U.S. v. Eichman,* 110 S. Ct. 2404, 1990 U.S. LEXIS 3048, is the one we wanted. We can read it, take notes from the screen, download the full decision, or have a printed copy of the decision mailed to us by LEXIS. If we don't want to pay the additional cost of downloading the decision or having a printed copy mailed to us (it costs two cents per line for either option), we can look it up in the Supreme Court's official

FIGURE 21-6   **Primary Network Options Menu**

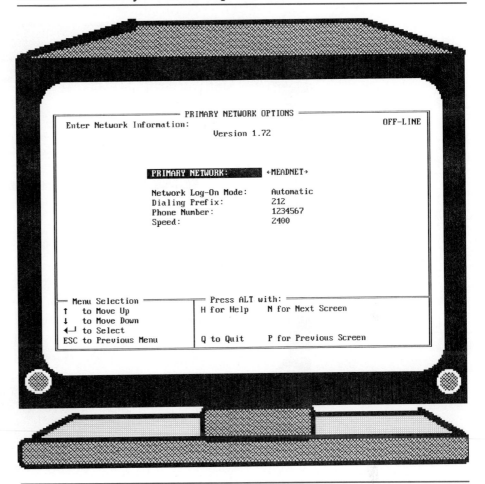

Before a user can connect to the LEXIS® service, he must select a primary network. The documentation lists a variety of networks that can be accessed via a local call from most large cities. Once a primary network is selected, its name and telephone number is entered into the research software by answering a few simple prompts. The research software uses this information to automatically connect a user's computer to the LEXIS® service through the selected network.

reporter—volume 110 at page 2404 (additional citations to other sources included by LEXIS for the same case are 110 L. Ed. 2d 287 and 58 U.S.L.W. 4744).

Searching LEXIS for statutory and secondary material is just as simple. I wanted to find my patent (showerhead with secondary liquid dispenser) in LEXIS's LEXPAT files. The simplest search would be for the inventor's name—LOPEZ, VICTOR D. But out of curiosity, I decided to search for the name of the company to which I'd assigned a 20 percent interest in my patent. A search for LAWRENCE PESKA AS-

FIGURE 21-7   **The Connect to LEXIS®/NEXIS® Services Option**

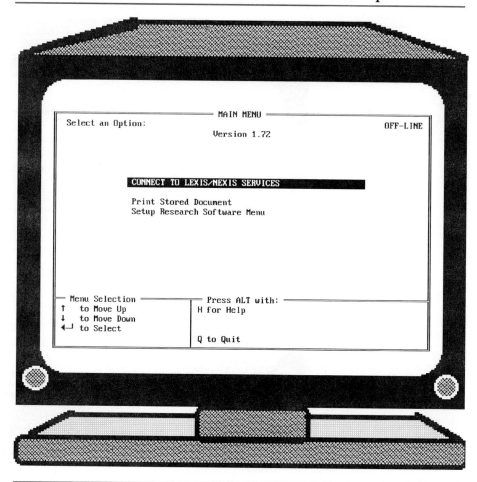

Once the user has configured research software, connecting to the LEXIS® service is simplicity itself: The Connect to LEXIS®/NEXIS® Services option is selected from the opening menu and the software does the rest: the proper network is accessed, the user's personal identification code is automatically transmitted, and an on-line connection is established in less than a minute.

SOCIATES found 361 patents—too many to search efficiently. I then selected the *modify search* option and limited the search with an additional criterion—AND SHOWER. In seconds, LEXIS informed me that there were nine cases meeting my search criteria (i.e., patents containing the words *Lawrence Peska Associates* and *shower*). Next, I browsed through the first page of each of the nine patents and found mine to be the seventh. Even though I purposely selected a less than efficient search (i.e., searching for the holder of a part interest in my patent rather than for my name), the entire search was completed in well under five minutes. I then downloaded the text of the patent for later use and compared it to my original; they were identical, but the downloaded version did not include the technical drawings that accompany

FIGURE 21-8   **Connecting to the LEXIS® Service**

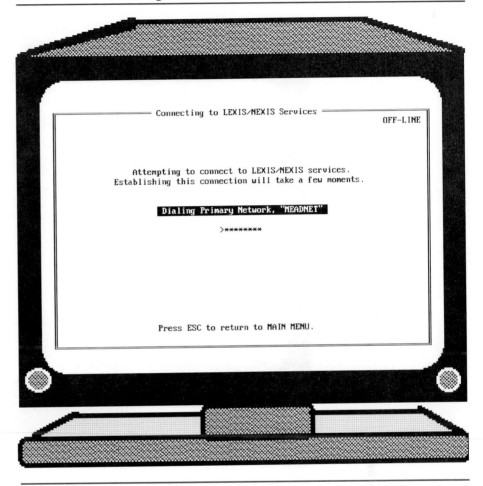

Once the Connect to LEXIS®/NEXIS® Services option is selected, the LEXIS 2000® research software takes over and automatically dials the preselected network and logs on to LEXIS® by entering the user's access number. In well under a minute, the user is connected to the LEXIS® service and can begin the research session.

the original. (Had I needed these, I could have instructed LEXIS to mail me a printed copy of the document.) The text of the patent as found in LEXIS follows:

3,964,686
Jun. 22, 1976

Showerhead with secondary liquid dispenser

INVENTOR: Lopez, Victor D., Woodside, New York

ASSIGNEE: Lawrence Peska Associates, Inc., New York, New York (12) A PART INTEREST

FIGURE 21–9   **Opening Screen for the LEXIS® Service**

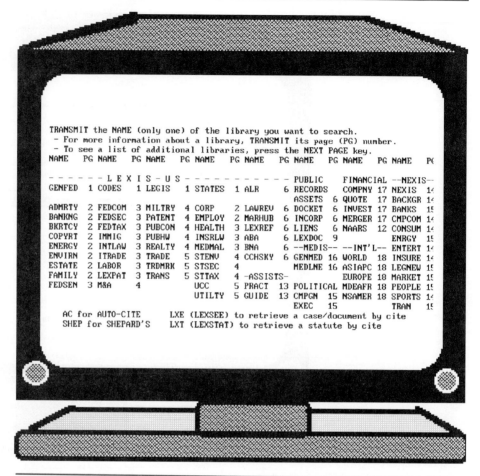

```
TRANSMIT the NAME (only one) of the library you want to search.
 - For more information about a library, TRANSMIT its page (PG) number.
 - To see a list of additional libraries, press the NEXT PAGE key.
NAME   PG NAME   PG NAME   PG NAME   PG NAME   PG NAME   PG NAME   PG

- - - - - L E X I S - U S - - - - - - - - - - - PUBLIC    FINANCIAL --NEXIS--
GENFED 1 CODES   1 LEGIS   1 STATES  1 ALR    6 RECORDS   COMPNY 17 NEXIS  1<
                                              ASSETS  6 QUOTE  17 BACKGR 1<
ADMRTY 2 FEDCOM  3 MILTRY  4 CORP    2 LAWREV 6 DOCKET  6 INVEST 17 BANKS  1!
BANKNG 2 FEDSEC  3 PATENT  4 EMPLOY  2 MARHUB 6 INCORP  6 MERGER 17 CMPCOM 1<
BKRTCY 2 FEDTAX  3 PUBCON  4 HEALTH  3 LEXREF 6 LIENS   6 NAARS  12 CONSUM 1<
COPYRT 2 IMMIG   3 PUBHW   4 INSRLW  3 ABA    6 LEXDOC  9              ENRGY  1!
ENERGY 2 INTLAW  3 REALTY  4 MEDMAL  3 BNA    6 --MEDIS-- --INT'L-- ENTERT 1<
ENVIRN 2 ITRADE  3 TRADE   5 STENV   4 CCHSKY 6 GENMED 16 WORLD  18 INSURE 1<
ESTATE 2 LABOR   3 TRDMRK  5 STSEC   4         MEDLNE 16 ASIAPC 18 LEGNEW 1!
FAMILY 2 LEXPAT  3 TRANS   5 STTAX   4 -ASSISTS-          EUROPE 18 MARKET 1!
FEDSEN 3 M&A     4         UCC     5 PRACT  13 POLITICAL MDEAFR 18 PEOPLE 1!
                          UTILTY  5 GUIDE  13 CMPGN  15 NSAMER 18 SPORTS 1<
                                             EXEC   15            TRAN   1!
    AC for AUTO-CITE      LXE (LEXSEE) to retrieve a case/document by cite
    SHEP for SHEPARD'S    LXT (LEXSTAT) to retrieve a statute by cite
```

A data base must be selected before research can begin. If, for example, one wishes to research federal law, the GENFED data base must be selected. On the other hand, if one wishes to research the law in one or more states, then STATES would be selected, followed by the state or states to which one wishes to limit the research. The process may appear complicated at first glance, but one becomes acclimated to the look and feel of the LEXIS® service in fairly short order. An excellent manual is available to guide even beginning users through the installation and use of the software; and knowledgeable support from a LEXIS® representative is always just a phone call away.

APPL-NO: 567,000

FILED: Apr. 10, 1975
INT-CL: [2] B05B 7#24

US-CL: 239#74; 239#315

CL: 239

SEARCH-FLD: 239#310, 315, 316, 71, 74

FIGURE 21-10   The Second of Two LEXIS® Service Opening Screens

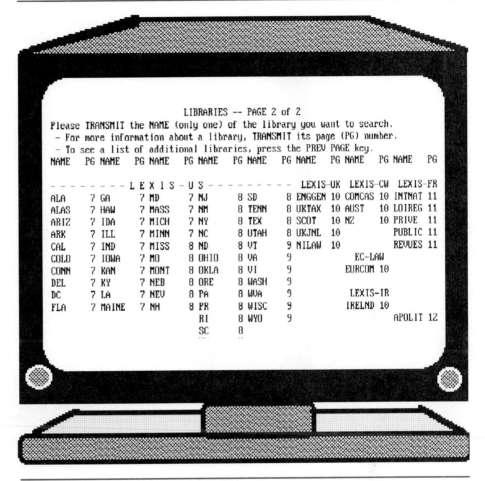

```
                    LIBRARIES -- PAGE 2 of 2
Please TRANSMIT the NAME (only one) of the library you want to search.
 - For more information about a library, TRANSMIT its page (PG) number.
 - To see a list of additional libraries, press the PREV PAGE key.
NAME   PG NAME   PG NAME   PG NAME   PG NAME   PG NAME   PG NAME   PG

- - - - - - - - L E X I S - U S - - - - - - - -  LEXIS-UK  LEXIS-CW  LEXIS-FR
ALA    7 GA     7 MD     7 NJ     8 SD     8 ENGGEN 10 COMCAS 10 INTNAT 11
ALAS   7 HAW    7 MASS   7 NM     8 TENN   8 UKTAX  10 AUST   10 LOIREG 11
ARIZ   7 IDA    7 MICH   7 NY     8 TEX    8 SCOT   10 NZ     10 PRIVE  11
ARK    7 ILL    7 MINN   7 NC     8 UTAH   8 UKJNL  10            PUBLIC 11
CAL    7 IND    7 MISS   8 ND     8 VT     9 NILAW  10            REVUES 11
COLO   7 IOWA   7 MO     8 OHIO   8 VA     9
CONN   7 KAN    7 MONT   8 OKLA   8 VI     9              EC-LAW
DEL    7 KY     7 NEB    8 ORE    8 WASH   9              EURCOM 10
DC     7 LA     7 NEV    8 PA     8 WVA    9
FLA    7 MAINE  7 NH     8 PR     8 WISC   9          LEXIS-IR
                         RI     8 WYO    9          IRELND 10
                         SC     8                       APOLIT 12
```

This continues the listing of the primary available data bases. Most of the data bases noted contain multiple secondary data bases within them. For example, by selecting NY as an option, data bases for New York cases and statutes become available, including NYCODE (comprehensive coverage of New York statutory law), NYTAX (New York tax law), and 21 others.

REF-CITED:

U.S. PATENT DOCUMENTS

2,504,506	4/1950	Du-For	239#315
2,580,696	1/1952	Novak	239#74
2,584,631	2/1952	Soss	239#316
2,620,234	12/1952	Schaich	239#315
2,795,460	6/1957	Bletcher et al.	239#315
3,788,553	1/1974	Heckman	239#315

PRIM-EXMR: Love, John J.

FIGURE 21-11   **The LEXIS®–UK Data Base**

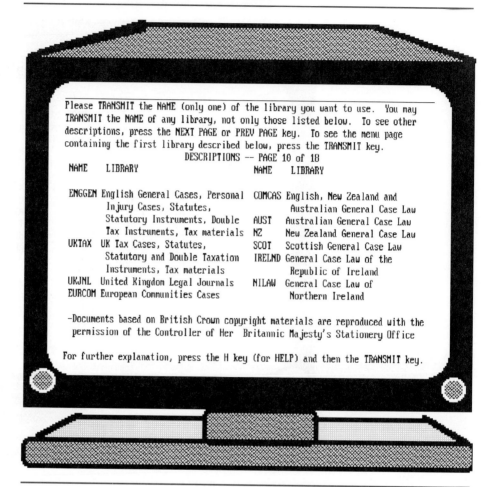

```
Please TRANSMIT the NAME (only one) of the library you want to use.  You may
TRANSMIT the NAME of any library, not only those listed below.  To see other
descriptions, press the NEXT PAGE or PREV PAGE key.  To see the menu page
containing the first library described below, press the TRANSMIT key.
                      DESCRIPTIONS -- PAGE 10 of 18
   NAME    LIBRARY                       NAME    LIBRARY

   ENGGEN  English General Cases, Personal   COMCAS  English, New Zealand and
           Injury Cases, Statutes,                   Australian General Case Law
           Statutory Instruments, Double    AUST    Australian General Case Law
           Tax Instruments, Tax materials   NZ      New Zealand General Case Law
   UKTAX   UK Tax Cases, Statutes,          SCOT    Scottish General Case Law
           Statutory and Double Taxation    IRELND  General Case Law of the
           Instruments, Tax materials               Republic of Ireland
   UKJNL   United Kingdom Legal Journals    NILAW   General Case Law of
   EURCOM  European Communities Cases               Northern Ireland

   -Documents based on British Crown copyright materials are reproduced with the
    permission of the Controller of Her  Britannic Majesty's Stationery Office

   For further explanation, press the H key (for HELP) and then the TRANSMIT key.
```

The LEXIS® Service is not limited in its scope to U.S. law; it also contains data bases on international law. Depicted here is the LEXIS®–UK data base, containing useful information on law in the United Kingdom.

ABST:

A shower head for shower baths including a compartment in which a hygienic liquid may be stored and selectively mixed into the water stream. A normally closed valve is positioned in the compartment and a valve operator disposed outside the shower head may selectively open the valve to dispense the liquid.

NO-OF-CLAIMS: 9

EXMPL-CLAIM: 1

NO-OF-FIGURES: 2

FIGURE 21-12 LEXIS® Document Delivery Options

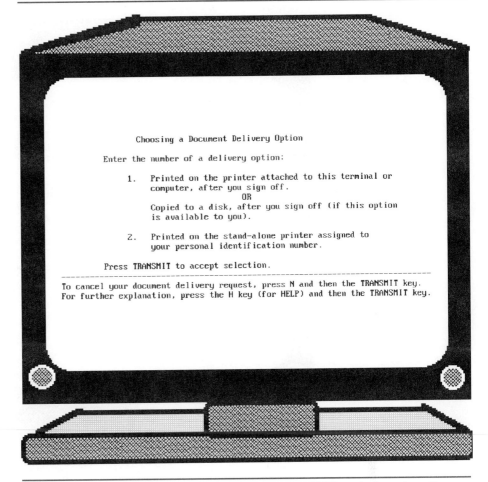

Attorneys or paralegals engaged in legal research using the LEXIS® service have the option of printing portions of relevant documents at any time during the research process. They can also select to have printed copies of relevant research material sent to them directly by the LEXIS® service or to have such information electronically stored in their computer's floppy or hard disks for future reference. There is an additional charge for such services.

NO-DRWNG-PP: 1

BACKGROUND OF THE INVENTION

This invention relates to showerhead attachments for shower baths and more particularly to a showerhead of this type wherein a quantity of a hygienic liquid may be selectively introduced into the stream of water flowing therethrough.

FIGURE 21–13 **Summary of LEXIS® Research Session**

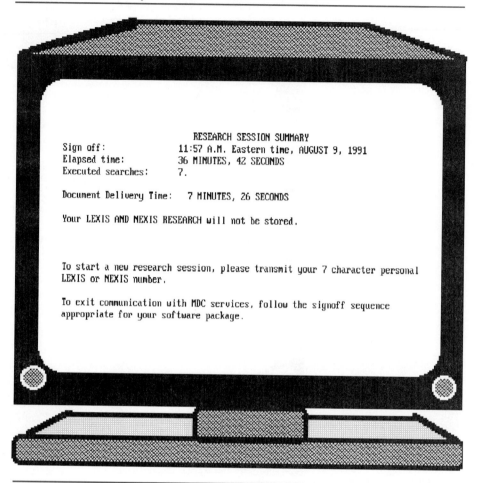

At the end of the research session, the LEXIS® service informs the researcher of the exact amount of time spent on-line and of the number of searches conducted. If the downloading of documents to disk was requested, the time taken by that transaction is also noted. At the end of the month, a detailed summary of all on-line usage charges incurred are forwarded to the user; each statement contains precise charges for each search, including the client's name—an extremely useful tool for client billing, since cost of on-line research is billable to the client, as well as the researcher's time in conducting the legal research and interpreting the results.

The inclusion of a hygienic liquid such as skin softening lotions, oils, or colognes into a tub bath is well known. In this manner the liquid can be dispersed over the entire body. This luxury, however, does not appear to be presently available to those who prefer the convenience and speed of a standing shower bath. The feature of introducing such liquids into the water stream while showering should add to the other conveniences of the shower bath. Moreover, since many people wash or shampoo their hair while showering, the capacity to introduce liquid shampoo into the stream of water would be additionally desirable.

SUMMARY OF THE INVENTION

Accordingly, it is a primary object of the present invention to provide a showerhead attachment that is capable of dispensing a hygienic liquid into the water stream.

It is a further object of this invention to provide a showerhead that includes a reservoir for storing a quantity of hygienic liquid and a dispensing means for selectively introducing the liquid into the water stream.

It is another object of this invention to provide a showerhead having a liquid storage reservoir and a valve means for selectively dispensing a controlled amount of the liquid into the stream of water.

The above objects as well as others, which will subsequently become clear, are achieved by providing a shower head attachment with a fillable reservoir for storing a hygienic liquid and a valve normally closing an orifice communicating the reservoir with the interior of the showerhead and operable to selectively open the orifice to dispense the liquid into the water stream. In the preferred embodiment the reservoir is formed in a thickened wall portion of the shower head body and a raised boss formed on the exterior of the body, and the valve includes a stem having an operator extending out of the shower head and biased into the closed position. Depression of the operator opens the valve to introduce liquid into the stream of water flowing in the shower head.

DRWDESC:
BRIEF DESCRIPTION OF THE DRAWINGS

Other objects and advantages of the invention will best be understood upon reading the following detailed description of the invention with the accompanying drawings, in which:

FIG. 1 is an elevational view of a shower head constructed in accordance with the principles of the present invention; and

FIG. 2 is a view similar to FIG. 1 with parts thereof broken away and in section for clarity in illustrating the invention.[2]
DETAILED DESCRIPTION OF THE PREFERRED EMBODIMENT

Referring now to the drawings, there is illustrated a shower head generally indicated at 10 and comprising a hollow casting or body structure diverging in configuration from an inlet end 12 to an outlet end 14. The shower head may be connected to a conventional plumbing fixture such as water pipe 16 by means of a coupling 18 having a fitting 20 threaded

---

[2]Figure 1 and Figure 2, as mentioned above, are not available in the LEXIS on-line data base, but a copy can be obtained from LEXIS by mail.

onto the pipe and a collar 22 threaded onto the inlet end of the shower head. The coupling 18 may include a conduit in a similarly shaped seat 28 sealed with rubber or the like. The ball and seat both, of course, have a passageway 30 through which the water may flow. The collar is loosely fitted about the ball 26 so the collar and the shower head can pivot with a universal swiveling motion to direct the water as desired. The outlet end 14 of the shower head includes a nozzle 32 which may be a conventional adjustable perforated plate or plurality of adjustable slit heads received in apertures, neither of which is illustrated, so that the spray of water may be controlably [sic] dispersed.

Intermediate the inlet end 12 and the outlet end 14 is a water dispersing chamber 34. In accordance with the preferred embodiment a wall 36 at one side of the shower head body in the vicinity of the chamber 34 is enlarged or thickened relative to the remainder of the body. Formed in this thickened wall 36 is a bore or cavity 38 that opens into the chamber 34 and which may be continuous with the hollow of an annular boss 40 that may be formed on the surface of the shower head. Preferrably [sic], the wall of the cavity 38 adjacent the chamber 34 is threaded at 42 to receive an externally threaded sleeve 44. The sleeve 44 has a central bore tapering in converging fashion from its upper portion 46 to a narrow orifice 48 and thence tapering in diverging fashion to an outer aperture 50 opening into the chamber 34. The cavity 38 together with the converging bore of the sleeve 44 form a reservoir for the storage of a hygienic liquid 52 such as skin softening lotions, cologne, shampoo or the like which may be dispensed into the water dispersing chamber 34 through the orifice 48. The purpose of the diverging section of the bore will hereinafter become clear.

In order to selectively dispense the liquid 52 from the reservoir the present invention provides a valve including a valve stem 54 extending centrally through the one end at a reservoir and connected at one end to a valve head 56 adjacent the chamber 34 and at the opposite end to an operator 58. The valve head 56 is positioned on the chamber side of the orifice and is tapered so as to be of a substantially truncated conical configuration of a size to fit within the diverging section of the bore of sleeve 44. The diverging section thus functions as a valve seat for the valve head 56 and may be of a material or coated with a material that acts to seal the bore when the valve head 56 is received therein. To enclose the reservoir there is provided a closure member which may comprise an internally threaded bonnet 60 adapted to be threadedly received on the upper portion of the boss 40. A slow return or delayed action spring 62 is coiled about the upper end of the stem 54 and is received within a recess 64 in the upper central wall of the bonnet 60 and a recess 66 in the bottom wall of the operator 58. The spring acts between the operator and the bonnet to urge the operator outwardly from the shower head, and thereby biases the valve head 56 into sealed position with the diverging portion of the bore of the sleeve 44 so as to close the orifice 48. Depression of the operator forces the stem 54 through the orifice and the valve head into the chamber 34 so as to open the orifice into the chamber.

Preferably a bushing 68 is positioned on a circumferential ledge 70 countersunk in the upper annulus of the boss 40 so as to provide a bearing surface for the stem 54. The stem 54 may be stepped as at 72 to act as a stop against a central annular portion 74 of the bushing 68 to prevent the valve head 56 from taking all the forces when the operator is released after depression. A gasket or washer 76 may be positioned between the outer circumferential edge of the bushing and the wall of the bonnet to prevent leakage of liquid past the bushing and down the threads of the bonnet. A further seal in the form of an "O" ring 78 may be positioned in a recess about the central bore of the bushing and the reduced portion of the valve stem 54.

In order to fill the reservoir and replenish the liquid therein when necessary, a passageway 80 is formed through a wall of the boss 40. The passageway 80 extends through a coupling 80 which may have a bulbous configuration formed on, or otherwise secured to, the boss. A preferably transparent plastic tube 84 is adapted to be received about the bulbous coupling 80 for universal pivotable movement, yet to provide a seal to prevent liquid, entering the tube, from escaping between the tube and outer surface of the coupling 80. Since the tube is transparent, the level of liquid in the reservoir may be indicated when the tube and the shower head are properly positioned, e.g., in the form illustrated, when the shower head is substantially horizontal and the tube is vertical. A cap 86 may be positioned on the open end of the tube 84 to prevent spillage when the shower head is pivoted.

In operation, when liquid L is desired to be mixed into the water W flowing through the chamber 34, the operator is depressed momentarily. Since the spring 62 returns slowly the liquid is dispensed over a longer period of time than the period of depression. Alternatively, the operator may be held for as long as required. Thus, the liquid is mixed with the water to be dispersed over the body of a shower bather.

Numerous alterations of the structure herein disclosed will suggest themselves to those skilled in the art. However, it is to be understood that the present disclosure relates to a preferred embodiment of the invention which is for purposes of illustration only and not to be construed as a limitation of the invention. All such modifications which do not depart from the spirit of the invention are intended to be included within the scope of the appended claims.

CLAIMS:
Having thus set forth the nature of the invention, what is claimed herein is:

1. In a showerhead comprising a hollow body member having an inlet at one end for connecting to a plumbing conduit to receive a stream of water, an outlet spaced from the inlet for discharging the water, and a dispensing chamber defined intermediate said inlet and outlet, a thickened

wall portion formed in the body member in the vicinity of said dispensing chamber, a reservoir comprising a cavity formed in said thickened wall portion and closure means for enclosing said cavity for storing a hygienic liquid, said thickened wall portion including an annular boss raised on the exterior of the body member, said boss having a passageway formed through a wall thereof, a filler port including a hollow tube disposed externally of the body member communicating with the reservoir for supplying liquid to the reservoir, coupling means connecting said tube to the boss with the hollow of the tube opening into the passageway, said reservoir having an orifice opening into said chamber, a valve normally closing the orifice, and a valve operator for selectively moving the valve to open the orifice to dispense said liquid into the chamber, whereby a controlled amount of said liquid is mixed with and discharged with the water.

2. In a shower head as recited in claim 1 wherein said valve comprises a valve head adapted to seal said orifice, a rod having one end connected to the valve head and a second end disposed outside the body member, said operator being secured to the second end of said rod, and biasing means for urging said valve head into sealing relation with said orifice.

3. In a shower head as recited in claim 1 wherein said valve comprises a valve head adapted to seal said opening, a rod having one end connected to the valve head and a second end disposed outside the body member, said operator being secured to said second end, and a spring disposed between the abutting said operator and said closure means for urging said operator and thereby said valve head into sealing relation with the orifice.

4. In a shower head as recited in claim 1 wherein said reservoir includes a sleeve positioned in the cavity adjacent the chamber, said orifice comprising a narrow opening in the sleeve.

5. In a shower head as recited in claim 3 wherein said valve head is positioned in said dispersing chamber, said rod being smaller than the orifice so as to pass freely therethrough and said spring is a coil spring normally urging the operator away from said closure means.

6. In a shower head as recited in claim 1 wherein said tube comprises a transparent plastic material, and said coupling means includes means for mounting said tube for universal pivotable movement relative to said boss.

7. In a showerhead comprising a hollow body member having an inlet at one end for connecting to a plumbing conduit to receive a stream of water, an outlet spaced from the inlet for discharging the water, and a dispensing chamber defined intermediate said inlet and outlet, a thickened wall portion formed in the body member in the vicinity of said dispens-

ing chamber, a reservoir comprising a cavity formed in said thickened wall portion and closure means for enclosing said cavity for storing a hygienic liquid, a filler port communicating with the reservoir for supplying liquid to the reservoir, said reservoir including a sleeve positioned in the cavity adjacent the chamber, said sleeve having an orifice opening into said chamber, a valve comprising a valve head, a rod having one end connected to the valve head and a second end disposed outside the body member, a spring for urging said valve head into normally sealing relationship with the orifice, and a valve operator secured to the second end of said rod for selectively moving the valve head to open the orifice to dispense said liquid into the chamber, whereby a controlled amount of said liquid is mixed with and discharged with the water.

8. In a showerhead as recited in claim 7 wherein said valve head is positioned in said dispensing chamber, said rod being smaller than the orifice so as to pass freely therethrough, and said spring is a coil spring normally urging the operator away from said closure means.

9. In a showerhead as recited in claim 8 wherein said spring is disposed between and abutting said operator and said closure member.

Advantages of LEXIS over Traditional Research Tools	The power, speed, and flexibility offered by LEXIS should be apparent by now. Its usefulness as a research tool cannot be overstated. The ability to conduct searches through the full text of legal opinions, statutes, and secondary material not only greatly speeds up traditional research but also allows the researcher to strategically search for precedent under criteria limited only by his or her imagination. By searching for specific words and limiting searches by logical operators, the researcher can sift through nearly the whole body of applicable law to find just the cases, statutes, or secondary materials that most closely meet his needs or most effectively bolster his arguments. Broad searches can be narrowed by adding, changing, or limiting search terms. It is even possible to tell LEXIS to search for words that appear within a set number of words from each other, as in the following example: CONTRACT W/10 CHILD AND NECESSARIES. This search request tells LEXIS to look for cases in which the word *contract* appears within 10 words of *child* and in which the word *necessaries* also appears. Such a search is likely to find a plethora of cases dealing with children's contracts for necessaries. If one were interested in finding cases in which children had contracted for an automobile under circumstances where the contract was found to be a necessary, and therefore not subject to renunciation by the child, one might alter the search as follows: CHILD AND CONTRACT W/10 AUTOMOBILE OR CAR AND NECESSARY. This search would find all cases that contained the words *child* and *contract* within 10 words of *automobile* or *car* and that

contained the word *necessary*. This search could be broadened even further by using the wild-card designator ? as follows: CHILD? AND CONTRACT? W/10 AUTOMOBILE? OR CAR AND NECESSAR?. The latter search would find all cases in which the words *child* with any possible ending (e.g., *child, children, child's, children's, childish,* etc.) and *contract* with any possible ending (e.g., *contract, contracting, contracted, contractor,* etc.) appeared within 10 words of *automobile* with any possible ending (e.g., *automobile, automobiles, automobile's, automobiles',* etc.) in any case that also contained the word *necessar* with any possible ending (e.g., *necessary, necessaries,* etc.).

By combining logical operators such as *AND, OR,* and *NOT* with the ability to search for words or phrases that appear within a certain number of words from each other, a researcher can broaden or narrow a search at will. LEXIS's full-text research capabilities also allow researchers to perform some types of research that would be impractical using traditional tools. For example, an attorney arguing a child custody case on appeal before justices Smith, Rivera, and Lee could easily read all decisions involving child custody by the three justices over the last several years. The following search is likely to yield all decisions by justices Lee, Rivera, or Smith over the past five years in the State of Moot's Superior Court dealing with child custody: CHILD? CUSTODY AND JUSTICE LEE OR JUSTICE SMITH OR JUSTICE RIVERA AND STATE OF MOOT SUPERIOR COURT AND 1992 OR 1991 OR 1990 OR 1989 OR 1987. In a matter of minutes, the researcher would have access to the relevant cases—something that could take days to compile using traditional research tools.

The Practice of Law and the Emerging Technologies

The move to ever-increasing computerization over the past decade has made its mark on the legal profession as it has on society as a whole. The trend will unquestionably continue in the future. The lawyer's legal pad is not yet obsolete, though the careful observer can see it begin to be supplanted by the notebook computer in the law library, the conference room, and even the courtroom. For a profession that depends so heavily on accessing, retrieving, and processing information, the computer is a godsend. As computers get smaller, cheaper, and ever more powerful (today's leading notebook computers boast greater processing power and speed than the most powerful desktop units of five years ago at one tenth the price), their continued integration into the legal profession is inevitable. Inexpensive laser printers that offer near typeset-quality output coupled with inexpensive mass data storage devices such as CD/ROM disks (compact disk read only memory disks that can store an entire encyclopedia of text and graphics in a format similar to audio CDs) and rewritable optical media can make powerful law libraries accessible to any legal practitioner at a modest cost. Add to this the ability to access gargantuan on-line data bases such as those offered by LEXIS and WESTLAW, and the greater accessibility of primary and secondary research material to attorneys and paralegals alike seems assured. Law libraries containing massive printed volumes of primary and secondary research material will begin to be supplanted by CD/ROM-based libraries offered to subscribers at reduced costs; digitally encoded CD/ROMs won't replace book-based libraries in the near future, but the latter will likely be relegated to public libraries and law schools. CD/ROMs are infinitely better suited to disseminate reported cases and statutes than bound books: CD/ROMs can be produced quicker and cheaper than books, are infinitely more durable, and when in a networked environment, can be used by more than one person at once. In addition, the text of reported cases that is in the public domain (when the comments and annotations added by the publishers are removed) can be directly imported into briefs without the need of retyping, photocopying, or scanning—the only options available when book-based reporters are used.

It is still possible today to conduct the practice of law without a computer. Indeed, some of the more conservative members of the legal profession are doing just that. But the future clearly demands that the new attorney and paralegal be prepared to use the existing and emerging technologies. As the cost of on-line legal research services such as LEXIS and WESTLAW continues to decline and law publishers inevitably move the legal library from paper to plastic, from book to CD/ROM and similar mass storage technologies, both attorneys and paralegals are well advised to learn to use both the existing and emerging research tools—they not only make the practice of law more efficient and effective, but they will soon be an inevitable fact of life.

Review Questions

1. What is the importance of legal research in the practice of law? Explain.
2. What are some problems associated with traditional printed law reporters?
3. What are some advantages of computer-assisted legal research? What two companies currently provide such services?
4. What are some disadvantages of computer-assisted legal research?
5. What is the likelihood that computerization will continue to grow in the practice of law? Explain.

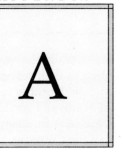

Constitution of the United States

Preamble

We the people of the United States, in order to form a more perfect Union, establish justice, insure domestic Tranquility, provide for the common defense, promote the general Welfare, and secure the Blessings of Liberty to ourselves and our Posterity, do ordain and establish this Constitution for the United States of America.

Article I

Section 1
All legislative Powers herein granted shall be vested in a Congress of the United States, which shall consist of a Senate and House of Representatives.

Section 2, Clause 1
The House of Representatives shall be composed of Members chosen every second Year by the People of the several States, and the Electors in each State shall have the Qualifications requisite for Electors of the most numerous Branch of the State Legislature.

Section 2, Clause 2
No person shall be a Representative who shall not have attained to the Age of twenty five Years, and been seven Years a Citizen of the United States, and who shall not, when elected, be an Inhabitant of that State in which he shall be chosen.

Section 2, Clause 3

Representatives and direct Taxes shall be apportioned among the several States which may be included within this Union, according to their respective Numbers, which shall be determined by adding to the whole Number of free Persons, including those bound to Service for a Term of Years, and excluding Indians not taxed, three-fifths of all other Persons. The actual Enumeration shall be made within three Years after the first Meeting of the Congress of the United States, and within every subsequent Term of ten Years in such Manner as they shall by Law direct. The Number of Representatives shall not exceed one for every thirty Thousand, but each State shall have at Least one Representative; and until such enumeration shall be made, the State of New Hampshire shall be entitled to chuse [*sic*] three, Massachusetts eight, Rhode Island and Providence Plantations one, Connecticut five, New York six, New Jersey four, Pennsylvania eight, Delaware one, Maryland six, Virginia ten, North Carolina five, South Carolina five, and Georgia three.

Section 2, Clause 4

When vacancies happen in the Representation from any State, the Executive Authority thereof shall issue Writs of Election to fill such Vacancies.

Section 2, Clause 5

The House of Representatives shall chuse [*sic*] their Speaker and other Officers; and shall have the sole Power of Impeachment.

Section 3, Clause 1

The Senate of the United States shall be composed of two Senators from each State, chosen by the Legislature thereof, for six Years; and each Senator shall have one Vote.

Section 3, Clause 2

Immediately after they shall be assembled in Consequence of the first Election, they shall be divided as equally as may be into three Classes. The Seats of the Senators of the first Class shall be vacated at the Expiration of the second Year, of the second Class at the Expiration of the fourth Year, and of the third Class at the Expiration of the sixth Year, so that one third may be chosen every second Year; [and if Vacancies happen by Resignation, or otherwise, during the Recess of the Legislature of any State, the Executive thereof may make temporary Appointments until the next Meeting of the Legislature, which shall then fill such Vacancies].

Section 3, Clause 3

No person shall be a Senator who shall not have attained to the Age of thirty years, and been nine Years a Citizen of the United States, and who shall not, when elected, be an Inhabitant of that State for which he shall be chosen.

Section 3, Clause 4
The Vice President of the United States shall be President of the Senate, but shall have no Vote, unless they be equally divided.

Section 3, Clause 5
The Senate shall chuse [*sic*] their other Officers, and also a President pro tempore, in the Absence of the Vice President, or when he shall exercise the Office of President of the United States.

Section 3, Clause 6
The Senate shall have the sole Power to try all Impeachments. When sitting for that Purpose, they shall be on Oath or Affirmation. When the President of the United States is tried, the Chief Justice shall preside: and no Person shall be convicted without the Concurrence of two thirds of the Members present.

Section 3, Clause 7
Judgment in Cases of Impeachment shall not extend further than to removal from Office, and disqualification to hold and enjoy any Office of honor, Trust or Profit under the United States: but the Party convicted shall nevertheless be liable and subject to Indictment, Trial, Judgment and Punishment, according to Law.

Section 4, Clause 1
The Times, Places and Manner of holding Elections for Senators and Representatives, shall be prescribed in each State by the Legislature thereof; but the Congress may at any time by Law make or alter such Regulations, except as to the Places of choosing Senators.

Section 4, Clause 2
The Congress shall assemble at least once in every Year, and such Meeting shall be on the [first Monday in December], unless they shall by Law appoint a different Day.

Section 5, Clause 1
Each House shall be the Judge of the Elections, Returns, and Qualifications of its own Members, and a Majority of each shall constitute a Quorum to do Business; but a smaller Number may adjourn from day to day, and may be authorized to compel the Attendance of absent Members, in such Manner, and under such Penalties as each House may provide.

Section 5, Clause 2
Each House may determine the Rules of its Proceedings, punish its Members for disorderly Behavior, and, with the Concurrence of two thirds, expel a Member.

Section 5, Clause 3

Each House shall keep a Journal of its Proceedings, and from time to time publish the same, excepting such Parts as may in their Judgment require Secrecy; and the Yeas and Nays of the Members of either House on any question shall, at the Desire of one fifth of those present, be entered on the Journal.

Section 5, Clause 4

Neither House, during the Session of Congress, shall, without the Consent of the other, adjourn for more than three days, nor to any other Place than that in which the two Houses shall be sitting.

Section 6, Clause 1

The Senators and Representatives shall receive a Compensation for their Services, to be ascertained by Law, and paid out of the Treasury of the United States. They shall in all Cases, except Treason, Felony and Breach of the Peace, be privileged from Arrest during their Attendance at the Session of their Respective Houses, and in going to and from the same; and for any Speech or Debate in either House, they shall not be questioned in any other Place.

Section 6, Clause 2

No Senator or Representative shall, during the Time for which he was elected, be appointed to any civil Office under the Authority of the United States, which shall have been created, or the Emoluments whereof shall have been encreased [*sic*] during such time; and no Person holding any Office under the United States, shall be a Member of either House during his Continuance in Office.

Section 7, Clause 1

All Bills for raising Revenue shall originate in the House of Representatives; but the Senate may propose or concur with Amendments as on other Bills.

Section 7, Clause 2

Every Bill which shall have passed the House of Representatives and the Senate, shall, before it become a Law, be presented to the President of the United States; If he approve he shall sign it, but if not he shall return it, with his Objections to that House in which it shall have originated, who shall enter the Objections at large on their Journal, and proceed to reconsider it. If after such Reconsideration two thirds of that House shall agree to pass the Bill, it shall be sent, together with the Objections, to the other House, by which it shall likewise be reconsidered, and if approved by two thirds of that House, it shall become a Law. But in all such Cases the Votes of both Houses shall be determined by Yeas and Nays, and the Names of the Persons voting for and against the Bill shall be entered on the Journal of each House respectively. If any Bill shall not be returned by the President within ten Days (Sundays excepted) after it shall have been presented to him, the Same shall be a Law, in like Manner as if he had signed it, unless the Congress by their Adjournment prevent its Return, in which Case it shall not be a Law.

Section 7, Clause 3

Every Order, Resolution, or Vote to which the Concurrence of the Senate and House of Representatives may be necessary (except on a question of adjournment) shall be presented to the President of the United States; and before the Same shall take Effect, shall be approved by him, or being disapproved by him, shall be repassed by two thirds of the Senate and House of Representatives, according to the Rules and Limitations prescribed in the Case of a Bill.

Section 8, Clause 1

The Congress shall have Power To lay and collect Taxes, Duties, Imposts and Excises, to pay the Debts and provide for the Common Defence [*sic*] and general Welfare of the United States; but all Duties, Imposts and Excises shall be uniform throughout the United States.

Section 8, Clause 2

To borrow money on the credit of the United States.

Section 8, Clause 3

To regulate commerce with foreign nations, and among the several States, and with the Indian tribes.

Section 8, Clause 4

To establish an uniform Rule of Naturalization, and uniform Laws on the subject of Bankruptcies throughout the United States. Section 8, Clause 5. Coinage, weights and measures.

To coin Money, regulate the Value thereof, and of foreign Coin, and fix the Standard of Weights and Measures.

Section 8, Clause 6

To provide for the Punishment of counterfeiting the Securities and current Coin of the United States.

Section 8, Clause 7

To establish Post Offices and post Roads.

Section 8, Clause 8

To promote the Progress of Science and useful Arts, by securing for limited Times to Authors and Inventors the exclusive Right to their respective Writings and Discoveries.

Section 8, Clause 9

To constitute tribunals inferior to the supreme Court.

Section 8, Clause 10

To define and punish Piracies and Felonies committed on the High Seas, and Offenses against the Law of Nations.

Section 8, Clause 11

To declare War, grant Letters of Marque and Reprisal, and make Rules concerning Captures on Land and Water.

Section 8, Clause 12

To raise and support Armies, but no Appropriation of Money to that Use shall be for a longer Term than two Years.

Section 8, Clause 13

To provide and maintain a Navy.

Section 8, Clause 14

To make Rules for the Government and Regulation of the land and naval Forces.

Section 8, Clause 15

To provide for calling forth the Militia to execute the Laws of the Union, suppress Insurrections and repel Invasions.

Section 8, Clause 16

To provide for organizing, arming, and disciplining, the Militia, and for governing such Part of them as may be employed in the Service of the United States, reserving to the States respectively, the Appointment of the Officers, and the Authority of training the Militia according to the discipline prescribed by Congress.

Section 8, Clause 17

To exercise exclusive Legislation in all Cases whatsoever, over such District (not exceeding ten Miles square) as may, by Cession of particular States, and the Acceptance of Congress, become the Seat of the Government of the United States, and to exercise like Authority over all Places purchased by the Consent of the Legislature of the State in which the Same shall be, for the Erection of Forts, Magazines, Arsenals, dock-Yards, and other needful Buildings.

Section 8, Clause 18

To make all Laws which shall be necessary and proper for carrying into Execution the foregoing Powers, and all other Powers vested by this Constitution in the Government of the United States, or in any Department or Officer thereof.

Section 9, Clause 1

The Migration or Importation of such Persons as any of the States now existing shall think proper to admit, shall not be prohibited by the Congress prior to the Year one thousand eight hundred and eight, but a Tax or duty may be imposed on such Importation, not exceeding ten dollars for each Person.

Section 9, Clause 2

The privilege of the writ of habeas corpus shall not be suspended, unless when in cases of rebellion or invasion the public safety may require it.

Section 9, Clause 3

No Bill of Attainder or ex post facto Law shall be passed.

Section 9, Clause 4

No Capitation, or other direct, Tax shall be laid, unless in Proportion to the Census or Enumeration herein before directed to be taken.

Section 9, Clause 5

No Tax or Duty shall be laid on Articles exported from any State.

Section 9, Clause 6

No Preference shall be given by any Regulation of Commerce or Revenue to the Ports of one State over those of another: nor shall Vessels bound to, or from, one State, be obliged to enter, clear, or pay Duties in another.

Section 9, Clause 7

No Money shall be drawn from the Treasury, but in Consequence of Appropriations made by Law; and a regular Statement and Account of the Receipts and Expenditures of all public Money shall be published from time to time.

Section 9, Clause 8

No Title of Nobility shall be granted by the United States: and no Person holding any Office of Profit or Trust under them, shall, without the Consent of the Congress, accept of any present, emolument, Office, or Title of any kind whatever from any King, Prince, or foreign State.

Section 10, Clause 1

No State shall enter into any Treaty, Alliance, or Confederation; grant Letters of Marque and Reprisal; coin Money; emit Bills of Credit; make any Thing but gold and silver Coin a Tender in Payment of Debts; pass any Bill of Attainder, ex post facto Law, or Law impairing the Obligation of Contracts, or grant any Title of Nobility.

Section 10, Clause 2

No State shall, without the Consent of the Congress, lay any Imposts or Duties on Imports or Exports, except what may be absolutely necessary for executing its inspection Laws: and the net Produce of all Duties and Imposts, laid by any State on Imports or Exports, shall be for the Use of the Treasury of the United States; and all such Laws shall be subject to the Revision and Control of the Congress.

Section 10, Clause 3
No State shall, without the Consent of Congress, lay any Duty of Tonnage, keep Troops, or Ships of War in time of Peace, enter into any Agreement or Compact with another State, or with a foreign Power, or engage in War, unless actually invaded, or in such imminent Danger as will not admit of delay.

Article II

Section 1, Clause 1
The executive Power shall be vested in a President of the United States of America. He shall hold his Office during the Term of four Years, and, together with the Vice President, chosen for the same Term, be elected, as follows:

Section 1, Clause 2
Each State shall appoint, in such Manner as the Legislature thereof may direct, a Number of Electors, equal to the whole Number of Senators and Representatives to which the State may be entitled in the Congress: but no Senator or Representative, or Person holding an Office of Trust or Profit under the United States, shall be appointed an Elector.

Section 1, Clause 3
The Electors shall meet in their repective States, and vote by Ballot for two Persons, of whom one at least shall not be an Inhabitant of the same State with themselves. And they shall make a List of all the Persons voted for, and of the Number of Votes for each; which List they shall sign and certify, and transmit sealed to the Seat of the Government of the United States, directed to the President of the Senate. The President of the Senate shall, in the Presence of the Senate and House of Representatives, open all the Certificates, and the Votes shall then be counted. The Person having the greatest Number of Votes shall be the President, if such Number be a Majority of the whole Number of Electors appointed; and if there be more than one who have such Majority, and have an equal Number of Votes, then the House of Representatives shall immediately chuse [*sic*] by Ballot one of them for President; and if no Person have a Majority, then from the five highest on the List the said House shall in like Manner chuse [*sic*] the President. But in chusing [*sic*] the President, the Votes shall be taken by States, the Representation from each State having one Vote; A quorum for this Purpose shall consist of a Member or Members from two thirds of the States, and a Majority of all the States shall be necessary to a Choice. In every Case, after the Choice of the President, the Person having the greater Number of Votes of the Electors shall be the Vice President. But if there should remain two or more who have equal Votes, the Senate shall chuse [*sic*] from them by Ballot the Vice President.

Section 1, Clause 4
The Congress may determine the Time of chusing [*sic.*] the Electors, and the Day on which they shall give their Votes; which Day shall be the same throughout the United States.

Section 1, Clause 5
No Person except a natural born Citizen, or a Citizen of the United States, at the time of the Adoption of this Constitution, shall be eligible to the Office of President; neither shall any Person be eligible to that Office who shall not have attained to the Age of thirty five Years, and been fourteen Years a Resident within the United States.

Section 1, Clause 6
In Case of the Removal of the President from Office, or of his Death, Resignation, or Inability to discharge the Powers and Duties of the said Office, the Same shall devolve on the Vice President, and the Congress may by Law provide for the Case of Removal, Death, Resignation, or Inability, both of the President and Vice President, declaring what Officer shall then act as President, and such Officer shall act accordingly, until the Disability be removed, or a President shall be elected.

Section 1, Clause 7
The President shall, at stated Times, receive for his Services, a Compensation, which shall neither be encreased [*sic*] nor diminished during the Period for which he shall have been elected, and he shall not receive within that Period any other Emolument from the United States, or any of them.

Section 1, Clause 8
Before he enter on the Execution of His Office, he shall take the following Oath or Affirmation:—"I do solemnly swear (or affirm) that I will faithfully execute the Office of President of the United States, and will to the best of my Ability, preserve, protect and defend the Constitution of the United States."

Section 2, Clause 1
The President shall be Commander in Chief of the Army and Navy of the United States, and of the Militia of the several States, when called into the actual Service of the United States; he may require the Opinion, in writing, of the principal Officer in each of the executive Departments, upon any Subject relating to the Duties of their respective Offices, and he shall have Power to grant Reprieves and Pardons for Offenses against the United States, except in Cases of Impeachment.

Section 2, Clause 2
He shall have Power, by and with the Advice and Consent of the Senate, to make Treaties, provided two thirds of the Senators present concur; and he shall nominate, and by and with the Advice and Consent of the Senate, shall appoint Ambassadors, other public Ministers and Consuls, Judges of the Supreme Court, and all other Officers of the United States, whose Appointments are not herein otherwise provided for, and which shall be established by Law: but the Congress may by Law vest the Appointment of such inferior Officers, as they think proper, in the President alone, in the Courts of Law, or in the Heads of Departments.

Section 2, Clause 3

The President shall have Power to fill up all Vacancies that may happen during the Recess of the Senate, by granting Commissions which shall expire at the End of their next Session.

Section 3

He shall from time to time give to the Congress Information of the State of the Union, and recommend to their Consideration such Measures as he shall judge necessary and expedient; he may, on extraordinary Occasions, convene both Houses, or either of them, and in Case of Disagreement between them, with Respect to the Time of Adjournment, he may adjourn them to such Time as he shall think proper; he shall receive Ambassadors and other public Ministers; he shall take Care that the Laws be faithfully executed, and shall Commission all the Officers of the United States.

Section 4

The President, Vice President and all civil Officers of the United States, shall be removed from Office on Impeachment for, and Conviction of, Treason, Bribery, or other high Crimes and Misdemeanors.

Article III

Section 1

The judicial Power of the United States, shall be vested in one supreme Court, and in such inferior Courts as the Congress may from time to time ordain and establish. The Judges, both of the supreme and inferior Courts, shall hold their Offices during good Behavior, and shall, at stated Times, receive for their Services, a Compensation, which shall not be diminished during their Continuance in Office.

Section 2, Clause 1

The judicial Power shall extend to all Cases, in Law and Equity, arising under this Constitution, the Laws of the United States, and Treaties made, or which shall be made, under their Authority,—to all Cases affecting Ambassadors, other public Ministers and Consuls;—to all Cases of admiralty and maritime Jurisdiction;—to Controversies to which the United States shall be a Party;—to Controversies between two or more States;—between a State and Citizens of another State;—between citizens of different States,—between citizens of the same State claiming Lands under Grants of different States, and between a State, or the Citizens thereof, and foreign States, Citizens or Subjects.

Section 2, Clause 2

In all Cases affecting Ambassadors, other public Ministers and Consuls, and those in which a State shall be Party, the supreme Court shall have original

Jurisdiction. In all the other Cases before mentioned, the supreme Court shall have appellate Jurisdiction, both as to Law and Fact, with such Exceptions, and under such Regulations as the Congress shall make.

Section 2, Clause 3

The Trial of all Crimes, except in Cases of Impeachment, shall be by Jury; and such Trial shall be held in the State where the said Crimes shall have been committed; but when not committed within any State, the Trial shall be at such Place or Places as the Congress may by Law have directed.

Section 3, Clause 1

Treason against the United States, shall consist only in levying War against them, or in adhering to their Enemies, giving them Aid and Comfort. No Person shall be convicted of Treason unless on the Testimony of two Witnesses to the same overt Act, or on Confession in open Court.

Section 3, Clause 2

The Congress shall have Power to declare the Punishment of Treason, but no Attainder of Treason shall work Corruption of Blood, or Forfeiture except during the Life of the Person attainted.

Article IV

Section 1

Full Faith and Credit shall be given in each State to the public Acts, Records, and judicial Proceedings of every other State. And the Congress may by general Laws prescribe the Manner in which such Acts, Records and Proceedings shall be proved, and the Effect thereof.

Section 2, Clause 1

The Citizens of each State shall be entitled to all Privileges and Immunities of Citizens in the several States.

Section 2, Clause 2

A Person charged in any State with Treason, Felony, or other Crime, who shall flee from Justice, and found in another State, shall on Demand of the executive Authority of the State from which he fled, be delivered up to be removed to the State having Jurisdiction of the Crime.

Section 2, Clause 3

No Person held to Service of Labour in one State, under the Laws thereof, escaping into another, shall, in Consequence of any Law or Regulation therein, be discharged from such Service or Labour, but shall be delivered upon Claim of the Party to whom such Service or Labour may be due.

Section 3, Clause 1

New States may be admitted by the Congress into this Union; but no new State shall be formed or erected within the Jurisdiction of any other State; nor any State be formed by the Junction of two or more States, or Parts of States, without the Consent of the Legislatures of the States concerned as well as of the Congress.

Section 3, Clause 2

The Congress shall have Power to dispose of and make all needful Rules and Regulations respecting the Territory or other Property belonging to the United States; and nothing in this Constitution shall be so construed as to Prejudice any Claims of the United States, or of any particular State.

Section 4

The United States shall guarantee to every State in this Union a Republican Form of Government, and shall protect each of them against Invasion; and on Application of the Legislature, or of the Executive (when the Legislature cannot be convened) against domestic Violence.

Article V

The Congress, whenever two thirds of both Houses shall deem it necessary, shall propose Amendments to this Constitution, or, on the Application of the Legislatures of two thirds of the several States, shall call a Convention for proposing Amendments, which, in either Case, shall be valid to all Intents and Purposes, as Part of this Constitution, when ratified by the Legislatures of three fourths of the several States, or by Convention in three fourths thereof, as the one or the other Mode of Ratification may be proposed by the Congress; Provided that no Amendment which may be made prior to the Year One thousand eight hundred and eight shall in any Manner affect the first and fourth Clauses in the Ninth Section of the first Article; and that no State, without its Consent, shall be deprived of its equal Suffrage in the Senate.

Article VI

Clause 1

All Debts contracted and Engagements entered into, before the Adoption of this Constitution, shall be as valid against the United States under this Constitution, as under the Confederation.

Clause 2

This Constitution, and the Laws of the United States which shall be made in Pursuance thereof; and all Treaties made, or which shall be made, under the

Authority of the United States, shall be the supreme Law of the Land; and the Judges in every State shall be bound thereby, any Thing in the Constitution or Laws of any State to the Contrary notwithstanding.

Clause 3

The Senators and Representatives before mentioned, and the Members of the several State Legislatures, and all executive and judicial Officers, both of the United States and of the several States, shall be bound by Oath or Affirmation, to support this Constitution; but no religious Test shall ever be required as a Qualification to any Office or public Trust under the United States.

Article VII

The Ratification of the Conventions of nine States, shall be sufficient for the Establishment of this Constitution between the States so ratifying the Same.

Amendments

Amendment 1

Congress shall make no law respecting an establishment of religion, or prohibiting the free exercise thereof; or abridging the freedom of speech, or of the press; or the right of the people peaceably to assemble, and to petition the Government for a redress of grievances.

Amendment 2

A well regulated Militia, being necessary to the security of a free State, the right of the people to keep and bear Arms, shall not be infringed.

Amendment 3

No Soldier shall, in time of peace be quartered in any house, without the consent of the Owner, nor in time of war, but in a manner to be prescribed by law.

Amendment 4

The right of the people to be secure in their persons, houses, papers, and effects, against unreasonable searches and seizures, shall not be violated, and no Warrants shall issue, but upon probable cause, supported by Oath or affirmation, and particularly describing the place to be searched, and the persons or things to be seized.

Amendment 5

No person shall be held to answer for a capital, or otherwise infamous crime, unless on a presentment or indictment of a Grand Jury, except in cases arising in the land or naval forces, or in the Militia, when in actual service in time of

War or public danger; nor shall any person be subject for the same offence [*sic*] to be twice put in jeopardy of life or limb; nor shall be compelled in any criminal case to be a witness against himself, nor be deprived of life, liberty, or property, without due process of law; nor shall private property be taken for public use, without just compensation.

Amendment 6
In all criminal prosecutions, the accused shall enjoy the right to a speedy and public trial, by an impartial jury of the State and district wherein the crime shall have been committed, which district shall have been previously ascertained by law, and to be informed of the nature and cause of the accusation; to be confronted with the witnesses against him; to have compulsory process for obtaining witnesses in his favor, and to have the Assistance of Counsel for his defense.

Amendment 7
In Suits at common law, where the value in controversy shall exceed twenty dollars, the right of trial by jury shall be preserved, and no fact tried by a jury shall be otherwise re-examined in any Court of the United States, than according to the rules of the common law.

Amendment 8
Excessive bail shall not be required, nor excessive fines imposed, nor cruel and unusual punishments inflicted.

Amendment 9
The enumeration in the Constitution, of certain rights, shall not be construed to deny or disparage others retained by the people.

Amendment 10
The powers not delegated to the United States by the Constitution, nor prohibited by it to the States, are reserved to the States respectively, or to the people.

Amendment 11
The Judicial power of the United States shall not be construed to extend to any suit in law or equity, commenced or prosecuted against one of the United States by Citizens of another State, or by Citizens or Subjects of any Foreign State.

Amendment 12
The Electors shall meet in their respective states, and vote by ballot for President and Vice-President, one of whom, at least, shall not be an inhabitant of the same state with themselves; they shall name in their ballots the person voted for as President, and in distinct ballots the person voted for as Vice-President, and they shall make distinct lists of all persons voted for as President, and of all persons voted for as Vice-President, and of the number of votes for each, which lists they shall sign and certify, and transmit sealed to

the seat of the government of the United States, directed to the President of the Senate;—the President of the Senate shall, in the presence of the Senate and House of Representatives, open all the certificates and the votes shall then be counted;—the person having the greatest number of votes for President, shall be the President, if such number be a majority of the whole number of Electors appointed; and if no person have such majority, then from the persons having the highest numbers not exceeding three on the list of those voted for as President, the House of Representatives shall choose immediately, by ballot, the President. But in choosing the President, the votes shall be taken by states, the representation from each state having one vote; a quorum for this purpose shall consist of a member or members from two-thirds of the states, and a majority of all the states shall be necessary to a choice. And if the House of Representatives shall not choose a President whenever the right of choice shall devolve upon them, before the fourth day of March next following, then the Vice-President shall act as President, as in the case of the death or other constitutional disability of the President.—The person having the greatest number of votes as Vice-President, shall be the Vice-President, if such number be a majority of the whole number of Electors appointed, and if no person have a majority, then from the two highest numbers on the list, the Senate shall choose the Vice-President; a quorum for the purpose shall consist of two-thirds of the whole number of Senators, and a majority of the whole number shall be necessary to a choice. But no person constitutionally ineligible to the office of President shall be eligible to that of Vice-President of the United States.

Amendment 13

Section 1.   Neither slavery nor involuntary servitude, except as a punishment for crime whereof the party shall have been duly convicted, shall exist within the United States, or any place subject to their jurisdiction.

Section 2.   Congress shall have power to enforce this article by appropriate legislation.

Amendment 14

Section 1.   All persons born or naturalized in the United States, and subject to the jurisdiction thereof, are citizens of the United States and of the State wherein they reside. No State shall make or enforce any law which shall abridge the privileges or immunities of citizens of the United States; nor shall any State deprive any person of life, liberty, or property, without due process of law; nor deny to any person within its jurisdiction the equal protection of the laws.

Section 2.   Representatives shall be apportioned among the several States according to their respective numbers, counting the whole number of persons in each State, excluding Indians not taxed. But when the right to vote at any election for the choice of electors for President and Vice-President of the

United States, Representatives in Congress, the Executive and Judicial officers of a State, or the members of the Legislature thereof, is denied to any of the male inhabitants of such State, being twenty-one years of age, and citizens of the United States, or in any way abridged, except for participation in rebellion, or other crime, the basis of representation therein shall be reduced in the proportion which the number of such male citizens shall bear to the whole number of male citizens twenty-one years of age in such State.

Section 3.   No person shall be a Senator or Representative in Congress, or Elector of President and Vice-President, or hold any office, civil or military, under the United States, or under any State, who, having previously taken an oath, as a member of Congress, or as an officer of the United States, or as a member of any State legislature, or as an executive or judicial officer of any State, to support the Constitution of the United States, shall have engaged in insurrection or rebellion against the same, or given aid or comfort to the enemies thereof. But Congress may by a vote of two-thirds of each House, remove such disability.

Section 4.   The validity of the public debt of the United States, authorized by law, including debts incurred for payment of pensions and bounties for services in suppressing insurrection or rebellion, shall not be questioned. But neither the United States nor any State shall assume or pay any debt or obligation incurred in aid of insurrection or rebellion against the United States, or any claim for the loss or emancipation of any slaves; but all such debts, obligations, and claims shall be held illegal and void.

Section 5.   The Congress shall have power to enforce, by appropriate legislation, the provisions of this article.

Amendment 15

Section 1.   The right of citizens of the United States to vote shall not be denied or abridged by the United States or by any State on account of race, color, or previous condition of servitude.

Section 2.   The Congress shall have power to enforce this article by appropriate legislation.

Amendment 16
The Congress shall have power to lay and collect taxes on incomes, from whatever source derived, without apportionment among the several States, and without regard to any census or enumeration.

Amendment 17
The Senate of the United States shall be composed of two Senators from each State, elected by the people thereof, for six years; and each Senator shall have one vote. The electors in each State shall have the qualifications requisite for electors of the most numerous branch of the State legislatures.

When vacancies happen in the representation of any State in the Senate, the executive authority of such State shall issue writs of election to fill such vacancies: Provided, That the legislature of any State may empower the executive thereof to make temporary appointment until the people fill the vacancies by election as the legislature may direct.

This amendment shall not be so construed as to affect the election or term of any Senator chosen before it becomes valid as part of the Constitution.

Amendment 18

Section 1. After one year from the ratification of this article the manufacture, sale, or transportation of intoxicating liquors within, the importation thereof into, or the exportation thereof from the United States and all territory subject to the jurisdiction thereof for beverage purposes is hereby prohibited.

Section 2. The Congress and the several States shall have concurrent power to enforce this article by appropriate legislation.

Section 3. This article shall be inoperative unless it shall have been ratified as an amendment to the Constitution by the legislatures of the several States, as provided in the Constitution, within seven years from the date of the submission hereof to the States by the Congress.

Amendment 19

Section 1. The right of citizens of the United States to vote shall not be denied or abridged by the United States or by any State on account of sex.

Section 2. Congress shall have power to enforce this article by appropriate legislation.

Amendment 20

Section 1. The terms of the President and Vice President shall end at noon on the 20th day of January, and the terms of Senators and Representatives at noon on the 3d day of January, of the years in which such terms would have ended if this article had not been ratified; and the terms of their successors shall then begin.

Section 2. The Congress shall assemble at least once in every year, and such meeting shall begin at noon on the 3d day of January, unless they shall by law appoint a different day.

Section 3. If, at the time fixed for the beginning of the term of the President, the President elect shall have died, the Vice President elect shall become President. If a President shall not have been chosen before the time fixed for the beginning of his term, or if the President elect shall have failed to qualify, then the Vice President elect shall act as President until a President shall have qualified; and the Congress may by law provide for the case wherein neither a President elect nor a Vice President elect shall have qualified, declaring who shall then act as President, or the manner in which one who is to act shall be selected, and such person shall act accordingly until a President or Vice President shall have qualified.

Section 4.   The Congress may by law provide for the case of the death of any of the persons from whom the House of Representatives may choose a President whenever the right of choice shall have devolved upon them, and for the case of the death of any of the persons from whom the Senate may choose a Vice President whenever the right of choice shall have devolved upon them.

Section 5.   Sections 1 and 2 shall take effect on the 15th day of October following the ratification of this article.

Section 6.   This article shall be inoperative unless it shall have been ratified as an amendment to the Constitution by the legislatures of three-fourths of the several States within seven years from the date of its submission.

Amendment 21

Section 1.   The eighteenth article of amendment to the Constitution of the United States is hereby repealed.

Section 2.   The transportation or importation into any State, Territory, or possession of the United States for delivery or use therein of intoxicating liquors, in violation of the laws thereof, is hereby prohibited.

Section 3.   This article shall be inoperative unless it shall have been ratified as an amendment to the Constitution by conventions in the several States, as provided in the Constitution, within seven years from the date of the submission hereof to the States by the Congress.

Amendment 22

Section 1.   No person shall be elected to the office of the President more than twice, and no person who has held the office of President, or acted as President, for more than two years of a term to which some other person was elected President shall be elected to the office of the President more than once. But this article shall not apply to any person holding the office of President when this article was proposed by the Congress, and shall not prevent any person who may be holding the office of President, or acting as President, during the term within which this article becomes operative from holding the office of President or acting as President during the remainder of such term.

Section 2.   This article shall be inoperative unless it shall have been ratified as an amendment to the Constitution by the legislatures of three-fourths of the several States within seven years from the date of its submission to the States by the Congress.

Amendment 23

Section 1. The District constituting the seat of Government of the United States shall appoint in such manner as the Congress may direct:

A number of electors of President and Vice President equal to the whole number of Senators and Representatives in Congress to which the District would be entitled if it were a State, but in no event more than the least populous State; they shall be in addition to those appointed by the States, but they shall be considered, for the purposes of the election of President and Vice President, to be electors appointed by a State; and they shall meet in the District and perform such duties as provided by the twelfth article of amendment.

Section 2. The Congress shall have power to enforce this article by appropriate legislation.

Amendment 24

Section 1. The right of citizens of the United States to vote in any primary or other election for President or Vice President, for electors for President or Vice President, or for Senator or Representative in Congress, shall not be denied or abridged by the United States or any State by reason of failure to pay any poll tax or other tax.

Section 2. The Congress shall have power to enforce this article by appropriate legislation.

Amendment 25

Section 1. In case of the removal of the President from office or of his death or resignation, the Vice President shall become President.

Section 2. Whenever there is a vacancy in the office of the Vice President, the President shall nominate a Vice President who shall take office upon confirmation by a majority vote of both Houses of Congress.

Section 3. Whenever the President transmits to the President pro tempore of the Senate and the Speaker of the House of Representatives his written declaration that he is unable to discharge the powers and duties of his office, and until he transmits to them a written declaration to the contrary, such powers and duties shall be discharged by the Vice President as Acting President.

Section 4. Whenever the Vice President and a majority of either the principal officers of the executive departments or of such other body as Congress may by law provide, transmit to the President pro tempore of the Senate and the Speaker of the House of Representatives their written declaration that the President is unable to discharge the powers and duties of his office, the Vice President shall immediately assume the powers and duties of the office as Acting President.

Thereafter, when the President transmits to the President pro tempore of the Senate and the Speaker of the House of Representatives his written declaration that no inability exists, he shall resume the powers and duties of his office unless the Vice President and a majority of either the principal officers of the executive department or of such other body as Congress may by law provide, transmit within four days to the President pro tempore of the Senate and the Speaker of the House of Representatives their written declaration that the President is unable to discharge the powers and duties of his office. Thereupon Congress shall decide the issue, assembling within forty-eight hours for that purpose if not in session. If the Congress, within twenty-one days after receipt of the latter written declaration, or, if Congress is not in session, within twenty-one days after Congress is required to assemble, determines by two-thirds vote of both Houses that the President is unable to discharge the powers and duties of his office, the Vice President shall continue to discharge the same as Acting President; otherwise, the President shall resume the powers and duties of his office.

Amendment 26

Section 1.   The right of citizens of the United States, who are eighteen years of age or older, to vote shall not be denied or abridged by the United States or by any State on account of age.

Section 2.   The Congress shall have power to enforce this article by appropriate legislation.

B

UNIFORM COMMERCIAL CODE ARTICLE 2–SALES

Selected Sections

§ 2–101. Short Title

This Article shall be known and may be cited as Uniform Commercial Code—Sales.

§ 2–102. Scope; Certain Security and Other Transactions Excluded From This Article

Unless the context otherwise requires, this Article applies to transactions in goods; it does not apply to any transaction which although in the form of an unconditional contract to sell or present sale is intended to operate only as a security transaction nor does this Article impair or repeal any statute regulating sales to consumers, farmers or other specified classes of buyers.

§ 2–103. Definitions and Index of Definitions

(1) In this Article unless the context otherwise requires

(a) "Buyer" means a person who buys or contracts to buy goods.

(b) "Good faith" in the case of a merchant means honesty in fact and the observance of reasonable commercial standards of fair dealing in the trade.

(c) "Receipt" of goods means taking physical possession of them.

(d) "Seller" means a person who sells or contracts to sell goods.

(2) Other definitions applying to this Article or to specified Parts thereof, and the sections in which they appear are:

"Acceptance". Section 2–606.

"Banker's credit". Section 2–325.

"Between merchants". Section 2–104.

"Cancellation". Section 2–106 (4).

"Commercial unit". Section 2–105.

"Confirmed credit". Section 2–325.

"Conforming to contract". Section 2–106.
"Contract for sale". Section 2–106.
"Cover". Section 2–712.
"Entrusting". Section 2–403.
"Financing agency". Section 2–104.
"Future goods". Section 2–105.
"Goods". Section 2–105.
"Identification". Section 2–501.
"Installment contract". Section 2–612.
"Letter of Credit". Section 2–325.
"Lot". Section 2–105.
"Merchant". Section 2–104.
"Overseas". Section 2–323.
"Person in position of seller". Section 2–707.
"Present sale". Section 2–106.
"Sale". Section 2–106.
"Sale on approval". Section 2–326.
"Sale or return". Section 2–326.
"Termination". Section 2–106.

§ 2–104. Definitions: "Merchant"; "Between Merchants"; "Financing Agency"

(1) "Merchant" means a person who deals in goods of the kind or otherwise by his occupation holds himself out as having knowledge or skill peculiar to the practices or goods involved in the transaction or to whom such knowledge or skill may be attributed by his employment of an agent or broker or other intermediary who by his occupation holds himself out as having such knowledge or skill.

(2) "Financing agency" means a bank, finance company or other person who in the ordinary course of business makes advances against goods or documents of title or who by arrangement with either the seller or the buyer intervenes in ordinary course to make or collect payment due or claimed under the contract for sale, as by purchasing or paying the seller's draft or making advances against it or by merely taking it for collection whether or not documents of title accompany the draft. "Financing agency" includes also a bank or other person who similarly intervenes between persons who are in the position of seller and buyer in respect to the goods (Section 2–707).

(3) "Between merchants" means in any transaction with respect to which both parties are chargeable with the knowledge or skill of merchants.

§ 2–105. Definitions: Transferability; "Goods"; "Future" Goods; "Lot"; "Commercial Unit"

(1) "Goods" means all things (including specially manufactured goods) which are movable at the time of identification to the contract for sale other than the money in which the price is to be paid, investment securities (Article

8) and things in action. "Goods" also includes the unborn young of animals and growing crops and other identified things attached to realty as described in the section on goods to be severed from realty (Section 2–107).

(2) Goods must be both existing and identified before any interest in them can pass. Goods which are not both existing and identified are "future" goods. A purported present sale of future goods or of any interest therein operates as a contract to sell.

(3) There may be a sale of a part interest in existing identified goods.

(4) An undivided share in an identified bulk of fungible goods is sufficiently identified to be sold although the quantity of the bulk is not determined. Any agreed proportion of such a bulk or any quantity thereof agreed upon by number, weight or other measure may to the extent of the seller's interest in the bulk be sold to the buyer who then becomes an owner in common.

(5) "Lot" means a parcel or a single article which is the subject matter of a separate sale or delivery, whether or not it is sufficient to perform the contract.

(6) "Commercial unit" means such a unit of goods as by commercial usage is a single whole for purposes of sale and division of which materially impairs its character or value on the market or in use. A commercial unit may be a single article (as a machine) or a set of articles (as a suit of furniture or an assortment of sizes) or a quantity (as a bale, gross, or carload) or any other unit treated in use or in the relevant market as a single whole.

§ 2–106. Definitions. "Contract"; "Agreement"; "Contract for Sale"; "Sale"; "Present Sale"; "Conforming" to Contract; "Termination"; "Cancellation"

(1) In this Article unless the context otherwise requires "contract" and "agreement" are limited to those relating to the present or future sale of goods. "Contract for sale" includes both a present sale of goods and a contract to sell goods at a future time. A "sale" consists in the passing of title from the seller to the buyer for a price (Section 2—401). A "present sale" means a sale which is accomplished by the making of the contract.

(2) Goods or conduct including any part of a performance are "conforming" or conform to the contract when they are in accordance with the obligations under the contract.

(3) "Termination" occurs when either party pursuant to a power created by agreement or law puts an end to the contract otherwise than for its breach. On "termination" all obligations which are still executory on both sides are discharged but any right based on prior breach or performance survives.

(4) "Cancellation" occurs when either party puts an end to the contract for breach by the other and its effect is the same as that of "termination" except that the canceling party also retains any remedy for breach of the whole contract or any unperformed balance.

§ 2–107. Goods to Be Severed From Realty: Recording

(1) A contract for the sale of minerals or the like (including oil and gas) or a structure or its materials to be removed from realty is a contract for the sale of goods within this Article if they are to be severed by the

seller but until severance a purported present sale thereof which is not effective as a transfer of an interest in land is effective only as a contract to sell.

(2) A contract for the sale apart from the land of growing crops or other things attached to realty and capable of severance without material harm thereto but not described in subsection (1) or of timber to be cut is a contract for the sale of goods within this Article whether the subject matter is to be severed by the buyer or by the seller even though it forms part of the realty at the time of contracting, and the parties can by identification effect a present sale before severance.

(3) The provisions of this section are subject to any third party rights provided by the law relating to realty records, and the contract for sale may be executed and recorded as a document transferring an interest in land and shall then constitute notice to third parties of the buyer's rights under the contract for sale.

§ 2–201. Formal Requirements; Statute of Frauds

(1) Except as otherwise provided in this section a contract for the sale of goods for the price of $500 or more is not enforceable by way of action or defense unless there is some writing sufficient to indicate that a contract for sale has been made between the parties and signed by the party against whom enforcement is sought or by his authorized agent or broker. A writing is not insufficient because it omits or incorrectly states a term agreed upon but the contract is not enforceable under this paragraph beyond the quantity of goods shown in such writing.

(2) Between merchants if within a reasonable time a writing in confirmation of the contract and sufficient against the sender is received and the party receiving it has reason to know its contents, it satisfies the requirements of subsection (1) against such party unless written notice of objection to its contents is given within ten days after it is received.

(3) A contract which does not satisfy the requirements of subsection (1) but which is valid in other respects is enforceable

(a) if the goods are to be specially manufactured for the buyer and are not suitable for sale to others in the ordinary course of the seller's business and the seller, before notice of repudiation is received and under circumstances which reasonably indicate that the goods are for the buyer, has made either a substantial beginning of their manufacture or commitments for their procurement; or

(b) if the party against whom enforcement is sought admits in his pleading, testimony or otherwise in court that a contract for sale was made, but the contract is not enforceable under this provision beyond the quantity of goods admitted; or

(c) with respect to goods for which payment has been made and accepted or which have been received and accepted (Section 2–606).

§ 2–202. Final Written Expression: Parol or Extrinsic Evidence

Terms with respect to which the confirmatory memoranda of the parties agree or which are otherwise set forth in a writing intended by the parties as a final expression of their agreement with respect to such terms as are included therein may not be contradicted by evidence of any prior agreement or of a contemporaneous oral agreement but may be explained or supplemented

> (a) by course of dealing or usage of trade (Section 1–205) or by course of performance (Section 2–208); and
>
> (b) by evidence of consistent additional terms unless the court finds the writing to have been intended also as a complete and exclusive statement of the terms of the agreement.

§ 2–203. Seals Inoperative

The affixing of a seal to a writing evidencing a contract for sale or an offer to buy or sell goods does not constitute the writing a sealed instrument and the law with respect to sealed instruments does not apply to such a contract or offer.

§ 2–204. Formation in General

(1) A contract for sale of goods may be made in any manner sufficient to show agreement, including conduct by both parties which recognizes the existence of such a contract.

(2) An agreement sufficient to constitute a contract for sale may be found even though the moment of its making is undetermined.

(3) Even though one or more terms are left open a contract for sale does not fail for indefiniteness if the parties have intended to make a contract and there is a reasonably certain basis for giving an appropriate remedy.

§ 2–205. Firm Offers

An offer by a merchant to buy or sell goods in a signed writing which by its terms gives assurance that it will be held open is not revocable, for lack of consideration, during the time stated or if no time is stated for a reasonable time, but in no event may such period of irrevocability exceed three months; but any such term of assurance on a form supplied by the offeree must be separately signed by the offeror.

§ 2–206. Offer and Acceptance in Formation of Contract

(1) Unless otherwise unambiguously indicated by the language or circumstances

> (a) an offer to make a contract shall be construed as inviting acceptance in any manner and by any medium reasonable in the circumstances;
>
> (b) an order or other offer to buy goods for prompt or current shipment shall be construed as inviting acceptance either by a prompt promise to ship or by the prompt or current shipment of conforming or non-conforming goods, but such a shipment of non-conforming goods does not constitute an acceptance if the seller seasonably notifies the buyer that the shipment is offered only as an accommodation to the buyer.

(2) Where the beginning of a requested performance is a reasonable mode of acceptance an offeror who is not notified of acceptance within a reasonable time may treat the offer as having lapsed before acceptance.

§ 2–207. Additional Terms in Acceptance or Confirmation

(1) A definite and seasonable expression of acceptance or a written confirmation which is sent within a reasonable time operates as an acceptance even though it states terms additional to or different from those offered or agreed upon, unless acceptance is expressly made conditional on assent to the additional or different terms.

(2) The additional terms are to be construed as proposals for addition to the contract. Between merchants such terms become part of the contract unless:

  (a) the offer expressly limits acceptance to the terms of the offer;

  (b) they materially alter it; or

  (c) notification of objection to them has already been given or is given within a reasonable time after notice of them is received.

(3) Conduct by both parties which recognizes the existence of a contract is sufficient to establish a contract for sale although the writings of the parties do not otherwise establish a contract. In such case the terms of the particular contract consist of those terms on which the writings of the parties agree, together with any supplementary terms incorporated under any other provisions of this Act.

§ 2–208. Course of Performance or Practical Construction

(1) Where the contract for sale involves repeated occasions for performance by either party with knowledge of the nature of the performance and opportunity for objection to it by the other, any course of performance accepted or acquiesced in without objection shall be relevant to determine the meaning of the agreement.

(2) The express terms of the agreement and any such course of performance, as well as any course of dealing and usage of trade, shall be construed whenever reasonable as consistent with each other; but when such construction is unreasonable, express terms shall control course of performance and course of performance shall control both course of dealing and usage of trade (Section 1–205).

(3) Subject to the provisions of the next section on modification and waiver, such course of performance shall be relevant to show a waiver or modification of any term inconsistent with such course of performance.

§ 2–209. Modification, Rescission and Waiver

(1) An agreement modifying a contract within this Article needs no consideration to be binding.

(2) A signed agreement which excludes modification or rescission except by a signed writing cannot be otherwise modified or rescinded, but except as between merchants such a requirement on a form supplied by the merchant must be separately signed by the other party.

(3) The requirements of the statute of frauds section of this Article (Section 2–201) must be satisfied if the contract as modified is within its provisions.

(4) Although an attempt at modification or rescission does not satisfy the requirements of subsection (2) or (3) it can operate as a waiver.

(5) A party who has made a waiver affecting an executory portion of the contract may retract the waiver by reasonable notification received by the other party that strict performance will be required of any term waived, unless the retraction would be unjust in view of a material change of position in reliance on the waiver.

§ 2–210. Delegation of Performance; Assignment of Rights

(1) A party may perform his duty through a delegate unless otherwise agreed or unless the other party has a substantial interest in having his original promisor perform or control the acts required by the contract. No delegation of performance relieves the party delegating of any duty to perform or any liability for breach.

(2) Unless otherwise agreed all rights of either seller or buyer can be assigned except where the assignment would materially change the duty of the other party, or increase materially the burden or risk imposed on him by his contract, or impair materially his chance of obtaining return performance. A right to damages for breach of the whole contract or a right arising out of the assignor's due performance of his entire obligation can be assigned despite agreement otherwise.

(3) Unless the circumstances indicate the contrary a prohibition of assignment of "the contract" is to be construed as barring only the delegation to the assignee of the assignor's performance.

(4) An assignment of "the contract" or of "all my rights under the contract" or an assignment in similar general terms is an assignment of rights and unless the language or the circumstances (as in an assignment for security) indicate the contrary, it is a delegation of performance of the duties of the assignor and its acceptance by the assignee constitutes a promise by him to perform those duties. This promise is enforceable by either the assignor or the other party to the original contract.

(5) The other party may treat any assignment which delegates performance as creating reasonable grounds for insecurity and may without prejudice to his rights against the assignor demand assurances from the assignee (Section 2–609).

§ 2–301. General Obligations of Parties

The obligation of the seller is to transfer and deliver and that of the buyer is to accept and pay in accordance with the contract.

§ 2–302. Unconscionable Contract or Clause

(1) If the court as a matter of law finds the contract or any clause of the contract to have been unconscionable at the time it was made the court may refuse to enforce the contract, or it may enforce the remainder of the contract without the unconscionable clause, or it may so limit the application of any unconscionable clause as to avoid any unconscionable result.

(2) When it is claimed or appears to the court that the contract or any clause thereof may be unconscionable the parties shall be afforded a reasonable opportunity to present evidence as to its commercial setting, purpose and effect to aid the court in making the determination.

§ 2–303. Allocation or Division of Risks

Where this Article allocates a risk or a burden as between the parties "unless otherwise agreed", the agreement may not only shift the allocation but may also divide the risk or burden.

§ 2–304. Price Payable in Money, Goods, Realty, or Otherwise

(1) The price can be made payable in money or otherwise. If it is payable in whole or in part in goods each party is a seller of the goods which he is to transfer.

(2) Even though all or part of the price is payable in an interest in realty the transfer of the goods and the seller's obligations with reference to them are subject to this Article, but not the transfer of the interest in realty or the transferor's obligations in connection therewith.

§ 2–305. Open Price Term

(1) The parties if they so intend can conclude a contract for sale even though the price is not settled. In such a case the price is a reasonable price at the time for delivery if

(a) nothing is said as to price; or

(b) the price is left to be agreed by the parties and they fail to agree; or

(c) the price is to be fixed in terms of some agreed market or other standard as set or recorded by a third person or agency and it is not so set or recorded.

(2) A price to be fixed by the seller or by the buyer means a price for him to fix in good faith.

(3) When a price left to be fixed otherwise than by agreement of the parties fails to be fixed through fault of one party the other may at his option treat the contract as canceled or himself fix a reasonable price.

(4) Where, however, the parties intend not to be bound unless the price be fixed or agreed and it is not fixed or agreed there is no contract. In such a case the buyer must return any goods already received or if unable so to do must pay their reasonable value at the time of delivery and the seller must return any portion of the price paid on account.

§ 2–306. Output, Requirements and Exclusive Dealings

(1) A term which measures the quantity by the output of the seller or the requirements of the buyer means such actual output or requirements as may occur in good faith, except that no quantity unreasonably disproportionate to any stated estimate or in the absence of a stated estimate to any normal or otherwise comparable prior output or requirements may be tendered or demanded.

(2) A lawful agreement by either the seller or the buyer for exclusive dealing in the kind of goods concerned imposes unless otherwise agreed an obligation by the seller to use best efforts to supply the goods and by the buyer to use best efforts to promote their sale.

§ 2–307. Delivery in Single Lot or Several Lots

Unless otherwise agreed all goods called for by a contract for sale must be tendered in a single delivery and payment is due only on such tender but where the circumstances give either party the right to make or demand delivery in lots the price if it can be apportioned may be demanded for each lot.

§ 2–308. Absence of Specified Place for Delivery

Unless otherwise agreed

(a) the place for delivery of goods is the seller's place of business or if he has none his residence; but

(b) in a contract for sale of identified goods which to the knowledge of the parties at the time of contracting are in some other place, that place is the place for their delivery; and

(c) documents of title may be delivered through customary banking channels.

§ 2–309. Absence of Specific Time Provisions; Notice of Termination

(1) The time for shipment or delivery or any other action under a contract if not provided in this Article or agreed upon shall be a reasonable time.

(2) Where the contract provides for successive performances but is indefinite in duration it is valid for a reasonable time but unless otherwise agreed may be terminated at any time by either party.

(3) Termination of a contract by one party except on the happening of an agreed event requires that reasonable notification be received by the other party and an agreement dispensing with notification is invalid if its operation would be unconscionable.

* * * *

§ 2–311. Options and Cooperation Respecting Performance

(1) An agreement for sale which is otherwise sufficiently definite (subsection (3) of Section 2–204) to be a contract is not made invalid by the fact that it leaves particulars of performance to be specified by one of the parties. Any such specification must be made in good faith and within limits set by commercial reasonableness.

(2) Unless otherwise agreed specifications relating to assortment of the goods are at the buyer's option and except as otherwise provided in subsections (1) (c) and (3) of Section 2–319 specifications or arrangements relating to shipment are at the seller's option.

(3) Where such specification would materially affect the other party's performance but is not seasonally made or where one party's cooperation is necessary to the agreed performance of the other but is not seasonably forthcoming, the other party in addition to all other remedies

(a) is excused for any resulting delay in his own performance; and

(b) may also either proceed to perform in any reasonable manner or after the time for a material part of his own performance treat the failure to specify or to cooperate as a breach by failure to deliver or accept the goods.

§ 2–312. Warranty of Title and Against Infringement; Buyer's Obligation Against Infringement

(1) Subject to subsection (2) there is in a contract for sale a warranty by the seller that

(a) the title conveyed shall be good, and its transfer rightful; and

(b) the goods shall be delivered free from any security interest or other lien or encumbrance of which the buyer at the time of contracting has no knowledge.

(2) A warranty under subsection (1) will be excluded or modified only by specific language or by circumstances which give the buyer reason to know that the person selling does not claim title in himself or that he is purporting to sell only such right or title as he or a third person may have.

(3) Unless otherwise agreed a seller who is a merchant regularly dealing in goods of the kind warrants that the goods shall be delivered free of the rightful claim of any third person by way of infringement or the like but a buyer who furnishes specifications to the seller must hold the seller harmless against any such claim which arises out of compliance with the specifications.

§ 2–313. Express Warranties by Affirmation, Promise, Description, Sample

(1) Express warranties by the seller are created as follows:

(a) Any affirmation of fact or promise made by the seller to the buyer which relates to the goods and becomes part of the basis of the bargain creates an express warranty that the goods shall conform to the affirmation or promise.

(b) Any description of the goods which is made part of the basis of the bargain creates an express warranty that the goods shall conform to the description.

(c) Any sample or model which is made part of the basis of the bargain creates an express warranty that the whole of the goods shall conform to the sample or model.

(2) It is not necessary to the creation of an express warranty that the seller use formal words such as "warrant" or "guarantee" or that he have a specific intention to make a warranty, but an affirmation merely of the value of the goods or a statement purporting to be merely the seller's opinion or commendation of the goods does not create a warranty.

§ 2–314. Implied Warranty: Merchantability; Usage of Trade

(1) Unless excluded or modified (Section 2–316), a warranty that the goods shall be merchantable is implied in a contract for their sale if the seller is a merchant with respect to goods of that kind. Under this section the serving for value of food or drink to be consumed either on the premises or elsewhere is a sale.

(2) Goods to be merchantable must be at least such as

(a) pass without objection in the trade under the contract description; and

(b) in the case of fungible goods, are of fair average quality within the description; and

(c) are fit for the ordinary purposes for which such goods are used; and

(d) run, within the variations permitted by the agreement, of even kind, quality and quantity within each unit and among all units involved; and

(e) are adequately contained, packaged, and labeled as the agreement may require; and

(f) conform to the promises or affirmations of fact made on the container or label if any.

(3) Unless excluded or modified (Section 2–316) other implied warranties may arise from course of dealing or usage of trade.

§ 2–315. Implied Warranty: Fitness for Particular Purpose

Where the seller at the time of contracting has reason to know any particular purpose for which the goods are required and that the buyer is relying on the seller's skill or judgment to select or furnish suitable goods, there is unless excluded or modified under the next section an implied warranty that the goods shall be fit for such purpose.

§ 2–316. Exclusion or Modification of Warranties

(1) Words or conduct relevant to the creation of an express warranty and words or conduct tending to negate or limit warranty shall be construed wherever reasonable as consistent with each other; but subject to the provisions of this Article on parol or extrinsic evidence (Section 2–202) negation or limitation is inoperative to the extent that such construction is unreasonable.

(2) Subject to subsection (3), to exclude or modify the implied warranty of merchantability or any part of it the language must mention merchantability and in case of a writing must be conspicuous, and to exclude or modify any implied warranty of fitness the exclusion must be by a writing and conspicuous. Language to exclude all implied warranties of fitness is sufficient if it states, for example, that "There are no warranties which extend beyond the description on the face hereof."

(3) Notwithstanding subsection (2)

(*a*) unless the circumstances indicate otherwise, all implied warranties are excluded by expressions like "as is", "with all faults" or other language which in common understanding calls the buyer's attention to the exclusion of warranties and makes plain that there is no implied warranty; and

(*b*) when the buyer before entering into the contract has examined the goods or the sample or model as fully as he desired or has refused to examine the goods there is no implied warranty with regard to defects which an examination ought in the circumstances to have revealed to him; and

(*c*) an implied warranty can also be excluded or modified by course of dealing or course of performance or usage of trade.

(4) Remedies for breach of warranty can be limited in accordance with the provisions of this Article on liquidation or limitation of damages and on contractual modification of remedy (Sections 2–718 and 2–719).

* * * *

§ 2–318. Third Party Beneficiaries of Warranties Express or Implied
A seller's warranty whether express or implied extends to any natural person if it is reasonable to expect that such person may use, consume or be affected by the goods and who is injured in person by breach of the warranty. A seller may not exclude or limit the operation of this section.

§ 2–319. F.O.B. and F.A.S. Terms
(1) Unless otherwise agreed the term F.O.B. (which means "free on board") at a named place, even though used only in connection with the stated price, is a delivery term under which

(*a*) when the term is F.O.B. the place of shipment, the seller must at that place ship the goods in the manner provided in this Article (Section 2–504) and bear the expense and risk of putting them into the possession of the carrier; or

(*b*) when the term is F.O.B. the place of destination, the seller must at his own expense and risk transport the goods to that place and there tender delivery of them in the manner provided in this Article (Section 2–503);

(*c*) when under either (a) or (b) the term is also F.O.B. vessel, car or other vehicle, the seller must in addition at his own expense and risk load the goods on board. If the term is F.O.B. vessel the buyer must name the vessel and in an appropriate case the seller must comply with the provisions of this Article on the form of bill of lading (Section 2–323).

(2) Unless otherwise agreed the term F.A.S. vessel (which means "free alongside") at a named port, even though used only in connection with the stated price, is a delivery term under which the seller must

(*a*) at his own expense and risk deliver the goods alongside the vessel in the manner usual in that port or on a dock designated and provided by the buyer; and

(b) obtain and tender a receipt for the goods in exchange for which the carrier is under a duty to issue a bill of lading.

(3) Unless otherwise agreed in any case falling within subsection (1) *(a)* or *(c)* or subsection (2) the buyer must seasonably give any needed instructions for making delivery, including when the term is F.A.S. or F.O.B. the loading berth of the vessel and in an appropriate case its name and sailing date. The seller may treat the failure of needed instructions as a failure of cooperation under this Article (Section 2–311). He may also at his option move the goods in p7 p73 any reasonable manner preparatory to delivery or shipment.

(4) Under the term F.O.B. vessel or F.A.S. unless otherwise agreed the buyer must make payment against tender of the required documents and the seller may not tender nor the buyer demand delivery of the goods in substitution for the documents.

§ 2–320. C.I.F. and C. & F. Terms

(1) The term C.I.F. means that the price includes in a lump sum the cost of the goods and the insurance and freight to the named destination. The term C. & F. or C.F. means that the price so includes cost and freight to the named destination.

(2) Unless otherwise agreed and even though used only in connection with the stated price and destination, the term C.I.F. destination or its equivalent requires the seller at his own expense and risk to

(a) put the goods into the possession of a carrier at the port for shipment and obtain a negotiable bill or bills of lading covering the entire transportation to the named destination; and

(b) load the goods and obtain a receipt from the carrier (which may be contained in the bill of lading) showing that the freight has been paid or provided for; and

(c) obtain a policy or certificate of insurance, including any war risk insurance, of a kind and on terms then current at the port of shipment in the usual amount, in the currency of the contract, shown to cover the same goods covered by the bill of lading and providing for payment of loss to the order of the buyer or for the account of whom it may concern; but the seller may add to the price the amount of the premium for any such war risk insurance; and

(d) prepare an invoice of the goods and procure any other documents required to effect shipment or to comply with the contract; and

(e) forward and tender with commercial promptness all the documents in due form and with any indorsement necessary to perfect the buyer's rights.

(3) Unless otherwise agreed the term C. & F. or its equivalent has the same effect and imposes upon the seller the same obligations and risks as a C.I.F. term except the obligation as to insurance.

(4) Under the term C.I.F. or C. & F. unless otherwise agreed the buyer must make payment against tender of the required documents and the seller may not tender nor the buyer demand delivery of the goods in substitution for the documents.

* * * *

§ 2–326. Sale on Approval and Sale or Return; Consignment Sales and Rights of Creditors

(1) Unless otherwise agreed, if delivered goods may be returned by the buyer even though they conform to the contract, the transaction is

    (a) a "sale on approval" if the goods are delivered primarily for use, and

    (b) a "sale or return" if the goods are delivered primarily for resale.

(2) Except as provided in subsection (3), goods held on approval are not subject to the claims of the buyer's creditors until acceptance; goods held on sale or return are subject to such claims while in the buyer's possession.

(3) Where goods are delivered to a person for sale and such person maintains a place of business at which he deals in goods of the kind involved, under a name other than the name of the person making delivery, then with respect to claims of creditors of the person conducting the business the goods are deemed to be on sale or return. The provisions of this subsection are applicable even though an agreement purports to reserve title to the person making delivery until payment or resale or uses such words as "on consignment" or "on memorandum". However, this subsection is not applicable if the person making delivery

    (a) complies with an applicable law providing for a consignor's interest or the like to be evidenced by a sign, or

    (b) establishes that the person conducting the business is generally known by his creditors to be substantially engaged in selling the goods of others, or

    (c) complies with the filing provisions of the Article on Secured Transactions (Article 9).

(4) Any "or return" term of a contract for sale is to be treated as a separate contract for sale within the statute of frauds section of this Article (Section 2–201) and as contradicting the sale aspect of the contract within the provisions of this Article on parol or extrinsic evidence (Section 2–202).

§ 2–327. Special Incidents of Sale on Approval and Sale or Return

(1) Under a sale on approval unless otherwise agreed

    (a) although the goods are identified to the contract the risk of loss and the title do not pass to the buyer until acceptance; and

    (b) use of the goods consistent with the purpose of trial is not acceptance but failure seasonably to notify the seller of election to return the goods is acceptance, and if the goods conform to the contract acceptance of any part is acceptance of the whole; and

    (c) after due notification of election to return, the return is at the seller's risk and expense but a merchant buyer must follow any reasonable instructions.

(2) Under a sale or return unless otherwise agreed

(*a*) the option to return extends to the whole or any commercial unit of the goods while in substantially their original condition, but must be exercised seasonably; and

(*b*) the return is at the buyer's risk and expense.

§ 2–328. Sale by Auction

(1) In a sale by auction if goods are put up in lots each lot is the subject of a separate sale.

(2) A sale by auction is complete when the auctioneer so announces by the fall of the hammer or in other customary manner. Where a bid is made while the hammer is falling in acceptance of a prior bid the auctioneer may in his discretion reopen the bidding or declare the goods sold under the bid on which the hammer was falling.

(3) Such a sale is with reserve unless the goods are in explicit terms put up without reserve. In an auction with reserve the auctioneer may withdraw the goods at any time until he announces completion of the sale. In an auction without reserve, after the auctioneer calls for bids on an article or lot, that article or lot cannot be withdrawn unless no bid is made within a reasonable time. In either case a bidder may retract his bid until the auctioneer's announcement of completion of the sale, but a bidder's retraction does not revive any previous bid.

(4) If the auctioneer knowingly receives a bid on the seller's behalf or the seller makes or procures such a bid, and notice has not been given that liberty for such bidding is reserved, the buyer may at his option avoid the sale or take the goods at the price of the last good faith bid prior to the completion of the sale. This subsection shall not apply to any bid at a forced sale.

§ 2–401. Passing of Title; Reservation for Security; Limited Application of This Section

Each provision of this Article with regard to the rights, obligations and remedies of the seller, the buyer, purchasers or other third parties applies irrespective of title to the goods except where the provision refers to such title. Insofar as situations are not covered by the other provisions of this Article and matters concerning title become material the following rules apply:

(1) Title to goods cannot pass under a contract for sale prior to their identification to the contract (Section 2–501), and unless otherwise explicitly agreed the buyer acquires by their identification a special property as limited by this Act. Any retention or reservation by the seller of the title (property) in goods shipped or delivered to the buyer is limited in effect to a reservation of a security interest. Subject to these provisions and to the provisions of the Article on Secured Transactions (Article 9), title to goods passes from the seller to the buyer in any manner and on any conditions explicitly agreed on by the parties.

(2) Unless otherwise explicitly agreed title passes to the buyer at the time and place at which the seller completes his performance with reference to the physical delivery of the goods, despite any reservation of a security interest and even though a document of title is to be delivered at a different time or place; and in particular and despite any reservation of a security interest by the bill of lading

(*a*) if the contract requires or authorizes the seller to send the goods to the buyer but does not require him to deliver them at destination, title passes to the buyer at the time and place of shipment; but

(*b*) if the contract requires delivery at destination, title passes on tender there.

(3) Unless otherwise explicitly agreed where delivery is to be made without moving the goods,

(*a*) if the seller is to deliver a document of title, title passes at the time when and the place where he delivers such documents; or

(*b*) if the goods are at the time of contracting already identified and no documents are to be delivered, title passes at the time and place of contracting.

(4) A rejection or other refusal by the buyer to receive or retain the goods, whether or not justified, or a justified revocation of acceptance revests title to the goods in the seller. Such revesting occurs by operation of law and is not a "sale".

§ 2–402. Rights of Seller's Creditors Against Sold Goods

(1) Except as provided in subsections (2) and (3), rights of unsecured creditors of the seller with respect to goods which have been identified to a contract for sale are subject to the buyer's rights to recover the goods under this Article (Sections 2–502 and 2–716).

(2) A creditor of the seller may treat a sale or an identification of goods to a contract for sale as void if as against him a retention of possession by the seller is fraudulent under any rule of law of the state where the goods are situated, except that retention of possession in good faith and current course of trade by a merchant-seller for a commercially reasonable time after a sale or identification is not fraudulent.

(3) Nothing in this Article shall be deemed to impair the rights of creditors of the seller

(*a*) under the provisions of the Article on Secured Transactions (Article 9); or

(*b*) where identification to the contract or delivery is made not in current course of trade but in satisfaction of or as security for a pre-existing claim for money, security or the like and is made under circumstances which under any rule of law of the state where the goods are situated would apart from this Article constitute the transaction a fraudulent transfer or voidable preference.

* * * *

§ 2–501. Insurable Interest in Goods; Manner of Identification of Goods

(1) The buyer obtains a special property and an insurable interest in goods by identification of existing goods as goods to which the contract refers even though the goods so identified are non-conforming and he has an option to return or reject them. Such identification can be made at any time and in any manner explicitly agreed to by the parties. In the absence of explicit agreement identification occurs

(*a*) when the contract is made if it is for the sale of goods already existing and identified;

(*b*) if the contract is for the sale of future goods other than those described in paragraph (c), when goods are shipped, marked or otherwise designated by the seller as goods to which the contract refers;

(*c*) when the crops are planted or otherwise become growing crops or the young are conceived if the contract is for the sale of unborn young to be born within twelve months after contracting or for the sale of crops to be harvested within twelve months or the next normal harvest season after contracting whichever is longer.

(2) The seller retains an insurable interest in goods so long as title to or any security interest in the goods remains in him and where the identification is by the seller alone he may until default or insolvency or notification to the buyer that the identification is final substitute other goods for those identified.

(3) Nothing in this section impairs any insurable interest recognized under any other statute or rule of law.

§ 2–502. Buyer's Right to Goods on Seller's Insolvency

(1) Subject to subsection (2) and even though the goods have not been shipped a buyer who has paid a part or all of the price of goods in which he has a special property under the provisions of the immediately preceding section may on making and keeping good a tender of any unpaid portion of their price recover them from the seller if the seller becomes insolvent within ten days after receipt of the first installment on their price.

(2) If the identification creating his special property has been made by the buyer he acquires the right to recover the goods only if they conform to the contract for sale.

§ 2–503. Manner of Seller's Tender of Delivery

(1) Tender of delivery requires that the seller put and hold conforming goods at the buyer's disposition and give the buyer any notification reasonably necessary to enable him to take delivery. The manner, time and place for tender are determined by the agreement and this Article, and in particular

(*a*) tender must be at a reasonable hour, and if it is of goods they must be kept available for the period reasonably necessary to enable the buyer to take possession; but

(*b*) unless otherwise agreed the buyer must furnish facilities reasonably suited to the receipt of the goods.

(2) Where the case is within the next section respecting shipment tender requires that the seller comply with its provisions.

(3) Where the seller is required to deliver at a particular destination tender requires that he comply with subsection (1) and also in any appropriate case tender documents as described in subsections (4) and (5) of this section.

(4) Where goods are in the possession of a bailee and are to be delivered without being moved

(*a*) tender requires that the seller either tender a negotiable document of title covering such goods or procure acknowledgment by the bailee of the buyer's right to possession of the goods; but

(*b*) tender to the buyer of a non-negotiable document of title or of a written direction to the bailee to deliver is sufficient tender unless the buyer seasonably objects, and receipt by the bailee of notification of the buyer's rights fixes those rights as against the bailee and all third persons; but risk of loss of the goods and of any failure by the bailee to honor the non-negotiable document of title or to obey the direction remains on the seller until the buyer has had a reasonable time to present the document or direction, and a refusal by the bailee to honor the document or to obey the direction defeats the tender.

(5) Where the contract requires the seller to deliver documents

(*a*) he must tender all such documents in correct form, except as provided in this Article with respect to bills of lading in a set (subsection (2) of Section 2–323); and

(*b*) tender through customary banking channels is sufficient and dishonor of a draft accompanying the documents constitutes non-acceptance or rejection.

§ 2–504. Shipment by Seller

Where the seller is required or authorized to send the goods to the buyer and the contract does not require him to deliver them at a particular destination, then unless otherwise agreed he must

(*a*) put the goods in the possession of such a carrier and make such a contract for their transportation as may be reasonable having regard to the nature of the goods and other circumstances of the case; and

(*b*) obtain and promptly deliver or tender in due form any document necessary to enable the buyer to obtain possession of the goods or otherwise required by the agreement or by usage of trade; and

(*c*) promptly notify the buyer of the shipment.

Failure to notify the buyer under paragraph (c) or to make a proper contract under paragraph (a) is a ground for rejection only if material delay or loss ensues.

* * * *

§ 2–507. Effect of Seller's Tender; Delivery on Condition

(1) Tender of delivery is a condition to the buyer's duty to accept the goods and, unless otherwise agreed, to his duty to pay for them. Tender entitles the seller to acceptance of the goods and to payment according to the contract.

(2) Where payment is due and demanded on the delivery to the buyer of goods or documents of title, his right as against the seller to retain or dispose of them is conditional upon his making the payment due.

* * * *

§ 2–509. Risk of Loss in the Absence of Breach

(1) Where the contract requires or authorizes the seller to ship the goods by carrier

> (a) if it does not require him to deliver them at a particular destination, the risk of loss passes to the buyer when the goods are duly delivered to the carrier even though the shipment is under reservation (Section 2–505); but
>
> (b) if it does require him to deliver them at a particular destination and the goods are there duly tendered while in the possession of the carrier, the risk of loss passes to the buyer when the goods are there duly so tendered as to enable the buyer to take delivery.

(2) Where the goods are held by a bailee to be delivered without being moved, the risk of loss passes to the buyer

> (a) on his receipt of a negotiable document of title covering the goods; or
>
> (b) on acknowledgment by the bailee of the buyer's right to possession of the goods; or
>
> (c) after his receipt of a non-negotiable document of title or other written direction to deliver, as provided in subsection (4) (b) of Section 2–503.

(3) In any case not within subsection (1) or (2), the risk of loss passes to the buyer on his receipt of the goods if the seller is a merchant; otherwise the risk passes to the buyer on tender of delivery.

(4) The provisions of this section are subject to contrary agreement of the parties and to the provisions of this Article on sale on approval (Section 2–327) and on effect of breach on risk of loss (Section 2–510).

§ 2–510. Effect of Breach on Risk of Loss

(1) Where a tender or delivery of goods so fails to conform to the contract as to give a right of rejection the risk of their loss remains on the seller until cure or acceptance.

(2) Where the buyer rightfully revokes acceptance he may to the extent of any deficiency in his effective insurance coverage treat the risk of loss as having rested on the seller from the beginning.

(3) Where the buyer as to conforming goods already identified to the contract for sale repudiates or is otherwise in breach before risk of their loss has passed to him, the seller may to the extent of any deficiency in his effective insurance coverage treat the risk of loss as resting on the buyer for a commercially reasonable time.

* * * *

§ 2–513. Buyer's Right to Inspection of Goods

(1) Unless otherwise agreed and subject to subsection (3), where goods are tendered or delivered or identified to the contract for sale, the buyer has a right before payment or acceptance to inspect them at any reasonable place

and time and in any reasonable manner. When the seller is required or authorized to send the goods to the buyer, the inspection may be after their arrival.

(2) Expenses of inspection must be borne by the buyer but may be recovered from the seller if the goods do not conform and are rejected.

(3) Unless otherwise agreed and subject to the provisions of this Article on C. I. F. contracts (subsection (3) of Section 2–321), the buyer is not entitled to inspect the goods before payment of the price when the contract provides

(a) for delivery "C. O. D." or on other like terms; or

(b) for payment against documents of title, except where such payment is due only after the goods are to become available for inspection.

(4) A place or method of inspection fixed by the parties is presumed to be exclusive but unless otherwise expressly agreed it does not postpone identification or shift the place for delivery or for passing the risk of loss. If compliance becomes impossible, inspection shall be as provided in this section unless the place or method fixed was clearly intended as an indispensable condition failure of which avoids the contract.

* * * *

§ 2–601. Buyer's Rights on Improper Delivery

Subject to the provisions of this Article on breach in installment contracts (Section 2–612) and unless otherwise agreed under the sections on contractual limitations of remedy (Sections 2–718 and 2–719), if the goods or the tender of delivery fail in any respect to conform to the contract, the buyer may

(a) reject the whole; or

(b) accept the whole; or

(c) accept any commercial unit or units and reject the rest.

§ 2–602. Manner and Effect of Rightful Rejection

(1) Rejection of goods must be within a reasonable time after their delivery or tender. It is ineffective unless the buyer seasonably notifies the seller.

(2) Subject to the provisions of the two following sections on rejected goods (Sections 2–603 and 2–604):

(a) after rejection any exercise of ownership by the buyer with respect to any commercial unit is wrongful as against the seller; and

(b) if the buyer has before rejection taken physical possession of goods in which he does not have a security interest under the provisions of this Article (subsection (3) of Section 2–711), he is under a duty after rejection to hold them with reasonable care at the seller's disposition for a time sufficient to permit the seller to remove them; but

(c) the buyer has no further obligations with regard to goods rightfully rejected.

(3) The seller's rights with respect to goods wrongfully rejected are governed by the provisions of this Article on seller's remedies in general (Section 2–703).

§ 2–603. Merchant Buyer's Duties as to Rightfully Rejected Goods

(1) Subject to any security interest in the buyer (subsection (3) of Section 2–711), when the seller has no agent or place of business at the market of rejection a merchant buyer is under a duty after rejection of goods in his possession or control to follow any reasonable instructions received from the seller with respect to the goods and in the absence of such instructions to make reasonable efforts to sell them for the seller's account if they are perishable or threaten to decline in value speedily. Instructions are not reasonable if on demand indemnity for expenses is not forthcoming.

(2) When the buyer sells goods under subsection (1), he is entitled to reimbursement from the seller or out of the proceeds for reasonable expenses of caring for and selling them, and if the expenses include no selling commission then to such commission as is usual in the trade or if there is none to a reasonable sum not exceeding ten per cent on the gross proceeds.

(3) In complying with this section the buyer is held only to good faith and good faith conduct hereunder is neither acceptance nor conversion nor the basis of an action for damages.

* * * *

§ 2–606. What Constitutes Acceptance of Goods

(1) Acceptance of goods occurs when the buyer

(a) after a reasonable opportunity to inspect the goods signifies to the seller that the goods are conforming or that he will take or retain them in spite of their non-conformity; or

(b) fails to make an effective rejection (subsection (1) of Section 2–602), but such acceptance does not occur until the buyer has had a reasonable opportunity to inspect them; or

(c) does any act inconsistent with the seller's ownership; but if such act is wrongful as against the seller it is an acceptance only if ratified by him.

(2) Acceptance of a part of any commercial unit is acceptance of that entire unit.

§ 2–607. Effect of Acceptance; Notice of Breach; Burden of Establishing Breach After Acceptance; Notice of Claim or Litigation to Person Answerable Over

(1) The buyer must pay at the contract rate for any goods accepted.

(2) Acceptance of goods by the buyer precludes rejection of the goods accepted and if made with knowledge of a non-conformity cannot be revoked because of it unless the acceptance was on the reasonable assumption that the non-conformity would be seasonably cured but acceptance does not of itself impair any other remedy provided by this Article for non-conformity.

(3) Where a tender has been accepted

(a) the buyer must within a reasonable time after he discovers or should have discovered any breach notify the seller of breach or be barred from any remedy; and

(b) if the claim is one for infringement or the like (subsection (3) of Section 2–312) and the buyer is sued as a result of such a breach he must so notify the seller within a reasonable time after he receives notice of the litigation or be barred from any remedy over for liability established by the litigation.

(4) The burden is on the buyer to establish any breach with respect to the goods accepted.

(5) Where the buyer is sued for breach of a warranty or other obligation for which his seller is answerable over

(a) he may give his seller written notice of the litigation. If the notice states that the seller may come in and defend and that if the seller does not do so he will be bound in any action against him by his buyer by any determination of fact common to the two litigations, then unless the seller after seasonable receipt of the notice does come in and defend he is so bound.

(b) if the claim is one for infringement or the like (subsection (3) of Section 2–312) the original seller may demand in writing that his buyer turn over to him control of the litigation including settlement or else be barred from any remedy over and if he also agrees to bear all expense and to satisfy any adverse judgment, then unless the buyer after seasonable receipt of the demand does turn over control the buyer is so barred.

(6) The provisions of subsection (3), (4) and (5) apply to any obligation of a buyer to hold the seller harmless against infringement or the like (subsection (3) of Section 2–312).

* * * *

§ 2–610. Anticipatory Repudiation

When either party repudiates the contract with respect to a performance not yet due the loss of which will substantially impair the value of the contract to the other, the aggrieved party may

(a) for a commercially reasonable time await performance by the repudiating party; or

(b) resort to any remedy for breach (Section 2–703 or Section 2–711), even though he has notified the repudiating party that he would await the latter's performance and has urged retraction; and

(c) in either case suspend his own performance or proceed in accordance with the provisions of this Article on the seller's right to identify goods to the contract notwithstanding breach or to salvage unfinished goods (Section 2–704)

* * * *

§ 2–612. "Installment Contract"; Breach

(1) An "installment contract" is one which requires or authorizes the delivery of goods in separate lots to be separately accepted, even though the contract contains a clause "each delivery is a separate contract" or its equivalent.

(2) The buyer may reject any installment which is non-conforming if the non-conformity substantially impairs the value of that installment and cannot be cured or if the non-conformity is a defect in the required documents; but if the non-conformity does not fall within subsection (3) and the seller gives adequate assurance of its cure the buyer must accept that installment.

(3) Whenever non-conformity or default with respect to one or more installments substantially impairs the value of the whole contract there is a breach of the whole. But the aggrieved party reinstates the contract if he accepts a non-conforming installment without seasonably notifying of cancellation or if he brings an action with respect only to past installments or demands performance as to future installments.

§ 2–613. Casualty to Identified Goods

Where the contract requires for its performance goods identified when the contract is made, and the goods suffer casualty without fault of either party before the risk of loss passes to the buyer, or in a proper case under a "no arrival, no sale" term (Section 2–324) then

- (*a*) if the loss is total the contract is avoided; and
- (*b*) if the loss is partial or the goods have so deteriorated as no longer to conform to the contract the buyer may nevertheless demand inspection and at his option either treat the contract as avoided or accept the goods with due allowance from the contract price for the deterioration or the deficiency in quantity but without further right against the seller.

§ 2–614. Substituted Performance

(1) Where without fault of either party the agreed berthing, loading, or unloading facilities fail or an agreed type of carrier becomes unavailable or the agreed manner of delivery otherwise becomes commercially impracticable but a commercially reasonable substitute is available, such substitute performance must be tendered and accepted.

(2) If the agreed means or manner of payment fails because of domestic or foreign governmental regulation, the seller may withhold or stop delivery unless the buyer provides a means or manner of payment which is commercially a substantial equivalent. If delivery has already been taken, payment by the means or in the manner provided by the regulation discharges the buyer's obligation unless the regulation is discriminatory, oppressive or predatory.

§ 2–615. Excuse by Failure of Presupposed Conditions

Except so far as a seller may have assumed a greater obligation and subject to the preceding section on substituted performance:

- (*a*) Delay in delivery or non-delivery in whole or in part by a seller who complies with paragraphs (b) and (c) is not a breach of his duty under a contract for sale if performance as agreed has been made impracticable by the occurrence of a contingency the non-occurrence of which was a basic assumption on which the contract was made or by compliance in good faith with any applicable foreign or domestic governmental regulation or order whether or not it later proves to be invalid.

(b) Where the causes mentioned in paragraph (a) affect only a part of the seller's capacity to perform, he must allocate production and deliveries among his customers but may at his option include regular customers not then under contract as well as his own requirements for further manufacture. He may so allocate in any manner which is fair and reasonable.

(c) The seller must notify the buyer seasonably that there will be delay or non-delivery and, when allocation is required under paragraph (b), of the estimated quota thus made available for the buyer.

* * * *

§ 2–703. Seller's Remedies in General

Where the buyer wrongfully rejects or revokes acceptance of goods or fails to make a payment due on or before delivery or repudiates with respect to a part or the whole, then with respect to any goods directly affected and, if the breach is of the whole contract (Section 2–612), then also with respect to the whole undelivered balance, the aggrieved seller may

(a) withhold delivery of such goods;

(b) stop delivery by any bailee as hereafter provided (Section 2–705);

(c) proceed under the next section respecting goods still unidentified to the contract;

(d) resell and recover damages as hereafter provided (Section 2–706);

(e) recover damages for non-acceptance (Section 2–708) or in a proper case the price (Section 2–709);

(f) cancel.

* * * *

§ 2–705. Seller's Stoppage of Delivery in Transit or Otherwise

(1) The seller may stop delivery of goods in the possession of a carrier or other bailee when he discovers the buyer to be insolvent (Section 2–702) and may stop delivery of carload, truckload, planeload or larger shipments of express or freight when the buyer repudiates or fails to make a payment due before delivery or if for any other reason the seller has a right to withhold or reclaim the goods.

(2) As against such buyer the seller may stop delivery until

(a) receipt of the goods by the buyer; or

(b) acknowledgment to the buyer by any bailee of the goods except a carrier that the bailee holds the goods for the buyer; or

(c) such acknowledgment to the buyer by a carrier by reshipment or as warehouseman; or

(d) negotiation to the buyer of any negotiable document of title covering the goods.

(3)

(a) To stop delivery the seller must so notify as to enable the bailee by reasonable diligence to prevent delivery of the goods.

(b) After such notification the bailee must hold and deliver the goods according to the directions of the seller but the seller is liable to the bailee for any ensuing charges or damages.

(c) If a negotiable document of title has been issued for goods the bailee is not obliged to obey a notification to stop until surrender of the document.

(d) A carrier who has issued a non-negotiable bill of lading is not obliged to obey a notification to stop received from a person other than the consignor.

* * * *

§ 2–708. Seller's Damages for Non-acceptance or Repudiation

(1) Subject to subsection (2) and to the provisions of this Article with respect to proof of market price (Section 2–723), the measure of damages for non-acceptance or repudiation by the buyer is the difference between the market price at the time and place for tender and the unpaid contract price together with any incidental damages provided in this Article (Section 2–710), but less expenses saved in consequence of the buyer's breach.

(2) If the measure of damages provided in subsection (1) is inadequate to put the seller in as good a position as performance would have done then the measure of damages is the profit (including reasonable overhead) which the seller would have made from full performance by the buyer, together with any incidental damages provided in this Article (Section 2–710), due allowance for costs reasonably incurred and due credit for payments or proceeds of resale.

§ 2–709. Action for the Price

(1) When the buyer fails to pay the price as it becomes due the seller may recover, together with any incidental damages under the next section, the price

(a) of goods accepted or of conforming goods lost or damaged within a commercially reasonable time after risk of their loss has passed to the buyer; and

(b) of goods identified to the contract if the seller is unable after reasonable effort to resell them at a reasonable price or the circumstances reasonably indicate that such effort will be unavailing.

(2) Where the seller sues for the price he must hold for the buyer any goods which have been identified to the contract and are still in his control except that if resale becomes possible he may resell them at any time prior to the collection of the judgment. The net proceeds of any such resale must be credited to the buyer and payment of the judgment entitles him to any goods not resold.

(3) After the buyer has wrongfully rejected or revoked acceptance of the goods or has failed to make a payment due or has repudiated (Section 2–610), a seller who is held not entitled to the price under this section shall nevertheless be awarded damages for non-acceptance under the preceding section.

§ 2–710. Seller's Incidental Damages

Incidental damages to an aggrieved seller include any commercially reasonable charges, expenses or commissions incurred in stopping delivery, in the transportation, care and custody of goods after the buyer's breach, in connection with return or resale of the goods or otherwise resulting from the breach.

§ 2–711. Buyer's Remedies in General; Buyer's Security Interest in Rejected Goods

(1) Where the seller fails to make delivery or repudiates or the buyer rightfully rejects or justifiably revokes acceptance then with respect to any goods involved, and with respect to the whole if the breach goes to the whole contract (Section 2–612), the buyer may cancel and whether or not he has done so may in addition to recovering so much of the price as has been paid

(a) "cover" and have damages under the next section as to all the goods affected whether or not they have been identified to the contract; or

(b) recover damages for non-delivery as provided in this Article (Section 2–713).

(2) Where the seller fails to deliver or repudiates the buyer may also

(a) if the goods have been identified recover them as provided in this Article (Section 2–502); or

(b) in a proper case obtain specific performance or replevy the goods as provided in this Article (Section 2–716).

(3) On rightful rejection or justifiable revocation of acceptance a buyer has a security interest in goods in his possession or control for any payments made on their price and any expenses reasonably incurred in their inspection, receipt, transportation, care and custody and may hold such goods and resell them in like manner as an aggrieved seller (Section 2–706).

§ 2–712. "Cover"; Buyer's Procurement of Substitute Goods

(1) After a breach within the preceding section the buyer may "cover" by making in good faith and without unreasonable delay any reasonable purchase of or contract to purchase goods in substitution for those due from the seller.

(2) The buyer may recover from the seller as damages the difference between the cost of cover and the contract price together with any incidental or consequential damages as hereinafter defined (Section 2–715), but less expenses saved in consequence of the seller's breach.

(3) Failure of the buyer to effect cover within this section does not bar him from any other remedy.

§ 2–713. Buyer's Damages for Non-Delivery or Repudiation

(1) Subject to the provisions of this Article with respect to proof of market price (Section 2–723), the measure of damages for non-delivery or repudiation by the seller is the difference between the market price at the time when the buyer learned of the breach and the contract price together with any incidental and consequential damages provided in this Article (Section 2–715), but less expenses saved in consequence of the seller's breach.

(2) Market price is to be determined as of the place for tender or, in cases of rejection after arrival or revocation of acceptance, as of the place of arrival.

§ 2–714. Buyer's Damages for Breach in Regard to Accepted Goods

(1) Where the buyer has accepted goods and given notification (subsection (3) of Section 2–607) he may recover as damages for any non-conformity of tender the loss resulting in the ordinary course of events from the seller's breach as determined in any manner which is reasonable.

(2) The measure of damages for breach of warranty is the difference at the time and place of acceptance between the value of the goods accepted and the value they would have had if they had been as warranted, unless special circumstances show proximate damages of a different amount.

(3) In a proper case any incidental and consequential damages under the next section may also be recovered.

§ 2–715. Buyer's Incidental and Consequential Damages

(1) Incidental damages resulting from the seller's breach include expenses reasonably incurred in inspection, receipt, transportation and care and custody of goods rightfully rejected, any commercially reasonable charges, expenses or commissions in connection with effecting cover and any other reasonable expense incident to the delay or other breach.

(2) Consequential damages resulting from the seller's breach include

(a) any loss resulting from general or particular requirements and needs of which the seller at the time of contracting had reason to know and which could not reasonably be prevented by cover or otherwise; and

(b) injury to person or property proximately resulting from any breach of warranty.

§ 2–716. Buyer's Right to Specific Performance or Replevin

(1) Specific performance may be decreed where the goods are unique or in other proper circumstances.

(2) The decree for specific performance may include such terms and conditions as to payment of the price, damages, or other relief as the court may deem just.

(3) The buyer has a right of replevin for goods identified to the contract if after reasonable effort he is unable to effect cover for such goods or the circumstances reasonably indicate that such effort will be unavailing or if the goods have been shipped under reservation and satisfaction of the security interest in them has been made or tendered.

* * * *

§ 2–718. Liquidation or Limitation of Damages; Deposits

(1) Damages for breach by either party may be liquidated in the agreement but only at an amount which is reasonable in the light of the anticipated or actual harm caused by the breach, the difficulties of proof of loss, and the inconvenience or nonfeasibility of otherwise obtaining an adequate remedy. A term fixing unreasonably large liquidated damages is void as a penalty.

(2) Where the seller justifiably withholds delivery of goods because of the buyer's breach, the buyer is entitled to restitution of any amount by which the sum of his payments exceeds

> (a) the amount to which the seller is entitled by virtue of terms liquidating the seller's damages in accordance with subsection (1), or
>
> (b) in the absence of such terms, twenty per cent of the value of the total performance for which the buyer is obligated under the contract or $500, whichever is smaller.

(3) The buyer's right to restitution under subsection (2) is subject to offset to the extent that the seller establishes

> (a) a right to recover damages under the provisions of this Article other than subsection (1), and
>
> (b) the amount or value of any benefits received by the buyer directly or indirectly by reason of the contract.

(4) Where a seller has received payment in goods their reasonable value or the proceeds of their resale shall be treated as payments for the purposes of subsection (2); but if the seller has notice of the buyer's breach before reselling goods received in part performance, his resale is subject to the conditions laid down in this Article on resale by an aggrieved seller (Section 2–706).

§ 2–719. Contractual Modification or Limitation of Remedy

(1) Subject to the provisions of subsections (2) and (3) of this section and of the preceding section on liquidation and limitation of damages,

> (a) the agreement may provide for remedies in addition to or in substitution for those provided in this Article and may limit or alter the measure of damages recoverable under this Article, as by limiting the buyer's remedies to return of the goods and repayment of the price or to repair and replacement of non-conforming goods or parts; and
>
> (b) resort to a remedy as provided is optional unless the remedy is expressly agreed to be exclusive, in which case it is the sole remedy.

(2) Where circumstances cause an exclusive or limited remedy to fail of its essential purpose, remedy may be had as provided in this Act.

(3) Consequential damages may be limited or excluded unless the limitation or exclusion is unconscionable. Limitation of consequential damages for injury to the person in the case of consumer goods is prima facie unconscionable but limitation of damages where the loss is commercial is not.

* * * *

§ 2–721. Remedies for Fraud

Remedies for material misrepresentation or fraud include all remedies available under this Article for non-fraudulent breach. Neither rescission or a claim for rescission of the contract for sale nor rejection or return of the goods shall bar or be deemed inconsistent with a claim for damages or other remedy.

* * * *

§ 2–725. Statute of Limitations in Contracts for Sale

(1) An action for breach of any contract for sale must be commenced within four years after the cause of action has accrued. By the original agreement the parties may reduce the period of limitation to not less than one year but may not extend it.

(2) A cause of action accrues when the breach occurs, regardless of the aggrieved party's lack of knowledge of the breach. A breach of warranty occurs when tender of delivery is made, except that where a warranty explicitly extends to future performance of the goods and discovery of the breach must await the time of such performance the cause of action accrues when the breach is or should have been discovered.

(3) Where an action commenced within the time limited by subsection (1) is so terminated as to leave available a remedy by another action for the same breach such other action may be commenced after the expiration of the time limited and within six months after the termination of the first action unless the termination resulted from voluntary discontinuance or from dismissal for failure or neglect to prosecute.

(4) This section does not alter the law on tolling of the statute of limitations nor does it apply to causes of action which have accrued before this Act becomes effective.

C

UNIFORM COMMERCIAL CODE ARTICLE 3– COMMERCIAL PAPER

[Selected Sections]

§ 3–101. Short Title

This Article shall be known and may be cited as Uniform Commercial Code-Commercial Paper.

§ 3–102. Definitions and Index of Definitions

(1) In this Article unless the context otherwise requires

(a) "Issue" means the first delivery of an instrument to a holder or a remitter.

(b) An "order" is a direction to pay and must be more than an authorization or request. It must identify the person to pay with reasonable certainty. It may be addressed to one or more such persons jointly or in the alternative but not in succession.

(c) A "promise" is an undertaking to pay and must be more than an acknowledgment of an obligation.

(d) "Secondary party" means a drawer or endorser.

(e) "Instrument" means a negotiable instrument.

(2) Other definitions applying to this Article and the sections in which they appear are:

"Acceptance". Section 3–410.

"Accommodation party". Section 3–415.

"Alteration". Section 3–407.

"Certificate of deposit". Section 3–104.

"Certification". Section 3–411.

"Check". Section 3–104.

"Definite time". Section 3–109.

"Dishonor". Section 3–507.

"Draft". Section 3–104.

"Holder in due course". Section 3–302.

"Negotiation". Section 3–202.

"Note". Section 3–104.

"Notice of dishonor". Section 3–508.

"On demand". Section 3–108.

"Presentment". Section 3–504.

"Protest". Section 3–509.

"Restrictive Indorsement". Section 3–205.

"Signature". Section 3–401.

* * * *

§ 3–103. Limitations on Scope of Article

(1) This Article does not apply to money, documents of title or investment securities.

* * * *

§ 3–104. Form of Negotiable Instruments; "Draft"; "Check"; "Certificate of Deposit"; "Note"

(1) Any writing to be a negotiable instrument within this Article must

(*a*) be signed by the maker or drawer; and

(*b*) contain an unconditional promise or order to pay a sum certain in money and no other promise, order, obligation or power given by the maker or drawer except as authorized by this Article; and

(*c*) be payable on demand or at a definite time; and

(*d*) be payable to order or to bearer.

(2) A writing which complies with the requirements of this section is

(*a*) a "draft" ("bill of exchange") if it is an order;

(*b*) a "check" if it is a draft drawn on a bank and payable on demand;

(*c*) a "certificate of deposit" if it is an acknowledgment by a bank of receipt of money with an engagement to repay it;

(*d*) a "note" if it is a promise other than a certificate of deposit.

(3) As used in other Articles of this Act, and as the context may require, the terms "draft", "check", "certificate of deposit" and "note" may refer to instruments which are not negotiable within this Article as well as to instruments which are so negotiable.

§ 3–105. When Promise or Order Unconditional

(1) A promise or order otherwise unconditional is not made conditional by the fact that the instrument

(*a*) is subject to implied or constructive conditions; or

(*b*) states its consideration, whether performed or promised, or the transaction which gave rise to the instrument, or that the promise or order is made or the instrument matures in accordance with or "as per" such transaction; or *(c)* refers to or states that it arises out of a separate agreement or refers to a separate agreement for rights as to prepayment or acceleration; or

    (d) states that it is drawn under a letter of credit; or

    (e) states that it is secured, whether by mortgage, reservation of title or otherwise; or

    (f) indicates a particular account to be debited or any other fund or source from which reimbursement is expected; or

    (g) is limited to payment out of a particular fund or the proceeds of a particular source, if the instrument is issued by a government or governmental agency or unit; or

    (h) is limited to payment out of the entire assets of a partnership, unincorporated association, trust or estate by or on behalf of which the instrument is issued.

    (2) A promise or order is not unconditional if the instrument

    (a) states that it is subject to or governed by any other agreement; or

    (b) states that it is to be paid only out of a particular fund or source except as provided in this section.

§ 3–106. Sum Certain

    (1) The sum payable is a sum certain even though it is to be paid

    (a) with a stated rate of interest or by stated installments; or

    (b) with stated different rates of interest before and after default or a specified date; or

    (c) with a stated discount or addition if paid before or after the date fixed for payment; or

    (d) with exchange or less exchange, whether at a fixed rate or at the current rate; or

    (e) with costs of collection or an attorney's fee or both upon default.

    (2) For the purposes of subsection one of this section "a stated rate of interest" shall also include a rate of interest that cannot be calculated by looking only to the instrument but which is readily ascertainable by a reference in the instrument to a published statute, regulation, rule of court, generally accepted commercial or financial index, compendium of interest rates, or announced rate of a named financial institution.

    (3) Nothing in this section shall validate any term which is otherwise illegal.

§ 3–107. Money

    (1) An instrument is payable in money if the medium of exchange in which it is payable is money at the time the instrument is made. An instrument payable in "currency" or "current funds" is payable in money.

(2) A promise or order to pay a sum stated in a foreign currency is for a sum certain in money and may be satisfied by payment of that number of dollars which the stated foreign currency will purchase at the buying sight rate for that currency on the day on which the instrument is payable, or, if payable on demand, on the day of demand.

§ 3–108. Payable on Demand

Instruments payable on demand include those payable at sight or on presentation and those in which no time for payment is stated.

§ 3–109. Definite Time

(1) An instrument is payable at a definite time if by its terms it is payable

(a) on or before a stated date or at a fixed period after a stated date; or

(b) at a fixed period after sight; or

(c) at a definite time subject to any acceleration; or

(d) at a definite time subject to extension at the option of the holder, or to extension to a further definite time at the option of the maker or acceptor or automatically upon or after a specified act or event.

(2) An instrument which by its terms is otherwise payable only upon an act or event uncertain as to time of occurrence is not payable at a definite time even though the act or event has occurred.

§ 3–110. Payable to Order

(1) An instrument is payable to order when by its terms it is payable to the order or assigns of any person therein specified with reasonable certainty, or to him or his order, or when it is conspicuously designated on its face as "exchange" or the like and names a payee. It may be payable to the order of

(a) the maker or drawer; or

(b) the drawee; or

(c) a payee who is not maker, drawer or drawee; or

(d) two or more payees together or in the alternative; or

(e) an estate, trust or fund, in which case it is payable to the order of the representative of such estate, trust or fund or his successors; or

(f) an office, or an officer by his title as such in which case it is payable to the principal but the incumbent of the office or his successors may act as if he or they were the holder; or

(g) a partnership or unincorporated association, in which case it is payable to the partnership or association and may be indorsed or transferred by any person thereto authorized.

(2) An instrument not payable to order is not made so payable by such words as "payable upon return of this instrument properly indorsed."

(3) An instrument made payable both to order and to bearer is payable to order unless the bearer words are handwritten or typewritten.

§ 3–111. Payable to Bearer

An instrument is payable to bearer when by its terms it is payable to

(a) bearer or the order of bearer; or

(b) a specified person or bearer; or

(c) "cash" or the order of "cash", or any other indication which does not purport to designate a specific payee.

§ 3–112. Terms and Omissions Not Affecting Negotiability

(1) The negotiability of an instrument is not affected by

(a) the omission of a statement of any consideration or of the place where the instrument is drawn or payable; or

(b) a statement that collateral has been given to secure obligations either on the instrument or otherwise of an obligor on the instrument or that in the case of default on those obligations the holder may realize on or dispose of the collateral; or

(c) a promise or power to maintain or protect collateral or to give additional collateral; or

(d) a term authorizing a confession of judgment on the instrument if it is not paid when due; or

(e) a term purporting to waive the benefit of any law intended for the advantage or protection of any obligor; or

(f) a term in a draft providing that the payee by indorsing or cashing it acknowledges full satisfaction of an obligation of the drawer; or

(g) a statement in a draft drawn in a set of parts (Section 3–801) to the effect that the order is effective only if no other part has been honored.

(2) Nothing in this section shall validate any term which is otherwise illegal.

§ 3–113. Seal

An instrument otherwise negotiable is within this Article even though it is under a seal.

§ 3–114. Date, Antedating, Postdating

(1) The negotiability of an instrument is not affected by the fact that it is undated, antedated or postdated.

(2) Where an instrument is antedated or postdated the time when it is payable is determined by the stated date if the instrument is payable on demand or at a fixed period after date.

(3) Where the instrument or any signature thereon is dated, the date is presumed to be correct.

§ 3–115. Incomplete Instruments

(1) When a paper whose contents at the time of signing show that it is intended to become an instrument is signed while still incomplete in any necessary respect it cannot be enforced until completed, but when it is completed in accordance with authority given it is effective as completed.

(2) If the completion is unauthorized the rules as to material alteration apply (Section 3–407), even though the paper was not delivered by the maker or drawer; but the burden of establishing that any completion is unauthorized is on the party so asserting.

§ 3–116. Instruments Payable to Two or More Persons
An instrument payable to the order of two or more persons

(a) if in the alternative is payable to any one of them and may be negotiated, discharged or enforced by any of them who has possession of it;

(b) if not in the alternative is payable to all of them and may be negotiated, discharged or enforced only by all of them.

* * * *

§ 3–118. Ambiguous Terms and Rules of Construction
The following rules apply to every instrument:

(a) Where there is doubt whether the instrument is a draft or a note the holder may treat it as either. A draft drawn on the drawer is effective as a note.

(b) Handwritten terms control typewritten and printed terms, and typewritten control printed.

(c) Words control figures except that if the words are ambiguous figures control.

(d) Unless otherwise specified a provision for interest means interest at the judgment rate at the place of payment from the date of the instrument, or if it is undated from the date of issue.

(e) Unless the instrument otherwise specifies two or more persons who sign as maker, acceptor or drawer or indorser and as a part of the same transaction are jointly and severally liable even though the instrument contains such words as "I promise to pay."

(f) Unless otherwise specified consent to extension authorizes a single extension for not longer than the original period. A consent to extension, expressed in the instrument, is binding on secondary parties and accommodation makers. A holder may not exercise his option to extend an instrument over the objection of a maker or acceptor or other party who in accordance with Section 3–604 tenders full payment when the instrument is due.

§ 3–119. Other Writings Affecting Instrument
(1) As between the obligor and his immediate obligee or any transferee the terms of an instrument may be modified or affected by any other written agreement executed as a part of the same transaction, except that a holder in due course is not affected by any limitation of his rights arising out of the separate written agreement if he had no notice of the limitation when he took the instrument.

(2) A separate agreement does not affect the negotiability of an instrument.

* * * *

§ 3–121. Instruments Payable at Bank

A note or acceptance which states that it is payable at a bank is the equivalent of a draft drawn on the bank payable when it falls due out of any funds of the maker or acceptor in current account or otherwise available for such payment.

§ 3–122. Accrual of Cause of Action

(1) A cause of action against a maker or an acceptor accrues

(a) in the case of a time instrument on the day after maturity;

(b) in the case of a demand instrument upon its date or, if no date is stated, on the date of issue.

(2) A cause of action against the obligor of a demand or time certificate of deposit accrues upon demand, but demand on a time certificate may not be made until on or after the date of maturity.

(3) A cause of action against a drawer of a draft or an indorser of any instrument accrues upon demand following dishonor of the instrument. Notice of dishonor is a demand.

(4) Unless an instrument provides otherwise, interest runs at the rate provided by law for a judgment

(a) in the case of a maker, acceptor or other primary obligor of a demand instrument, from the date of demand;

(b) in all other cases from the date of accrual of the cause of action.

§ 3–201. Transfer: Right to Indorsement

(1) Transfer of an instrument vests in the transferee such rights as the transferor has therein, except that a transferee who has himself been a party to any fraud or illegality affecting the instrument or who as a prior holder had notice of a defense or claim against it cannot improve his position by taking from a later holder in due course.

(2) A transfer of a security interest in an instrument vests the foregoing rights in the transferee to the extent of the interest transferred.

(3) Unless otherwise agreed any transfer for value of an instrument not then payable to bearer gives the transferee the specifically enforceable right to have the unqualified indorsement of the transferor. Negotiation takes effect only when the indorsement is made and until that time there is no presumption that the transferee is the owner.

§ 3–202. Negotiation

(1) Negotiation is the transfer of an instrument in such form that the transferee becomes a holder. If the instrument is payable to order it is negotiated by delivery with any necessary indorsement; if payable to bearer it is negotiated by delivery.

(2) An indorsement must be written by or on behalf of the holder and on the instrument or on a paper so firmly affixed thereto as to become a part thereof.

(3) An indorsement is effective for negotiation only when it conveys the entire instrument or any unpaid residue. If it purports to be of less it operates only as a partial assignment.

(4) Words of assignment, condition, waiver, guaranty, limitation or disclaimer of liability and the like accompanying an indorsement do not affect its character as an indorsement.

§ 3–203. Wrong or Misspelled Name

Where an instrument is made payable to a person under a misspelled name or one other than his own he may indorse in that name or his own or both; but signature in both names may be required by a person paying or giving value for the instrument.

§ 3–204. Special Indorsement; Blank Indorsement

(1) A special indorsement specifies the person to whom or to whose order it makes the instrument payable. Any instrument specially indorsed becomes payable to the order of the special indorsee and may be further negotiated only by his indorsement.

(2) An indorsement in blank specifies no particular indorsee and may consist of a mere signature. An instrument payable to order and indorsed in blank becomes payable to bearer and may be negotiated by delivery alone until specially indorsed.

(3) The holder may convert a blank indorsement into a special indorsement by writing over the signature of the indorser in blank any contract consistent with the character of the indorsement.

§ 3–205. Restrictive Indorsements

An indorsement is restrictive which either

- (a) is conditional; or
- (b) purports to prohibit further transfer of the instrument; or
- (c) includes the words "for collection", "for deposit", "pay any bank", or like terms signifying a purpose of deposit or collection; or
- (d) otherwise states that it is for the benefit or use of the indorser or of another person.

§ 3–206. Effect of Restrictive Indorsement

(1) No restrictive indorsement prevents further transfer or negotiation of the instrument.

(2) An intermediary bank, or a payor bank which is not the depositary bank, is neither given notice nor otherwise affected by a restrictive indorsement of any person except the bank's immediate transferor or the person presenting for payment.

(3) Except for an intermediary bank, any transferee under an indorsement which is conditional or includes the words "for collection", "for deposit", "pay any bank", or like terms (subparagraphs (a) and (c) of Section 3–205) must pay or apply any value given by him for or on the security of the instrument consistently with the indorsement and to the extent that he does so he becomes a holder for value. In addition such transferee is a holder in due course if he otherwise complies with the requirements of Section 3–302 on what constitutes a holder in due course.

(4) The first taker under an indorsement for the benefit of the indorser or another person (subparagraph (d) of Section 3–205) must pay or apply any value given by him for or on the security of the instrument consistently with the indorsement and to the extent that he does so he becomes a holder for value. In addition such taker is a holder in due course if he otherwise complies with the requirements of Section 3–302 on what constitutes a holder in due course. A later holder for value is neither given notice nor otherwise affected by such restrictive indorsement unless he has knowledge that a fiduciary or other person has negotiated the instrument in any transaction for his own benefit or otherwise in breach of duty (subsection (2) of Section 3–304).

§ 3–207. Negotiation Effective Although It May Be Rescinded

(1) Negotiation is effective to transfer the instrument although the negotiation is

> *(a)* made by an infant, a corporation exceeding its powers, or any other person without capacity; or
>
> *(b)* obtained by fraud, duress or mistake of any kind; or
>
> *(c)* part of an illegal transaction; or
>
> *(d)* made in breach of duty.

(2) Except as against a subsequent holder in due course such negotiation is in an appropriate case subject to rescission, the declaration of a constructive trust or any other remedy permitted by law.

* * * *

§ 3–301. Rights of a Holder

The holder of an instrument whether or not he is the owner may transfer or negotiate it and, except as otherwise provided in Section 3–603 on payment or satisfaction, discharge it or enforce payment in his own name.

§ 3–302. Holder in Due Course

(1) A holder in due course is a holder who takes the instrument

> *(a)* for value; and
>
> *(b)* in good faith; and
>
> *(c)* without notice that it is overdue or has been dishonored or of any defense against or claim to it on the part of any person.

(2) A payee may be a holder in due course.

(3) A holder does not become a holder in due course of an instrument:

    (*a*) by purchase of it at judicial sale or by taking it under legal process; or

    (*b*) by acquiring it in taking over an estate; or

    (*c*) by purchasing it as part of a bulk transaction not in regular course of business of the transferor.

    (4) A purchaser of a limited interest can be a holder in due course only to the extent of the interest purchased.

§ 3–303. Taking for Value

A holder takes the instrument for value

    (*a*) to the extent that the agreed consideration has been performed or that he acquires a security interest in or a lien on the instrument otherwise than by legal process; or

    (*b*) when he takes the instrument in payment of or as security for an antecedent claim against any person whether or not the claim is due; or

    (*c*) when he gives a negotiable instrument for it or makes an irrevocable commitment to a third person.

§ 3–304. Notice to Purchaser

    (1) The purchaser has notice of a claim or defense if

    (*a*) the instrument is so incomplete, bears such visible evidence of forgery or alteration, or is otherwise so irregular as to call into question its validity, terms or ownership or to create an ambiguity as to the party to pay; or

    (*b*) the purchaser has notice that the obligation of any party is voidable in whole or in part, or that all parties have been discharged.

    (2) The purchaser has notice of a claim against the instrument when he has knowledge that a fiduciary has negotiated the instrument in payment of or as security for his own debt or in any transaction for his own benefit or otherwise in breach of duty.

    (3) The purchaser has notice that an instrument is overdue if he has reason to know

    (*a*) that any part of the principal amount is overdue or that there is an uncured default in payment of another instrument of the same series; or

    (*b*) that acceleration of the instrument has been made; or

    (*c*) that he is taking a demand instrument after demand has been made or more than a reasonable length of time after its issue. A reasonable time for a check drawn and payable within the states and territories of the United States and the District of Columbia is presumed to be thirty days.

    (4) Knowledge of the following facts does not of itself give the purchaser notice of a defense or claim

(*a*) that the instrument is antedated or postdated;

(*b*) that it was issued or negotiated in return for an executory promise or accompanied by a separate agreement, unless the purchaser has notice that a defense or claim has arisen from the terms thereof;

(*c*) that any party has signed for accommodation;

(*d*) that an incomplete instrument has been completed, unless the purchaser has notice of any improper completion;

(*e*) that any person negotiating the instrument is or was a fiduciary;

(*f*) that there has been default in payment of interest on the instrument or in payment of any other instrument, except one of the same series.

(5) The filing or recording of a document does not of itself constitute notice within the provisions of this Article to a person who would otherwise be a holder in due course.

(6) To be effective notice must be received at such time and in such manner as to give a reasonable opportunity to act on it.

(7) In any event, to constitute notice of a claim or defense, the purchaser must have knowledge of the claim or defense or knowledge of such facts that his action in taking the instrument amounts to bad faith.

§ 3–305. Rights of a Holder in Due Course

To the extent that a holder is a holder in due course he takes the instrument free from

(1) all claims to it on the part of any person; and

(2) all defenses of any party to the instrument with whom the holder has not dealt except

(*a*) infancy, to the extent that it is a defense to a simple contract; and

(*b*) such other incapacity, or duress, or illegality of the transaction, as renders the obligation of the party a nullity; and

(*c*) such misrepresentation as has induced the party to sign the instrument with neither knowledge nor reasonable opportunity to obtain knowledge of its character or its essential terms; and

(*d*) discharge in insolvency proceedings; and

(*e*) any other discharge of which the holder has notice when he takes the instrument.

§ 3–306. Rights of One Not Holder in Due Course

Unless he has the rights of a holder in due course any person takes the instrument subject to

(*a*) all valid claims to it on the part of any person; and

(*b*) all defenses of any party which would be available in an action on a simple contract; and

(*c*) the defenses of want or failure of consideration, non-performance of any condition precedent, non-delivery, or delivery for a special purpose (Section 3–408); and

(d) the defense that he or a person through whom he holds the instrument acquired it by theft, or that payment or satisfaction to such holder would be inconsistent with the terms of a restrictive indorsement. The claim of any third person to the instrument is not otherwise available as a defense to any party liable thereon unless the third person himself defends the action for such party.

§ 3–307. Burden of Establishing Signatures, Defenses and Due Course

(1) Unless specifically denied in the pleadings each signature on an instrument is admitted. When the effectiveness of a signature is put in issue

(a) the burden of establishing it is on the party claiming under the signature; but

(b) the signature is presumed to be genuine or authorized except where the action is to enforce the obligation of a purported signer who has died or become incompetent before proof is required.

(2) When signatures are admitted or established, production of the instrument entitles a holder to recover on it unless the defendant establishes a defense.

(3) After it is shown that a defense exists a person claiming the rights of a holder in due course has the burden of establishing that he or some person under whom he claims is in all respects a holder in due course.

§ 3–401. Signature

(1) No person is liable on an instrument unless his signature appears thereon.

(2) A signature is made by use of any name, including any trade or assumed name, upon an instrument, or by any word or mark used in lieu of a written signature.

§ 3–402. Signature in Ambiguous Capacity

Unless the instrument clearly indicates that a signature is made in some other capacity it is an indorsement.

§ 3–403. Signature by Authorized Representative

(1) A signature may be made by an agent or other representative, and his authority to make it may be established as in other cases of representation. No particular form of appointment is necessary to establish such authority.

(2) An authorized representative who signs his own name to an instrument

(a) is personally obligated if the instrument neither names the person represented nor shows that the representative signed in a representative capacity;

(b) except as otherwise established between the immediate parties, is personally obligated if the instrument names the person represented but does not show that the representative signed in a representative capacity, or if the instrument does not name the person represented but does show that the representative signed in a representative capacity.

(3) Except as otherwise established the name of an organization preceded or followed by the name and office of an authorized individual is a signature made in a representative capacity.

§ 3–404. Unauthorized Signatures

(1) Any unauthorized signature is wholly inoperative as that of the person whose name is signed unless he ratifies it or is precluded from denying it; but it operates as the signature of the unauthorized signer in favor of any person who in good faith pays the instrument or takes it for value.

(2) Any unauthorized signature may be ratified for all purposes of this Article. Such ratification does not of itself affect any rights of the person ratifying against the actual signer.

§ 3–405. Impostors; Signature in Name of Payee

(1) An indorsement by any person in the name of a named payee is effective if

(a) an impostor by use of the mails or otherwise has induced the maker or drawer to issue the instrument to him or his confederate in the name of the payee; or

(b) a person signing as or on behalf of a maker or drawer intends the payee to have no interest in the instrument; or

(c) an agent or employee of the maker or drawer has supplied him with the name of the payee intending the latter to have no such interest.

(2) Nothing in this section shall affect the criminal or civil liability of the person so indorsing.

§ 3–406. Negligence Contributing to Alteration or Unauthorized Signature

Any person who by his negligence substantially contributes to a material alteration of the instrument or to the making of an unauthorized signature is precluded from asserting the alteration or lack of authority against a holder in due course or against a drawee or other payor who pays the instrument in good faith and in accordance with the reasonable commercial standards of the drawee's or payor's business.

§ 3–407. Alteration

(1) Any alteration of an instrument is material which changes the contract of any party thereto in any respect, including any such change in

(a) the number or relations of the parties; or

(b) an incomplete instrument, by completing it otherwise than as authorized; or

(c) the writing as signed, by adding to it or by removing any part of it.

(2) As against any person other than a subsequent holder in due course

(a) alteration by the holder which is both fraudulent and material discharges any party whose contract is thereby changed unless that party assents or is precluded from asserting the defense;

(b) no other alteration discharges any party and the instrument may be enforced according to its original tenor, or as to incomplete instruments according to the authority given.

(3) A subsequent holder in due course may in all cases enforce the instrument according to its original tenor, and when an incomplete instrument has been completed, he may enforce it as completed.

§ 3–408. Consideration

Want or failure of consideration is a defense as against any person not having the rights of a holder in due course (Section 3-305), except that no consideration is necessary for an instrument or obligation thereon given in payment of or as security for an antecedent obligation of any kind. Nothing in this section shall be taken to displace any statute outside this Act under which a promise is enforceable notwithstanding lack or failure of consideration. Partial failure of consideration is a defense pro tanto whether or not the failure is in an ascertained or liquidated amount.

* * * *

§ 3–410. Definition and Operation of Acceptance

(1) Acceptance is the drawee's signed engagement to honor the draft as presented. It must be written on the draft, and may consist of his signature alone. It becomes operative when completed by delivery or notification.

(2) A draft may be accepted although it has not been signed by the drawer or is otherwise incomplete or is overdue or has been dishonored.

(3) Where the draft is payable at a fixed period after sight and the acceptor fails to date his acceptance the holder may complete it by supplying a date in good faith.

§ 3–411. Certification of a Check

(1) Certification of a check is acceptance. Where a holder procures certification the drawer and all prior indorsers are discharged.

(2) Unless otherwise agreed a bank has no obligation to certify a check.

(3) A bank may certify a check before returning it for lack of proper indorsement. If it does so the drawer is discharged.

* * * *

§ 3–413. Contract of Maker, Drawer and Acceptor

(1) The maker or acceptor engages that he will pay the instrument according to its tenor at the time of his engagement or as completed pursuant to Section 3–115 on incomplete instruments.

(2) The drawer engages that upon dishonor of the draft and any necessary notice of dishonor or protest he will pay the amount of the draft to the holder or to any indorser who takes it up. The drawer may disclaim this liability by drawing without recourse.

(3) By making, drawing or accepting the party admits as against all subsequent parties including the drawee the existence of the payee and his then capacity to indorse.

§ 3–414. Contract of Indorser; Order of Liability

(1) Unless the indorsement otherwise specifies (as by such words as "without recourse") every indorser engages that upon dishonor and any necessary notice of dishonor and protest he will pay the instrument according to its tenor at the time of his indorsement to the holder or to any subsequent indorser who takes it up, even though the indorser who takes it up was not obligated to do so.

(2) Unless they otherwise agree indorsers are liable to one another in the order in which they indorse, which is presumed to be the order in which their signatures appear on the instrument.

§ 3–415. Contract of Accommodation Party

(1) An accommodation party is one who signs the instrument in any capacity for the purpose of lending his name to another party to it.

(2) When the instrument has been taken for value before it is due the accommodation party is liable in the capacity in which he has signed even though the taker knows of the accommodation.

(3) As against a holder in due course and without notice of the accommodation oral proof of the accommodation is not admissible to give the accommodation party the benefit of discharges dependent on his character as such. In other cases the accommodation character may be shown by oral proof.

(4) An indorsement which shows that it is not in the chain of title is notice of its accommodation character.

(5) An accommodation party is not liable to the party accommodated, and if he pays the instrument has a right of recourse on the instrument against such party.

(6) An accommodation party warrants to any subsequent holder who is not the party accommodated and who takes the instrument in good faith that

(a) all signatures are genuine or authorized; and

(b) the instrument has not been materially altered; and

(c) all prior parties had capacity to contract; and

(d) he has no knowledge of any insolvency proceeding instituted with respect to the maker or acceptor or the drawer of an unaccepted instrument.

§ 3–416. Contract of Guarantor

(1) "Payment guaranteed" or equivalent words added to a signature mean that the signer engages that if the instrument is not paid when due he will pay it according to its tenor without resort by the holder to any other party.

(2) "Collection guaranteed" or equivalent words added to a signature mean that the signer engages that if the instrument is not paid when due he will pay it according to its tenor, but only after the holder has reduced his

claim against the maker or acceptor to judgment and execution has been returned unsatisfied, or after the maker or acceptor has become insolvent or it is otherwise apparent that it is useless to proceed against him.

(3) Words of guaranty which do not otherwise specify guarantee payment.

(4) No words of guaranty added to the signature of a sole maker or acceptor affect his liability on the instrument. Such words added to the signature of one of two or more makers or acceptors create a presumption that the signature is for the accommodation of the others.

(5) When words of guaranty are used presentment, notice of dishonor and protest are not necessary to charge the user.

(6) Any guaranty written on the instrument is enforceable notwithstanding any statute of frauds.

§ 3–417. Warranties on Presentment and Transfer

(1) Any person who obtains payment or acceptance and any prior transferor warrants to a person who in good faith pays or accepts that

(a) he has a good title to the instrument or is authorized to obtain payment or acceptance on behalf of one who has a good title; and

(b) he has no knowledge that the signature of the maker or drawer is unauthorized, except that this warranty is not given by a holder in due course acting in good faith
(i) to a maker with respect to the maker's own signature; or
(ii) to a drawer with respect to the drawer's own signature, whether or not the drawer is also the drawee; or
(iii) to an acceptor of a draft if the holder in due course took the draft after the acceptance or obtained the acceptance without knowledge that the drawer's signature was unauthorized; and

(c) the instrument has not been materially altered, except that this warranty is not given by a holder in due course acting in good faith
(i) to the maker of a note; or
(ii) to the drawer of a draft whether or not the drawer is also the drawee; or
(iii) to the acceptor of a draft with respect to an alteration made prior to the acceptance if the holder in due course took the draft after the acceptance, even though the acceptance provided "payable as originally drawn" or equivalent terms; or
(iv) to the acceptor of a draft with respect to an alteration made after the acceptance.

(2) Any person who transfers an instrument and receives consideration warrants to his transferee and if the transfer is by indorsement to any subsequent holder who takes the instrument in good faith that

(a) he has a good title to the instrument or is authorized to obtain payment or acceptance on behalf of one who has a good title and the transfer is otherwise rightful; and

(b) all signatures are genuine or authorized; and

(c) the instrument has not been materially altered; and

(*d*) no defense of any party is good against him; and

(*e*) he has no knowledge of any insolvency proceeding instituted with respect to the maker or acceptor or the drawer of an unaccepted instrument.

(3) By transferring "without recourse" the transferor limits the obligation stated in subsection (2) (d) to a warranty that he has no knowledge of such a defense.

(4) A selling agent or broker who does not disclose the fact that he is acting only as such gives the warranties provided in this section, but if he makes such disclosure warrants only his good faith and authority.

§ 3–418. Finality of Payment or Acceptance

Except for recovery of bank payments as provided in the Article on Bank Deposits and Collections (Article 4) and except for liability for breach of warranty on presentment under the preceding section, payment or acceptance of any instrument is final in favor of a holder in due course, or a person who has in good faith changed his position in reliance on the payment.

* * * *

§ 3–501. When Presentment, Notice of Dishonor, and Protest Necessary or Permissible

(1) Unless excused (Section 3–511) presentment is necessary to charge secondary parties as follows:

(*a*) presentment for acceptance is necessary to charge the drawer and indorsers of a draft where the draft so provides, or is payable elsewhere than at the residence or place of business of the drawee, or its date of payment depends upon such presentment. The holder may at his option present for acceptance any other draft payable at a stated date;

(*b*) presentment for payment is necessary to charge any indorser;

(*c*) in the case of any drawer, the acceptor of a draft payable at a bank or the maker of a note payable at a bank, presentment for payment is necessary, but failure to make presentment discharges such drawer, acceptor or maker only as stated in Section 3–502 (1) (b).

(2) Unless excused (Section 3–511)

(*a*) notice of any dishonor is necessary to charge any indorser;

(*b*) in the case of any drawer, the acceptor of a draft payable at a bank or the maker of a note payable at a bank, notice of any dishonor is necessary, but failure to give such notice discharges such drawer, acceptor or maker only as stated in Section 3–502 (1) (b).

(3) Unless excused (Section 3–511) protest of any dishonor is necessary to charge the drawer and indorsers of any draft which on its face appears to be drawn or payable outside of the states and territories of the United States and the District of Columbia. The holder may at his option make protest of any dishonor of any other instrument and in the case of a foreign draft may on insolvency of the acceptor before maturity make protest for better security.

(4) Notwithstanding any provision of this section, neither presentment nor notice of dishonor nor protest is necessary to charge an indorser who has indorsed an instrument after maturity.

§ 3–502. Unexcused Delay; Discharge

(1) Where without excuse any necessary presentment or notice of dishonor is delayed beyond the time when it is due

   (a) any indorser is discharged; and

   (b) any drawer or the acceptor of a draft payable at a bank or the maker of a note payable at a bank who because the drawee or payor bank becomes insolvent during the delay is deprived of funds maintained with the drawee or payor bank to cover the instrument may discharge his liability by written assignment to the holder of his rights against the drawee or payor bank in respect of such funds, but such drawer, acceptor or maker is not otherwise discharged.

(2) Where without excuse a necessary protest is delayed beyond the time when it is due any drawer or indorser is discharged.

§ 3–503. Time of Presentment

(1) Unless a different time is expressed in the instrument the time for any presentment is determined as follows:

   (a) where an instrument is payable at or a fixed period after a stated date any presentment for acceptance must be made on or before the date it is payable;

   (b) where an instrument is payable after sight it must either be presented for acceptance or negotiated within a reasonable time after date or issue whichever is later;

   (c) where an instrument shows the date on which it is payable presentment for payment is due on that date;

   (d) where an instrument is accelerated presentment for payment is due within a reasonable time after the acceleration;

   (e) with respect to the liability of any secondary party presentment for acceptance or payment of any other instrument is due within a reasonable time after such party becomes liable thereon.

(2) A reasonable time for presentment is determined by the nature of the instrument, any usage of banking or trade and the facts of the particular case. In the case of an uncertified check which is drawn and payable within the United States and which is not a draft drawn by a bank the following are presumed to be reasonable periods within which to present for payment or to initiate bank collection:

   (a) with respect to the liability of the drawer, thirty days after date or issue whichever is later; and

   (b) with respect to the liability of an endorser, seven days after his indorsement.

(3) Where any presentment is due on a day which is not a full business day for either the person making presentment or the party to pay or accept, presentment is due on the next following day which is a full business day for both parties.

(4) Presentment to be sufficient must be made at a reasonable hour, and if at a bank during its banking day.

§ 3–504. How Presentment Made

(1) Presentment is a demand for acceptance or payment made upon the maker, acceptor, drawee or other payor by or on behalf of the holder.

(2) Presentment may be made

(a) by mail, in which event the time of presentment is determined by the time of receipt of the mail; or

(b) through a clearing house; or

(c) at the place of acceptance or payment specified in the instrument or if there be none at the place of business or residence of the party to accept or pay. If neither the party to accept or pay nor anyone authorized to act for him is present or accessible at such place presentment is excused.

(3) It may be made

(a) to any one of two or more makers, acceptors, drawees or other payors; or

(b) to any person who has authority to make or refuse the acceptance or payment.

(4) A draft accepted or a note made payable at a bank in the United States must be presented at such bank.

(5) In the cases described in Section 4–210 presentment may be made in the manner and with the result stated in that section.

§ 3–505. Rights of Party to Whom Presentment Is Made

(1) The party to whom presentment is made may without dishonor require

(a) exhibition of the instrument; and

(b) reasonable identification of the person making presentment and evidence of his authority to make it if made for another; and

(c) that the instrument be produced for acceptance or payment at a place specified in it, or if there be none at any place reasonable in the circumstances; and

(d) a signed receipt on the instrument for any partial or full payment and its surrender upon full payment.

(2) Failure to comply with any such requirement invalidates the presentment but the person presenting has a reasonable time in which to comply and the time for acceptance or payment runs from the time of compliance.

§ 3–506. Time Allowed for Acceptance or Payment

(1) Acceptance may be deferred without dishonor until the close of the next business day following presentment. The holder may also in a good faith effort to obtain acceptance and without either dishonor of the instrument or discharge of secondary parties allow postponement of acceptance for an additional business day.

(2) Except as a longer time is allowed in the case of documentary drafts drawn under a letter of credit, and unless an earlier time is agreed to by the party to pay, payment of an instrument may be deferred without dishonor pending reasonable examination to determine whether it is properly payable, but payment must be made in any event before the close of business on the day of presentment.

§ 3–507. Dishonor; Holder's Right of Recourse; Term Allowing Re-Presentment

(1) An instrument is dishonored when

(a) a necessary or optional presentment is duly made and due acceptance or payment is refused or cannot be obtained within the prescribed time or in case of bank collections the instrument is seasonably returned by the midnight deadline (Section 4–301); or

(b) presentment is excused and the instrument is not duly accepted or paid.

(2) Subject to any necessary notice of dishonor and protest, the holder has upon dishonor an immediate right of recourse against the drawers and indorsers.

(3) Return of an instrument for lack of proper indorsement is not dishonor.

(4) A term in a draft or an indorsement thereof allowing a stated time for re-presentment in the event of any dishonor of the draft by nonacceptance if a time draft or by nonpayment if a sight draft gives the holder as against any secondary party bound by the term an option to waive the dishonor without affecting the liability of the secondary party and he may present again up to the end of the stated time.

§ 3–508. Notice of Dishonor

(1) Notice of dishonor may be given to any person who may be liable on the instrument by or on behalf of the holder or any party who has himself received notice, or any other party who can be compelled to pay the instrument. In addition an agent or bank in whose hands the instrument is dishonored may give notice to his principal or customer or to another agent or bank from which the instrument was received.

(2) Any necessary notice must be given by a bank before its midnight deadline and by any other person before midnight of the third business day after dishonor or receipt of notice of dishonor.

(3) Notice may be given in any reasonable manner. It may be oral or written and in any terms which identify the instrument and state that it has been dishonored. A misdescription which does not mislead the party notified does not vitiate the notice. Sending the instrument bearing a stamp, ticket or writing stating that acceptance or payment has been refused or sending a notice of debit with respect to the instrument is sufficient.

(4) Written notice is given when sent although it is not received.

(5) Notice to one partner is notice to each although the firm has been dissolved.

(6) When any party is in insolvency proceedings instituted after the issue of the instrument notice may be given either to the party or to the representative of his estate.

(7) When any party is dead or incompetent notice may be sent to his last known address or given to his personal representative.

(8) Notice operates for the benefit of all parties who have rights on the instrument against the party notified.

§ 3–509. Protest; Noting for Protest

(1) A protest is a certificate of dishonor made under the hand and seal of a United States consul or vice consul or a notary public or other person authorized to certify dishonor by the law of the place where dishonor occurs. It may be made upon information satisfactory to such person.

(2) The protest must identify the instrument and certify either that due presentment has been made or the reason why it is excused and that the instrument has been dishonored by nonacceptance or nonpayment.

(3) The protest may also certify that notice of dishonor has been given to all parties or to specified parties.

(4) Subject to subsection (5) any necessary protest is due by the time that notice of dishonor is due.

(5) If, before protest is due, an instrument has been noted for protest by the officer to make protest, the protest may be made at any time thereafter as of the date of the noting.

§ 3–510. Evidence of Dishonor and Notice of Dishonor

The following are admissible as evidence and create a presumption of dishonor and of any notice of dishonor therein shown:

(a) a document regular in form as provided in the preceding section which purports to be a protest;

(b) the purported stamp or writing of the drawee, payor bank or presenting bank on the instrument or accompanying it stating that acceptance or payment has been refused for reasons consistent with dishonor;

(c) any book or record of the drawee, payor bank, or any collecting bank kept in the usual course of business which shows dishonor, even though there is no evidence of who made the entry.

§ 3–511. Waived or Excused Presentment, Protest or Notice of Dishonor or Delay Therein

(1) Delay in presentment, protest or notice of dishonor is excused when the party is without notice that it is due or when the delay is caused by circumstances beyond his control and he exercises reasonable diligence after the cause of the delay ceases to operate.

(2) Presentment or notice or protest as the case may be is entirely excused when

(a) the party to be charged has waived it expressly or by implication either before or after it is due; or

(b) such party has himself dishonored the instrument or has countermanded payment or otherwise has no reason to expect or right to require that the instrument be accepted or paid; or

(c) by reasonable diligence the presentment or protest cannot be made or the notice given.

(3) Presentment is also entirely excused when

(a) the maker, acceptor or drawee of any instrument except a documentary draft is dead or in insolvency proceedings instituted after the issue of the instrument; or

(b) acceptance or payment is refused but not for want of proper presentment.

(4) Where a draft has been dishonored by nonacceptance a later presentment for payment and any notice of dishonor and protest for nonpayment are excused unless in the meantime the instrument has been accepted.

(5) A waiver of protest is also a waiver of presentment and of notice of dishonor even though protest is not required.

(6) Where a waiver of presentment or notice or protest is embodied in the instrument itself it is binding upon all parties; but where it is written above the signature of an indorser it binds him only.

* * * *

§ 3–602. Effect of Discharge Against Holder in Due Course

No discharge of any party provided by this Article is effective against a subsequent holder in due course unless he has notice thereof when he takes the instrument.

* * * *

§ 3–605. Cancellation and Renunciation

(1) The holder of an instrument may even without consideration discharge any party

(a) in any manner apparent on the face of the instrument or the indorsement, as by intentionally cancelling the instrument or the party's signature by destruction or mutilation, or by striking out the party's signature; or

(b) by renouncing his rights by a writing signed and delivered or by surrender of the instrument to the party to be discharged.

(2) Neither cancellation nor renunciation without surrender of the instrument affects the title thereto.

* * * *

§ 3–804. Lost, Destroyed or Stolen Instruments

The owner of an instrument which is lost, whether by destruction, theft or otherwise, may maintain an action in his own name and recover from any party liable thereon upon due proof of his ownership, the facts which prevent his production of the instrument and its terms. The court shall require security, in an amount fixed by the court not less than twice the amount allegedly unpaid on the instrument, indemnifying the defendant, his heirs, personal representatives, successors and assigns against loss, including costs and expenses, by reason of further claims on the instrument, but this provision does not apply where an action is prosecuted or defended by the state or by a public officer in its behalf.

§ 3–805. Instruments Not Payable to Order or to Bearer

This Article applies to any instrument whose terms do not preclude transfer and which is otherwise negotiable within this Article but which is not payable to order or to bearer, except that there can be no holder in due course of such an instrument.

GLOSSARY

acceptance   An agreement to enter into a contract under the terms of the offer.

accession   An increase in the value of property by the addition of new material or by the expense of labor in its improvement, and the owner's right to that increase in value.

accidentally   An event that occurs without anyone being at fault is said to happen accidentally.

accord   An agreement supported by new consideration to discharge an unfulfilled contract.

accord and satisfaction   The execution or performance of the accord constitutes satisfaction. This method of discharging a claim bars a suit.

acquittal   A finding of not guilty by judgment of the court.

Act for the Prevention of Fraud and Perjuries   A statute that seeks to prevent fraudulent contracts by requiring certain types of contracts to be in writing and signed by the participating parties. This act is commonly known as the statute of frauds.

active fraud   The intentional misrepresentation of important facts in order to propel others to take action that causes harm.

active ratification   An overt act by a minor that indicates the intention to honor a contract.

adhesion contracts   A preprinted contract that a consumer must accept or reject in its entirety.

administrator/administratrix   A man or woman appointed by the court to settle the estate of a deceased person.

administrative law judge   A person, usually an employee of a federal or state agency, who is empowered to render decisions in administrative hearings.

admission in pleadings   The acknowledgment in a formal statement of the terms of an oral contract for goods worth $500 or more, which then becomes legally binding.

adult   A man or woman who has reached legal age.

adverse possession   The legal acquisition of land through open, continuous, and exclusive possession of it for a statutorily mandated period of time.

agency by operation of law   The relationship of agent and principal that is derived from public policy rather than a formal agreement between the two parties.

agent   A person authorized to conduct business for another person, who is known as the principal.

aggravated battery   The harmful or offensive touching of another person causing serious injury, or an offense performed with a deadly weapon.

aggravated kidnapping   The unlawful confining, transporting, or hiding of a person for the purpose of obtaining a ransom, committing a sexual assault, or any other criminal purpose.

animals   A nonhuman, multicellular organism that is not a plant or fungus.

anti-injunction act   A statute that disallows injunctions in labor disputes except under special circumstances.

antitrust law   A federal or state statute that prevents the formation of monopolies or agreements in restraint of trade.

apparent authority   The presumption of authority retained by an agent after the agent's power to conduct business has been terminated and which continues to exist until all third parties have been notified.

appeal   The action of taking a case to a higher court to determine the validity of the judgment of a lower court.

appellate jurisdiction   The right of a court to hear cases on appeal to determine if there was any error in the application of the law.

appropriation of a person's name or likeness for commercial use   One of the four categories of action constituting invasion of privacy.

arson   A felony committed by maliciously burning down any structure belonging to another or one's own house with intent to defraud an insurer.

assault   The act of intentionally causing someone to fear that he or she is about to become the victim of battery, or an incompleted battery.

assignable rights   The benefits of a contract that can be transferred to a third party providing the assignment does not substantially change the burden to the obligor.

assignment of a lease   The transfer of all rights and responsibilities in a rental property to a third party for the full duration of a lease period.

assignment of contract   The practice of transferring rights under a contract from one or both parties to a third party.

assumption of risk   The rule that participating in a dangerous activity at one's own risk bars that person from suing for damages if an injury occurs.

attorney in fact   Any person who holds a power of attorney that authorizes her to act on another's behalf.

bailee   A person entrusted with the property of another.

bailment   The legal relationship that arises out of the temporary transfer of personal property for a specific purpose from one person to another.

bailment for the sole benefit of the bailee   A bailment in which the person entrusted with the property is the sole beneficiary.

bailment for the sole benefit of the bailor   A bailment in which the bailor alone benefits from entrusting his or her property to the bailee.

bailor   The person who entrusts his or her property into the care of another.

bank draft   A bill of exchange drawn by one bank on another bank.

bankruptcy   The proceedings by which a court legally declares a person or business unable to pay its debts and assumes control over all assets belonging to that person or business in order to distribute those assets to the creditors.

battery   The act of intentionally touching someone in a harmful or offensive manner without the person's consent.

bearer instrument   A negotiable instument that is payable to cash, to the bearer, or to no specific person.

beneficiary   The person for whom a trust is created, or the recipient of income or property from a will or an insurance policy.

bequest   A gift of personal property designated in a will.

bilateral contract   An agreement entered into by two parties who each promise to undertake some future action.

bill of attainder   A legislative act that confers punishment without a judicial trial.

bill of lading   A contract issued by a transportation agency listing the goods to be shipped, acknowledging their receipt and the method of delivery.

Bill of Rights   The first 10 amendments to the U.S. Constitution.

bill of sale   A written statement that attests to the transfer of property from one party to another.

blackmail   The act of obtaining or attempting to obtain property by threatening to disclose discrediting information.

blank indorsement   The payee's signing of the back of a note or draft without indicating to whom the draft or note is to be paid.

bona fide   A Latin term meaning in good faith. True.

breach   A failure to observe the terms of a contract.

bribery   The unlawful receipt of payment or anything of value in exchange for official action.

brief   The summary of arguments filed by a lawyer for the information of the court.

burglary   The act of breaking and entering any structure for the purpose of committing a crime.

business contract   A legal agreement relating to the buying and selling of goods and services.

business law   The regulations and statutes governing all aspects of commercial transactions.

capital   The net assets of a business.

capital felony   A crime punishable by death.

carrier   A person or company that transports goods.

carrier contracts   An agreement that states the terms by which goods are to be delivered by someone other than the seller.

cashier's check A draft drawn by a bank on itself.

casualty to identified goods The damage done to purchased goods that may nullify or alter the sales agreement depending on the extent of the damage.

caveat emptor A Latin phrase meaning let the buyer beware.

cease and desist An official order by a court or administrative agency to discontinue a practice.

centralized management The concentration of authority in a corporation represented by a board of directors elected by stockholders.

certificate of incorporation A certificate filed with the appropriate state agency listing the name, purpose, addresses, and other required information relating to a corporation.

certificate of deposit A note issued by a commercial bank or savings and loan association.

certified check A draft that is certified or guaranteed by the bank on which it is drawn.

chattels Personal property.

check A draft by a bank's depositor indicating a sum of money to be drawn on his or her account.

civil law A legal system based on written codes of behavior.

Civil Rights Act An act passed in 1964 outlawing discrimination against employees based on race, color, religion, national origin, or gender.

class A felony A crime punishable by maximum imprisonment of more than 15 years.

class A misdemeanor A crime punishable by a fine or imprisonment of six months to one year.

class B felony A crime punishable by imprisonment of 7 to 15 years.

class B misdemeanor A crime punishable by a fine or imprisonment of up to six months.

class C felony A crime punishable by imprisonment of one to seven years.

classification of crimes The division of crimes into categories according to their seriousness.

Clayton Act An act of Congress passed in 1914 to prevent unfair trade practices and, by doing so, to enhance competition.

closed shop The requirement that new employees be union members as a condition of employment.

closely held corporation A small, privately held corporation whose shares are not traded on any stock exchange.

code A body of laws or rules of conduct.

Code of Hammurabi A set of laws attributed to Hammurabi, a king of Babylon in the 18th century B.C.

commercial impracticability The condition that occurs when the performance of a contract becomes too difficult or too expensive to carry out.

commercial paper A written negotiable instrument that is either a note, draft, check, or certificate of deposit.

common law A system of laws based on common customs and traditions.

comparative negligence The practice in some states of allowing a plaintiff who is contributorily negligent to recover partial damages in a lawsuit.

compensatory damages A money award meant to provide restitution to the victim of a breach of contract.

computer crime An unlawful act committed by using a computer.

computerized legal research The method of conducting legal research using the commercial services of a legal data base.

conforming goods Goods of the type, quality, and condition deemed acceptable under the contract.

consideration Anything of legal value that induces parties to enter into a contract.

constructive notice The public notification of an agency's termination, accomplished by placing a legal notice to that effect in a newspaper of general circulation in the area the principal does business.

contempt of court The punishable act of showing disrespect for the authority and dignity of the court.

contract A legally enforceable promise between two or more people under which each receives some benefit.

contract for necessities A contract involving items deemed essential for a minor or dependent person.

contract involving the commission of a tort or a crime A contract that is unenforceable because it requires the commission of a crime.

contractual duties The work or service one is bound to accomplish in order to fulfill a contract.

contractual right The entitlement a party is to receive as consideration under a contract.

contributory negligence A plaintiff's partial responsibility for negligence that may invalidate his or her ability to sue for damages.

conversion A tort that permanently deprives another of the use or enjoyment of her or his personal property.

copyright The exclusive right of an author or publisher to the use of the author's material during the author's lifetime and continuing for an established period of time after the author's death.

Copyright Act of 1976 An act that mandates that an author's work automatically obtains a copyright when published with the word *copyright* or the letter *c* followed by the year published. Subsequent to this act being passed, it was no longer necessary to apply to the U.S. Copyright Office for copyright protection.

corporate bylaws An internal corporate code created and adopted by the corporation's board of directors.

corporate entity The quality of a corporation having a separate existence or becoming an artificial person in the eyes of the law.

corporate name The stated name of a corporation that must be different and unlike the names of other existing corporations so as not to confuse the public.

corporation A business organization that is a legal entity apart from the individuals who own and manage it.

corpus juris civilis A Latin phrase meaning "the body of the civil law," more commonly called the Justinian Code.

course of dealing The previous conduct by the parties of a contract, establishing a common basis of understanding for interpreting specific contract provisions and the conduct of the parties.

course of performance (practical construction) The provision in a contract for the sale of goods that requires repeated performance over a period of time.

court of appeals The federal or state intermediate courts that hear appeals of cases from lower courts and administrative agencies.

court of original jurisdiction The first court in which a case is tried.

covenant of quiet enjoyment The implied understanding in a rental agreement that the renter will be allowed to enjoy the rented property free from outside interference preventable by the landlord.

creating easements The use of one of four methods to establish access to one's land by the limited use of another's land.

creator of the trust The owner of the property that has been given in trust for another's benefit.

crime A violation of a local, state, or federal law.

crime against a person A violation of the law that results in harm or death of a person or persons.

crime against judicial procedure A violation of the law such as perjury and bribery that seeks to undermine the integrity of the legal process.

crime against property A crime that involves the unlawful taking or harming of property.

criminal law The system of determining guilt and punishing people for crimes against society.

criminal motive The reason for committing a crime, but which is not an element of the crime under the law.

criteria for defining commercial paper The conditions under which a note, draft, check, or certificate of deposit is deemed legal under the Uniform Commercial Code.

damages The money collected as compensation for injury, loss, or illegal action.

death or incapacity The condition by which a contract for personal services is discharged, namely the death or physical incapacity of the person who was to fulfill the contract.

decedent A person who has died with or without a valid will.

deed A legal document by which the owner of property holds or conveys title to that land.

defamation A tort arising from a published false statement about someone that causes harm to his or her reputation.

default The failure to perform a duty or appear in court when required.

defendant The party accused in a court of law.

defense The arguments brought by the defendant and his or her lawyer in justification of his or her actions.

defense of property The act of protecting one's property. Defense of property is allowed under law by using reasonable but not deadly force.

defenses to criminal liability The arguments by the defense that either the crime was not committed by the defendant or that the defendant was not capable of criminal intent.

defenses to negligence The circumstances that avoid or reduce liability, namely contributory negligence, comparative negligence, and assumption of risk.

delegable duties The duties required to fulfill a contract that may legally be transferred to another person.

delegatee The person who agrees to assume the performance of the obligor's duties on his or her behalf.

delegatee's duties The contractual duties that the delegatee agrees to perform for the obligor.

delegator The original obligor under a contract who assigns his or her performance to a third party.

delegator's duties The obligation of the original obligor to ensure that the delegatee has fulfilled all the requirements of the contract.

delivery The transfer of goods or documents to another's possession.

deposition The recorded testimony of a witness taken under oath outside of court in preparation for a trial.

destination contract A contract involving delivery of goods with a provision stating that the seller is responsible for loss of those goods until delivery is made, whereupon the risk passes to buyer.

devise   A gift of real property by will.

devisee   A person who receives property under a will.

disaffirmance   The exercise of a minor's right to invalidate any contract in which he or she is involved.

discharge of contract   The satisfaction or performance of the duties of a contract or any other circumstances that release both parties from the contract.

district court   The federal trial court in each U.S. district.

domicile   A person's home or the state in which a corporation was incorporated.

dominant tenement   The land benefiting from an easement.

donative intent   The requirement in law that a donor's motive for making a gift be detached, disinterested generosity and that the donor be mentally competent.

draft   An unconditional written, signed order by the drawer that the drawee pay a certain sum of money to the payee.

duress   The use of force or compulsion.

Durham Rule   A rule of law also known as the New Hampshire Rule; it stipulates that a defendant cannot be found guilty if he or she establishes that the crime was the product of a mental illness or defect.

duty of care   The responsibility not to infringe on another's rights by either intentionally or carelessly causing him or her harm.

easement   The right to use the land of another for a specific, limited purpose, such as access to one's own land.

easement by express grant   An easement executed and recorded in a deed.

easement by implication   An easement that is not specifically noted in the deed but is created by the necessity of an easement to reach the land.

easement by prescription   An easement that comes into effect by the use of another's land openly, exclusively, and continuously for an extended period of time, usually 20 years.

easement by reservation   An easement created when the original owner of the land reserves the right to use his or her land, after its sale, for a specific purpose.

easement in gross   The right to use part or all of another's land for a specific purpose unrelated to the use of adjoining or other land.

election of remedies   The necessity that the victim of a breach of contract choose the remedy when more than one type of compensation for the breach is available.

elements of a crime   The two essential components that determine whether or not a crime has been committed. These are that an illegal physical act or wrongful

omission has been committed and that there was a wrongful state of mind or intent to commit the crime.

embezzlement   The conversion or improper use of another's property that is lawfully in one's possession.

eminent domain   The right of government to take private property for public use and compensate the owner for the reasonable value of that land.

Employees Retirement Income Security Act (ERISA)   An act passed in 1974 that requires employers who provide pension plans to protect their employee's fiduciary interests and make periodic reports on pension funds to the secretary of labor.

endorsement   *See* indorsement, which is the preferred legal term.

enforceable agreement   A legal contract between two or more parties.

entrapment   The act of convincing or manipulating someone into committing a crime in order to arrest that person for the crime.

equal dignities rule   The requirement that agents receive a signed statement of authority from a principal for any action requiring that agent's signature to an agreement.

equitable   A term meaning just, fair, or proper.

estate   The real and personal property belonging to a person. The quality of interest one has in property.

estoppel   The prevention of someone from affirming or denying a fact if it is contrary to that person's previous affirmation or denial.

eviction   The expulsion or removal of a tenant from one's premises by legal procedure.

evidence   The objects or written statements of witnesses that are presented to the court to make clear a point of fact or argument.

executed contract   An agreement that has been completed to the satisfaction of both parties.

executor/executrix   A man or woman designated in a will to carry out the terms of a will.

executory contract   A contract that has not yet been fully performed by both parties.

express contract   An actual agreement between the parties either orally or in writing.

express warranty   A seller's guarantee that goods will be as represented.

extortion   The use of threats to obtain property.

ex post facto   A Latin phrase meaning retroactively.

ex post facto law   A law exacting punishment for past conduct that was previously legal.

fact pattern   A brief synopsis of the essential facts of the case.

fair employment practice acts The laws passed to prevent discrimination in employment due to race, religion, national origin, or gender.

Fair Labor Standards Act A federal act that set a minimum wage, maximum 40-hour workweek for industries engaging in interstate commerce; it also prohibited labor of children under 16 in most employments and under 18 in dangerous occupations.

fair use doctrine The provision in copyright law that allows individuals to copy parts of copyrighted material strictly for their own use.

false imprisonment The intentional and unjustifiable act of preventing someone from moving about.

family court A court in which matters pertaining to families are adjudicated.

Federal Trade Commission (FTC) The agency created by an act of 1914 that is empowered to prevent unfair competition and unfair or deceptive trade practices. By subsequent amendments, the FTC has the power to investigate federal antitrust statute violations, define unfair trade practices, and issue cease and desist orders.

Federal Trade Commission Act of 1914 The statute that created the Federal Trade Commission.

fee simple The absolute ownership of property.

felony The most serious type of crime, punishable by more than one year in prison.

fiduciary relationship A relationship based on trust.

fixtures The things permanently attached to land.

forbearance and adequacy of consideration The first term, forbearance, refers to an agreement to refrain from doing a legal act for a period of time. Adequacy of consideration refers to the fairness of the amount paid for the goods or service rendered. However, if the amount of the consideration has been agreed upon, it can only be a judicial issue if it involves a fraudulent claim.

forgery The fraudulent writing or altering of any document that has legal significance.

formal contract A written or oral agreement that follows a specific form and must be signed or witnessed.

fraud An intentional misrepresentation that occurs when one person makes a false statement about an important fact to induce another to take action that causes harm.

fraud in the execution A misrepresentation that makes the innocent party unaware he or she is entering into a contract.

fraud in the inducement A misrepresentation concerning the subject matter of the contract.

frustration of purpose The instance of an unforeseeable event that makes the completion of the contract pointless and therefore allows the contract to be discharged.

fungible goods Goods that are homogeneous in nature and that can be divided into interchangeable units of the same grade, for example grain or gasoline.

future interests The nonpossessory interests in real property that can become possessory interests in the future upon a given event.

FOB and FAS shipping contracts The first term, FOB, stands for free on board and refers to the obligation of the buyer to pay freight charges. FAS stands for free along side and refers to the obligation of the buyer to pay loading and transportation fees on any goods received.

general partner A man or woman who is active in a business in which he or she has full responsibility and shares in its profits and risks.

general partnership A partnership of fully shared ownership and liability in which each partner shares the responsibility of management.

general warranty deed A deed in which the property is free from outside claims, guaranteeing clear title to the grantee.

genuine assent An agreement to a contract by an adult of sound mind with full knowledge of the terms and nature of the contract.

gift causa mortis A gift made in anticipation of impending death that is revokable if death does not occur.

gifts The transfer of properties and the interest in those properties to another out of detached and disinterested generosity.

gifts made in contemplation of death *See* gift causa mortis.

goods Tangible, movable objects that can be owned.

grantor The owner of the property given over into trust for another's benefit.

holder A person possessing an order instrument that names him or her as payee or a person possessing a bearer instrument.

holder in due course A person who takes a negotiable instrument for value, in good faith, and without knowledge that it has been dishonored, is overdue, or has any claims against it.

homicide The unjustified taking of a human life.

illusory promise A promise in a contract that does not obligate action.

implied contract A contract formed from persons' actions rather than from words or writing.

impossibility of performance The physical inability to fulfill a contract.

impracticability of performance The provision in some states that allows a contract to be discharged if it is too expensive or too difficult to carry out, providing the difficulty or expense was unforeseen.

in the heat of passion The qualification of a crime of violence that is committed during rage and therefore not premeditated.

incidental beneficiary A third party to a contract who is not a primary beneficiary but who benefits economically.

incorporators A person who files a certificate of incorporation that meets the legal requirements of the state in which the business is incorporated.

indorsing The act of signing one's name as payee on a negotiable instrument.

indorsement The signature of the payee on a negotiable instrument, in order to further negotiate.

infancy The state of being considered too young to be liable for criminal activity. The age varies from one jurisdiction to another. Most states consider children under 14 to be incapable of framing the necessary intent to commit a crime.

injunction An order from the court prohibiting an activity.

innocent trespasser A person who takes or uses property in good faith not realizing it belongs to another, or one who innocently wanders onto another's land.

insanity A mental condition that prevents a person from making reasonable decisions or understanding the consequences of his or her own actions.

instrument A formal document.

insurable interest The acquisition of sufficient interest in goods under contract to make them insurable against damage or loss by the buyer.

intangible personal property Personal property that cannot be touched, for example, a copyright.

intended beneficiary A party whom a contract expressly names as beneficiary.

intent The purpose of the person committing an act.

intentional With purpose, deliberate.

intentional infliction of emotional distress The willful infliction of suffering through outrageous, extreme behavior.

intentional tort The willful infringement on another's rights that causes injury.

intentional tort against a person A willful act against a person that causes them personal injury.

intentional tort against property A willful act that results in the intrusion on or violation of the ownership of one's property.

inter vivos A Latin term meaning between the living.

inter vivos trust A trust established during the grantor's lifetime.

intestate The condition of a person who dies without leaving a legal will.

intoxication The state of a person who is under the influence of drugs or alcohol and is incapable of making competent decisions.

intrusion into a person's seclusion The willful invasion of a person's right of privacy.

invasion of privacy A tort that involves one or more of four categories: appropriation of another's name for commercial use, intrusion into a person's seclusion, placing a person in false light, or public disclosure of private facts.

involuntary intoxication The state of inebriation that occurs when a person is forced to take or takes by accident drugs or alcohol.

involuntary manslaughter A death resulting from a criminally negligent act or a killing that occurs during the commission of a misdemeanor.

irresistible impulse A provision of defense by insanity that describes the inability to refrain from committing a crime.

joint tenancy The ownership of land in common with another person with the provision that when one person dies, the other inherits full ownership.

judge A person who is appointed or elected to hear and decide cases in a court of law.

judicial review The power of a court to interpret and rule on statutes enacted by such bodies as Congress and state and local legislatures.

jurisdiction The authority of a court to hear and decide cases brought before it.

justice of the peace court A lower court of limited jurisdiction where minor criminal offenses are adjudicated.

Justinian Code The code of ancient civil laws consolidated by the Byzantine Emperor Justinian I around 533 A.D.

juvenile court A court that has authority to hear cases involving minors.

kidnapping The act of unlawfully detaining, transporting, or hiding a person against his or her will.

Labor-Management Relations Act of 1947 The act that amended the National Labor Relations Act to include provisions protecting employers from unfair labor practices of unions. Also known as the Taft-Hartley Act.

Labor-Management Reporting and Disclosure Act of 1959 The act that set regulations for internal procedures of unions such as elections. Also known as the Landrum-Griffin Act.

lack of capacity   The inability of minors, mental incompetents, and intoxicated persons to give full assent in a contractual agreement.

landlord   The person who owns property leased to another.

landlord's responsibilities   The duties of a landlord to exercise reasonable care, to provide necessary services for her or his tenants, and to maintain the property in habitable condition.

landlord's rights   The rights of a landlord, for example, to receive the agreed-upon rent, to be notified of damage to his or her property, and any other rights designated by contract between the landlord and his or her tenants.

Landrum-Griffin Act   *See* Labor-Management Reporting and Disclosure Act of 1959.

larceny   The taking and carrying away of the property of another by theft or fraud.

law   A rule of conduct established and enforced by a governmental body.

lease   A contract between a landlord and tenant specifying the terms by which a tenant may use the landlord's property and the payment due for such use.

legacy   The property designated in a will to be transferred to another's ownership.

legal duty   The obligation of all persons to respect the rights of others as specified by law.

legality   The quality of conforming with existing laws.

lessee   A tenant or person leasing property.

lessor   The owner of property leased to another. Synonymous with landlord.

liability of indorser   The responsibility of the person who indorses a negotiable instrument to honor payment of it if not honored by the drawee or maker.

liability without fault   The responsibility under tort law for a person to pay damages even though he or she has not intentionally caused harm. This liability generally occurs in three categories: damage done by wild animals, damage done by defective products, or damage occurring because of ultrahazardous activities.

libel   A written false statement about someone that causes harm to that person's reputation.

life estate   An ownership interest in realty that lasts only for a person's lifetime.

life insurance   A system of protection from loss by which a person contracts to make regular payments to a company in return for a stipulated sum of money to be paid to a named beneficiary upon the death of insured.

life tenant   A person who owns an interest in realty that lasts for his or her lifetime.

limitations on statutes creating new crimes   The constitutionally mandated rules that govern the creation of new crimes by Congress and state legislatures. They include the following mandates: any conduct to be labeled criminal must be specific and understandable to the general public, laws may not be retroactive, laws may not punish without trial, and laws may not contradict the U.S. Constitution.

limited partnership   The participation of a person in a business under an agreement that limits both his or her management role and liability for the debts of the business.

litigation   The act of carrying out a lawsuit.

locus sigilli   A Latin phrase meaning in place of seal. Some states allow any mark, the word *seal,* or the letters L.S. (for locus sigilli) to be used in place of a seal on a formal contract.

lost property   Personal goods that are missing.

majority   1. The greater part of the total number. 2. The condition of having reached full legal age.

malice   Evil intent.

malpractice   The misconduct or unprofessional treatment by someone in a professional or official position.

merchant   A person who makes her or his living in the buying and selling of goods.

merchantable   The condition of goods meeting the criteria that allows them to be sold, namely that they are not contrary to the contract description; that, if fungible, they are of fair or average quality; that they are fit for the purposes for which they are intended; and that they are properly labeled and conform to factual descriptions on the label.

merchant's firm offer   An offer of a set price for goods, which is written and signed by a merchant and irrevocable for the period of time specified in the offer or, if no specific period is stated, for a reasonable time. The maximum duration of a firm offer is three months under the Uniform Commercial Code.

minor   A person who has not yet reached full legal age.

minor's contract   A contract entered into by a person who has not reached legal age. In most states, such a contract is voidable at the minor's option.

mirror image rule   The provision in common law that an acceptance of a contract is valid only if the contract reflects the offer exactly.

misdemeanor   A type of crime less serious than a felony, punishable by a fine or imprisonment of up to one year; examples are prostitution and disorderly conduct.

model penal code test   The test for insanity adopted by the American Law Institute that determines if the defendant suffers from mental disease preventing her or him from distinguishing between right and wrong or from conforming to the law; if so determined, insanity excuses criminal conduct.

money order   An instrument issued for a fee by a bank or post office stating that the payee is to be paid a specified sum of money.

murder   The unjustified and premeditated killing of another human being with malice.

mutual benefit bailment   A bailment where both the bailor and the bailee receive some tangible benefit.

mutual mistake   A mistake made by both parties to a contract that prevents the contract from being formed.

M'Naughten Rule   The rule of law stating that a defendant who suffers from a mental disease that prevented her or him at the time of the crime from understanding the wrongfulness of her or his actions is excused from criminal liability.

National Conference of Commissioners on Uniform State Laws   The commissioners who drafted the Uniform Commercial Code to unify state laws affecting commerce into a single code that all states could accept.

National Labor Relations Act of 1932   The act that established the National Labor Relations Board and gave employees the right to engage in collective bargaining and to strike. Also known as the Wagner Act.

National Labor Relations Board   The national board established by the National Labor Relations Act to oversee union elections and prevent unfair labor practices by employers.

necessaries   Essential commodities such as food, clothing, shelter, and medical care.

necessity   *See* necessaries.

negligence   The failure to act with reasonable care that results in harming others.

negotiable instrument   *See* commercial paper.

negotiation   The formal name given to the legal transfer of ownership from one holder to another.

New Hampshire rule   *See* the Durham rule.

nominal damages   An award of damages in name only, usually one dollar.

nonconforming goods   Goods that are defective or that do not conform to the contract describing them.

nonfreehold   A nonpossessory interest in land that gives its holder the right to use the land but no ownership interest in it.

nonpossessory interest in land   *See* nonfreehold.

Norris-LaGuardia Act of 1932   The act that gave employees the right to engage in peaceful strikes, picketing, and/or boycotts.

note   An unconditional promise to pay a certain sum of money to a named payee or bearer, payable on a specific date or on demand.

novation   An obligee's agreement to allow a delegatee to perform a contract in circumstances under which a delegation would not otherwise be allowed.

nuisance   An action or thing that endangers, annoys, or harms people.

nuncupative will   An oral will, recognized under certain circumstances in many states.

objective impossibility of performance   The requirement that the excuse of impossibility of performance used to discharge a contract can be judged objectively rather than subjectively.

obligation   An agreement by which one person is bound to make payment or provide services to another.

obligee   The person to whom the obligor owes a duty of performance under a contract.

obligor   The person required to perform under a contract.

obstruction of justice   An action that leads to interference with the administration of justice, such as bribery of public officials, influence peddling, or jury tampering.

obtaining a property interest   The procuring of interest in personal property either by the purchase or manufacture of the property.

Occupational Safety and Health Act of 1970 (OSHA)   The act that ensured employees a safe work environment by establishing safety standards and creating a mechanism for their enforcement.

offer   An invitation to another to enter into a contract.

offer and acceptance of the sales contract   An offer may be accepted by any reasonable means unless the method of acceptance is specifically stated in the offer or the circumstances dictate acceptance in a specific manner.

operation of law   The principles of law that supercede contracts, behavior, or transactions between parties without the active participation of the parties involved.

order paper   A negotiable instrument payable to the order of a specific person or company.

ordinance   A regulation or law usually passed by a municipality.

original jurisdiction   The authority of a court to hear a case at its inception.

ownership of stolen property The ownership of stolen property remains with the true owner from whom the property was originally stolen, regardless of how many times the property is transferred.

parol evidence Oral evidence.

parol evidence rule A rule stating that once parties have set down the terms of their agreement in writing, no oral evidence may be used to modify or change the terms of the written agreement unless fraud, duress, or mistake at the time of the writing is alleged.

parole A release from prison conditional upon certain behavior.

partner One of two or more persons who together own and/or manage a business.

partnership An association of two or more competent persons who carry on a business as co-owners for profit.

partnership agreement A contract stipulating the terms of a partnership. This contract can be oral, written, or even implied by the actions of the parties over a period of time.

partnership dissolution The termination of a partnership, which may occur because of the desire of any one partner, at a specified date, upon a given event, or by operation of law.

partnership formation An agreement between two or more persons to join together for the purpose of operating a business.

passive fraud The act of participating in a misrepresentation by failing to speak the truth when one has a duty to speak because of a relationship of trust.

passive ratification The ratification of a contract involving a minor that occurs automatically after a reasonable period of time has passed once the minor has reached the age of consent, unless the minor takes action to disaffirm the contract.

past consideration The previous performance that is used as the basis for a contract. Generally, contracts based on past consideration are unenforceable because there is no present value in such services.

patent An exclusive right issued to an inventor by the Patent and Trademark Office to profit from his or her invention for 17 years.

payee The person to whom an instrument is made payable.

per capita The proviso in a will to equally distribute property to the named surviving beneficiaries.

per stirpes The proviso in a will to distribute property equally among the testator's children; if any child dies before the testator, that child's share passes to his or her descendants.

performance The execution of one's obligations under a contract.

periodic tenancy The contracted occupancy of another's property that continues for a specific period of time, at the end of which it is automatically renewed unless either the tenant or owner gives proper notice of his or her wish to terminate the tenancy.

perjury The act of willfully or maliciously taking a false oath in regard to a material fact in a judicial proceeding.

personal jurisdiction The authority of a court over the person of a defendant as opposed to over his or her property.

personal property Anything capable of being owned, whether tangible or intangible, other than real estate.

piercing of the corporate veil A court's act of ignoring the existence of a dummy corporation to hold the creator of the dummy corporation liable.

placing a person in a false light The act of assigning socially unfavorable attributes to a person or claiming that a person has taken actions he or she has not taken.

plaintiff A person who brings an action in a court.

pleadings The formal statements made to the court regarding claims, allegations, or defenses.

possession of personal property The holding of property, which by itself does not convey to the holder good title or ownership rights.

possessory interests in land The varying degrees of ownership of real estate, ranging from an absolute right to use and dispose of land to qualified interests.

preexisting duty A performance that one was obligated to execute prior to the formation of a contract.

principal The person on whose behalf an agent acts.

product liability The manufacturers and retailers of commercial products may be held responsible for damage done by products they make and/or sell if the products are so defective as to be unreasonably dangerous to intended users. Products that by their nature are hazardous, such as guns or razor blades, are excluded from this liability unless defects make them unpredictably dangerous.

profit 1. A nonpossessory right in real estate giving the holder the privilege of entering another's land to remove something such as soil or water. 2. A benefit or gain.

promisee The person to whom the promise is made.

promisor The person making the promise.

promissory note *See* note.

prosecution The initiation of legal proceedings against a person.

provisions for acceptance The requirement that for an

acceptance to be valid it must be made by the offeree, be unequivocal, and be communicated to the offeror.

provisions for revocation   The rule under contract law that an offeror can revoke an offer any time before it is accepted, but once an offeree accepts the offer, it cannot be revoked except with the consent of both parties.

proxy   1. A person who has been given the authority to act for another. 2. A written authorization allowing one stockholder to vote for another.

public disclosure of private facts   The publishing of facts about someone that a reasonable person would find objectionable, for example, publishing that an adult is a bed wetter. *See* invasion of privacy.

public corporation   A corporation created for the administration of public affairs.

public domain   The state of being free from copyright or patent and therefore available for anyone's use.

public figure   A person who is well known.

pure comparative negligence   The provision in some states that parties who are more than 50 percent negligent may recover damages according to the percentage of their fault. Thus, if it is determined that a party is 90 percent negligent, she or he may recover 10 percent of the damages suffered.

quasi contract   An obligation for performance similar to that made under a contract and enforceable as if by contract.

quitclaim deed   A deed or other legal paper by which a person gives up whatever property right he has to specific property to another.

rape   The act of forced sexual intercourse with a woman by a man, not her husband, without her effective consent, or if the act is committed while the woman is drugged, underage, or overcome by duress or threats.

ratification   A person or group's formal consent or approval of a previously unauthorized action on its behalf.

real defense   A defense that is effective against all parties, including holders in due course of negotiable instruments.

real property   The same as real estate. Real property consists of land, the buildings on it, and the natural assets of the land, such as minerals or water.

recording statute   The requirement that all transfers of real property be recorded with the proper authorities to protect the rights of the grantee. Thus, in the case of the same property being sold to two different persons, the one who recorded the title first would be the true owner.

reform   A judicial order to change a contract to eliminate an illegal provision.

release   An agreement not to sue that serves to discharge a contract, provided the agreement is supported by new consideration.

remainder   A future or residuary interest in an estate, such as land, that is conveyed to party A during his or her lifetime, which then devolves to party B or his or her heirs after party A's death.

remedies for breach   The compensatory damages or specific performance that seek to return the injured party to the position he or she was in before the breach occurred.

rent   The money paid to a landlord for the use of leased property or to contract for the use of another's property.

renunciation of authority   The act of an agent terminating his agency relationship.

requirement contract   An agreement under which the promisor agrees to purchase whatever quantity of a product he will need either over a period of time or to complete a specific job. For example, a gasoline station owner agreeing to purchase from a particular supplier all the gasoline he needs during a six-month period.

rescission   A mutual agreement to nullify a binding contract, provided the parties have freely entered into it.

residuary interest   *See* future interests.

restraint of trade   The unlawful practices that limit the free market, such as unfair competition, price-fixing, or monopolies.

Retirement Equity Act of 1984   The act that permits an employee to leave the work force for up to five consecutive years and still retain eligibility for pension rights. The act also stipulates that an employee's spouse who is eligible for benefits must sign a waiver before the employee may give up the survivor's annuity option that the act requires.

reversion   The return of an estate to the grantor or his or her heirs after the period of the grant is over.

revocation of authority   The termination of the agency relationship by the principal.

right of survivorship   The right of a tenant in a joint tenancy to inherit ownership of the land in the event the other tenant dies.

right to petition   The right to ask the court to make a judgment, for example, a joint tenant's right to ask the court to partition or divide up land among the different owners.

risk of loss   The determination of who is liable for the loss or damage of goods between the time a contract is set up and when the goods are delivered to the buyer. The Uniform Commercial Code has set out guidelines defining when the buyer, carrier, or seller is liable.

robbery The taking of another's property by force or threat of force with the intention of permanently depriving its owner of it.

Robinson-Patman Act of 1936 An act passed as a supplement to the Clayton Antitrust Act that prohibits businesses from discriminating in the price charged to buyers of goods of similar grade and quality when that discrimination lessens competition. Price differentials are allowed if the seller can prove the difference is due to shipping costs or a good faith attempt to meet a competitor's lower price. The act also allows injured businesses to sue for three times the amount of their actual losses.

sale The transfer of goods from a seller to a buyer in exchange for consideration, usually money.

satisfaction The settlement or discharge of a debt or obligation.

scienter A Latin term meaning knowingly.

seal A mark traditionally made by a signet ring on sealing wax that identifies the document as belonging to a particular person; currently, any mark or symbol adopted by a company or individual.

self-defense The use of reasonable force to protect oneself against another's aggression.

seller's obligations The duty of a seller to tender conforming goods; when delivery is specified, it must be made with sufficient notice and at a reasonable hour.

servient tenement A piece of land burdened by an easement.

settlor of a trust A person who creates a trust.

Sherman Antitrust Act of 1890 The act that made it a felony to enter into contracts that result in the restraint of trade among the states or with foreign countries. The act also makes it a felony to monopolize or attempt to monopolize any part of interstate or international trade or commerce. It allows civil remedies to individuals for injury by illegal antitrust activities, namely the ability to sue for three times the actual damages.

shipment by seller through carrier An agreement by a seller to ship goods through a carrier, who then discharges the seller's duties under the contract.

simple battery A misdemeanor consisting of the harmful or offensive touching of a person.

simple contract An oral or written agreement that does not follow a specific form.

slander The act of making a false statement about someone that tends to harm the person's reputation. Slander is spoken as opposed to libel, which is written.

small claims court A court that hears civil cases involving small dollar amounts, typically not exceeding $5,000.

Social Security Act of 1935 The federal act that created a mechanism to provide old-age, unemployment, and/or disability insurance for most employees.

sources of the law The statutes passed by bodies such as the U.S. Congress and state legislatures, decisions handed down by federal and state judges, and regulations and administrative decisions of state and federal agencies.

specially manufactured goods Goods made to an individual's specifications, therefore not suitable for general sale. Oral contracts for specially manufactured goods are fully enforceable regardless of price.

specific performance The requirement, decreed by a court of equity, for performance of the exact terms of a contract.

statute of frauds *See* Act for the Prevention of Fraud and Perjuries.

statutes The laws enacted by a legislative body.

statutory rape The act of engaging in sexual intercourse with a woman under the age of consent.

stock The shares of ownership in a corporation or the certificates of ownership representing them.

stockholder A person who has an ownership interest in a corporation.

strict liability *See* liability without fault.

strike The refusal of employees to work in order to compel their employer to grant them certain benefits.

subchapter S corporations The Internal Revenue Code classification of small businesses that allows them to avoid paying corporate taxes. To qualify for this status, businesses must comply with specific conditions enumerated in the IRS code.

subject matter jurisdiction The authority of a court to hear a certain type of case, for example, traffic court, family court.

sublease The lease by a tenant to a third party of a part of a rental property or of the entire rental property for a part of the tenant's lease period.

subpoena An order from the court to appear as a witness.

substituted performance The requirement that a seller provide a commercially reasonable substitute for the transportation of goods if the agreed-upon method becomes unavailable. The buyer must agree to the substitution, providing the failure of the original transportation method has occurred through no fault of the seller.

supernumerary In excess of the usually required or necessary number, such as an extra witness to a will.

Supreme Court The highest court in most states or the federal government. The Supreme Court of the United States makes final decisions on all cases it hears, and its decisions take precedence over those made by any other court.

surrogate court   The court where matters relating to trusts and estates are heard.

Taft-Hartley Act   *See* the Labor-Management Relations Act of 1947.

tangible personal property   A person's personal property that has a physical existence and can be touched, for example, a car or a book.

tenancy   The property occupied by a renter, the amount of time a renter occupies the property, or the possession of lands by any type of title.

tenancy at sufferance   The condition of a tenant who remains in possession of property at the expiration of the tenancy without the landlord's consent.

tenancy at will   A tenancy agreement in which the tenancy can be terminated at any time without previous notice either at the tenant's will or the landlord's.

tenancy by the entirety   A form of joint tenancy reserved for property owned by husbands and wives. This form, which is recognized in fewer than half of the states, requires that consent of both husband and wife be obtained before the property can be transferred.

tenancy for years   A contractual agreement in which the landowner gives a tenant the right to occupy and use the realty for a set period in exchange for consideration such as rent.

tenancy from term to term   *See* periodic tenancy.

tenancy in common   A tenant agreement in which each tenant owns a proportionate interest in the land. Each tenant can transfer his or her right in the land to anyone else during his or her lifetime or by will upon his or her death.

tenant   The person who rents or leases land from a landlord. Also known as a lessee.

tenant's responsibilities   The duties of a tenant to pay the agreed-upon rent, to make minor repairs, and to notify the landlord of any damage to the property. The tenant may also be responsible for additional duties specified in the rental agreement.

tenant's rights   A tenant has the right to occupy property that is habitable and free from dangerous defects and to enjoy such occupancy free from outside interference preventable by the landlord.

term tenancy   *See* tenancy for years.

testamentary trust   A trust set up after the grantor's death through provisions made in a will.

testate   The condition of a person who has died with a legal will.

testator/testatrix   The maker of a will.

third-party beneficiary   A person other than the prin-

cipal parties to a contract who stands to benefit from it.

tort feasor   A person who is guilty of a tort.

tort   A wrongful act not involving a breach of contract that infringes on the rights of another either intentionally or carelessly and causes harm.

totten trust   A trust set up by a depositor who deposits money in a bank account in her or his own name as trustee for a third-party beneficiary. During the grantor's lifetime, this trust is revocable at any time; but upon the grantor's death, the beneficiary is entitled to the trust corpus.

trademark   A symbol, graphic image, word, or name attached to a manufacturer's product that distinguishes it from similar products on the market.

traffic court   A lower court where traffic violations are adjudicated.

trespass   The unlawful invasion of another's rights, person, or property.

trespass to land   An intentional physical intrusion onto the land of another without the owner's consent.

trespass to personal property   An intentional act against or use of someone's personal property without the owner's consent.

trust   A legal arrangement where property is held by someone for the benefit of another.

trust corpus   The body or underlying property of the trust.

trustee   The person who is entrusted to hold property for the benefit of another.

types of indorsements   An indorsement may be blank, special, or restrictive. The different types refer to whether the indorsement is open-ended, specific, or conditional.

types of torts   A tort can be intentional, negligent, or one of strict liability.

types of wills   The most common and acceptable form of will is one that is written, signed, and witnessed. There are also nuncupative (oral) and holographic (written in the testator's hand) wills.

ultrahazardous activity   An extremely dangerous activity, for example, working with explosives.

unenforceable contract   An agreement that is not legally binding.

Uniform Commercial Code (UCC)   The statute drafted by the National Conference of Commissioners on Uniform State Laws and adopted in full in all states except Louisiana, which has adopted it in part. This code unifies the laws governing interstate commerce and trade throughout the United States.

unilateral contract   A contract in which one party

makes a promise to the other that can only be accepted by the other's performance rather than a promise in return; for example, when a father offers his son $500 (the promise) to stop smoking for two years (the performance).

union shop   An employment practice in which employees are required to join a union after they are hired.

usage of trade   A practice having such regularity of observance in a place, vocation, or trade so as to justify an expectation that it will be observed with respect to all subsequent transactions.

usurious contract   A contract that is unenforceable because the borrower has agreed to pay a greater rate of interest than that allowed by law.

usury   The practice of lending money at higher interest rates than those allowed by law.

valid   Having legal force.

validity of a will   A will is legally binding if it conforms to the legal requirements for wills in the jurisdiction in which it was made. In most cases, wills must be signed, witnessed, and published.

value   The amount of money which something is worth; the intrinsic worth of an object or service.

verdict   The finding of members of a jury in a case brought before them.

violation   The least serious type of criminal conduct, for example, exceeding the speed limit in a car.

voidable   Having justification to be nullified.

voluntary intoxication   The intentional use of an intoxicating substance such as drugs or alcohol to the point of incapacity.

voluntary manslaughter   The intentional taking of a human life with adequate provocation.

voluntary modification   The Uniform Commercial Code holds that changes to sales contracts are legal and binding if made in good faith by both parties even if there is no additional consideration.

Wagner Act   *See* National Labor Relations Act of 1932.

warehouse receipt   A document of title that entitles the bearer to pick up goods at a warehouse.

warranty   A promise that goods will conform to facts made about them.

warranty of presentment and transfer   The implied warranty made by all transferors of negotiable instruments upon presentation for payment, for example, the warranty implied when one pays by check that the check is good.

waste   The destruction of property by a tenant.

wild animal   An animal that can never be fully tamed, for example, a lion or a rattlesnake.

will   A legal document in which a person states how and to whom his or her property is to be transferred upon his or her death.

winding up of a partnership   The transactions conducted by the partners to close out the business after the dissolution of a partnership, for example, selling assets, filling existing orders, and paying off creditors.

with reserve   A term used in auction sales to indicate that the auctioneer or seller reserves the right to withdraw the item at any time before accepting a bid.

without reserve   A term used in auction sales to indicate that any bid will be accepted and the item will go to the highest bidder.

writ   A formal document issued by a court ordering or prohibiting some action.

writ of certiorari   An order from the Supreme Court of the United States to a lower court demanding that court forward the record of a particular case for its review.

Index

B

C